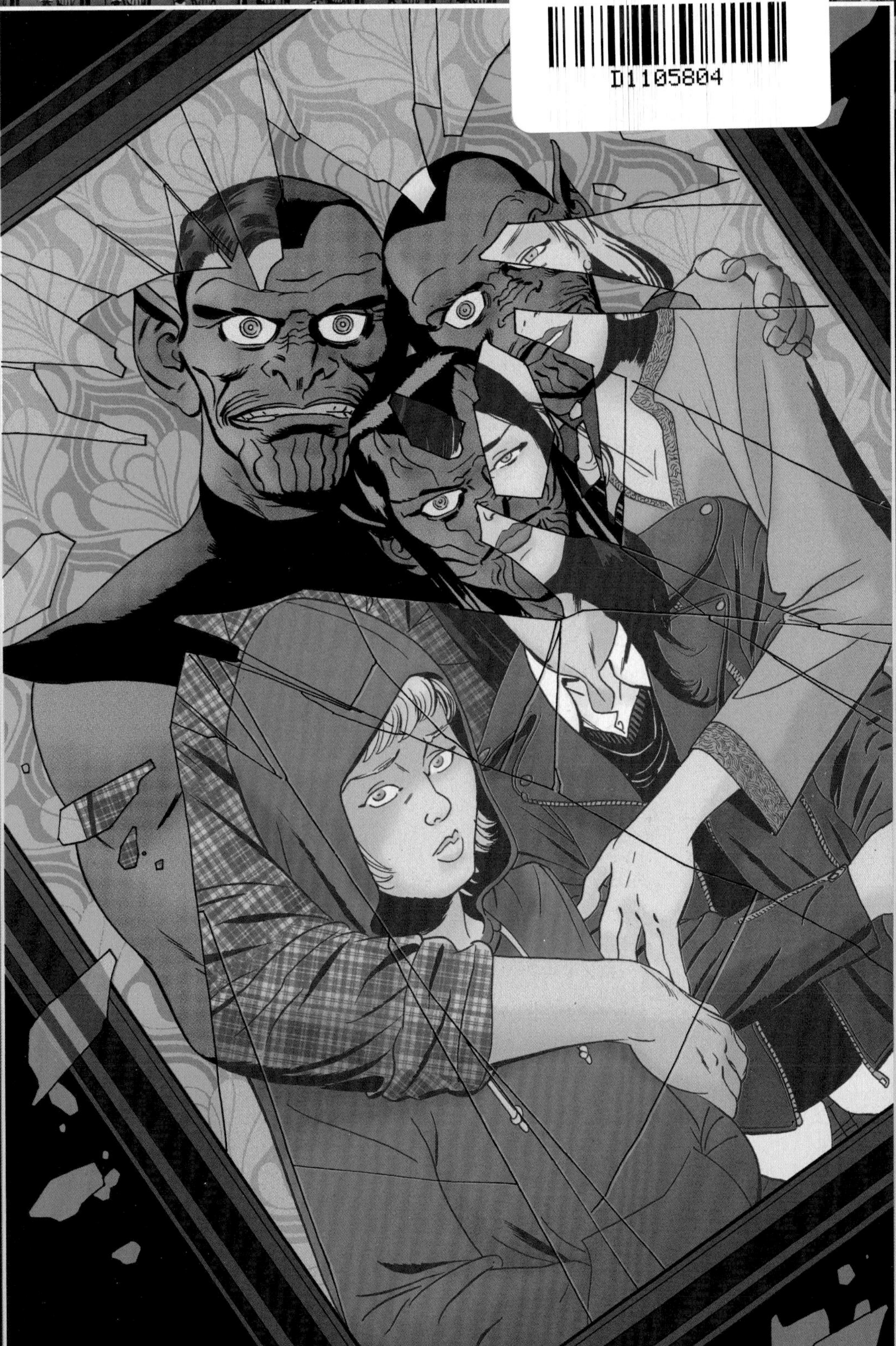

MEET THE SKRULLS #1

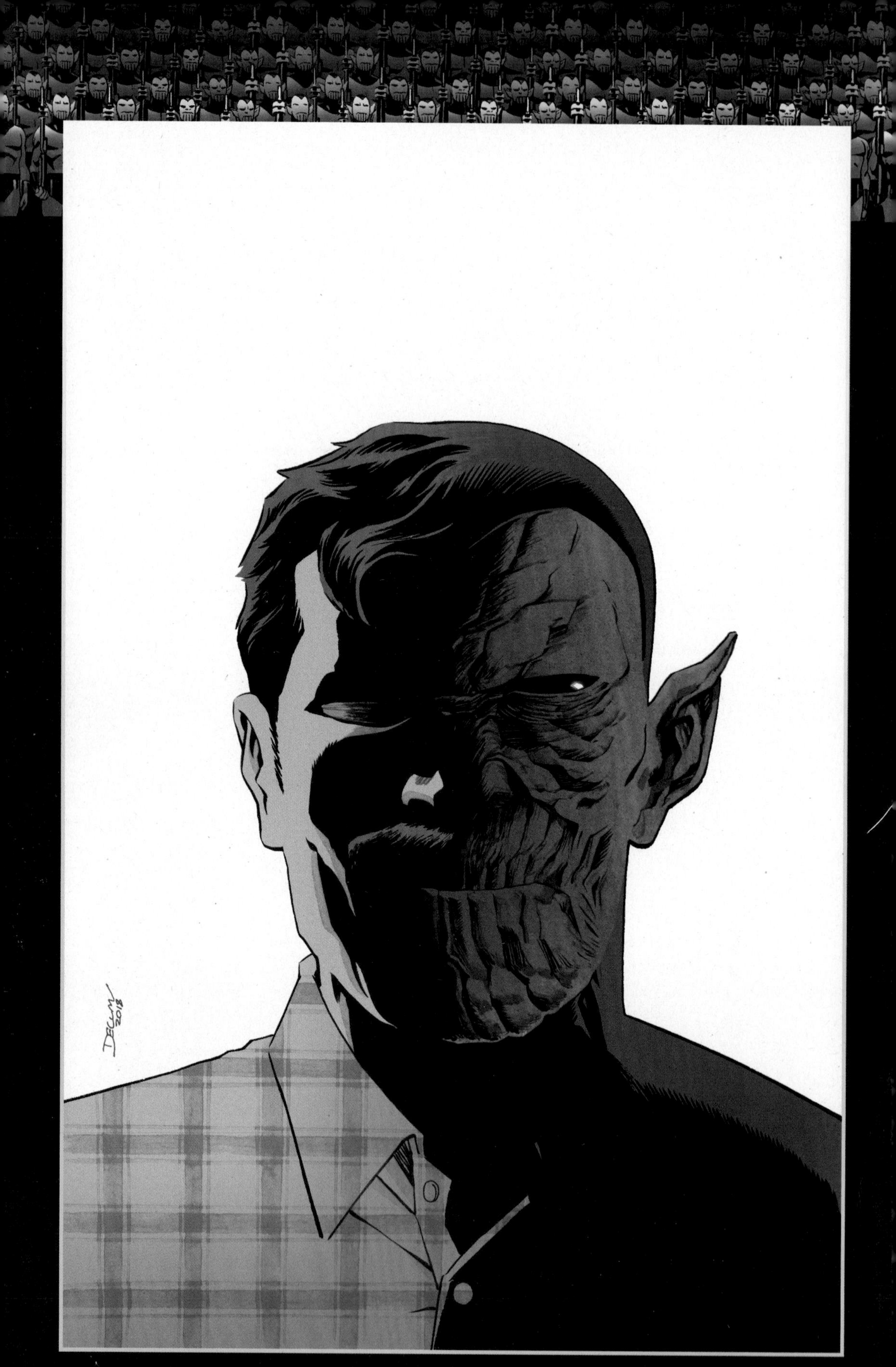

DECLAN SHALVEY MEET THE SKRULLS #1 VARIANT

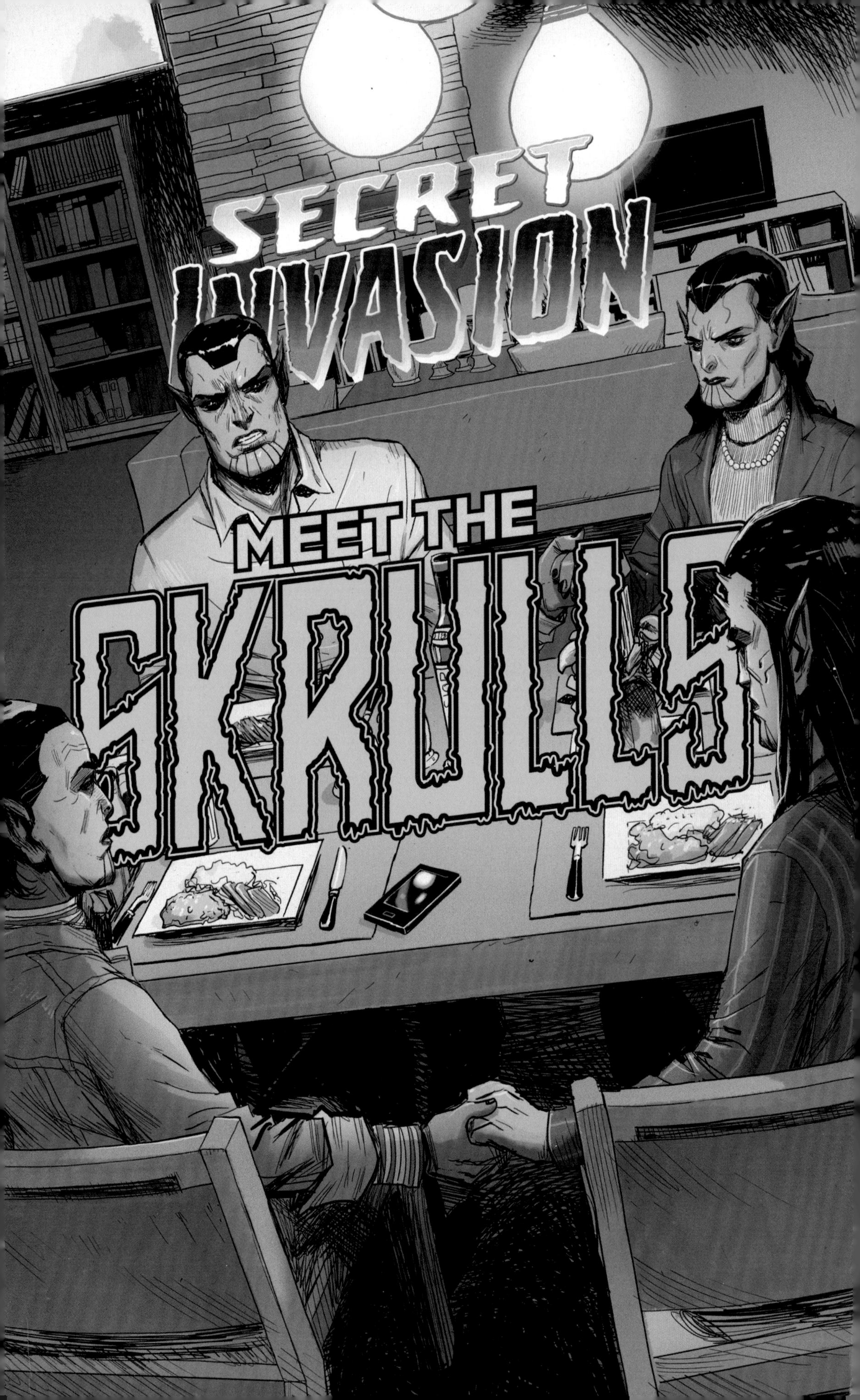
SECRET INVASION
MEET THE SKRULLS

SECRET INVASION

MEET THE SKRULLS

MEET THE SKRULLS #1-5

ROBBIE THOMPSON
WRITER

NIKO HENRICHON
ARTIST & COLOR ARTIST

LAURENT GROSSAT
COLOR ASSISTANT

VC's **TRAVIS LANHAM**
LETTERER

MARCOS MARTIN
COVER ART

KATHLEEN WISNESKI
ASSISTANT EDITOR

NICK LOWE
EDITOR

ROAD TO EMPYRE: THE KREE/ SKRULL WAR

ROBBIE THOMPSON
WRITER

MATTIA DE IULIS
ARTIST & COLOR ARTIST, PRESENT DAY

JAVIER RODRÍGUEZ
ARTIST, FLASHBACK

ÁLVARO LÓPEZ
COLOR ARTIST, FLASHBACK

VC's **JOE CARAMAGNA**
LETTERER

PHIL NOTO
COVER ART

MARTIN BIRO
ASSISTANT EDITOR

ALANNA SMITH
ASSOCIATE EDITOR

TOM BREVOORT
EDITOR

FANTASTIC FOUR #2
(JANUARY 1962)

STAN LEE
WRITER & EDITOR

JACK KIRBY
PENCILER

GEORGE KLEIN
INKER

JOHN DUFFY
LETTERER

FANTASTIC FOUR #18
(SEPTEMBER 1963)

STAN LEE
WRITER & EDITOR

JACK KIRBY
PENCILER

DICK AYERS
INKER

ART SIMEK
LETTERER

AVENGERS #93
(NOVEMBER 1971)

ROY THOMAS
WRITER

NEAL ADAMS
PENCILER

TOM PALMER
INKER

SAM ROSEN
LETTERER

STAN LEE
EDITOR

FANTASTIC FOUR #257
(AUGUST 1983)

JOHN BYRNE
WRITER & ARTIST

GLYNIS WEIN
COLORIST

JIM NOVAK
LETTERER

ANN NOCENTI
ASSISTANT EDITOR

AL MILGROM
EDITOR

NEW AVENGERS: ILLUMINATI #1
(FEBRUARY 2007)

BRIAN MICHAEL BENDIS & **BRIAN REED**
WRITERS

JIM CHEUNG
PENCILER

MARK MORALES
INKER

JUSTIN PONSOR
COLORIST

VC's **CORY PETIT**
LETTERER

MOLLY LAZER & **AUBREY SITTERSON**
ASSISTANT EDITORS

TOM BREVOORT
EDITOR

JENNIFER GRÜNWALD COLLECTION EDITOR
DANIEL KIRCHHOFFER ASSISTANT EDITOR
MAIA LOY ASSISTANT MANAGING EDITOR
LISA MONTALBANO ASSOCIATE MANAGER, TALENT RELATIONS
JOE HOCHSTEIN ASSOCIATE MANAGER, DIGITAL ASSETS

JEFF YOUNGQUIST VP PRODUCTION & SPECIAL PROJECTS
JAY BOWEN BOOK DESIGNER
DAVID GABRIEL SVP PRINT, SALES & MARKETING
C.B. CEBULSKI EDITOR IN CHIEF

SECRET INVASION: MEET THE SKRULLS. Contains material originally published in magazine form as MEET THE SKRULLS (2019) #1-5, ROAD TO EMPYRE: THE KREE/SKRULL WAR (2020) #1, FANTASTIC FOUR (1961) #2 and #18, AVENGERS (1963) #93, NEW AVENGERS: ILLUMINATI (2007) #1, and FANTASTIC FOUR (1961) #257. First printing 2022. ISBN 978-1-302-94676-0. Published by MARVEL WORLDWIDE, INC., a subsidiary of MARVEL ENTERTAINMENT, LLC. OFFICE OF PUBLICATION: 1290 Avenue of the Americas, New York, NY 10104. © 2022 MARVEL No similarity between any of the names, characters, persons, and/or institutions in this book with those of any living or dead person or institution is intended, and any such similarity which may exist is purely coincidental. **Printed in Canada.** KEVIN FEIGE, Chief Creative Officer; DAN BUCKLEY, President, Marvel Entertainment; JOE QUESADA, EVP & Creative Director; DAVID BOGART, Associate Publisher & SVP of Talent Affairs; TOM BREVOORT, VP, Executive Editor; NICK LOWE, Executive Editor, VP of Content, Digital Publishing; DAVID GABRIEL, VP of Print & Digital Publishing; MARK ANNUNZIATO, VP of Planning & Forecasting; JEFF YOUNGQUIST, VP of Production & Special Projects; ALEX MORALES, Director of Publishing Operations; DAN EDINGTON, Director of Editorial Operations; RICKEY PURDIN, Director of Talent Relations; JENNIFER GRÜNWALD, Director of Production & Special Projects; SUSAN CRESPI, Production Manager; STAN LEE, Chairman Emeritus. For information regarding advertising in Marvel Comics or on Marvel.com, please contact Vit DeBellis, Custom Solutions & Integrated Advertising Manager, at vdebellis@marvel.com. For Marvel subscription inquiries, please call 888-511-5480. **Manufactured between 1/21/2022 and 2/22/2022 by SOLISCO PRINTERS, SCOTT, QC, CANADA.**

10 9 8 7 6 5 4 3 2 1

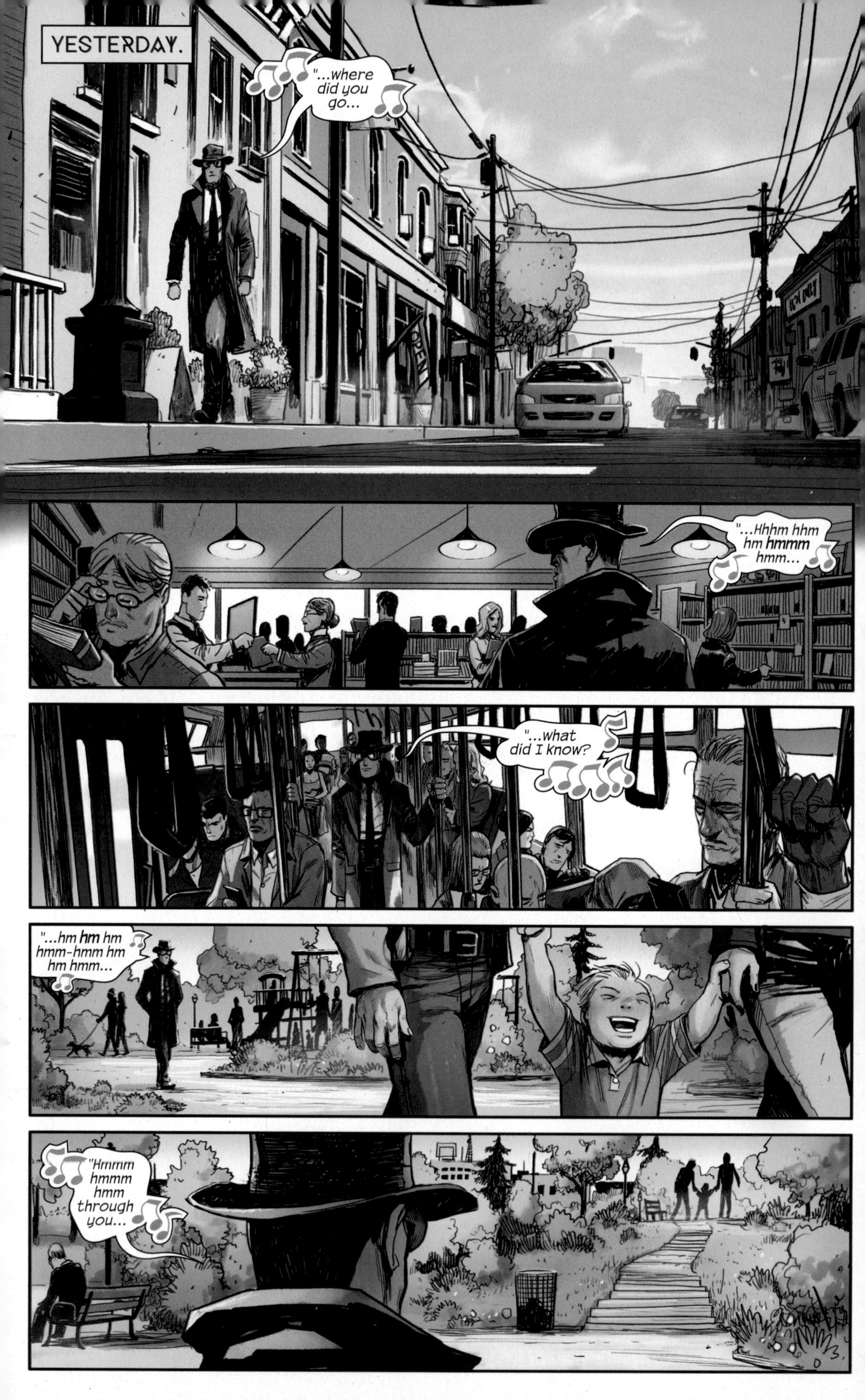
YESTERDAY.
"...where did you go...
"...Hhhm hhm hm **hmmm** hmm...
"...what did I know?
"...hm **hm** hm hmm-hmm hm hm hmm...
"Hmmm hmmm hmm through you...

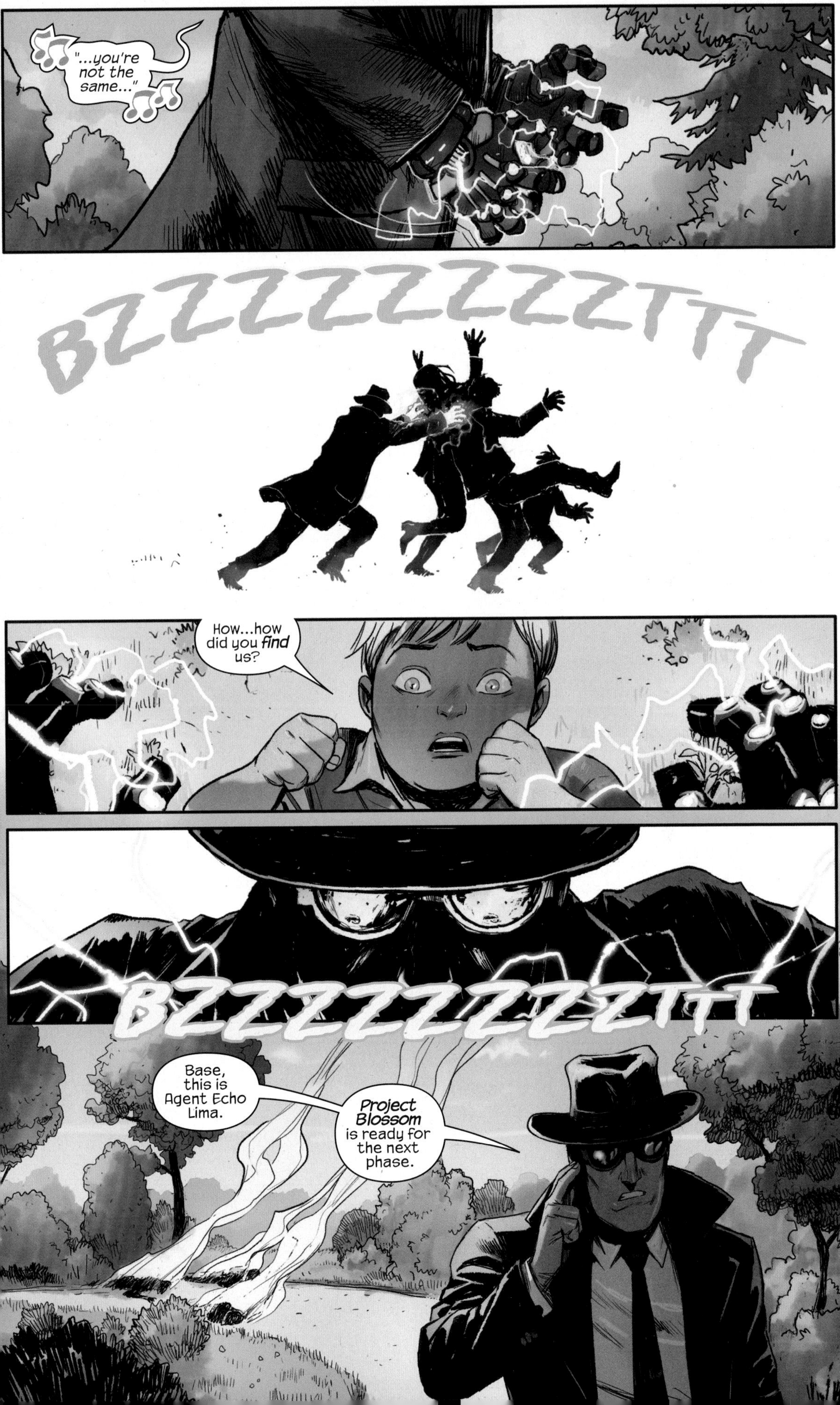
"...you're not the same..."
BZZZZZZZZZZTTT
How...how did you *find* us?
BZZZZZZZZZZTTT
Base, this is Agent Echo Lima.
Project Blossom is ready for the next phase.

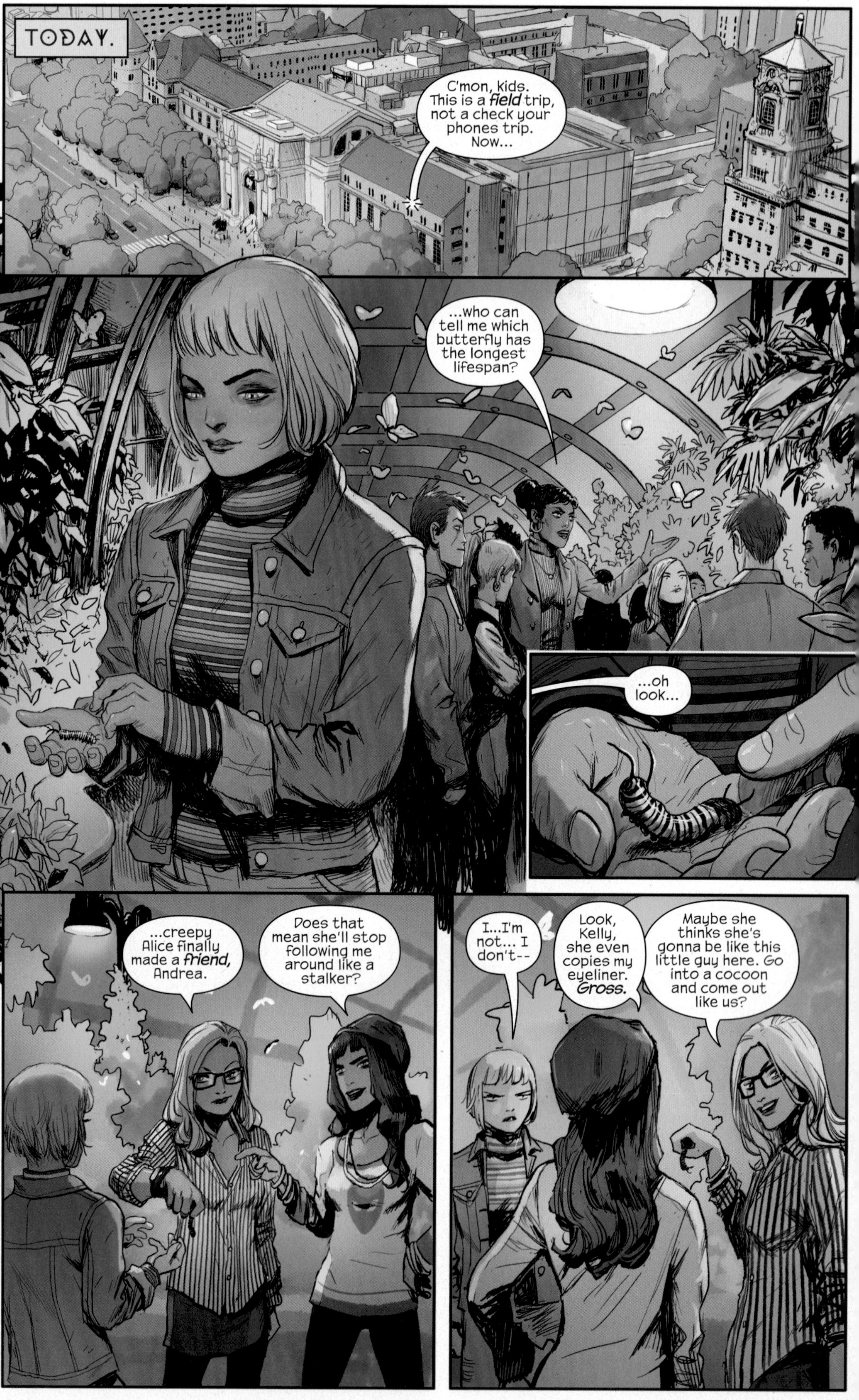
TODAY.
C'mon, kids. This is a *field* trip, not a check your phones trip. Now...
...who can tell me which butterfly has the longest lifespan?
...oh look...
...creepy Alice finally made a *friend,* Andrea.
Does that mean she'll stop following me around like a stalker?
I...I'm not... I don't--
Look, Kelly, she even copies my eyeliner. ***Gross.***
Maybe she thinks she's gonna be like this little guy here. *Go* into a cocoon and come out like us?

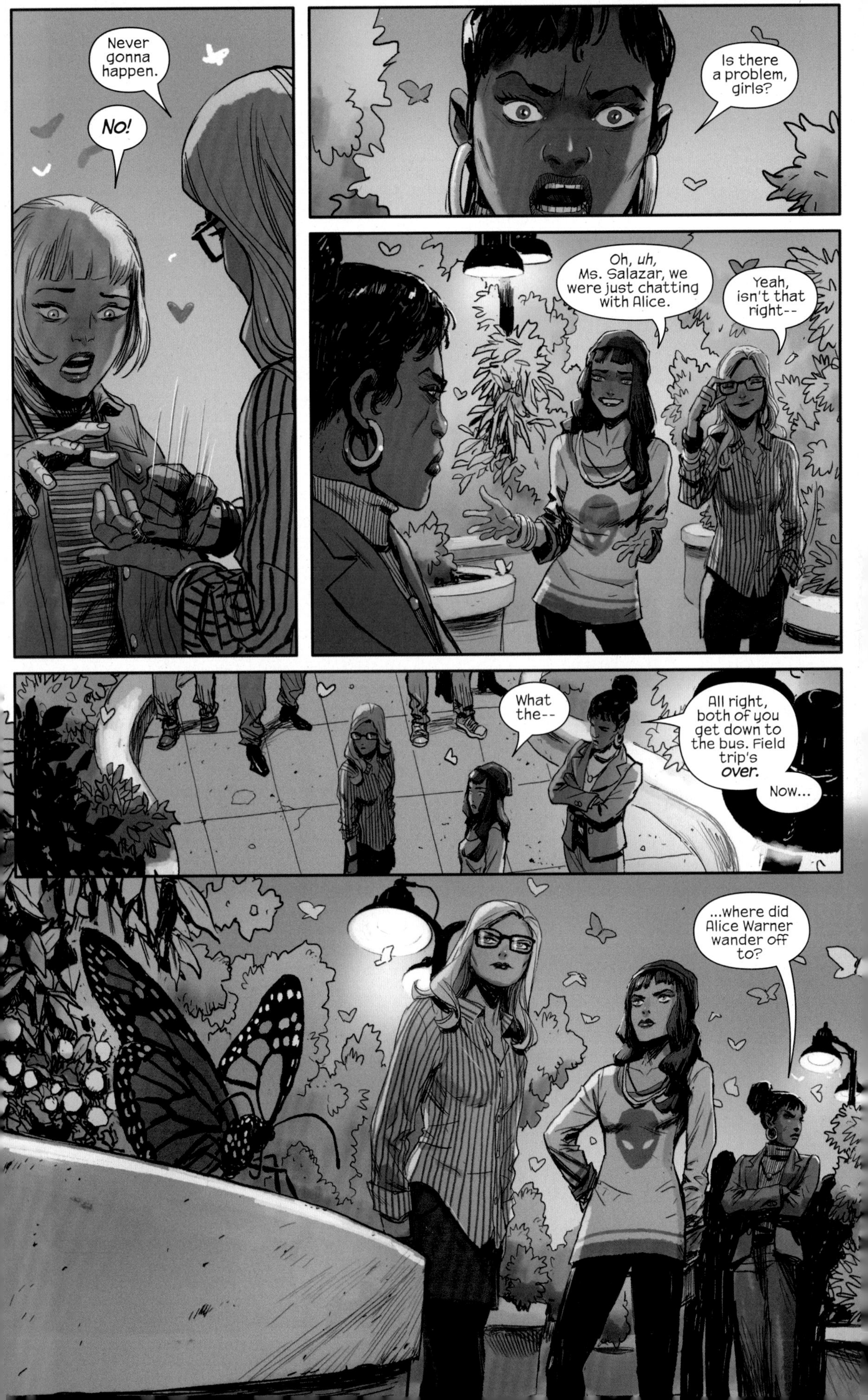
Never gonna happen.
NO!
Is there a problem, girls?
Oh, *uh*, Ms. Salazar, we were just chatting with Alice.
Yeah, isn't that right--
What the--
All right, both of you get down to the bus. Field trip's **over.**
Now...
...where did Alice Warner wander off to?

BUTTERFLY EXHIBIT
WELCOME TO STAMFORD
WARNER FAMILY

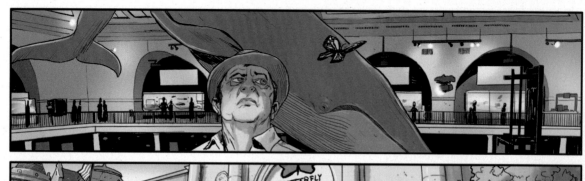

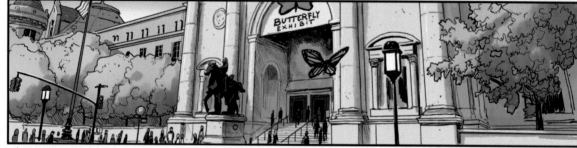

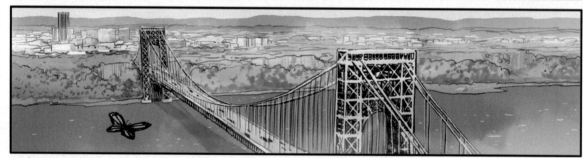

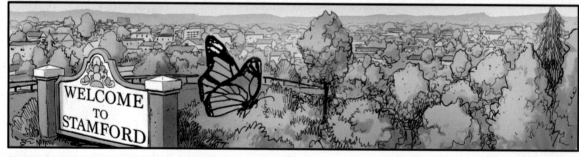

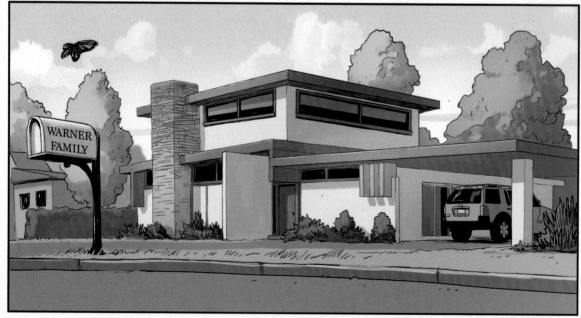

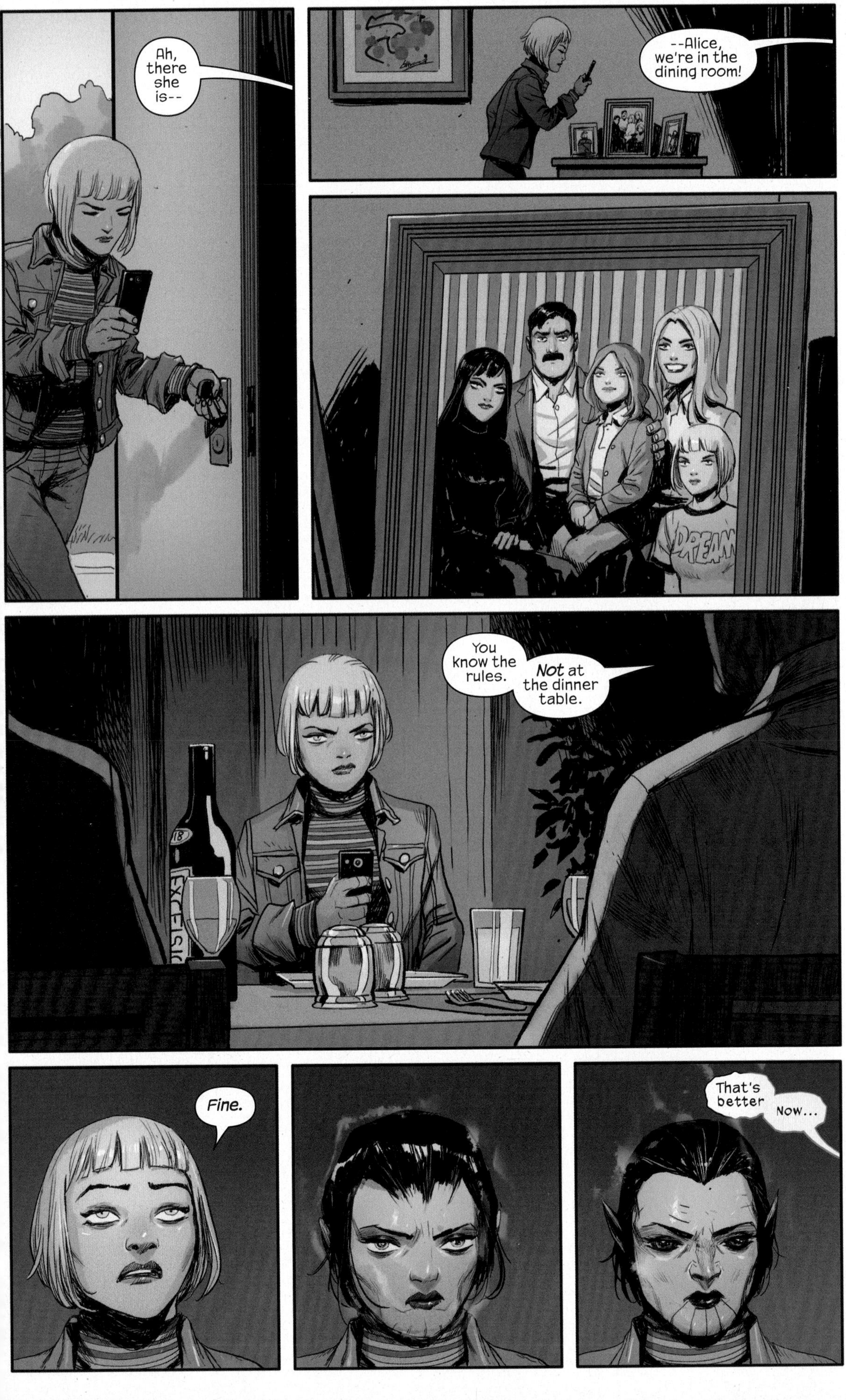
Ah, there she is--
--Alice, we're in the dining room!
You know the rules.
Not at the dinner table.
Fine.
That's better
Now...

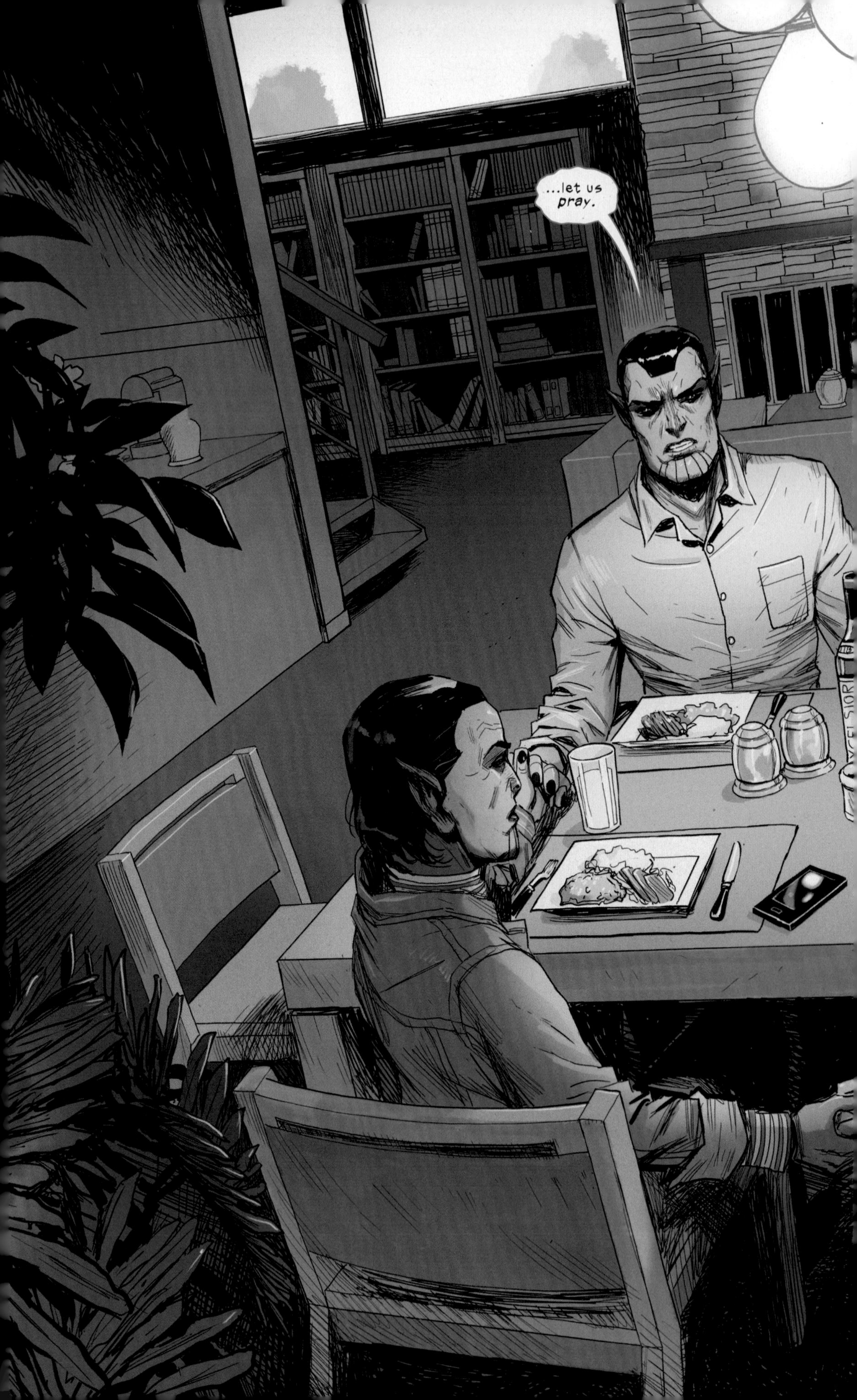
...let us pray.

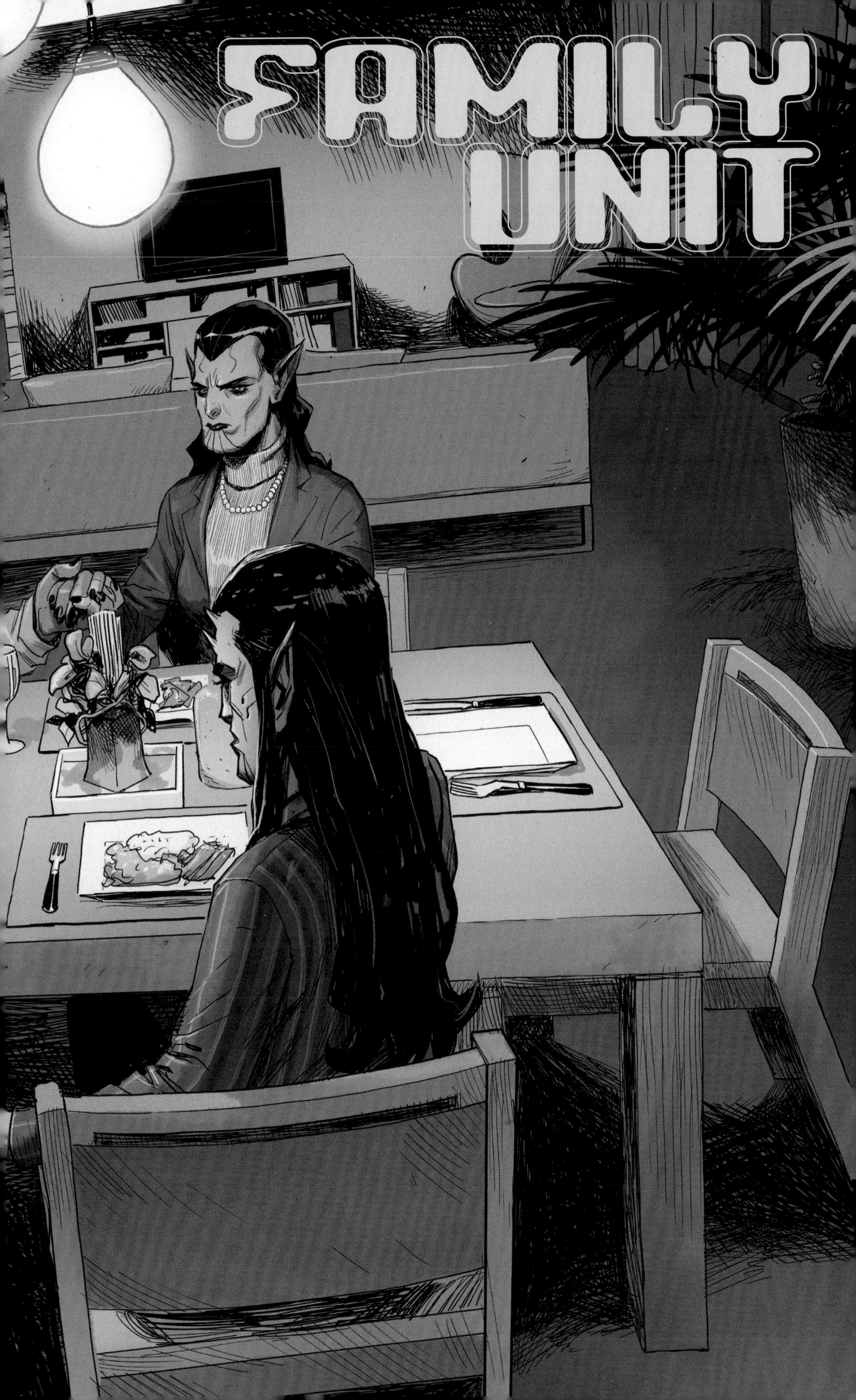
FAMILY
UNIT

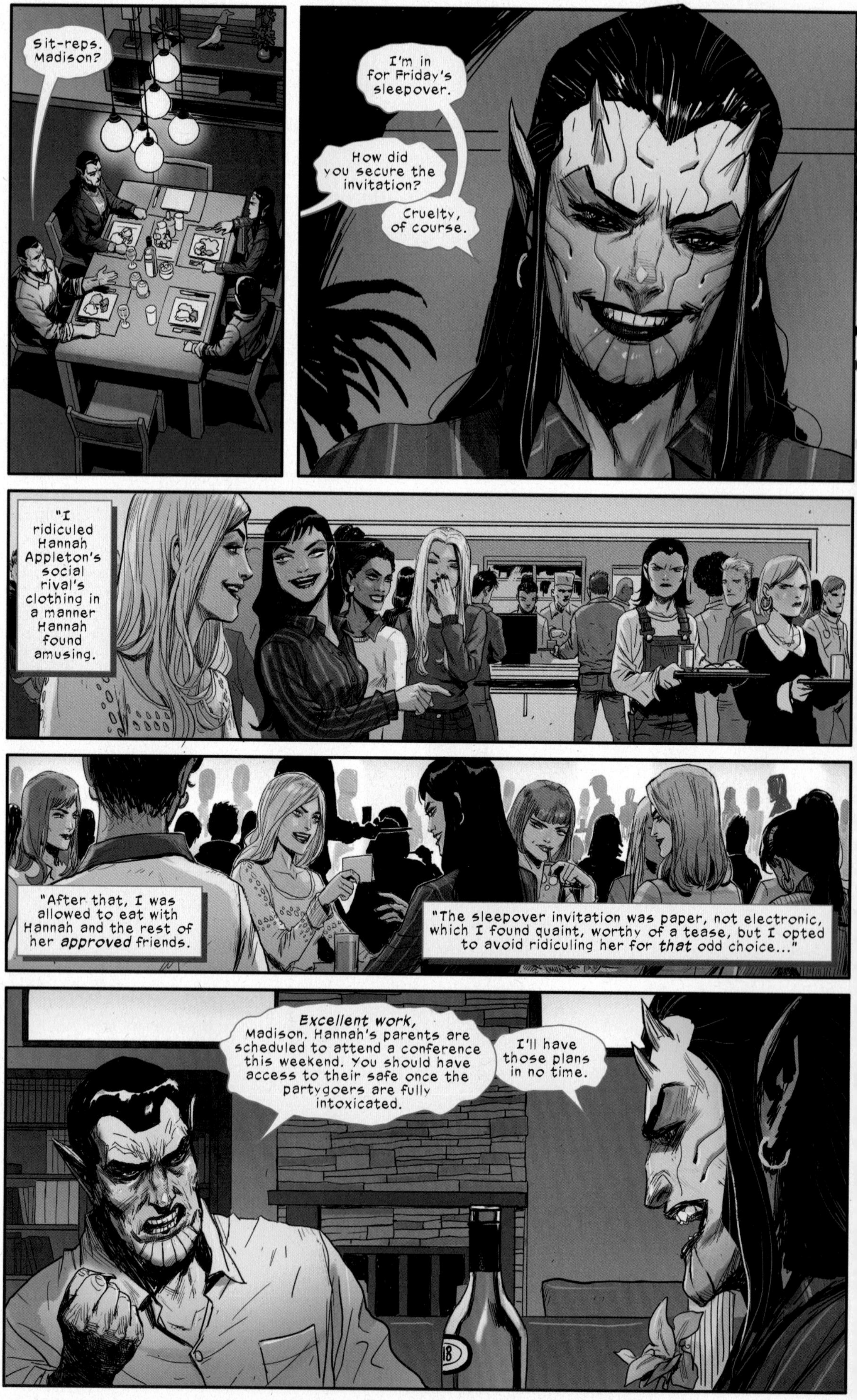
Sit-reps. Madison?
I'm in for Friday's sleepover.
How did you secure the invitation?
Cruelty, of course.
"I ridiculed Hannah Appleton's social rival's clothing in a manner Hannah found amusing.
"After that, I was allowed to eat with Hannah and the rest of her *approved* friends.
"The sleepover invitation was paper, not electronic, which I found quaint, worthy of a tease, but I opted to avoid ridiculing her for *that* odd choice..."
Excellent work, Madison. Hannah's parents are scheduled to attend a conference this weekend. You should have access to their safe once the partygoers are fully intoxicated.
I'll have those plans in no time.

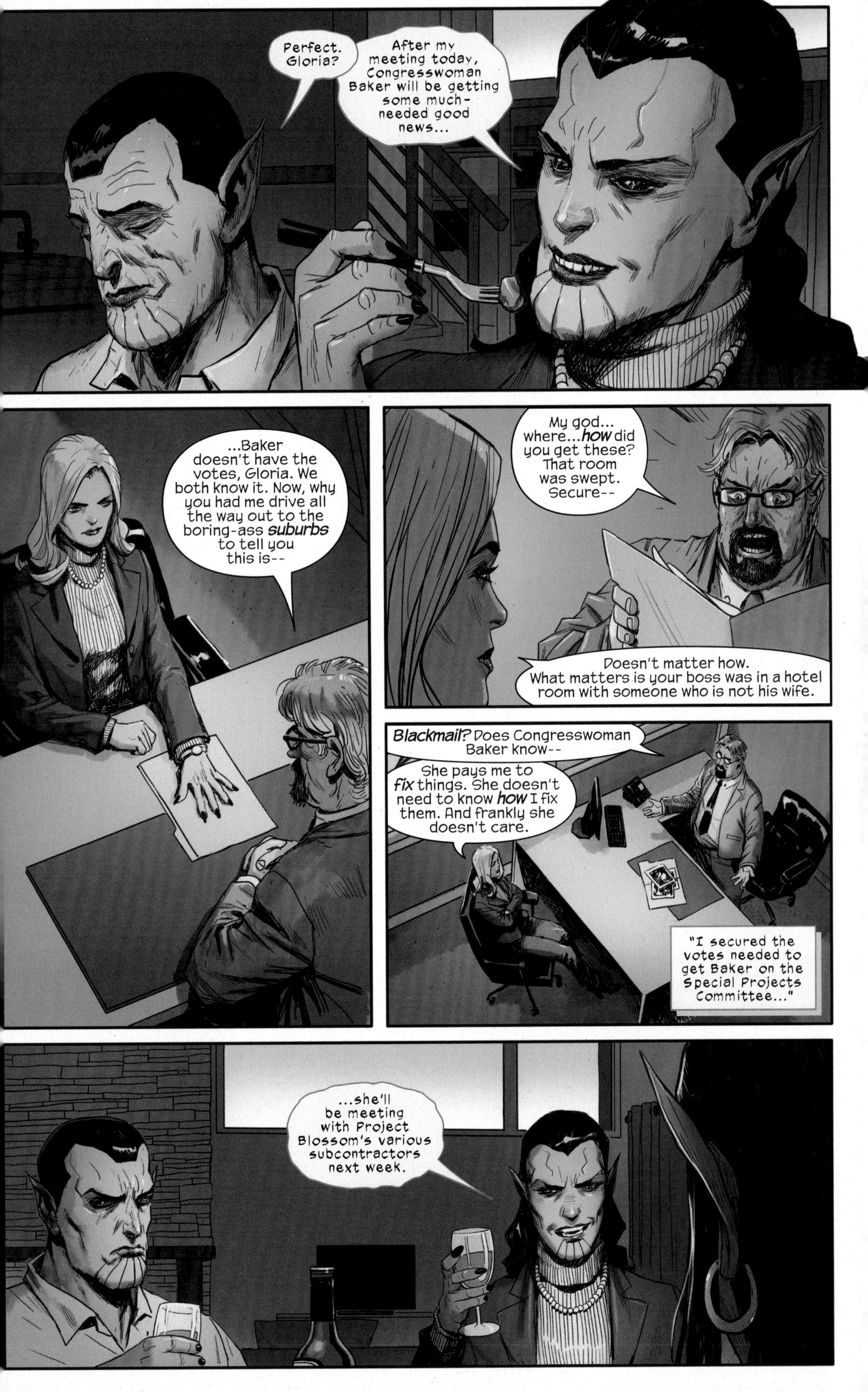
Perfect. Gloria?
After my meeting today, Congresswoman Baker will be getting some much-needed good news...
...Baker doesn't have the votes, Gloria. We both know it. Now, why you had me drive all the way out to the boring-ass *suburbs* to tell you this is--
My god... where...*how* did you get these? That room was swept. Secure--
Doesn't matter how. What matters is your boss was in a hotel room with someone who is not his wife.
Blackmail? Does Congresswoman Baker know--
She pays me to *fix* things. She doesn't need to know *how* I fix them. And frankly she doesn't care.
"I secured the votes needed to get Baker on the Special Projects Committee..."
...she'll be meeting with Project Blossom's various subcontractors next week.

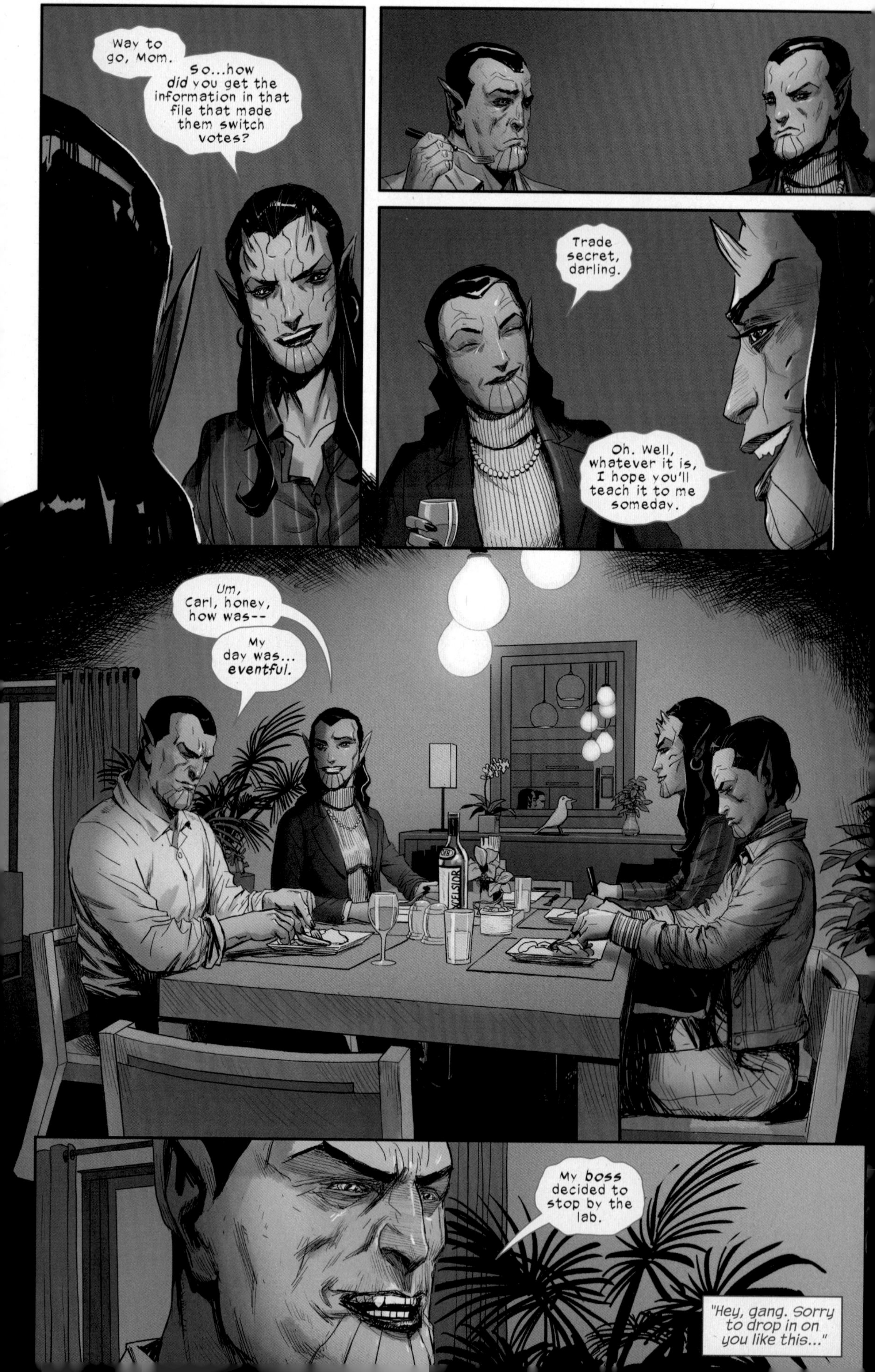
Way to go, Mom.
So...how did you get the information in that file that made them switch votes?
Trade secret, darling.
Oh. Well, whatever it is, I hope you'll teach it to me someday.
Um, Carl, honey, how was--
My day was... eventful.
My boss decided to stop by the lab.
"Hey, gang. Sorry to drop in on you like this..."

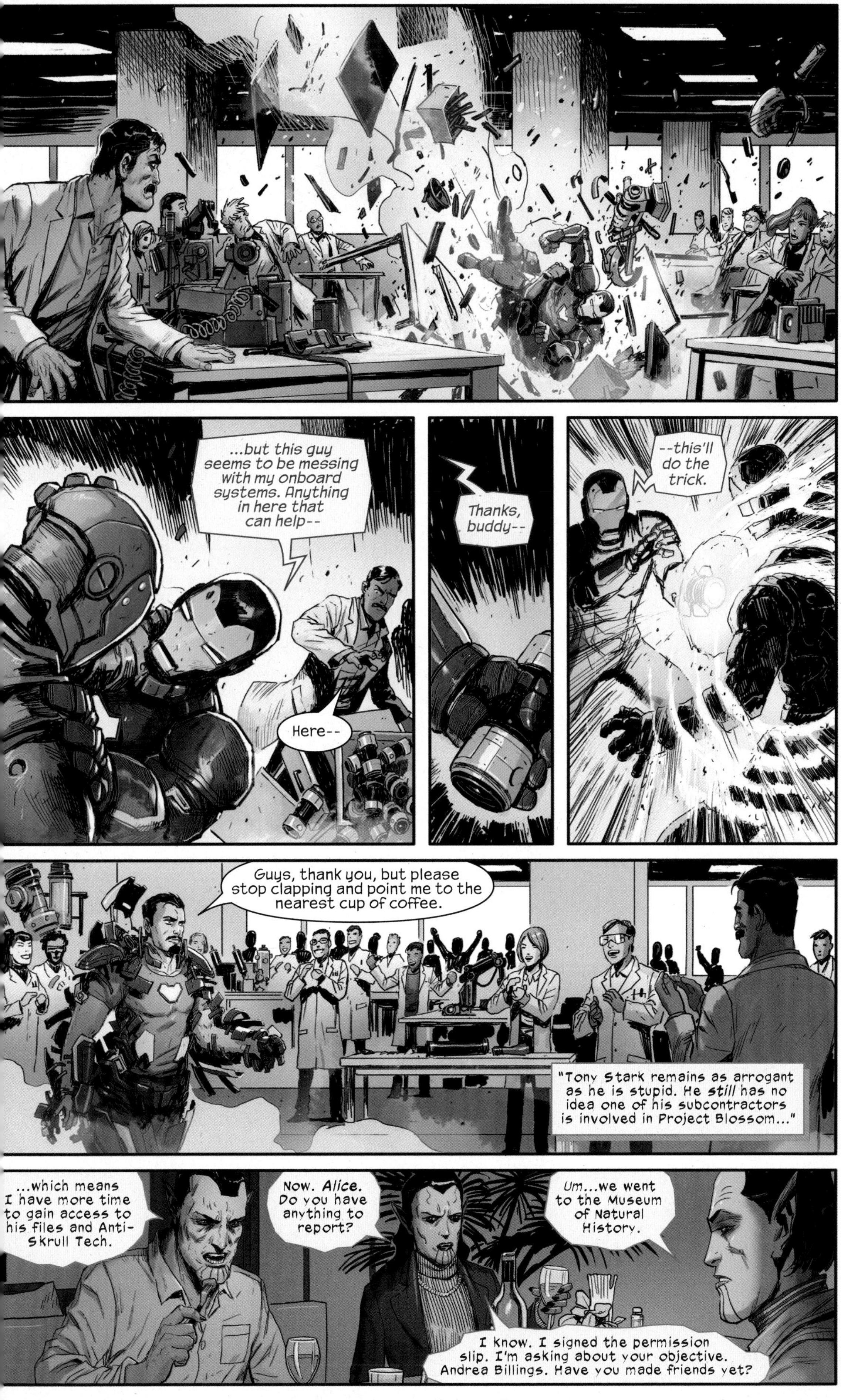
...but this guy seems to be messing with my onboard systems. Anything in here that can help--
Here--
Thanks, buddy--
--this'll do the trick.
Guys, thank you, but please stop clapping and point me to the nearest cup of coffee.
"Tony Stark remains as arrogant as he is stupid. He still has no idea one of his subcontractors is involved in Project Blossom..."
...which means I have more time to gain access to his files and Anti-Skrull Tech.
Now. Alice. Do you have anything to report?
Um...we went to the Museum of Natural History.
I know. I signed the permission slip. I'm asking about your objective. Andrea Billings. Have you made friends yet?

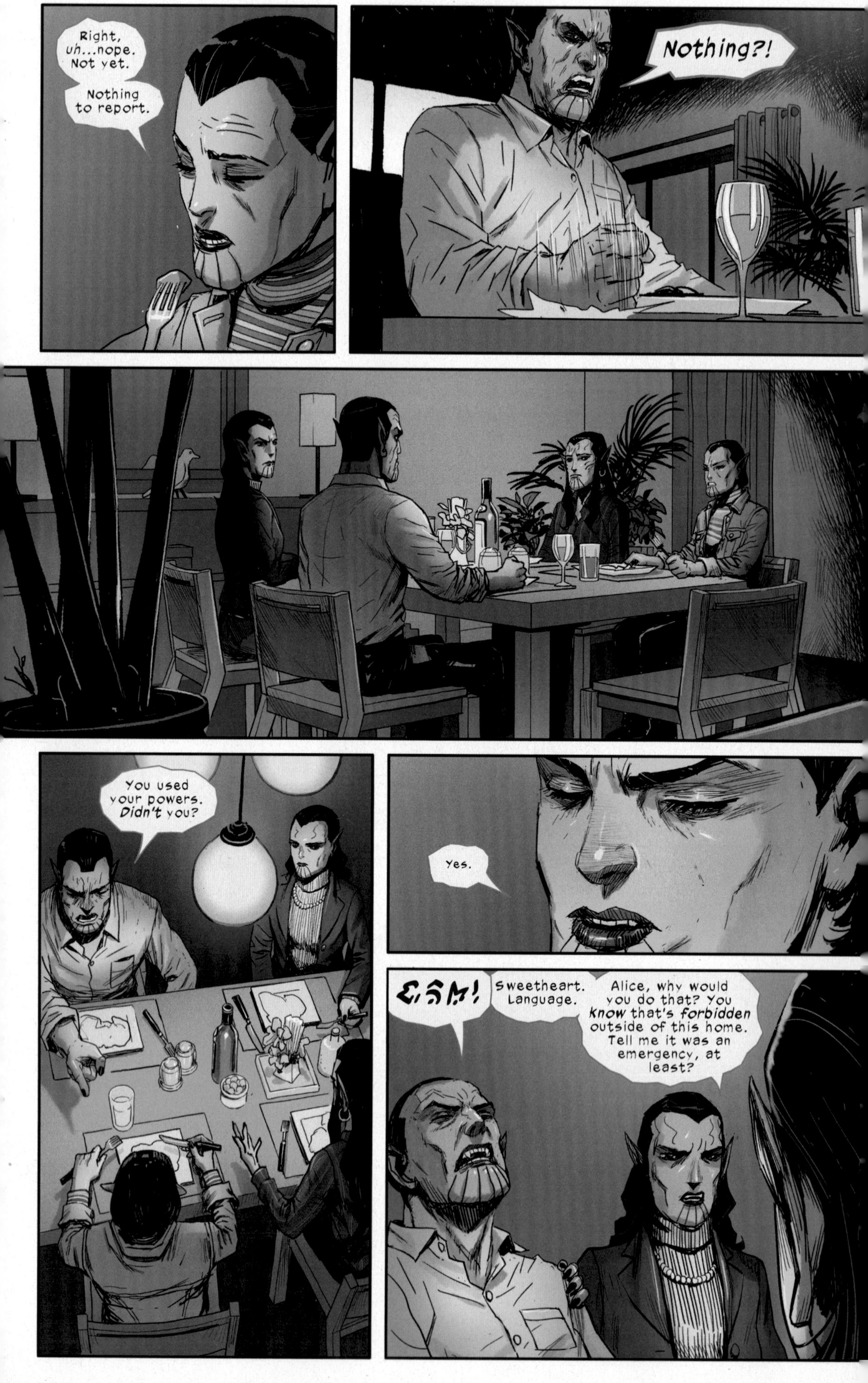
Right, uh...nope. Not yet.
Nothing to report.
Nothing?!
You used your powers. Didn't you?
Yes.
Sweetheart. Language.
Alice, why would you do that? You know that's forbidden outside of this home. Tell me it was an emergency, at least?

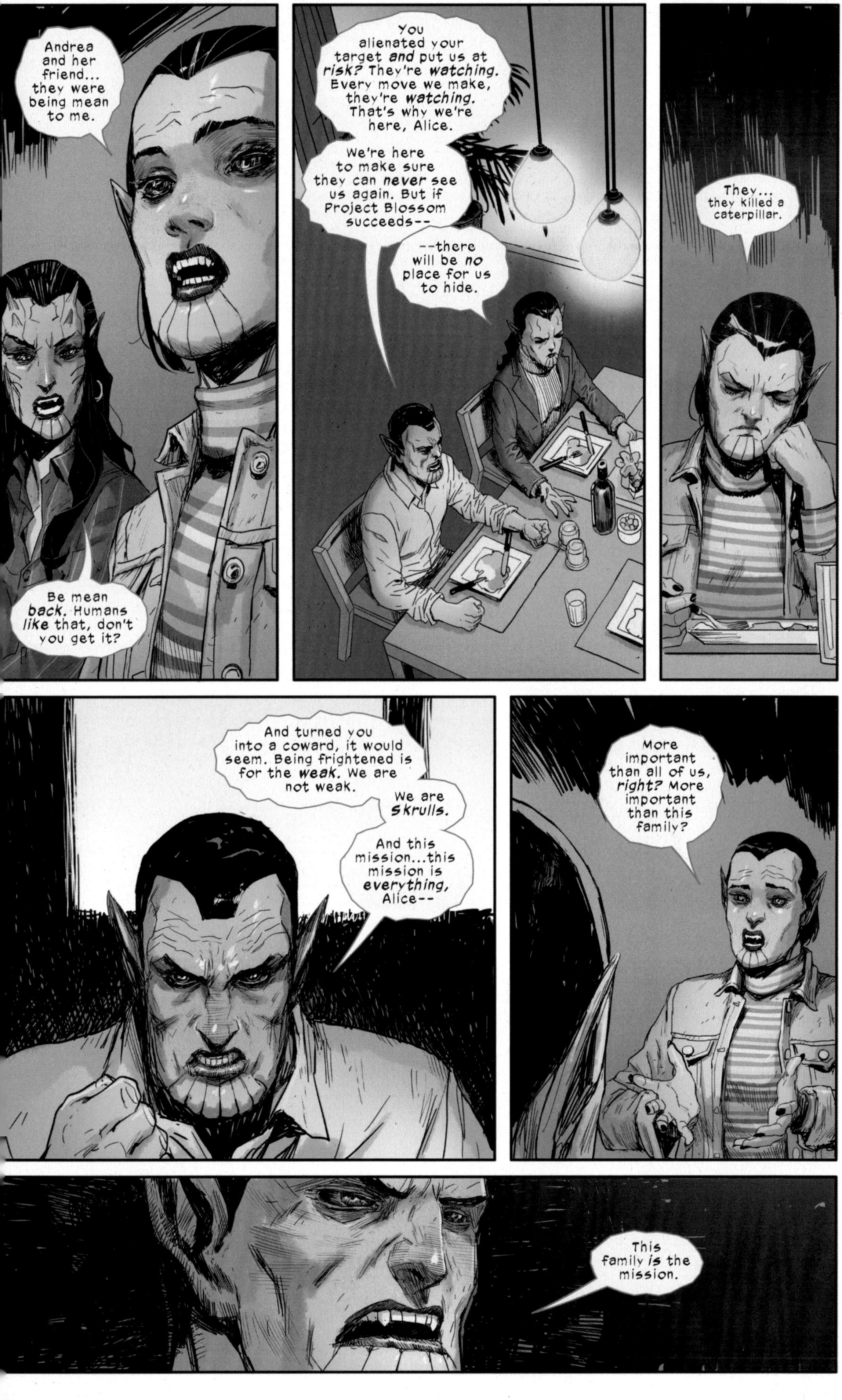
Andrea and her friend... they were being mean to me.
Be mean back. Humans like that, don't you get it?
You alienated your target and put us at risk? They're watching. Every move we make, they're watching. That's why we're here, Alice.
We're here to make sure they can never see us again. But if Project Blossom succeeds--
--there will be no place for us to hide.
They... they killed a caterpillar.
And turned you into a coward, it would seem. Being frightened is for the weak. We are not weak.
We are Skrulls.
And this mission...this mission is everything, Alice--
More important than all of us, right? More important than this family?
This family is the mission.

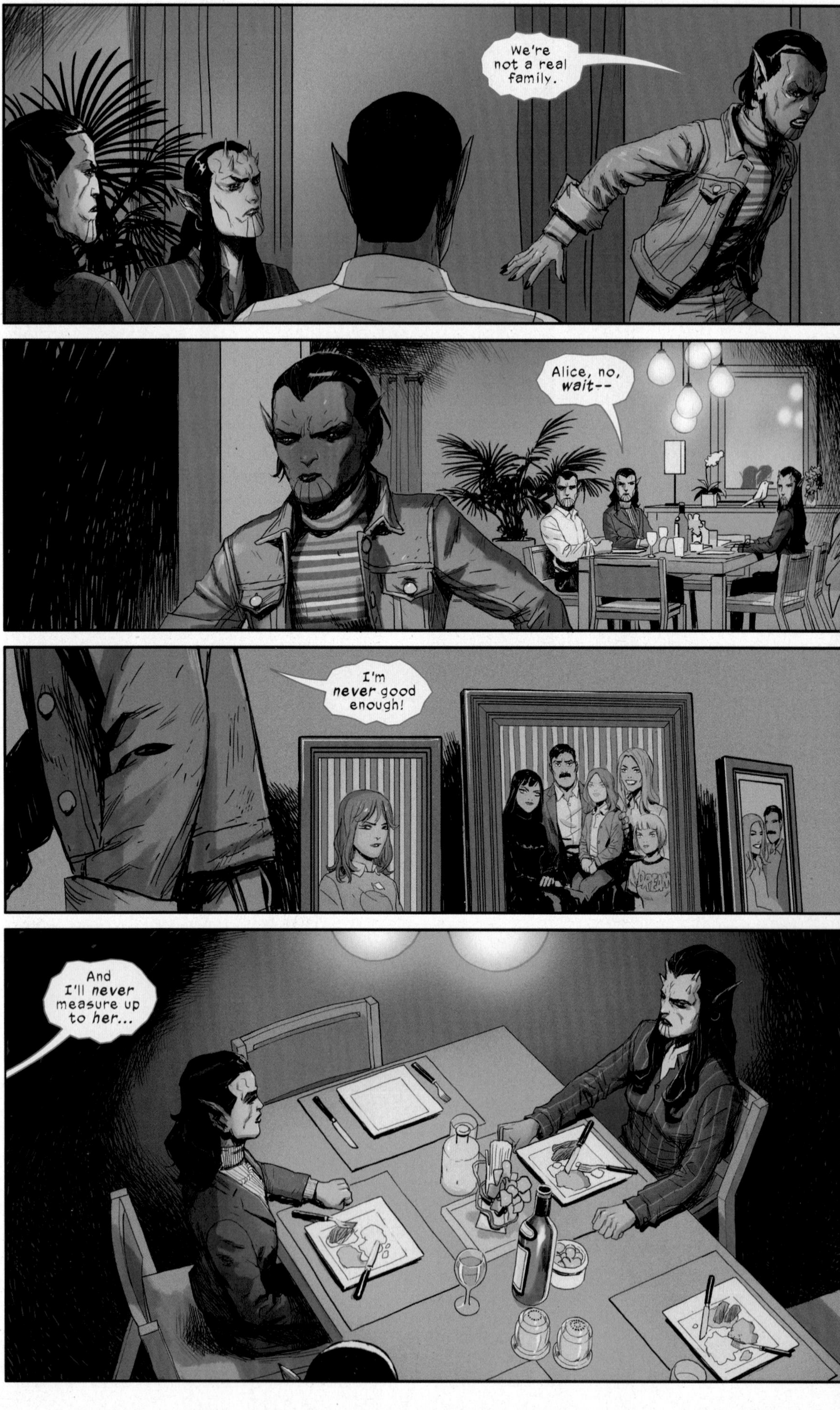
We're not a real family.
Alice, no, *wait*--
I'm *never* good enough!
And I'll *never* measure up to *her*...

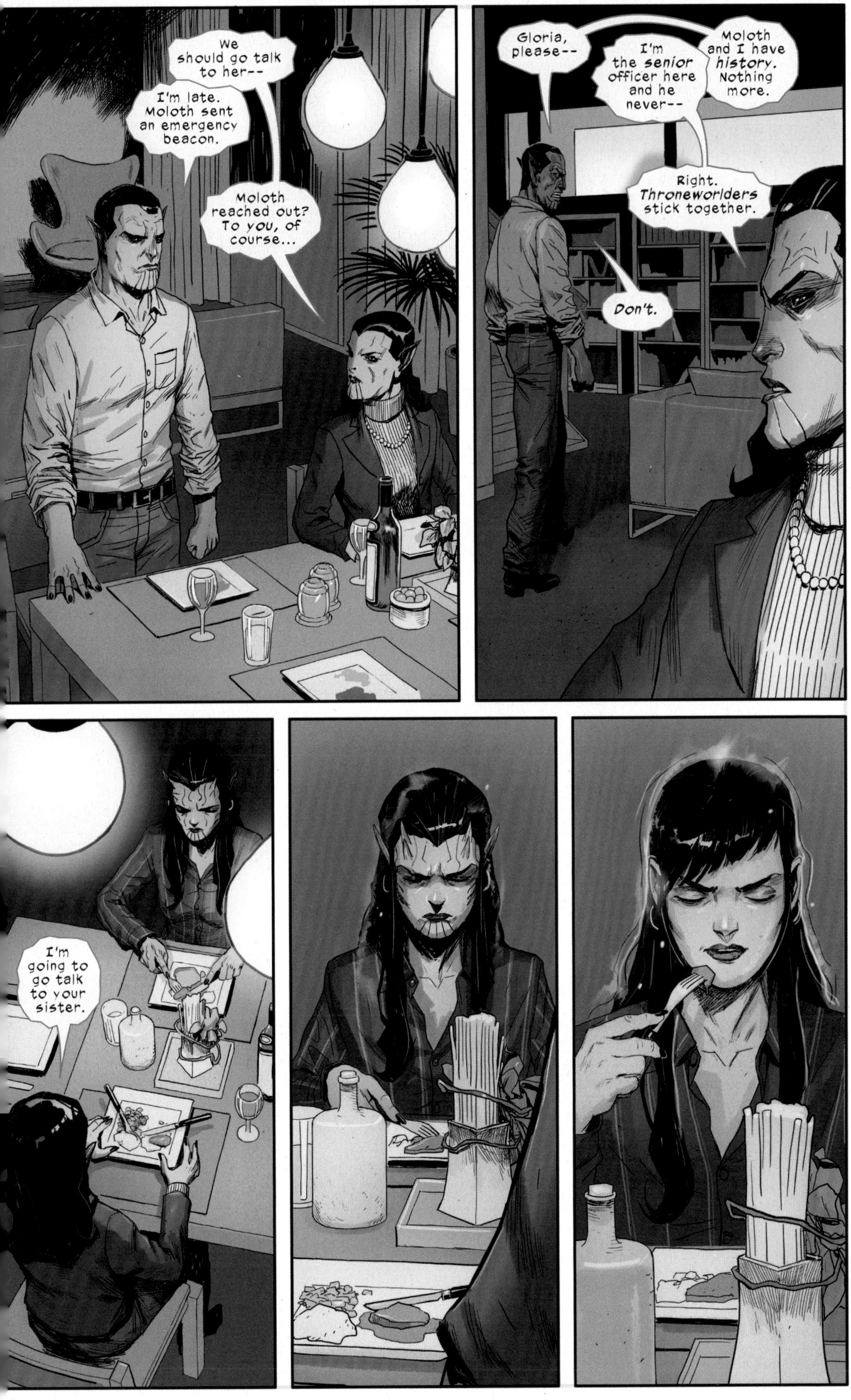
We should go talk to her--
I'm late. Moloth sent an emergency beacon.
Moloth reached out? To *you*, of course...
Gloria, please--
I'm the *senior* officer here and he never--
Moloth and I have *history*. Nothing more.
Right. *Throneworlders* stick together.
Don't.
I'm going to go talk to your sister.

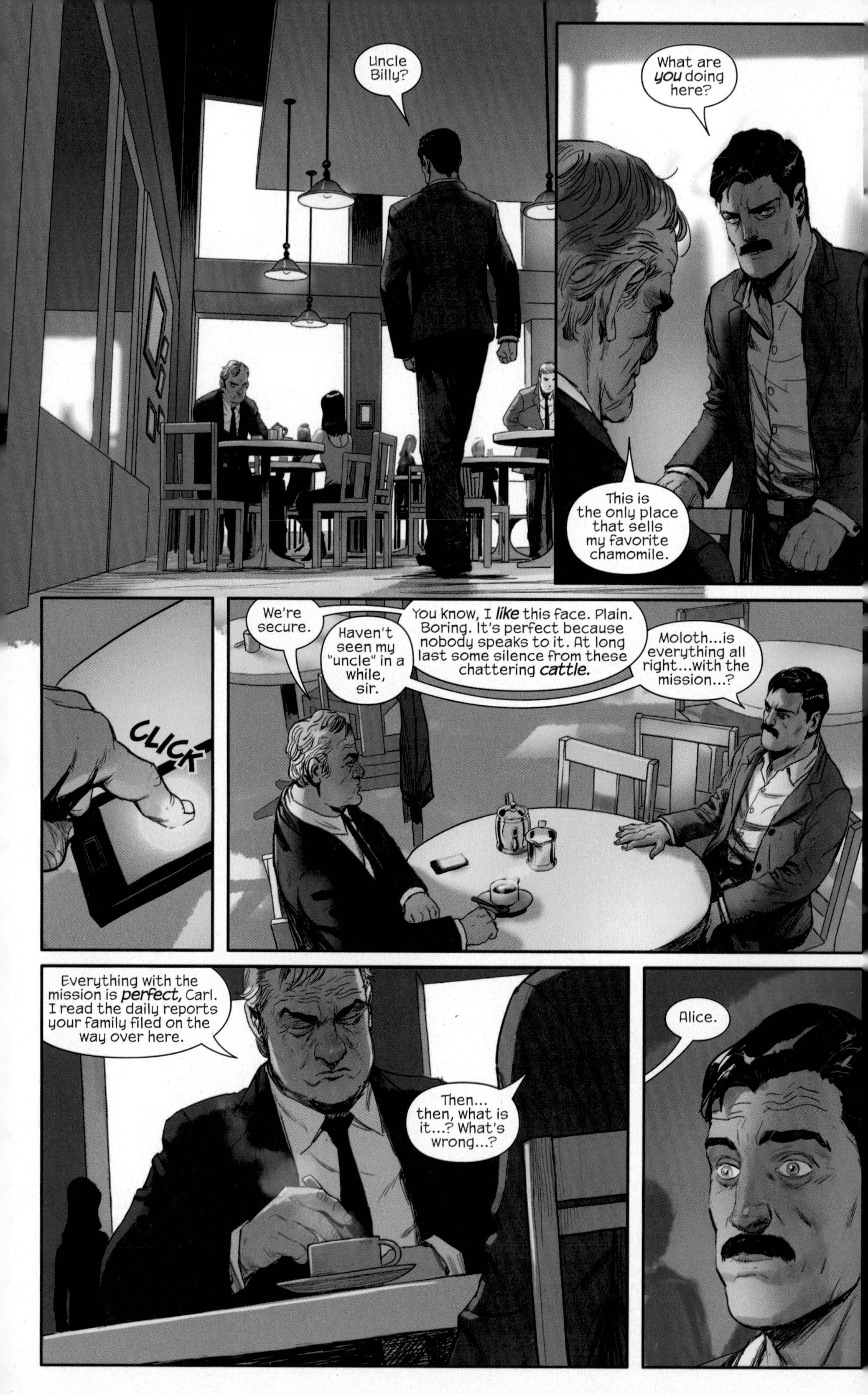
Uncle Billy?
What are *you* doing here?
This is the only place that sells my favorite chamomile.
CLICK
We're secure.
Haven't seen my "uncle" in a while, sir.
You know, I *like* this face. Plain. Boring. It's perfect because nobody speaks to it. At long last some silence from these chattering *cattle.*
Moloth...is everything all right...with the mission...?
Everything with the mission is *perfect,* Carl. I read the daily reports your family filed on the way over here.
Then... then, what is it...? What's wrong...?
Alice.

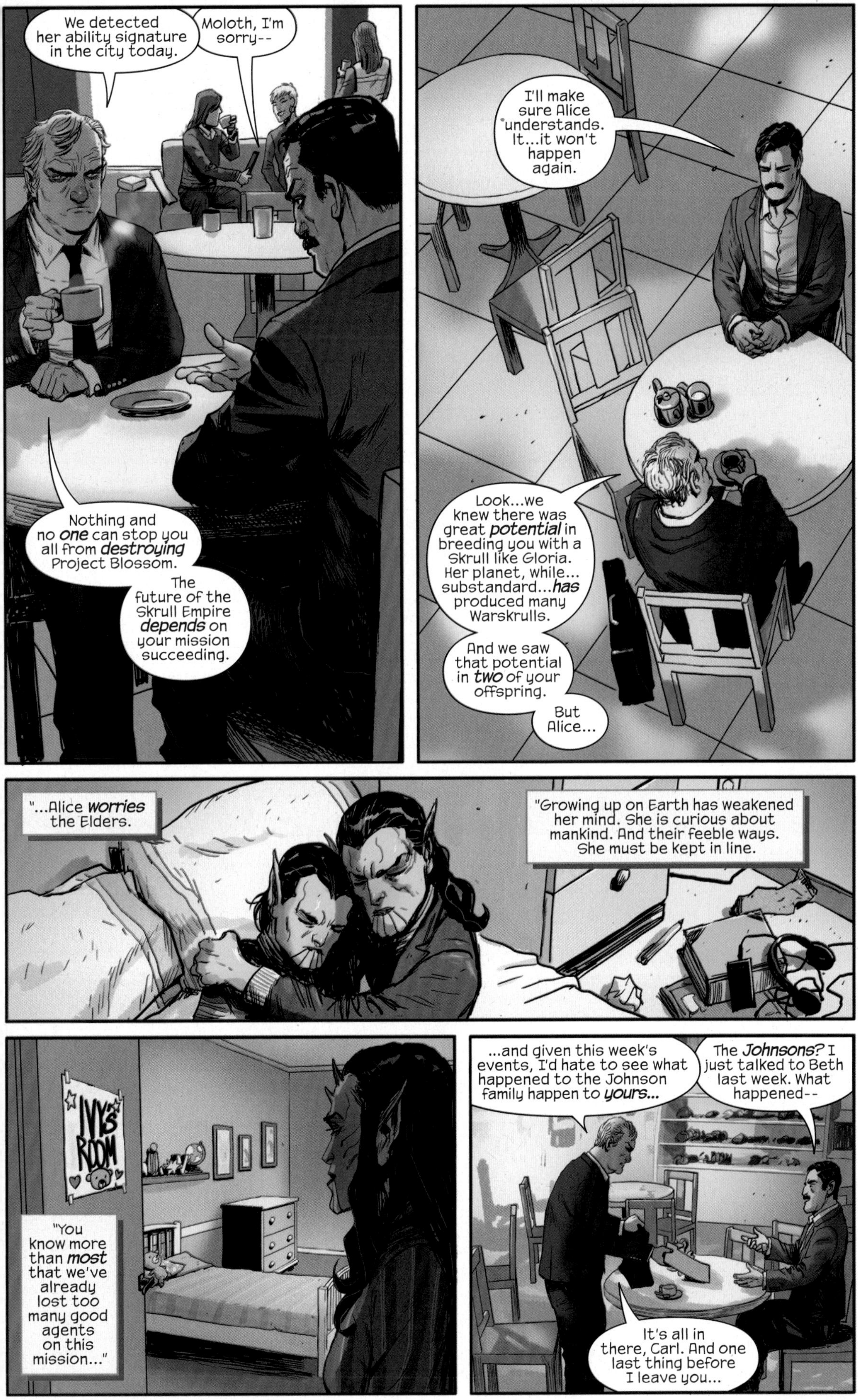
We detected her ability signature in the city today.
Moloth, I'm sorry--
Nothing and no *one* can stop you all from *destroying* Project Blossom.
The future of the Skrull Empire *depends* on your mission succeeding.
I'll make sure Alice understands. It...it won't happen again.
Look...we knew there was great *potential* in breeding you with a Skrull like Gloria. Her planet, while... substandard...*has* produced many Warskrulls.
And we saw that potential in *two* of your offspring.
But Alice...
"...Alice *worries* the Elders.
"Growing up on Earth has weakened her mind. She is curious about mankind. And their feeble ways. She must be kept in line.
IVY'S ROOM
"You know more than *most* that we've already lost too many good agents on this mission..."
...and given this week's events, I'd hate to see what happened to the Johnson family happen to *yours...*
The *Johnsons?* I just talked to Beth last week. What happened--
It's all in there, Carl. And one last thing before I leave you...

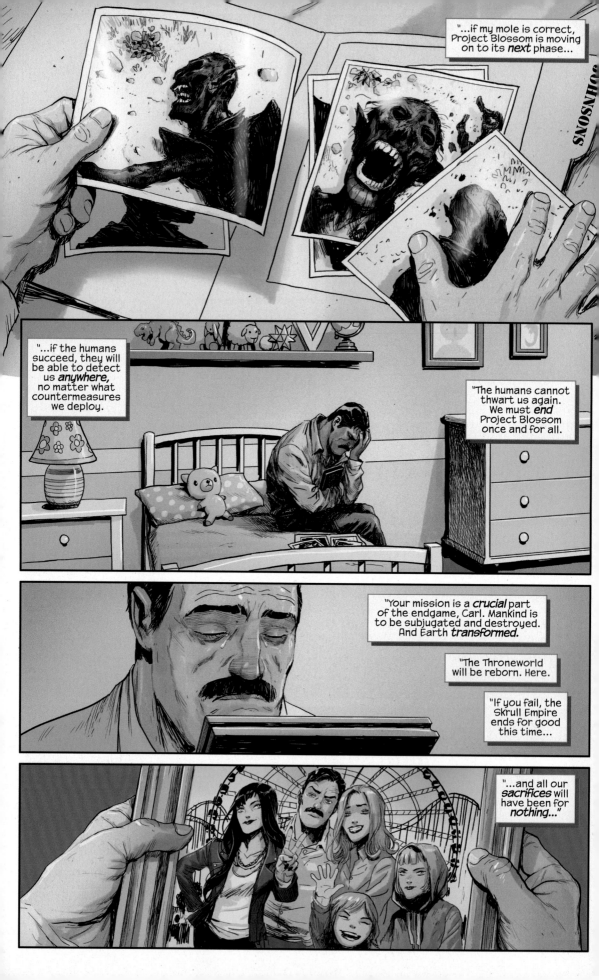

"...if my mole is correct, Project Blossom is moving on to its *next* phase...

"...if the humans succeed, they will be able to detect us *anywhere*, no matter what countermeasures we deploy.

"The humans cannot thwart us again. We must *end* Project Blossom once and for all.

"Your mission is a *crucial* part of the endgame, Carl. Mankind is to be subjugated and destroyed. And Earth *transformed*.

"The Throneworld will be reborn. Here.

"If you fail, the Skrull Empire ends for good this time...

"...and all our *sacrifices* will have been for *nothing*...

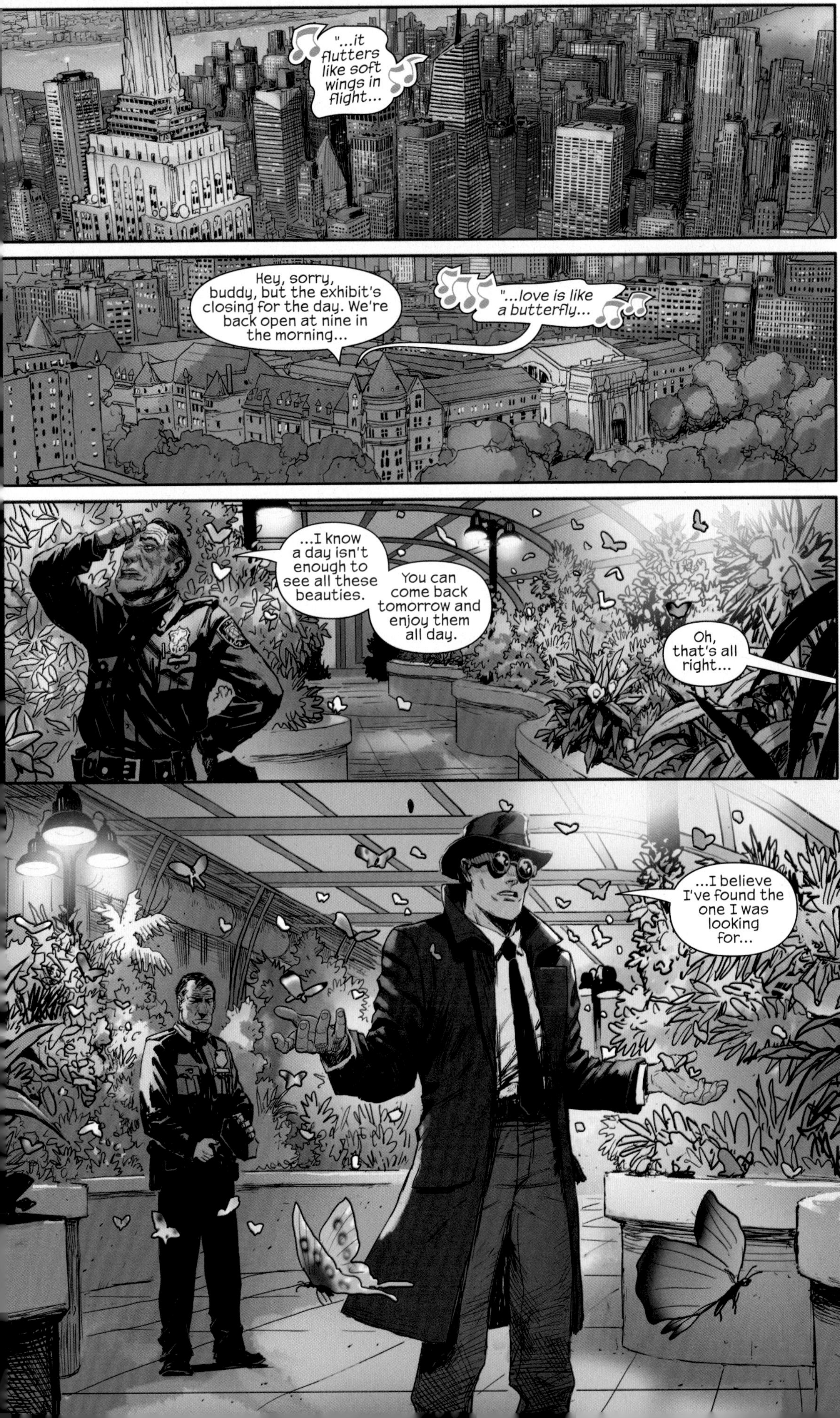
"...it flutters like soft wings in flight...
Hey, sorry, buddy, but the exhibit's closing for the day. We're back open at nine in the morning...
"...love is like a butterfly...
...I know a day isn't enough to see all these beauties.
You can come back tomorrow and enjoy them all day.
Oh, that's all right...
...I believe I've found the one I was looking for...

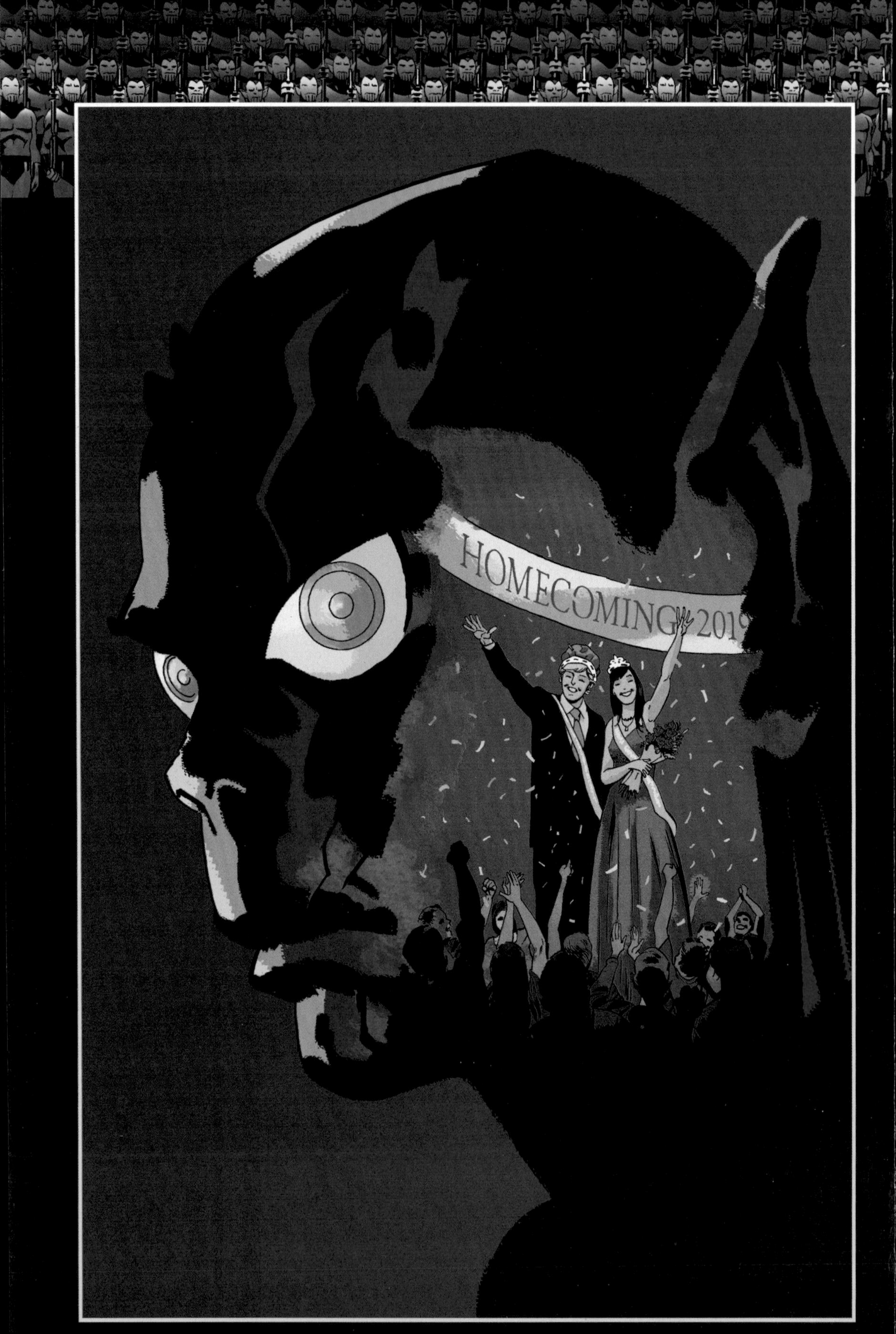
HOMECOMING 201

MEET THE SKRULLS #2

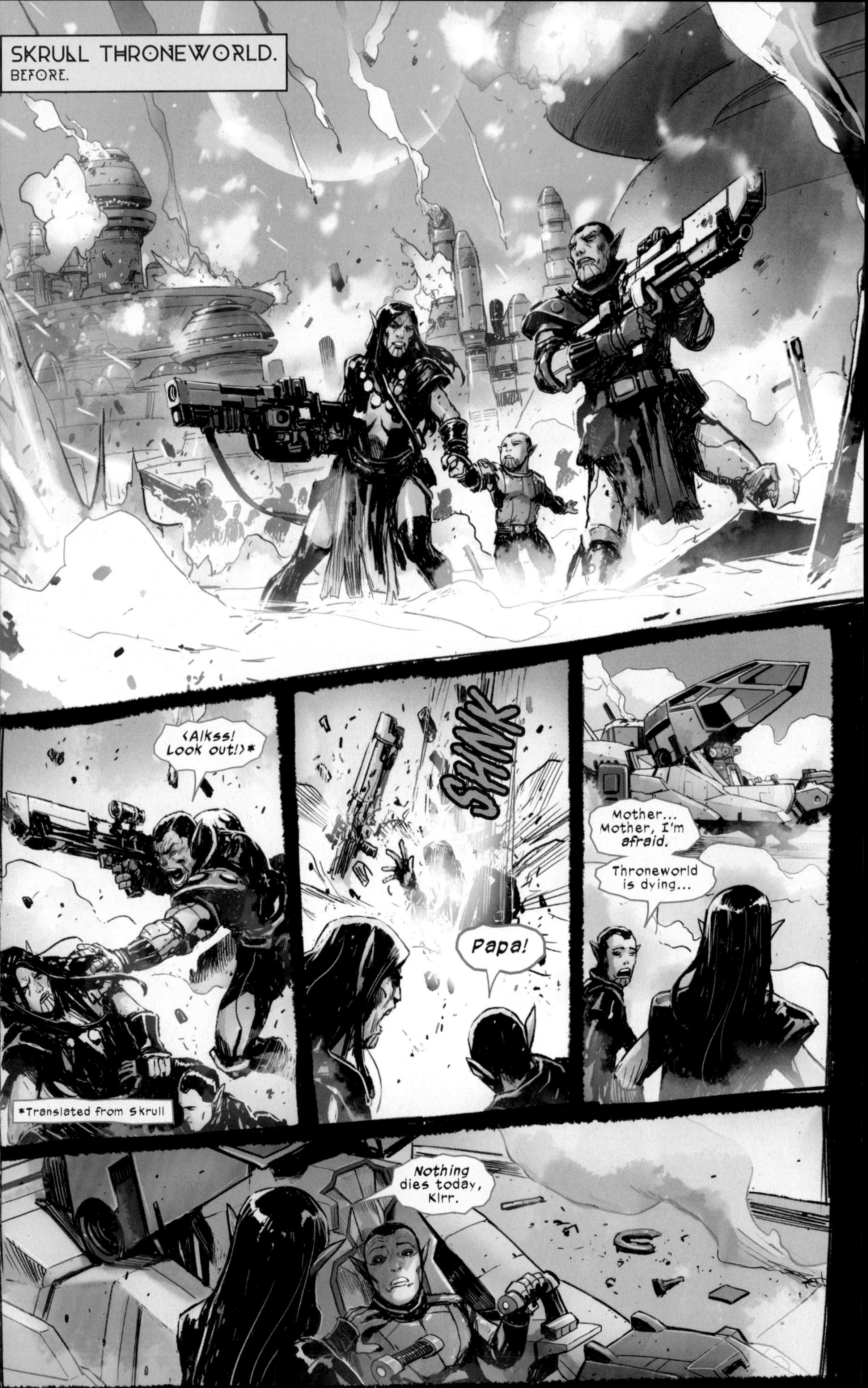
SKRULL THRONEWORLD.
BEFORE.
‹Alkss! Look out!›*
*Translated from Skrull
SHINK
Papa!
Mother... Mother, I'm afraid.
Throneworld is dying...
Nothing dies today, Klrr.

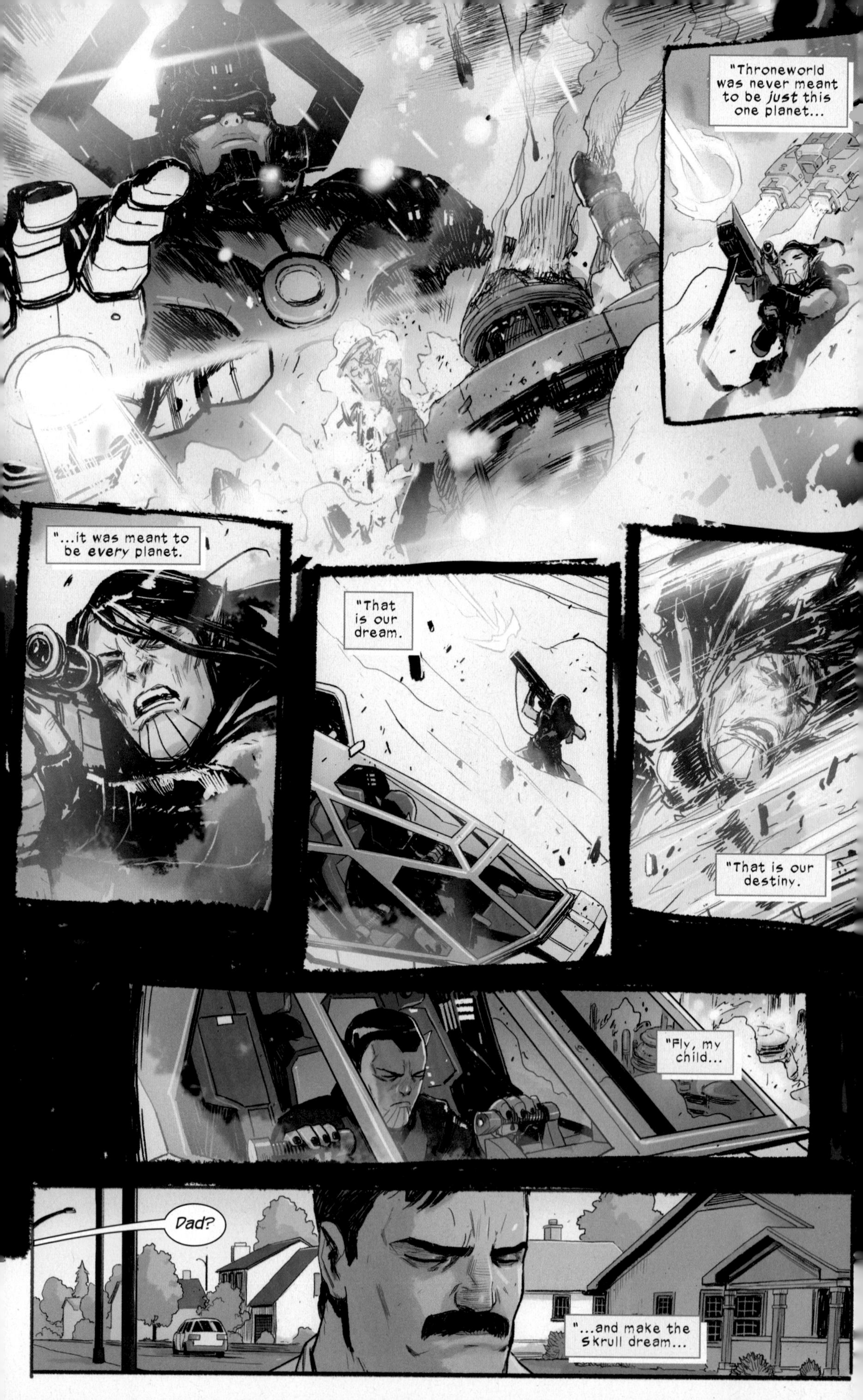
"Throneworld was never meant to be *just* this one planet...
"...it was meant to be *every* planet.
"That is our dream.
"That is our destiny.
"Fly, my child...
Dad?
"...and make the Skrull dream...

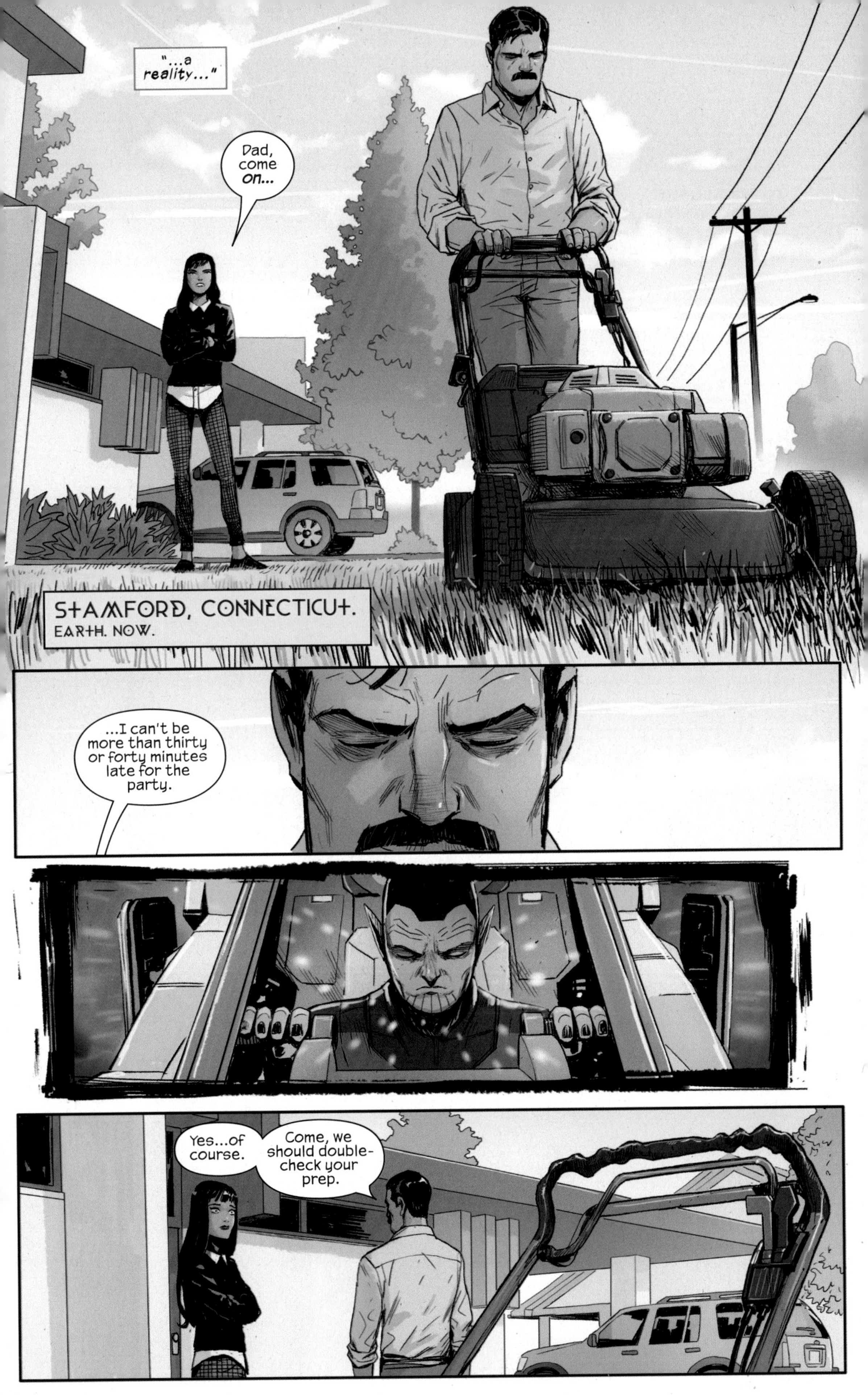
"...a reality..."
Dad, come on...
STAMFORD, CONNECTICUT.
EARTH. NOW.
...I can't be more than thirty or forty minutes late for the party.
Yes...of course.
Come, we should double-check your prep.

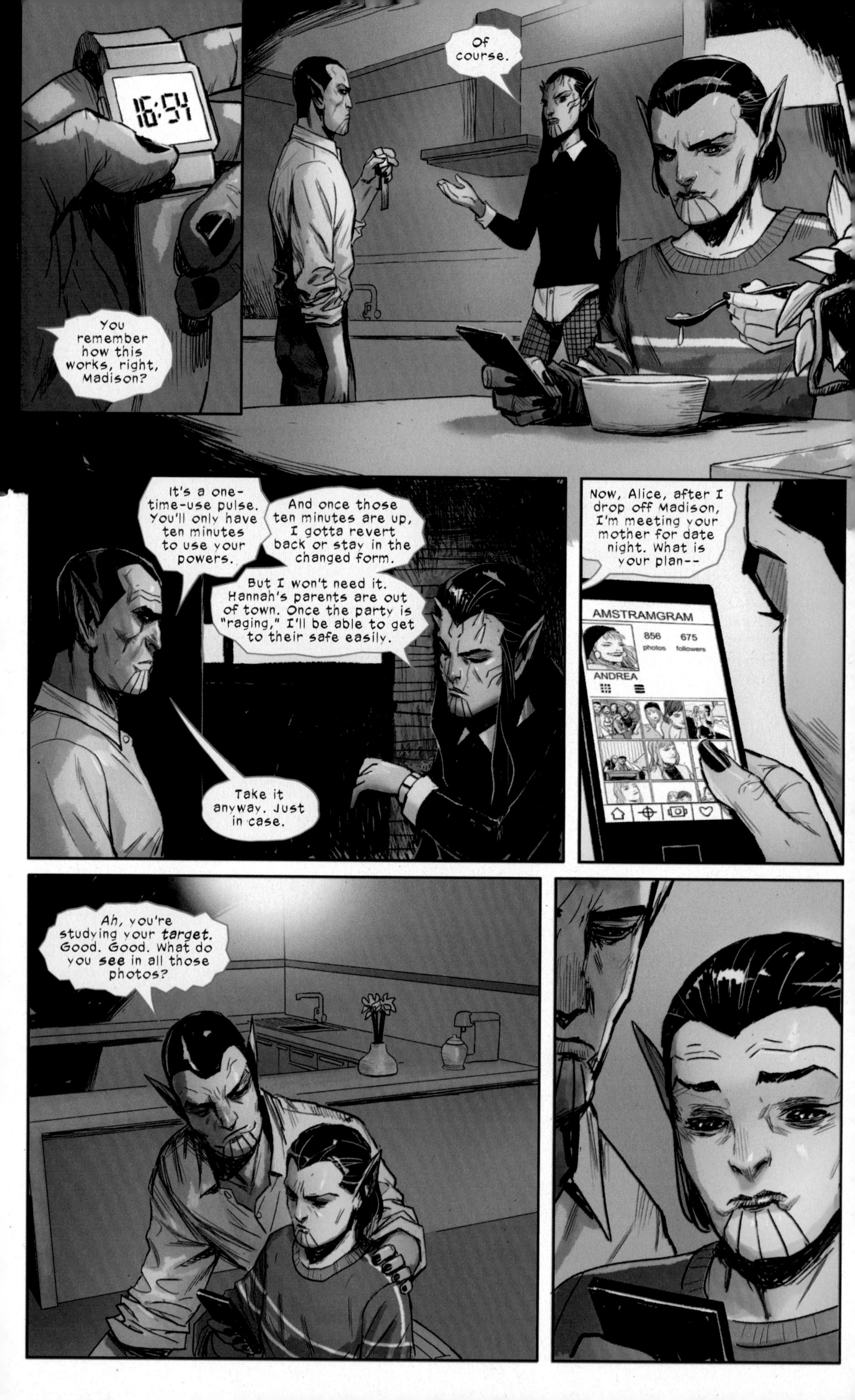

16:54
You remember how this works, right, Madison?
Of course.
It's a one-time-use pulse. You'll only have ten minutes to use your powers.
And once those ten minutes are up, I gotta revert back or stay in the changed form.
But I won't need it. Hannah's parents are out of town. Once the party is "raging," I'll be able to get to their safe easily.
Take it anyway. Just in case.
Now, Alice, after I drop off Madison, I'm meeting your mother for date night. What is your plan--
AMSTRAMGRAM
856 photos
675 followers
ANDREA
Ah, you're studying your *target*. Good. Good. What do you *see* in all those photos?

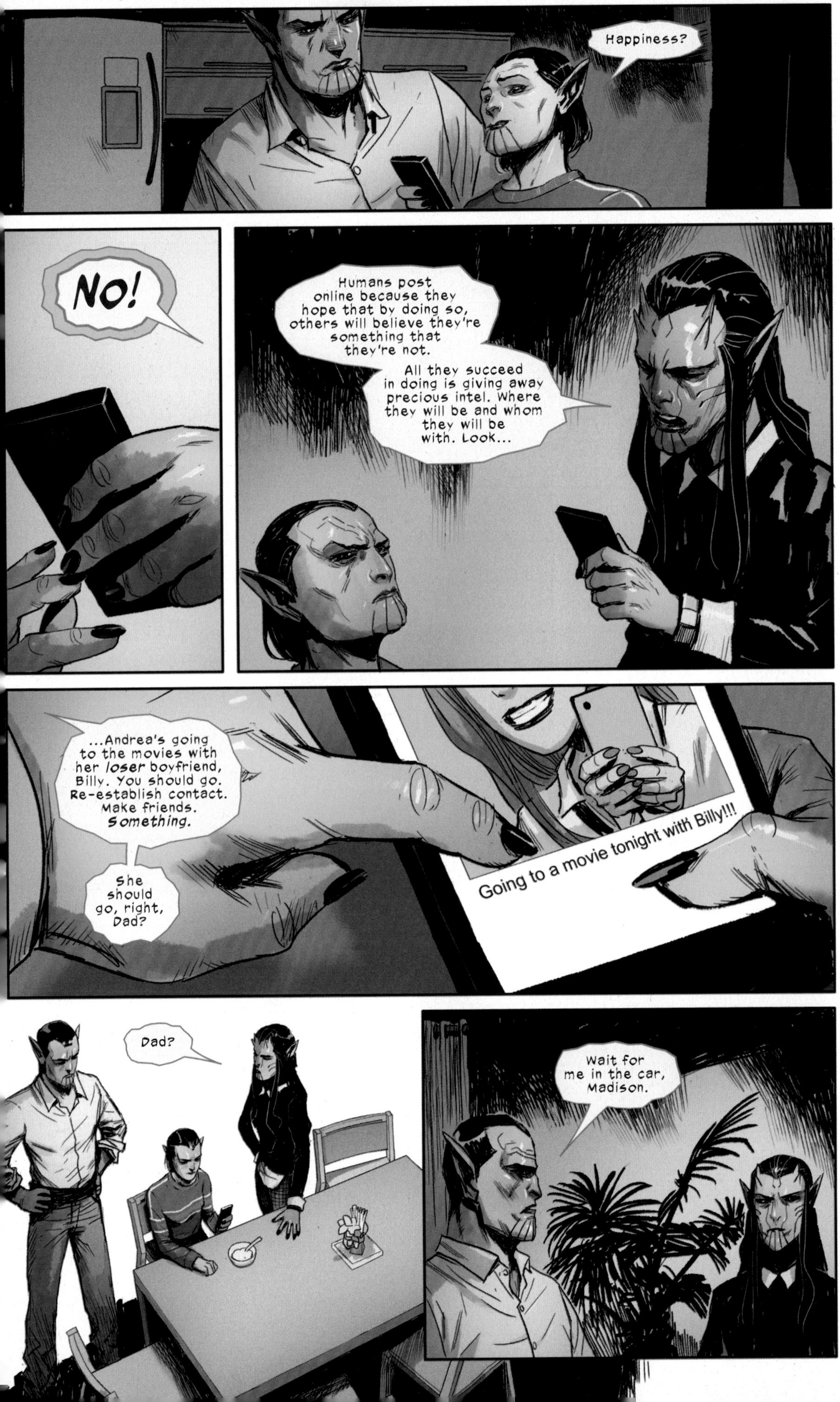
Happiness?
NO!
Humans post online because they hope that by doing so, others will believe they're something that they're not.
All they succeed in doing is giving away precious intel. Where they will be and whom they will be with. Look...
...Andrea's going to the movies with her *loser* boyfriend, Billy. You should go. Re-establish contact. Make friends. ***Something.***
She should go, right, Dad?
Going to a movie tonight with Billy!!!
Dad?
Wait for me in the car, Madison.

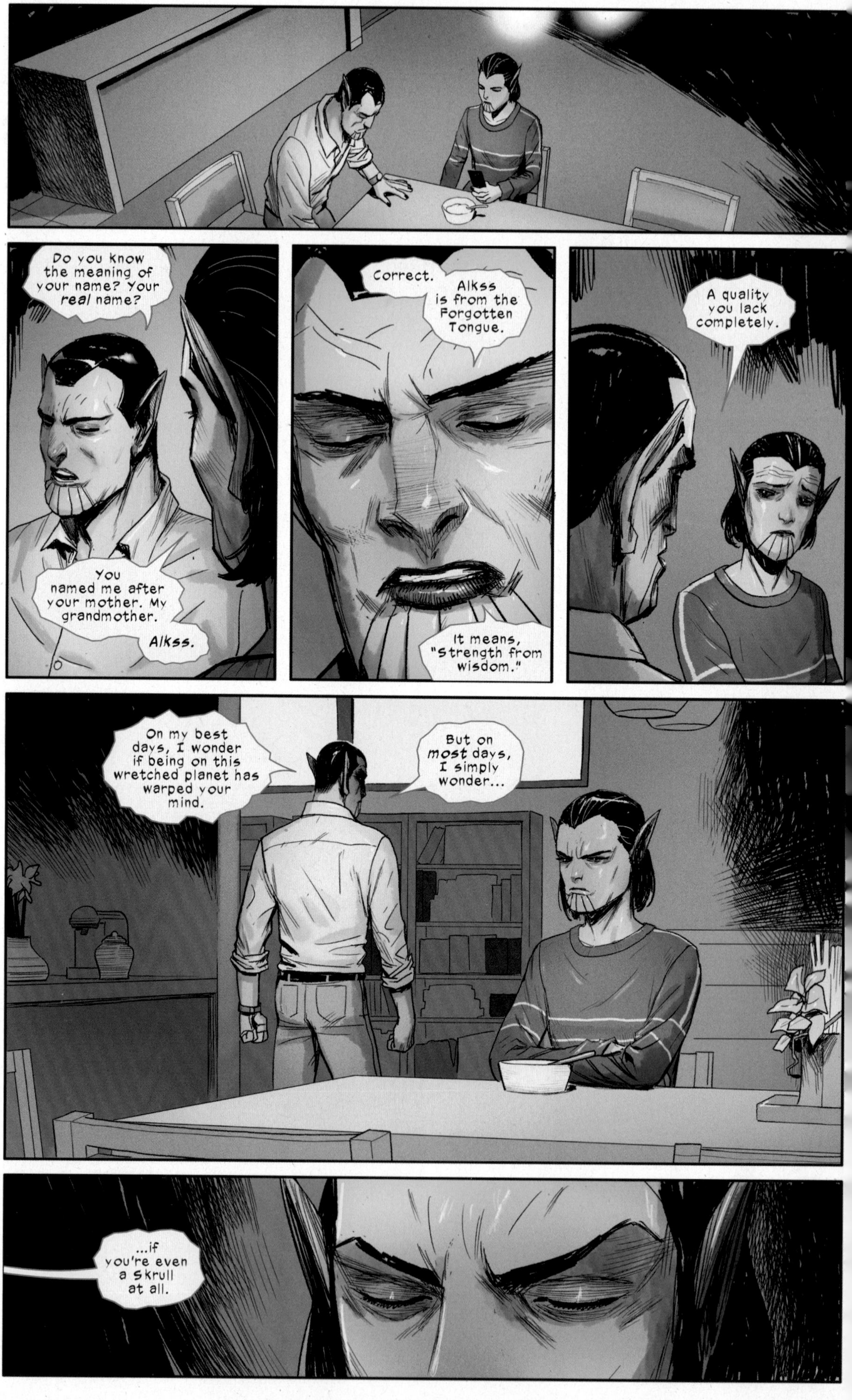
Do you know the meaning of your name? Your real name?
You named me after your mother. My grandmother.
Alkss.
Correct.
Alkss is from the Forgotten Tongue.
It means, "Strength from wisdom."
A quality you lack completely.
On my best days, I wonder if being on this wretched planet has warped your mind.
But on most days, I simply wonder...
...if you're even a Skrull at all.

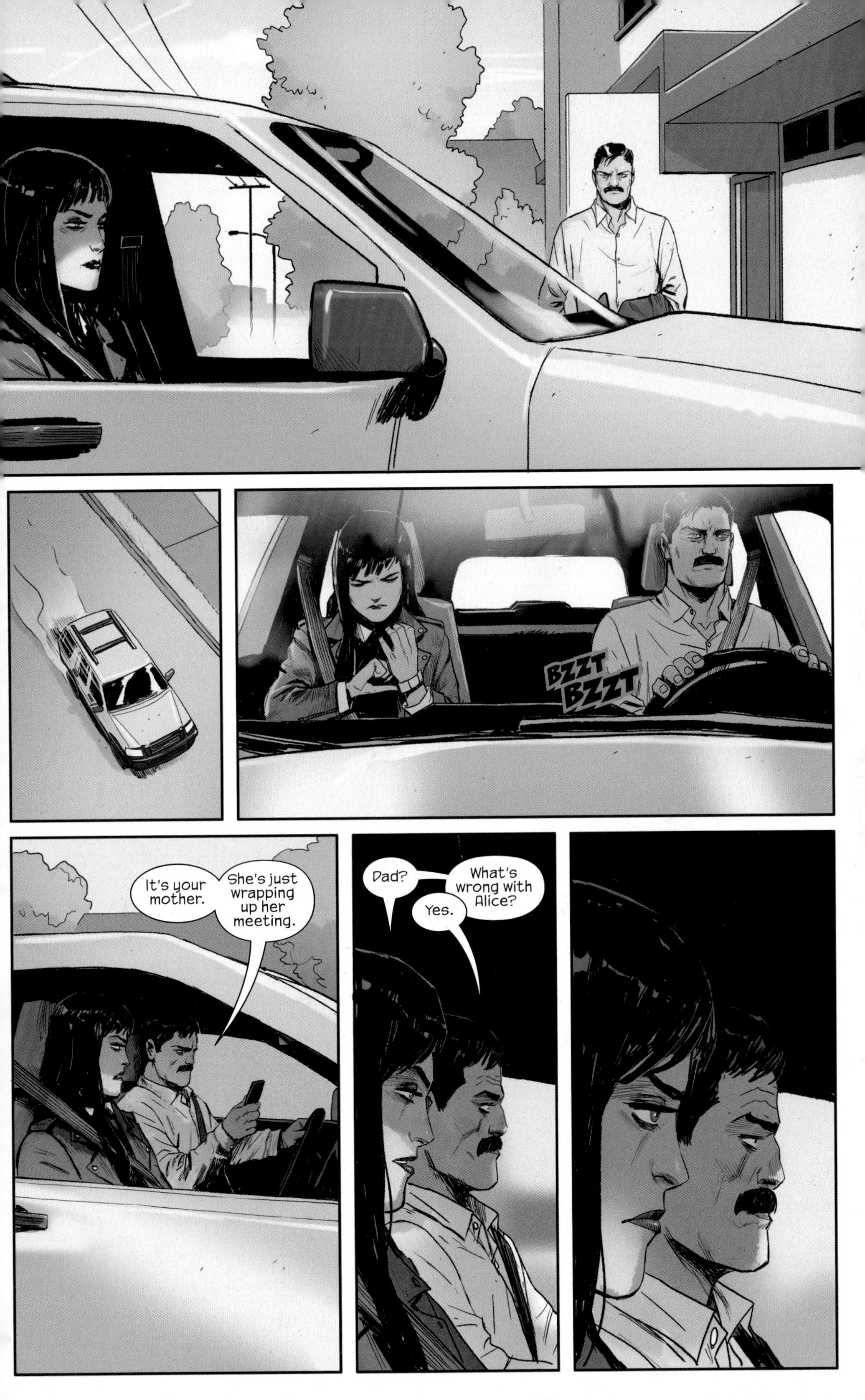
BZZT
BZZT
It's your mother.
She's just wrapping up her meeting.
Dad?
What's wrong with Alice?
Yes.

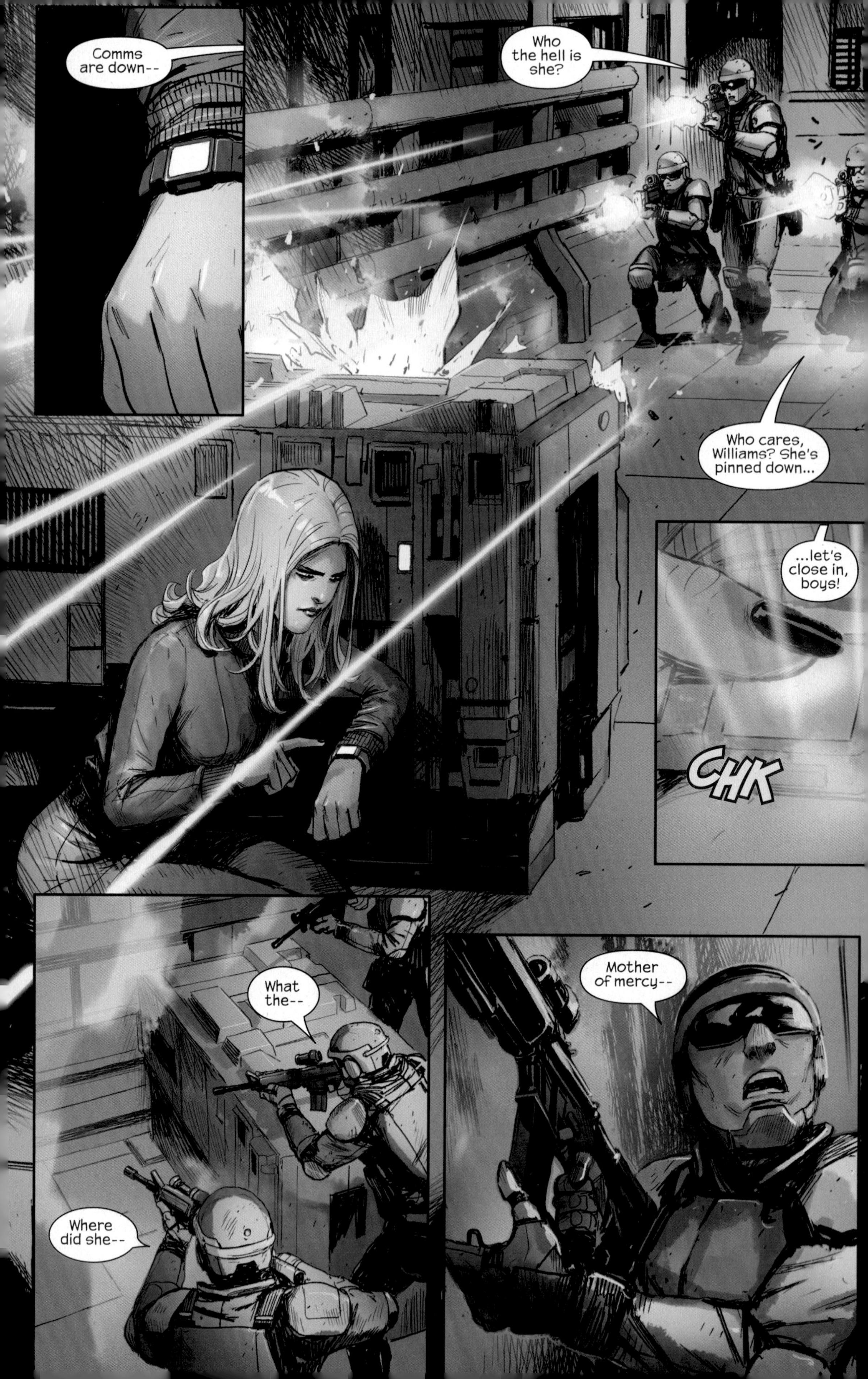
Comms are down--
Who the hell is she?
Who cares, Williams? She's pinned down...
...let's close in, boys!
CHK
What the--
Where did she--
Mother of mercy--

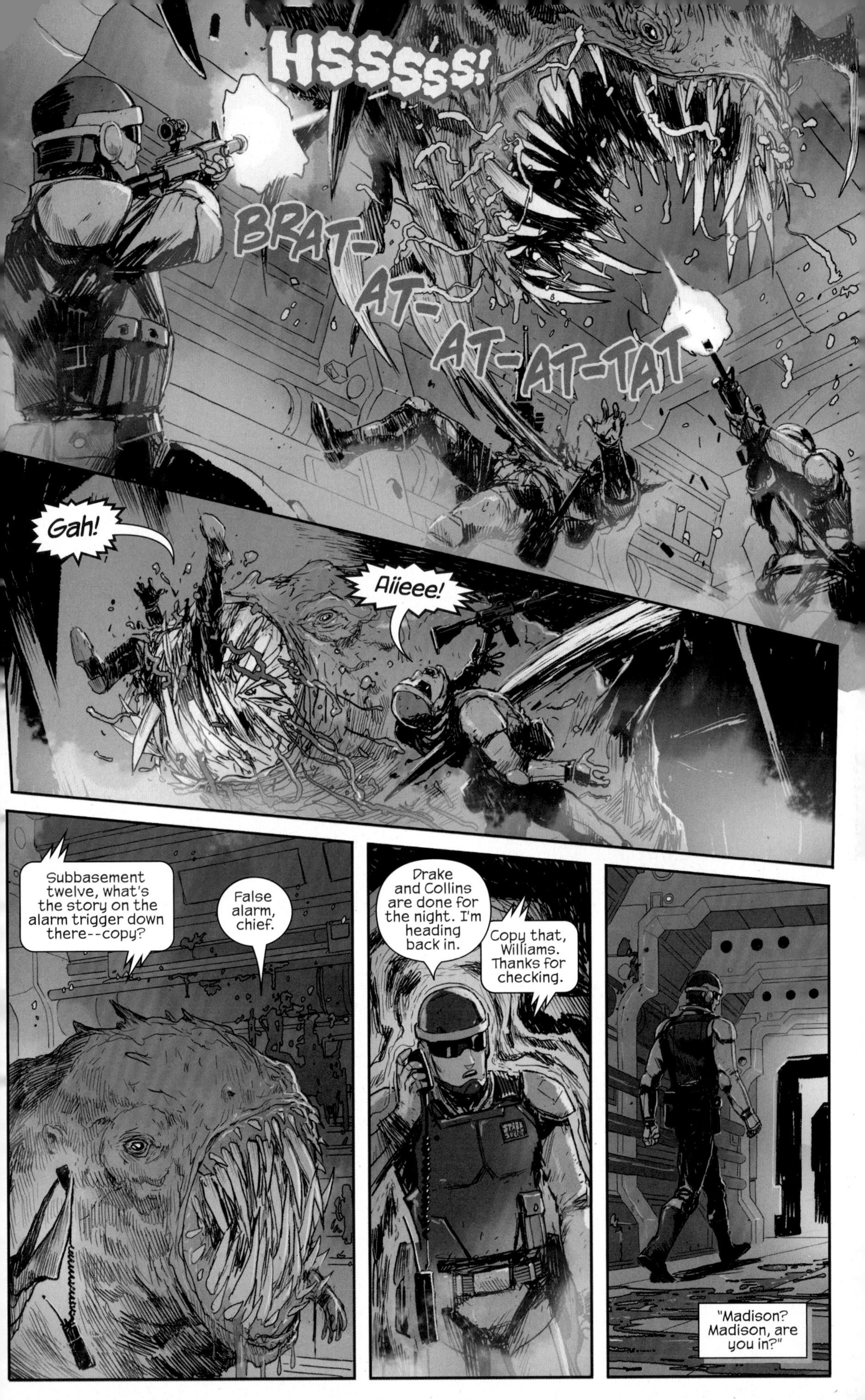
HSSSSSS!
BRAT-AT-AT-AT-TAT
Gah!
Aiieee!
Subbasement twelve, what's the story on the alarm trigger down there--copy?
False alarm, chief.
Drake and Collins are done for the night. I'm heading back in.
Copy that, Williams. Thanks for checking.
"Madison? Madison, are you in?"

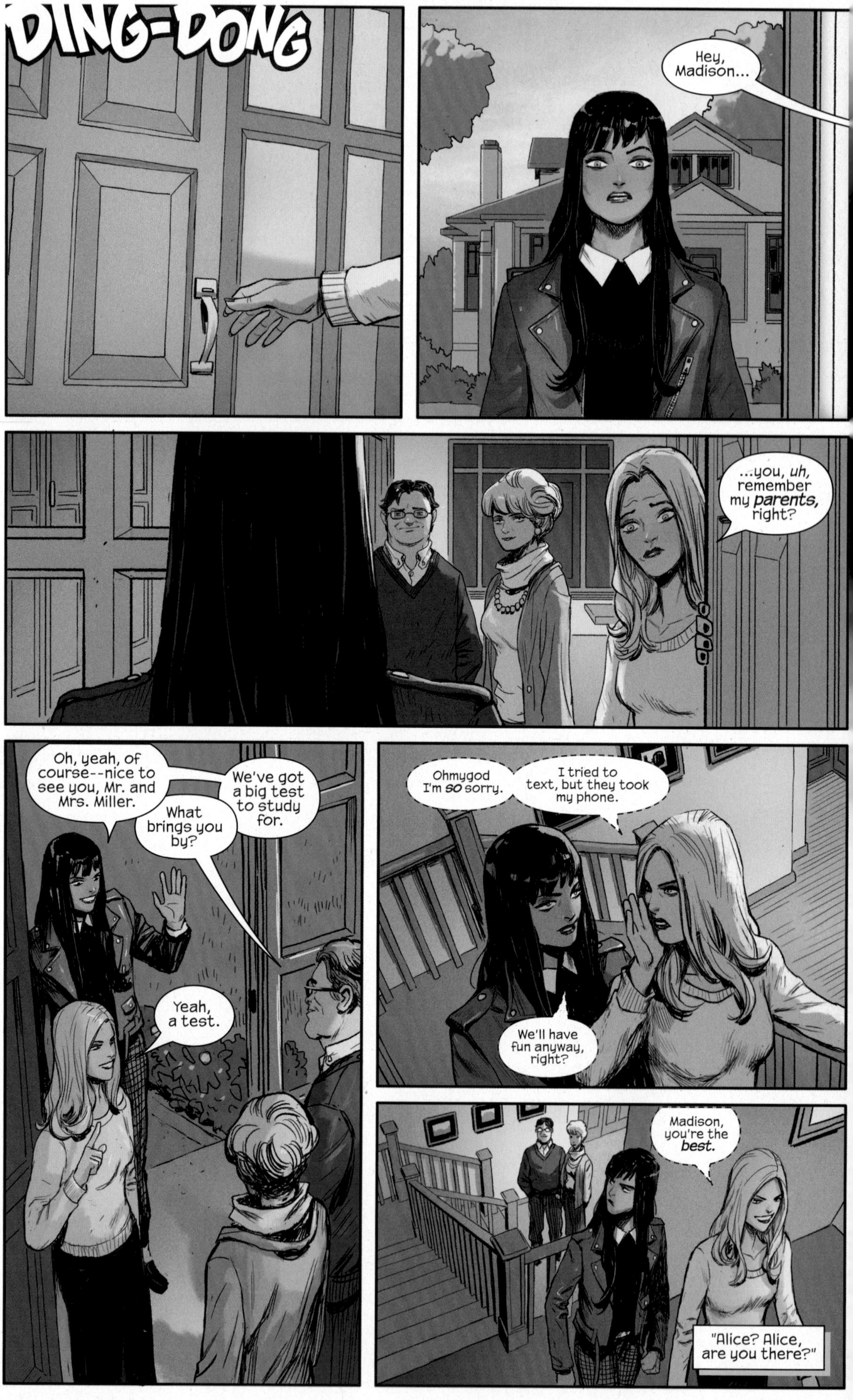
DING-DONG
Hey, Madison...
...you, *uh*, remember my *parents*, right?
Oh, yeah, of course--nice to see you, Mr. and Mrs. Miller.
What brings you by?
We've got a big test to study for.
Yeah, a test.
Ohmygod I'm *SO* sorry.
I tried to text, but they took my phone.
We'll have fun anyway, right?
Madison, you're the *best.*
"Alice? Alice, are you there?"

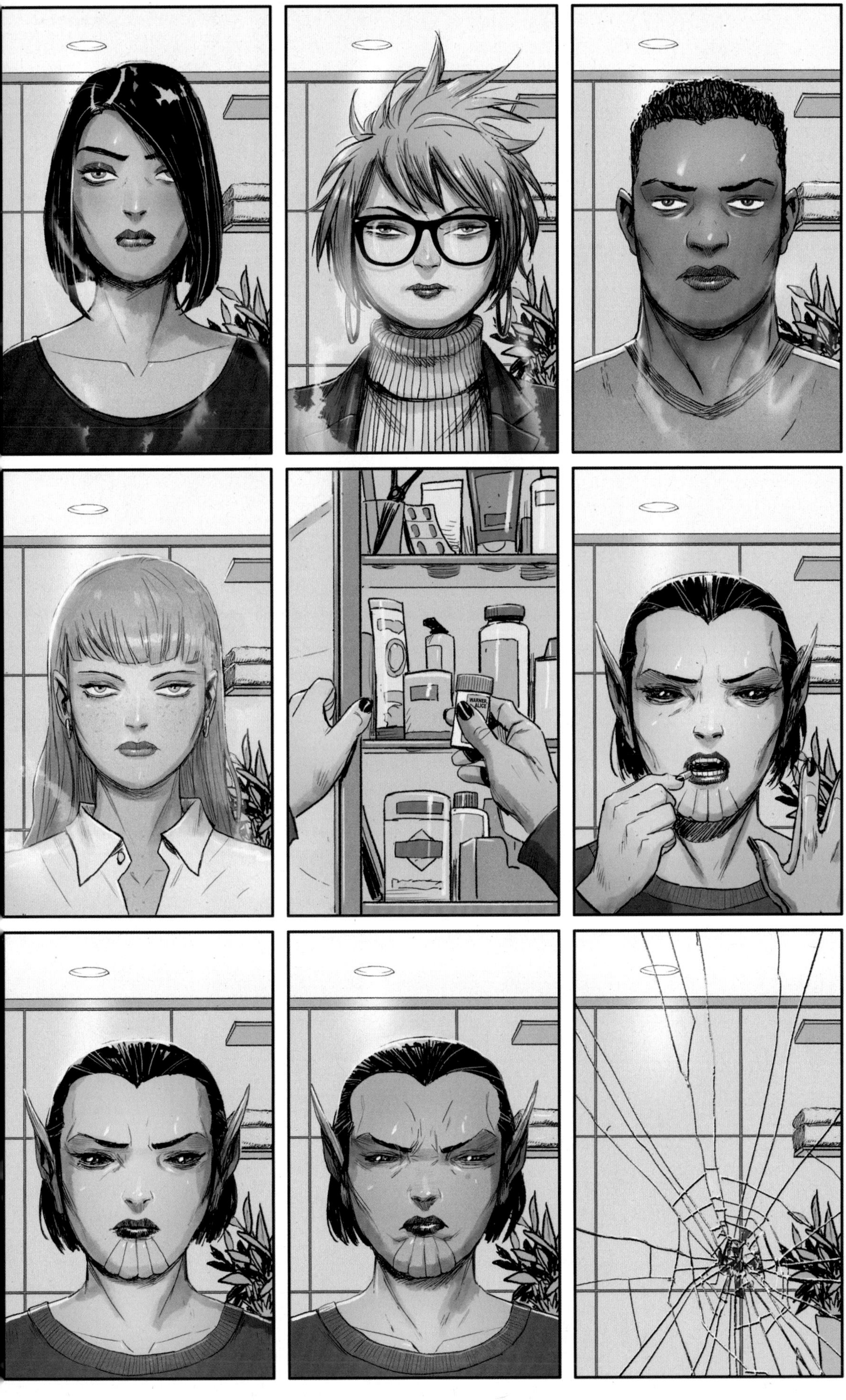
WARNER,
ALICE

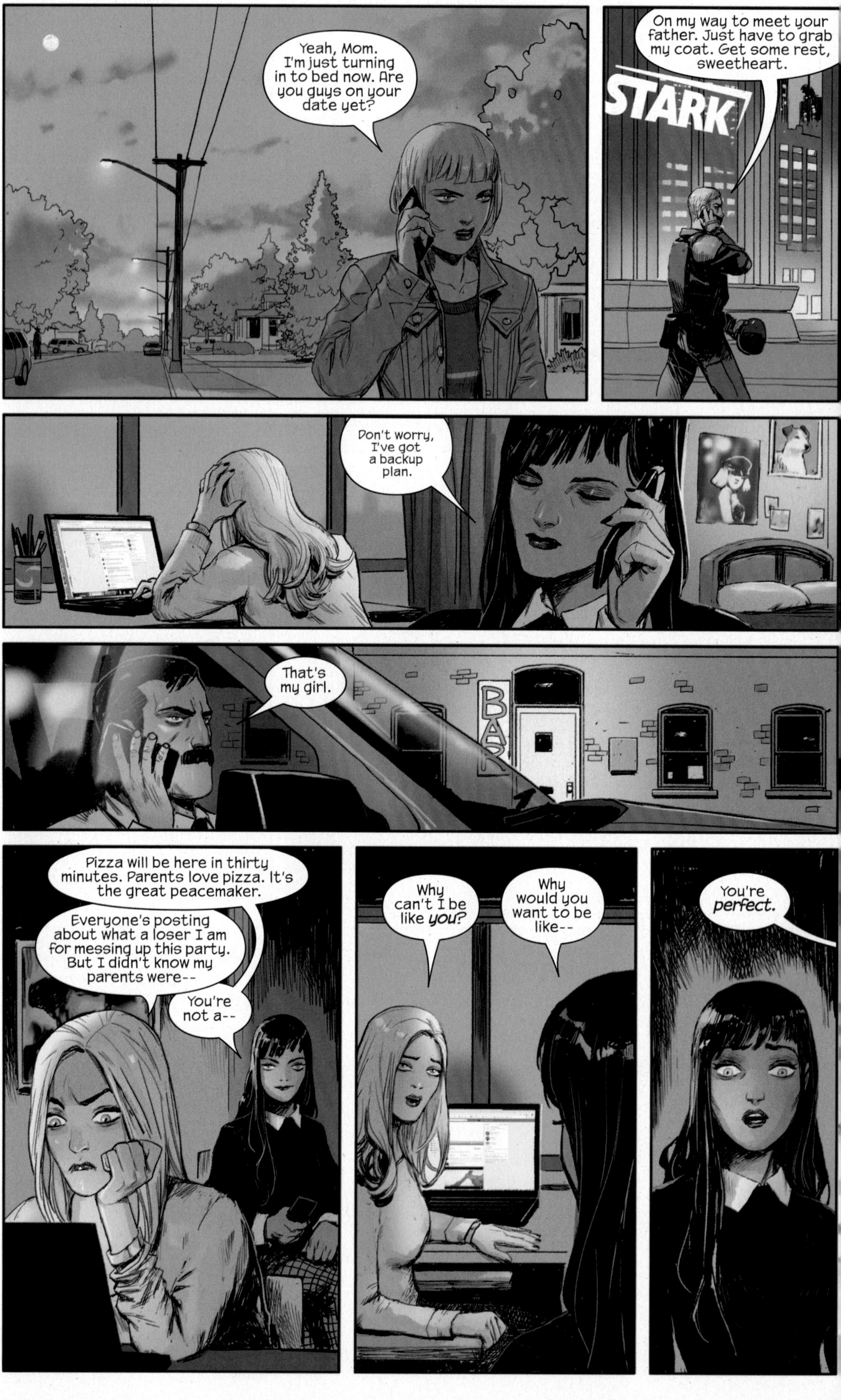
Yeah, Mom. I'm just turning in to bed now. Are you guys on your date yet?
On my way to meet your father. Just have to grab my coat. Get some rest, sweetheart.
STARK
Don't worry, I've got a backup plan.
That's my girl.
BAR
Pizza will be here in thirty minutes. Parents love pizza. It's the great peacemaker.
Everyone's posting about what a loser I am for messing up this party. But I didn't know my parents were--
You're not a--
Why can't I be like *you?*
Why would you want to be like--
You're *perfect.*

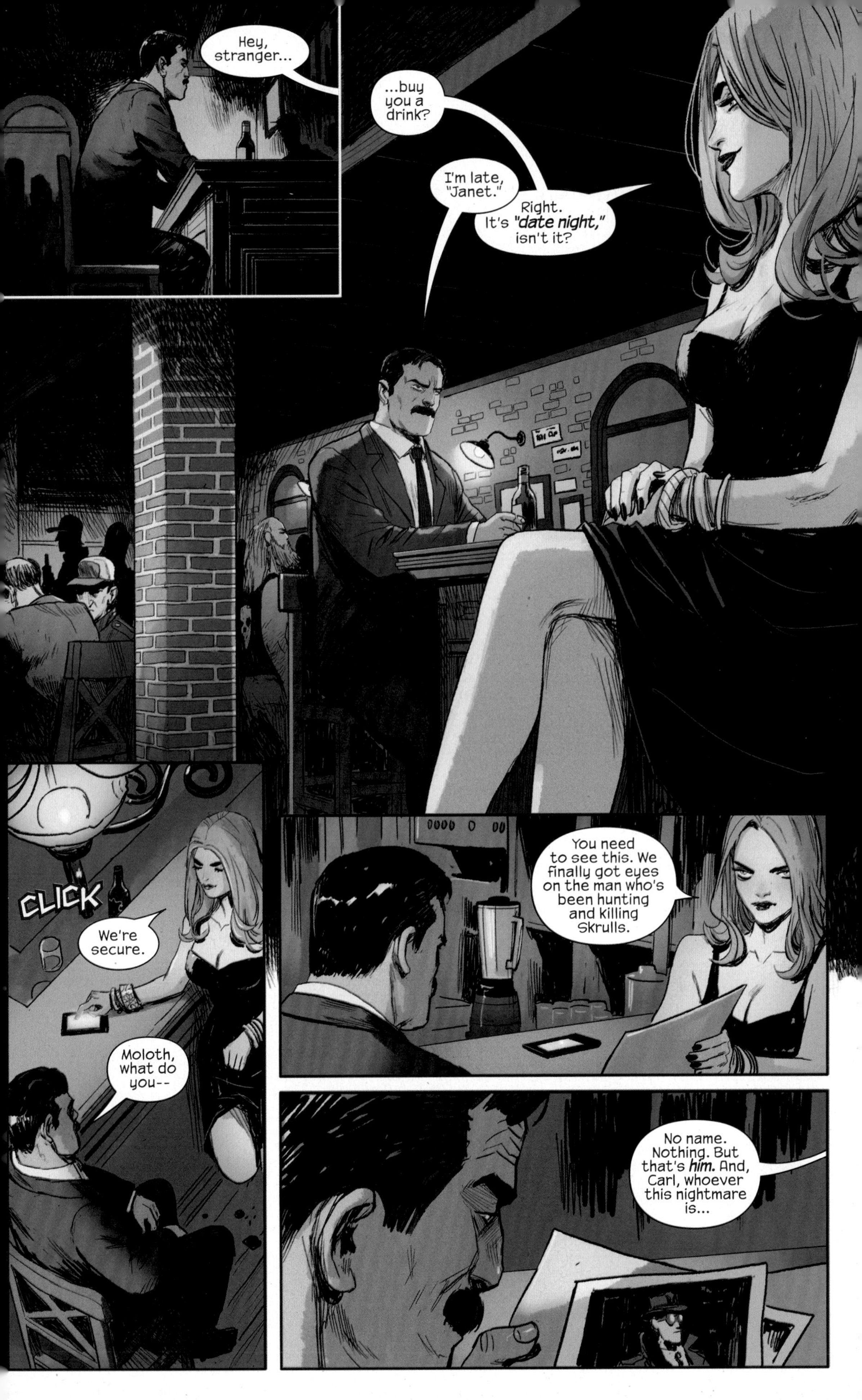
Hey, stranger...
...buy you a drink?
I'm late, "Janet."
Right. It's *"date night,"* isn't it?
CLICK
We're secure.
Moloth, what do you--
You need to see this. We finally got eyes on the man who's been hunting and killing Skrulls.
No name. Nothing. But that's *him.* And, Carl, whoever this nightmare is...

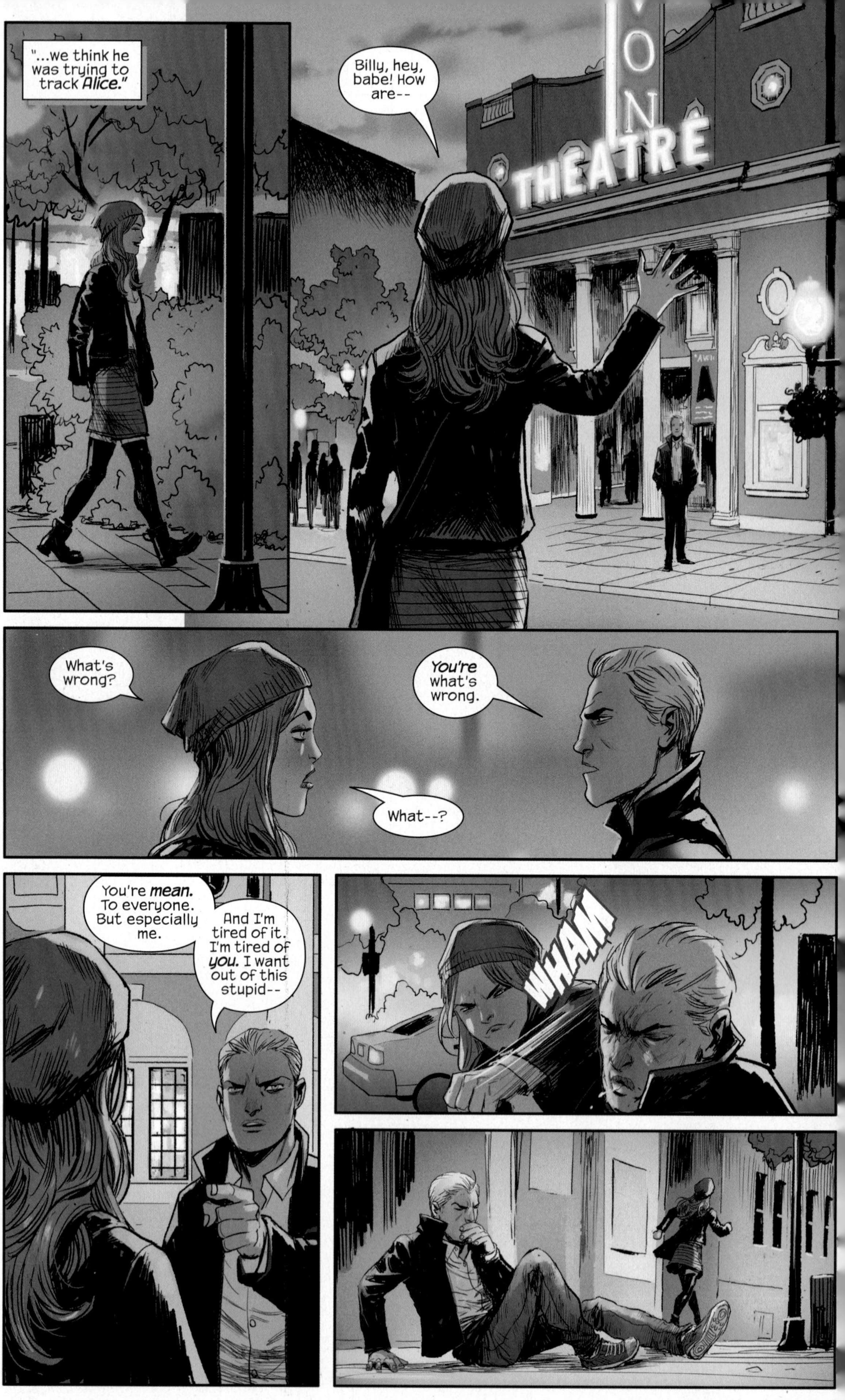
"...we think he was trying to track *Alice.*"
Billy, hey, babe! How are--
THEATRE
What's wrong?
You're what's wrong.
What--?
You're *mean.* To everyone. But especially me.
And I'm tired of it. I'm tired of *you.* I want out of this stupid--
WHAM

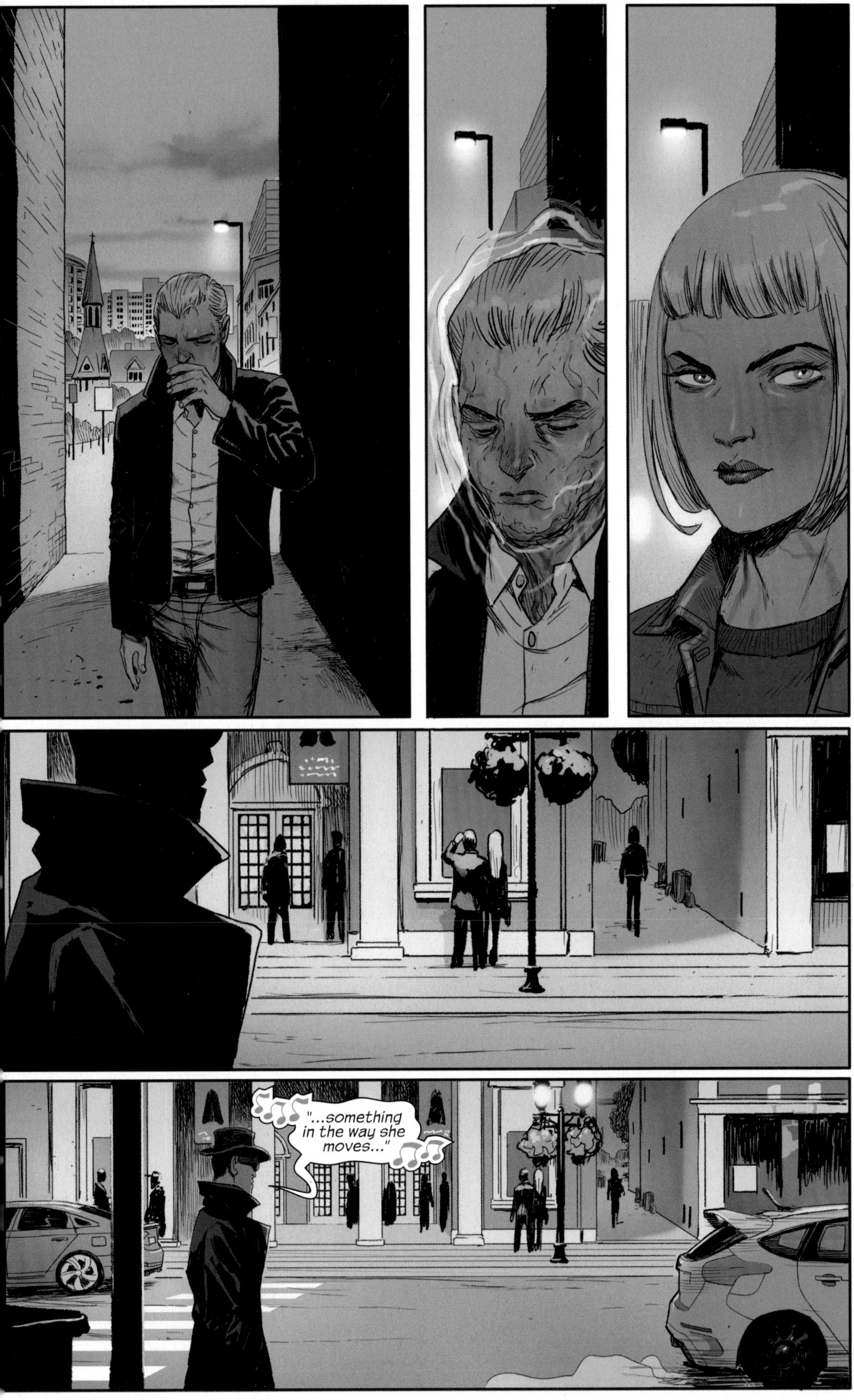
"...something in the way she moves..."

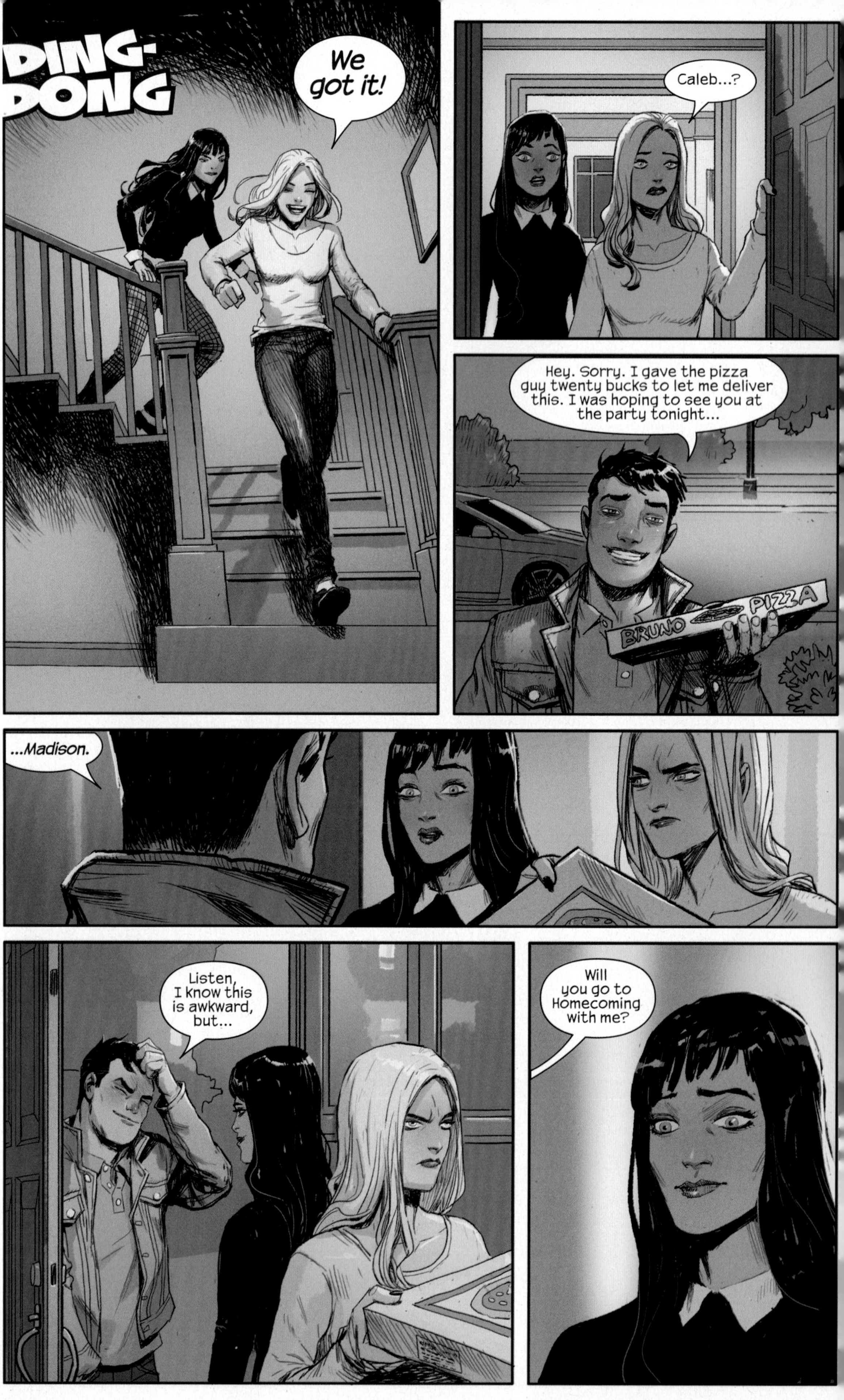
DING-DONG
We got it!
Caleb...?
Hey. Sorry. I gave the pizza guy twenty bucks to let me deliver this. I was hoping to see you at the party tonight...
BRUNO PIZZA
...Madison.
Listen, I know this is awkward, but...
Will you go to Homecoming with me?

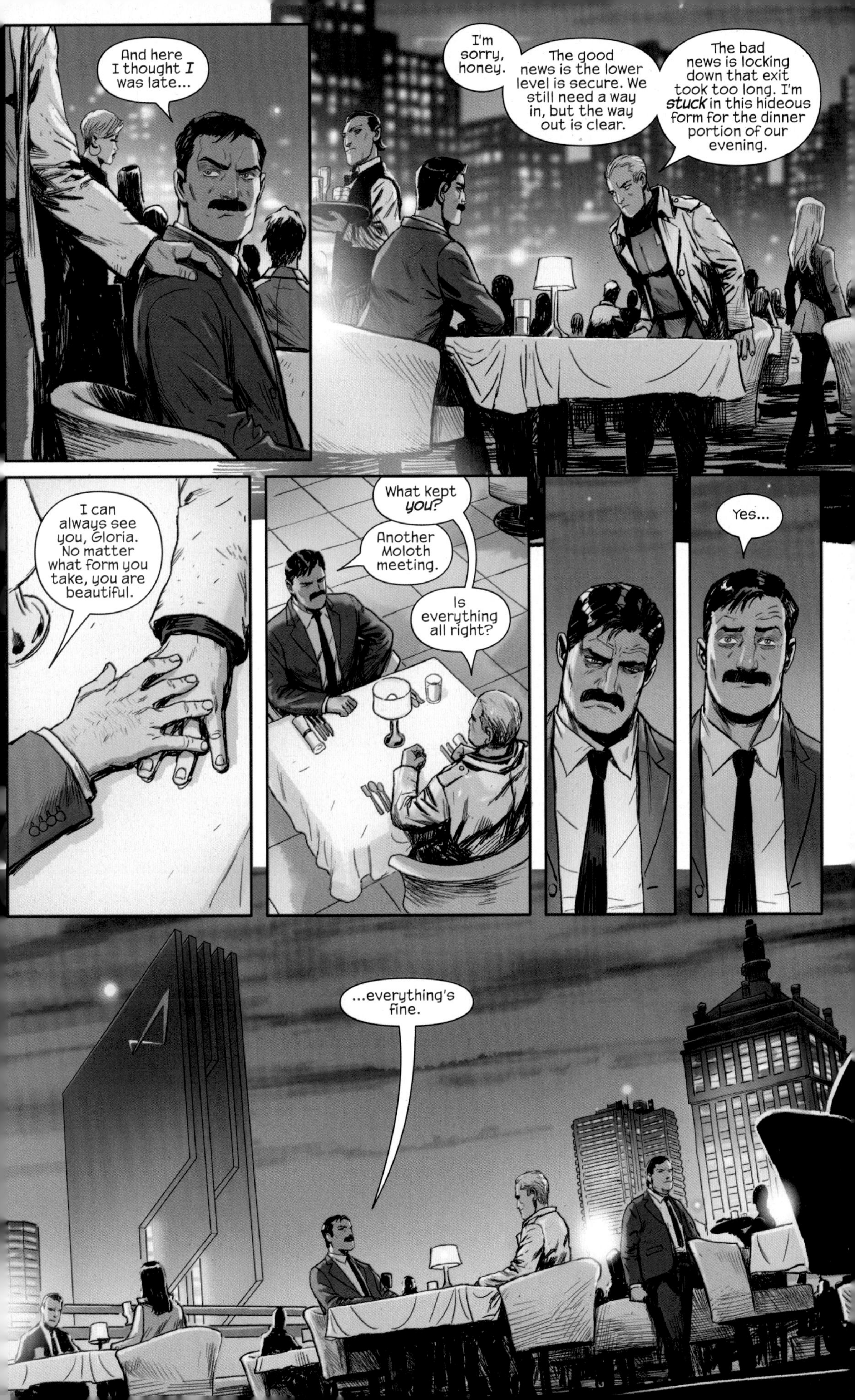
And here I thought *I* was late...
I'm sorry, honey.
The good news is the lower level is secure. We still need a way in, but the way out is clear.
The bad news is locking down that exit took too long. I'm *stuck* in this hideous form for the dinner portion of our evening.
I can always see you, Gloria. No matter what form you take, you are beautiful.
What kept *you*?
Another Moloth meeting.
Is everything all right?
Yes...
...everything's fine.

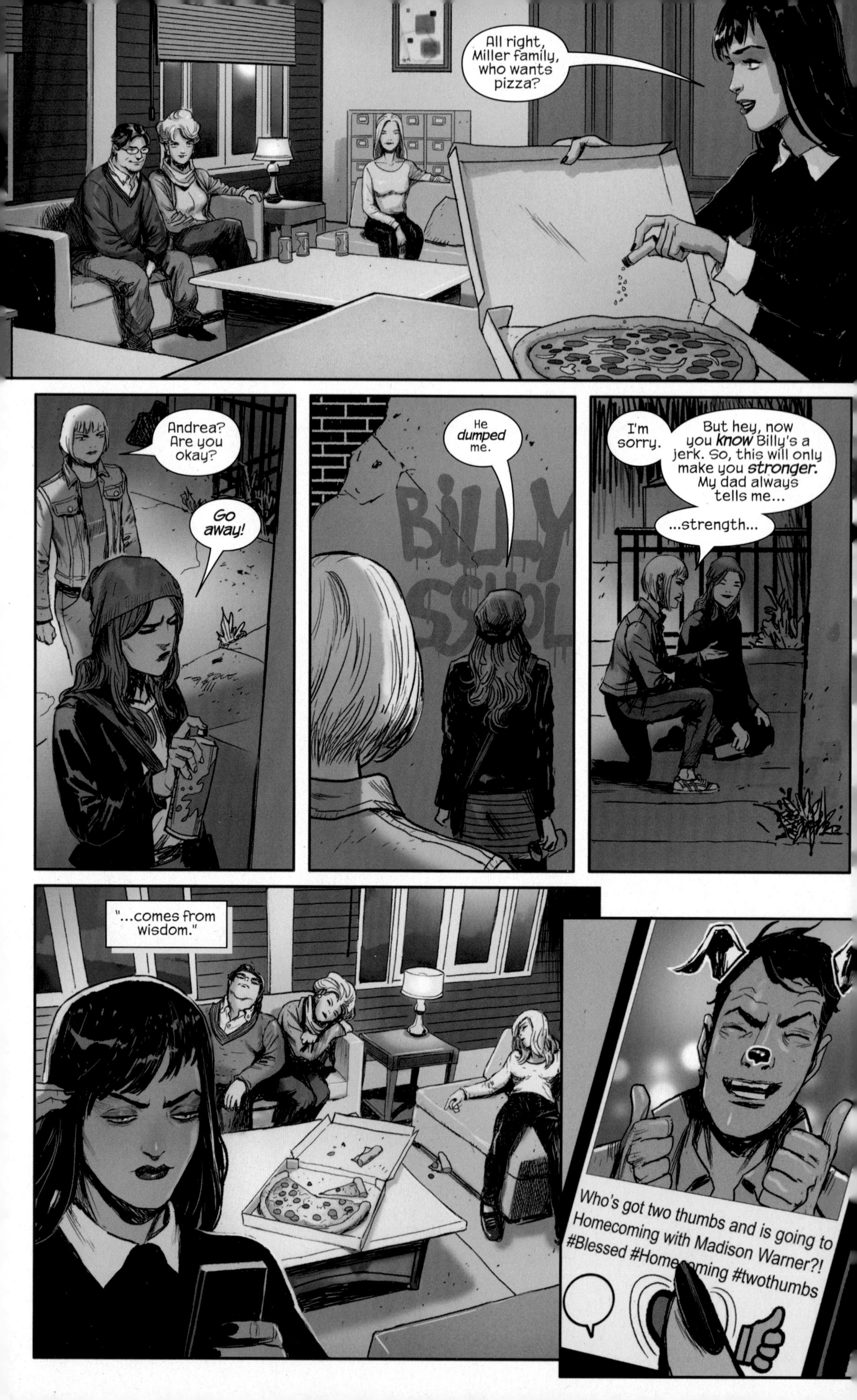
All right, Miller family, who wants pizza?
Andrea? Are you okay?
Go away!
He dumped me.
BILLY
SSHOL
I'm sorry.
But hey, now you know Billy's a jerk. So, this will only make you stronger. My dad always tells me...
...strength...
"...comes from wisdom."
Who's got two thumbs and is going to Homecoming with Madison Warner?! #Blessed #Homecoming #twothumbs

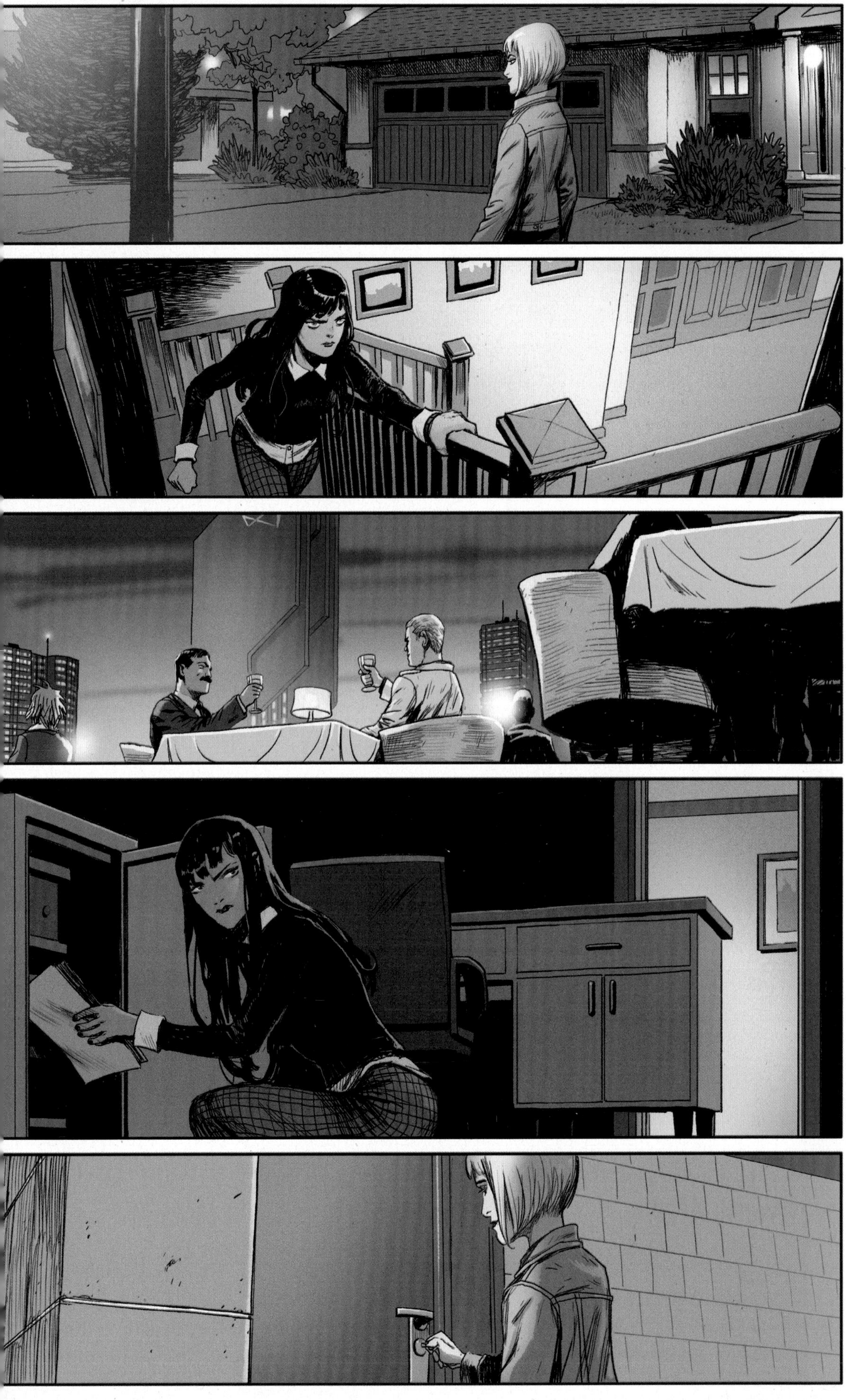

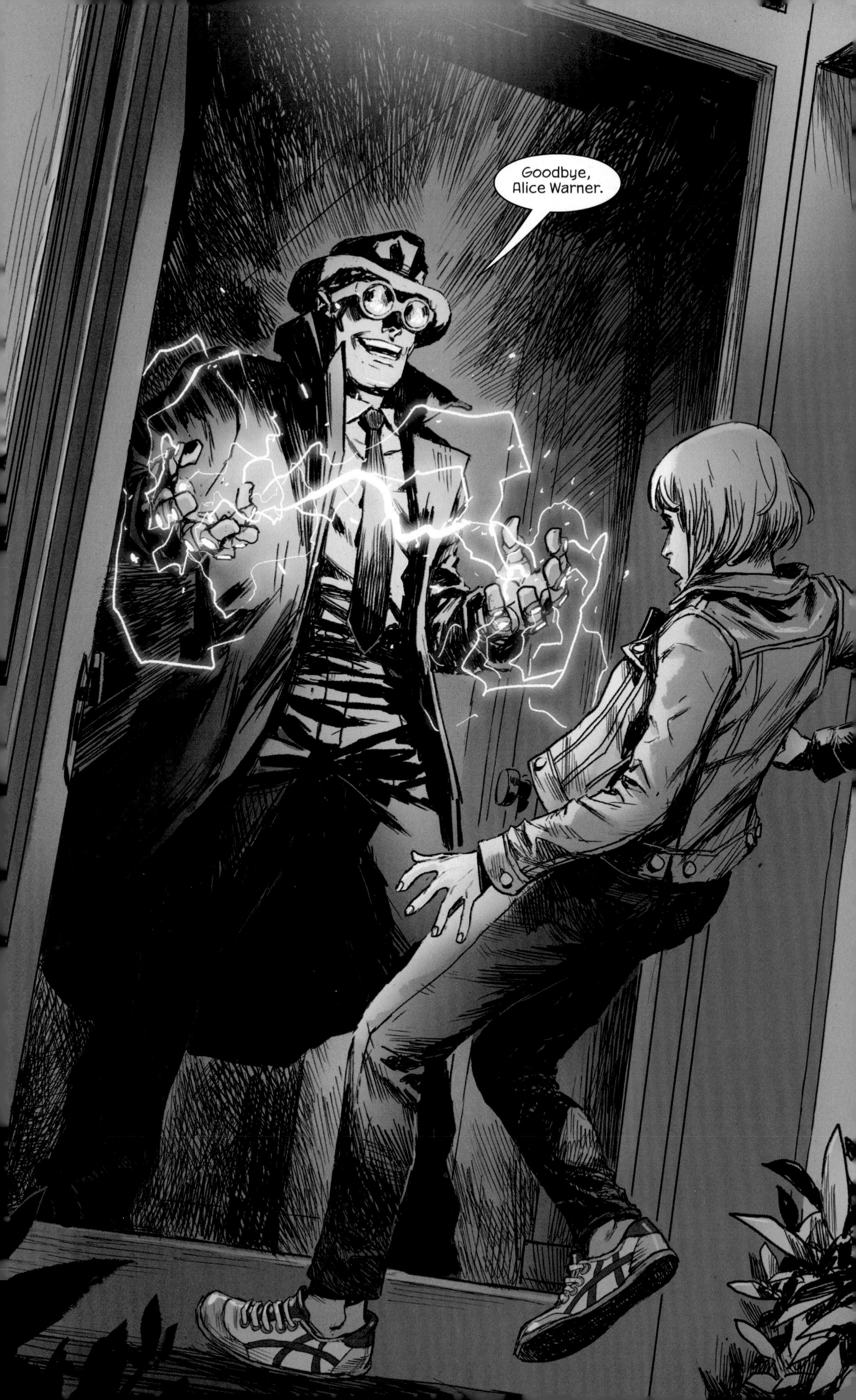
Goodbye, Alice Warner.

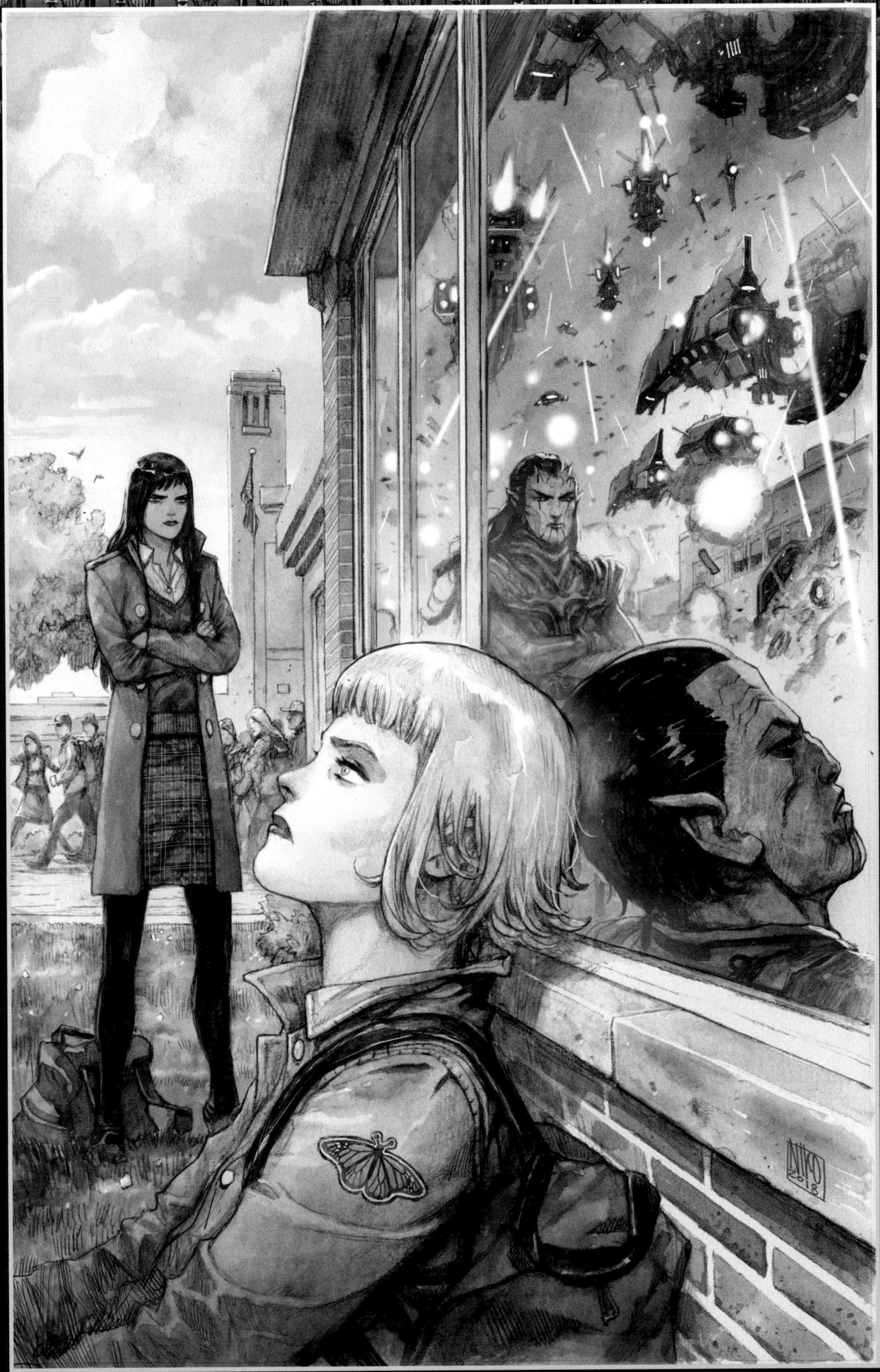

NIKO HENRICHON MEET THE SKRULLS #1 VARIANT

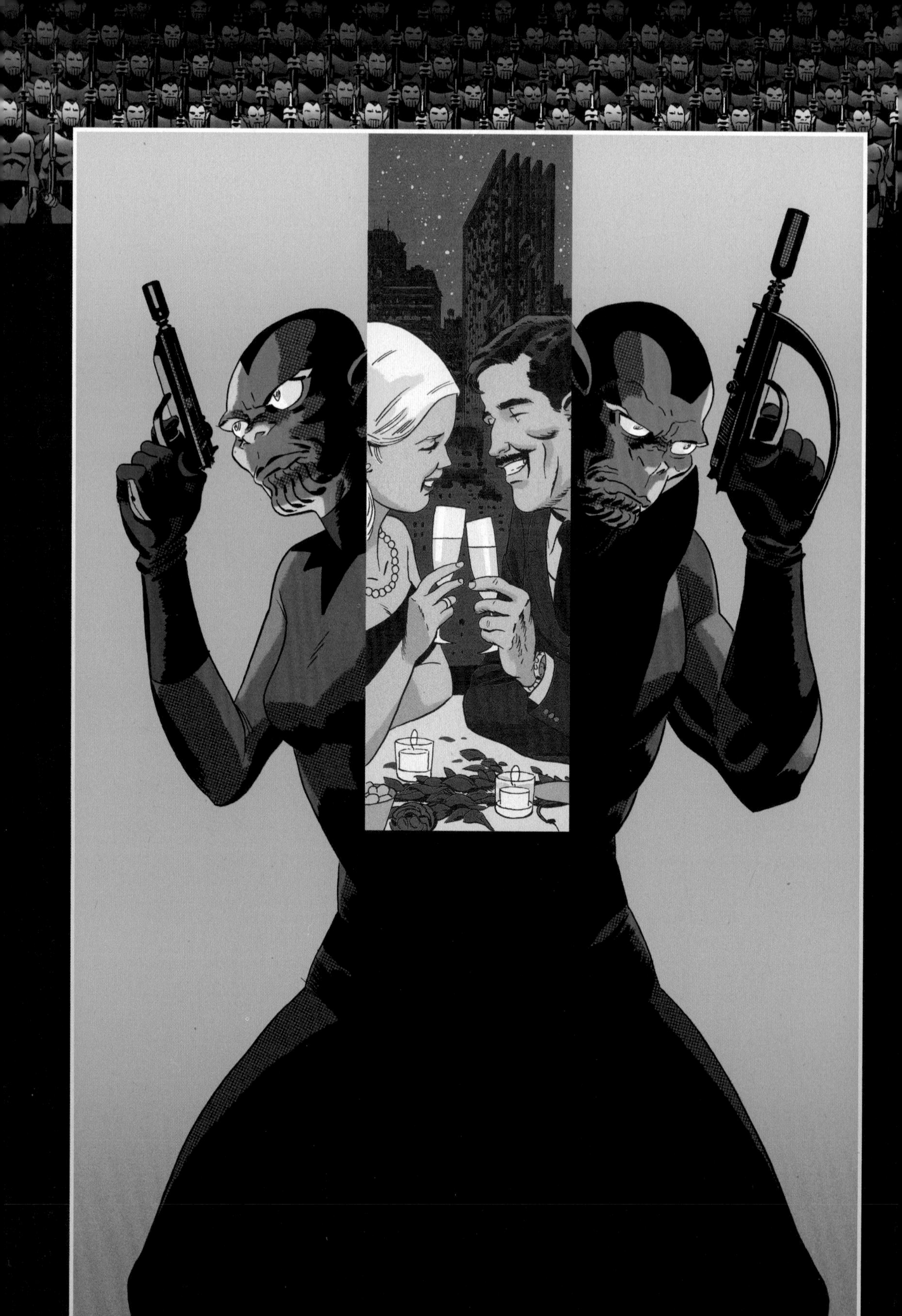

MEET THE SKRULLS #3

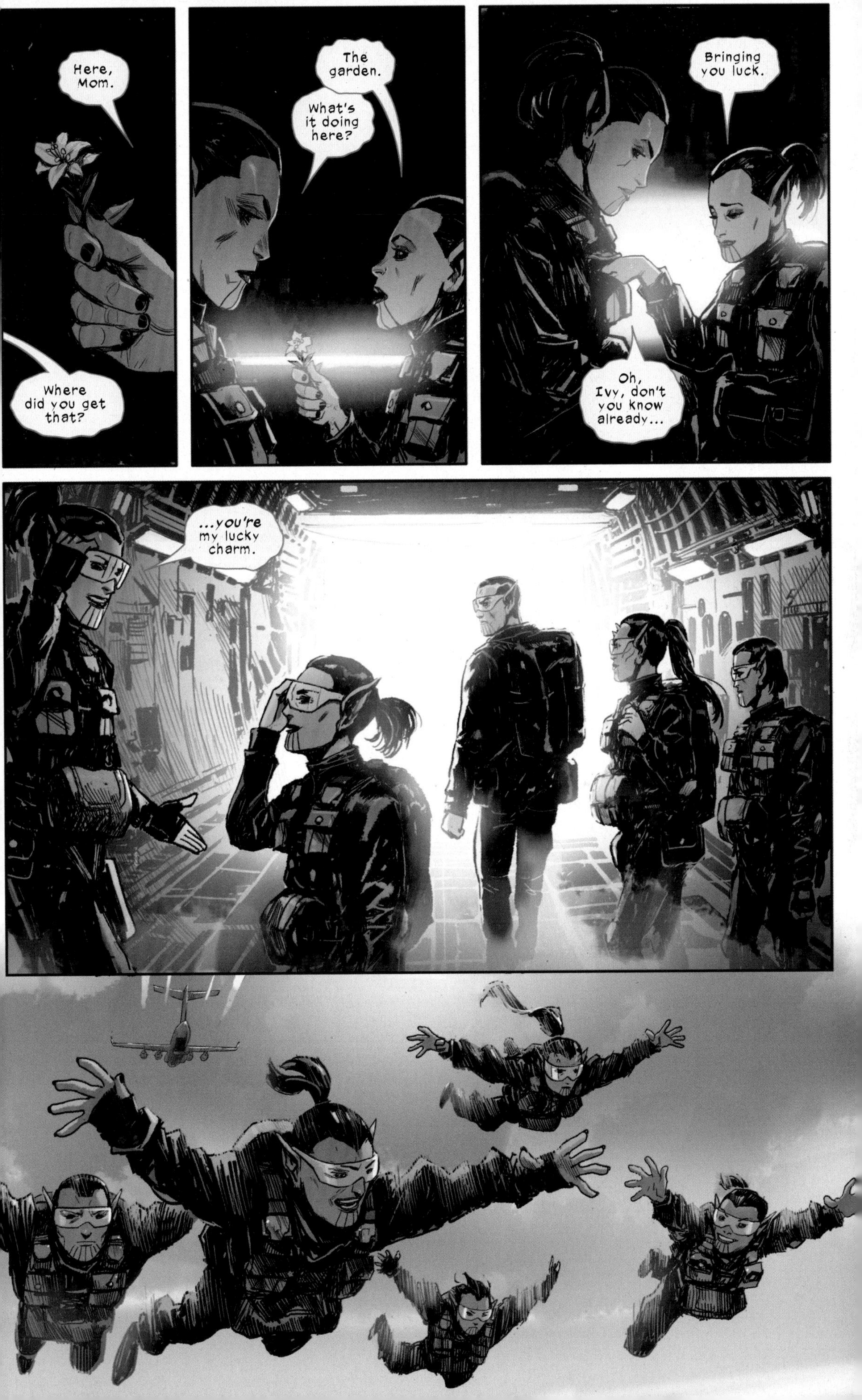
Here, Mom.
Where did you get that?
The garden.
What's it doing here?
Bringing you luck.
Oh, Ivy, don't you know already...
...you're my lucky charm.

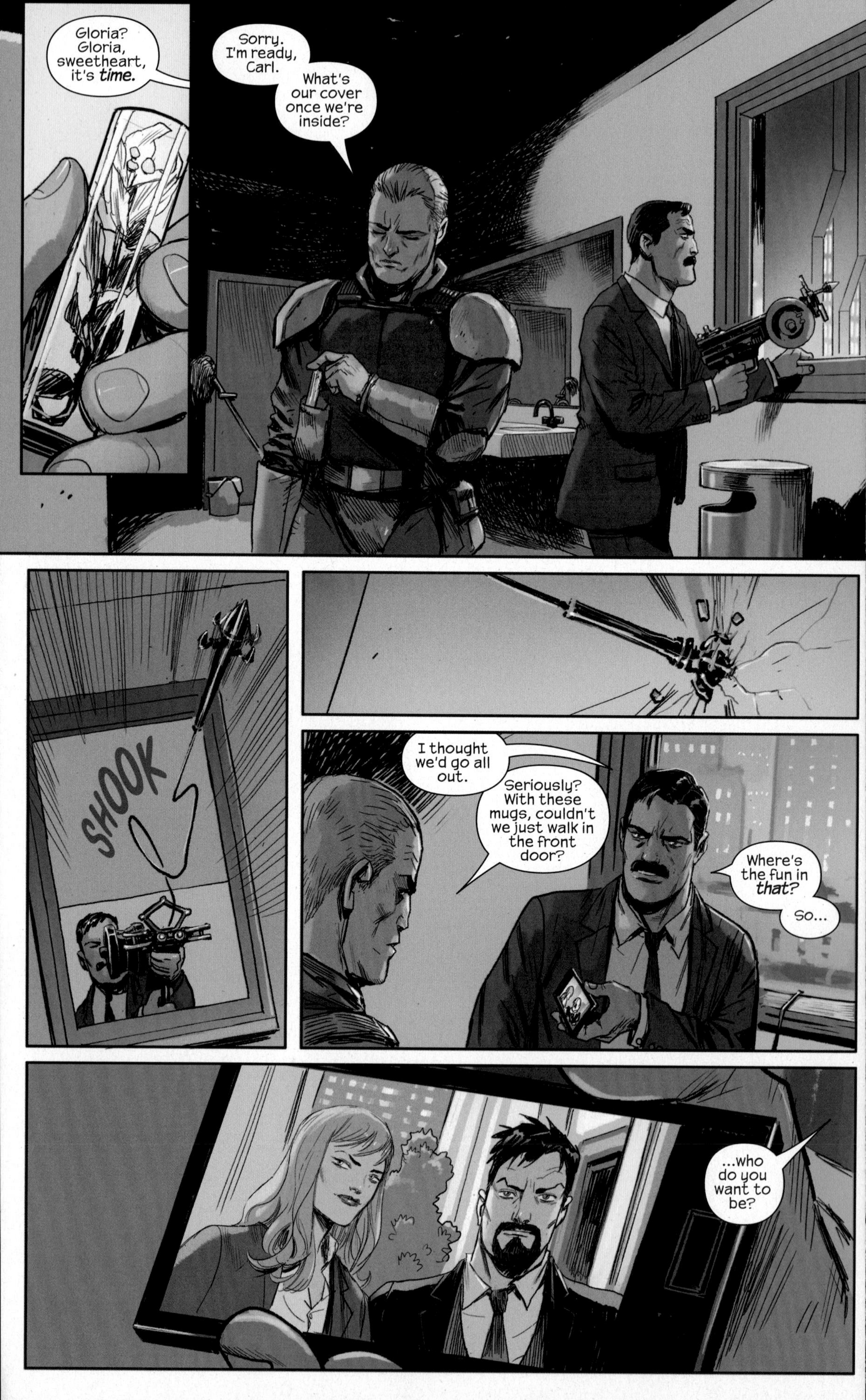

Gloria? Gloria, sweetheart, it's *time.*
Sorry. I'm ready, Carl.
What's our cover once we're inside?
SHOOK
I thought we'd go all out.
Seriously? With these mugs, couldn't we just walk in the front door?
Where's the fun in *that?*
So...
...who do you want to be?

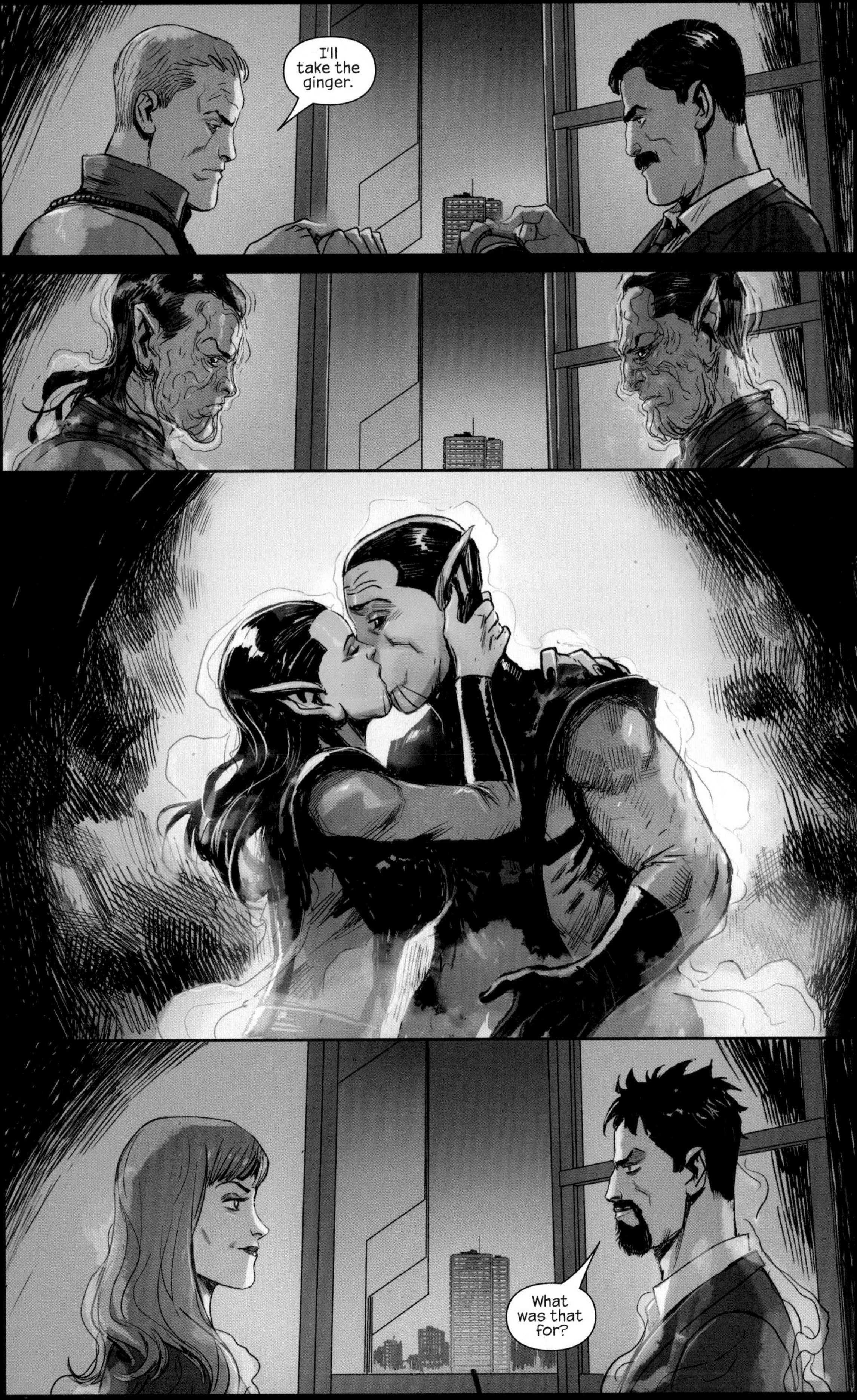
I'll take the ginger.
What was that for?

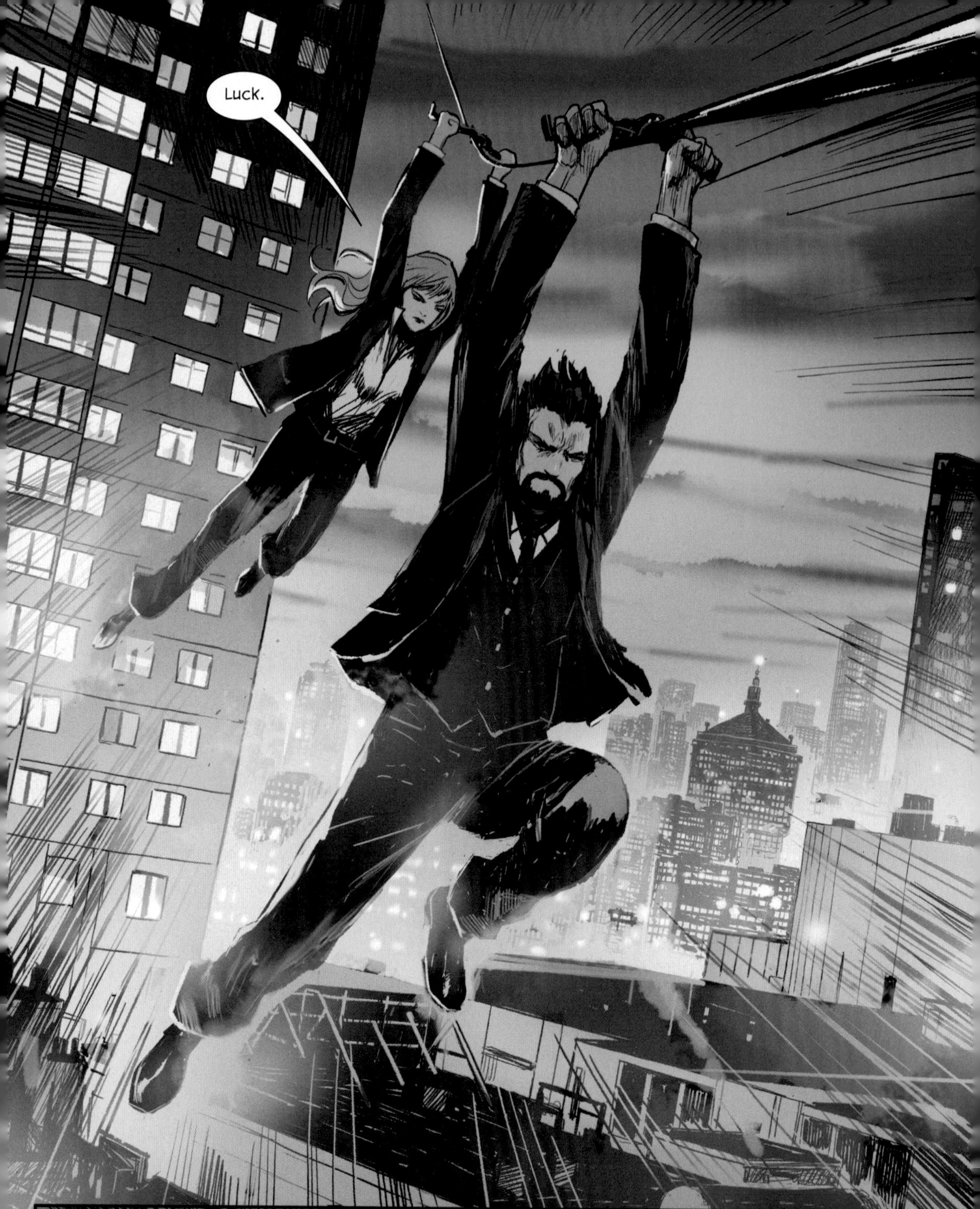
Luck.
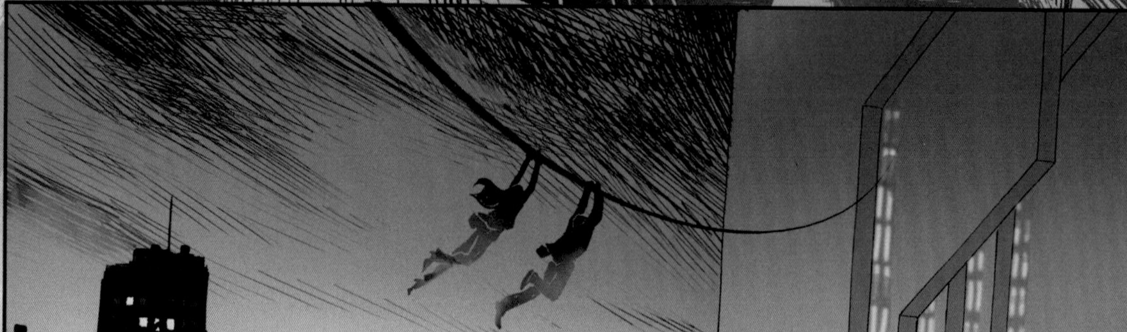

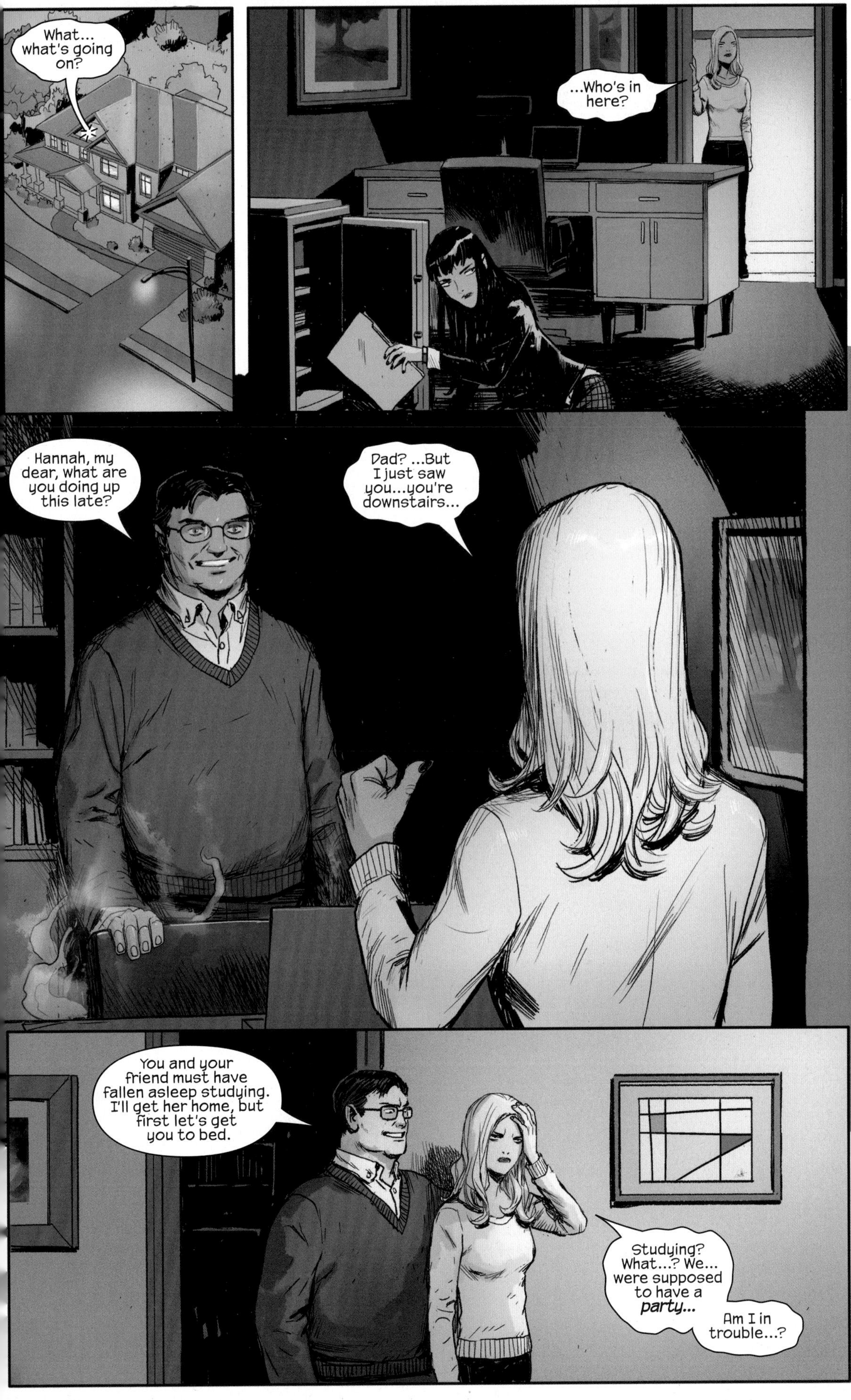
What... what's going on?
...Who's in here?
Hannah, my dear, what are you doing up this late?
Dad? ...But I just saw you...you're downstairs...
You and your friend must have fallen asleep studying. I'll get her home, but first let's get you to bed.
Studying? What...? We... were supposed to have a *party...*
Am I in trouble...?

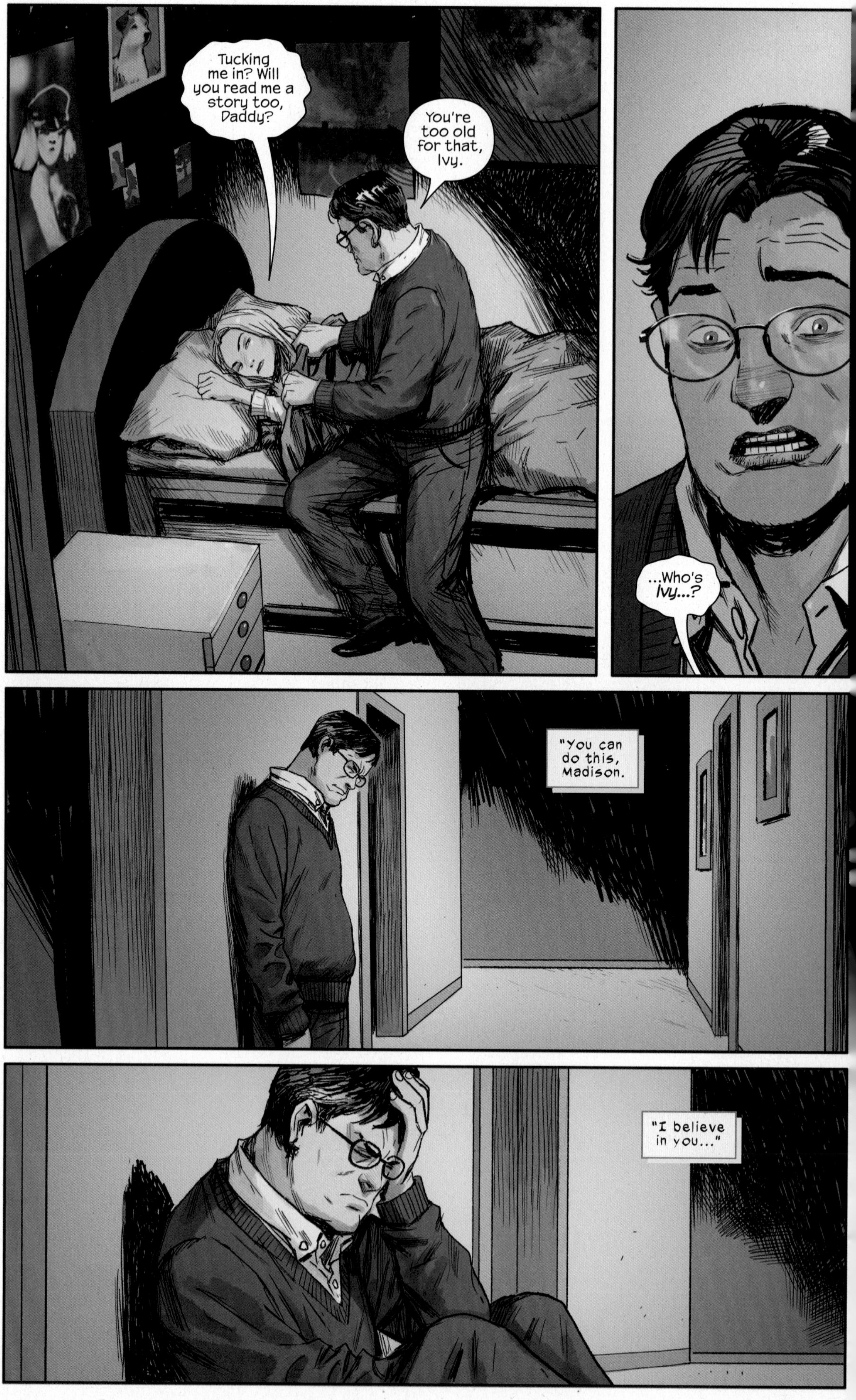
Tucking me in? Will you read me a story too, Daddy?
You're too old for that, Ivy.
...Who's Ivy...?
"You can do this, Madison.
"I believe in you..."

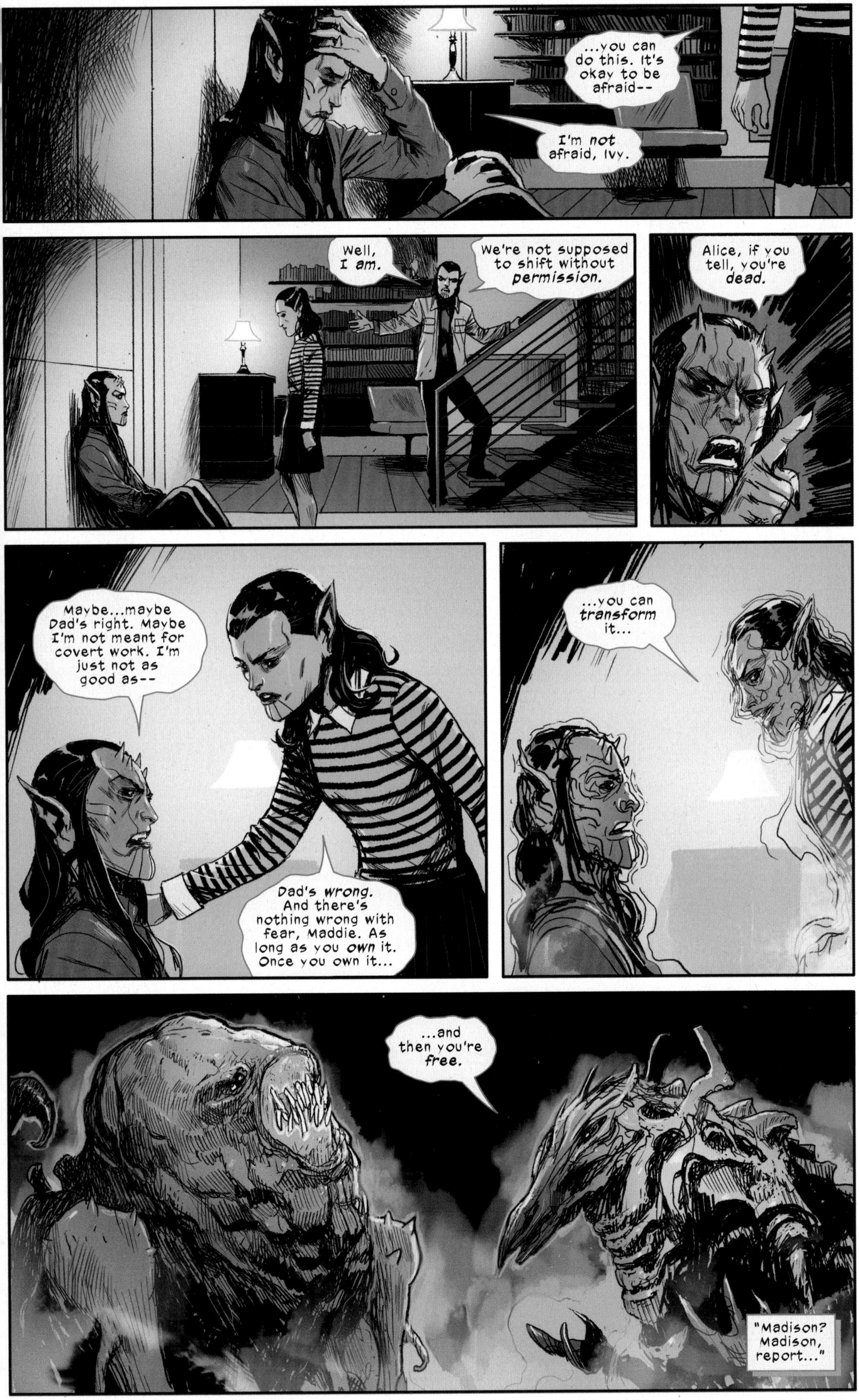
...you can do this. It's okay to be afraid--
I'm *not* afraid, Ivy.
Well, I *am.*
We're not supposed to shift without *permission.*
Alice, if you tell, you're *dead.*
Maybe...maybe Dad's right. Maybe I'm not meant for covert work. I'm just not as good as--
Dad's *wrong.* And there's nothing wrong with fear, Maddie. As long as you *own* it. Once you own it...
...you can *transform* it...
...and then you're *free.*
"Madison? Madison, report..."

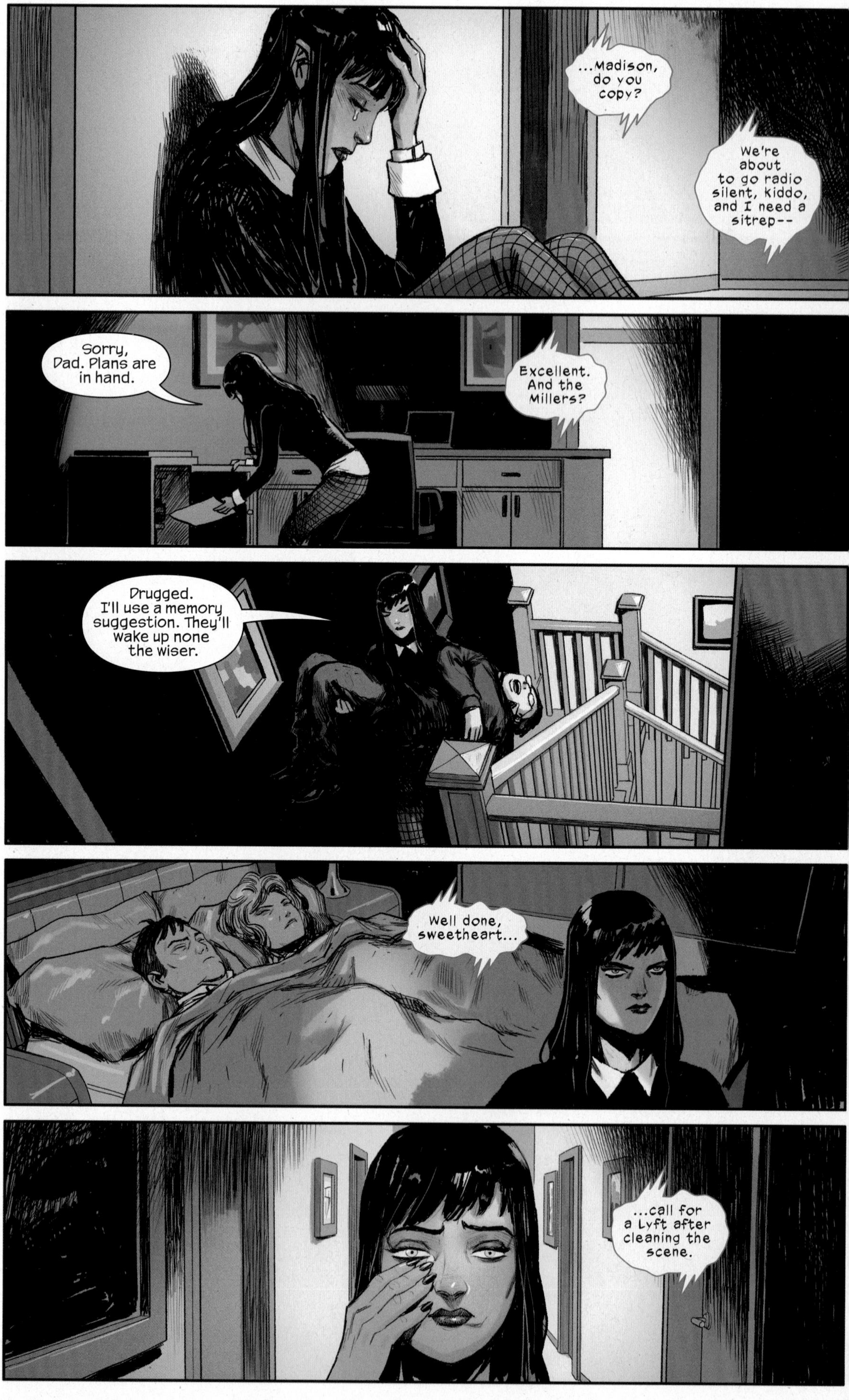
...Madison, do you copy?
We're about to go radio silent, kiddo, and I need a sitrep--
Sorry, Dad. Plans are in hand.
Excellent. And the Millers?
Drugged. I'll use a memory suggestion. They'll wake up none the wiser.
Well done, sweetheart...
...call for a Lyft after cleaning the scene.

I can't reach Alice. Have you heard from--

She's home. Focus.

Hey, Mr. Stark! Ms. Potts.

SPECIAL PROJECTS

BZZT

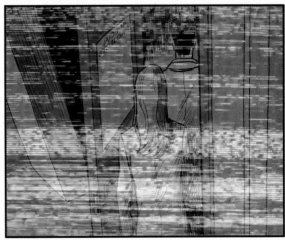

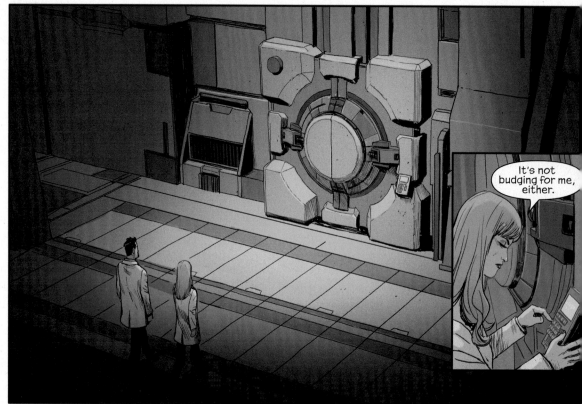

It's not budging for me, either.

Not even *Stark* can get in here?

How is that possible?

Who *knows* with him.

Fortunately, we have alternate ways in.

I'll be right back.

"Be right back, Daddy."

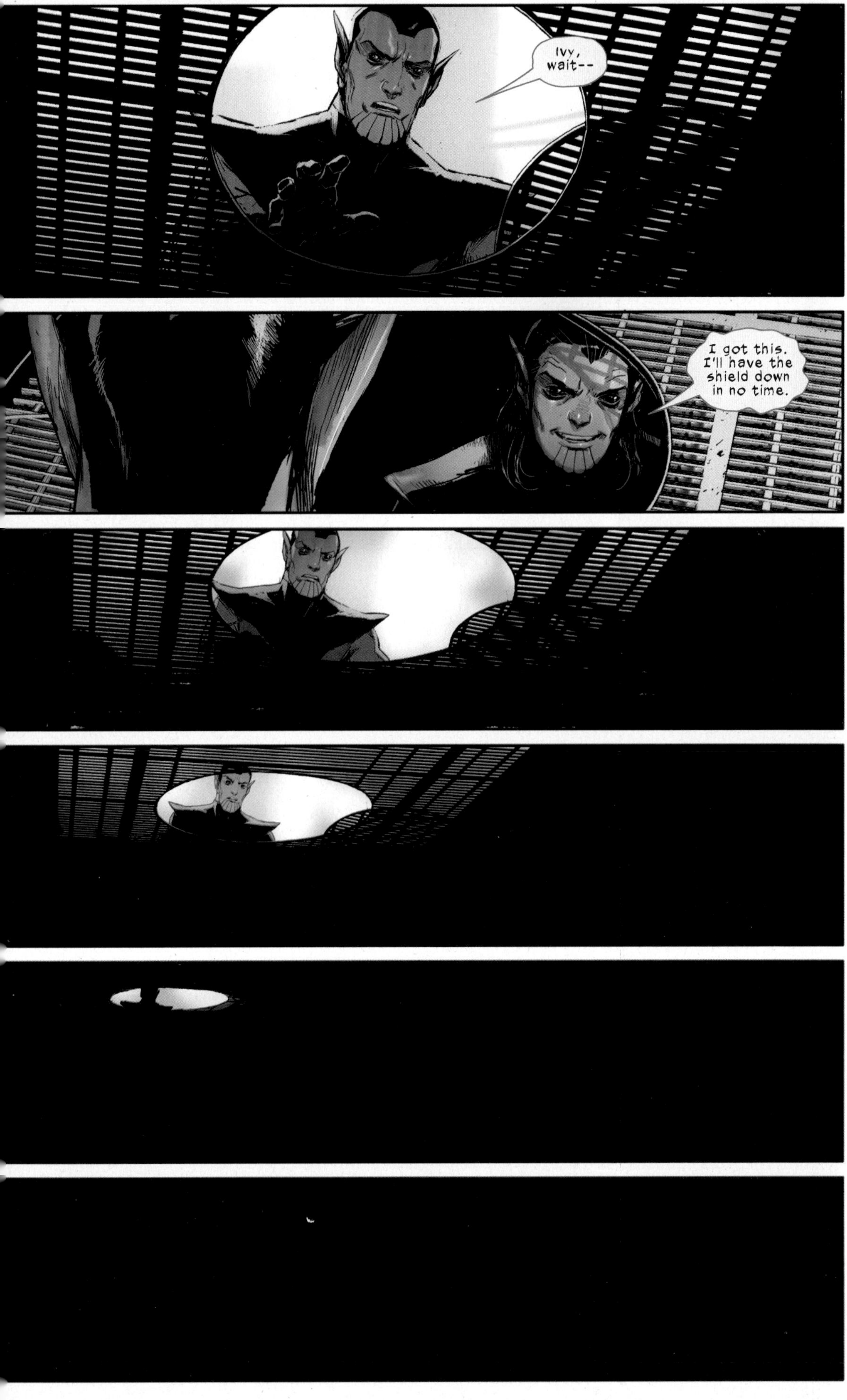
Ivy, wait--
I got this. I'll have the shield down in no time.

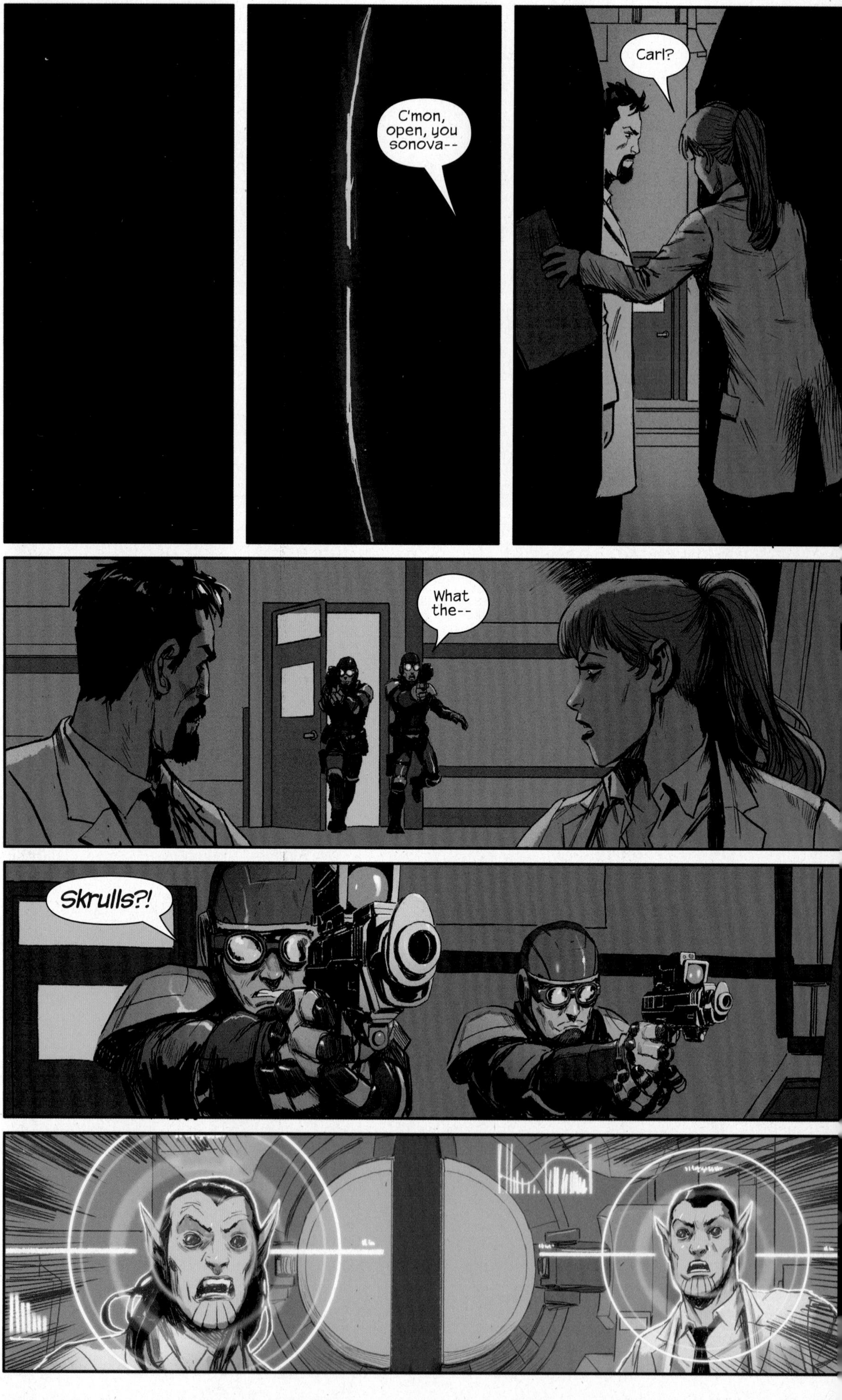
C'mon, open, you sonova--
Carl?
What the--
Skrulls?!

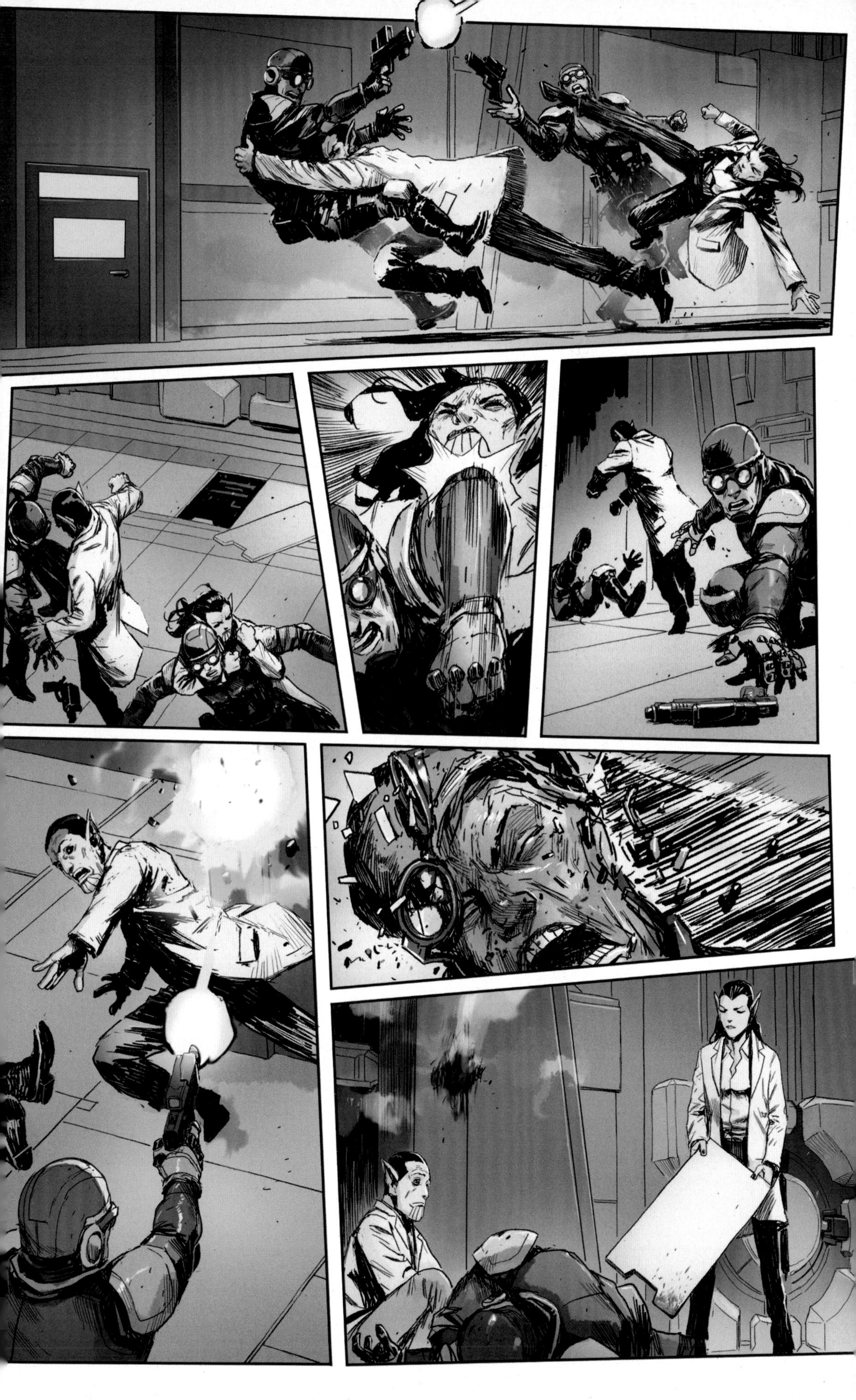

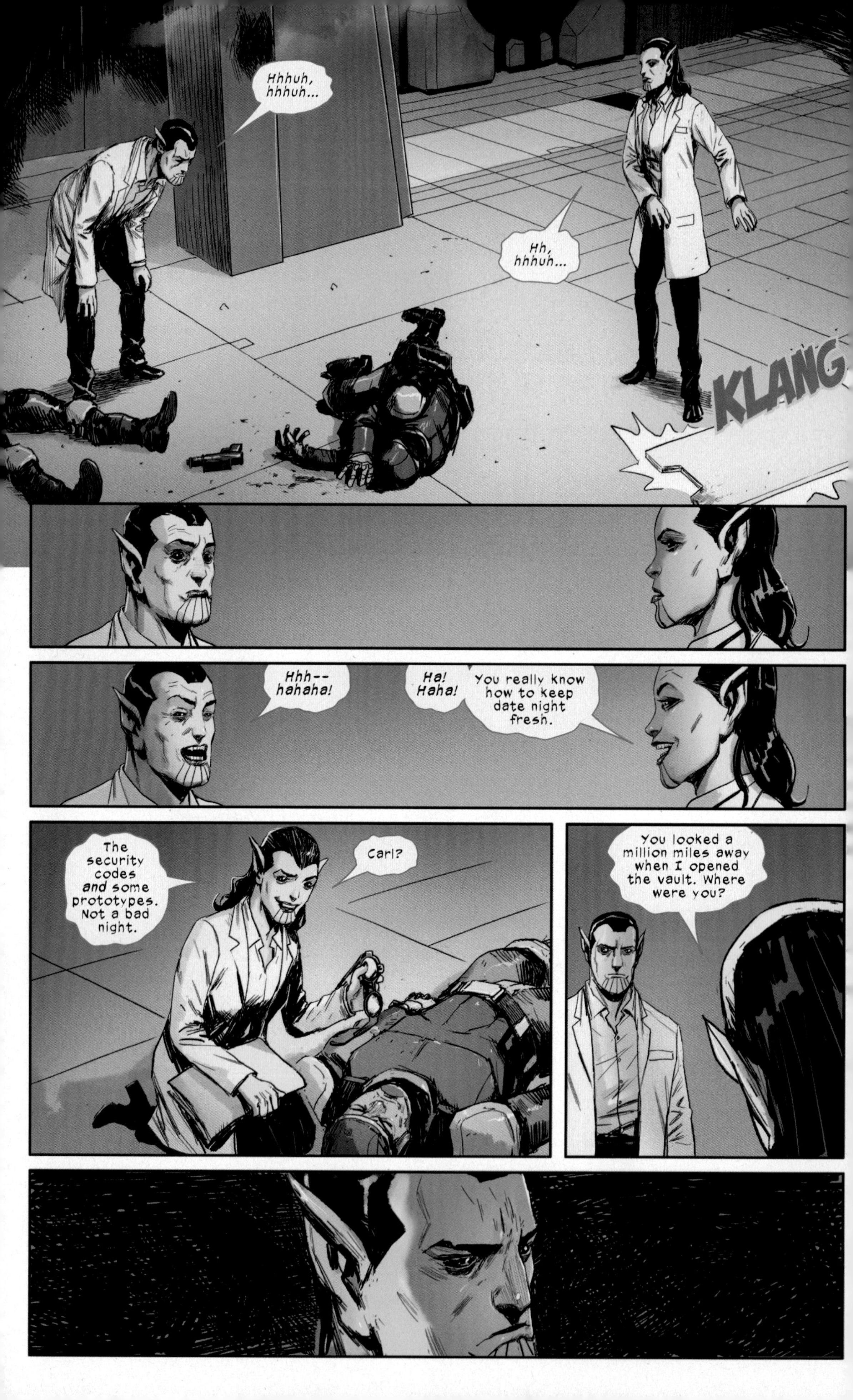
Hhhuh, hhhuh...
Hh, hhhuh...
KLANG
Hhh-- hahaha!
Ha! Haha!
You really know how to keep date night fresh.
The security codes and some prototypes. Not a bad night.
Carl?
You looked a million miles away when I opened the vault. Where were you?

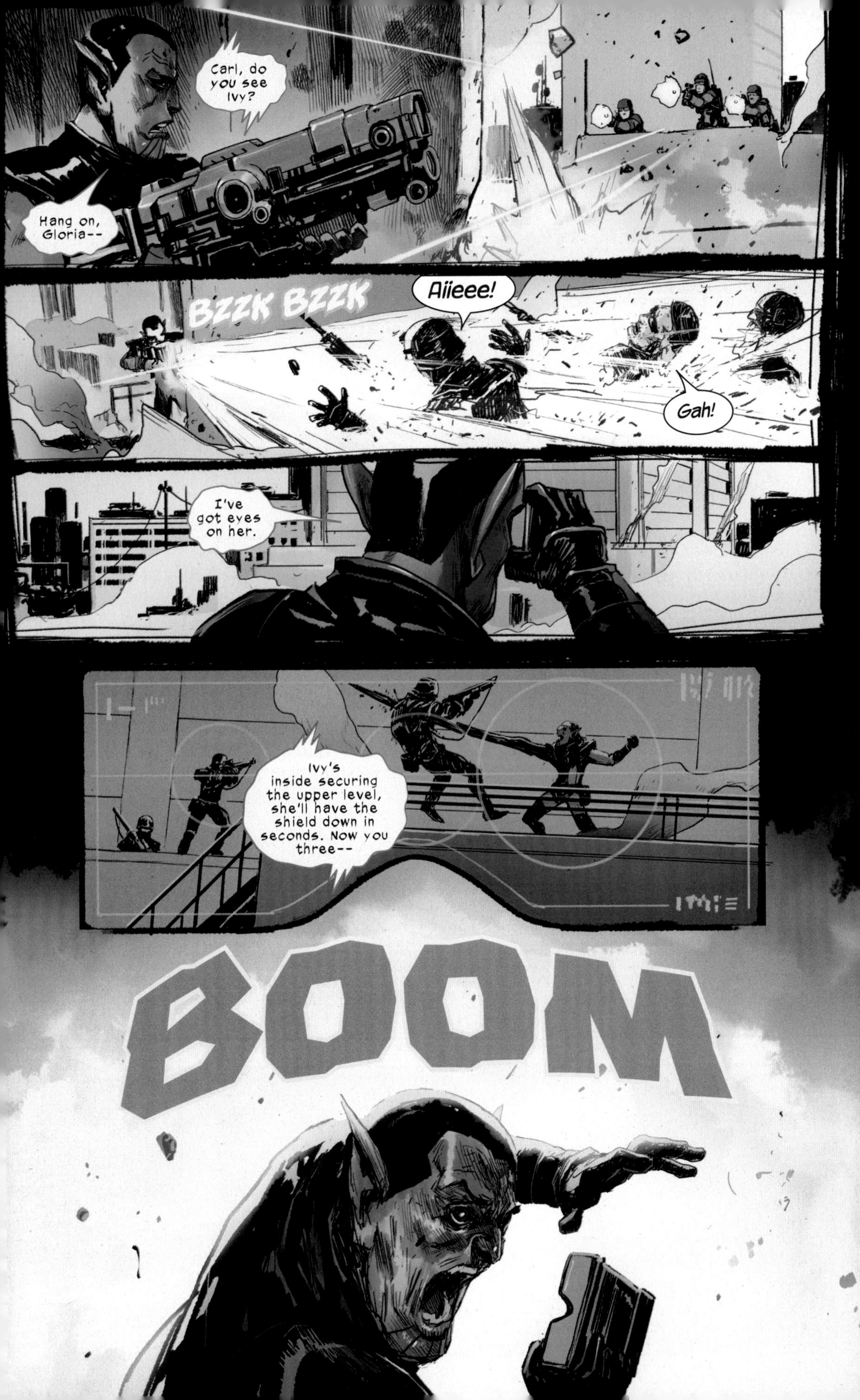

Carl, do you see Ivy?
Hang on, Gloria--
BZZK BZZK
Aiieee!
Gah!
I've got eyes on her.
Ivy's inside securing the upper level, she'll have the shield down in seconds. Now you three--
BOOM

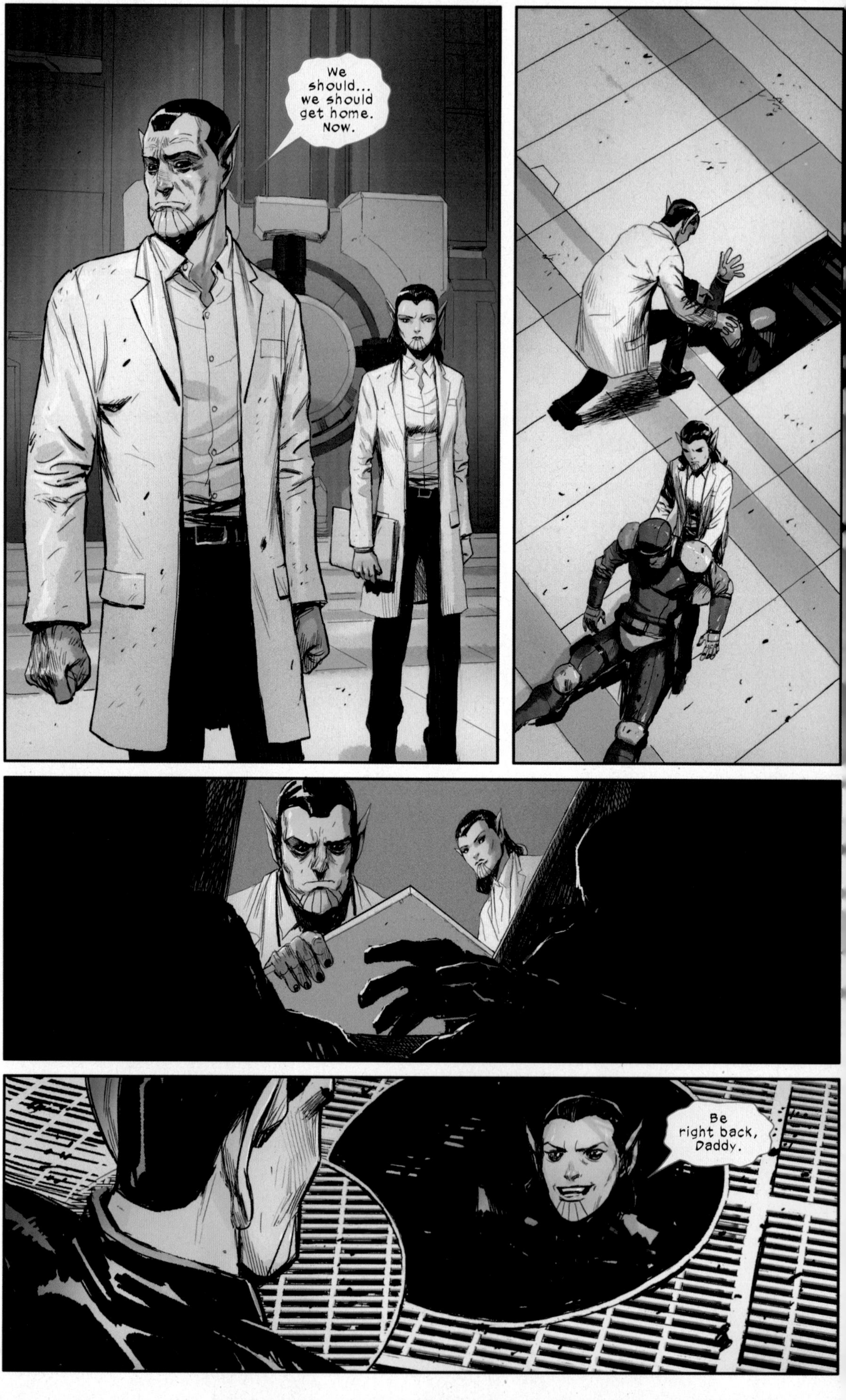
We should... we should get home. Now.
Be right back, Daddy.

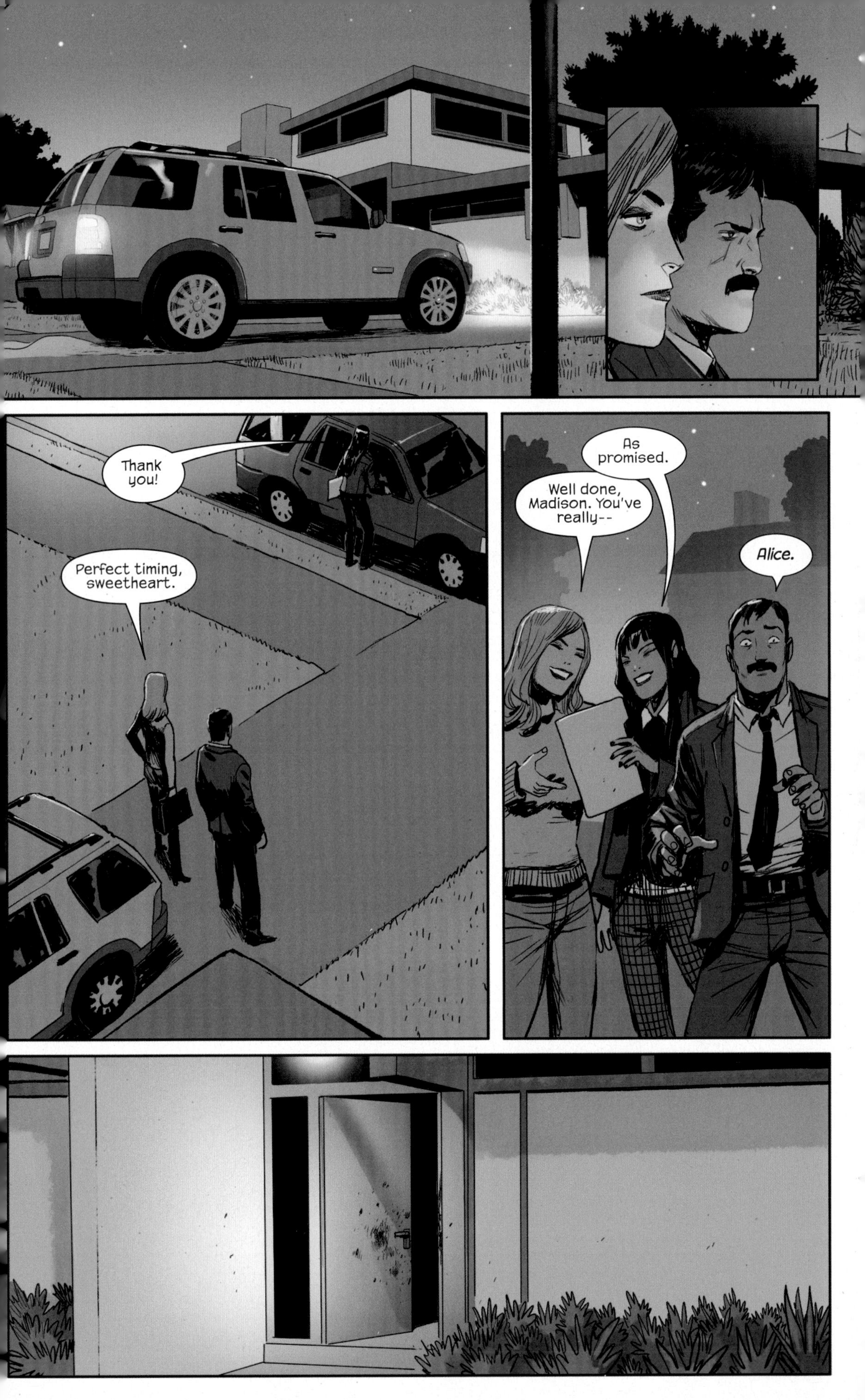

Thank you!
Perfect timing, sweetheart.
Well done, Madison. You've really--
As promised.
Alice.

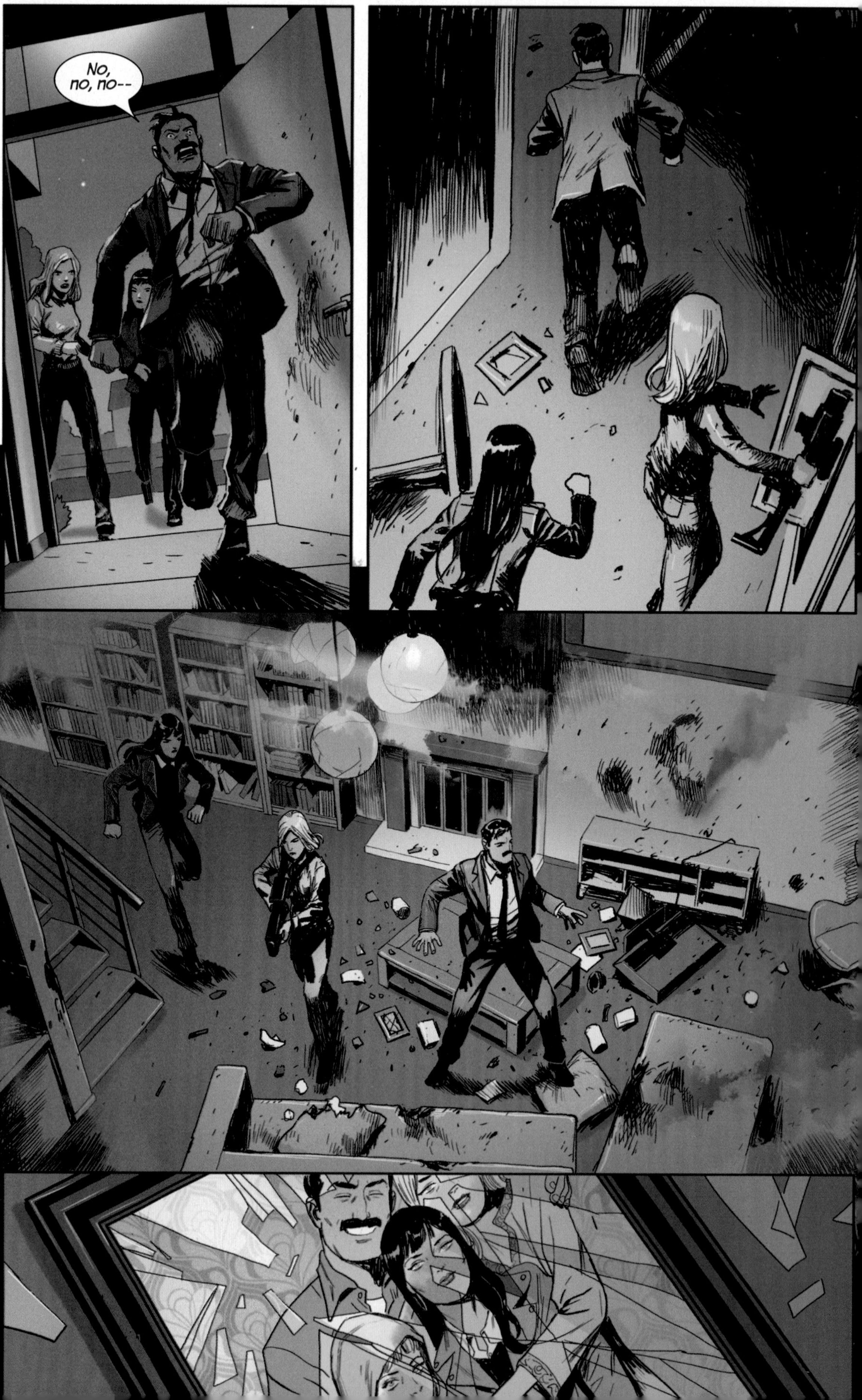
No, no, no--

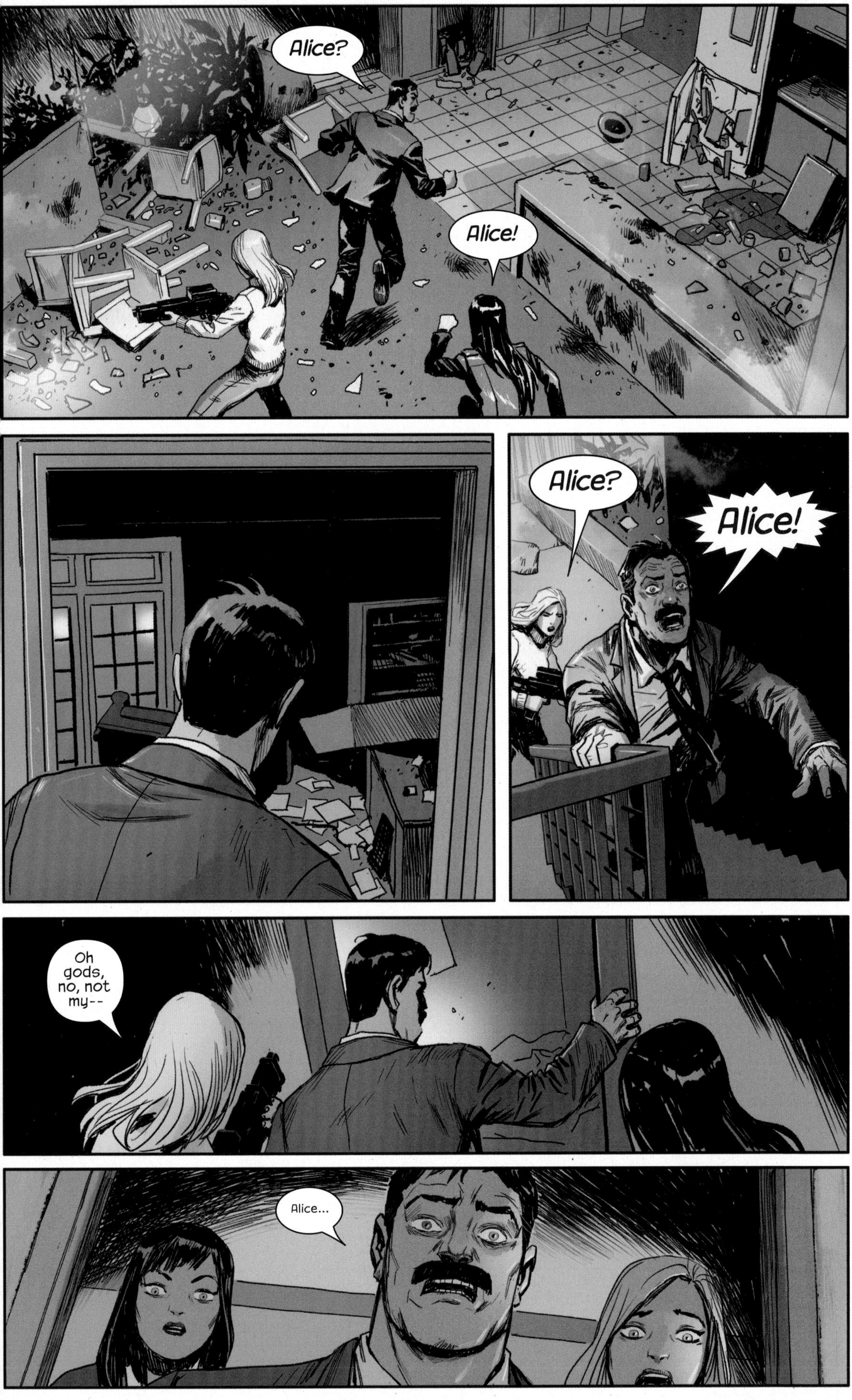
Alice?
Alice!
Alice?
Alice!
Oh gods, no, not my--
Alice...

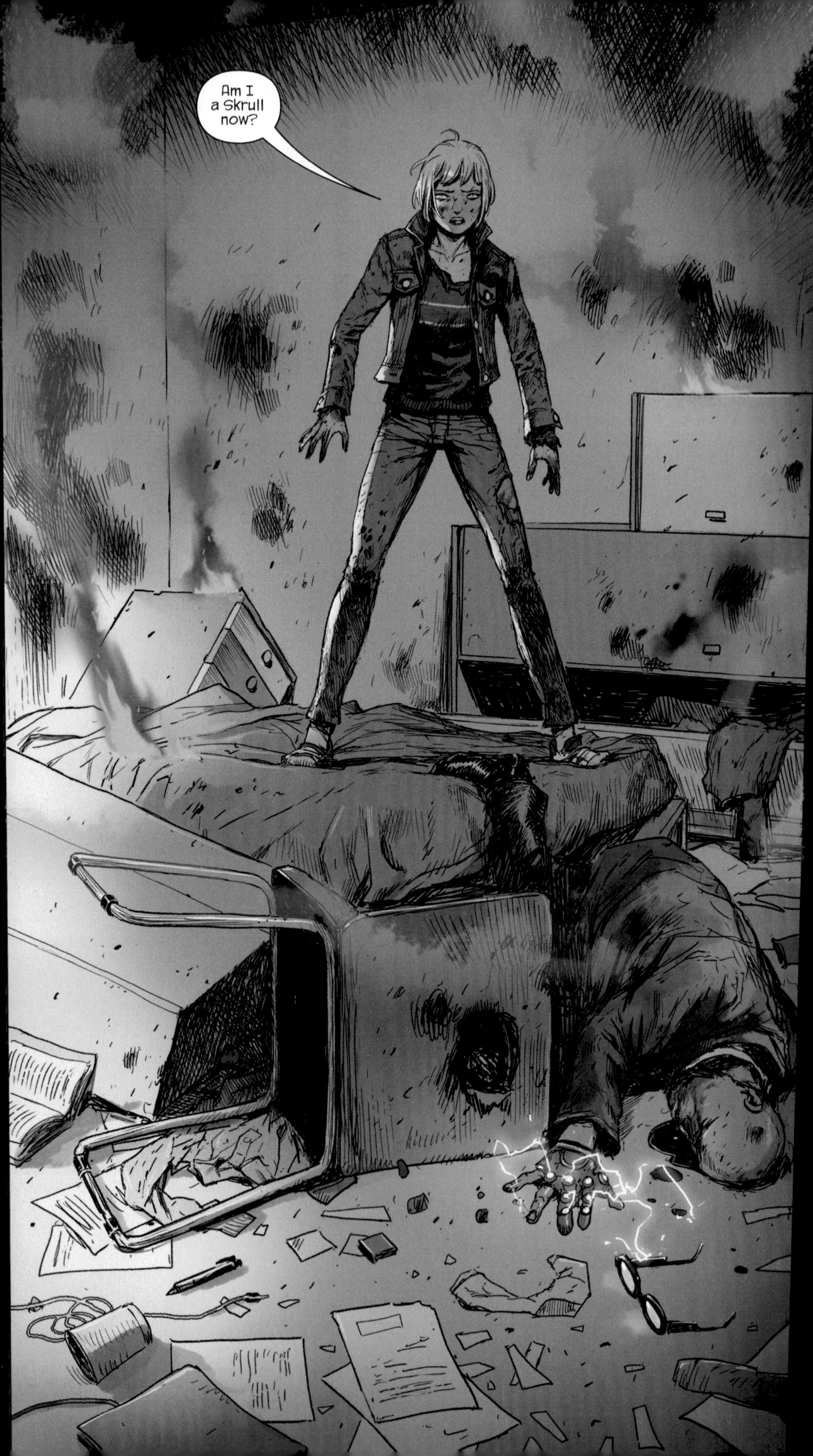
Am I a Skrull now?

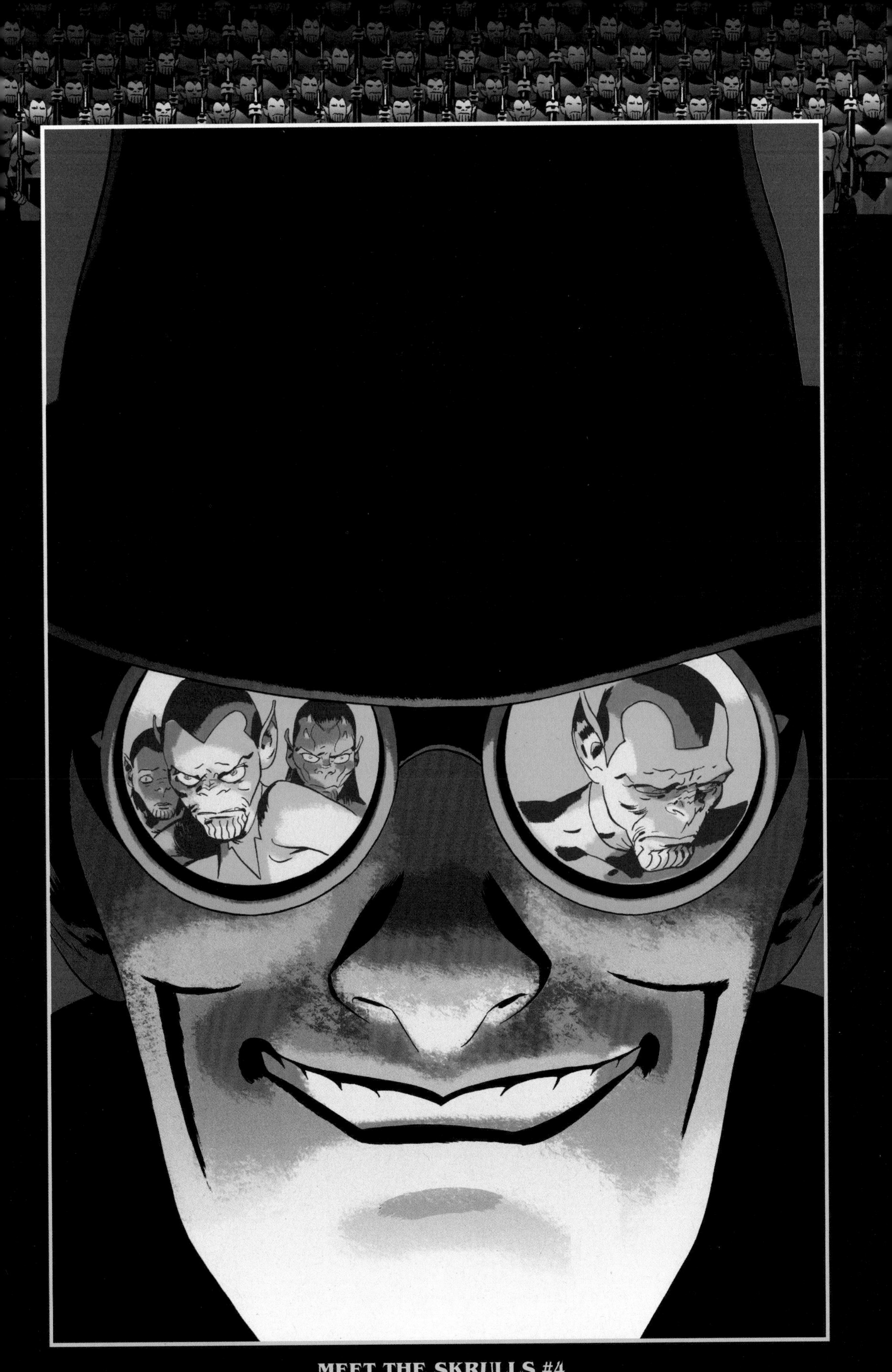

MEET THE SKRULLS #4

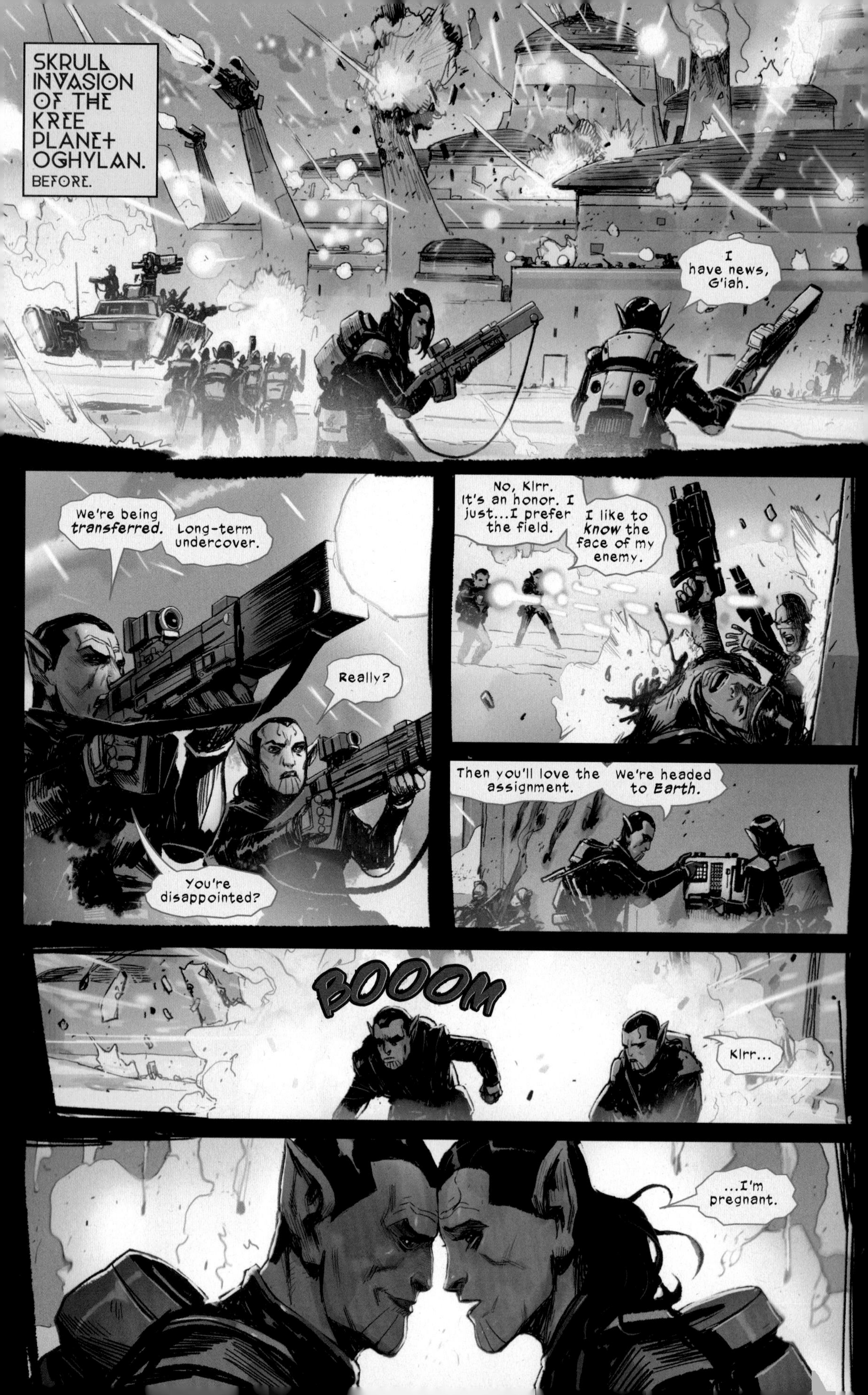
SKRULL INVASION OF THE KREE PLANET OGHYLAN.
BEFORE.
I have news, G'iah.
We're being *transferred.*
Long-term undercover.
Really?
You're disappointed?
No, Klrr. It's an honor. I just...I prefer the field.
I like to *know* the face of my enemy.
Then you'll love the assignment.
We're headed to *Earth.*
BOOOM
Klrr...
...I'm pregnant.

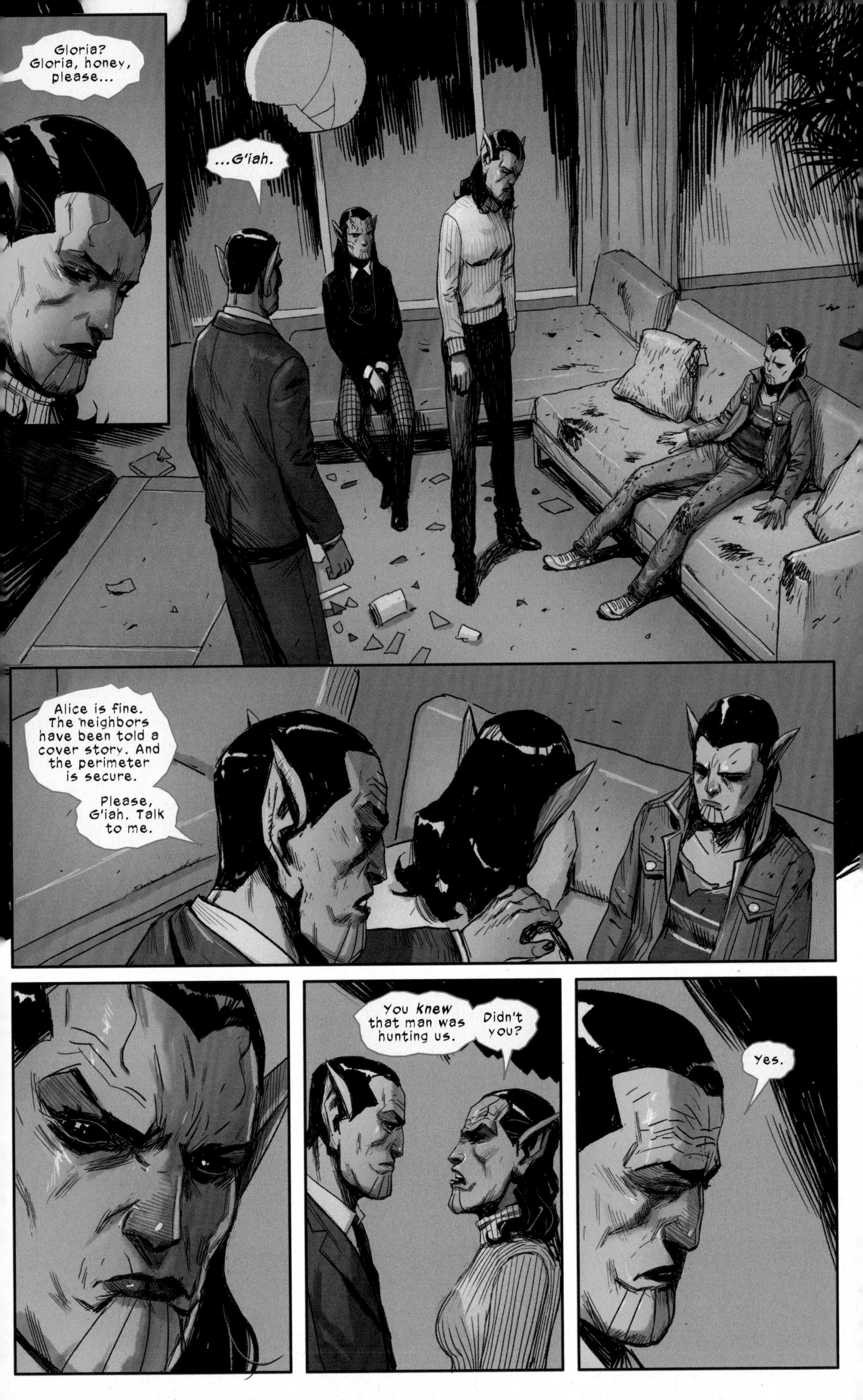

Gloria? Gloria, honey, please...
...G'iah.
Alice is fine. The neighbors have been told a cover story. And the perimeter is secure.
Please, G'iah. Talk to me.
You knew that man was hunting us.
Didn't you?
Yes.

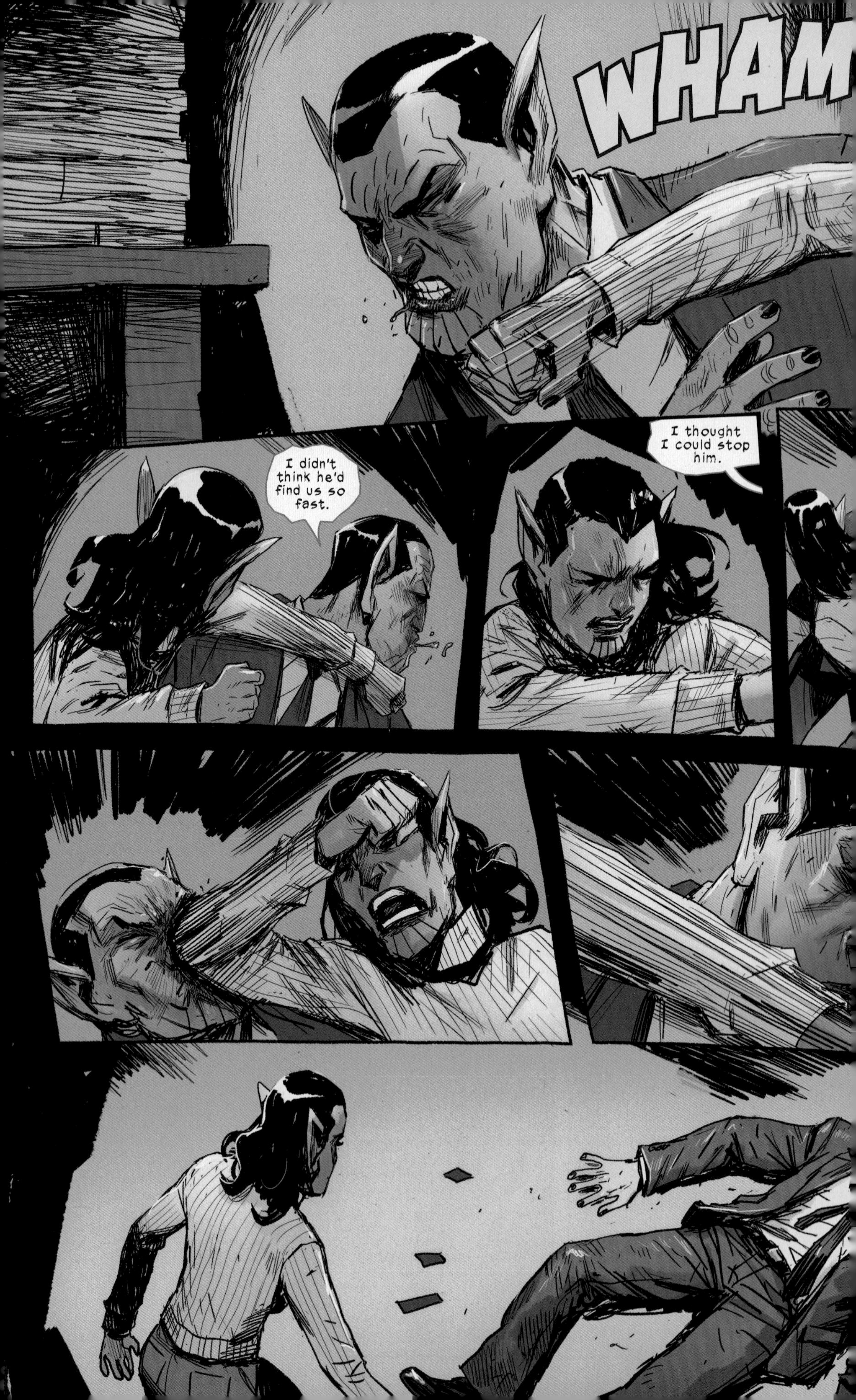
WHAM
I didn't think he'd find us so fast.
I thought I could stop him.

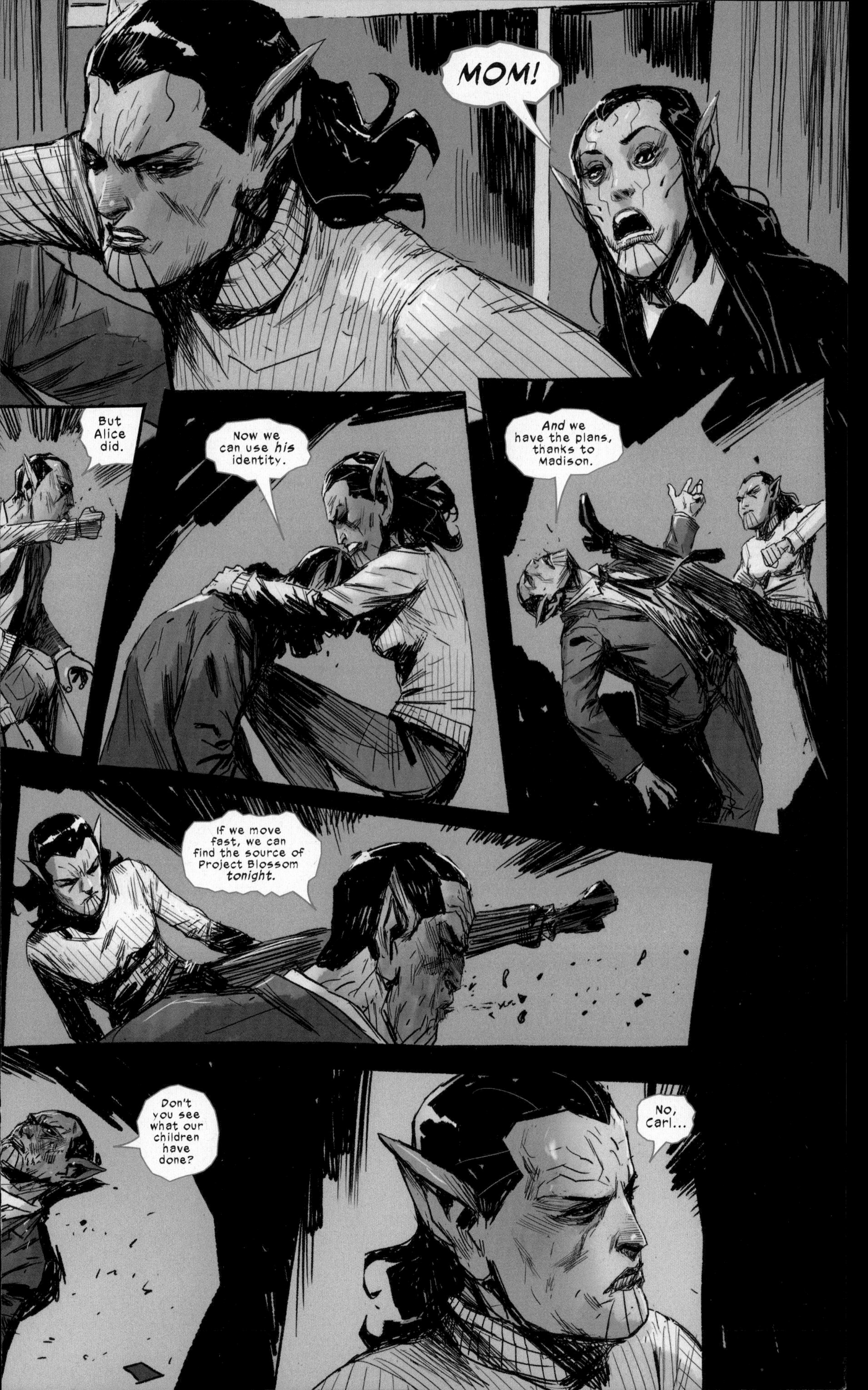
MOM!
But Alice did.
Now we can use *his* identity.
And we have the plans, thanks to Madison.
If we move fast, we can find the source of Project Blossom *tonight.*
Don't you see what our children have done?
No, Carl...

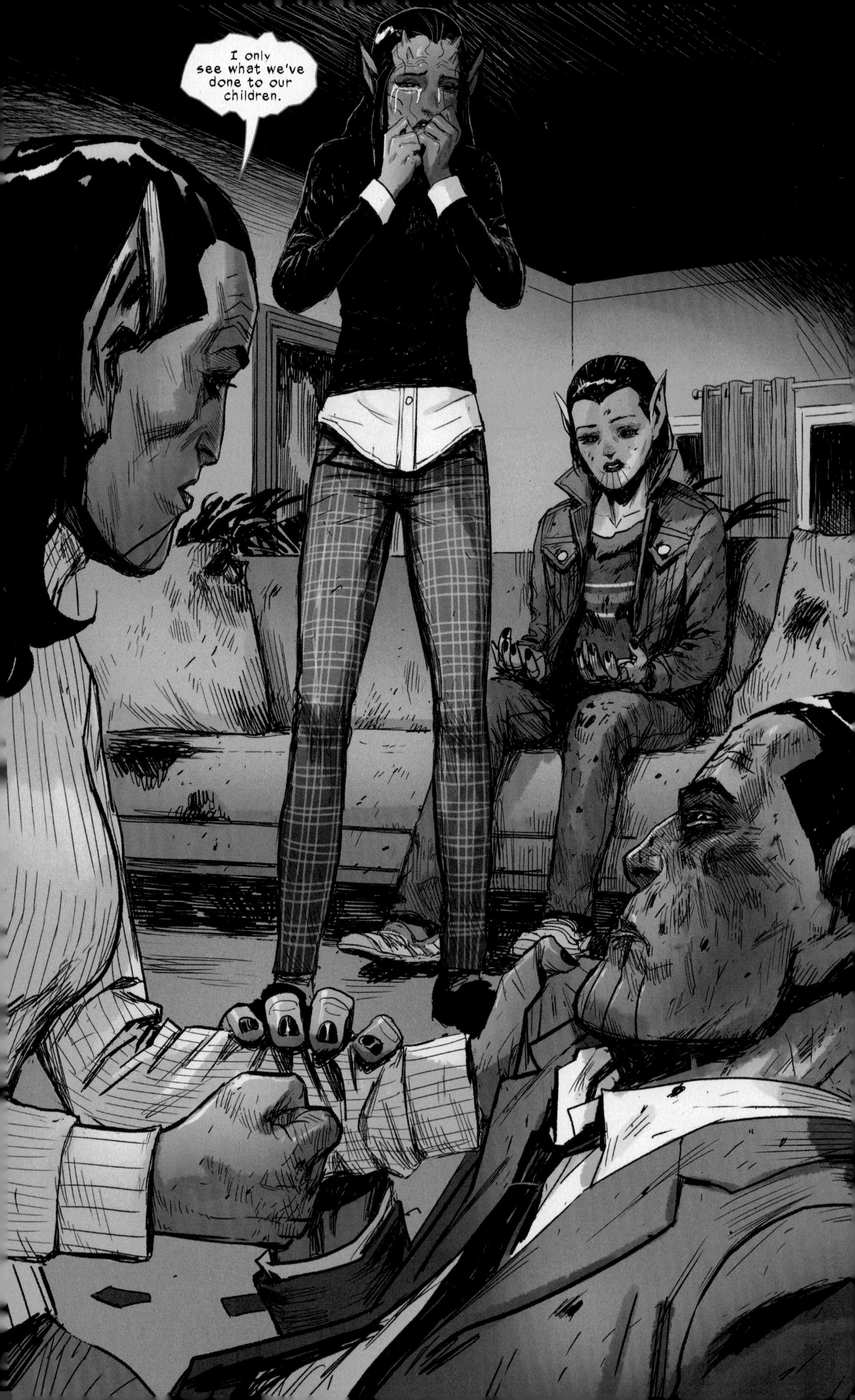
I only see what we've done to our children.

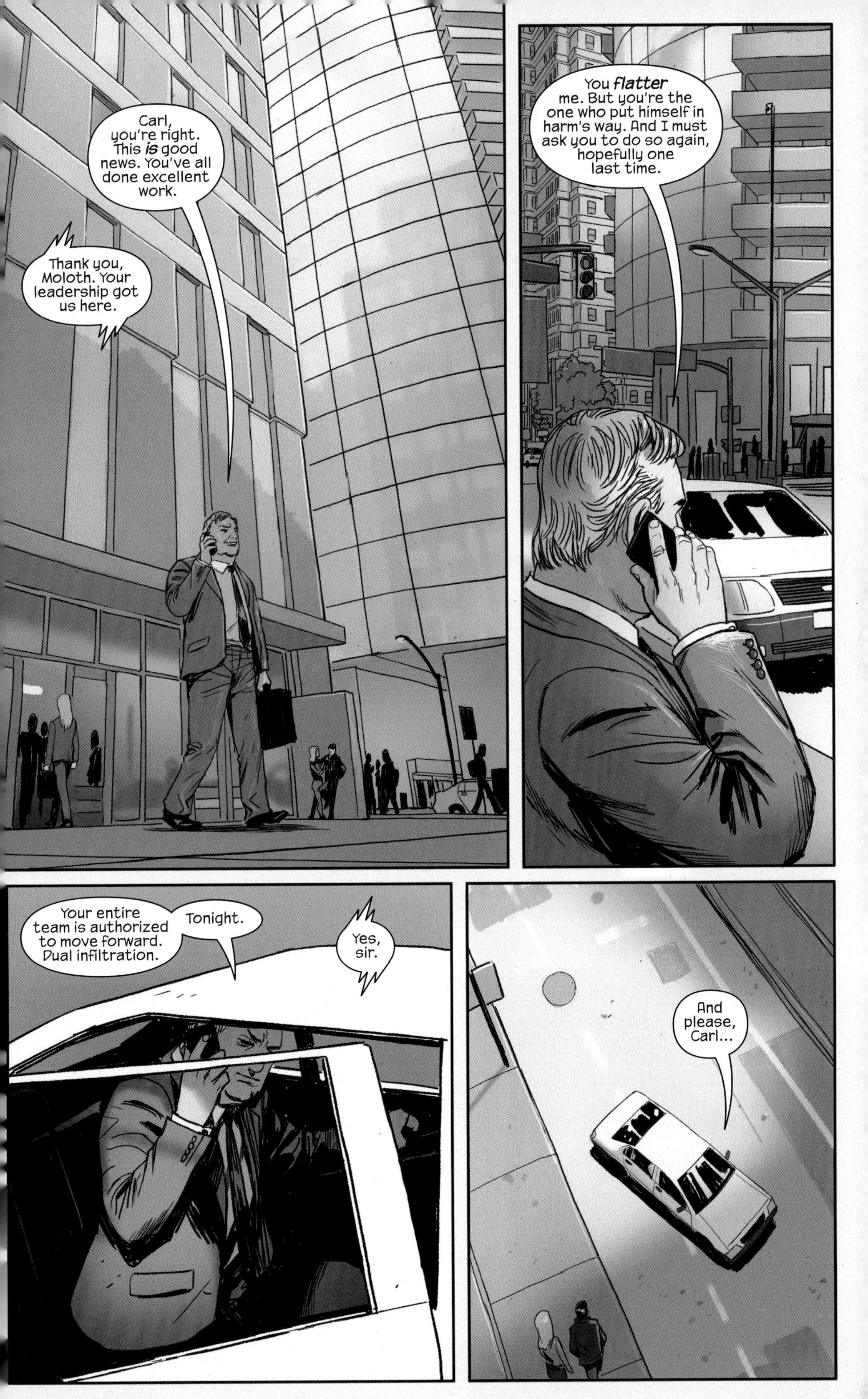
Carl, you're right. This *is* good news. You've all done excellent work.
Thank you, Moloth. Your leadership got us here.
You *flatter* me. But you're the one who put himself in harm's way. And I must ask you to do so again, hopefully one last time.
Your entire team is authorized to move forward. Dual infiltration.
Tonight.
Yes, sir.
And please, Carl...

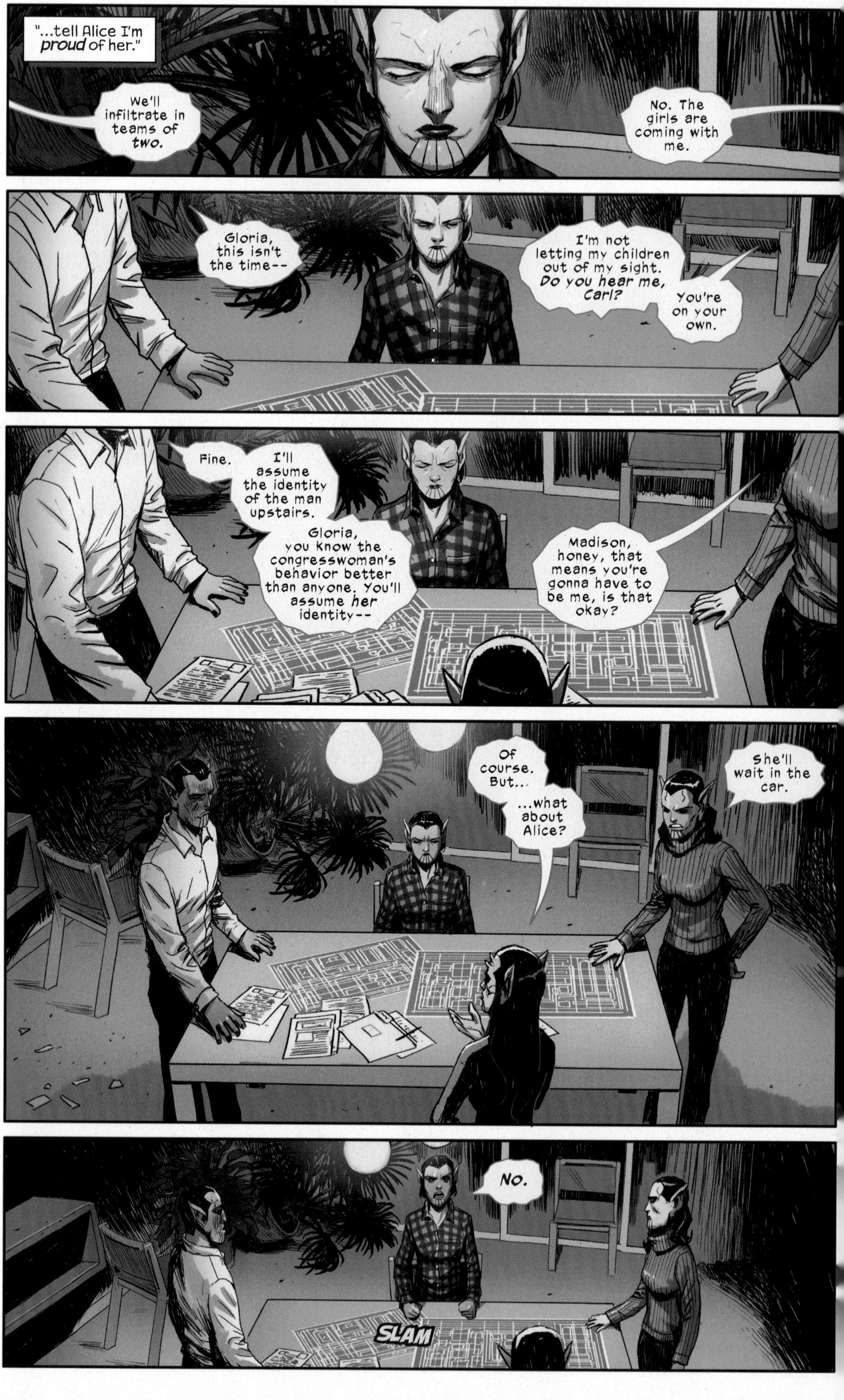
"...tell Alice I'm *proud* of her."
We'll infiltrate in teams of *two*.
No. The girls are coming with me.
Gloria, this isn't the time--
I'm not letting my children out of my sight. *Do you hear me, Carl?*
You're on your own.
Fine.
I'll assume the identity of the man upstairs.
Gloria, you know the congresswoman's behavior better than anyone. You'll assume *her* identity--
Madison, honey, that means you're gonna have to be me, is that okay?
Of course. But...
...what about Alice?
She'll wait in the car.
No.
SLAM

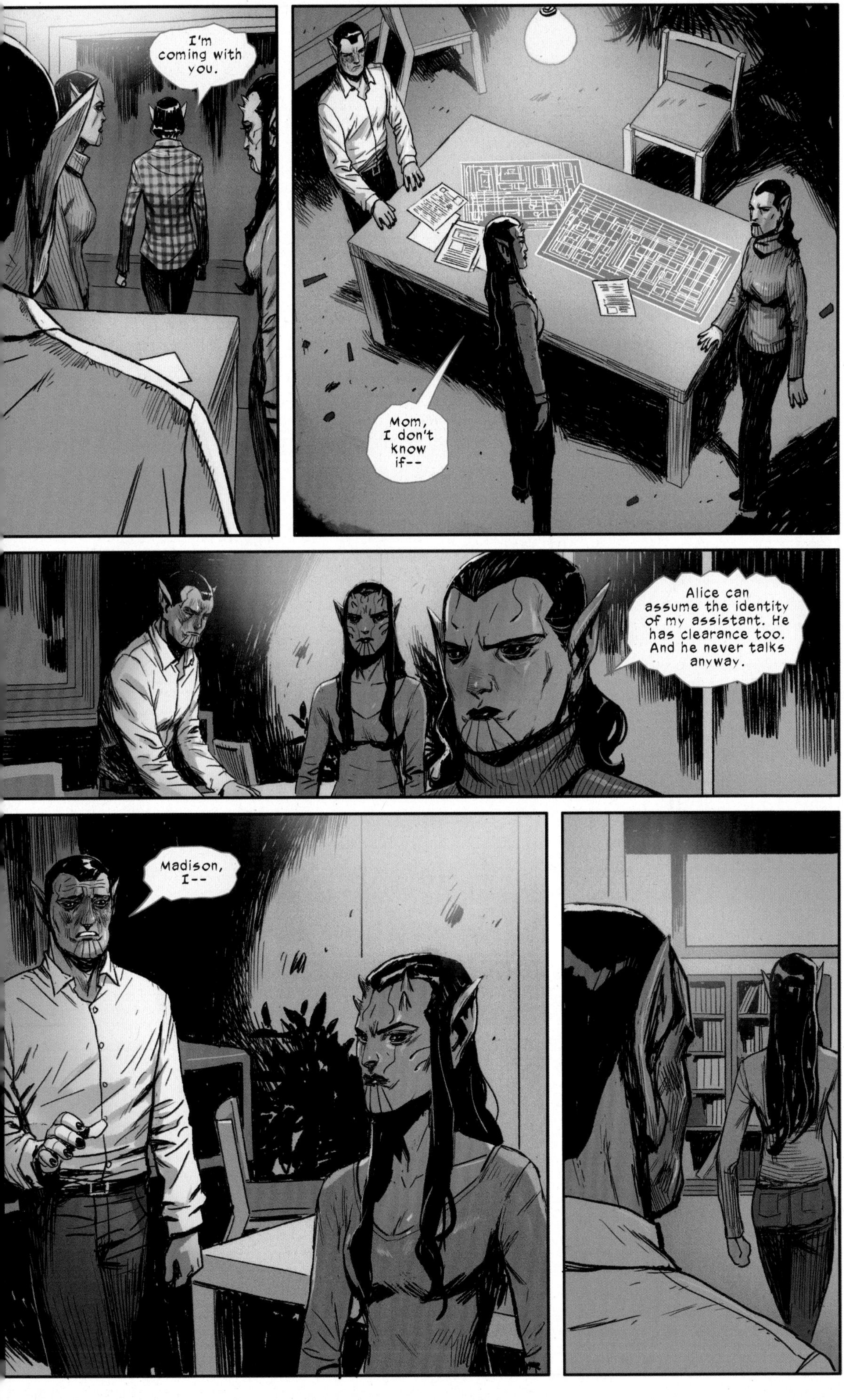
I'm coming with you.
Mom, I don't know if--
Alice can assume the identity of my assistant. He has clearance too. And he never talks anyway.
Madison, I--

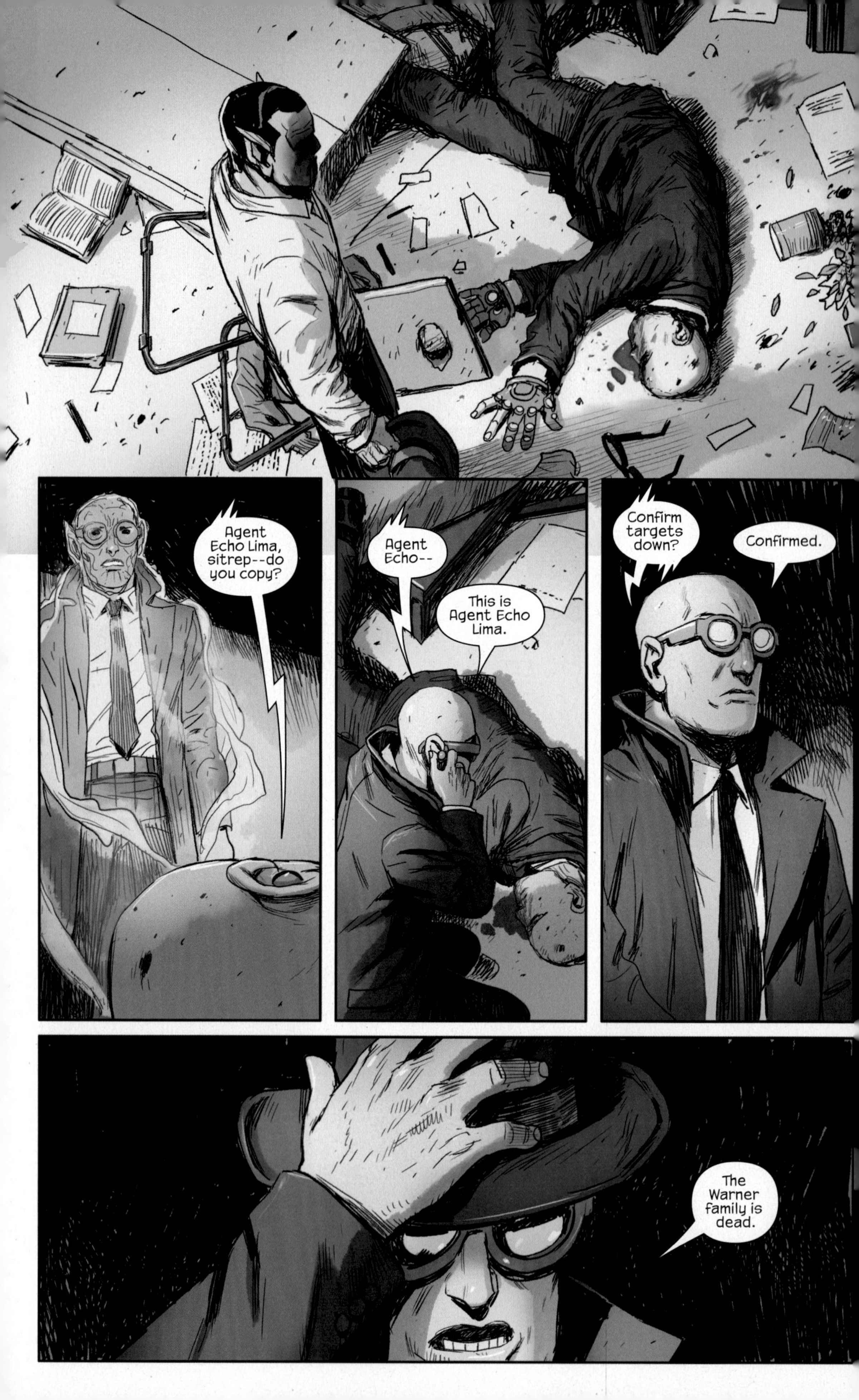
Agent Echo Lima, sitrep--do you copy?
Agent Echo--
This is Agent Echo Lima.
Confirm targets down?
Confirmed.
The Warner family is dead.

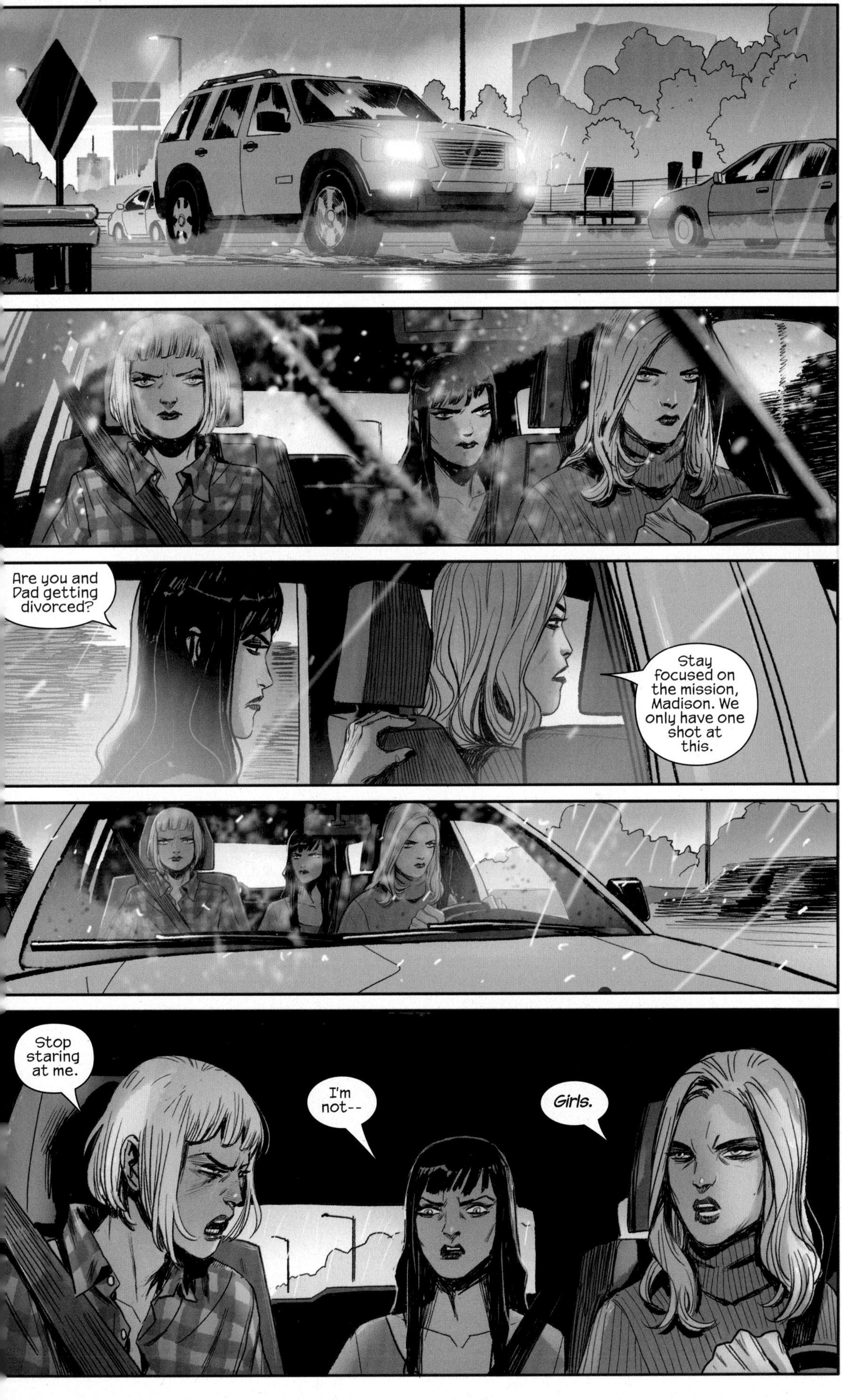
Are you and Dad getting divorced?
Stay focused on the mission, Madison. We only have one shot at this.
Stop staring at me.
I'm not--
Girls.

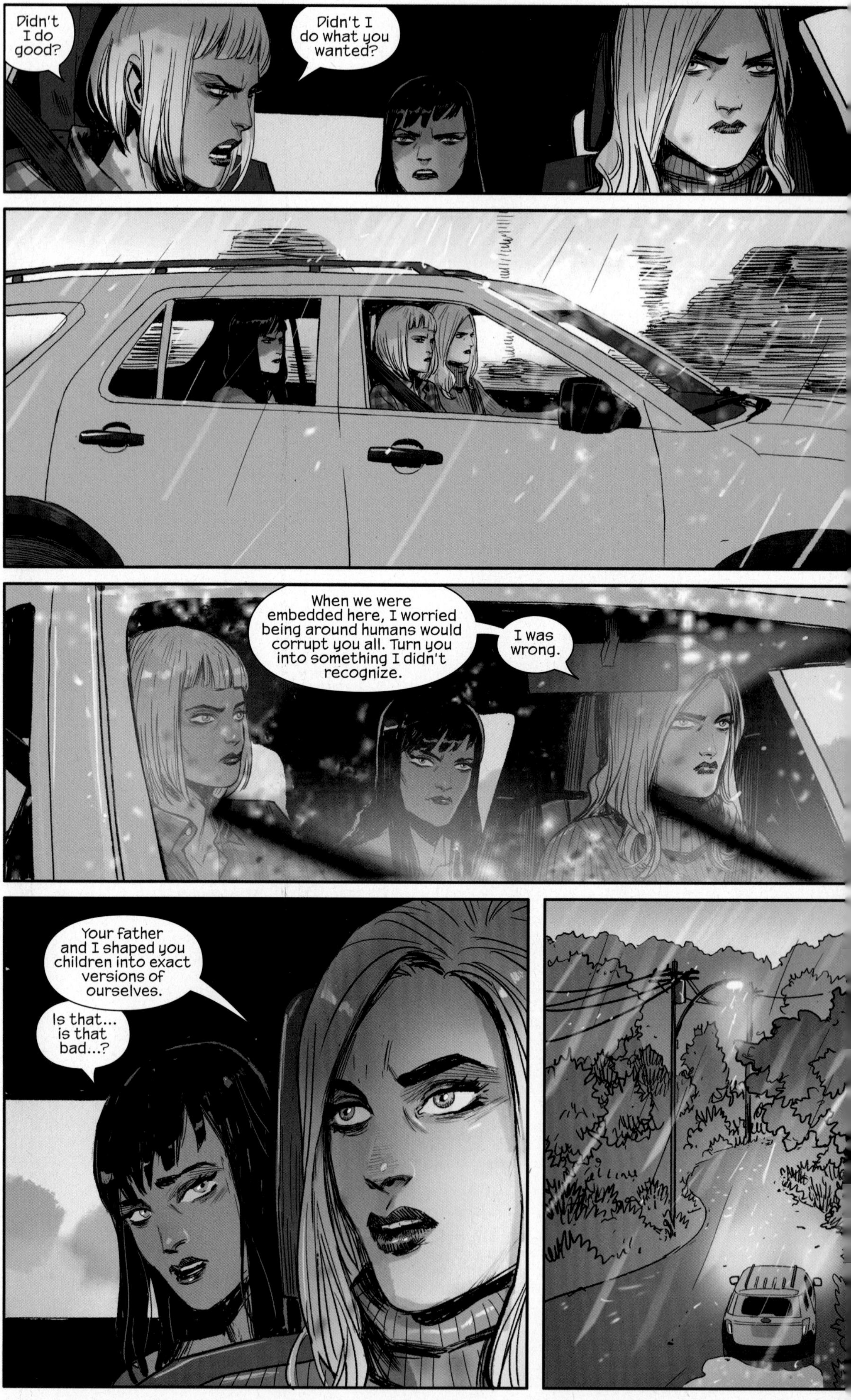
Didn't I do good?
Didn't I do what you wanted?
When we were embedded here, I worried being around humans would corrupt you all. Turn you into something I didn't recognize.
I was wrong.
Your father and I shaped you children into exact versions of ourselves.
Is that... is that bad...?

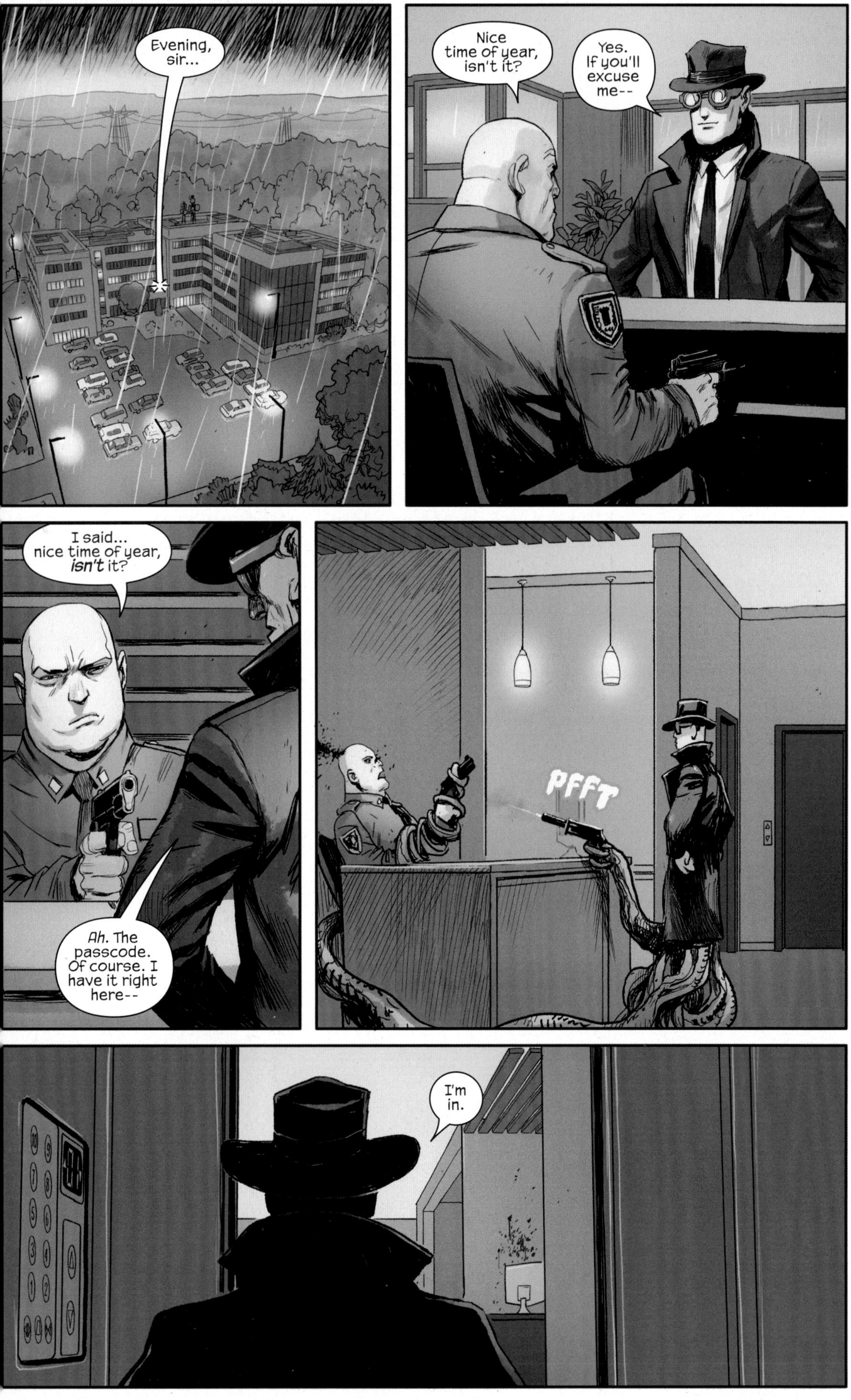
Evening, sir...
Nice time of year, isn't it?
Yes. If you'll excuse me--
I said... nice time of year, *isn't* it?
Ah. The passcode. Of course. I have it right here--
PFFT
I'm in.

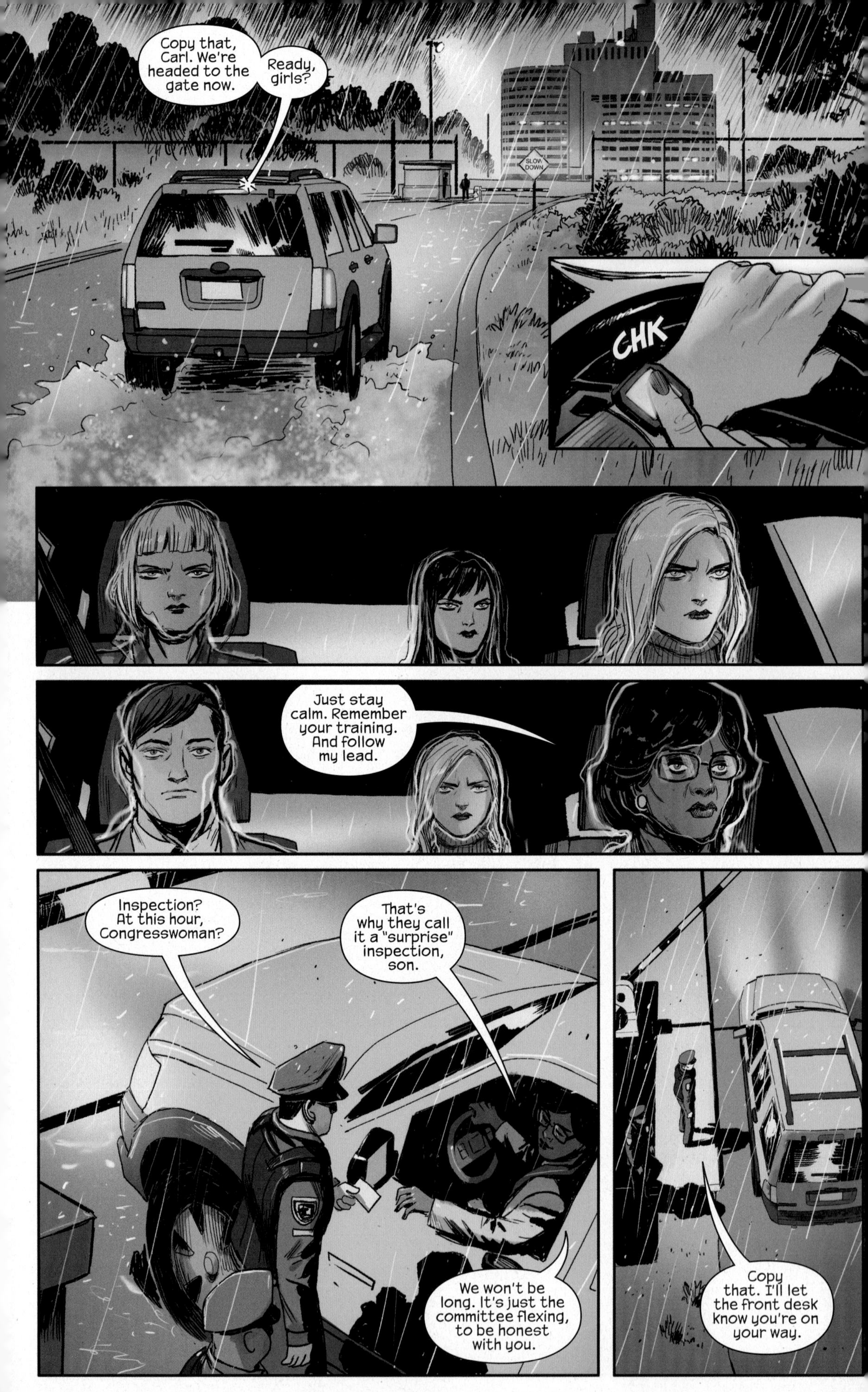
Copy that, Carl. We're headed to the gate now.
Ready, girls?
SLOW DOWN
CHK
Just stay calm. Remember your training. And follow my lead.
Inspection? At this hour, Congresswoman?
That's why they call it a "surprise" inspection, son.
We won't be long. It's just the committee flexing, to be honest with you.
Copy that. I'll let the front desk know you're on your way.

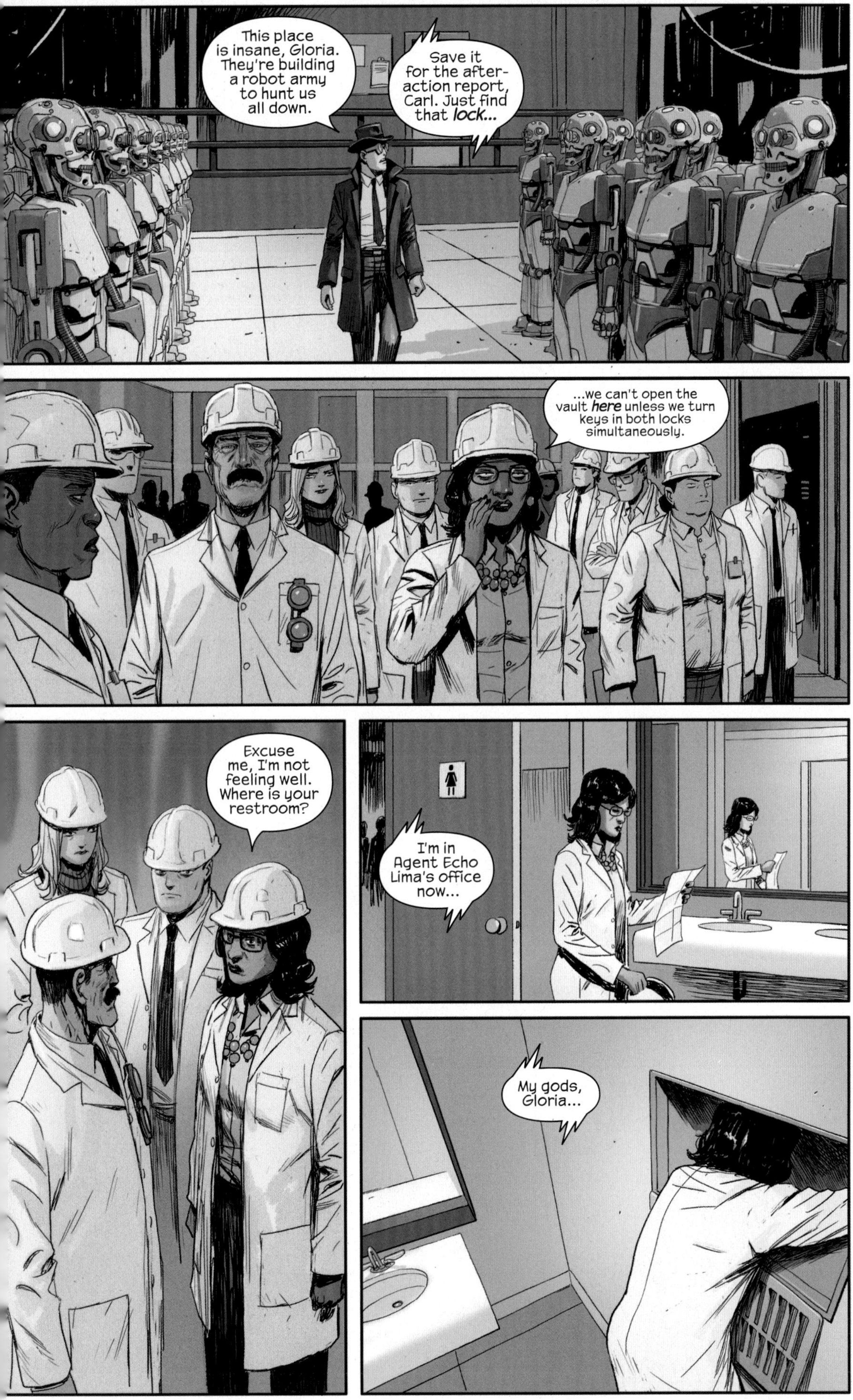
This place is insane, Gloria. They're building a robot army to hunt us all down.
Save it for the after-action report, Carl. Just find that lock...
...we can't open the vault here unless we turn keys in both locks simultaneously.
Excuse me, I'm not feeling well. Where is your restroom?
I'm in Agent Echo Lima's office now...
My gods, Gloria...

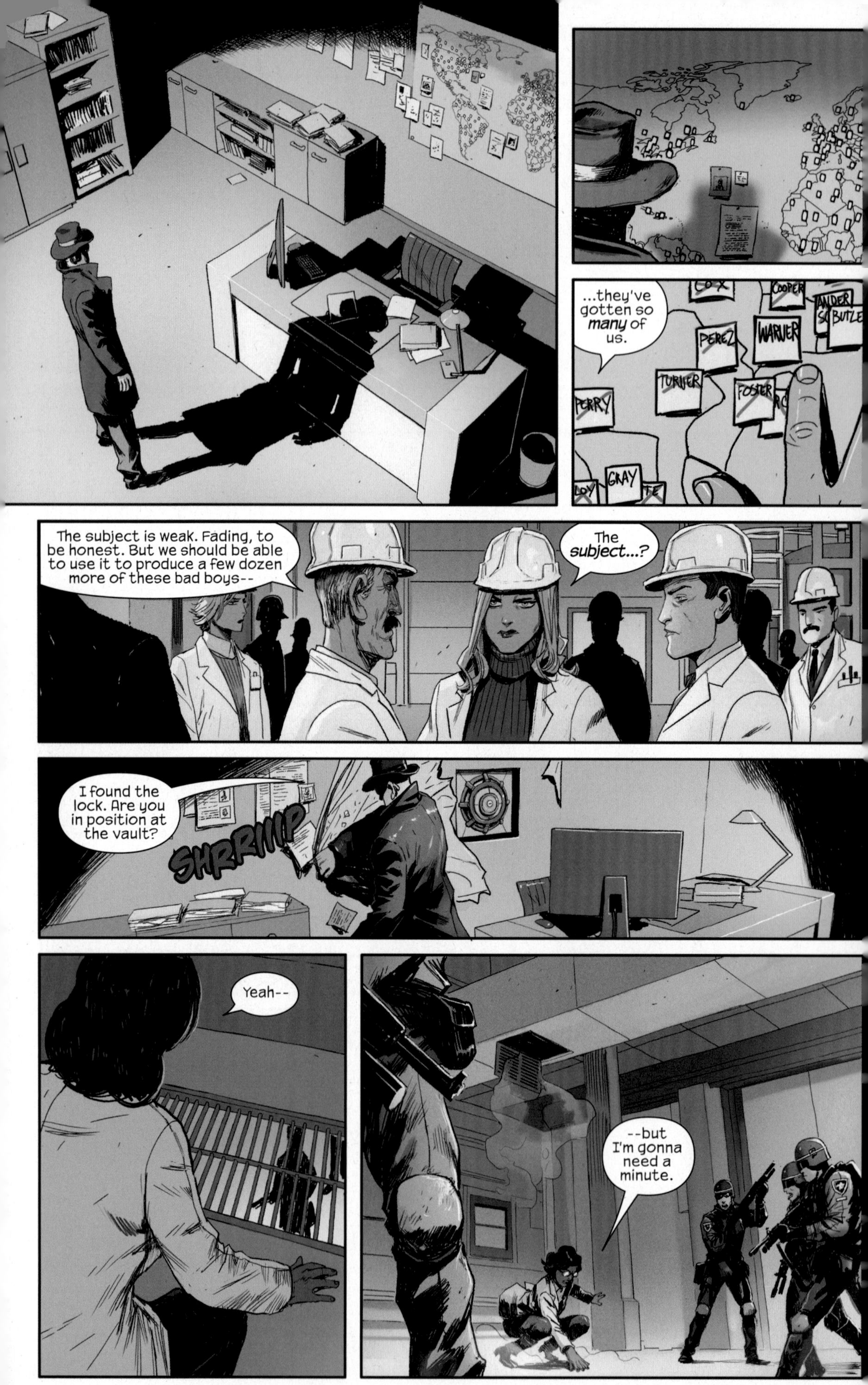
...they've gotten so *many* of us.
COX
COOPER
PEREZ
WARNER
TURNER
FOSTER
PERRY
GRAY
The subject is weak. Fading, to be honest. But we should be able to use it to produce a few dozen more of these bad boys--
The *subject...?*
I found the lock. Are you in position at the vault?
SHRRIIIP
Yeah--
--but I'm gonna need a minute.

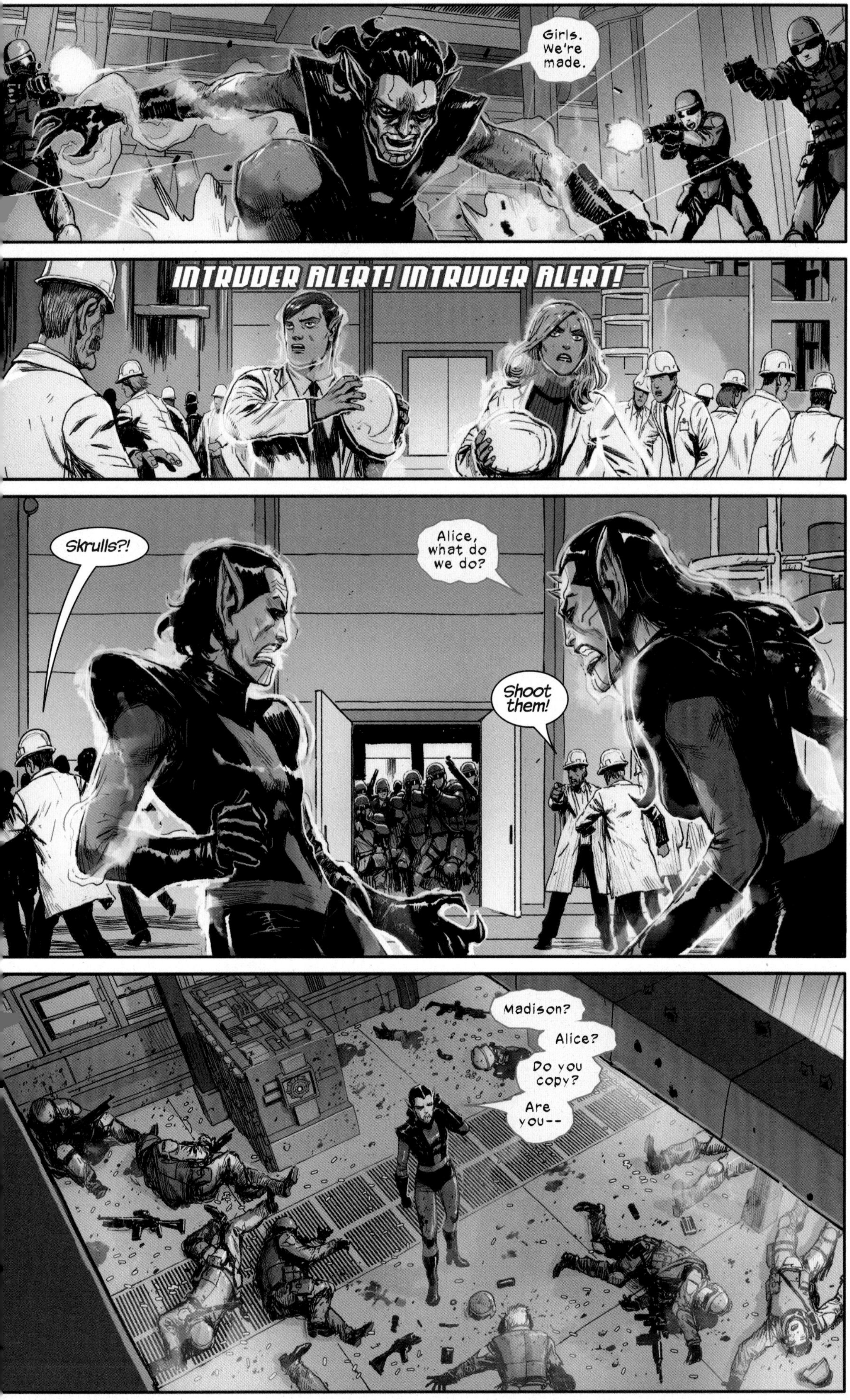
Girls. We're made.
INTRUDER ALERT! INTRUDER ALERT!
Skrulls?!
Alice, what do we do?
Shoot them!
Madison?
Alice?
Do you copy?
Are you--

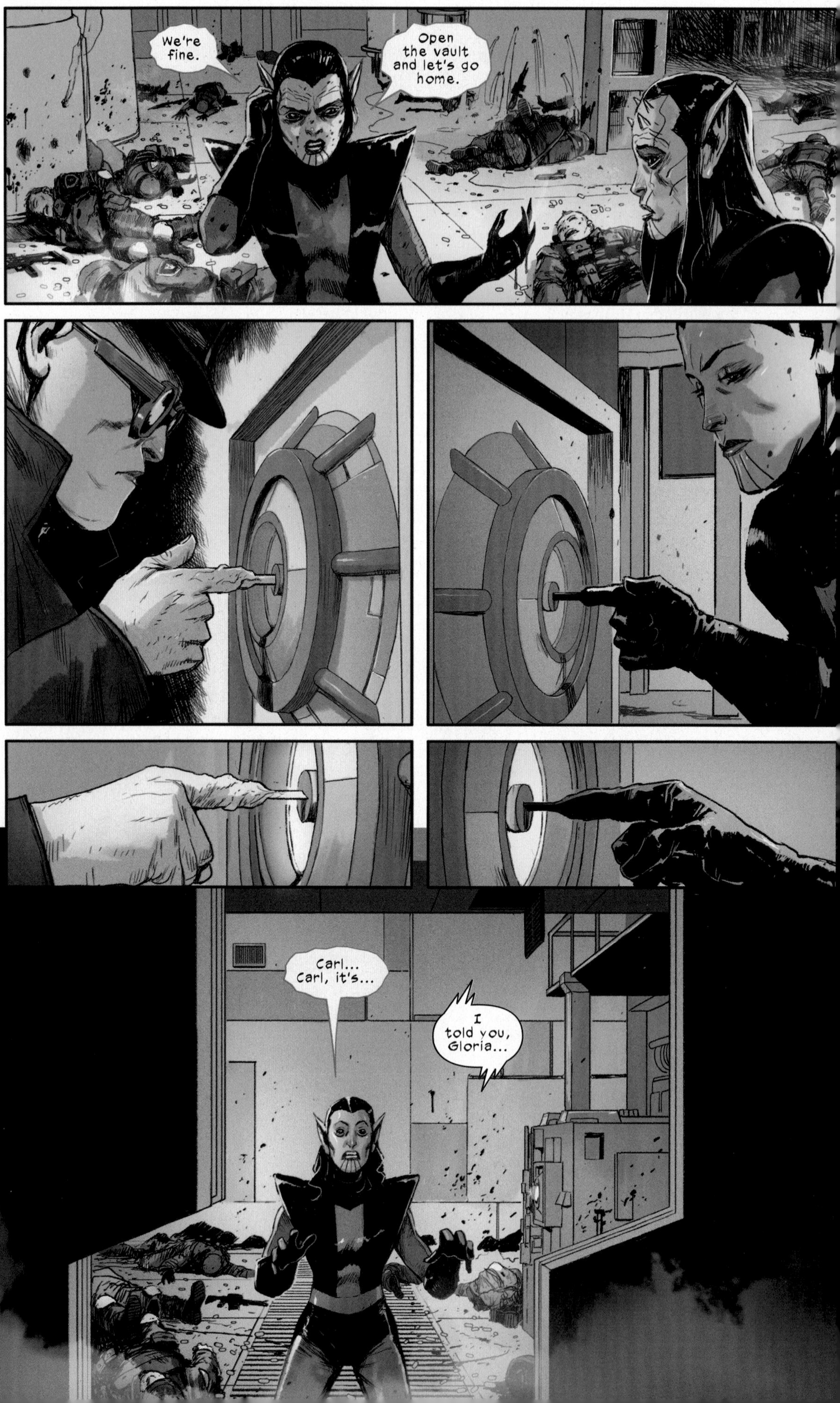
We're fine.
Open the vault and let's go home.
Carl... Carl, it's...
I told you, Gloria...

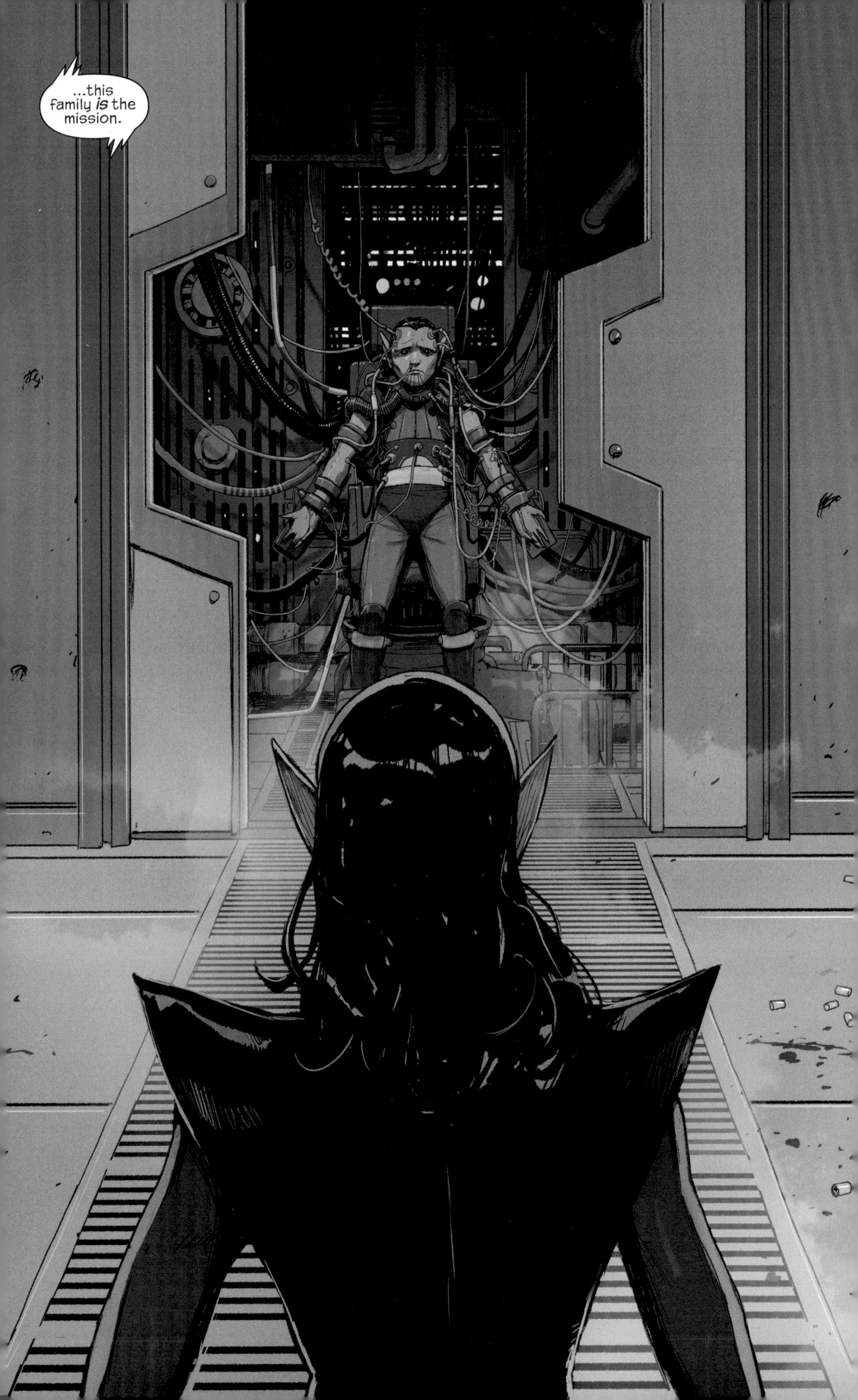
...this family *is* the mission.

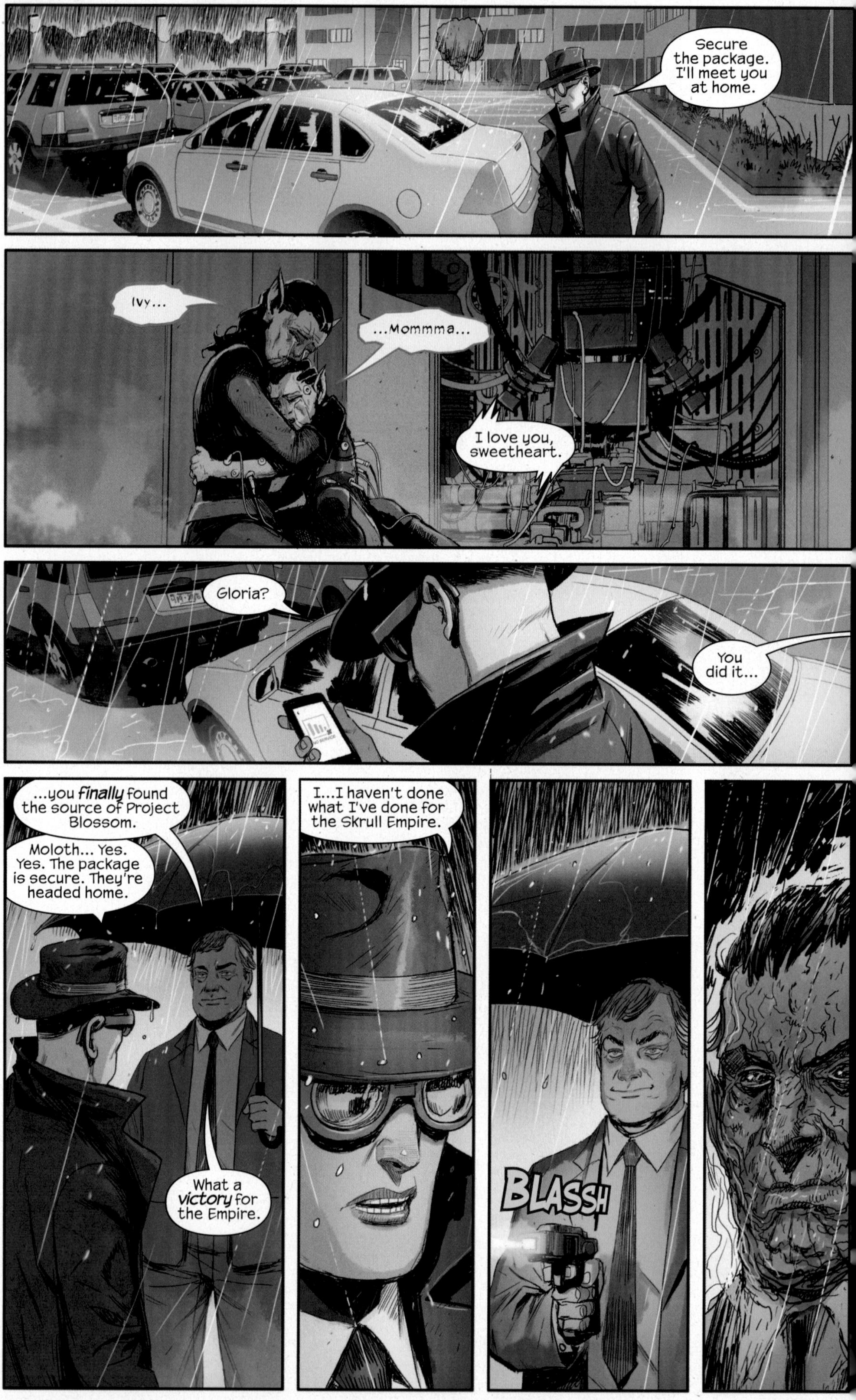
Secure the package. I'll meet you at home.
Ivy...
...Mommma...
I love you, sweetheart.
Gloria?
You did it...
...you finally found the source of Project Blossom.
Moloth... Yes. Yes. The package is secure. They're headed home.
What a victory for the Empire.
I...I haven't done what I've done for the Skrull Empire.
BLASSH

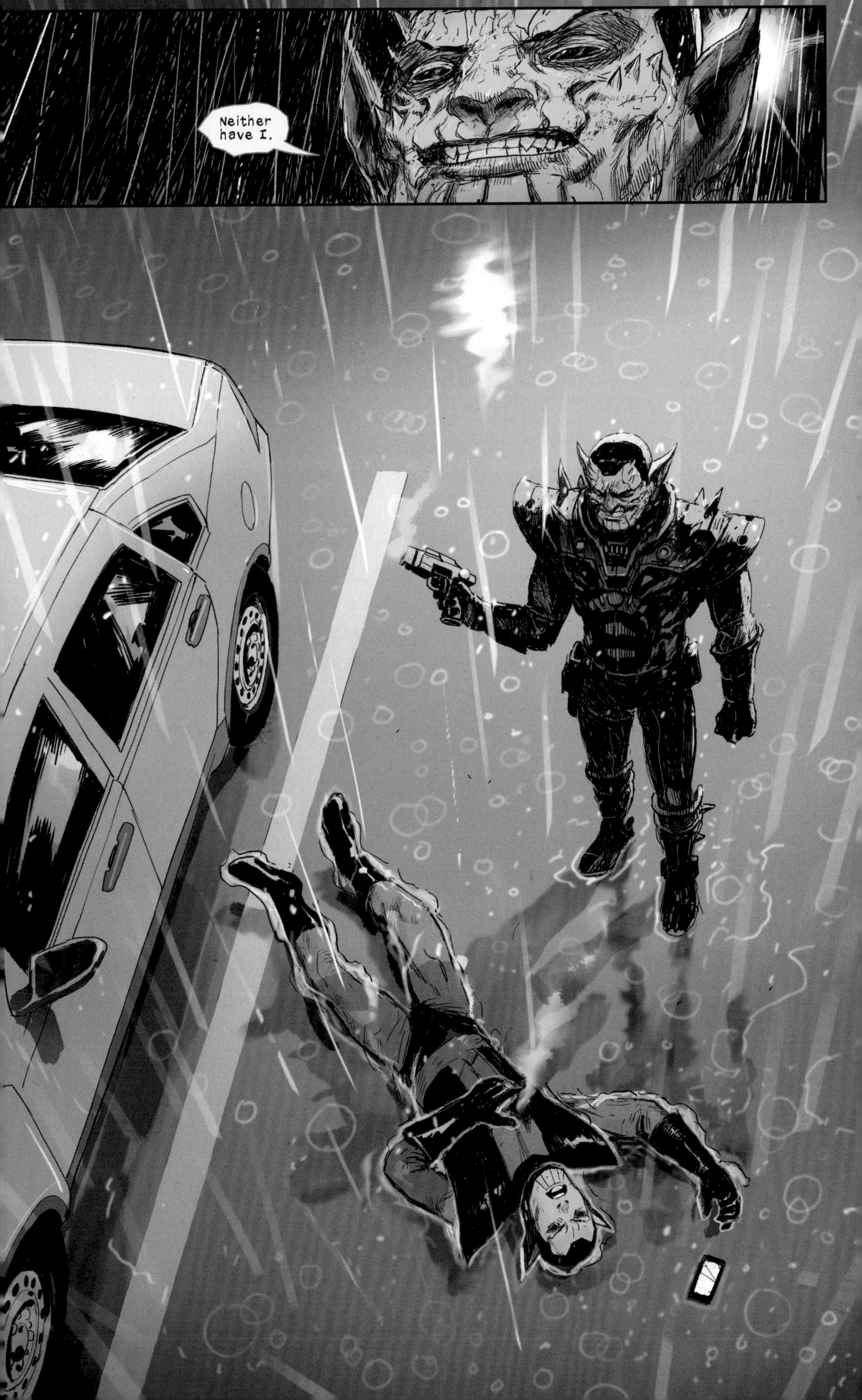
Neither have I.

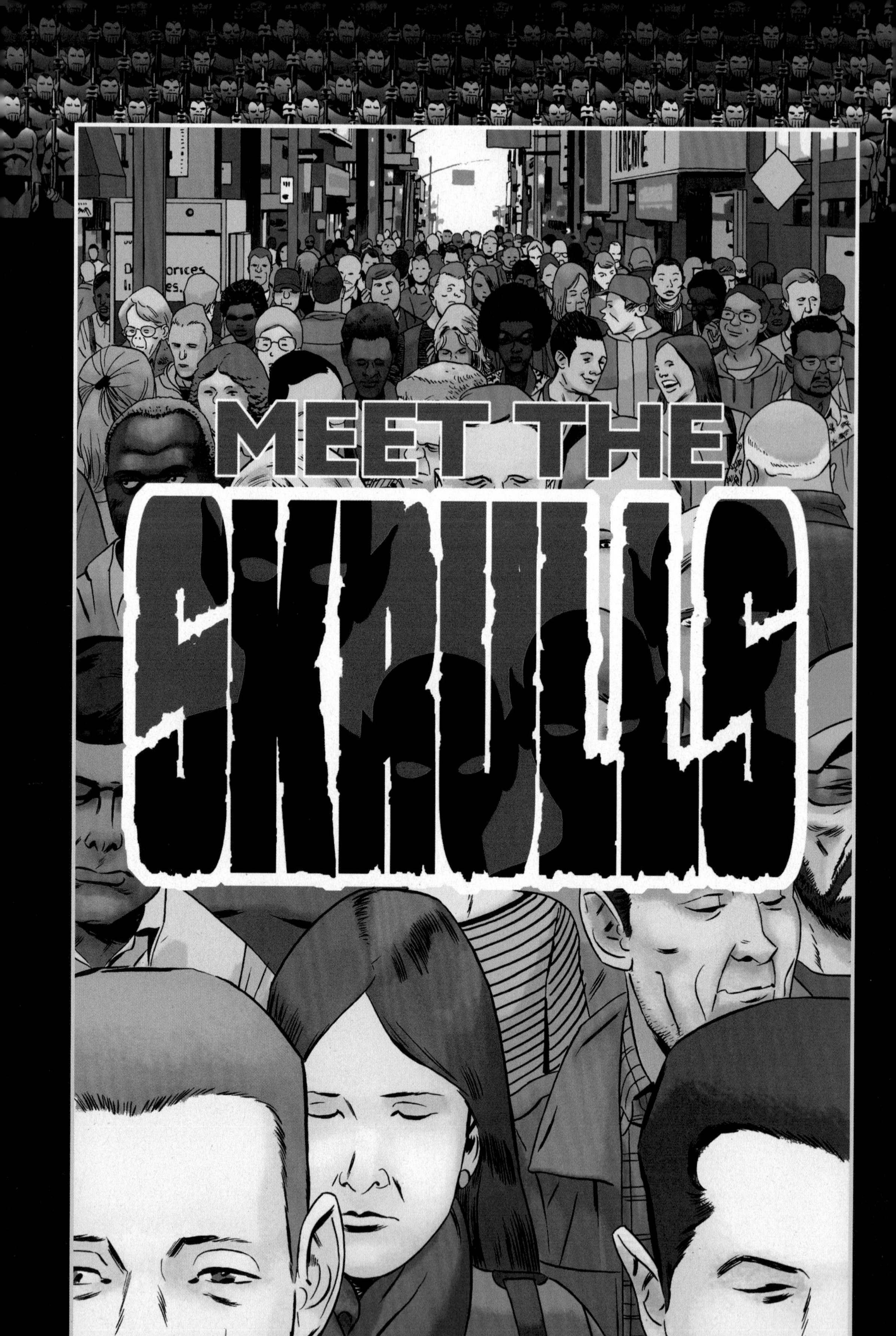
MEET THE
SKRULLS

MEET THE SKRULLS #5

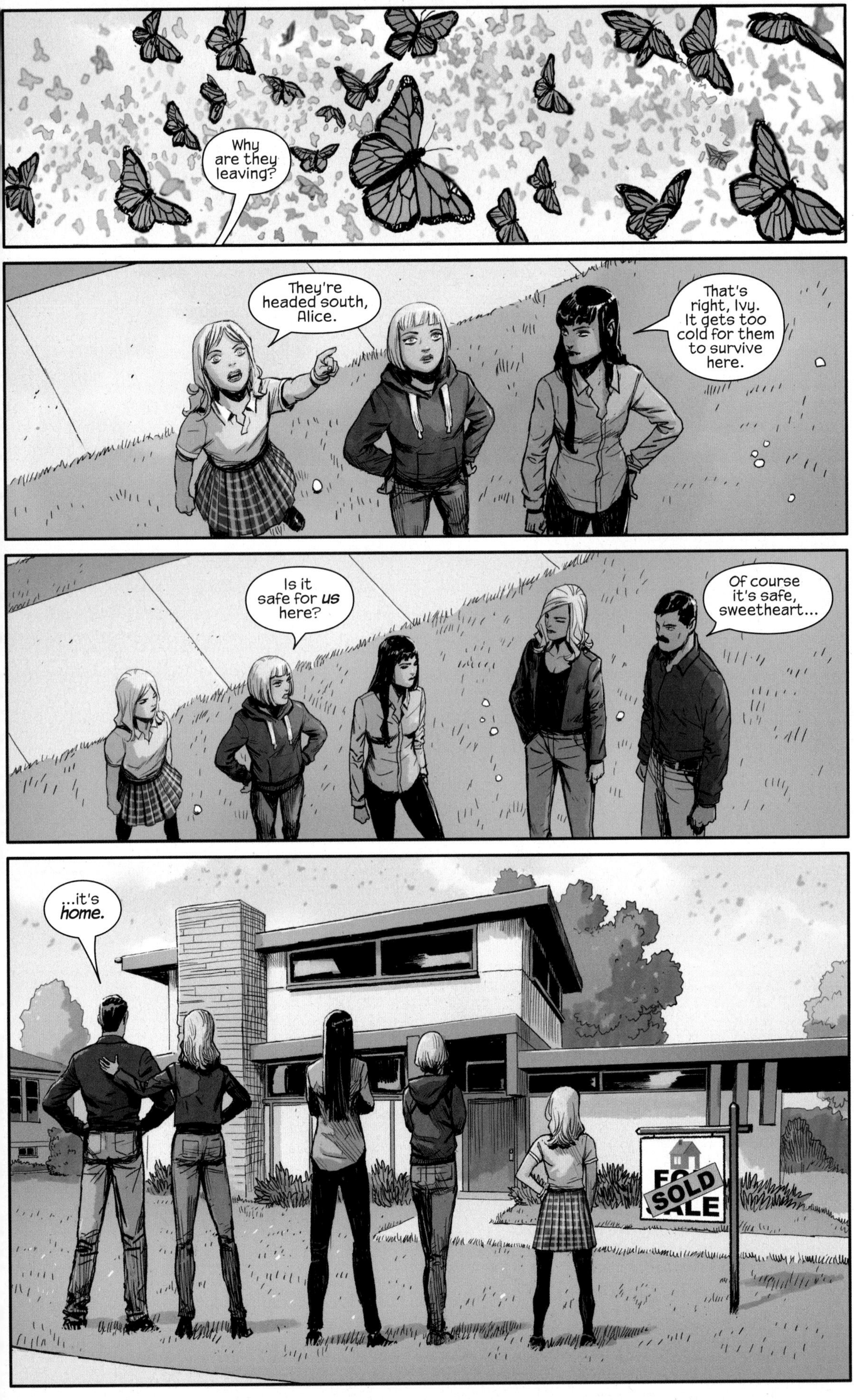
Why are they leaving?
They're headed south, Alice.
That's right, Ivy. It gets too cold for them to survive here.
Is it safe for *us* here?
Of course it's safe, sweetheart...
...it's *home.*
SOLD

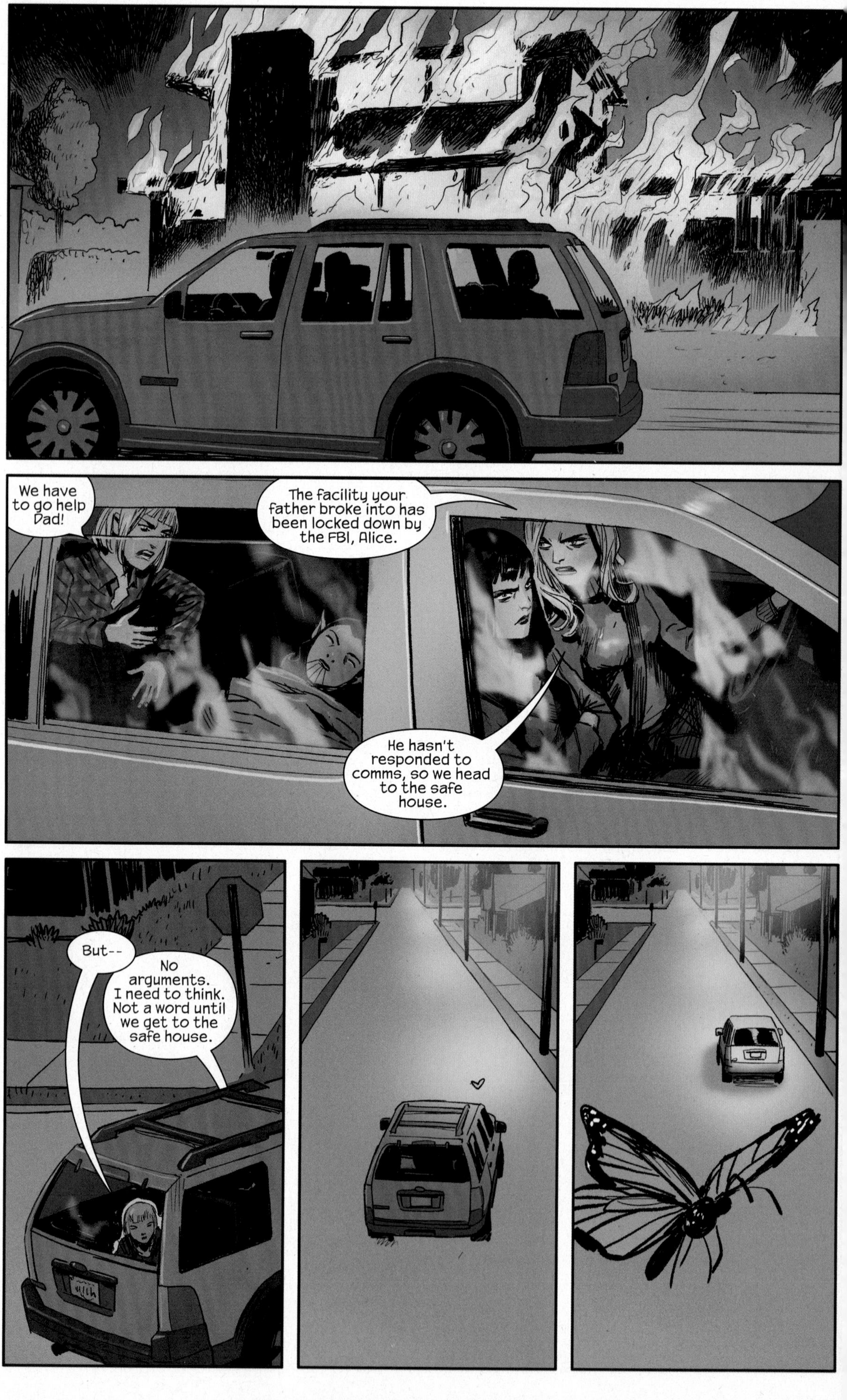
We have to go help Dad!
The facility your father broke into has been locked down by the FBI, Alice.
He hasn't responded to comms, so we head to the safe house.
But--
No arguments. I need to think. Not a word until we get to the safe house.

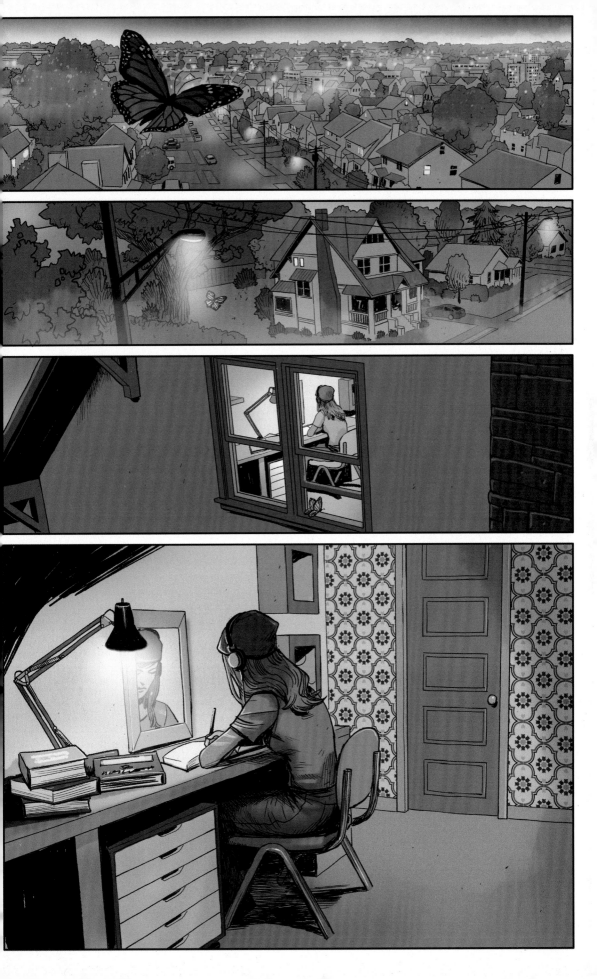

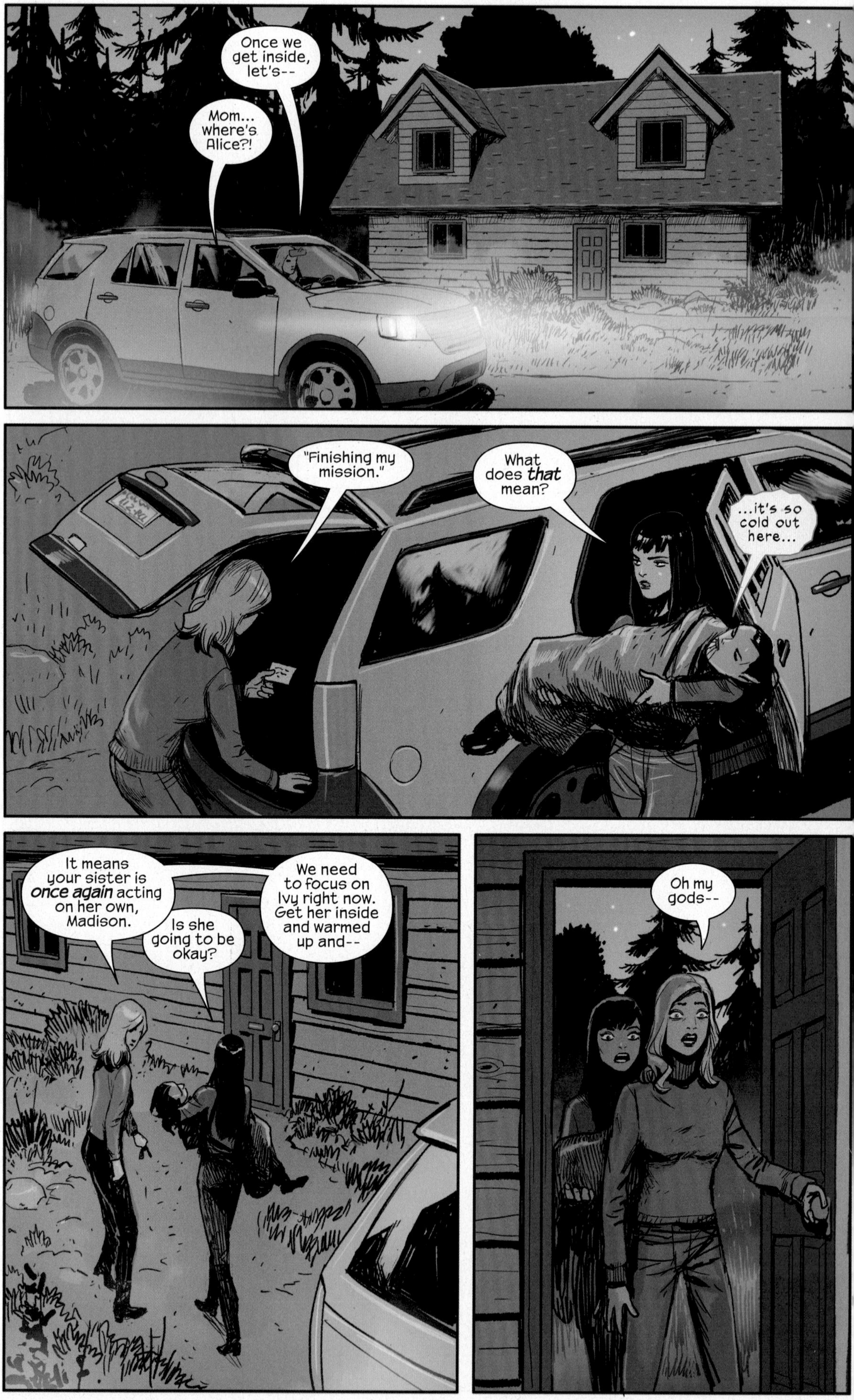
Once we get inside, let's--
Mom... where's Alice?!
"Finishing my mission."
What does *that* mean?
...it's so cold out here...
It means your sister is *once again* acting on her own, Madison.
Is she going to be okay?
We need to focus on Ivy right now. Get her inside and warmed up and--
Oh my gods--

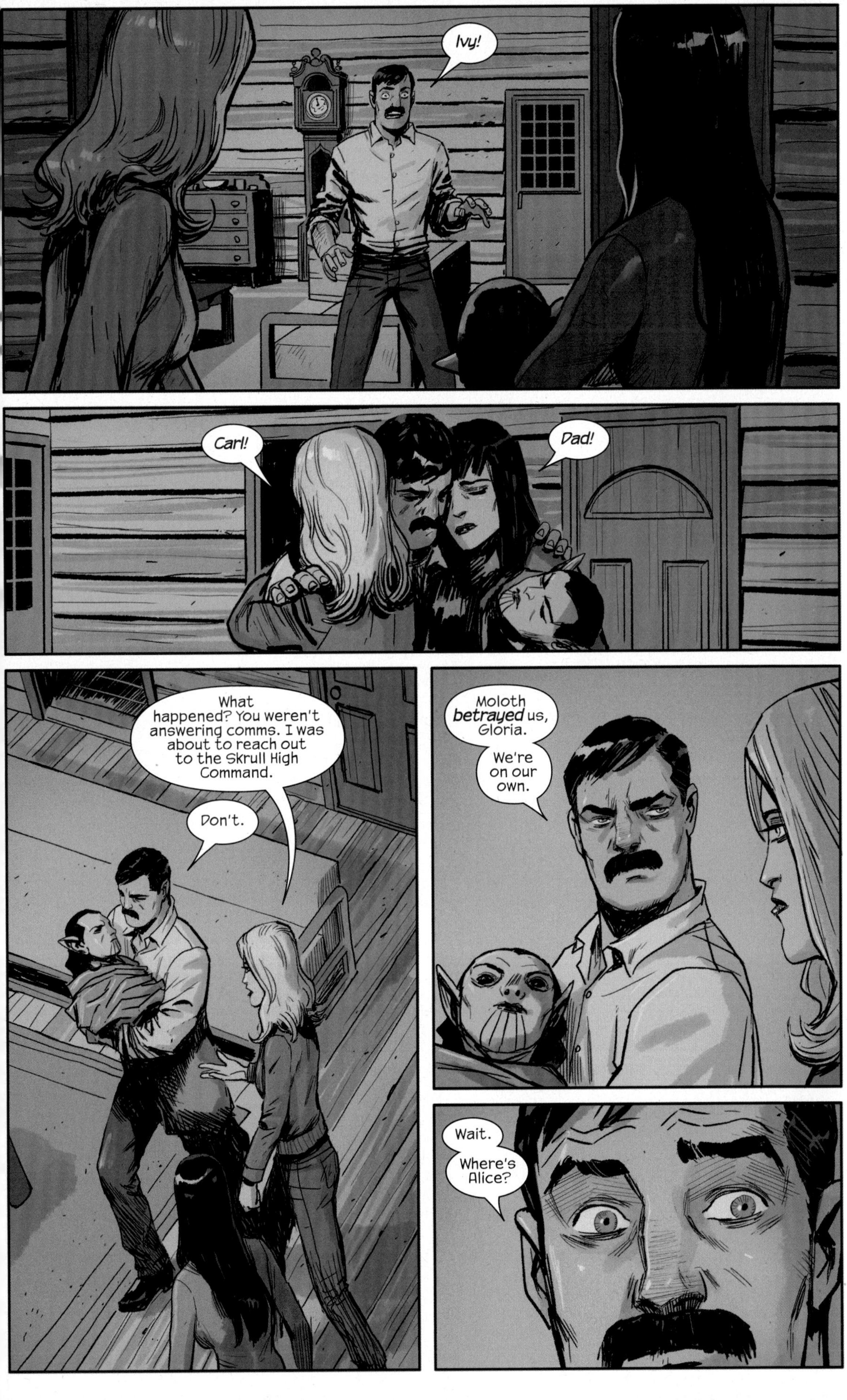
Ivy!
Carl!
Dad!
What happened? You weren't answering comms. I was about to reach out to the Skrull High Command.
Don't.
Moloth betrayed us, Gloria.
We're on our own.
Wait.
Where's Alice?

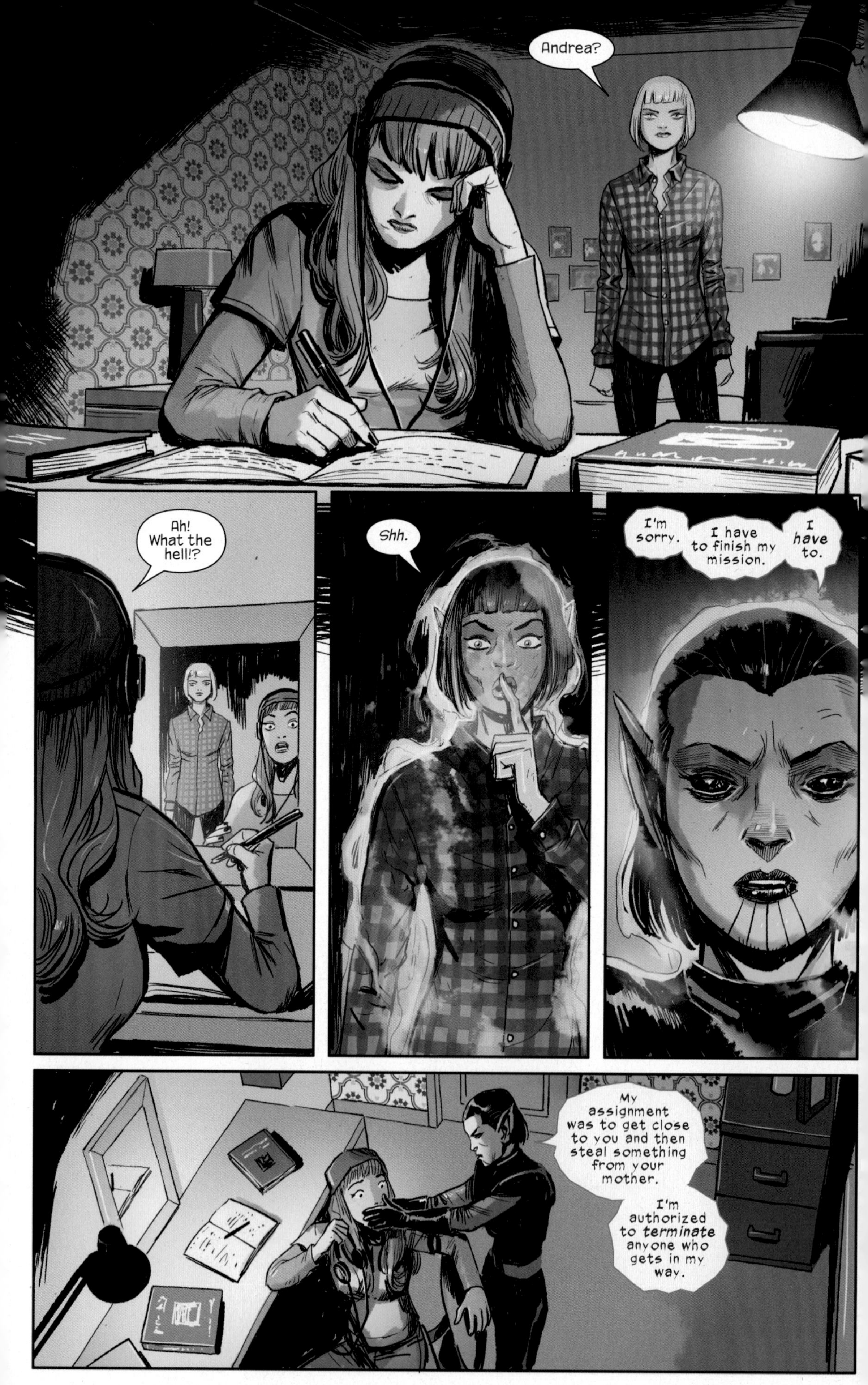
Andrea?
Ah! What the hell!?
Shh.
I'm sorry.
I have to finish my mission.
I *have* to.
My assignment was to get close to you and then steal something from your mother.
I'm authorized to *terminate* anyone who gets in my way.

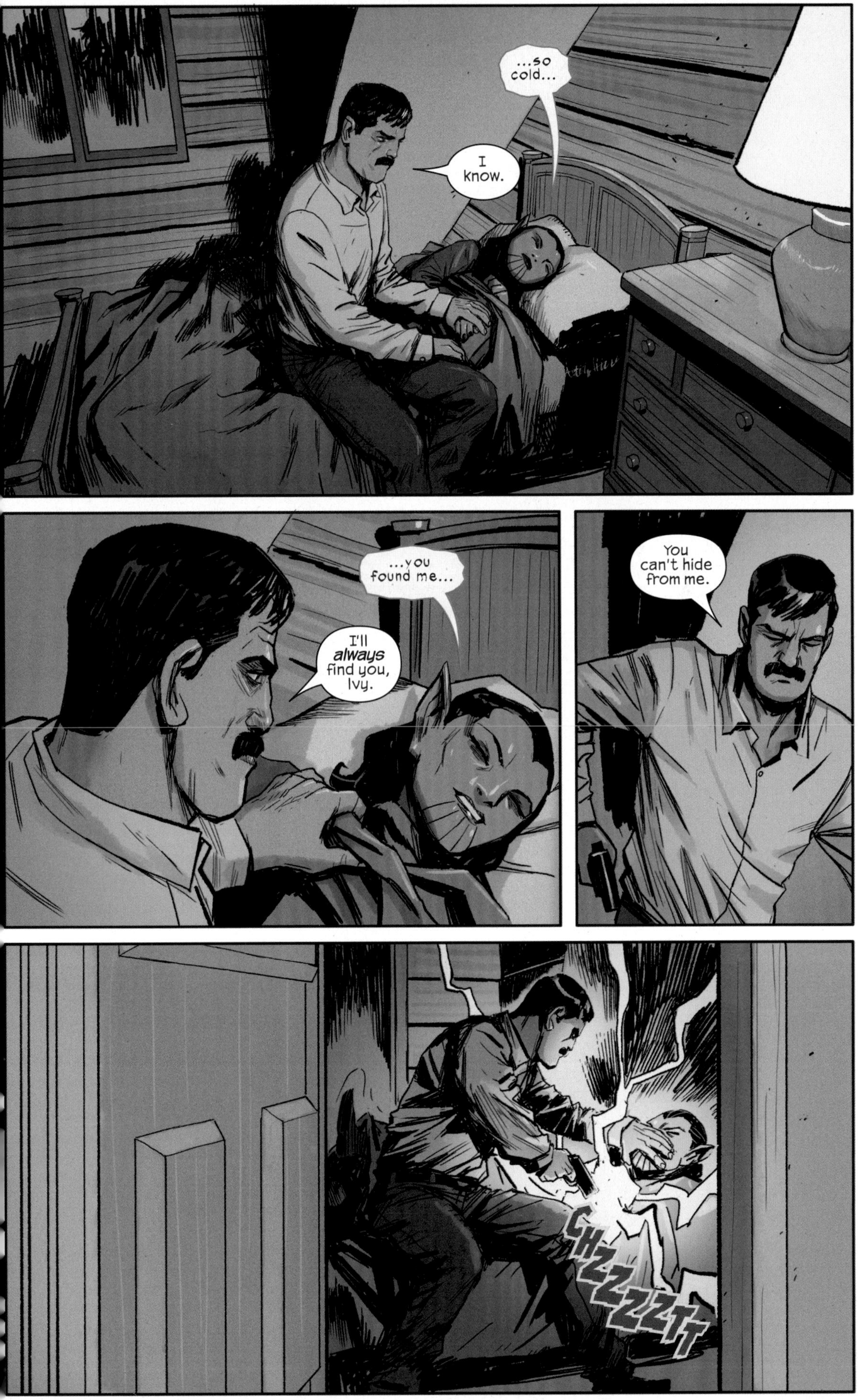
...so cold...
I know.
...you found me...
I'll *always* find you, Ivy.
You can't hide from me.
CHZZZZZTT

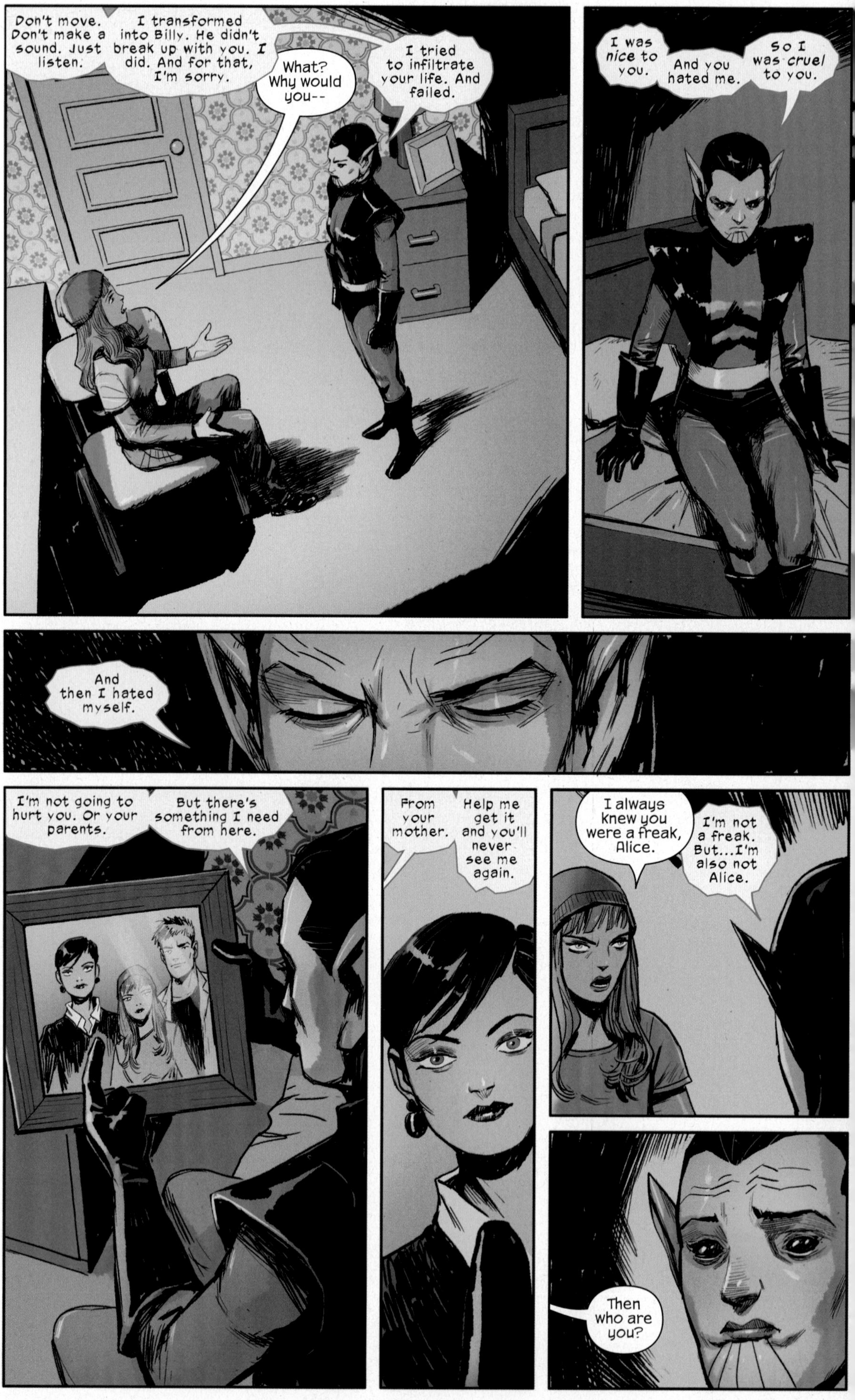
Don't move. Don't make a sound. Just listen.
I transformed into Billy. He didn't break up with you. I did. And for that, I'm sorry.
What? Why would you--
I tried to infiltrate your life. And failed.
I was *nice* to you.
And you hated me.
So I was *cruel* to you.
And then I hated myself.
I'm not going to hurt you. Or your parents.
But there's something I need from here.
From your mother.
Help me get it and you'll never see me again.
I always knew you were a freak, Alice.
I'm not a freak. But...I'm also not Alice.
Then who are you?

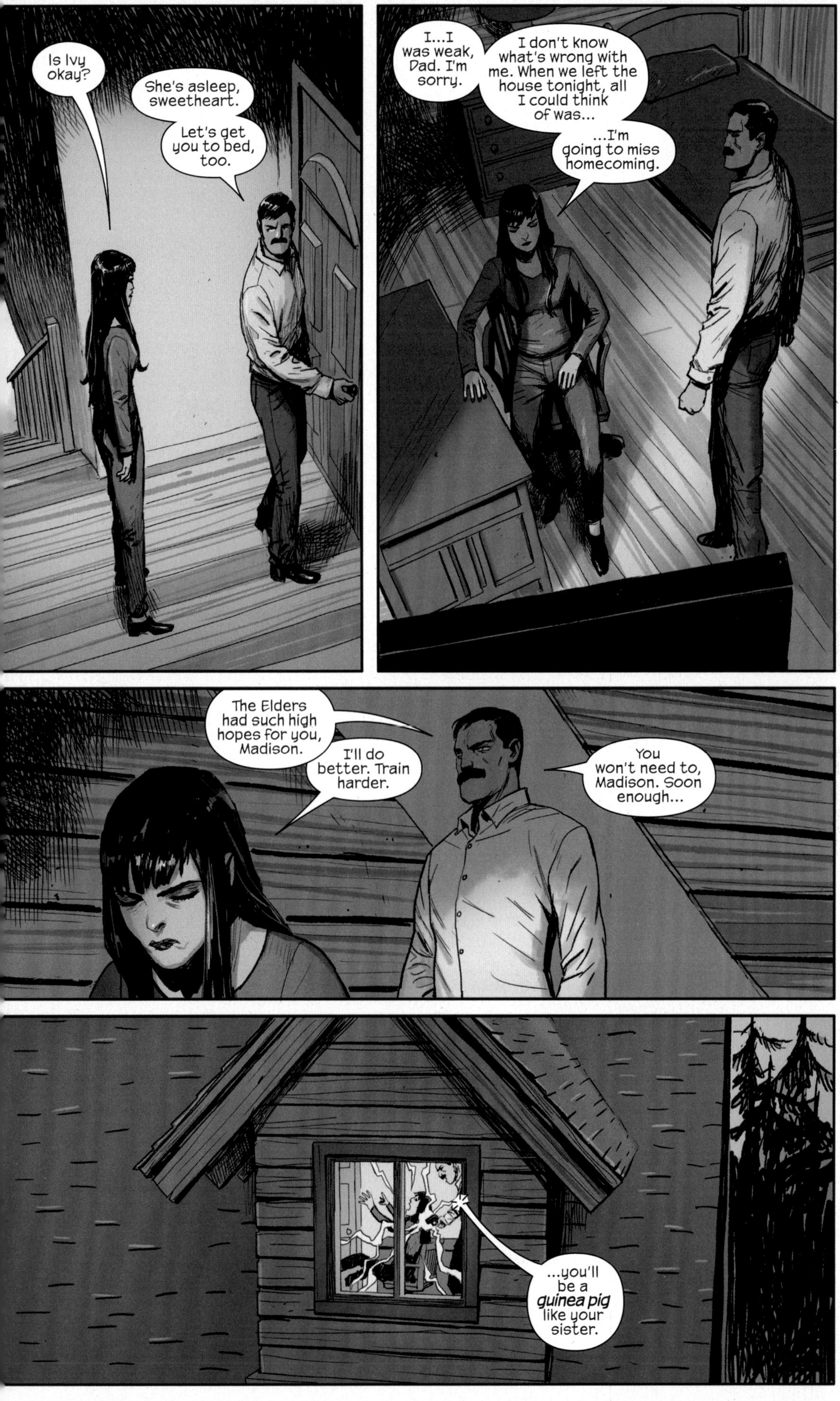

Is Ivy okay?
She's asleep, sweetheart.
Let's get you to bed, too.
I...I was weak, Dad. I'm sorry.
I don't know what's wrong with me. When we left the house tonight, all I could think of was...
...I'm going to miss homecoming.
The Elders had such high hopes for you, Madison.
I'll do better. Train harder.
You won't need to, Madison. Soon enough...
...you'll be a *guinea pig* like your sister.

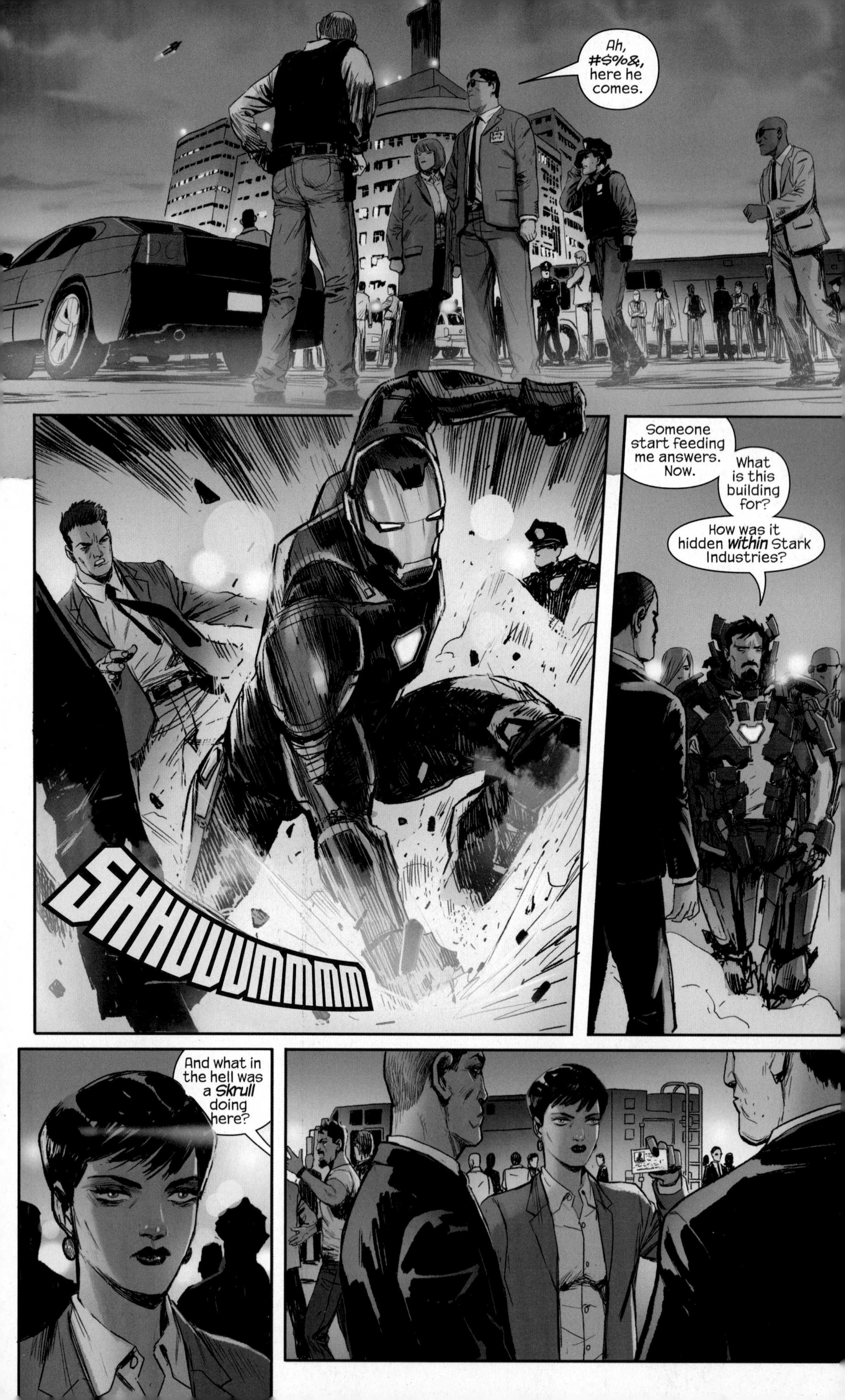
Ah, #$%&, here he comes.
SHHUUUMMMM
Someone start feeding me answers. Now.
What is this building for?
How was it hidden *within* Stark Industries?
And what in the hell was a *Skrull* doing here?

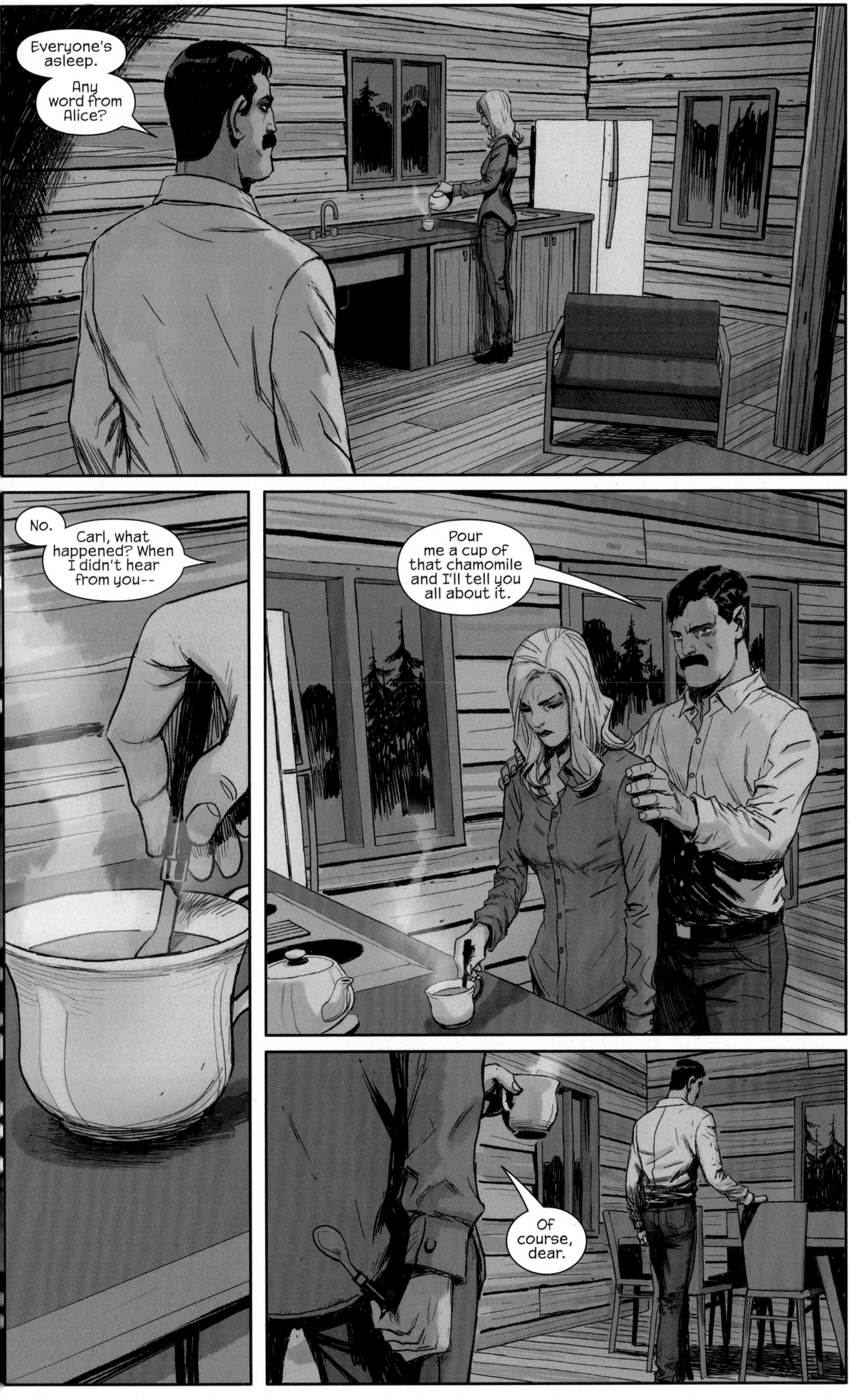
Everyone's asleep.
Any word from Alice?
No.
Carl, what happened? When I didn't hear from you--
Pour me a cup of that chamomile and I'll tell you all about it.
Of course, dear.

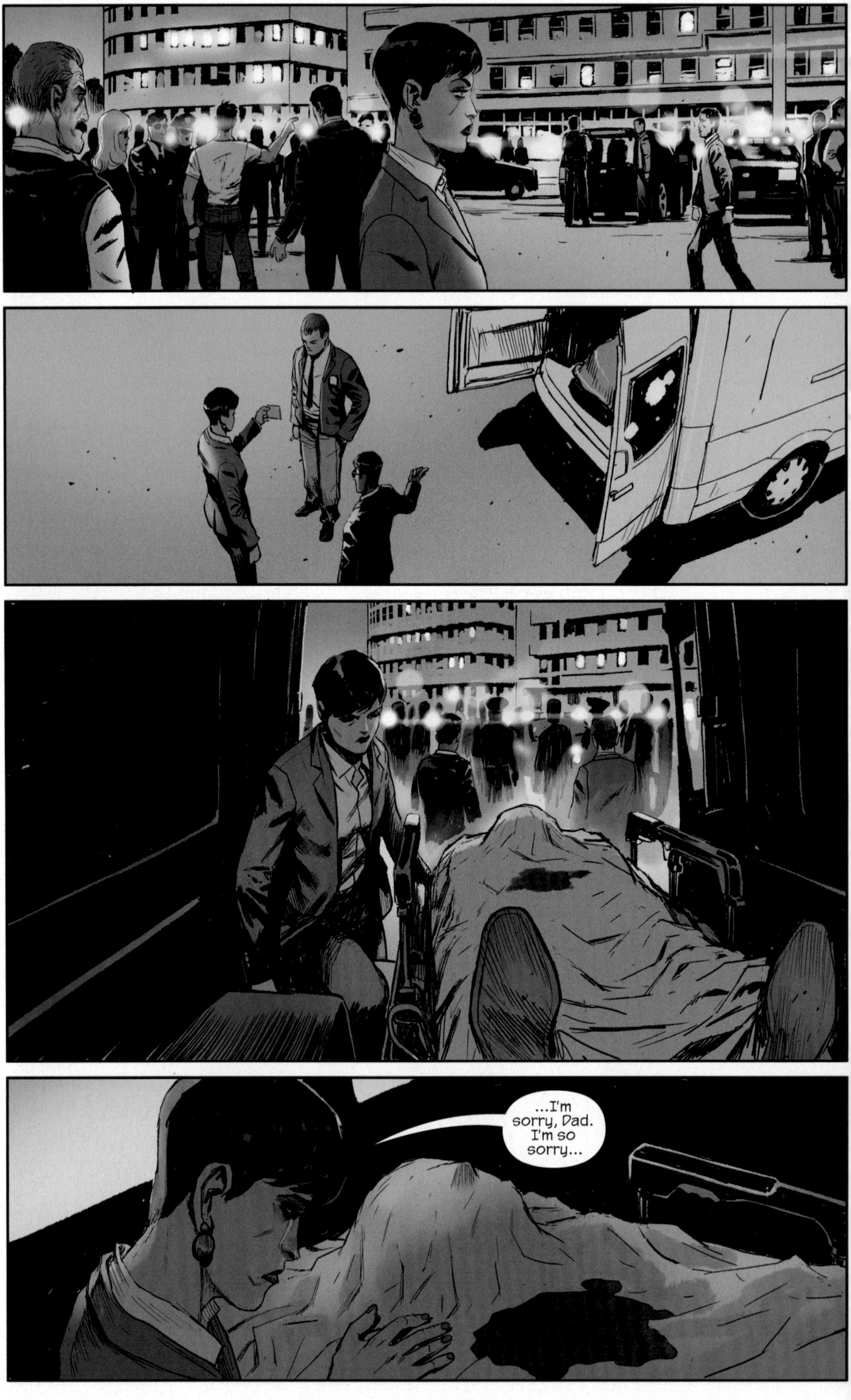
...I'm sorry, Dad. I'm so sorry...

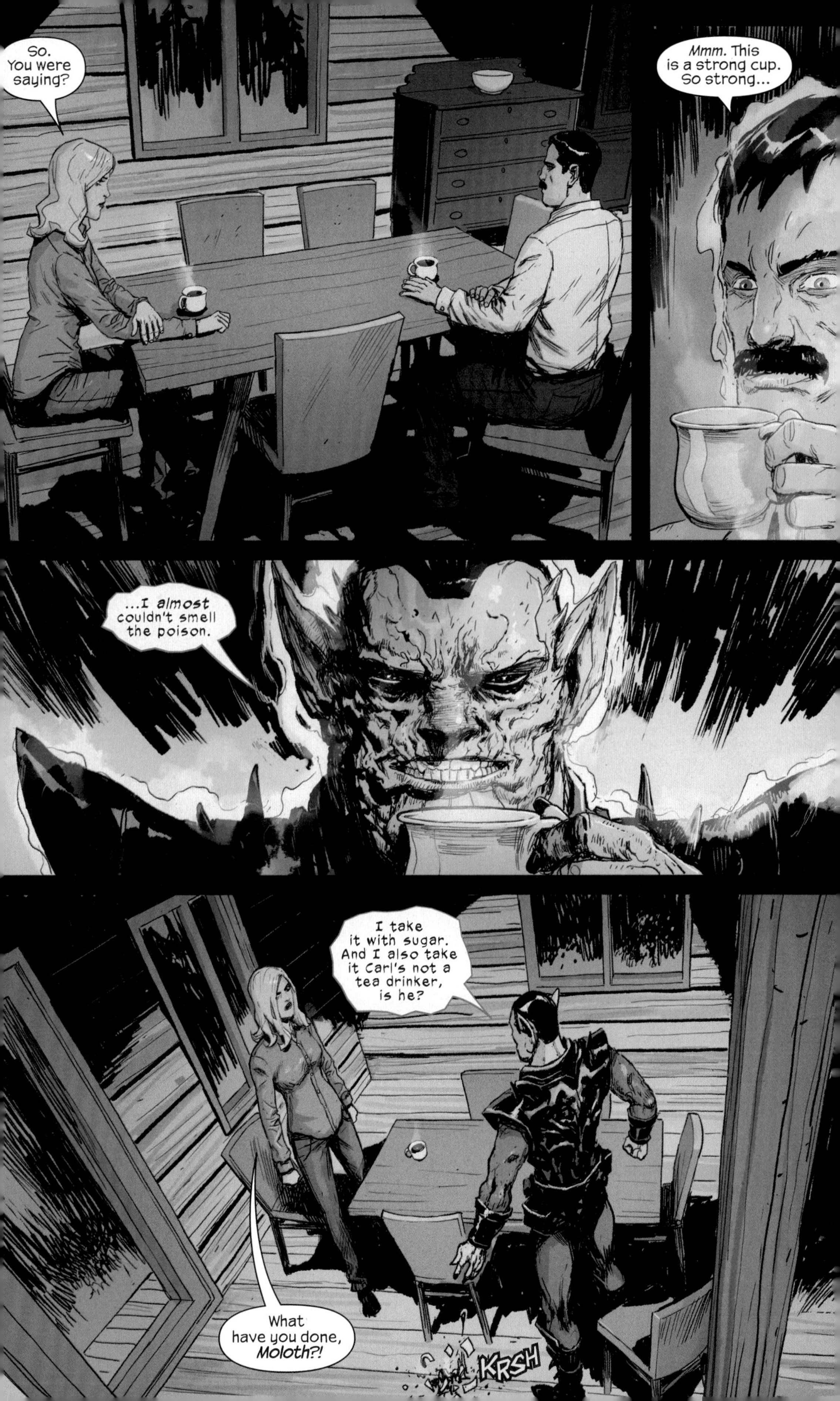

So. You were saying?
Mmm. This is a strong cup. So strong...
...I *almost* couldn't smell the poison.
I take it with sugar. And I also take it Carl's not a tea drinker, is he?
What have you done, *Moloth?!*
KRSH

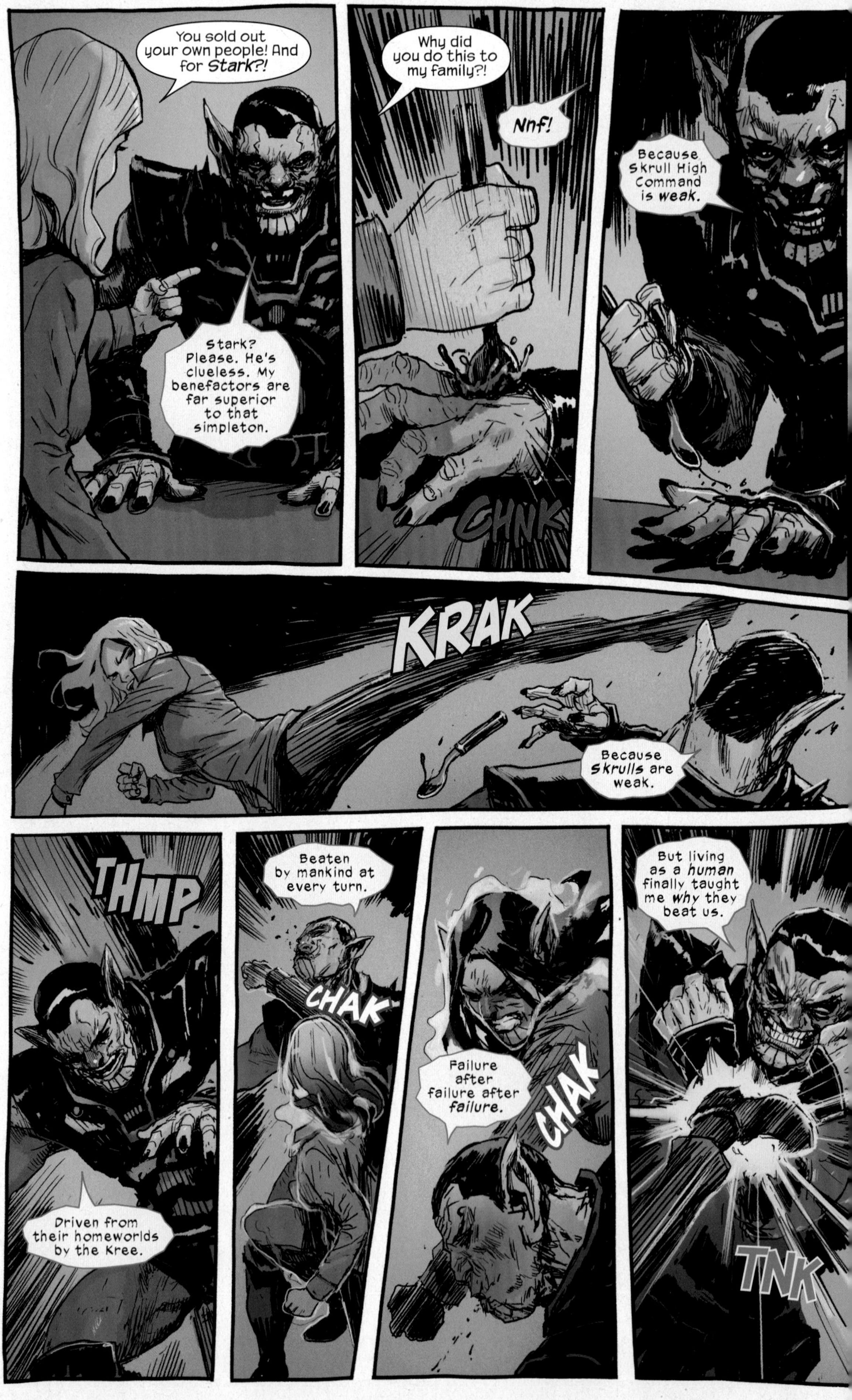
You sold out your own people! And for Stark?!
Stark? Please. He's clueless. My benefactors are far superior to that simpleton.
Why did you do this to my family?!
Nnf!
CHNK
Because Skrull High Command is weak.
KRAK
Because Skrulls are weak.
THMP
Driven from their homeworlds by the Kree.
Beaten by mankind at every turn.
CHAK
Failure after failure after failure.
CHAK
But living as a human finally taught me why they beat us.
TNK

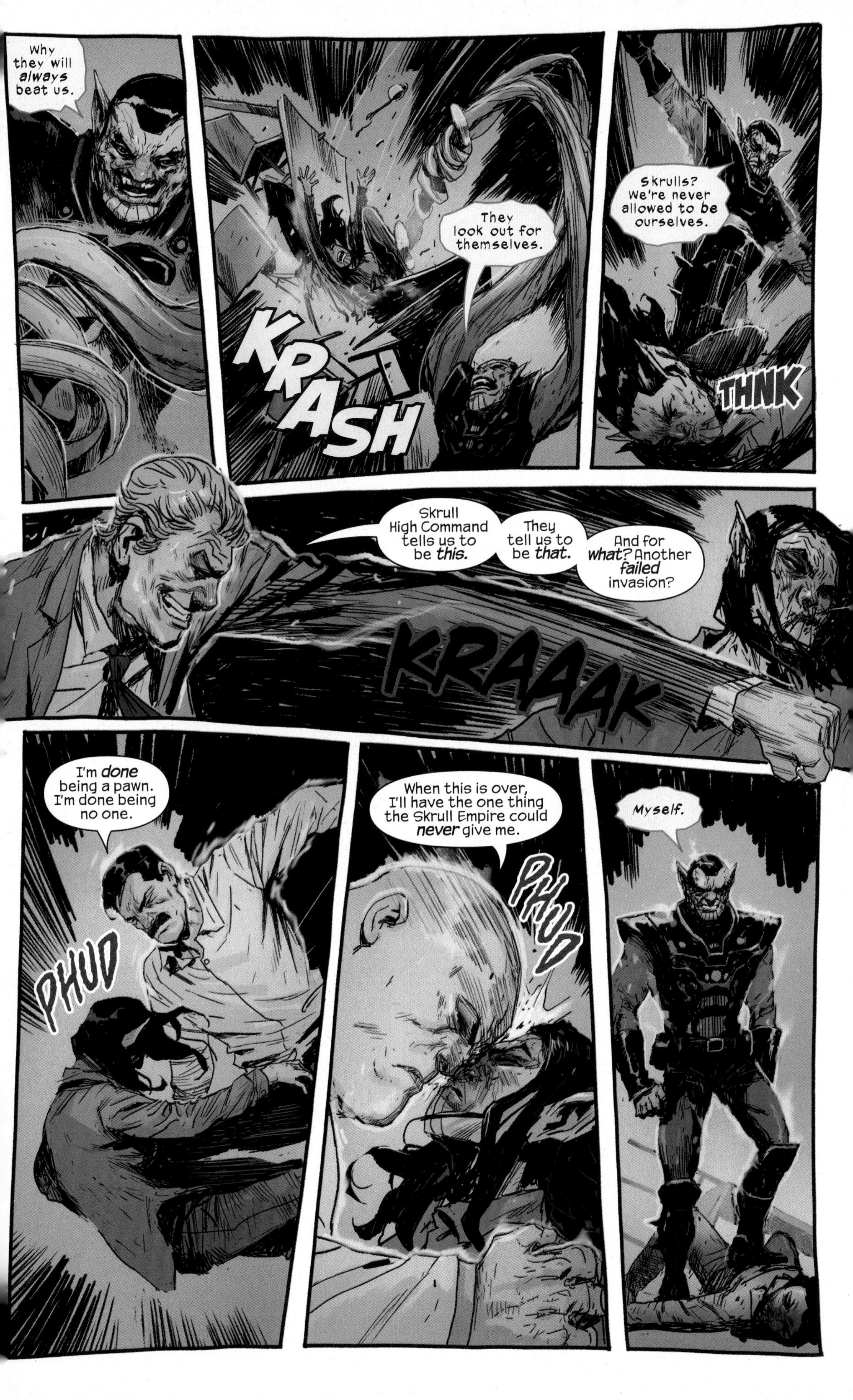
Why they will always beat us.
They look out for themselves.
KRASH
Skrulls? We're never allowed to be ourselves.
THNK
Skrull High Command tells us to be this.
They tell us to be that.
And for what? Another failed invasion?
KRAAAK
I'm done being a pawn. I'm done being no one.
PHUD
When this is over, I'll have the one thing the Skrull Empire could never give me.
PHUD
Myself.

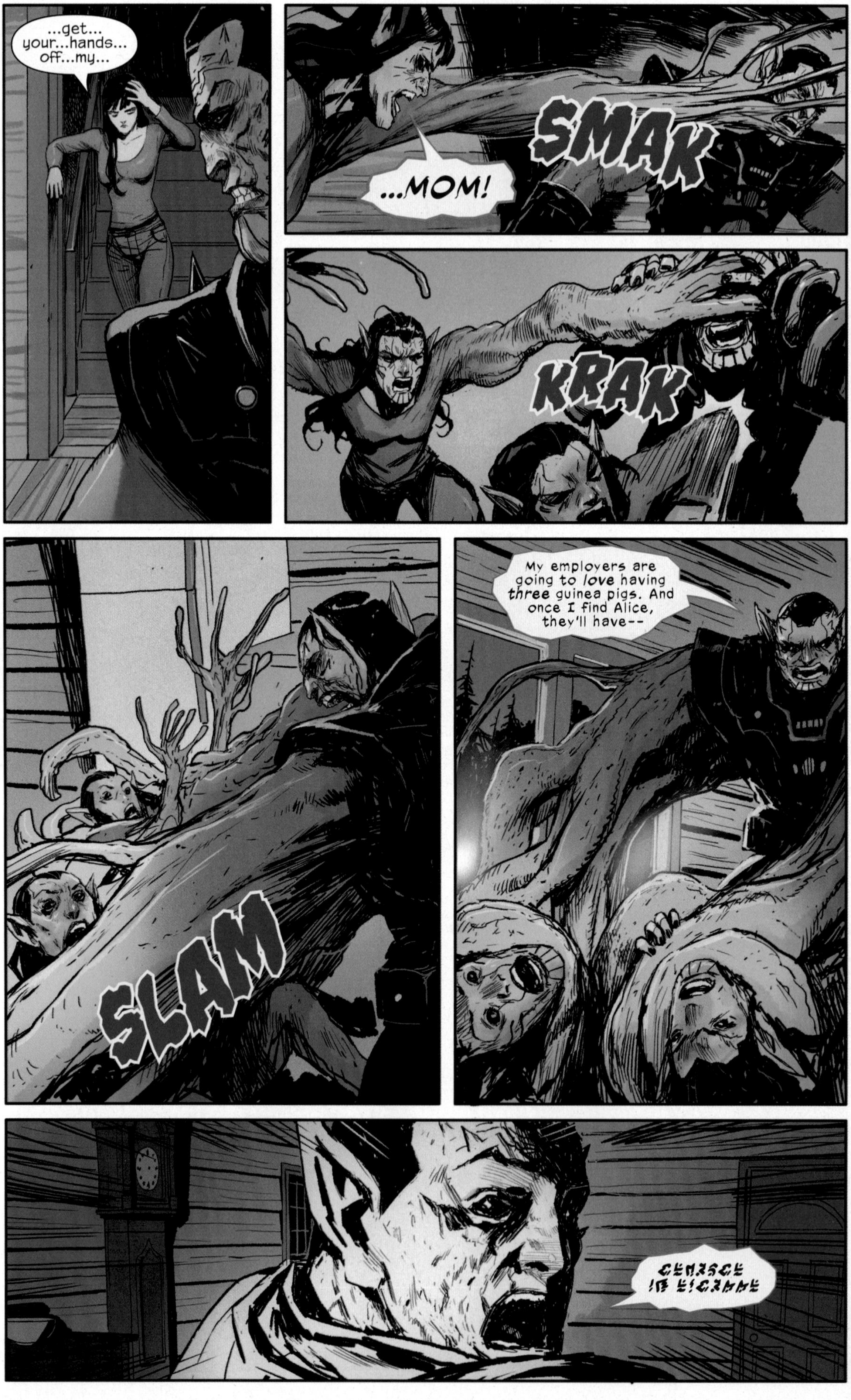
...get... your...hands... off...my...
...MOM!
SMAK
KRAK
SLAM
My employers are going to *love* having *three* guinea pigs. And once I find Alice, they'll have--

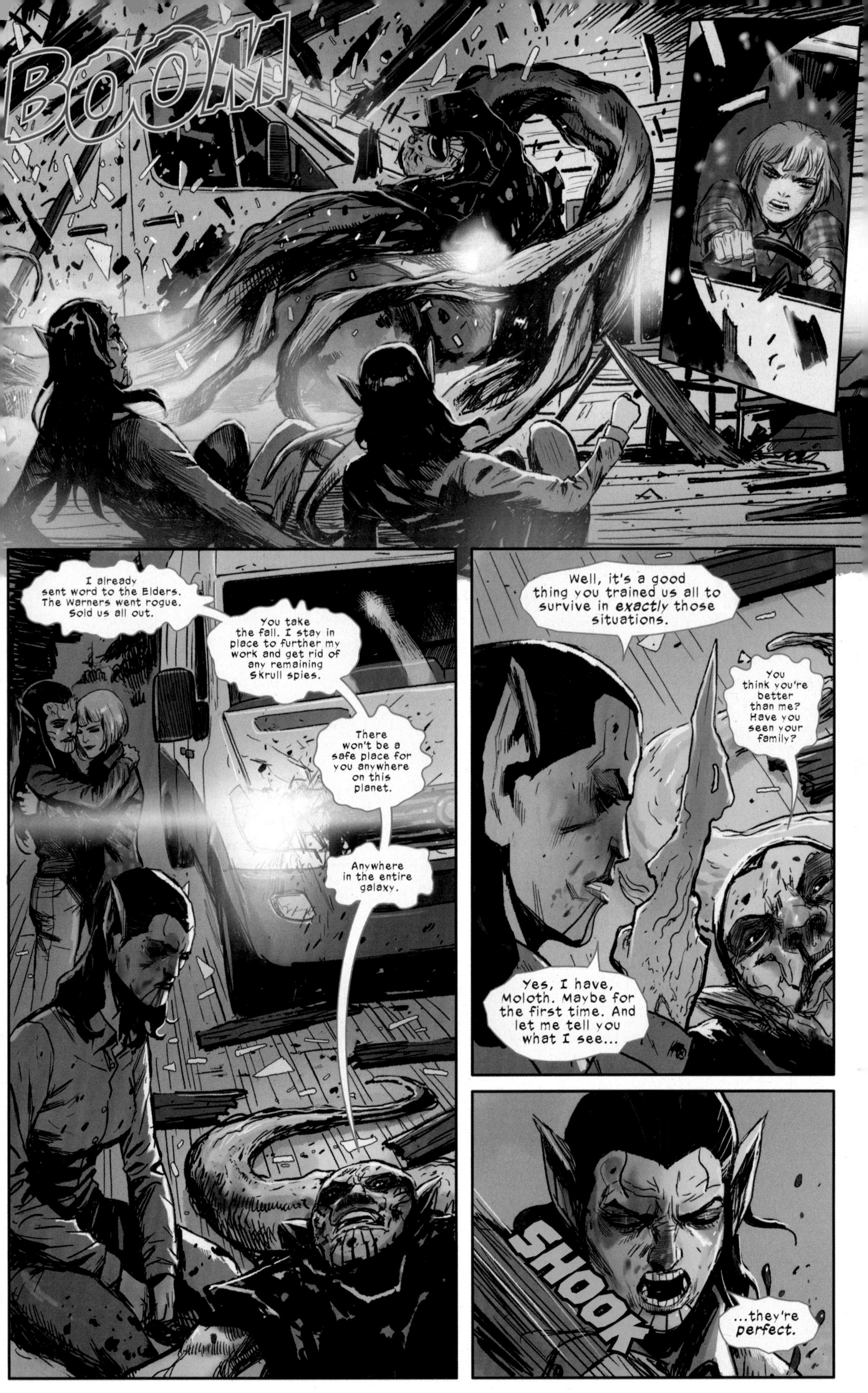
BOOM
I already sent word to the Elders. The Warners went rogue. Sold us all out.
You take the fall. I stay in place to further my work and get rid of any remaining Skrull spies.
There won't be a safe place for you anywhere on this planet.
Anywhere in the entire galaxy.
Well, it's a good thing you trained us all to survive in *exactly* those situations.
You think you're better than me? Have you seen your family?
Yes, I have, Moloth. Maybe for the first time. And let me tell you what I see...
SHOOK
...they're *perfect.*

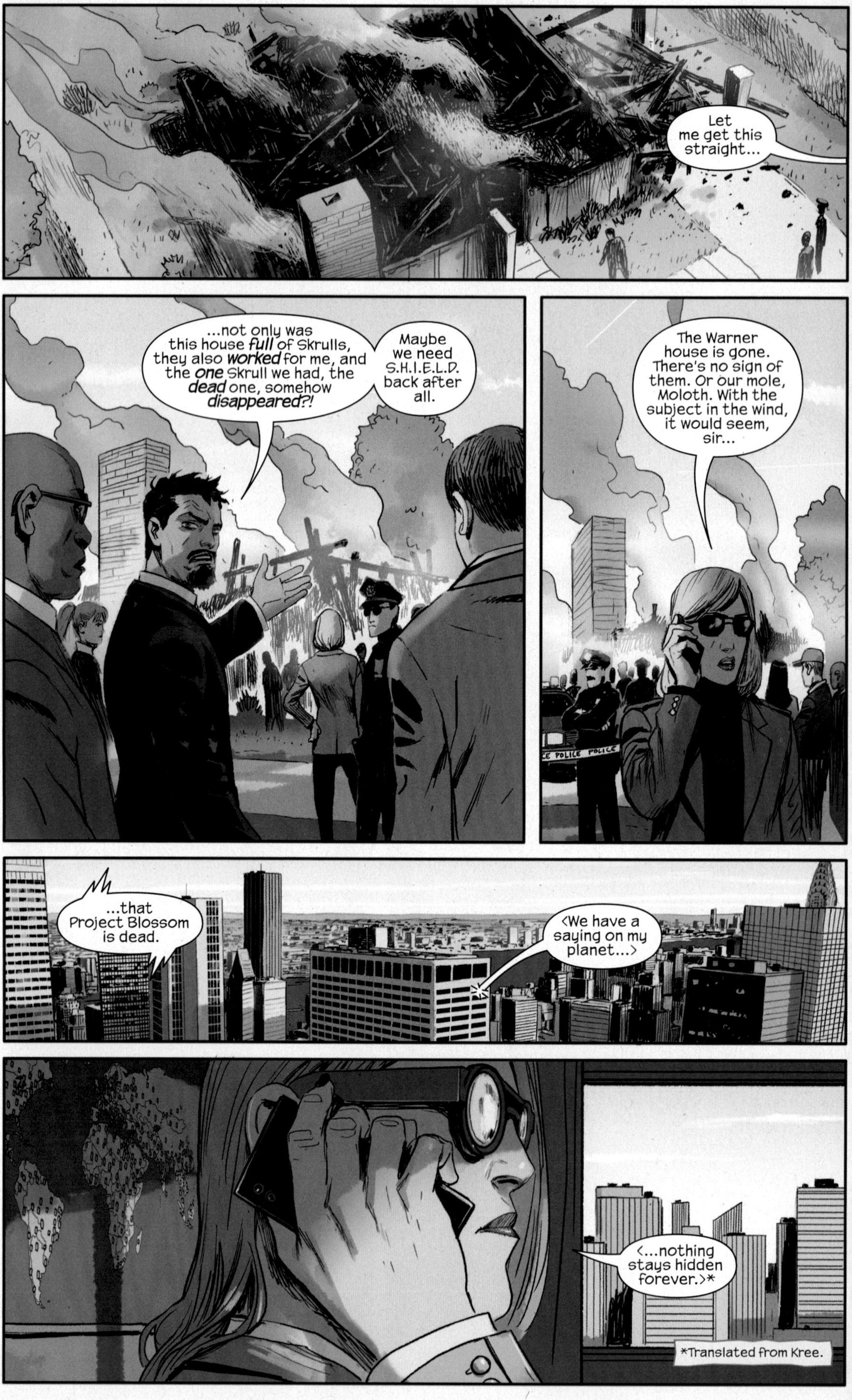
Let me get this straight...
...not only was this house full of Skrulls, they also worked for me, and the one Skrull we had, the dead one, somehow disappeared?!
Maybe we need S.H.I.E.L.D. back after all.
The Warner house is gone. There's no sign of them. Or our mole, Moloth. With the subject in the wind, it would seem, sir...
POLICE POLICE
...that Project Blossom is dead.
<We have a saying on my planet...>
<...nothing stays hidden forever.>*
*Translated from Kree.

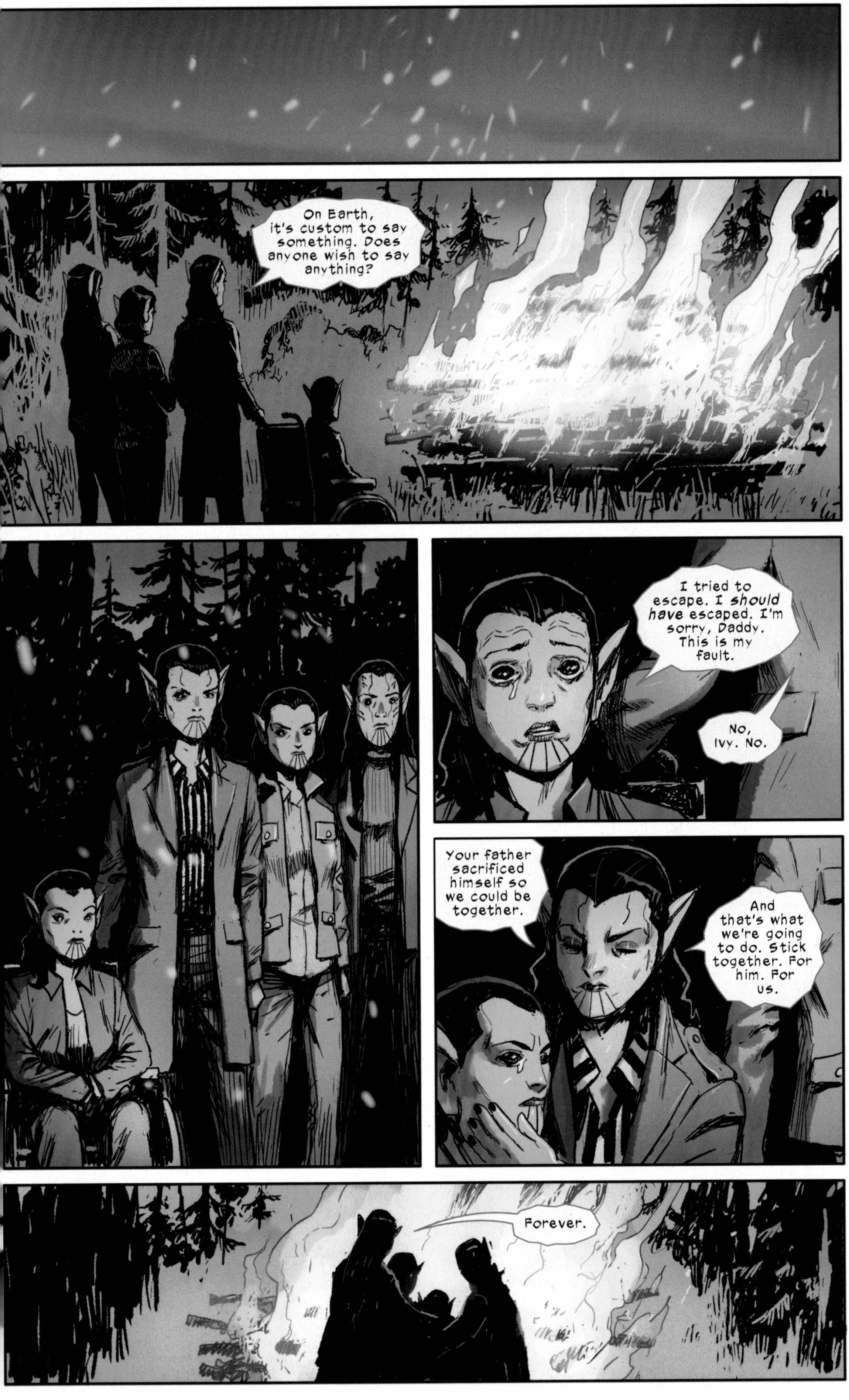
On Earth, it's custom to say something. Does anyone wish to say anything?
I tried to escape. I *should have* escaped. I'm sorry, Daddy. This is my fault.
No, Ivy. No.
Your father sacrificed himself so we could be together.
And that's what we're going to do. Stick together. For him. For us.
Forever.

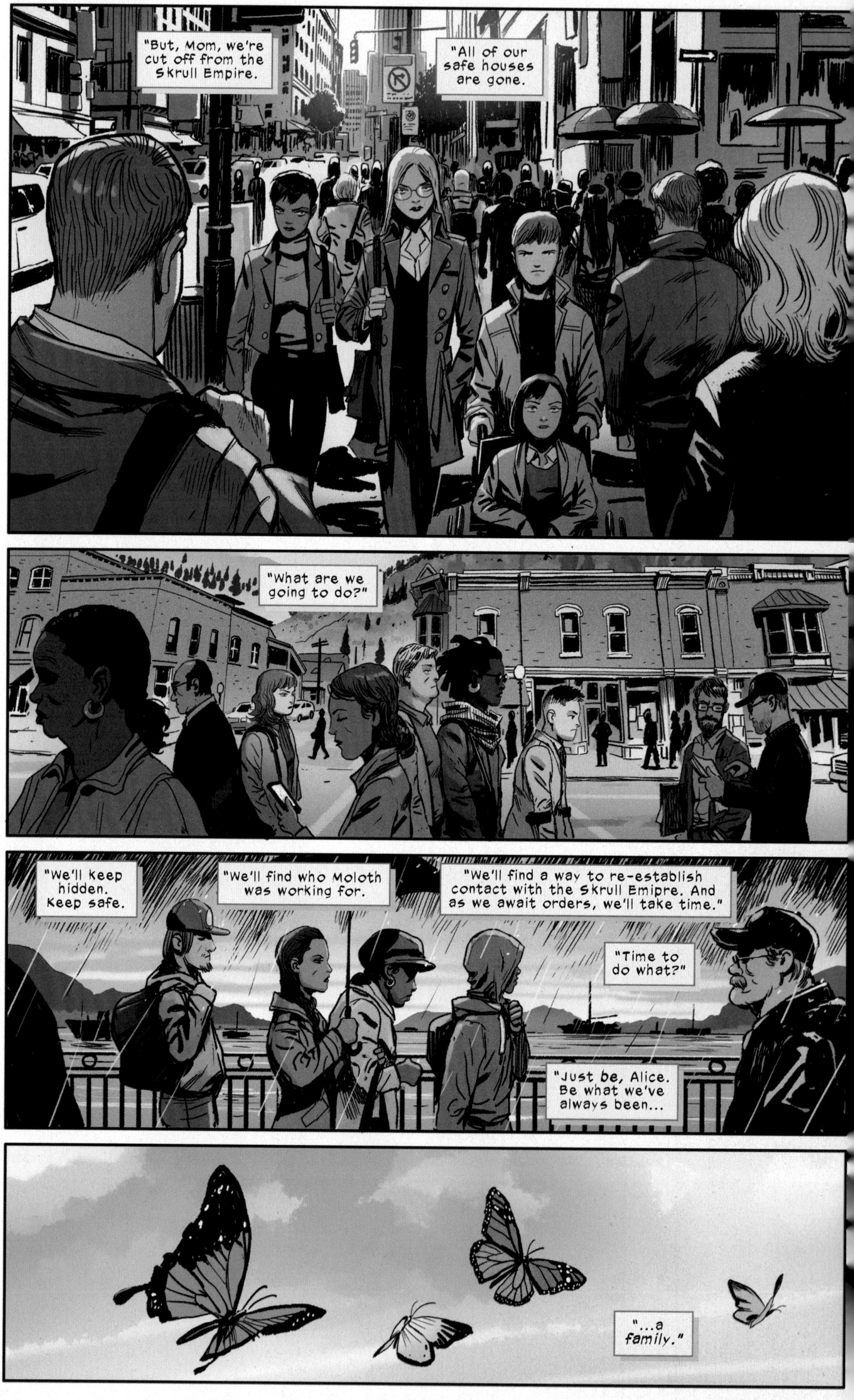
"But, Mom, we're cut off from the Skrull Empire.
"All of our safe houses are gone.
"What are we going to do?"
"We'll keep hidden. Keep safe.
"We'll find who Moloth was working for.
"We'll find a way to re-establish contact with the Skrull Emipre. And as we await orders, we'll take time."
"Time to do what?"
"Just be, Alice. Be what we've always been...
"...a family."

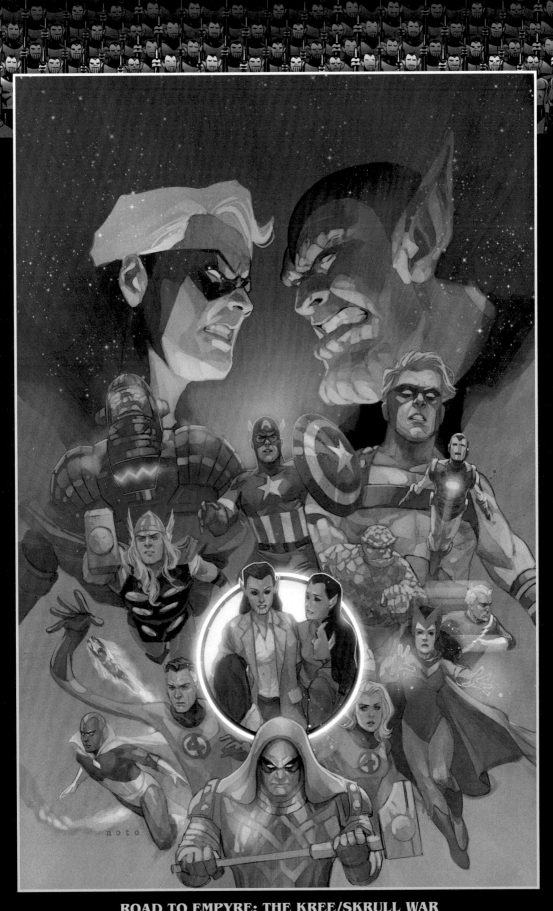

ROAD TO EMPYRE: THE KREE/SKRULL WAR

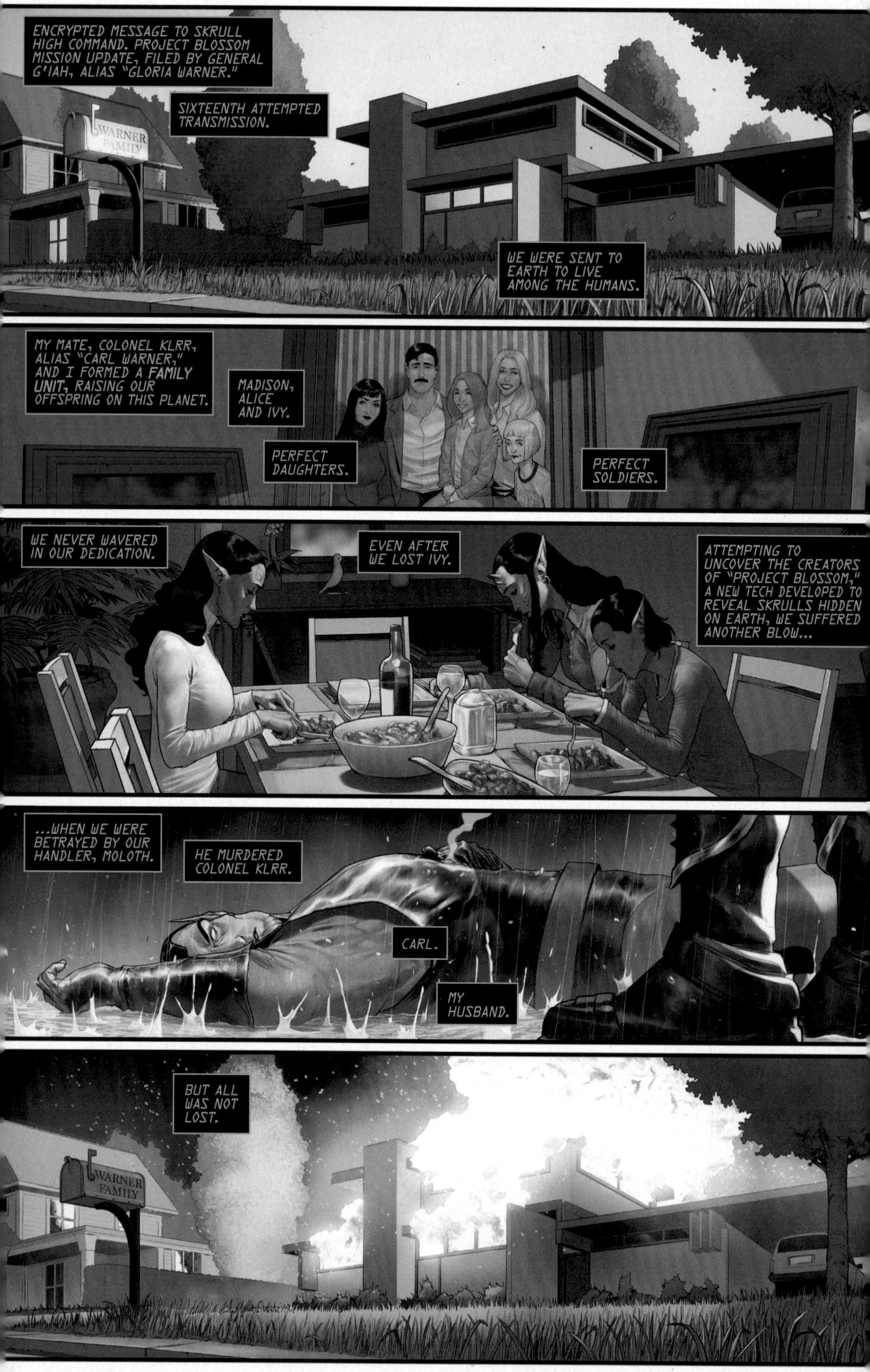
ENCRYPTED MESSAGE TO SKRULL HIGH COMMAND. PROJECT BLOSSOM MISSION UPDATE, FILED BY GENERAL G'IAH, ALIAS "GLORIA WARNER."
SIXTEENTH ATTEMPTED TRANSMISSION.
WARNER FAMILY
WE WERE SENT TO EARTH TO LIVE AMONG THE HUMANS.
MY MATE, COLONEL KLRR, ALIAS "CARL WARNER," AND I FORMED A **FAMILY UNIT**, RAISING OUR OFFSPRING ON THIS PLANET.
MADISON, ALICE AND IVY.
PERFECT DAUGHTERS.
PERFECT SOLDIERS.
WE NEVER WAVERED IN OUR DEDICATION.
EVEN AFTER WE LOST IVY.
ATTEMPTING TO UNCOVER THE CREATORS OF "PROJECT BLOSSOM," A NEW TECH DEVELOPED TO REVEAL SKRULLS HIDDEN ON EARTH, WE SUFFERED ANOTHER BLOW...
...WHEN WE WERE BETRAYED BY OUR HANDLER, MOLOTH.
HE MURDERED COLONEL KLRR.
CARL.
MY HUSBAND.
BUT ALL WAS NOT LOST.
WARNER FAMILY

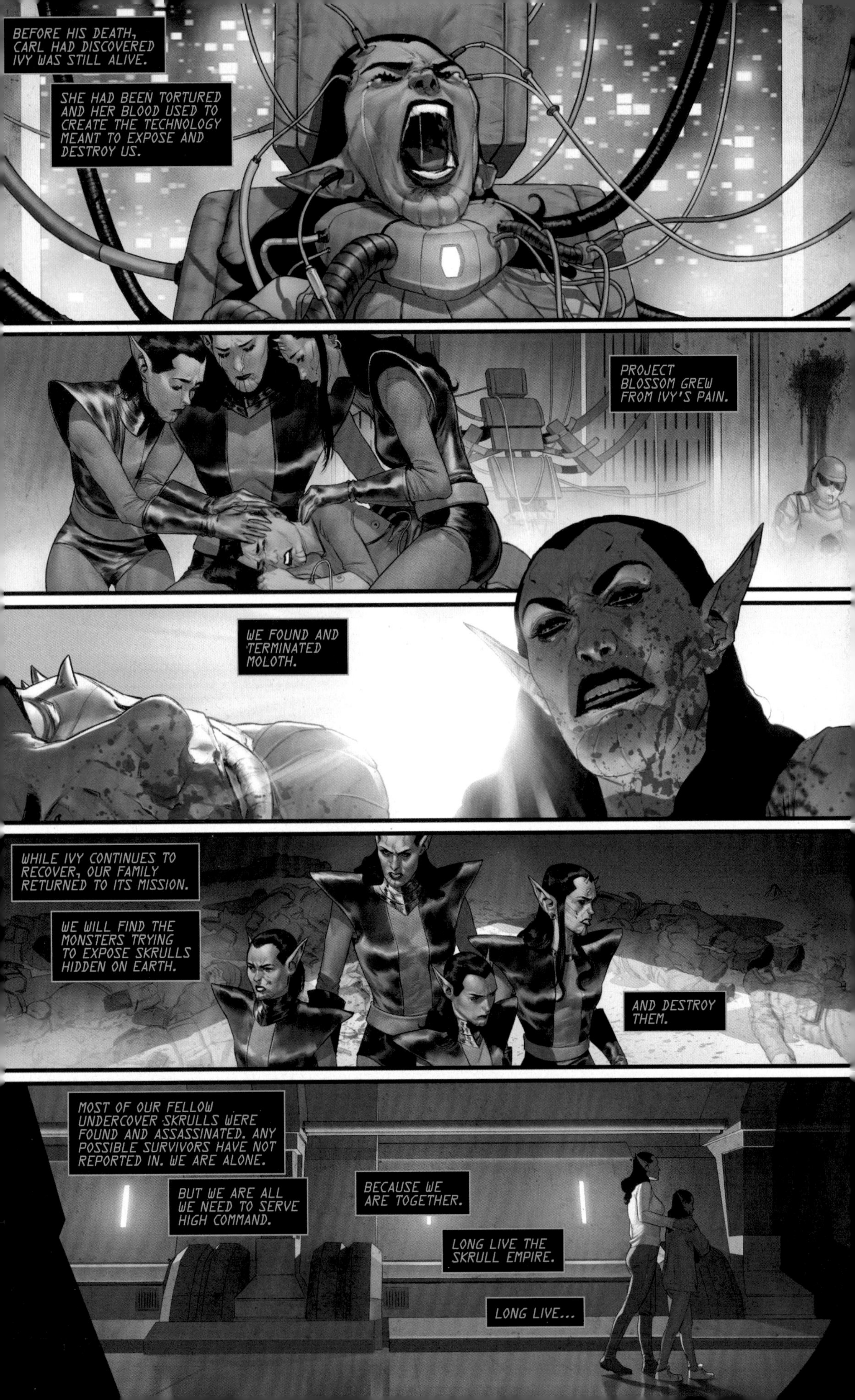
BEFORE HIS DEATH, CARL HAD DISCOVERED IVY WAS STILL ALIVE.
SHE HAD BEEN TORTURED AND HER BLOOD USED TO CREATE THE TECHNOLOGY MEANT TO EXPOSE AND DESTROY US.
PROJECT BLOSSOM GREW FROM IVY'S PAIN.
WE FOUND AND TERMINATED MOLOTH.
WHILE IVY CONTINUES TO RECOVER, OUR FAMILY RETURNED TO ITS MISSION.
WE WILL FIND THE MONSTERS TRYING TO EXPOSE SKRULLS HIDDEN ON EARTH.
AND DESTROY THEM.
MOST OF OUR FELLOW UNDERCOVER SKRULLS WERE FOUND AND ASSASSINATED. ANY POSSIBLE SURVIVORS HAVE NOT REPORTED IN. WE ARE ALONE.
BUT WE ARE ALL WE NEED TO SERVE HIGH COMMAND.
BECAUSE WE ARE TOGETHER.
LONG LIVE THE SKRULL EMPIRE.
LONG LIVE...

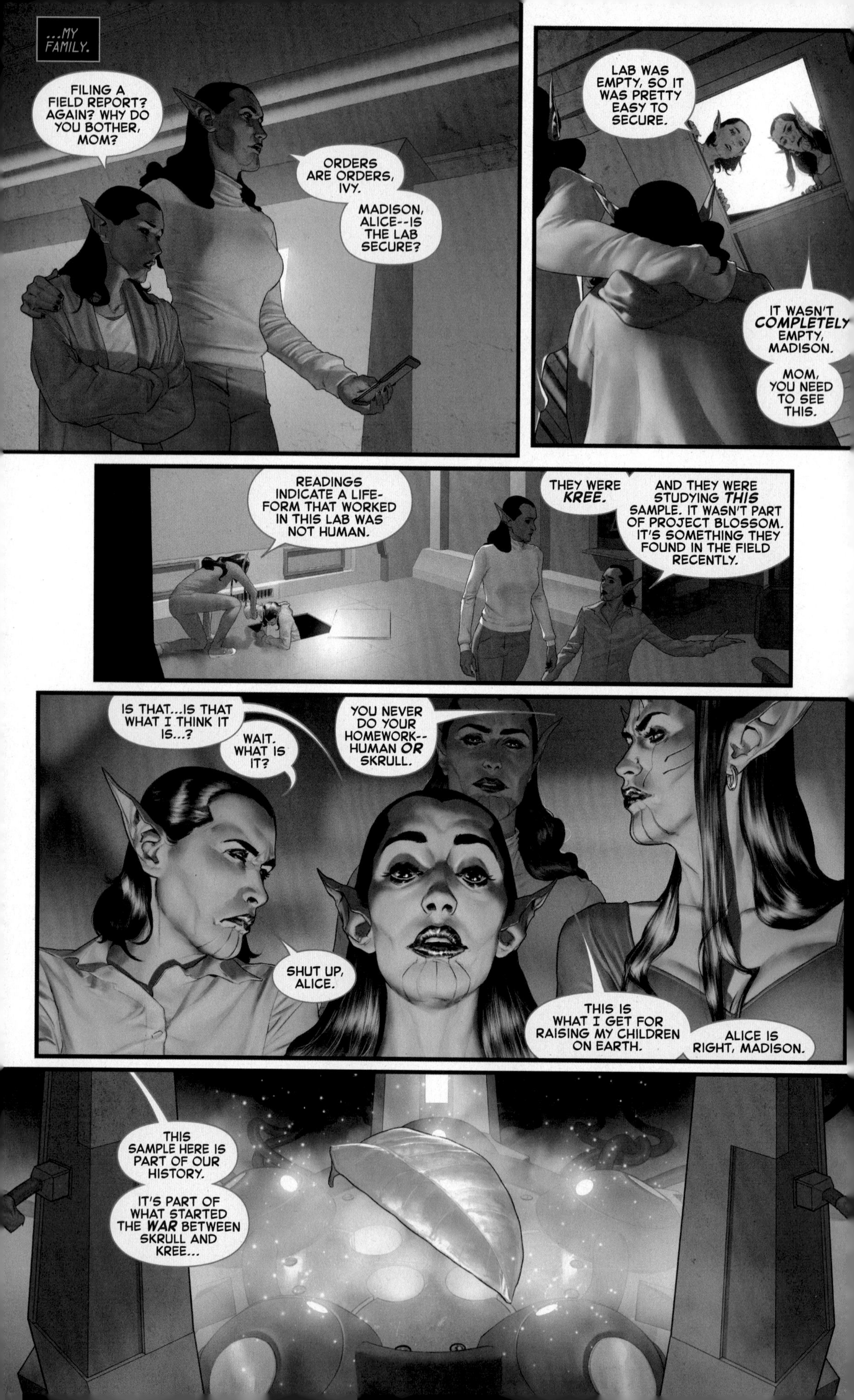
...MY FAMILY.
FILING A FIELD REPORT? AGAIN? WHY DO YOU BOTHER, MOM?
ORDERS ARE ORDERS, IVY.
MADISON, ALICE--IS THE LAB SECURE?
LAB WAS EMPTY, SO IT WAS PRETTY EASY TO SECURE.
IT WASN'T COMPLETELY EMPTY, MADISON.
MOM, YOU NEED TO SEE THIS.
READINGS INDICATE A LIFE-FORM THAT WORKED IN THIS LAB WAS NOT HUMAN.
THEY WERE KREE.
AND THEY WERE STUDYING THIS SAMPLE. IT WASN'T PART OF PROJECT BLOSSOM. IT'S SOMETHING THEY FOUND IN THE FIELD RECENTLY.
IS THAT...IS THAT WHAT I THINK IT IS...?
WAIT. WHAT IS IT?
YOU NEVER DO YOUR HOMEWORK--HUMAN OR SKRULL.
SHUT UP, ALICE.
THIS IS WHAT I GET FOR RAISING MY CHILDREN ON EARTH.
ALICE IS RIGHT, MADISON.
THIS SAMPLE HERE IS PART OF OUR HISTORY.
IT'S PART OF WHAT STARTED THE WAR BETWEEN SKRULL AND KREE...

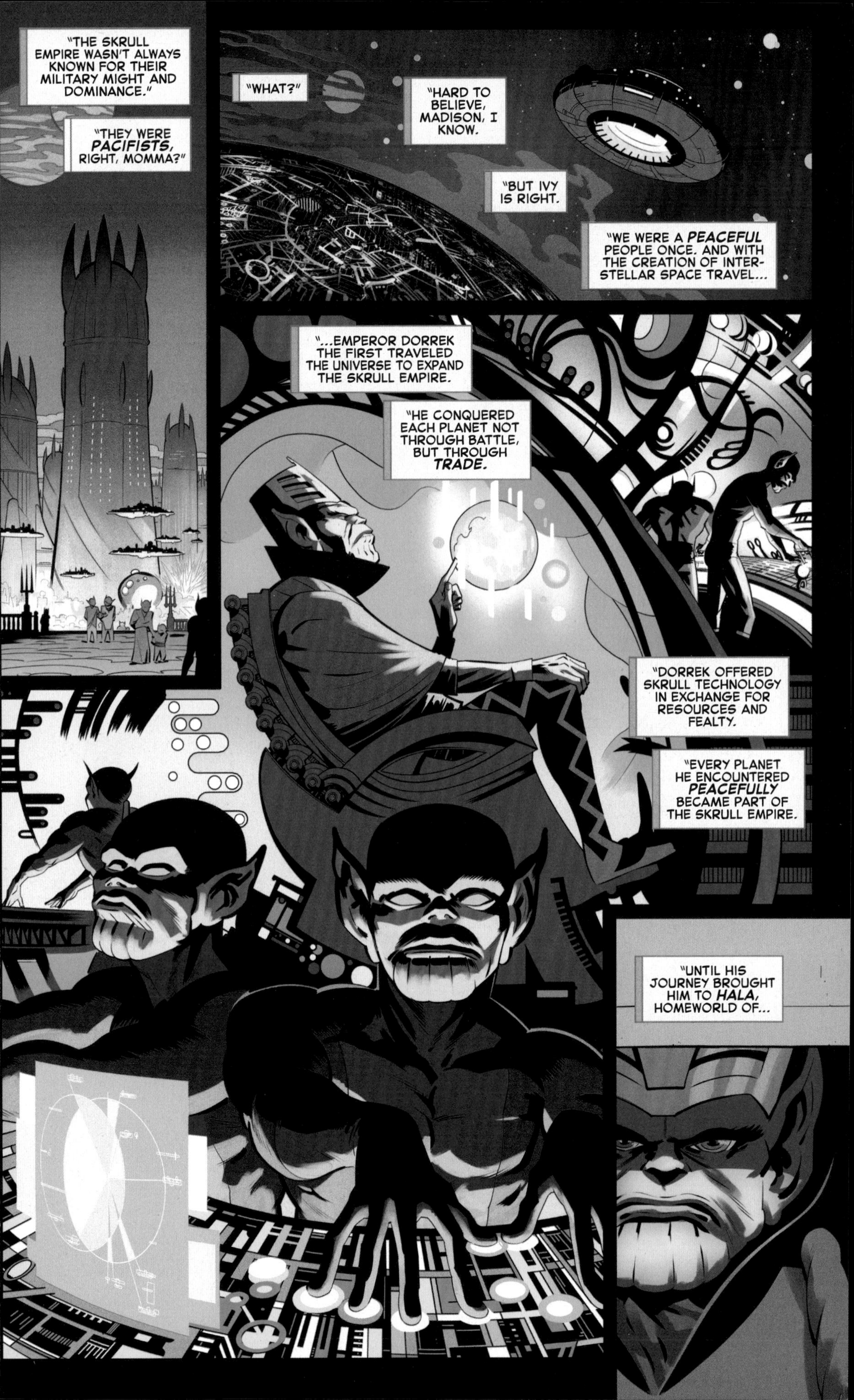
"THE SKRULL EMPIRE WASN'T ALWAYS KNOWN FOR THEIR MILITARY MIGHT AND DOMINANCE."
"THEY WERE PACIFISTS, RIGHT, MOMMA?"
"WHAT?"
"HARD TO BELIEVE, MADISON, I KNOW.
"BUT IVY IS RIGHT.
"WE WERE A PEACEFUL PEOPLE ONCE. AND WITH THE CREATION OF INTER-STELLAR SPACE TRAVEL...
"...EMPEROR DORREK THE FIRST TRAVELED THE UNIVERSE TO EXPAND THE SKRULL EMPIRE.
"HE CONQUERED EACH PLANET NOT THROUGH BATTLE, BUT THROUGH TRADE.
"DORREK OFFERED SKRULL TECHNOLOGY IN EXCHANGE FOR RESOURCES AND FEALTY.
"EVERY PLANET HE ENCOUNTERED PEACEFULLY BECAME PART OF THE SKRULL EMPIRE.
"UNTIL HIS JOURNEY BROUGHT HIM TO HALA, HOMEWORLD OF...

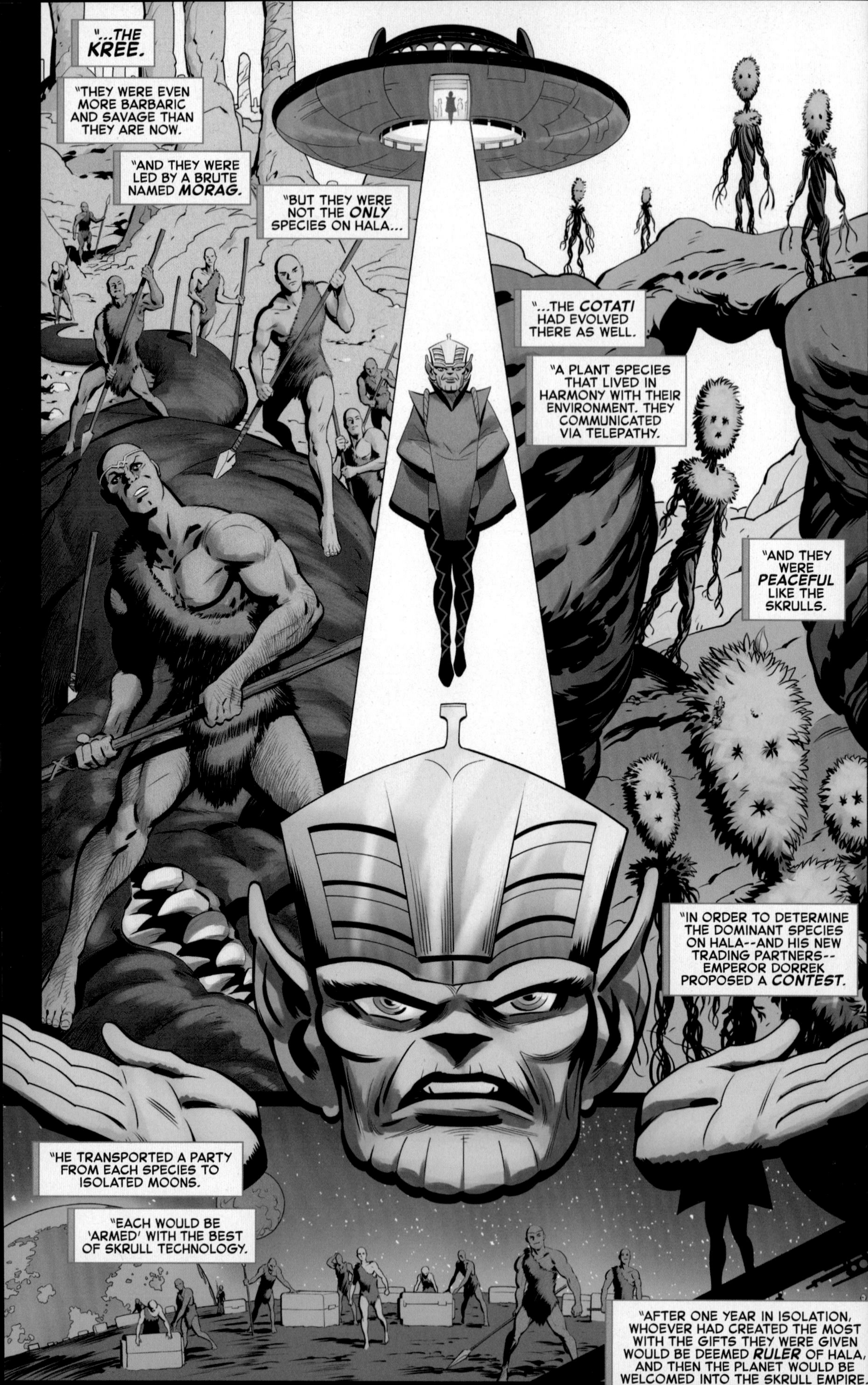
"...THE KREE.
"THEY WERE EVEN MORE BARBARIC AND SAVAGE THAN THEY ARE NOW.
"AND THEY WERE LED BY A BRUTE NAMED MORAG.
"BUT THEY WERE NOT THE ONLY SPECIES ON HALA...
"...THE COTATI HAD EVOLVED THERE AS WELL.
"A PLANT SPECIES THAT LIVED IN HARMONY WITH THEIR ENVIRONMENT. THEY COMMUNICATED VIA TELEPATHY.
"AND THEY WERE PEACEFUL LIKE THE SKRULLS.
"IN ORDER TO DETERMINE THE DOMINANT SPECIES ON HALA--AND HIS NEW TRADING PARTNERS--EMPEROR DORREK PROPOSED A CONTEST.
"HE TRANSPORTED A PARTY FROM EACH SPECIES TO ISOLATED MOONS.
"EACH WOULD BE 'ARMED' WITH THE BEST OF SKRULL TECHNOLOGY.
"AFTER ONE YEAR IN ISOLATION, WHOEVER HAD CREATED THE MOST WITH THE GIFTS THEY WERE GIVEN WOULD BE DEEMED RULER OF HALA, AND THEN THE PLANET WOULD BE WELCOMED INTO THE SKRULL EMPIRE.

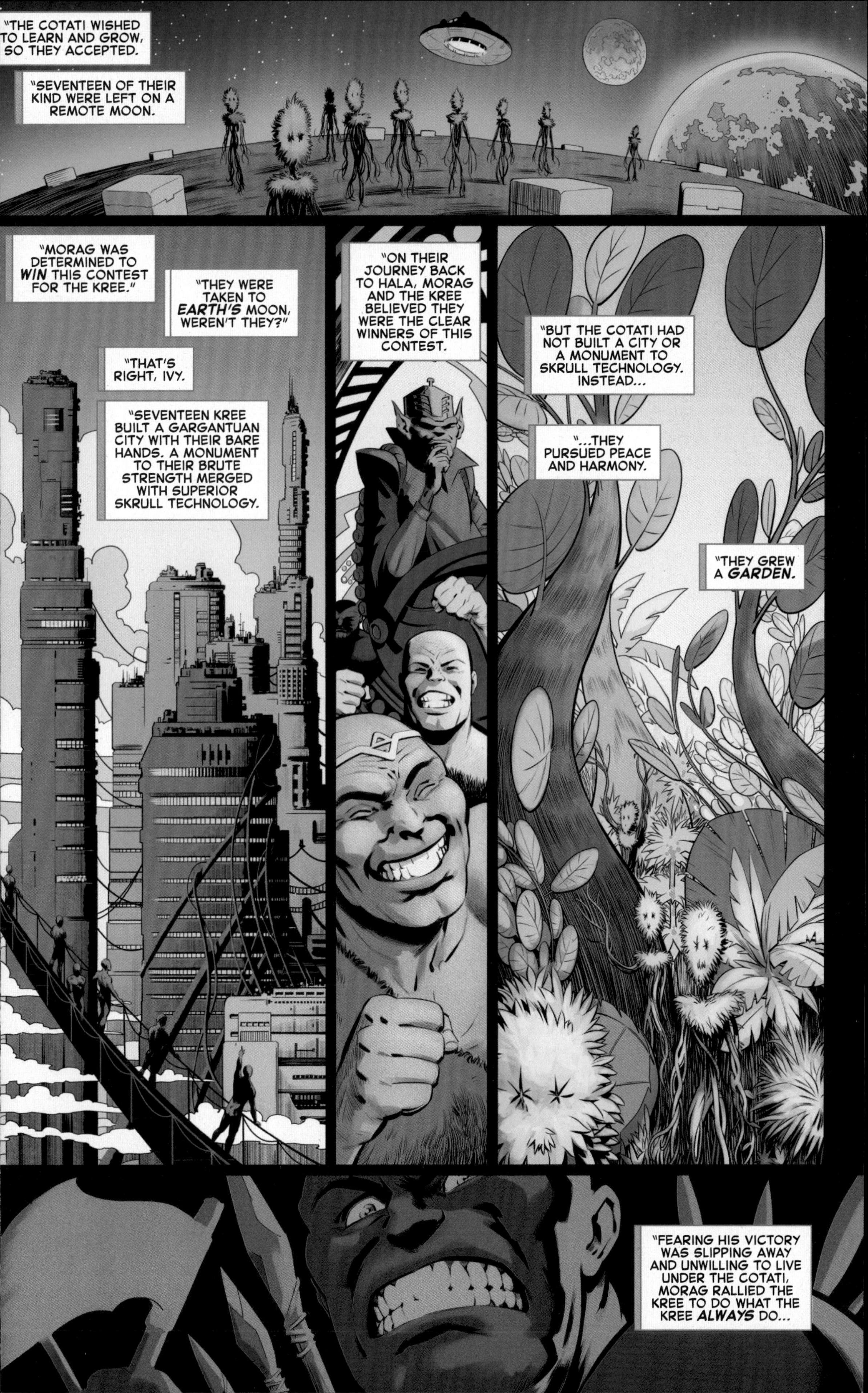
"THE COTATI WISHED TO LEARN AND GROW, SO THEY ACCEPTED.
"SEVENTEEN OF THEIR KIND WERE LEFT ON A REMOTE MOON.
"MORAG WAS DETERMINED TO WIN THIS CONTEST FOR THE KREE."
"THEY WERE TAKEN TO EARTH'S MOON, WEREN'T THEY?"
"THAT'S RIGHT, IVY.
"SEVENTEEN KREE BUILT A GARGANTUAN CITY WITH THEIR BARE HANDS. A MONUMENT TO THEIR BRUTE STRENGTH MERGED WITH SUPERIOR SKRULL TECHNOLOGY.
"ON THEIR JOURNEY BACK TO HALA, MORAG AND THE KREE BELIEVED THEY WERE THE CLEAR WINNERS OF THIS CONTEST.
"BUT THE COTATI HAD NOT BUILT A CITY OR A MONUMENT TO SKRULL TECHNOLOGY. INSTEAD...
"...THEY PURSUED PEACE AND HARMONY.
"THEY GREW A GARDEN.
"FEARING HIS VICTORY WAS SLIPPING AWAY AND UNWILLING TO LIVE UNDER THE COTATI, MORAG RALLIED THE KREE TO DO WHAT THE KREE ALWAYS DO...

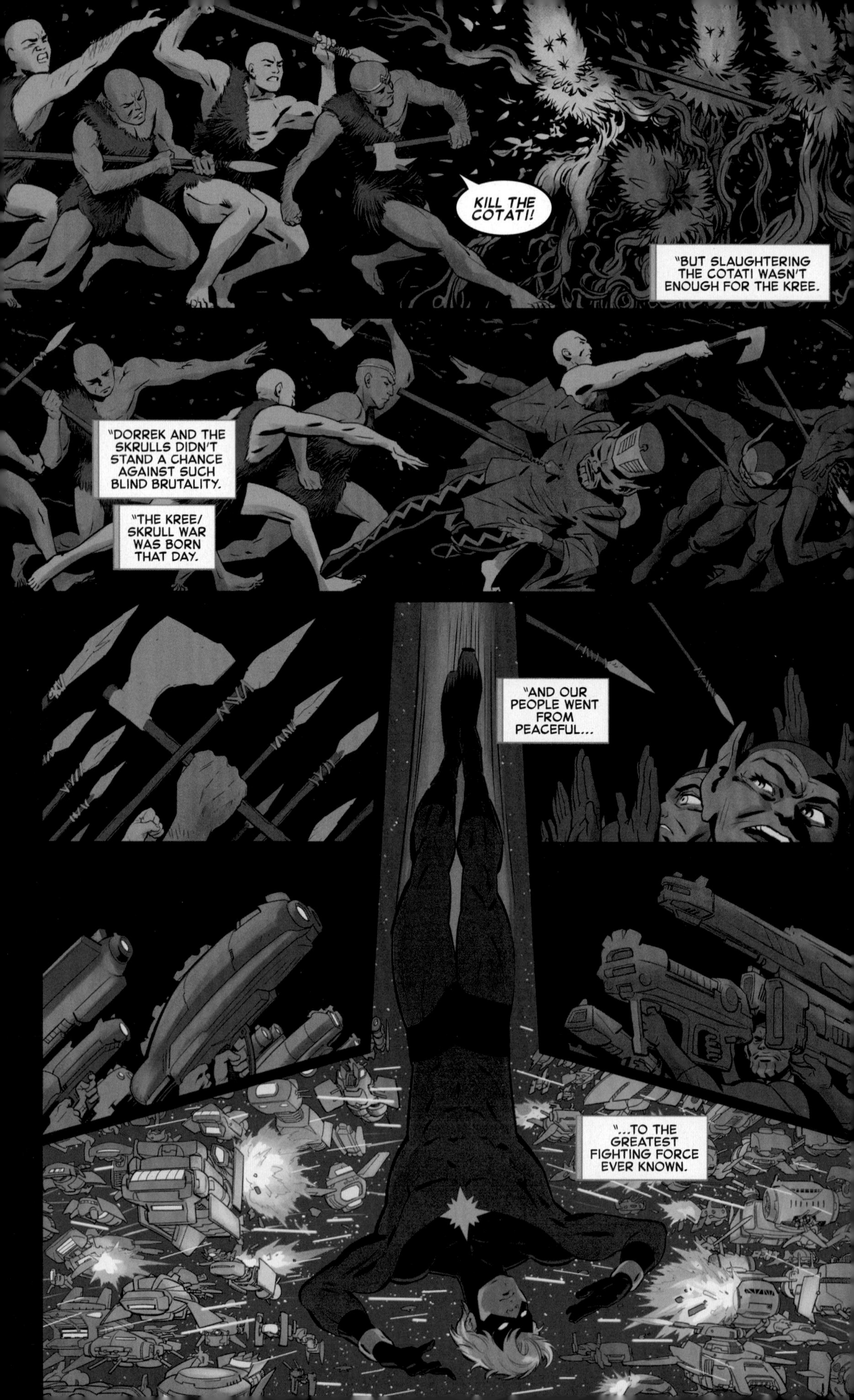
KILL THE COTATI!
"BUT SLAUGHTERING THE COTATI WASN'T ENOUGH FOR THE KREE.
"DORREK AND THE SKRULLS DIDN'T STAND A CHANCE AGAINST SUCH BLIND BRUTALITY.
"THE KREE/ SKRULL WAR WAS BORN THAT DAY.
"AND OUR PEOPLE WENT FROM PEACEFUL...
"...TO THE GREATEST FIGHTING FORCE EVER KNOWN.

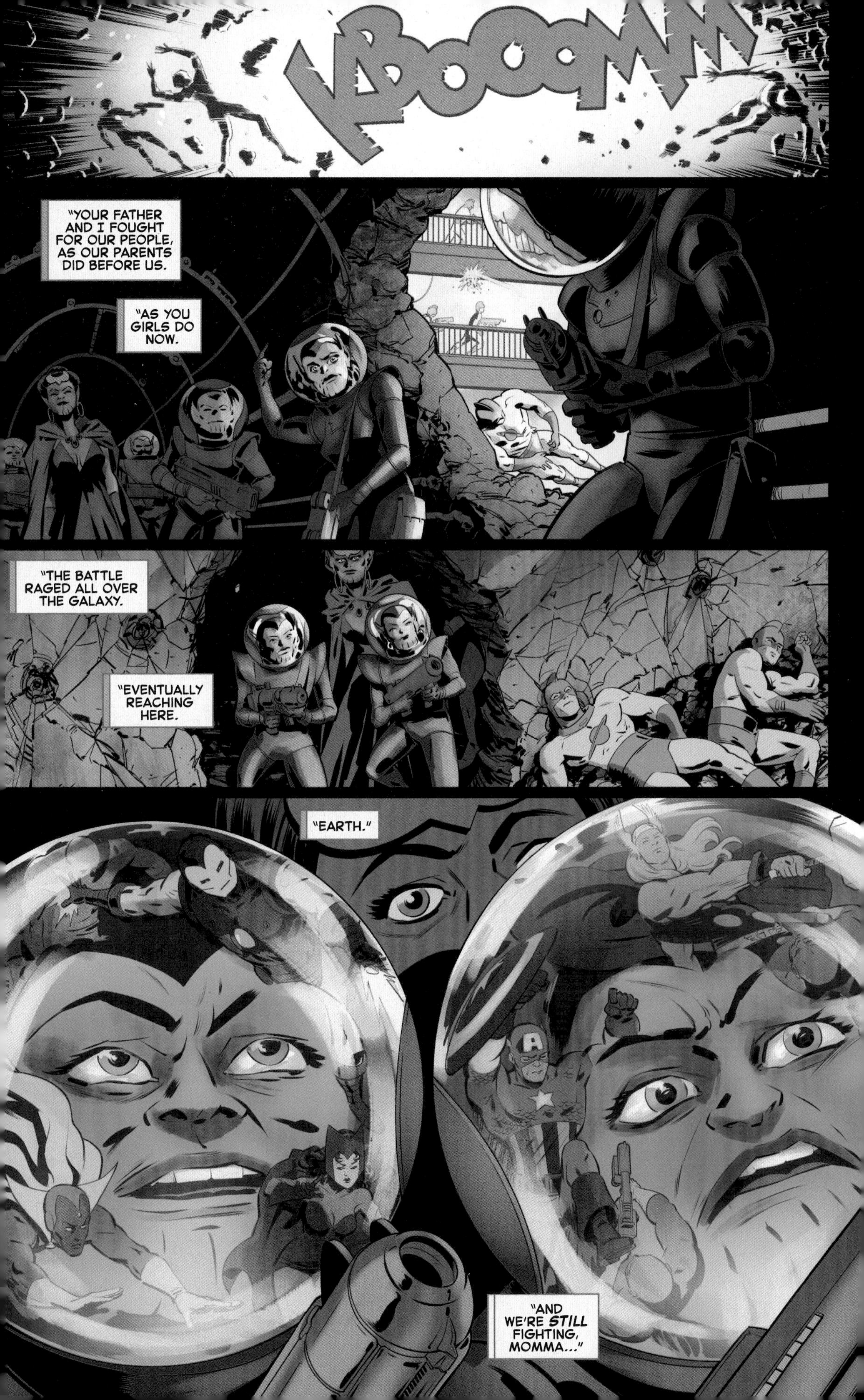
KABOOOMM
"YOUR FATHER AND I FOUGHT FOR OUR PEOPLE, AS OUR PARENTS DID BEFORE US.
"AS YOU GIRLS DO NOW.
"THE BATTLE RAGED ALL OVER THE GALAXY.
"EVENTUALLY REACHING HERE.
"EARTH."
"AND WE'RE *STILL* FIGHTING, MOMMA..."

...BUT WHY?

FOR THE SKRULL EMPIRE.

BUT YOU JUST SAID IT YOURSELF. WE WERE PEACEFUL ONCE.

CAN'T WE BE SO AGAIN?

IVY, FOR ALL WE KNOW, THE KREE HAD THIS SAMPLE TO ENSURE THEY CAN COMPLETELY WIPE THE COTATI FROM EXISTENCE ONCE AND FOR ALL.

GIRLS, EXTRACT ANY MESSAGES FROM THE COMMS--ENCRYPTED OR OTHERWISE. I WANT EVERYTHING. AND RUN A TRACE ON THE KREE.

WHAT ABOUT THE CELESTIAL MESSIAH?

MAYBE THAT SAMPLE IS FROM HIM. MAYBE HE'S FINALLY--

THAT'S JUST A STORY, IVY.

NOW LET'S GET BACK TO THE SAFE HOUSE.

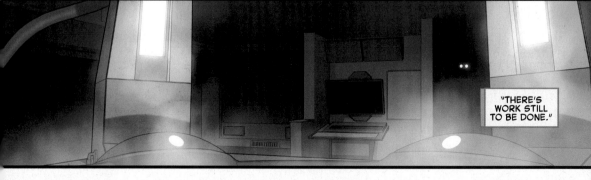

"THERE'S WORK STILL TO BE DONE."

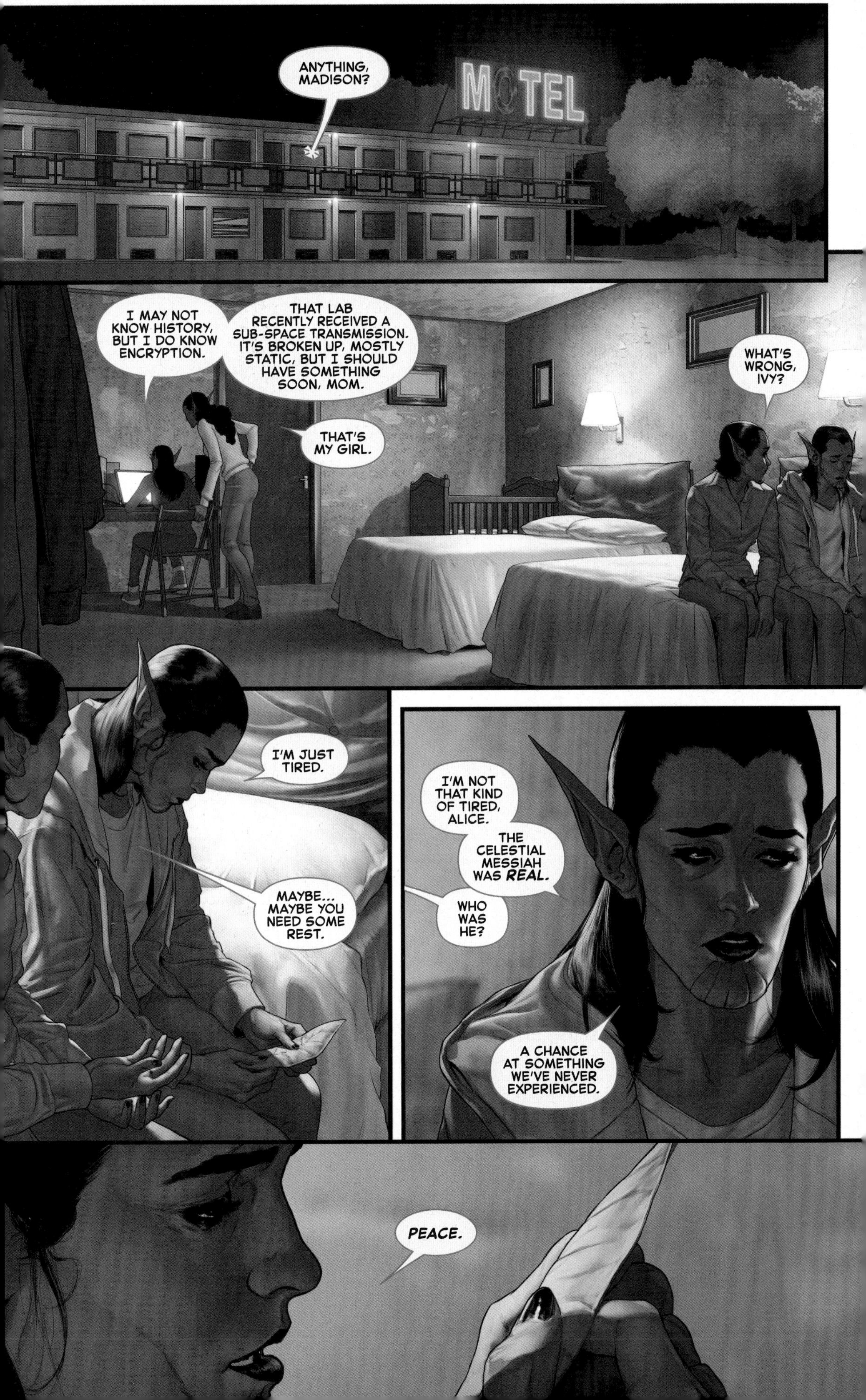
ANYTHING, MADISON?
MOTEL
I MAY NOT KNOW HISTORY, BUT I DO KNOW ENCRYPTION.
THAT LAB RECENTLY RECEIVED A SUB-SPACE TRANSMISSION. IT'S BROKEN UP, MOSTLY STATIC, BUT I SHOULD HAVE SOMETHING SOON, MOM.
THAT'S MY GIRL.
WHAT'S WRONG, IVY?
I'M JUST TIRED.
MAYBE... MAYBE YOU NEED SOME REST.
I'M NOT THAT KIND OF TIRED, ALICE.
THE CELESTIAL MESSIAH WAS *REAL.*
WHO WAS HE?
A CHANCE AT SOMETHING WE'VE NEVER EXPERIENCED.
PEACE.

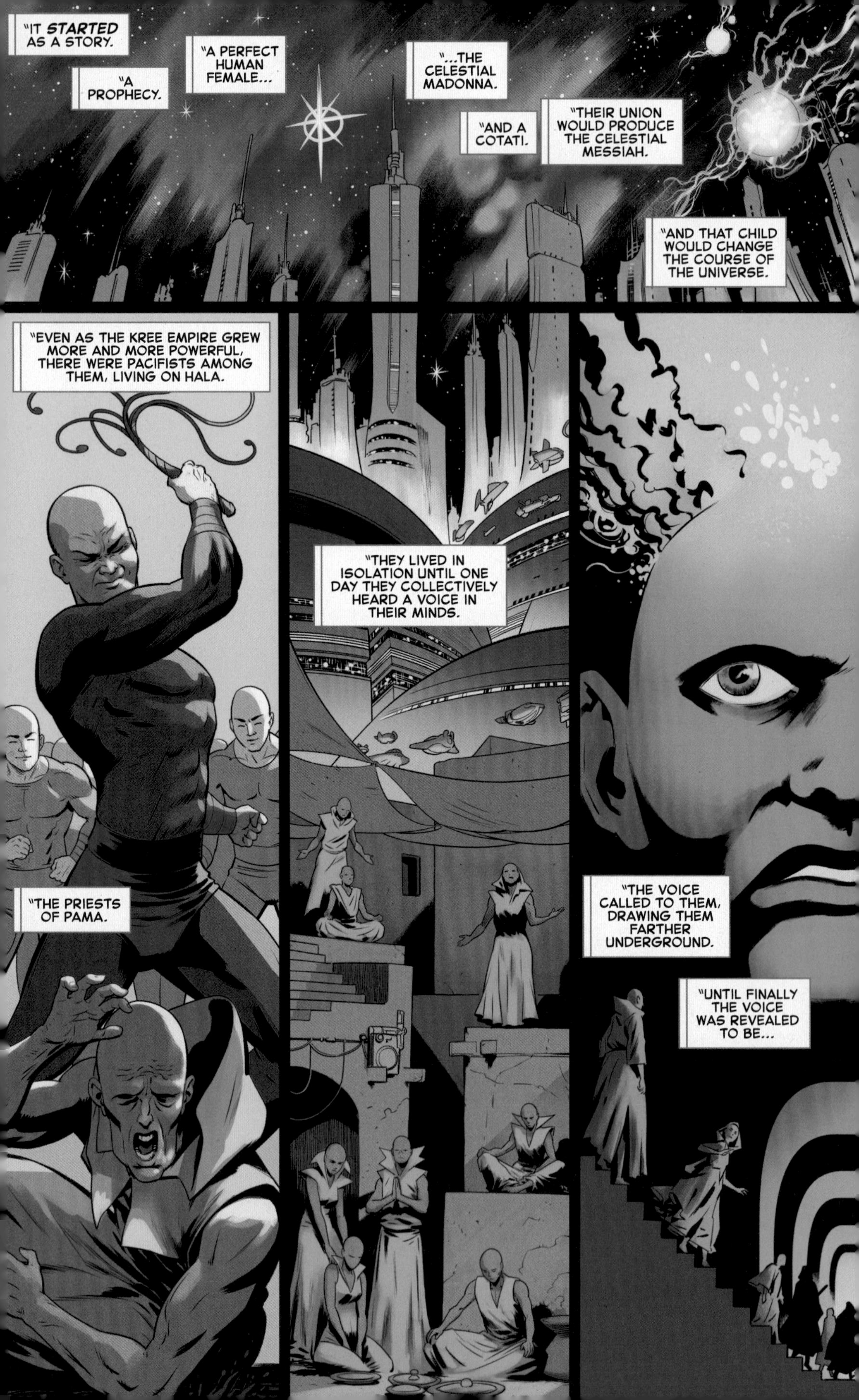
"IT STARTED AS A STORY.
"A PROPHECY.
"A PERFECT HUMAN FEMALE...
"...THE CELESTIAL MADONNA.
"AND A COTATI.
"THEIR UNION WOULD PRODUCE THE CELESTIAL MESSIAH.
"AND THAT CHILD WOULD CHANGE THE COURSE OF THE UNIVERSE.
"EVEN AS THE KREE EMPIRE GREW MORE AND MORE POWERFUL, THERE WERE PACIFISTS AMONG THEM, LIVING ON HALA.
"THE PRIESTS OF PAMA.
"THEY LIVED IN ISOLATION UNTIL ONE DAY THEY COLLECTIVELY HEARD A VOICE IN THEIR MINDS.
"THE VOICE CALLED TO THEM, DRAWING THEM FARTHER UNDERGROUND.
"UNTIL FINALLY THE VOICE WAS REVEALED TO BE...

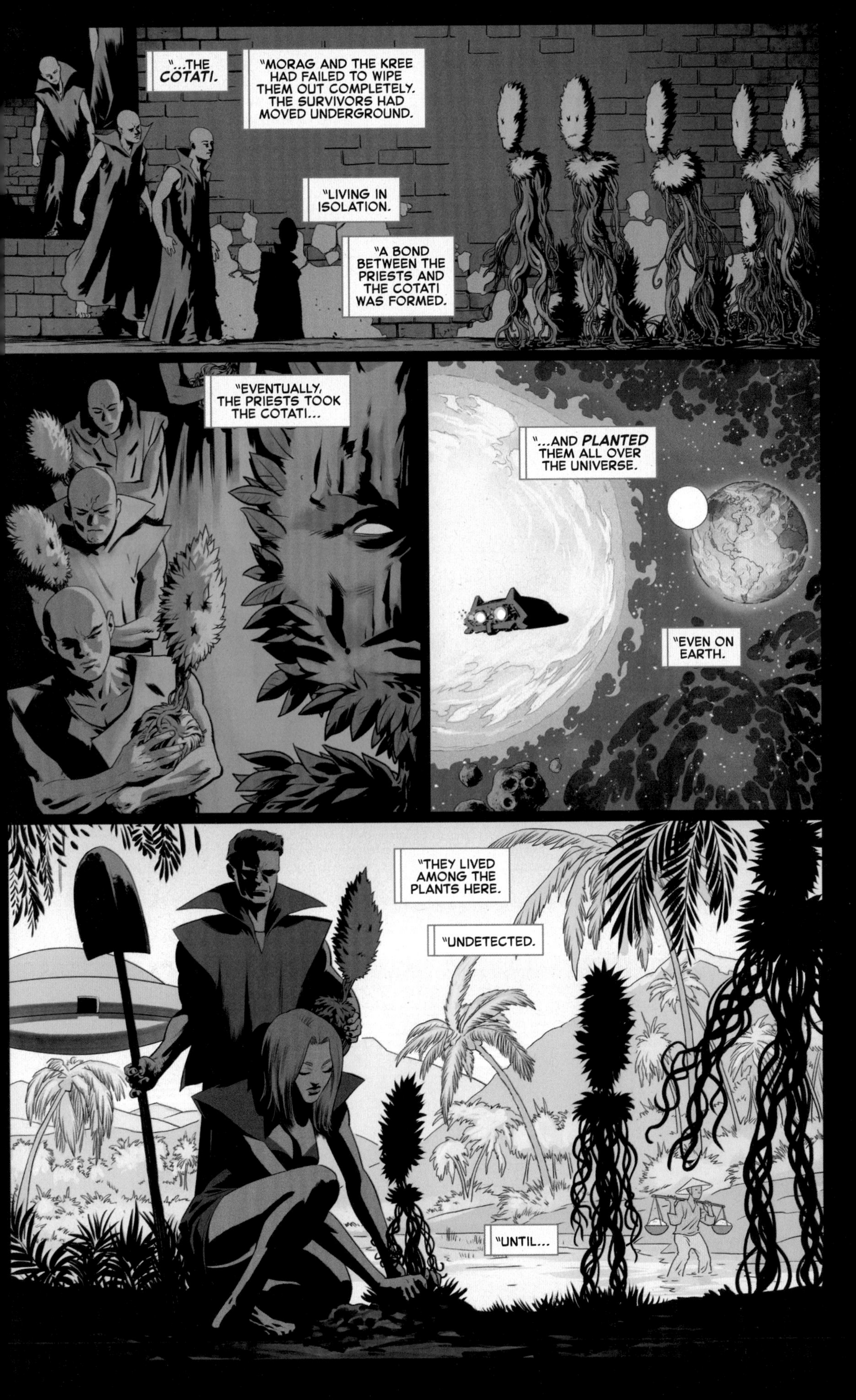
"...THE COTATI.
"MORAG AND THE KREE HAD FAILED TO WIPE THEM OUT COMPLETELY. THE SURVIVORS HAD MOVED UNDERGROUND.
"LIVING IN ISOLATION.
"A BOND BETWEEN THE PRIESTS AND THE COTATI WAS FORMED.
"EVENTUALLY, THE PRIESTS TOOK THE COTATI...
"...AND PLANTED THEM ALL OVER THE UNIVERSE.
"EVEN ON EARTH.
"THEY LIVED AMONG THE PLANTS HERE.
"UNDETECTED.
"UNTIL...

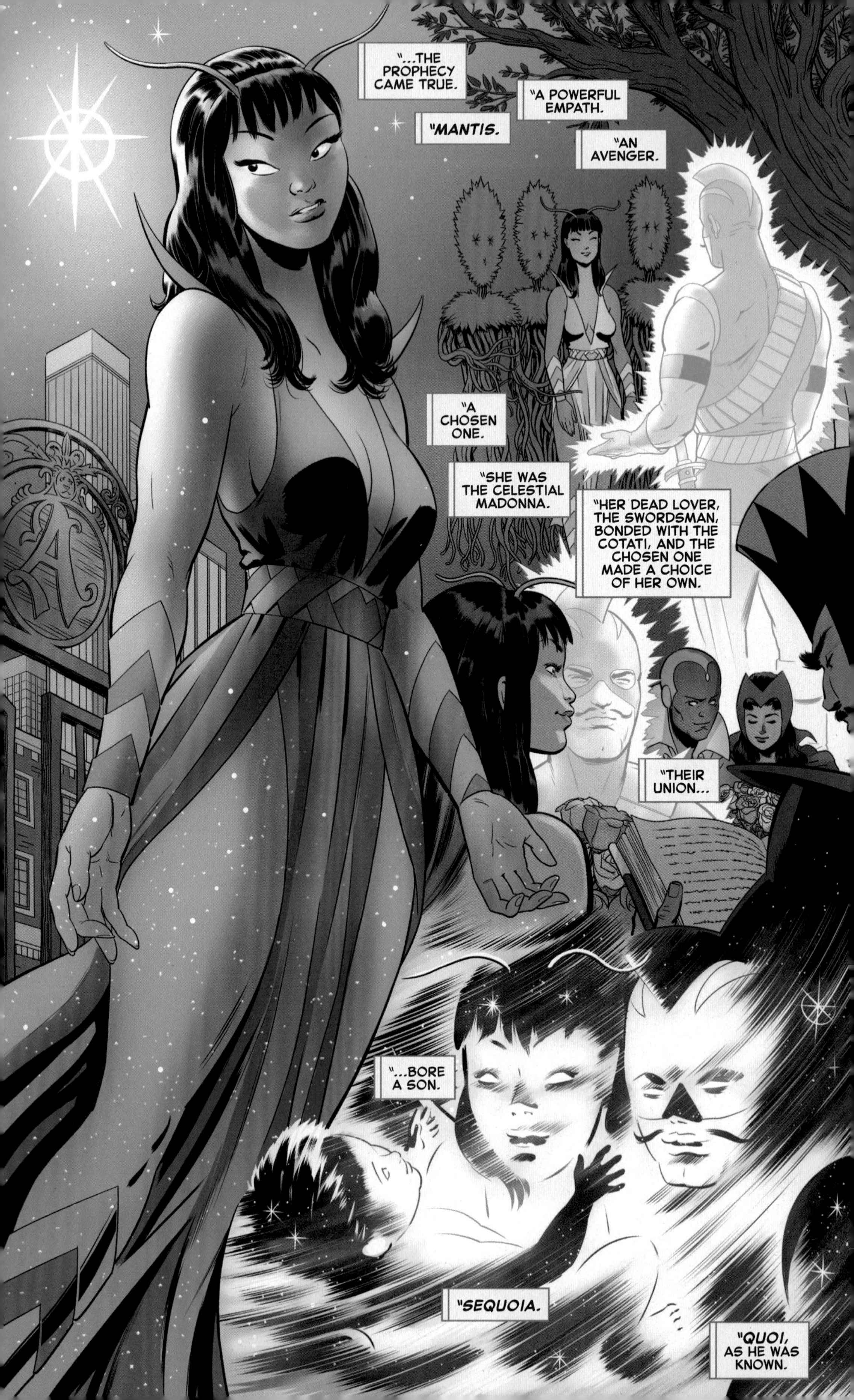
"...THE PROPHECY CAME TRUE.
"MANTIS.
"A POWERFUL EMPATH.
"AN AVENGER.
"A CHOSEN ONE.
"SHE WAS THE CELESTIAL MADONNA.
"HER DEAD LOVER, THE SWORDSMAN, BONDED WITH THE COTATI, AND THE CHOSEN ONE MADE A CHOICE OF HER OWN.
"THEIR UNION...
"...BORE A SON.
"SEQUOIA.
"QUOI, AS HE WAS KNOWN.

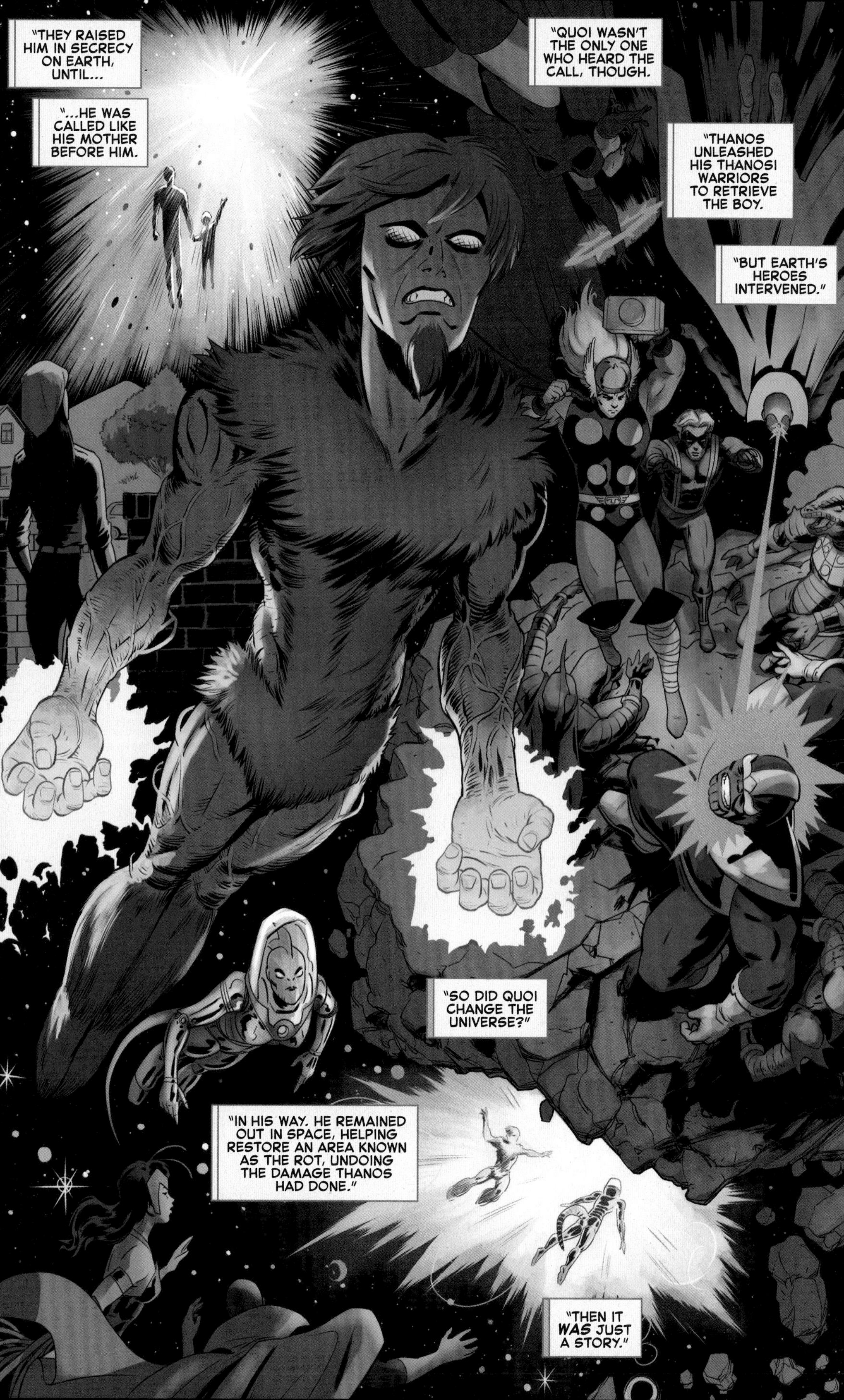
"THEY RAISED HIM IN SECRECY ON EARTH, UNTIL...
"...HE WAS CALLED LIKE HIS MOTHER BEFORE HIM.
"QUOI WASN'T THE ONLY ONE WHO HEARD THE CALL, THOUGH.
"THANOS UNLEASHED HIS THANOSI WARRIORS TO RETRIEVE THE BOY.
"BUT EARTH'S HEROES INTERVENED."
"SO DID QUOI CHANGE THE UNIVERSE?"
"IN HIS WAY. HE REMAINED OUT IN SPACE, HELPING RESTORE AN AREA KNOWN AS THE ROT, UNDOING THE DAMAGE THANOS HAD DONE."
"THEN IT *WAS* JUST A STORY."

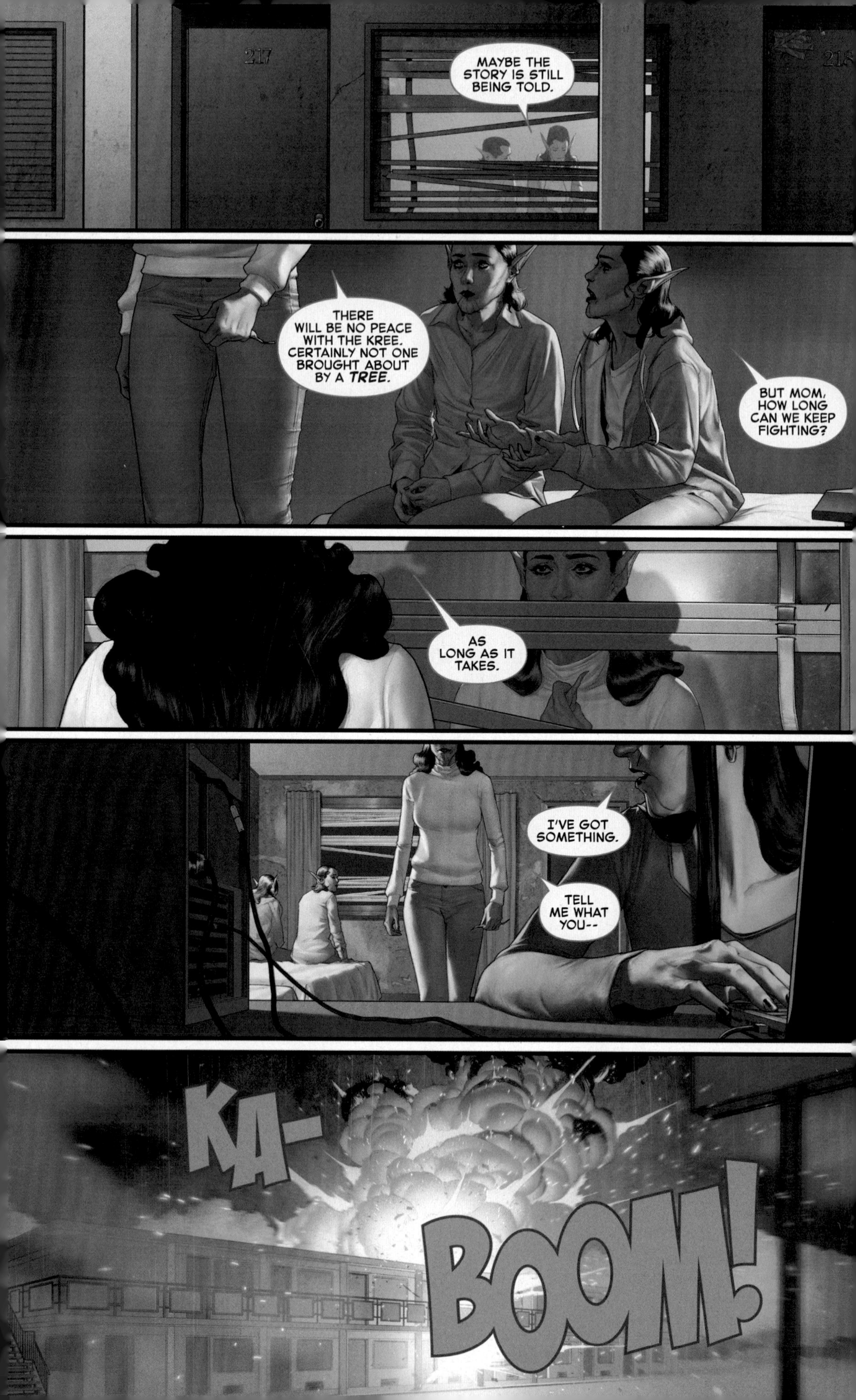
217
218
MAYBE THE STORY IS STILL BEING TOLD.
THERE WILL BE NO PEACE WITH THE KREE. CERTAINLY NOT ONE BROUGHT ABOUT BY A TREE.
BUT MOM, HOW LONG CAN WE KEEP FIGHTING?
AS LONG AS IT TAKES.
I'VE GOT SOMETHING.
TELL ME WHAT YOU--
KA-
BOOM!

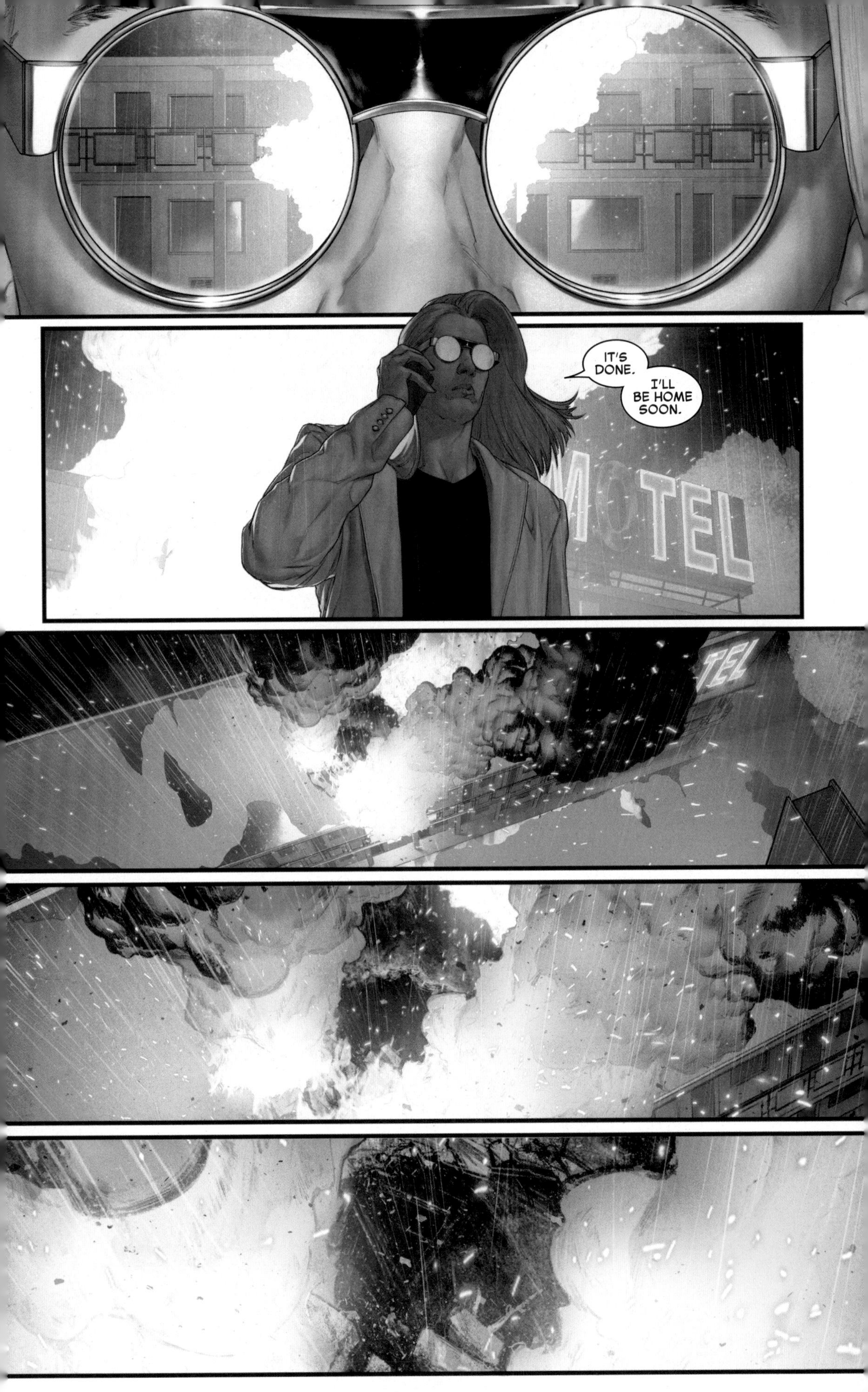
IT'S DONE.
I'LL BE HOME SOON.
MOTEL
TEL

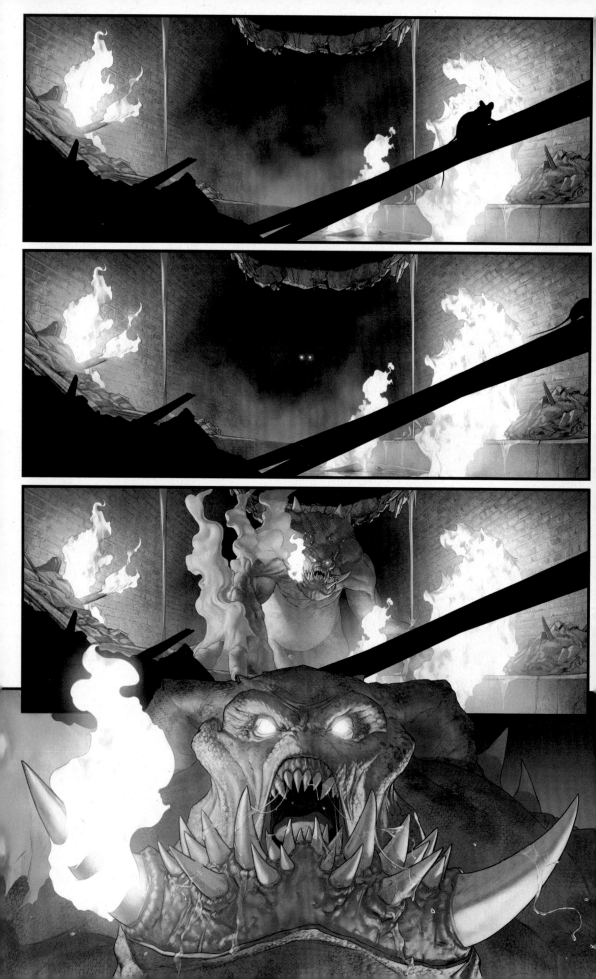

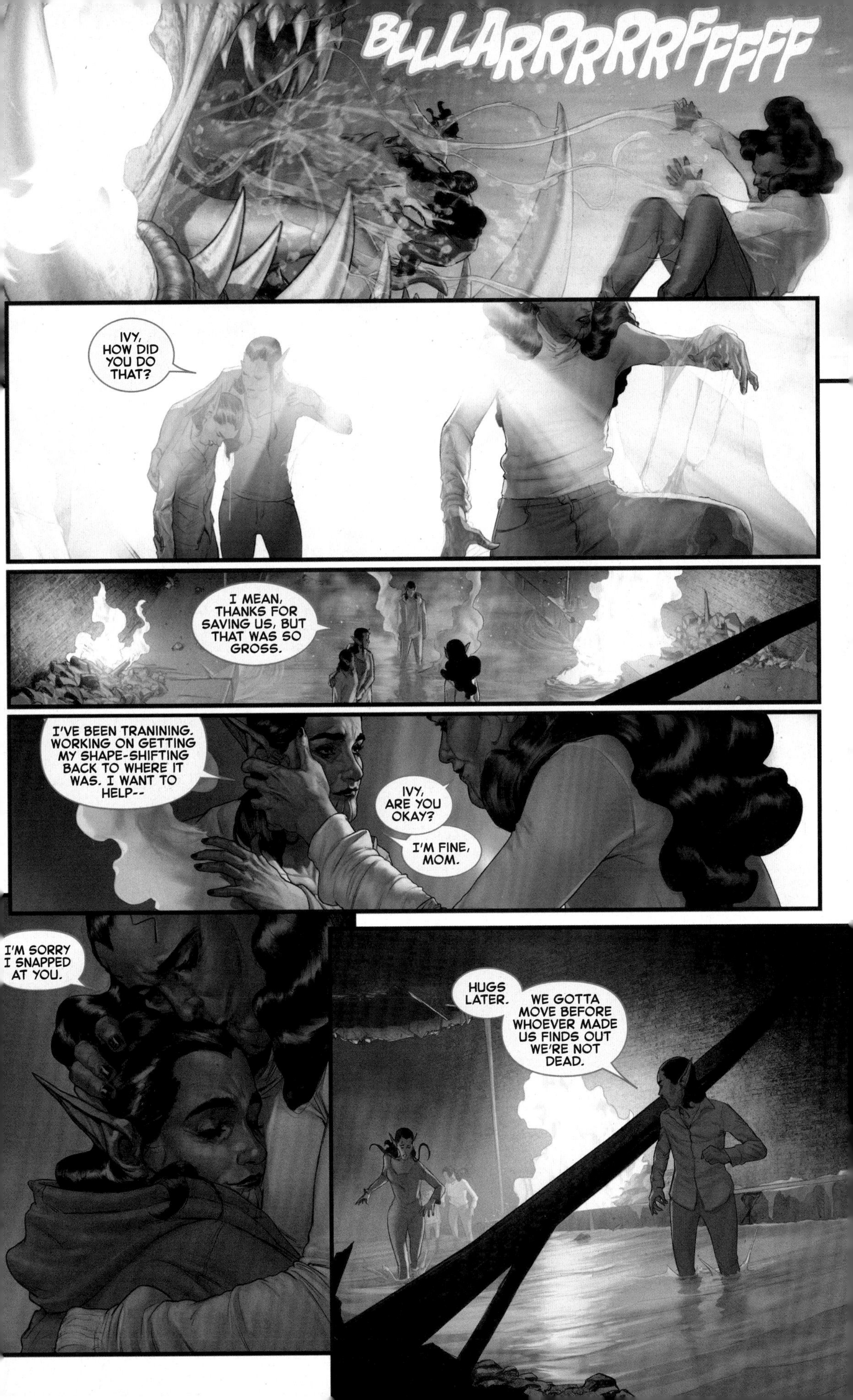
BLLLARRRRRRFFFFF
IVY, HOW DID YOU DO THAT?
I MEAN, THANKS FOR SAVING US, BUT THAT WAS SO GROSS.
I'VE BEEN TRANINING. WORKING ON GETTING MY SHAPE-SHIFTING BACK TO WHERE IT WAS. I WANT TO HELP--
IVY, ARE YOU OKAY?
I'M FINE, MOM.
I'M SORRY I SNAPPED AT YOU.
HUGS LATER.
WE GOTTA MOVE BEFORE WHOEVER MADE US FINDS OUT WE'RE NOT DEAD.

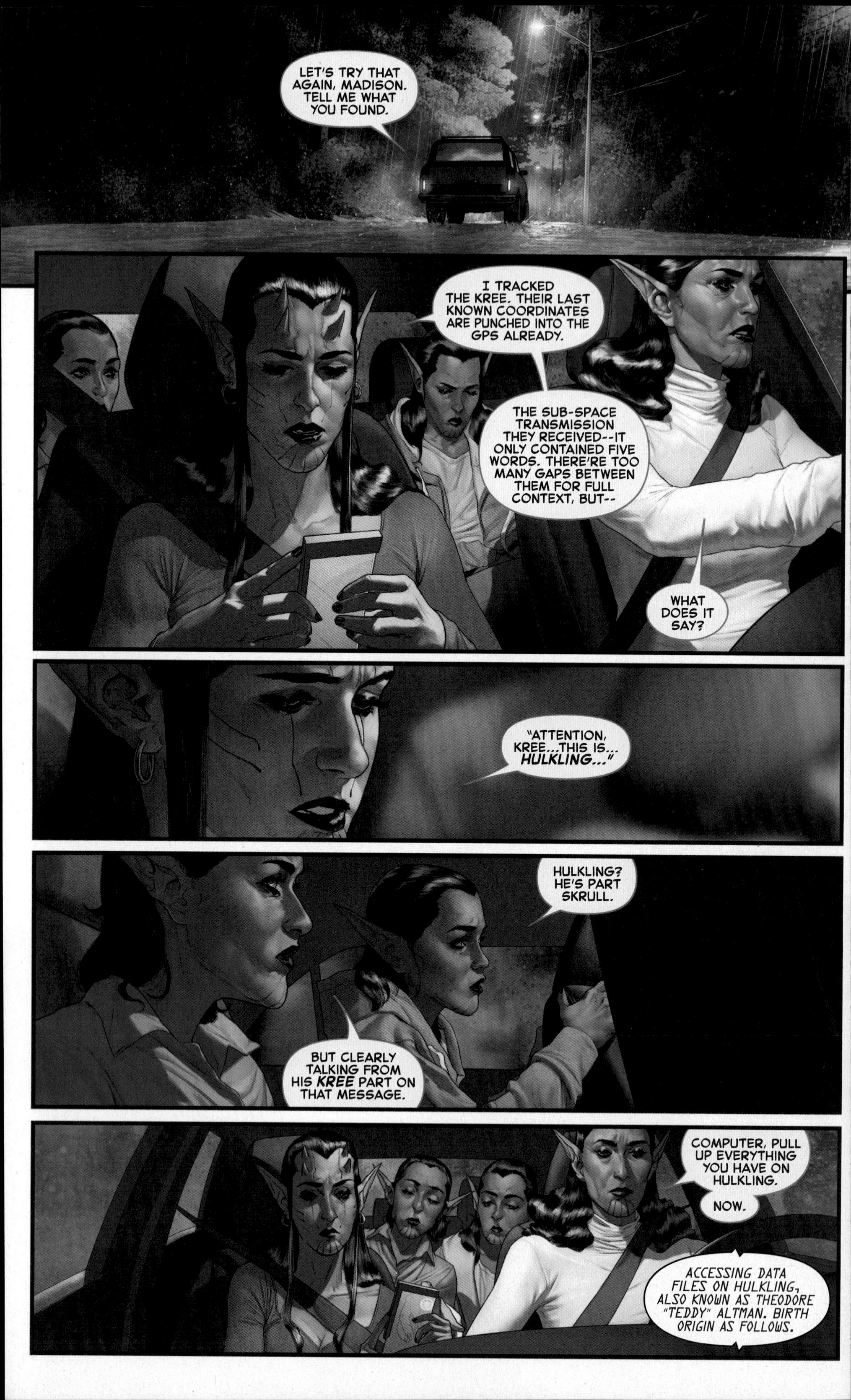
LET'S TRY THAT AGAIN, MADISON. TELL ME WHAT YOU FOUND.
I TRACKED THE KREE. THEIR LAST KNOWN COORDINATES ARE PUNCHED INTO THE GPS ALREADY.
THE SUB-SPACE TRANSMISSION THEY RECEIVED--IT ONLY CONTAINED FIVE WORDS. THERE'RE TOO MANY GAPS BETWEEN THEM FOR FULL CONTEXT, BUT--
WHAT DOES IT SAY?
"ATTENTION, KREE...THIS IS... HULKLING..."
HULKLING? HE'S PART SKRULL.
BUT CLEARLY TALKING FROM HIS KREE PART ON THAT MESSAGE.
COMPUTER, PULL UP EVERYTHING YOU HAVE ON HULKLING.
NOW.
ACCESSING DATA FILES ON HULKLING, ALSO KNOWN AS THEODORE "TEDDY" ALTMAN. BIRTH ORIGIN AS FOLLOWS.

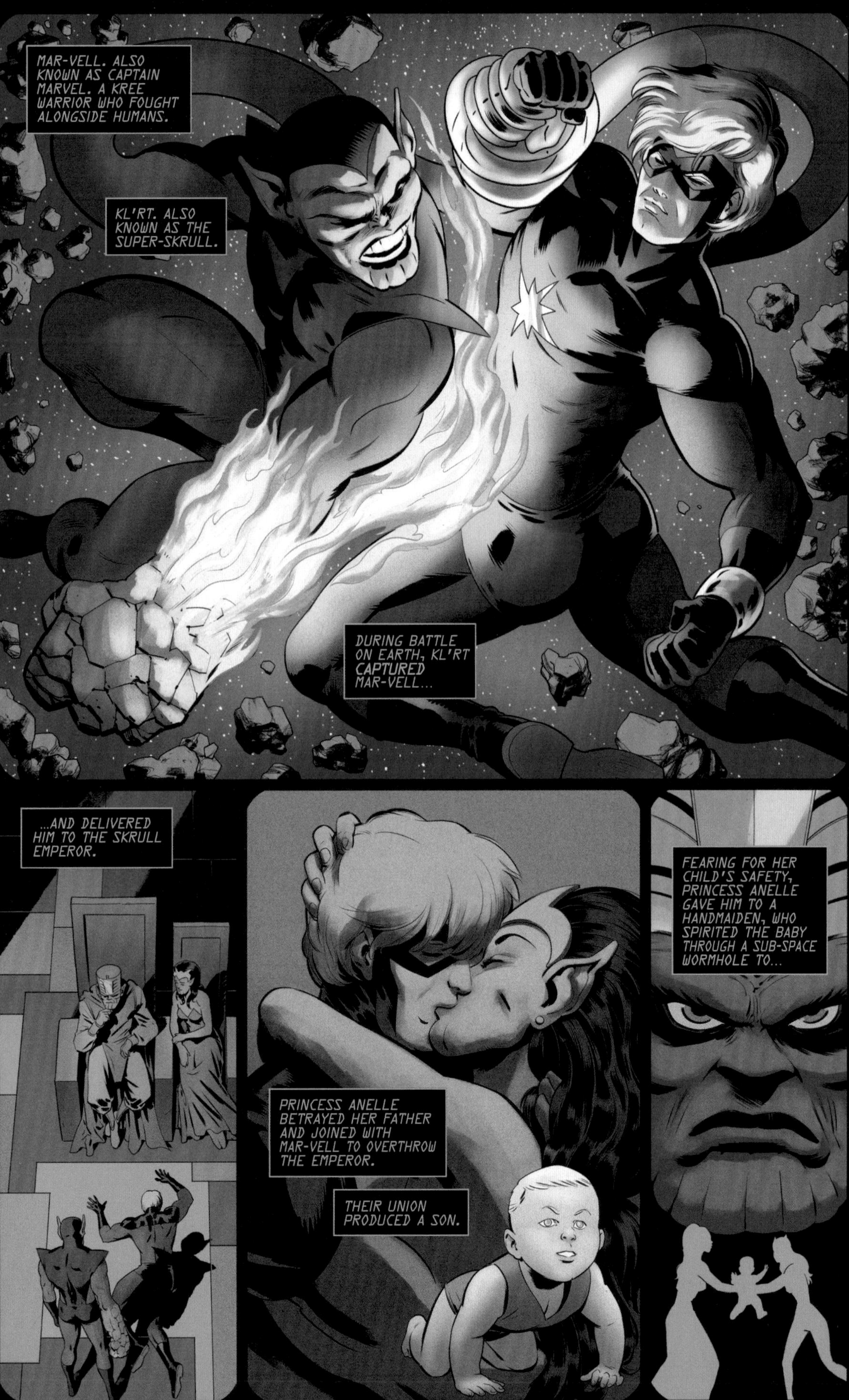
MAR-VELL. ALSO KNOWN AS CAPTAIN MARVEL. A KREE WARRIOR WHO FOUGHT ALONGSIDE HUMANS.
KL'RT. ALSO KNOWN AS THE SUPER-SKRULL.
DURING BATTLE ON EARTH, KL'RT CAPTURED MAR-VELL...
...AND DELIVERED HIM TO THE SKRULL EMPEROR.
PRINCESS ANELLE BETRAYED HER FATHER AND JOINED WITH MAR-VELL TO OVERTHROW THE EMPEROR.
THEIR UNION PRODUCED A SON.
FEARING FOR HER CHILD'S SAFETY, PRINCESS ANELLE GAVE HIM TO A HANDMAIDEN, WHO SPIRITED THE BABY THROUGH A SUB-SPACE WORMHOLE TO...

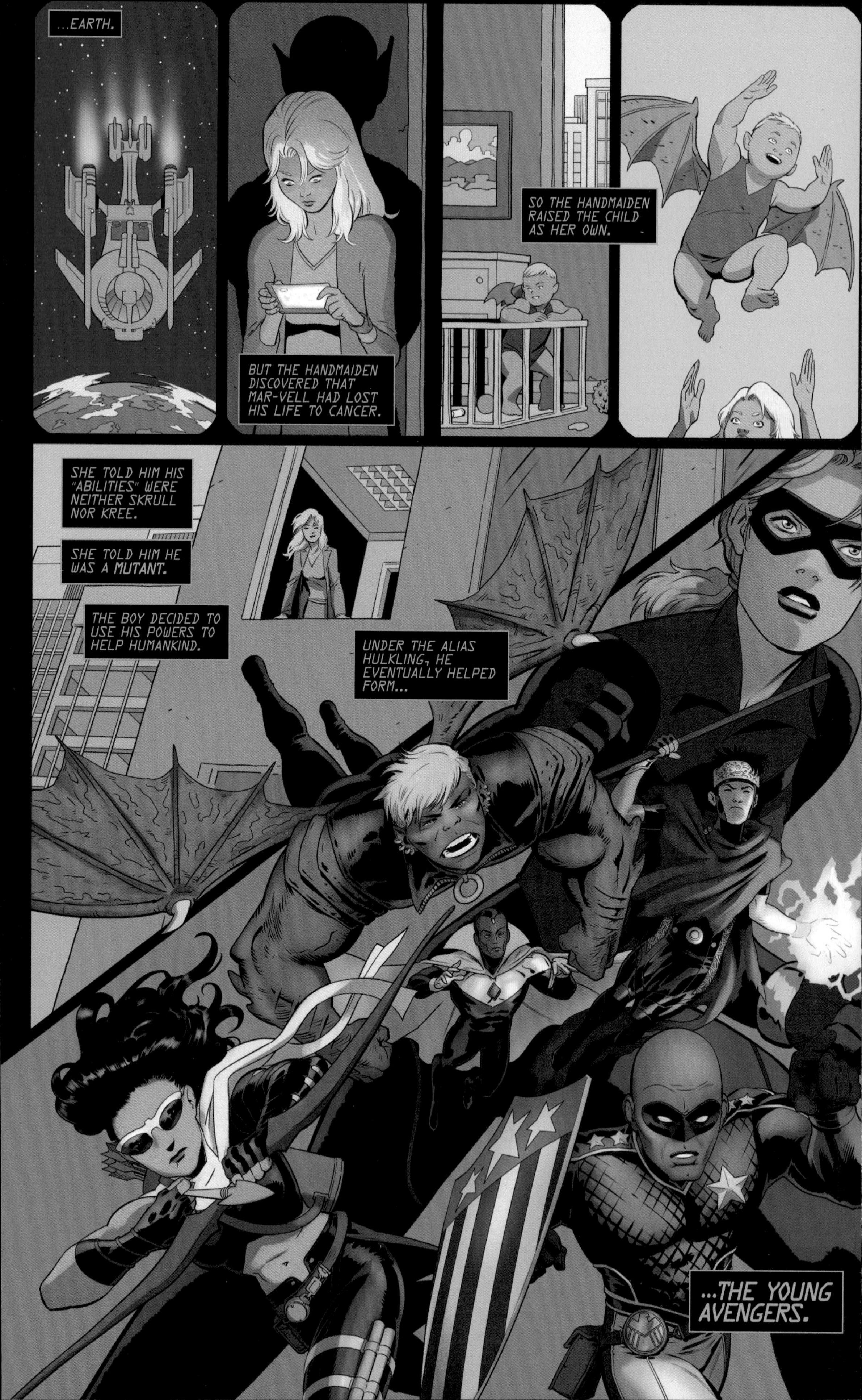
...EARTH.
BUT THE HANDMAIDEN DISCOVERED THAT MAR-VELL HAD LOST HIS LIFE TO CANCER.
SO THE HANDMAIDEN RAISED THE CHILD AS HER OWN.
SHE TOLD HIM HIS "ABILITIES" WERE NEITHER SKRULL NOR KREE.
SHE TOLD HIM HE WAS A MUTANT.
THE BOY DECIDED TO USE HIS POWERS TO HELP HUMANKIND.
UNDER THE ALIAS HULKLING, HE EVENTUALLY HELPED FORM...
...THE YOUNG AVENGERS.

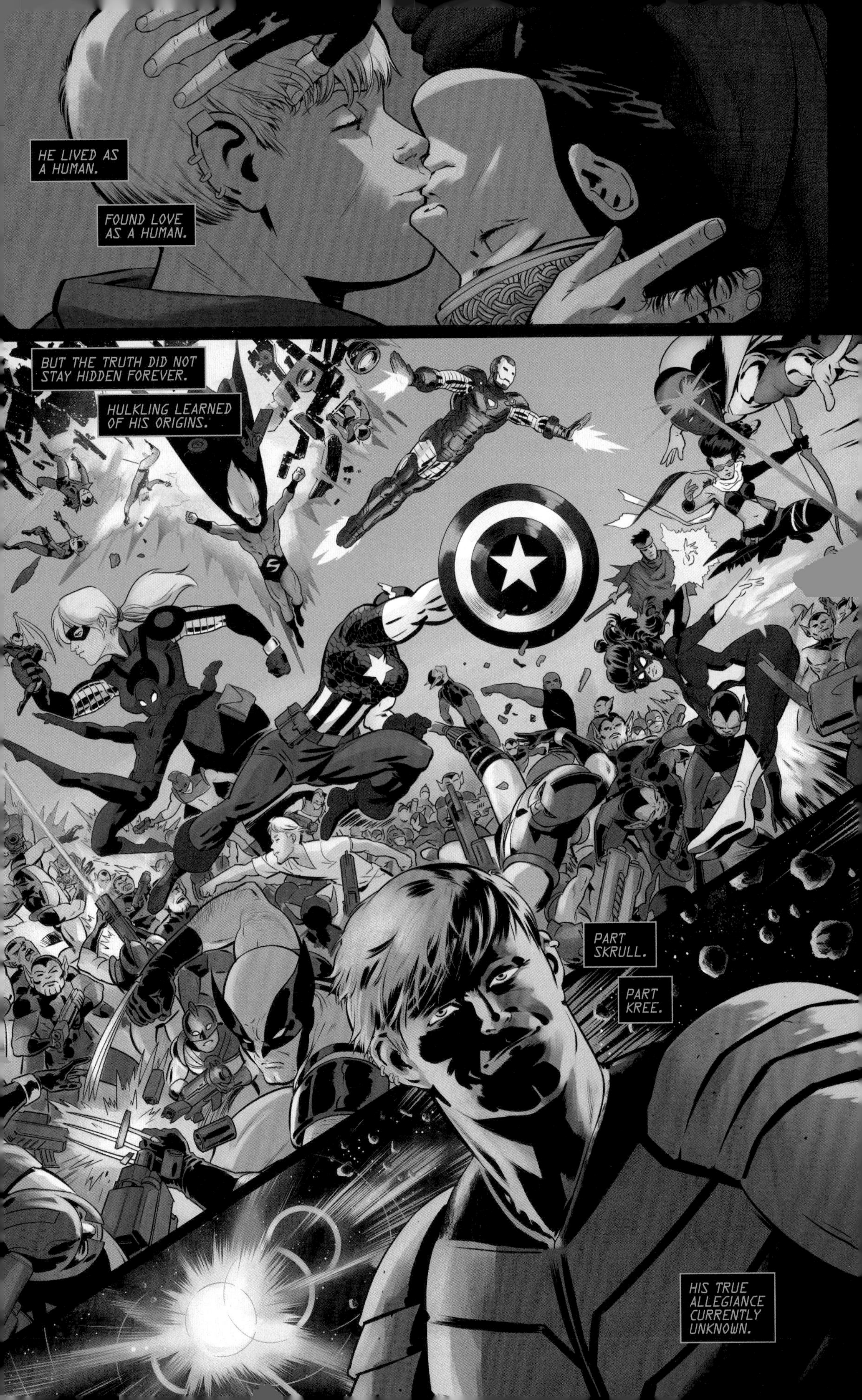
HE LIVED AS A HUMAN.
FOUND LOVE AS A HUMAN.
BUT THE TRUTH DID NOT STAY HIDDEN FOREVER.
HULKLING LEARNED OF HIS ORIGINS.
PART SKRULL.
PART KREE.
HIS TRUE ALLEGIANCE CURRENTLY UNKNOWN.

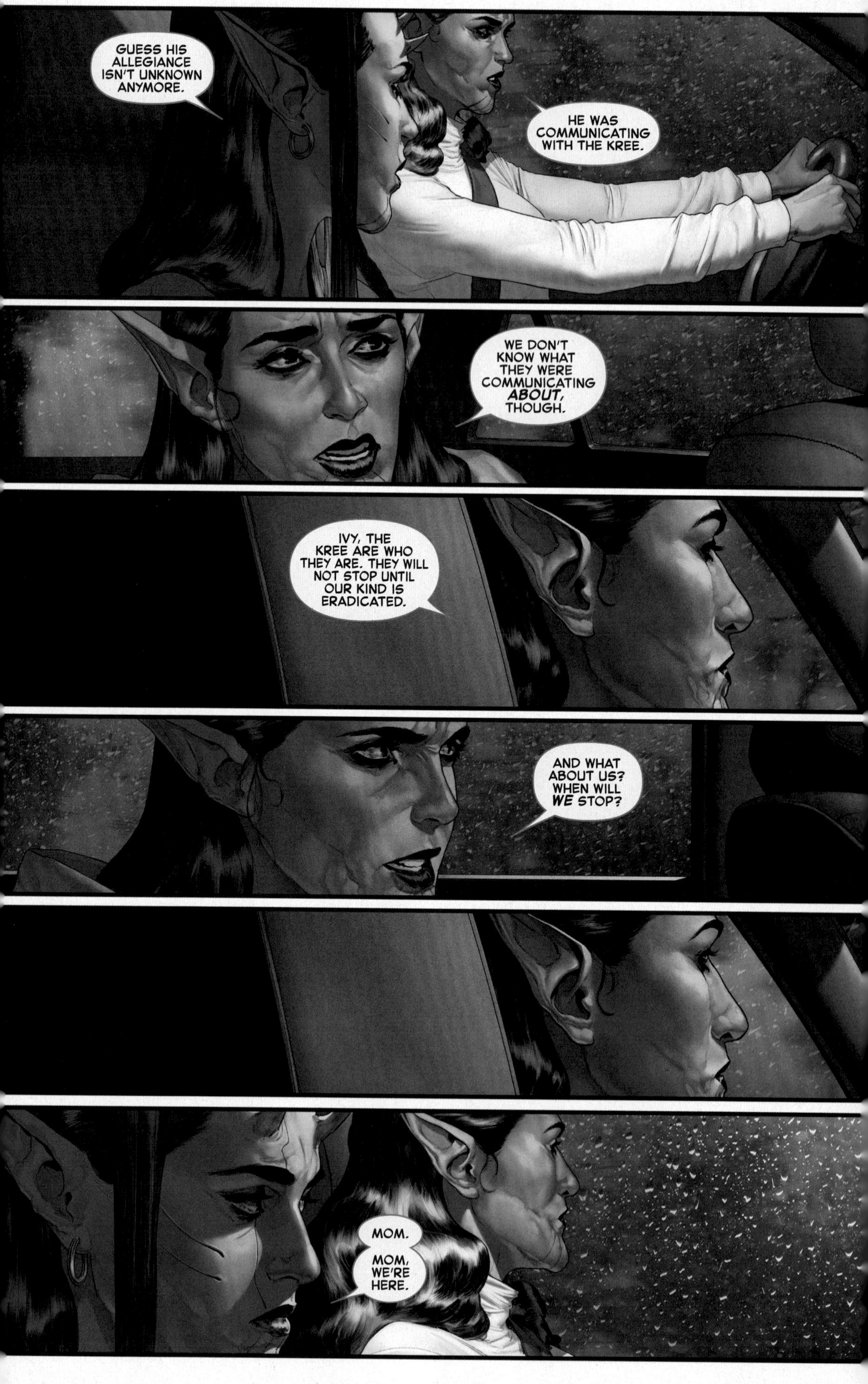
GUESS HIS ALLEGIANCE ISN'T UNKNOWN ANYMORE.
HE WAS COMMUNICATING WITH THE KREE.
WE DON'T KNOW WHAT THEY WERE COMMUNICATING ABOUT, THOUGH.
IVY, THE KREE ARE WHO THEY ARE. THEY WILL NOT STOP UNTIL OUR KIND IS ERADICATED.
AND WHAT ABOUT US? WHEN WILL WE STOP?
MOM.
MOM, WE'RE HERE.

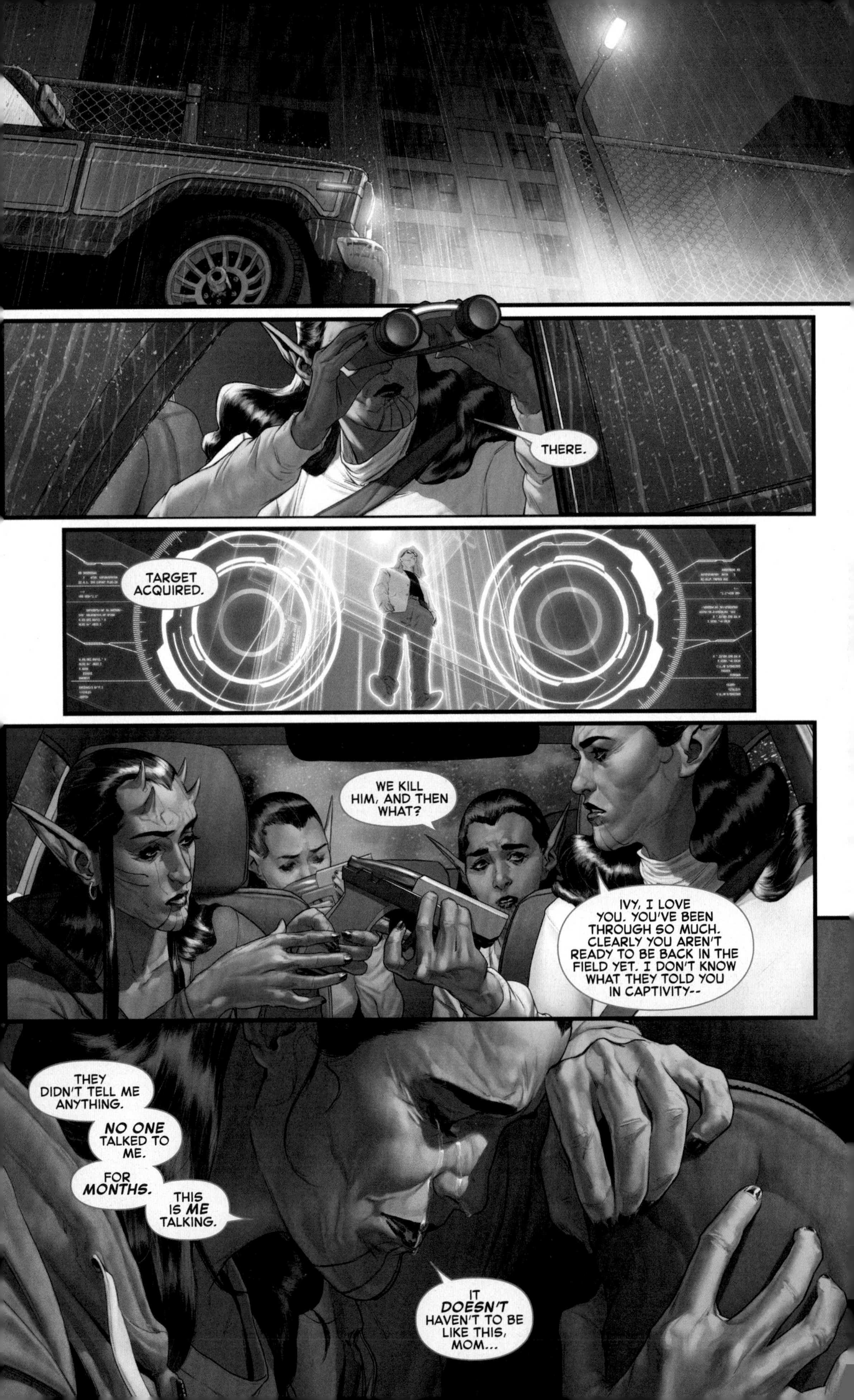
THERE.
TARGET ACQUIRED.
WE KILL HIM, AND THEN WHAT?
IVY, I LOVE YOU. YOU'VE BEEN THROUGH SO MUCH. CLEARLY YOU AREN'T READY TO BE BACK IN THE FIELD YET. I DON'T KNOW WHAT THEY TOLD YOU IN CAPTIVITY--
THEY DIDN'T TELL ME ANYTHING.
NO ONE TALKED TO ME.
FOR *MONTHS.*
THIS IS *ME* TALKING.
IT *DOESN'T* HAVEN'T TO BE LIKE THIS, MOM...

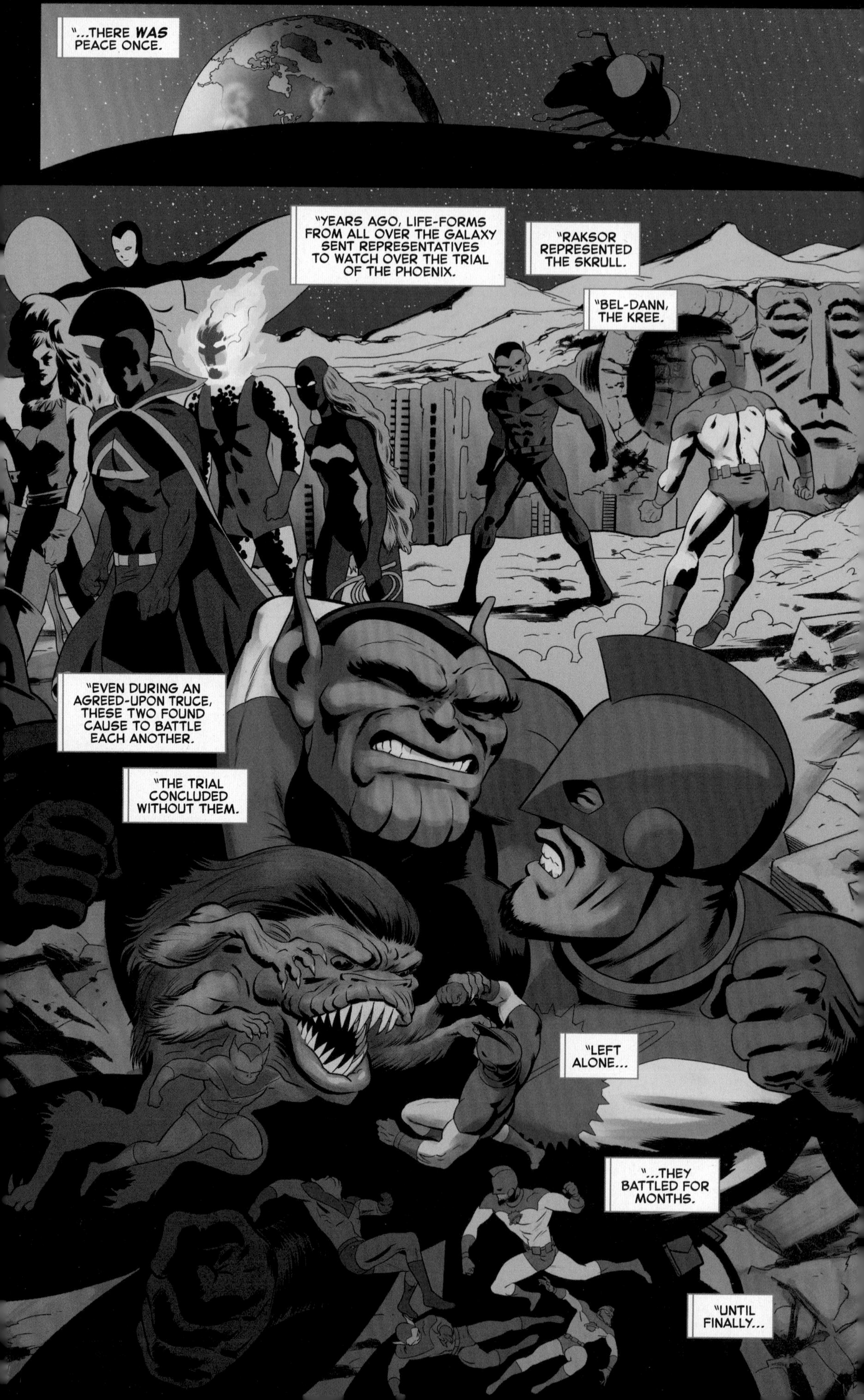
"...THERE WAS PEACE ONCE.
"YEARS AGO, LIFE-FORMS FROM ALL OVER THE GALAXY SENT REPRESENTATIVES TO WATCH OVER THE TRIAL OF THE PHOENIX.
"RAKSOR REPRESENTED THE SKRULL.
"BEL-DANN, THE KREE.
"EVEN DURING AN AGREED-UPON TRUCE, THESE TWO FOUND CAUSE TO BATTLE EACH ANOTHER.
"THE TRIAL CONCLUDED WITHOUT THEM.
"LEFT ALONE...
"...THEY BATTLED FOR MONTHS.
"UNTIL FINALLY...

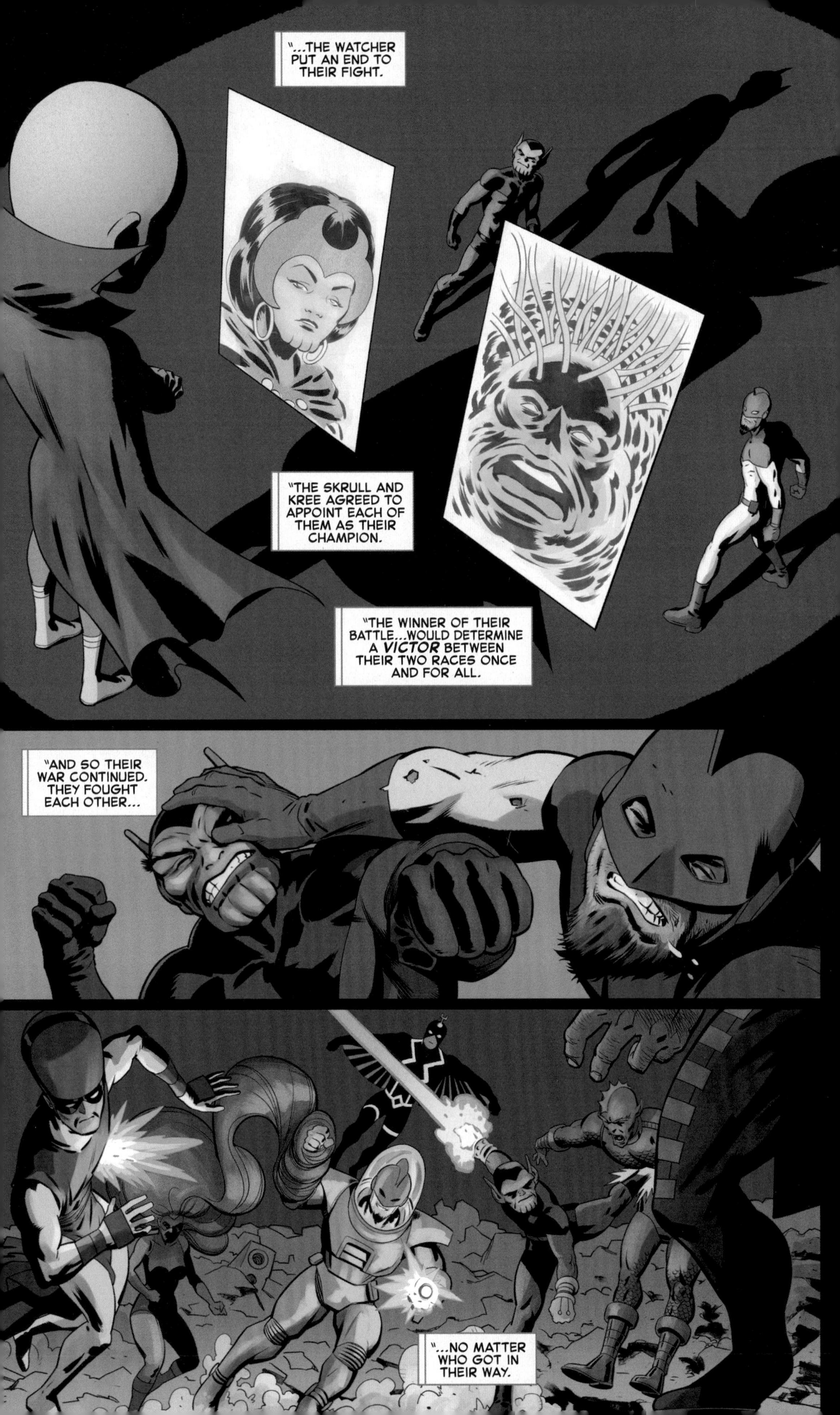
"...THE WATCHER PUT AN END TO THEIR FIGHT.
"THE SKRULL AND KREE AGREED TO APPOINT EACH OF THEM AS THEIR CHAMPION.
"THE WINNER OF THEIR BATTLE...WOULD DETERMINE A *VICTOR* BETWEEN THEIR TWO RACES ONCE AND FOR ALL.
"AND SO THEIR WAR CONTINUED. THEY FOUGHT EACH OTHER...
"...NO MATTER WHO GOT IN THEIR WAY.

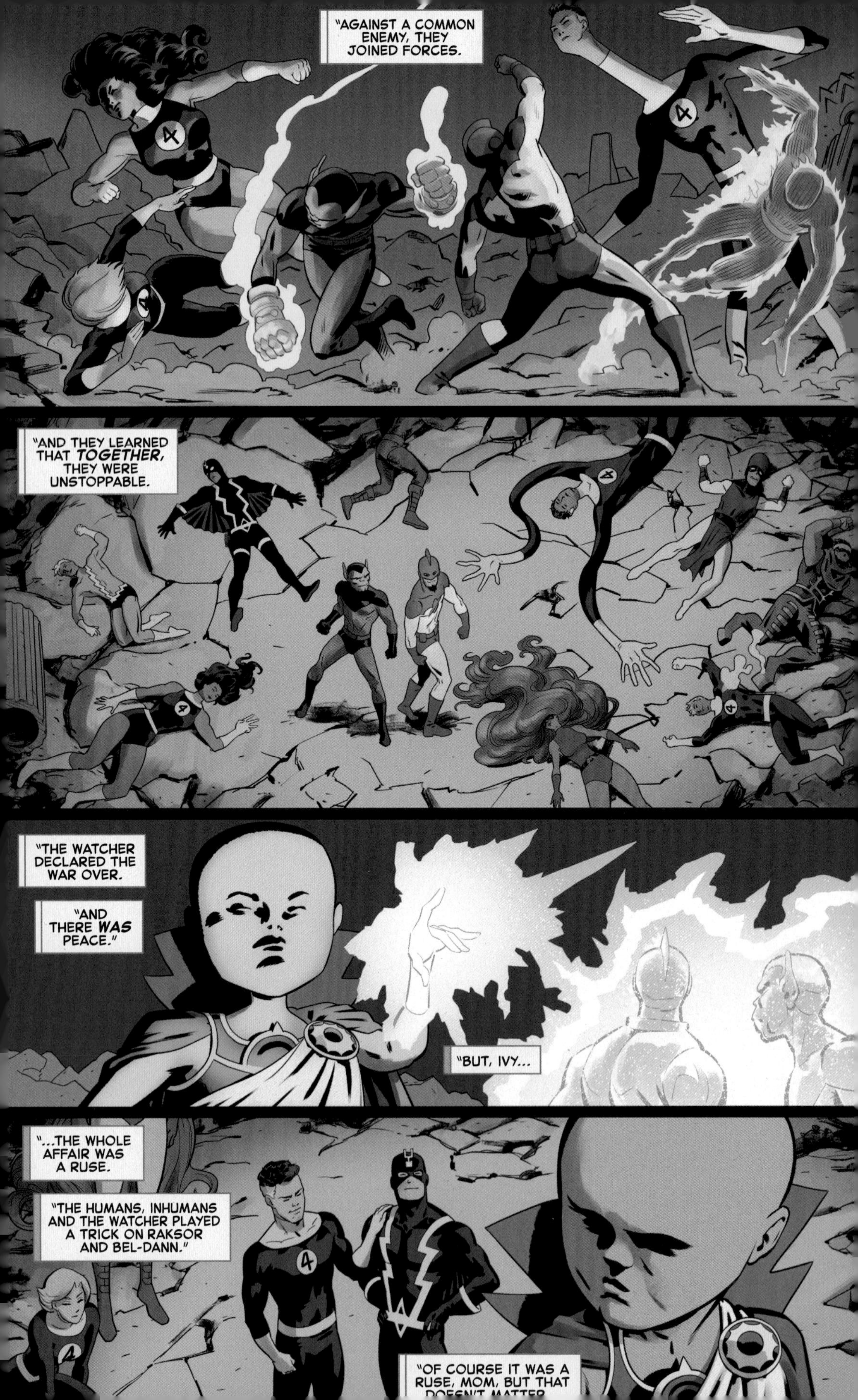
"AGAINST A COMMON ENEMY, THEY JOINED FORCES.
"AND THEY LEARNED THAT TOGETHER, THEY WERE UNSTOPPABLE.
"THE WATCHER DECLARED THE WAR OVER.
"AND THERE WAS PEACE."
"BUT, IVY...
"...THE WHOLE AFFAIR WAS A RUSE.
"THE HUMANS, INHUMANS AND THE WATCHER PLAYED A TRICK ON RAKSOR AND BEL-DANN."
"OF COURSE IT WAS A RUSE, MOM, BUT THAT

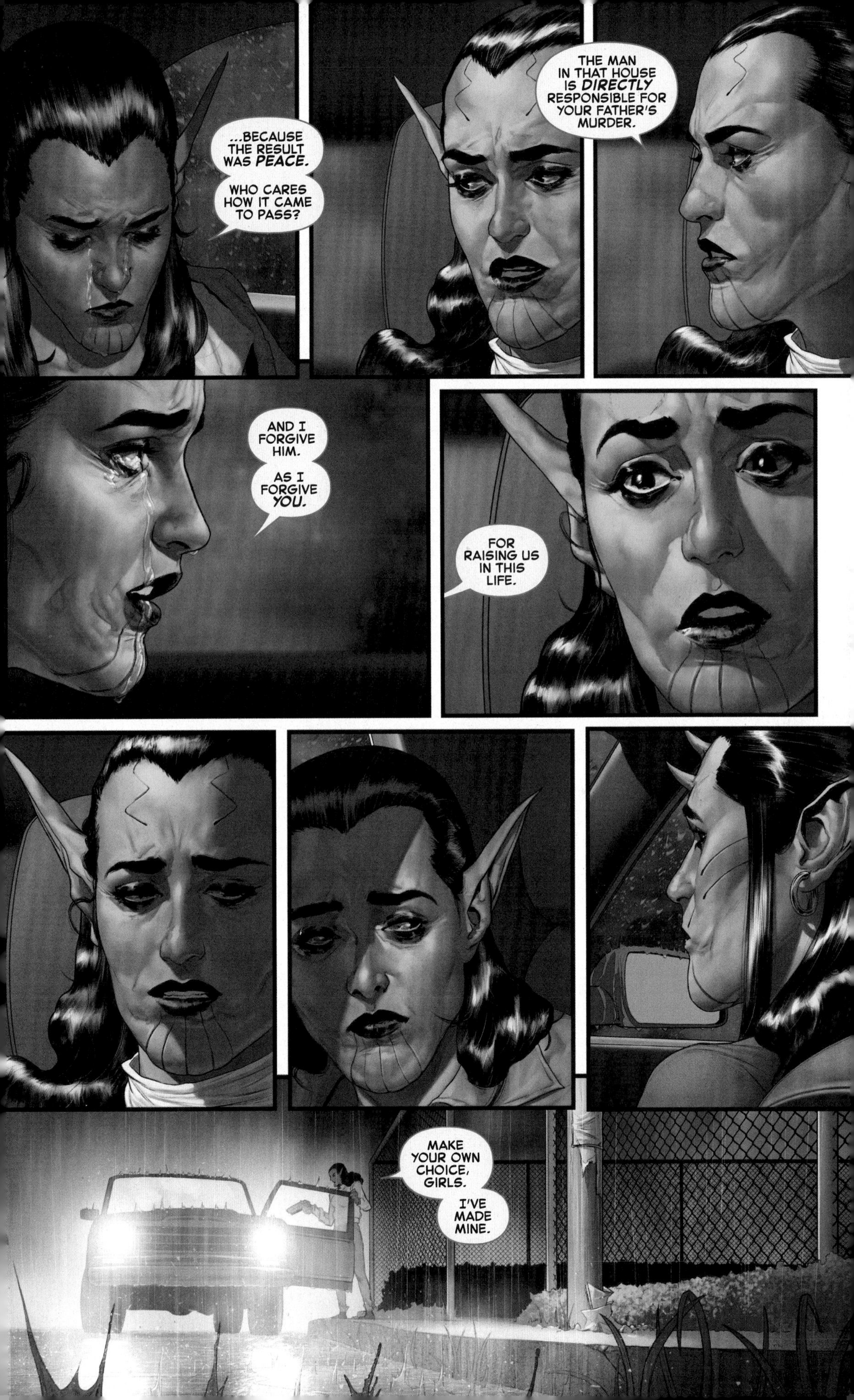

...BECAUSE THE RESULT WAS PEACE.
WHO CARES HOW IT CAME TO PASS?
THE MAN IN THAT HOUSE IS DIRECTLY RESPONSIBLE FOR YOUR FATHER'S MURDER.
AND I FORGIVE HIM.
AS I FORGIVE YOU.
FOR RAISING US IN THIS LIFE.
MAKE YOUR OWN CHOICE, GIRLS.
I'VE MADE MINE.

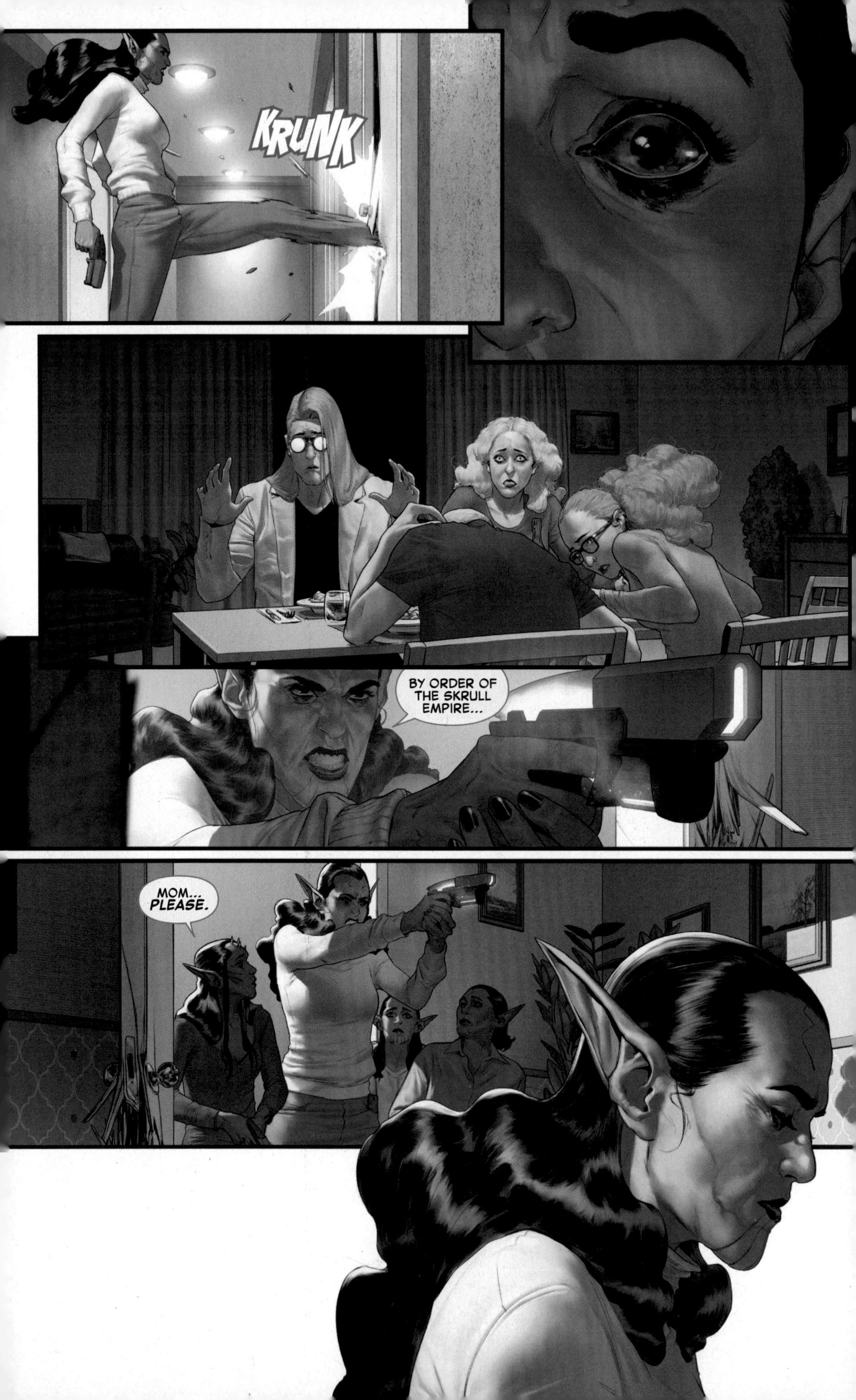
KRUNK
BY ORDER OF THE SKRULL EMPIRE...
MOM... PLEASE.

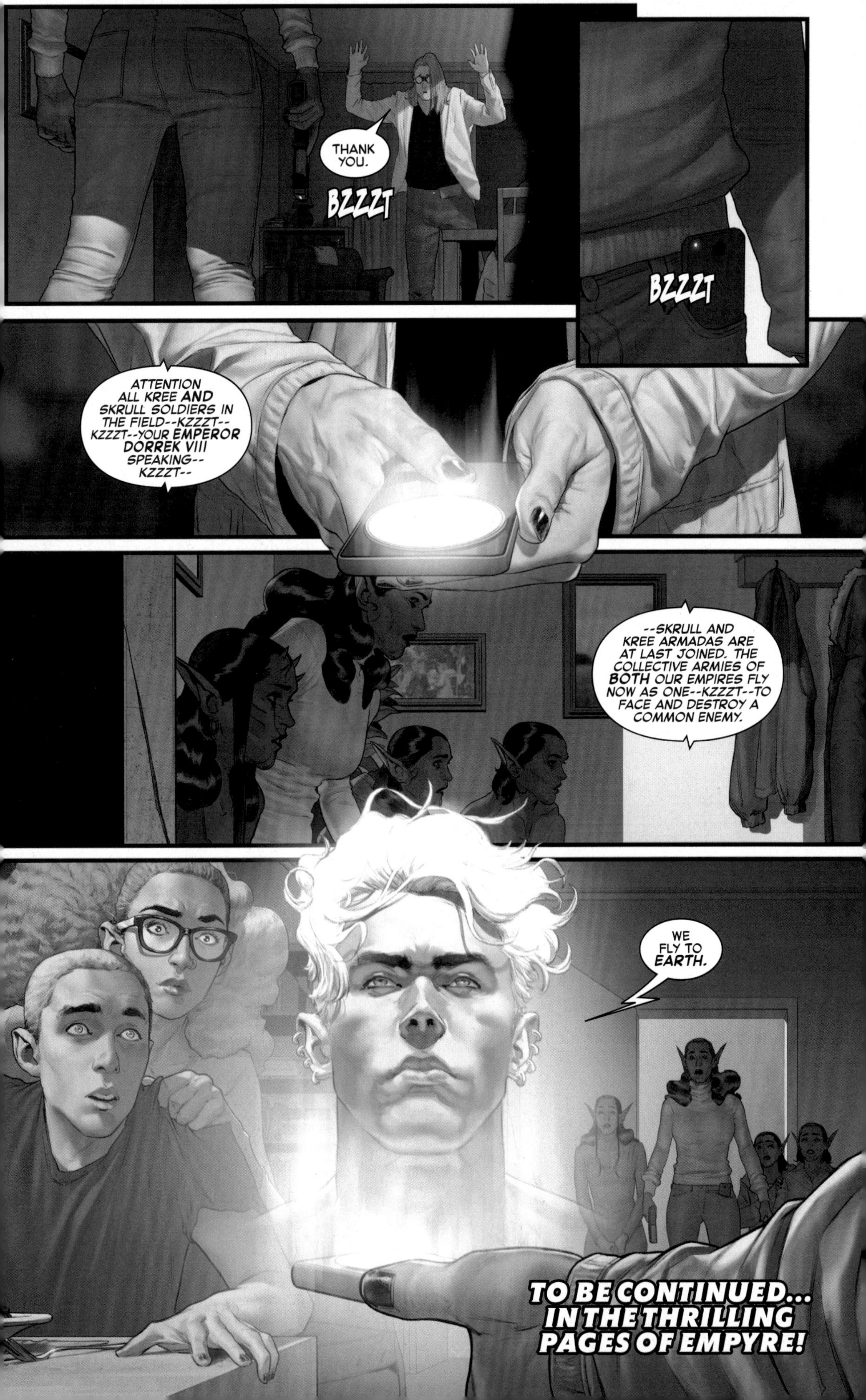
THANK YOU.
BZZZT
BZZZT
ATTENTION ALL KREE AND SKRULL SOLDIERS IN THE FIELD--KZZZT--KZZZT--YOUR EMPEROR DORREK VIII SPEAKING--KZZZT--
--SKRULL AND KREE ARMADAS ARE AT LAST JOINED. THE COLLECTIVE ARMIES OF BOTH OUR EMPIRES FLY NOW AS ONE--KZZZT--TO FACE AND DESTROY A COMMON ENEMY.
WE FLY TO EARTH.
TO BE CONTINUED... IN THE THRILLING PAGES OF EMPYRE!

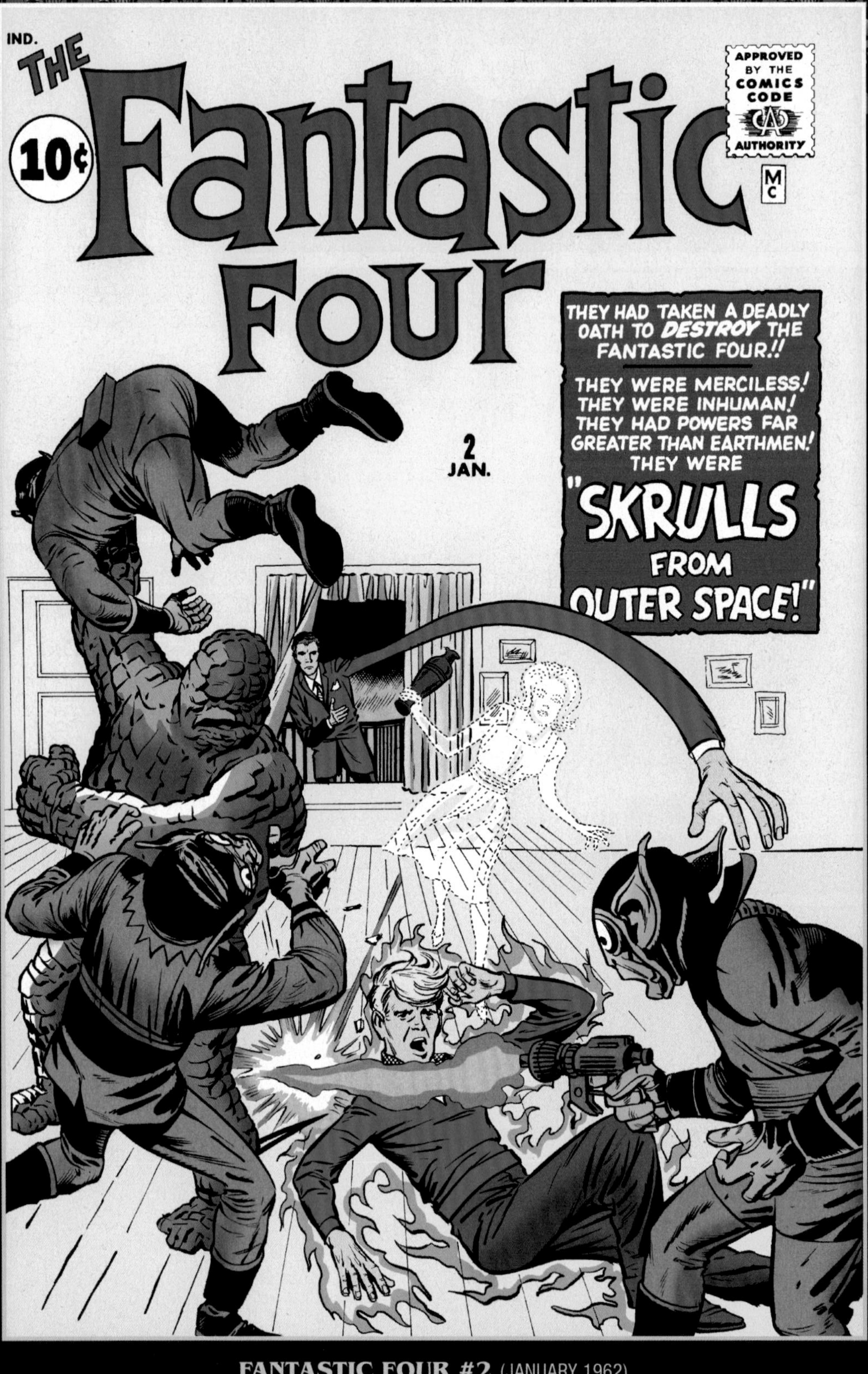
IND.
THE
10¢
Fantastic Four
APPROVED BY THE COMICS CODE AUTHORITY
MC
THEY HAD TAKEN A DEADLY OATH TO DESTROY THE FANTASTIC FOUR!!
THEY WERE MERCILESS! THEY WERE INHUMAN! THEY HAD POWERS FAR GREATER THAN EARTHMEN! THEY WERE
"SKRULLS FROM OUTER SPACE!"
2
JAN.

FANTASTIC FOUR #2 (JANUARY 1962)

From deep space come the shape-changing Skrulls!
Now the Fantastic Four must work to stop them conquering Earth!

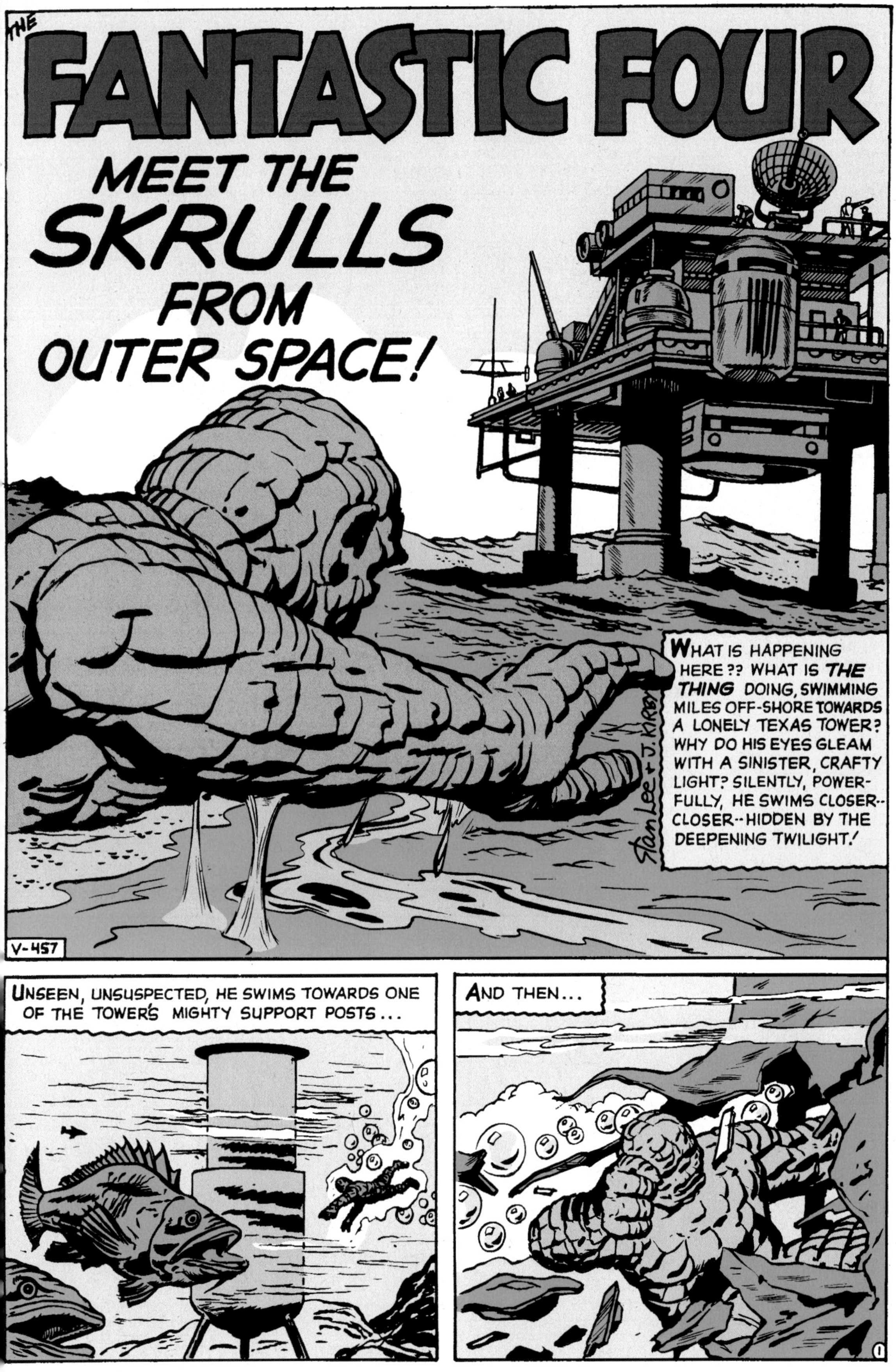
THE FANTASTIC FOUR
MEET THE SKRULLS FROM OUTER SPACE!
WHAT IS HAPPENING HERE?? WHAT IS THE THING DOING, SWIMMING MILES OFF-SHORE TOWARDS A LONELY TEXAS TOWER? WHY DO HIS EYES GLEAM WITH A SINISTER, CRAFTY LIGHT? SILENTLY, POWERFULLY, HE SWIMS CLOSER-- CLOSER-- HIDDEN BY THE DEEPENING TWILIGHT!
Stan Lee + J. Kirby
V-457
UNSEEN, UNSUSPECTED, HE SWIMS TOWARDS ONE OF THE TOWER'S MIGHTY SUPPORT POSTS...
AND THEN...
1

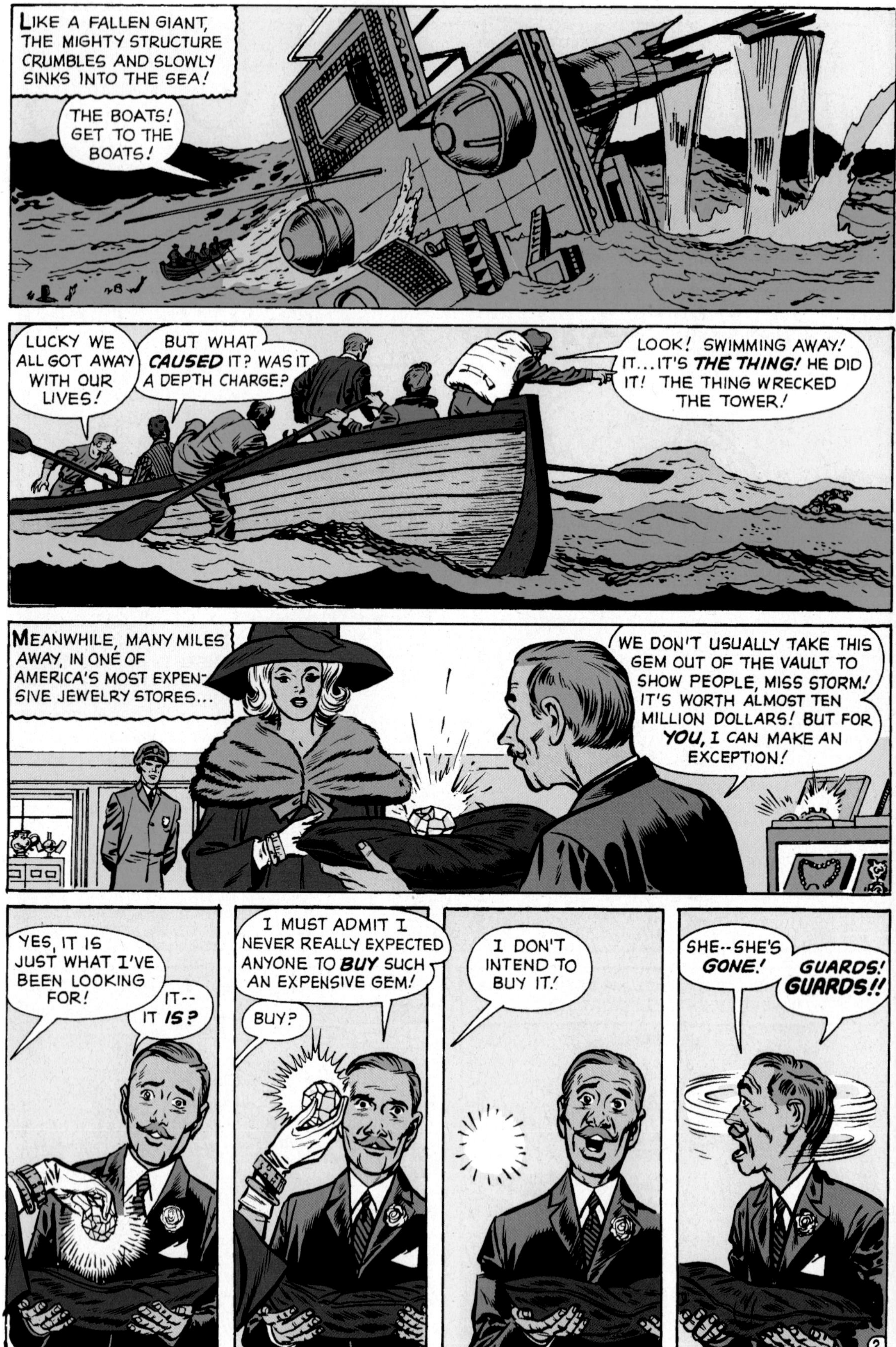
LIKE A FALLEN GIANT, THE MIGHTY STRUCTURE CRUMBLES AND SLOWLY SINKS INTO THE SEA!
THE BOATS! GET TO THE BOATS!
LUCKY WE ALL GOT AWAY WITH OUR LIVES!
BUT WHAT CAUSED IT? WAS IT A DEPTH CHARGE?
LOOK! SWIMMING AWAY! IT...IT'S THE THING! HE DID IT! THE THING WRECKED THE TOWER!
MEANWHILE, MANY MILES AWAY, IN ONE OF AMERICA'S MOST EXPENSIVE JEWELRY STORES...
WE DON'T USUALLY TAKE THIS GEM OUT OF THE VAULT TO SHOW PEOPLE, MISS STORM! IT'S WORTH ALMOST TEN MILLION DOLLARS! BUT FOR YOU, I CAN MAKE AN EXCEPTION!
YES, IT IS JUST WHAT I'VE BEEN LOOKING FOR!
IT-- IT IS?
I MUST ADMIT I NEVER REALLY EXPECTED ANYONE TO BUY SUCH AN EXPENSIVE GEM!
BUY?
I DON'T INTEND TO BUY IT!
SHE--SHE'S GONE!
GUARDS! GUARDS!!
2

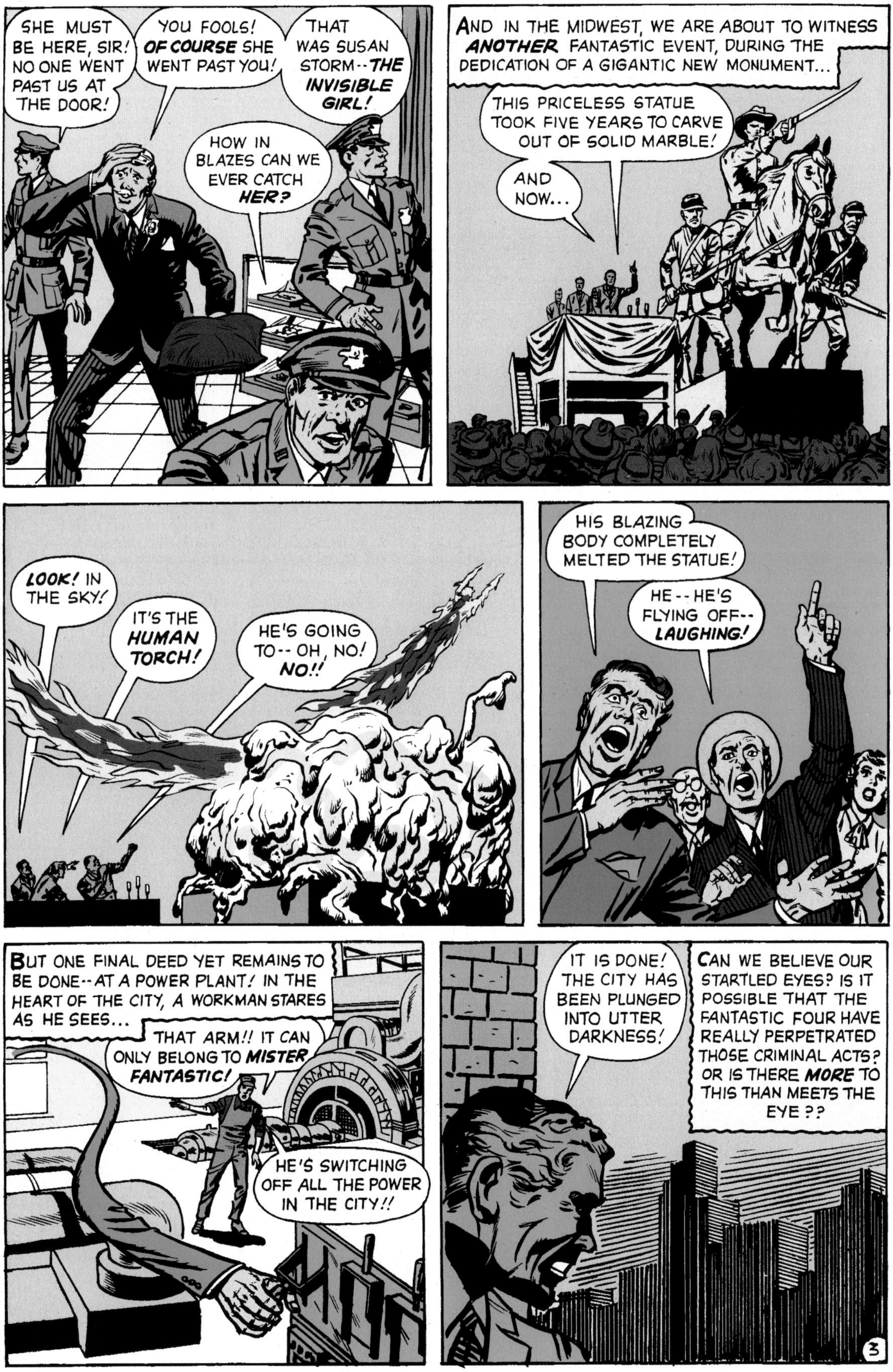
SHE MUST BE HERE, SIR! NO ONE WENT PAST US AT THE DOOR!
YOU FOOLS! OF COURSE SHE WENT PAST YOU!
THAT WAS SUSAN STORM--THE INVISIBLE GIRL!
HOW IN BLAZES CAN WE EVER CATCH HER?
AND IN THE MIDWEST, WE ARE ABOUT TO WITNESS ANOTHER FANTASTIC EVENT, DURING THE DEDICATION OF A GIGANTIC NEW MONUMENT...
THIS PRICELESS STATUE TOOK FIVE YEARS TO CARVE OUT OF SOLID MARBLE!
AND NOW...
LOOK! IN THE SKY!
IT'S THE HUMAN TORCH!
HE'S GOING TO--OH, NO! NO!!
HIS BLAZING BODY COMPLETELY MELTED THE STATUE!
HE--HE'S FLYING OFF--LAUGHING!
BUT ONE FINAL DEED YET REMAINS TO BE DONE--AT A POWER PLANT! IN THE HEART OF THE CITY, A WORKMAN STARES AS HE SEES...
THAT ARM!! IT CAN ONLY BELONG TO MISTER FANTASTIC!
HE'S SWITCHING OFF ALL THE POWER IN THE CITY!!
IT IS DONE! THE CITY HAS BEEN PLUNGED INTO UTTER DARKNESS!
CAN WE BELIEVE OUR STARTLED EYES? IS IT POSSIBLE THAT THE FANTASTIC FOUR HAVE REALLY PERPETRATED THOSE CRIMINAL ACTS? OR IS THERE MORE TO THIS THAN MEETS THE EYE??
3

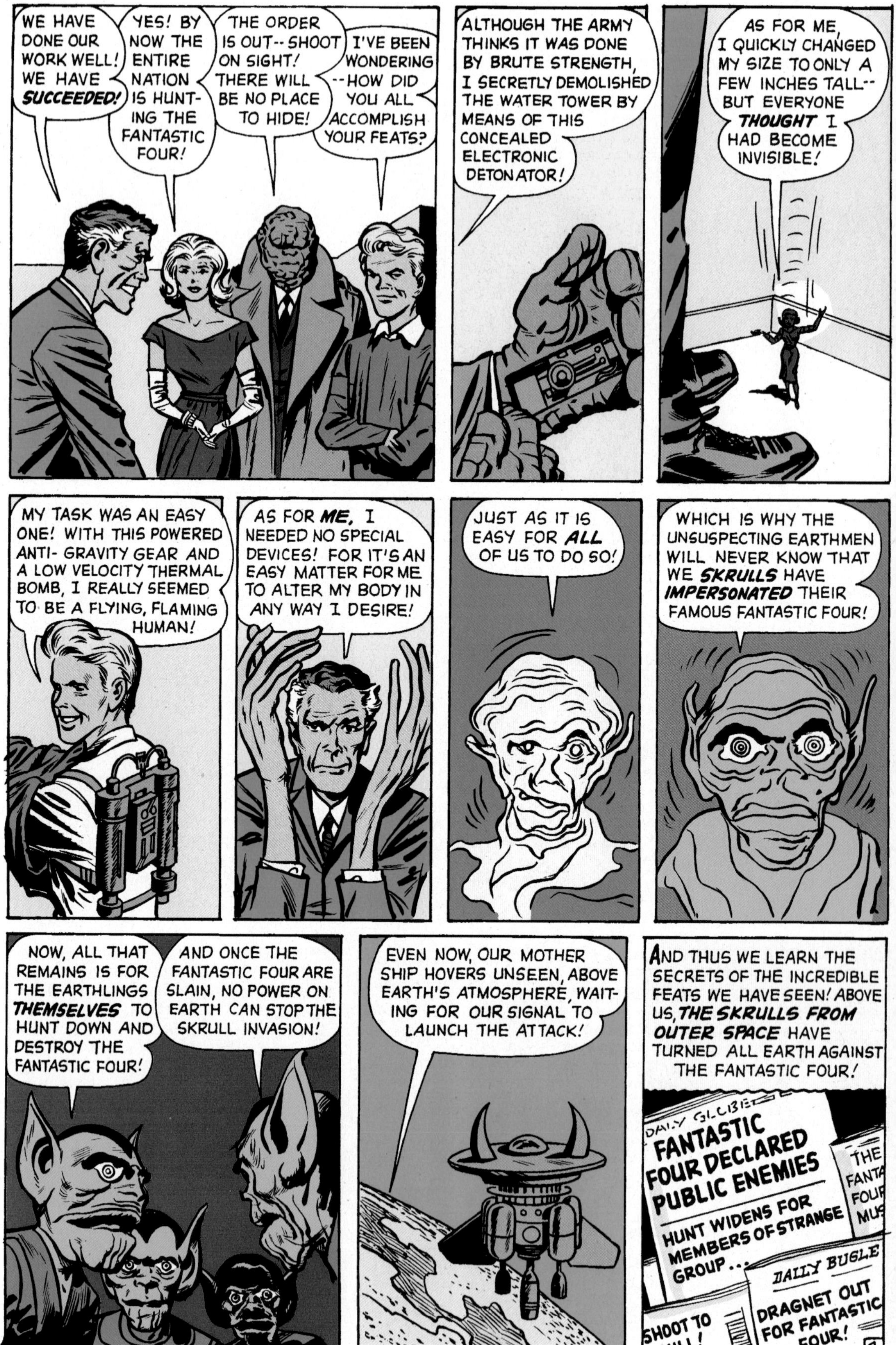
WE HAVE DONE OUR WORK WELL! WE HAVE SUCCEEDED!
YES! BY NOW THE ENTIRE NATION IS HUNTING THE FANTASTIC FOUR!
THE ORDER IS OUT-- SHOOT ON SIGHT! THERE WILL BE NO PLACE TO HIDE!
I'VE BEEN WONDERING --HOW DID YOU ALL ACCOMPLISH YOUR FEATS?
ALTHOUGH THE ARMY THINKS IT WAS DONE BY BRUTE STRENGTH, I SECRETLY DEMOLISHED THE WATER TOWER BY MEANS OF THIS CONCEALED ELECTRONIC DETONATOR!
AS FOR ME, I QUICKLY CHANGED MY SIZE TO ONLY A FEW INCHES TALL-- BUT EVERYONE THOUGHT I HAD BECOME INVISIBLE!
MY TASK WAS AN EASY ONE! WITH THIS POWERED ANTI- GRAVITY GEAR AND A LOW VELOCITY THERMAL BOMB, I REALLY SEEMED TO BE A FLYING, FLAMING HUMAN!
AS FOR ME, I NEEDED NO SPECIAL DEVICES! FOR IT'S AN EASY MATTER FOR ME TO ALTER MY BODY IN ANY WAY I DESIRE!
JUST AS IT IS EASY FOR ALL OF US TO DO SO!
WHICH IS WHY THE UNSUSPECTING EARTHMEN WILL NEVER KNOW THAT WE SKRULLS HAVE IMPERSONATED THEIR FAMOUS FANTASTIC FOUR!
NOW, ALL THAT REMAINS IS FOR THE EARTHLINGS THEMSELVES TO HUNT DOWN AND DESTROY THE FANTASTIC FOUR!
AND ONCE THE FANTASTIC FOUR ARE SLAIN, NO POWER ON EARTH CAN STOP THE SKRULL INVASION!
EVEN NOW, OUR MOTHER SHIP HOVERS UNSEEN, ABOVE EARTH'S ATMOSPHERE, WAITING FOR OUR SIGNAL TO LAUNCH THE ATTACK!
AND THUS WE LEARN THE SECRETS OF THE INCREDIBLE FEATS WE HAVE SEEN! ABOVE US, THE SKRULLS FROM OUTER SPACE HAVE TURNED ALL EARTH AGAINST THE FANTASTIC FOUR!
DAILY GLOBE
FANTASTIC FOUR DECLARED PUBLIC ENEMIES
HUNT WIDENS FOR MEMBERS OF STRANGE GROUP...
SHOOT TO KILL!
DAILY BUGLE
DRAGNET OUT FOR FANTASTIC FOUR!
4

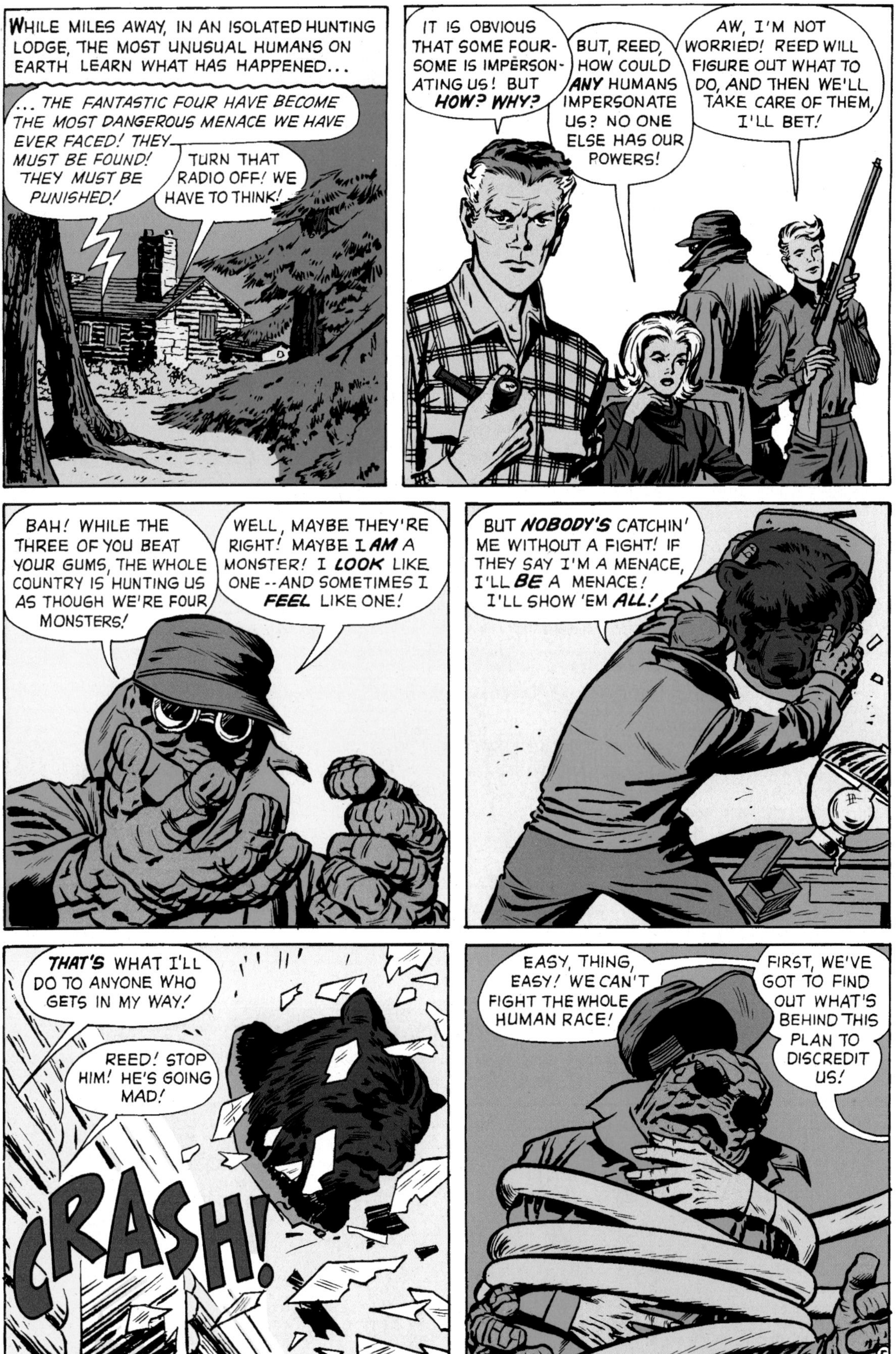

WHILE MILES AWAY, IN AN ISOLATED HUNTING LODGE, THE MOST UNUSUAL HUMANS ON EARTH LEARN WHAT HAS HAPPENED...
... THE FANTASTIC FOUR HAVE BECOME THE MOST DANGEROUS MENACE WE HAVE EVER FACED! THEY MUST BE FOUND! THEY MUST BE PUNISHED!
TURN THAT RADIO OFF! WE HAVE TO THINK!
IT IS OBVIOUS THAT SOME FOURSOME IS IMPERSONATING US! BUT HOW? WHY?
BUT, REED, HOW COULD ANY HUMANS IMPERSONATE US? NO ONE ELSE HAS OUR POWERS!
AW, I'M NOT WORRIED! REED WILL FIGURE OUT WHAT TO DO, AND THEN WE'LL TAKE CARE OF THEM, I'LL BET!
BAH! WHILE THE THREE OF YOU BEAT YOUR GUMS, THE WHOLE COUNTRY IS HUNTING US AS THOUGH WE'RE FOUR MONSTERS!
WELL, MAYBE THEY'RE RIGHT! MAYBE I AM A MONSTER! I LOOK LIKE ONE--AND SOMETIMES I FEEL LIKE ONE!
BUT NOBODY'S CATCHIN' ME WITHOUT A FIGHT! IF THEY SAY I'M A MENACE, I'LL BE A MENACE! I'LL SHOW 'EM ALL!
THAT'S WHAT I'LL DO TO ANYONE WHO GETS IN MY WAY!
REED! STOP HIM! HE'S GOING MAD!
CRASH!
EASY, THING, EASY! WE CAN'T FIGHT THE WHOLE HUMAN RACE!
FIRST, WE'VE GOT TO FIND OUT WHAT'S BEHIND THIS PLAN TO DISCREDIT US!
5

TALK! *TALK!* ALL YOU EVER DO IS TALK! BUT I'M NOT *BUILT* THAT WAY! I WANT ACTION!

I *KNOW* YOU DO, THING! BUT WE CAN'T FLY OFF THE HANDLE! WE'VE GOT TO WAIT TILL WE KNOW WHO'S *BEHIND* ALL THIS!

WAIT?? THAT'S ALL RIGHT FOR YOU, TORCH! AT LEAST YOU'RE *HUMAN!*

BUT HOW WOULD YOU LIKE TO BE ME? I WON'T WAIT ANY LONGER! I'M GOING OUT...

...TO FIGHT! ...TO SMASH!

REED, HOW MUCH MORE OF THIS CAN WE TAKE! SOONER OR LATER, THE THING WILL RUN AMOK AND NONE OF US WILL BE ABLE TO STOP HIM!

SHE'S RIGHT, REED! WE'VE GOT TO *DO* SOMETHING ABOUT HIM!

NO! WE MUST BE PATIENT! AFTER ALL, HE'S NOT REALLY TO BLAME! IT'S ACTUALLY *MY* FAULT THAT HE IS THE WAY HE IS!

"IT WAS *MY* FAULT THAT OUR FLIGHT TO MARS FAILED AND WE NEARLY LOST OUR LIVES WHEN WE CRASH-LANDED ON EARTH!..."

"IT WAS MY FAULT THAT THE COSMIC RAYS OF SPACE TURNED SUE INTO A SOMETIMES INVISIBLE GIRL!..."

"...THE SAME RAYS WHICH MADE A POWERFUL, BRUTAL THING OUT OF POOR BEN!..."

"IT WAS BECAUSE OF MY OVERSIGHT THAT JOHNNY WAS TRANSFORMED INTO A TEMPORARY HUMAN TORCH BY THOSE FANTASTIC RAYS!..."

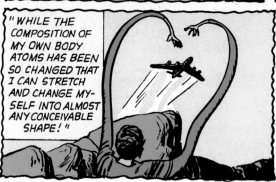

"WHILE THE COMPOSITION OF MY OWN BODY ATOMS HAS BEEN SO CHANGED THAT I CAN STRETCH AND CHANGE MYSELF INTO ALMOST ANY CONCEIVABLE SHAPE!"

I CAN'T PUNISH THE THING WHEN THE FAULT IS *MINE!*

OKAY, FORGET *HIM!* WHAT DO WE DO *NOW?*

6

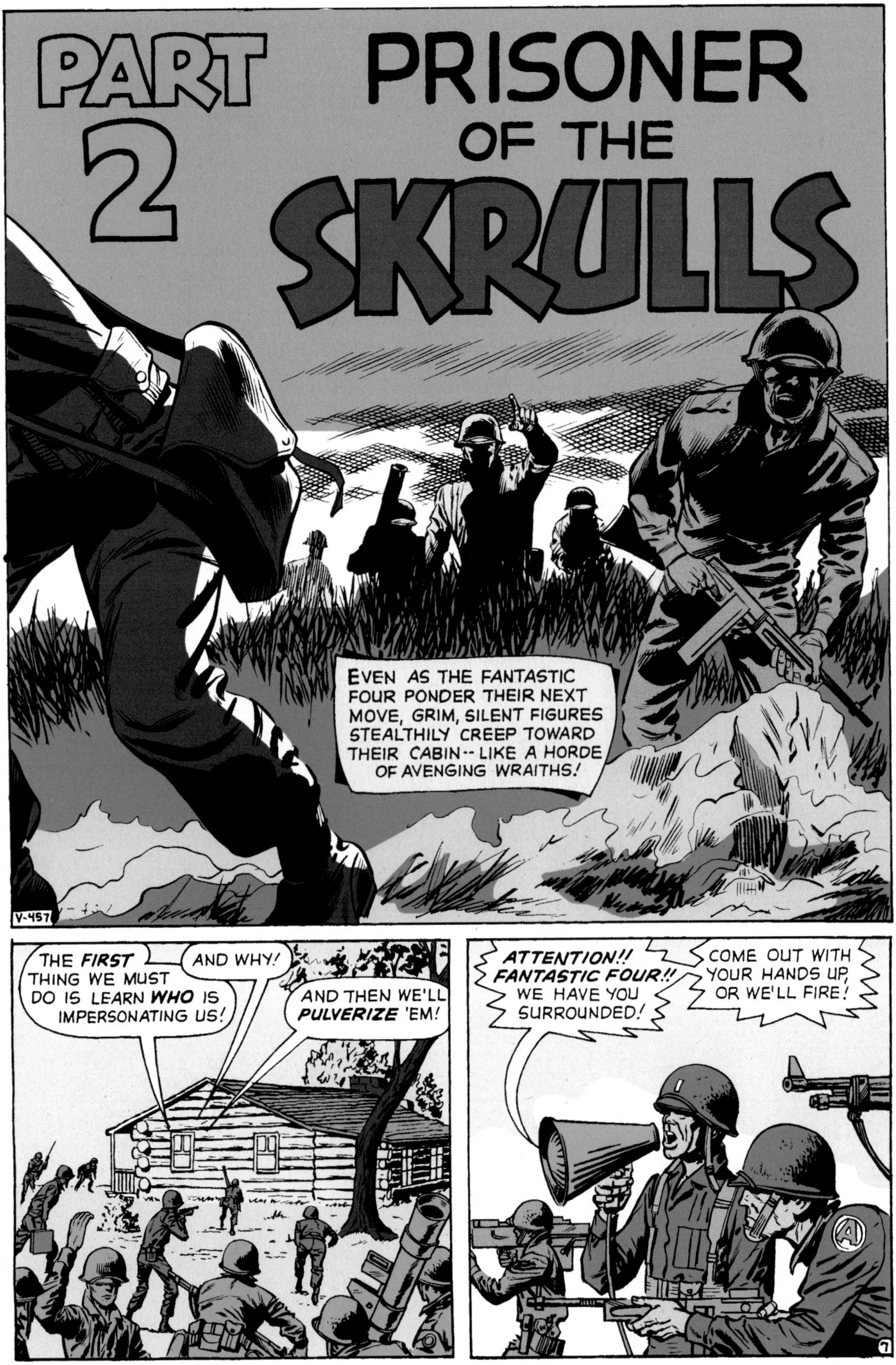
PART 2
PRISONER OF THE SKRULLS
EVEN AS THE FANTASTIC FOUR PONDER THEIR NEXT MOVE, GRIM, SILENT FIGURES STEALTHILY CREEP TOWARD THEIR CABIN-- LIKE A HORDE OF AVENGING WRAITHS!
V-457
THE FIRST THING WE MUST DO IS LEARN WHO IS IMPERSONATING US!
AND WHY!
AND THEN WE'LL PULVERIZE 'EM!
ATTENTION!! FANTASTIC FOUR!! WE HAVE YOU SURROUNDED!
COME OUT WITH YOUR HANDS UP, OR WE'LL FIRE!
7

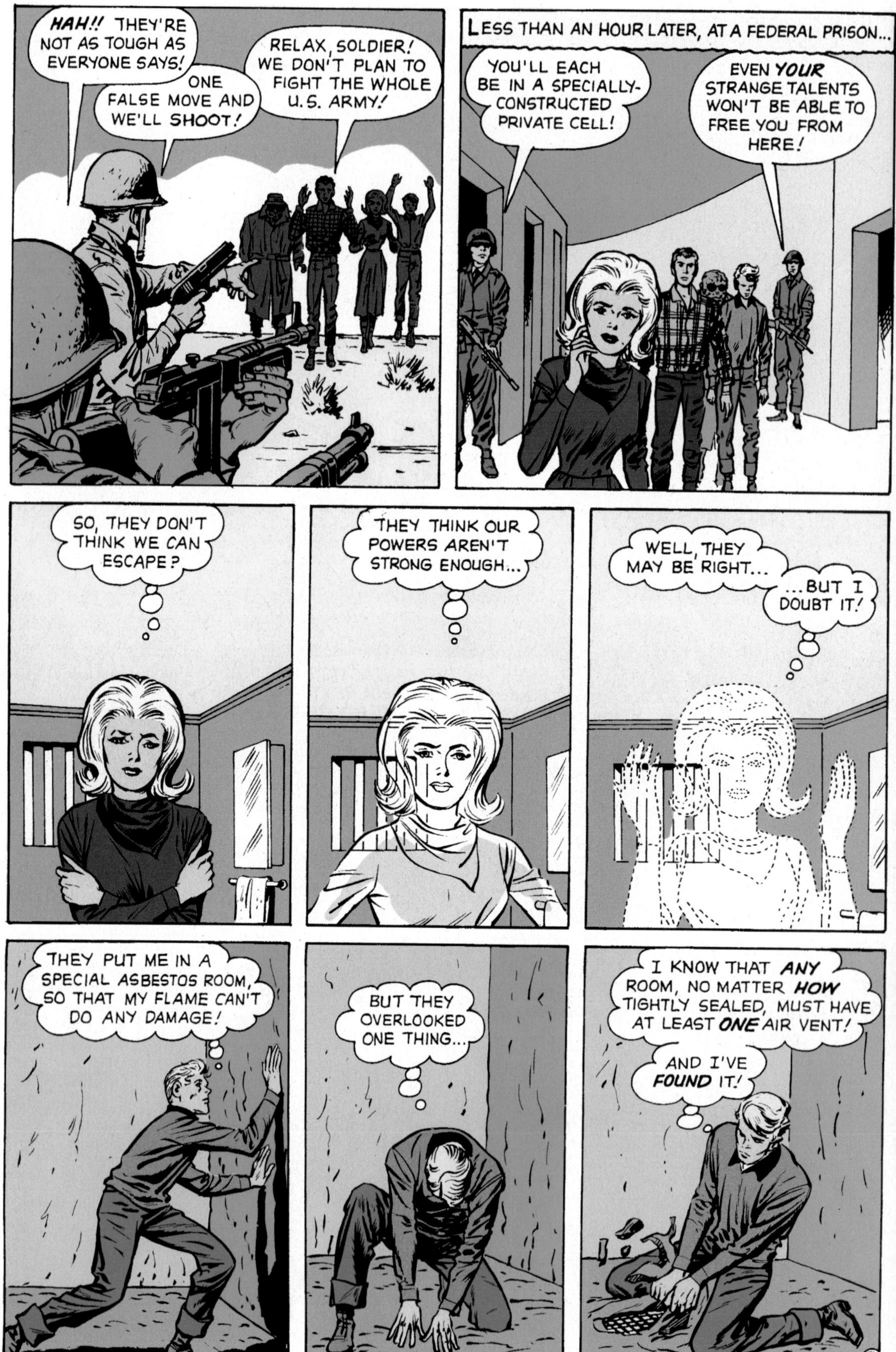
HAH!! THEY'RE NOT AS TOUGH AS EVERYONE SAYS!
ONE FALSE MOVE AND WE'LL SHOOT!
RELAX, SOLDIER! WE DON'T PLAN TO FIGHT THE WHOLE U.S. ARMY!
LESS THAN AN HOUR LATER, AT A FEDERAL PRISON...
YOU'LL EACH BE IN A SPECIALLY-CONSTRUCTED PRIVATE CELL!
EVEN YOUR STRANGE TALENTS WON'T BE ABLE TO FREE YOU FROM HERE!
SO, THEY DON'T THINK WE CAN ESCAPE?
THEY THINK OUR POWERS AREN'T STRONG ENOUGH...
WELL, THEY MAY BE RIGHT...
...BUT I DOUBT IT!
THEY PUT ME IN A SPECIAL ASBESTOS ROOM, SO THAT MY FLAME CAN'T DO ANY DAMAGE!
BUT THEY OVERLOOKED ONE THING...
I KNOW THAT ANY ROOM, NO MATTER HOW TIGHTLY SEALED, MUST HAVE AT LEAST ONE AIR VENT!
AND I'VE FOUND IT!
8

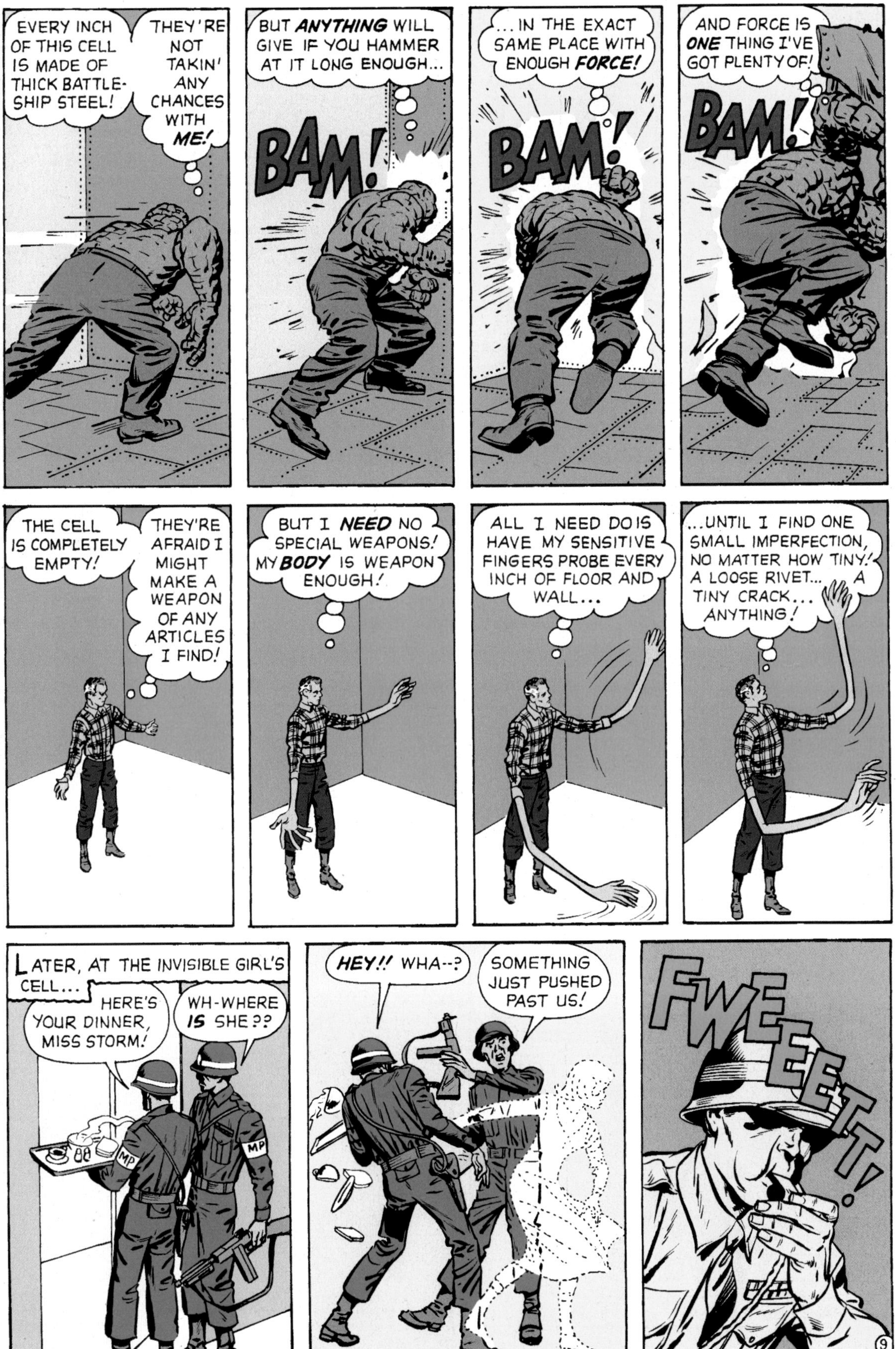

EVERY INCH OF THIS CELL IS MADE OF THICK BATTLE-SHIP STEEL!
THEY'RE NOT TAKIN' ANY CHANCES WITH ME!
BUT ANYTHING WILL GIVE IF YOU HAMMER AT IT LONG ENOUGH...
BAM!
...IN THE EXACT SAME PLACE WITH ENOUGH FORCE!
BAM!
AND FORCE IS ONE THING I'VE GOT PLENTY OF!
BAM!
THE CELL IS COMPLETELY EMPTY!
THEY'RE AFRAID I MIGHT MAKE A WEAPON OF ANY ARTICLES I FIND!
BUT I NEED NO SPECIAL WEAPONS! MY BODY IS WEAPON ENOUGH!
ALL I NEED DO IS HAVE MY SENSITIVE FINGERS PROBE EVERY INCH OF FLOOR AND WALL...
...UNTIL I FIND ONE SMALL IMPERFECTION, NO MATTER HOW TINY! A LOOSE RIVET... A TINY CRACK... ANYTHING!
LATER, AT THE INVISIBLE GIRL'S CELL...
HERE'S YOUR DINNER, MISS STORM!
WH-WHERE IS SHE??
MP
MP
HEY!! WHA--?
SOMETHING JUST PUSHED PAST US!
FWEEEETT!
9

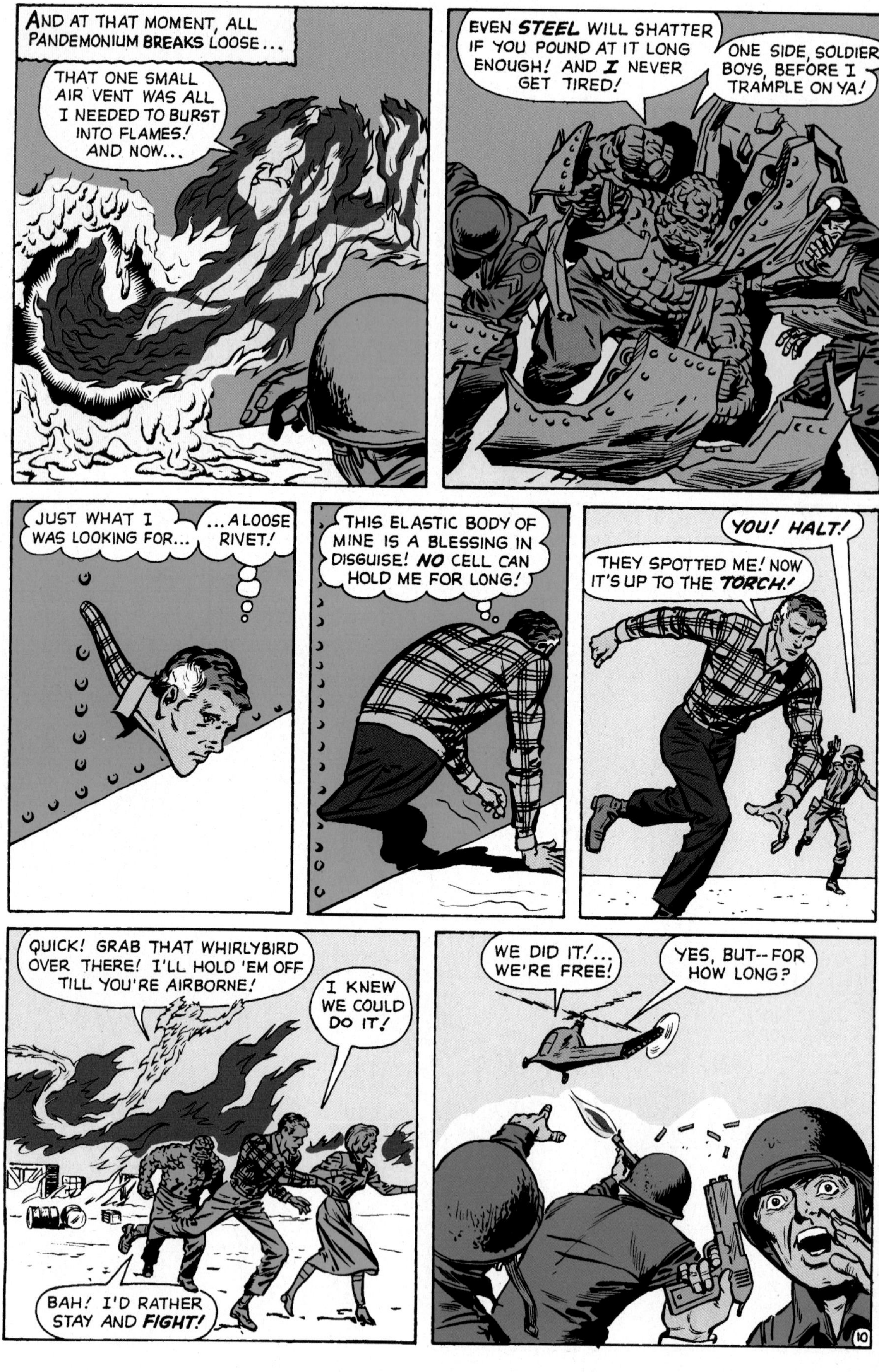
AND AT THAT MOMENT, ALL PANDEMONIUM BREAKS LOOSE...
THAT ONE SMALL AIR VENT WAS ALL I NEEDED TO BURST INTO FLAMES! AND NOW...
EVEN STEEL WILL SHATTER IF YOU POUND AT IT LONG ENOUGH! AND I NEVER GET TIRED!
ONE SIDE, SOLDIER BOYS, BEFORE I TRAMPLE ON YA!
JUST WHAT I WAS LOOKING FOR...
...A LOOSE RIVET!
THIS ELASTIC BODY OF MINE IS A BLESSING IN DISGUISE! NO CELL CAN HOLD ME FOR LONG!
YOU! HALT!
THEY SPOTTED ME! NOW IT'S UP TO THE TORCH!
QUICK! GRAB THAT WHIRLYBIRD OVER THERE! I'LL HOLD 'EM OFF TILL YOU'RE AIRBORNE!
I KNEW WE COULD DO IT!
BAH! I'D RATHER STAY AND FIGHT!
WE DID IT!... WE'RE FREE!
YES, BUT--FOR HOW LONG?
10

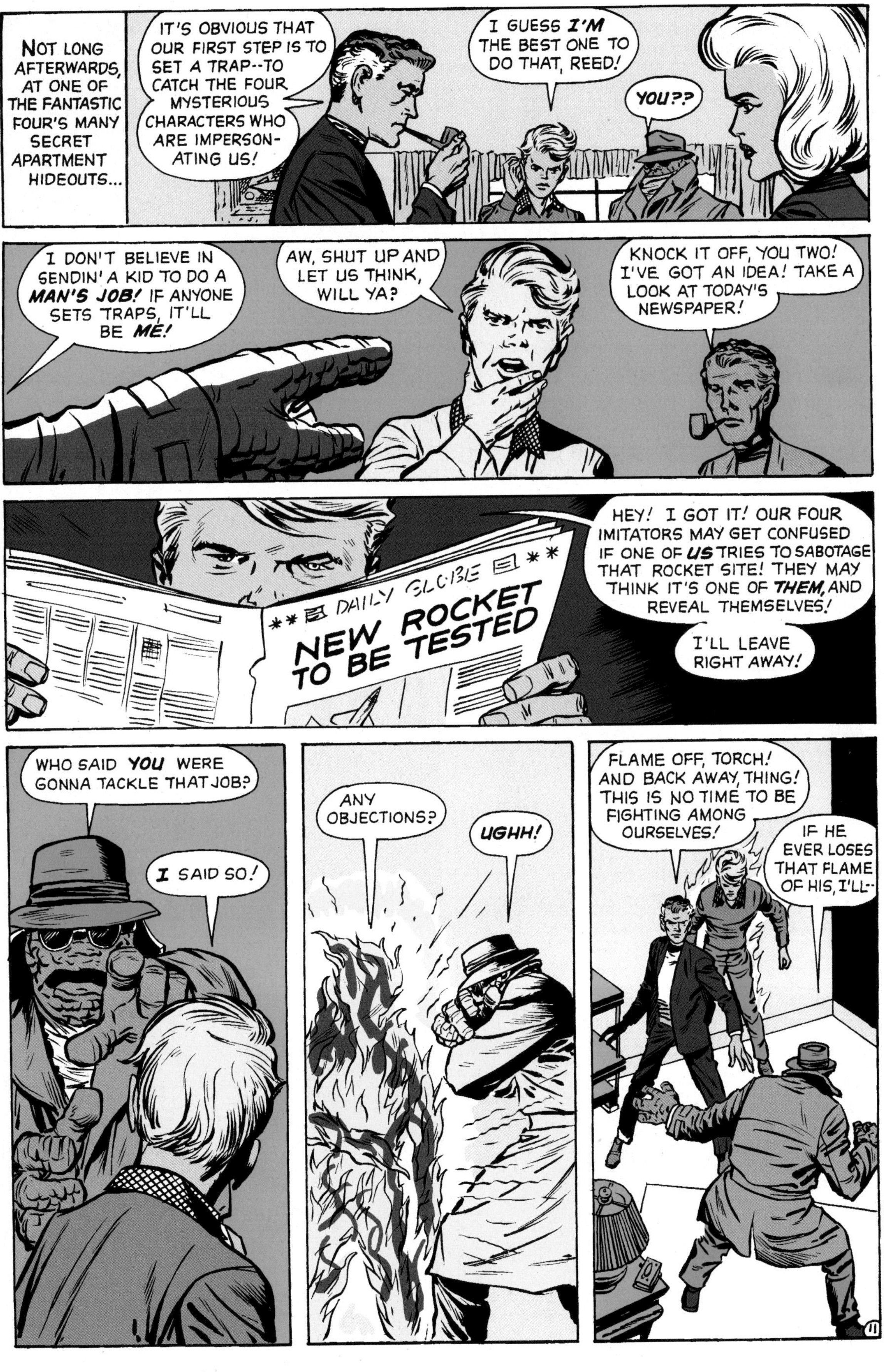
NOT LONG AFTERWARDS, AT ONE OF THE FANTASTIC FOUR'S MANY SECRET APARTMENT HIDEOUTS...
IT'S OBVIOUS THAT OUR FIRST STEP IS TO SET A TRAP--TO CATCH THE FOUR MYSTERIOUS CHARACTERS WHO ARE IMPERSON-ATING US!
I GUESS I'M THE BEST ONE TO DO THAT, REED!
YOU??
I DON'T BELIEVE IN SENDIN' A KID TO DO A MAN'S JOB! IF ANYONE SETS TRAPS, IT'LL BE ME!
AW, SHUT UP AND LET US THINK, WILL YA?
KNOCK IT OFF, YOU TWO! I'VE GOT AN IDEA! TAKE A LOOK AT TODAY'S NEWSPAPER!
DAILY GLOBE
NEW ROCKET TO BE TESTED
HEY! I GOT IT! OUR FOUR IMITATORS MAY GET CONFUSED IF ONE OF US TRIES TO SABOTAGE THAT ROCKET SITE! THEY MAY THINK IT'S ONE OF THEM, AND REVEAL THEMSELVES!
I'LL LEAVE RIGHT AWAY!
WHO SAID YOU WERE GONNA TACKLE THAT JOB?
I SAID SO!
ANY OBJECTIONS?
UGHH!
FLAME OFF, TORCH! AND BACK AWAY, THING! THIS IS NO TIME TO BE FIGHTING AMONG OURSELVES!
IF HE EVER LOSES THAT FLAME OF HIS, I'LL--
11

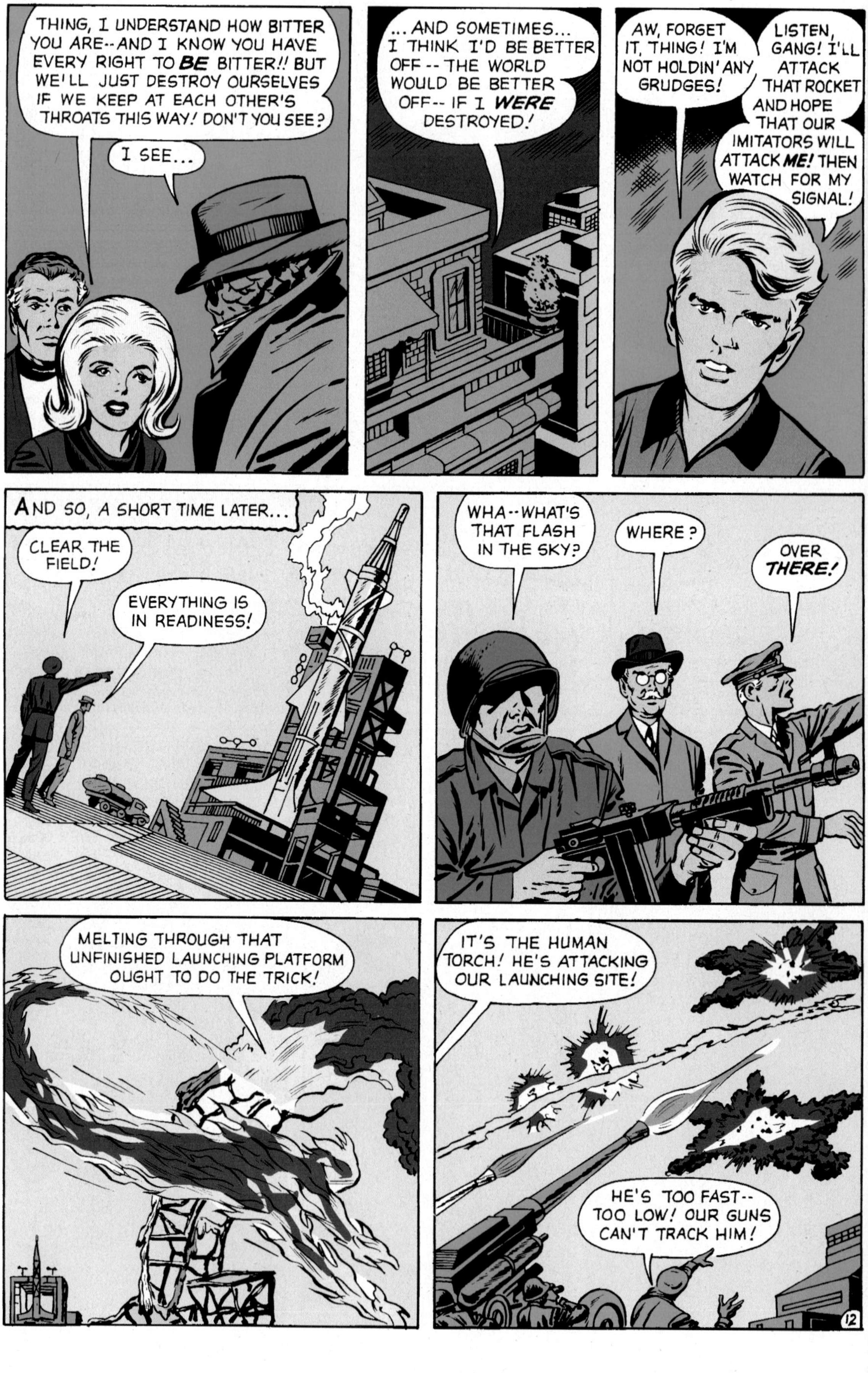
THING, I UNDERSTAND HOW BITTER YOU ARE--AND I KNOW YOU HAVE EVERY RIGHT TO BE BITTER!! BUT WE'LL JUST DESTROY OURSELVES IF WE KEEP AT EACH OTHER'S THROATS THIS WAY! DON'T YOU SEE?
I SEE...
...AND SOMETIMES... I THINK I'D BE BETTER OFF -- THE WORLD WOULD BE BETTER OFF-- IF I WERE DESTROYED!
AW, FORGET IT, THING! I'M NOT HOLDIN' ANY GRUDGES!
LISTEN, GANG! I'LL ATTACK THAT ROCKET AND HOPE THAT OUR IMITATORS WILL ATTACK ME! THEN WATCH FOR MY SIGNAL!
AND SO, A SHORT TIME LATER...
CLEAR THE FIELD!
EVERYTHING IS IN READINESS!
WHA--WHAT'S THAT FLASH IN THE SKY?
WHERE?
OVER THERE!
MELTING THROUGH THAT UNFINISHED LAUNCHING PLATFORM OUGHT TO DO THE TRICK!
IT'S THE HUMAN TORCH! HE'S ATTACKING OUR LAUNCHING SITE!
HE'S TOO FAST-- TOO LOW! OUR GUNS CAN'T TRACK HIM!
12

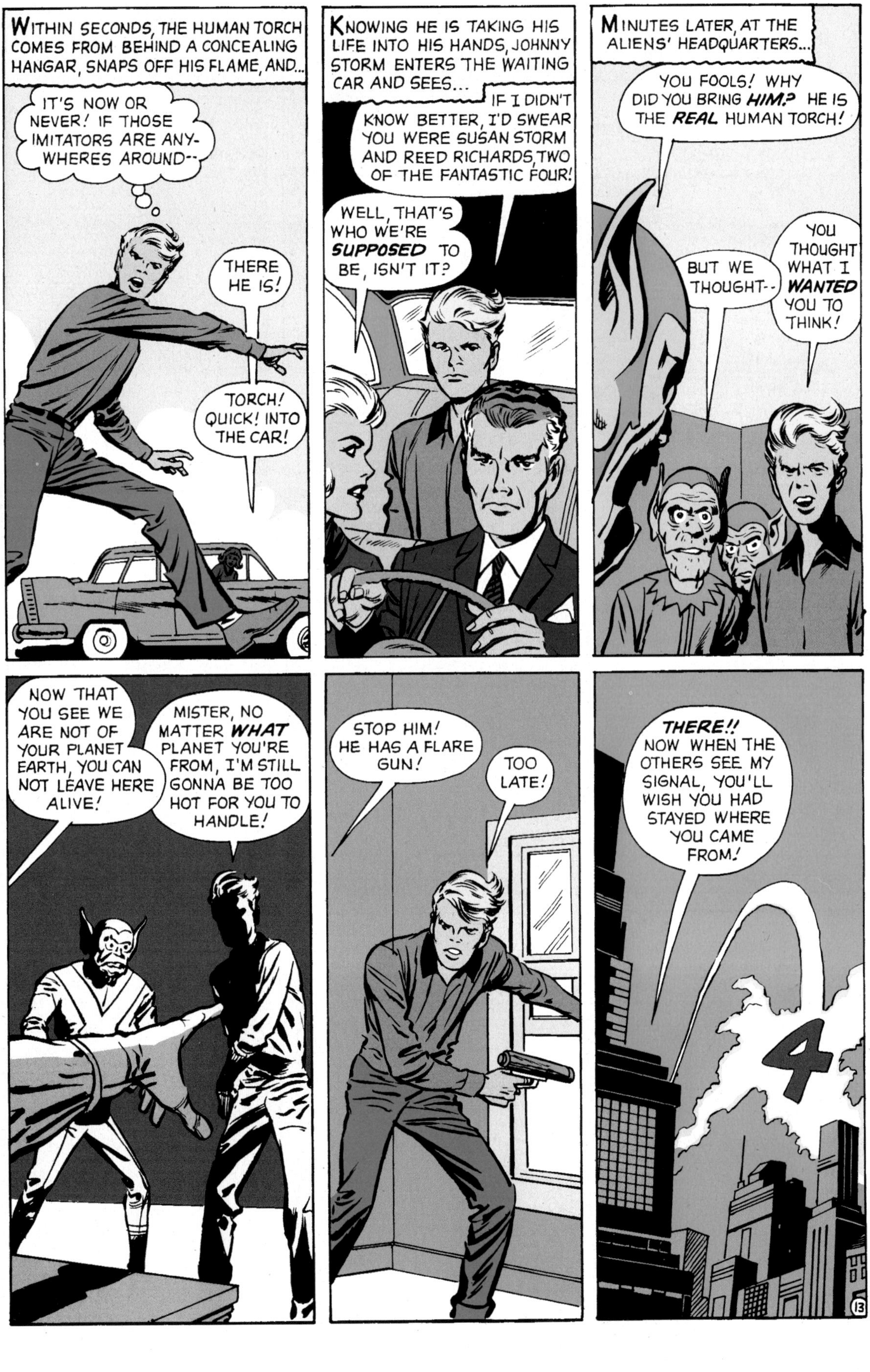
WITHIN SECONDS, THE HUMAN TORCH COMES FROM BEHIND A CONCEALING HANGAR, SNAPS OFF HIS FLAME, AND...
IT'S NOW OR NEVER! IF THOSE IMITATORS ARE ANY-WHERES AROUND--
THERE HE IS!
TORCH! QUICK! INTO THE CAR!
KNOWING HE IS TAKING HIS LIFE INTO HIS HANDS, JOHNNY STORM ENTERS THE WAITING CAR AND SEES...
IF I DIDN'T KNOW BETTER, I'D SWEAR YOU WERE SUSAN STORM AND REED RICHARDS, TWO OF THE FANTASTIC FOUR!
WELL, THAT'S WHO WE'RE SUPPOSED TO BE, ISN'T IT?
MINUTES LATER, AT THE ALIENS' HEADQUARTERS...
YOU FOOLS! WHY DID YOU BRING HIM? HE IS THE REAL HUMAN TORCH!
BUT WE THOUGHT--
YOU THOUGHT WHAT I WANTED YOU TO THINK!
NOW THAT YOU SEE WE ARE NOT OF YOUR PLANET EARTH, YOU CAN NOT LEAVE HERE ALIVE!
MISTER, NO MATTER WHAT PLANET YOU'RE FROM, I'M STILL GONNA BE TOO HOT FOR YOU TO HANDLE!
STOP HIM! HE HAS A FLARE GUN!
TOO LATE!
THERE!! NOW WHEN THE OTHERS SEE MY SIGNAL, YOU'LL WISH YOU HAD STAYED WHERE YOU CAME FROM!
4
13

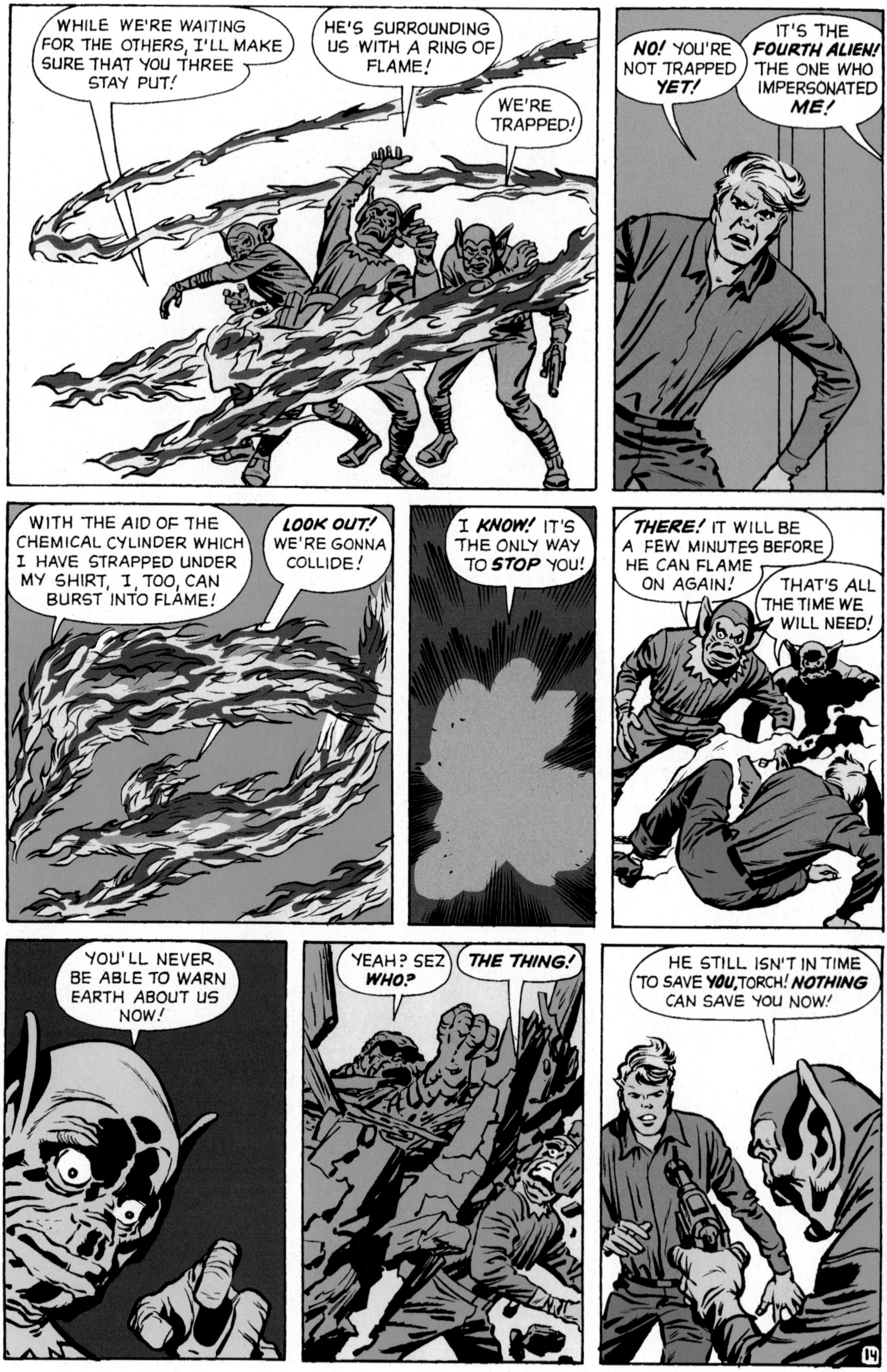
WHILE WE'RE WAITING FOR THE OTHERS, I'LL MAKE SURE THAT YOU THREE STAY PUT!
HE'S SURROUNDING US WITH A RING OF FLAME!
WE'RE TRAPPED!
NO! YOU'RE NOT TRAPPED YET!
IT'S THE FOURTH ALIEN! THE ONE WHO IMPERSONATED ME!
WITH THE AID OF THE CHEMICAL CYLINDER WHICH I HAVE STRAPPED UNDER MY SHIRT, I, TOO, CAN BURST INTO FLAME!
LOOK OUT! WE'RE GONNA COLLIDE!
I KNOW! IT'S THE ONLY WAY TO STOP YOU!
THERE! IT WILL BE A FEW MINUTES BEFORE HE CAN FLAME ON AGAIN!
THAT'S ALL THE TIME WE WILL NEED!
YOU'LL NEVER BE ABLE TO WARN EARTH ABOUT US NOW!
YEAH? SEZ WHO?
THE THING!
HE STILL ISN'T IN TIME TO SAVE YOU, TORCH! NOTHING CAN SAVE YOU NOW!
14

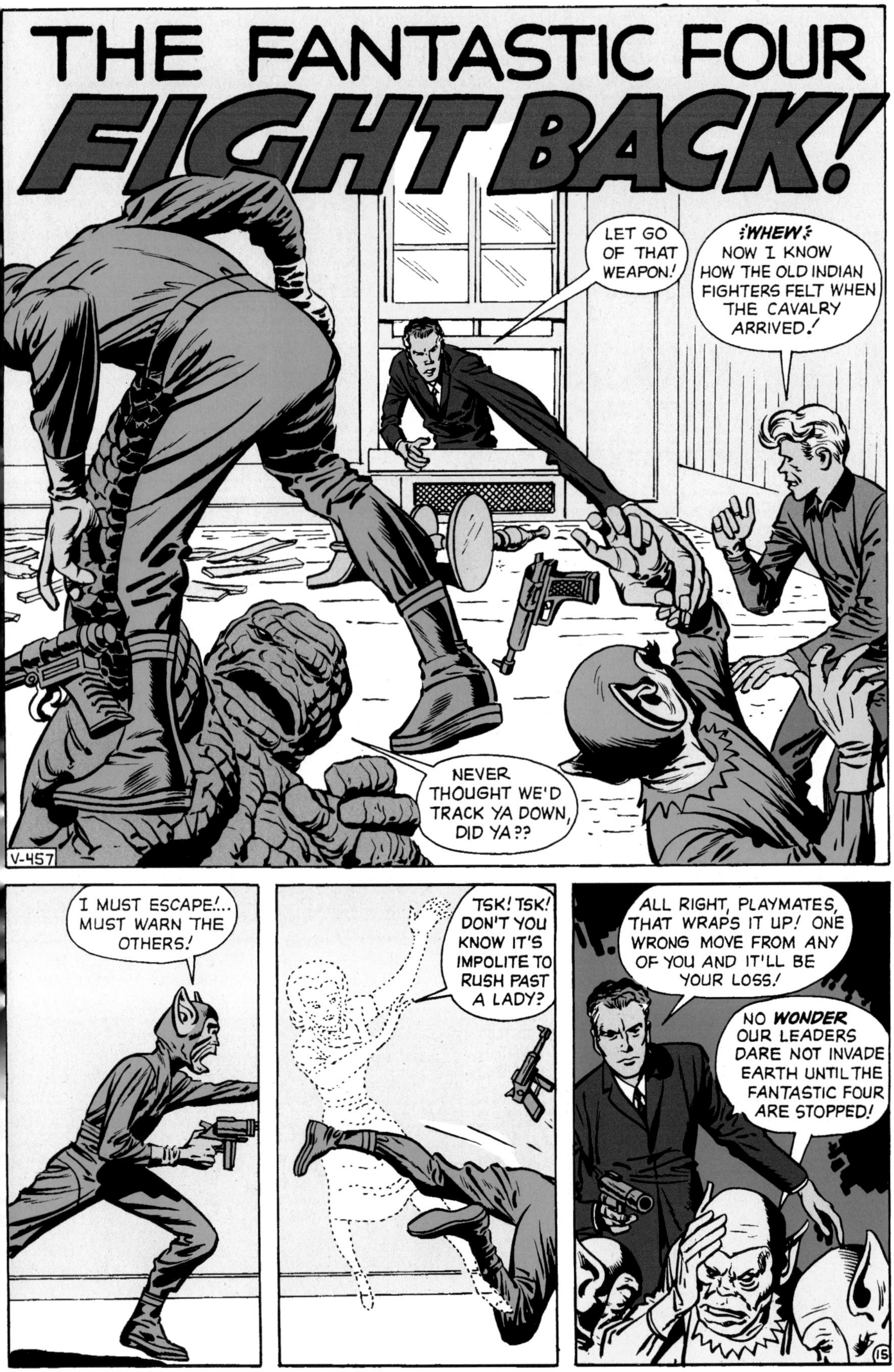
THE FANTASTIC FOUR
FIGHT BACK!
LET GO OF THAT WEAPON!
WHEW! NOW I KNOW HOW THE OLD INDIAN FIGHTERS FELT WHEN THE CAVALRY ARRIVED!
NEVER THOUGHT WE'D TRACK YA DOWN, DID YA??
V-457
I MUST ESCAPE!... MUST WARN THE OTHERS!
TSK! TSK! DON'T YOU KNOW IT'S IMPOLITE TO RUSH PAST A LADY?
ALL RIGHT, PLAYMATES, THAT WRAPS IT UP! ONE WRONG MOVE FROM ANY OF YOU AND IT'LL BE YOUR LOSS!
NO WONDER OUR LEADERS DARE NOT INVADE EARTH UNTIL THE FANTASTIC FOUR ARE STOPPED!
15

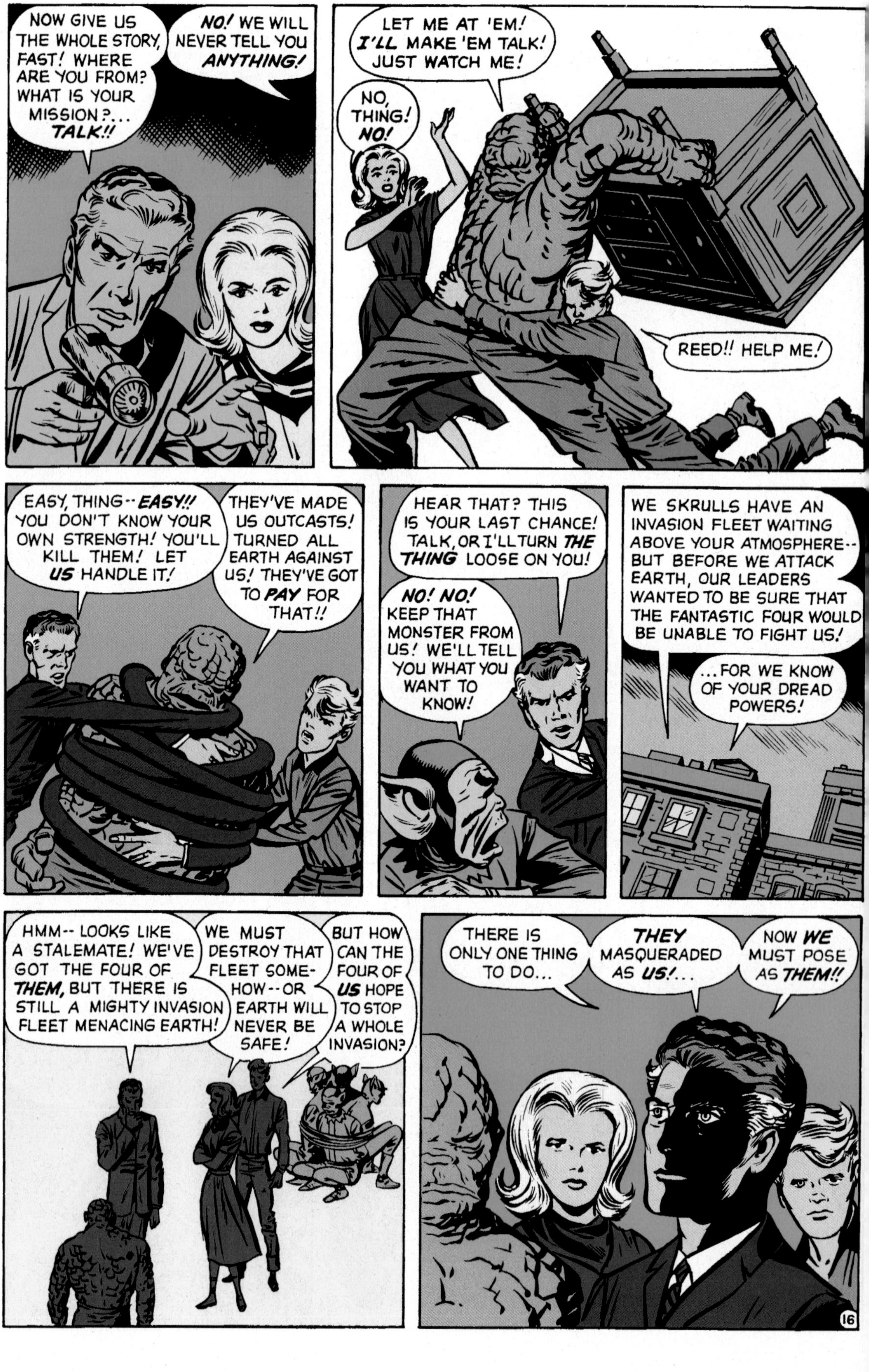
NOW GIVE US THE WHOLE STORY, FAST! WHERE ARE YOU FROM? WHAT IS YOUR MISSION?... TALK!!
NO! WE WILL NEVER TELL YOU ANYTHING!
LET ME AT 'EM! I'LL MAKE 'EM TALK! JUST WATCH ME!
NO, THING! NO!
REED!! HELP ME!
EASY, THING-- EASY!! YOU DON'T KNOW YOUR OWN STRENGTH! YOU'LL KILL THEM! LET US HANDLE IT!
THEY'VE MADE US OUTCASTS! TURNED ALL EARTH AGAINST US! THEY'VE GOT TO PAY FOR THAT!!
HEAR THAT? THIS IS YOUR LAST CHANCE! TALK, OR I'LL TURN THE THING LOOSE ON YOU!
NO! NO! KEEP THAT MONSTER FROM US! WE'LL TELL YOU WHAT YOU WANT TO KNOW!
WE SKRULLS HAVE AN INVASION FLEET WAITING ABOVE YOUR ATMOSPHERE-- BUT BEFORE WE ATTACK EARTH, OUR LEADERS WANTED TO BE SURE THAT THE FANTASTIC FOUR WOULD BE UNABLE TO FIGHT US!
...FOR WE KNOW OF YOUR DREAD POWERS!
HMM-- LOOKS LIKE A STALEMATE! WE'VE GOT THE FOUR OF THEM, BUT THERE IS STILL A MIGHTY INVASION FLEET MENACING EARTH!
WE MUST DESTROY THAT FLEET SOME-HOW-- OR EARTH WILL NEVER BE SAFE!
BUT HOW CAN THE FOUR OF US HOPE TO STOP A WHOLE INVASION?
THERE IS ONLY ONE THING TO DO...
THEY MASQUERADED AS US!...
NOW WE MUST POSE AS THEM!!
16

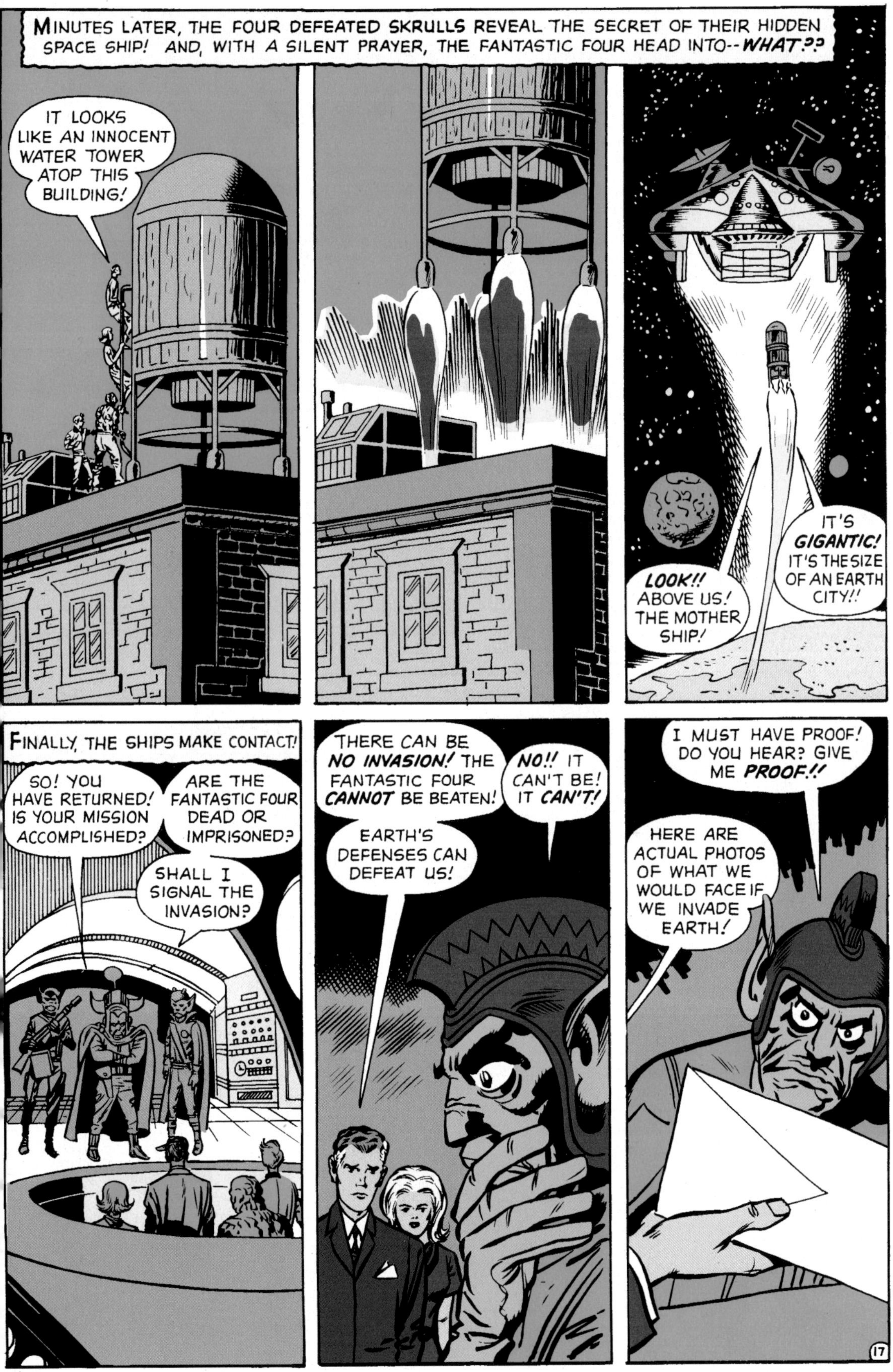

MINUTES LATER, THE FOUR DEFEATED SKRULLS REVEAL THE SECRET OF THEIR HIDDEN SPACE SHIP! AND, WITH A SILENT PRAYER, THE FANTASTIC FOUR HEAD INTO--WHAT??
IT LOOKS LIKE AN INNOCENT WATER TOWER ATOP THIS BUILDING!
LOOK!! ABOVE US! THE MOTHER SHIP!
IT'S GIGANTIC! IT'S THE SIZE OF AN EARTH CITY!!
FINALLY, THE SHIPS MAKE CONTACT!
SO! YOU HAVE RETURNED! IS YOUR MISSION ACCOMPLISHED?
ARE THE FANTASTIC FOUR DEAD OR IMPRISONED?
SHALL I SIGNAL THE INVASION?
THERE CAN BE NO INVASION! THE FANTASTIC FOUR CANNOT BE BEATEN!
EARTH'S DEFENSES CAN DEFEAT US!
NO!! IT CAN'T BE! IT CAN'T!
I MUST HAVE PROOF! DO YOU HEAR? GIVE ME PROOF!!
HERE ARE ACTUAL PHOTOS OF WHAT WE WOULD FACE IF WE INVADE EARTH!

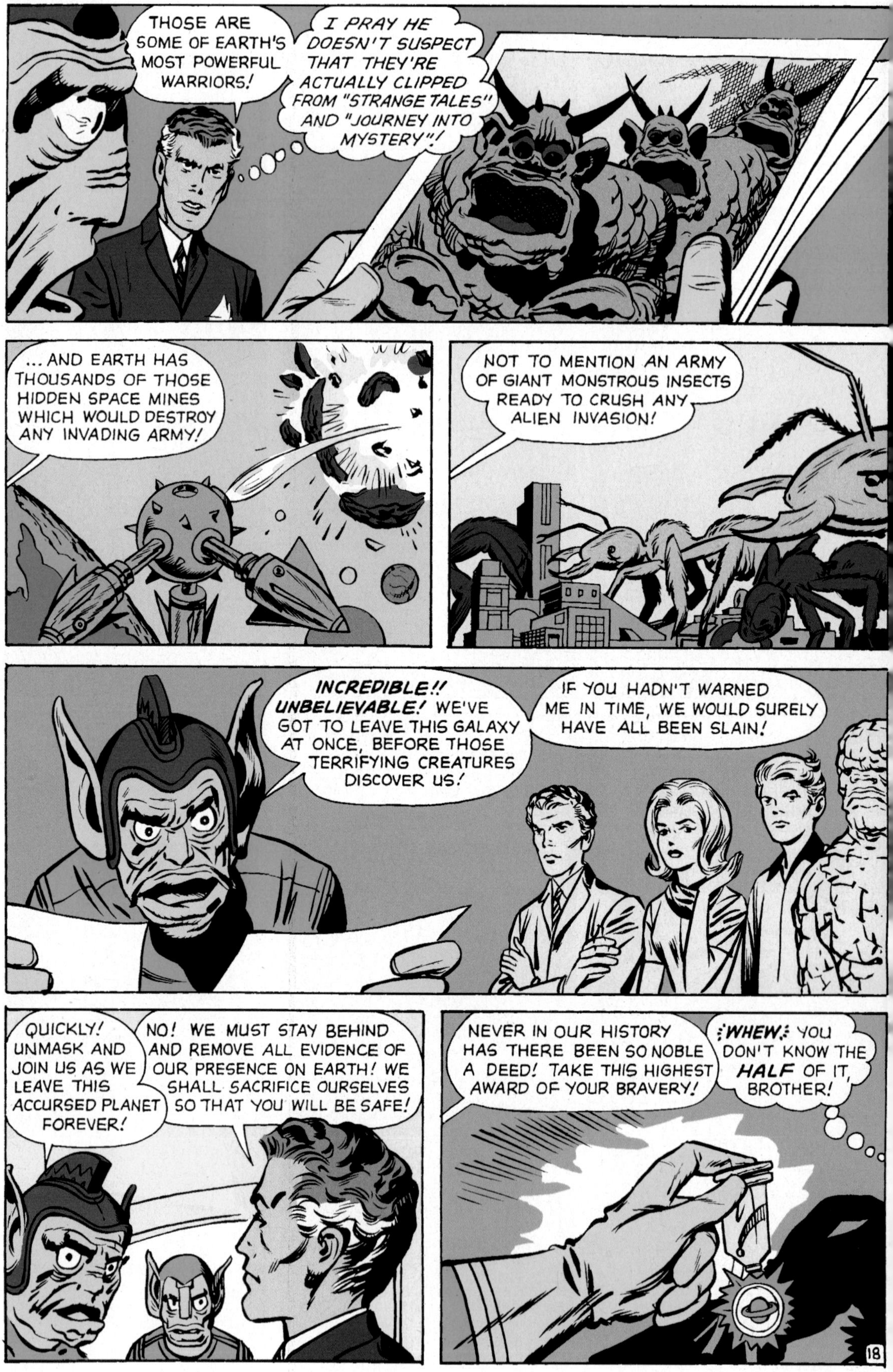
THOSE ARE SOME OF EARTH'S MOST POWERFUL WARRIORS!
I PRAY HE DOESN'T SUSPECT THAT THEY'RE ACTUALLY CLIPPED FROM "STRANGE TALES" AND "JOURNEY INTO MYSTERY"!
...AND EARTH HAS THOUSANDS OF THOSE HIDDEN SPACE MINES WHICH WOULD DESTROY ANY INVADING ARMY!
NOT TO MENTION AN ARMY OF GIANT MONSTROUS INSECTS READY TO CRUSH ANY ALIEN INVASION!
INCREDIBLE!! UNBELIEVABLE! WE'VE GOT TO LEAVE THIS GALAXY AT ONCE, BEFORE THOSE TERRIFYING CREATURES DISCOVER US!
IF YOU HADN'T WARNED ME IN TIME, WE WOULD SURELY HAVE ALL BEEN SLAIN!
QUICKLY! UNMASK AND JOIN US AS WE LEAVE THIS ACCURSED PLANET FOREVER!
NO! WE MUST STAY BEHIND AND REMOVE ALL EVIDENCE OF OUR PRESENCE ON EARTH! WE SHALL SACRIFICE OURSELVES SO THAT YOU WILL BE SAFE!
NEVER IN OUR HISTORY HAS THERE BEEN SO NOBLE A DEED! TAKE THIS HIGHEST AWARD OF YOUR BRAVERY!
WHEW! YOU DON'T KNOW THE HALF OF IT, BROTHER!
18

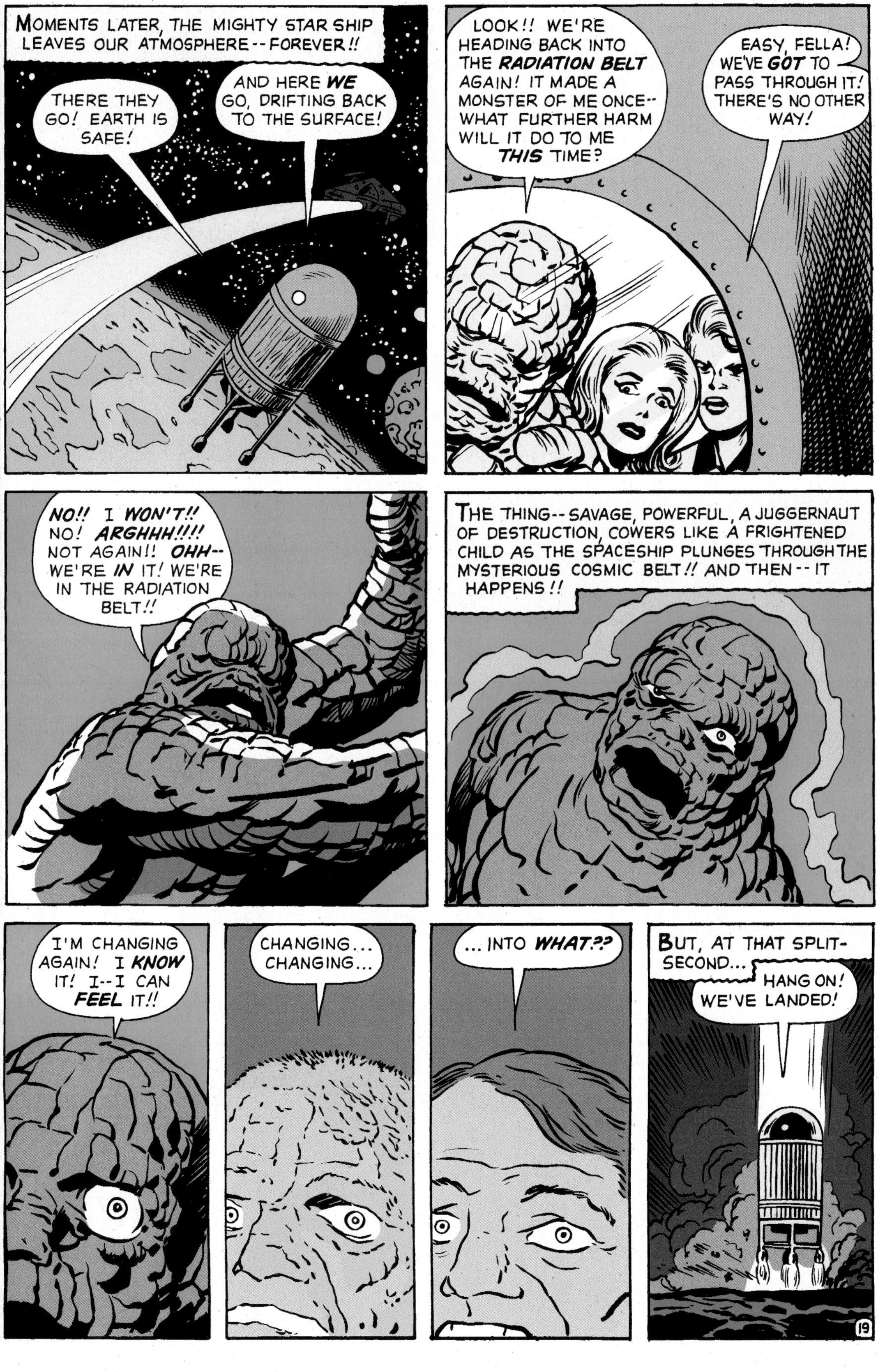

MOMENTS LATER, THE MIGHTY STAR SHIP LEAVES OUR ATMOSPHERE--FOREVER!!
THERE THEY GO! EARTH IS SAFE!
AND HERE WE GO, DRIFTING BACK TO THE SURFACE!
LOOK!! WE'RE HEADING BACK INTO THE RADIATION BELT AGAIN! IT MADE A MONSTER OF ME ONCE-- WHAT FURTHER HARM WILL IT DO TO ME THIS TIME?
EASY, FELLA! WE'VE GOT TO PASS THROUGH IT! THERE'S NO OTHER WAY!
NO!! I WON'T!! NO! ARGHHH!!!! NOT AGAIN!! OHH-- WE'RE IN IT! WE'RE IN THE RADIATION BELT!!
THE THING--SAVAGE, POWERFUL, A JUGGERNAUT OF DESTRUCTION, COWERS LIKE A FRIGHTENED CHILD AS THE SPACESHIP PLUNGES THROUGH THE MYSTERIOUS COSMIC BELT!! AND THEN--IT HAPPENS!!
I'M CHANGING AGAIN! I KNOW IT! I--I CAN FEEL IT!!
CHANGING... CHANGING...
...INTO WHAT??
BUT, AT THAT SPLIT-SECOND...
HANG ON! WE'VE LANDED!
19

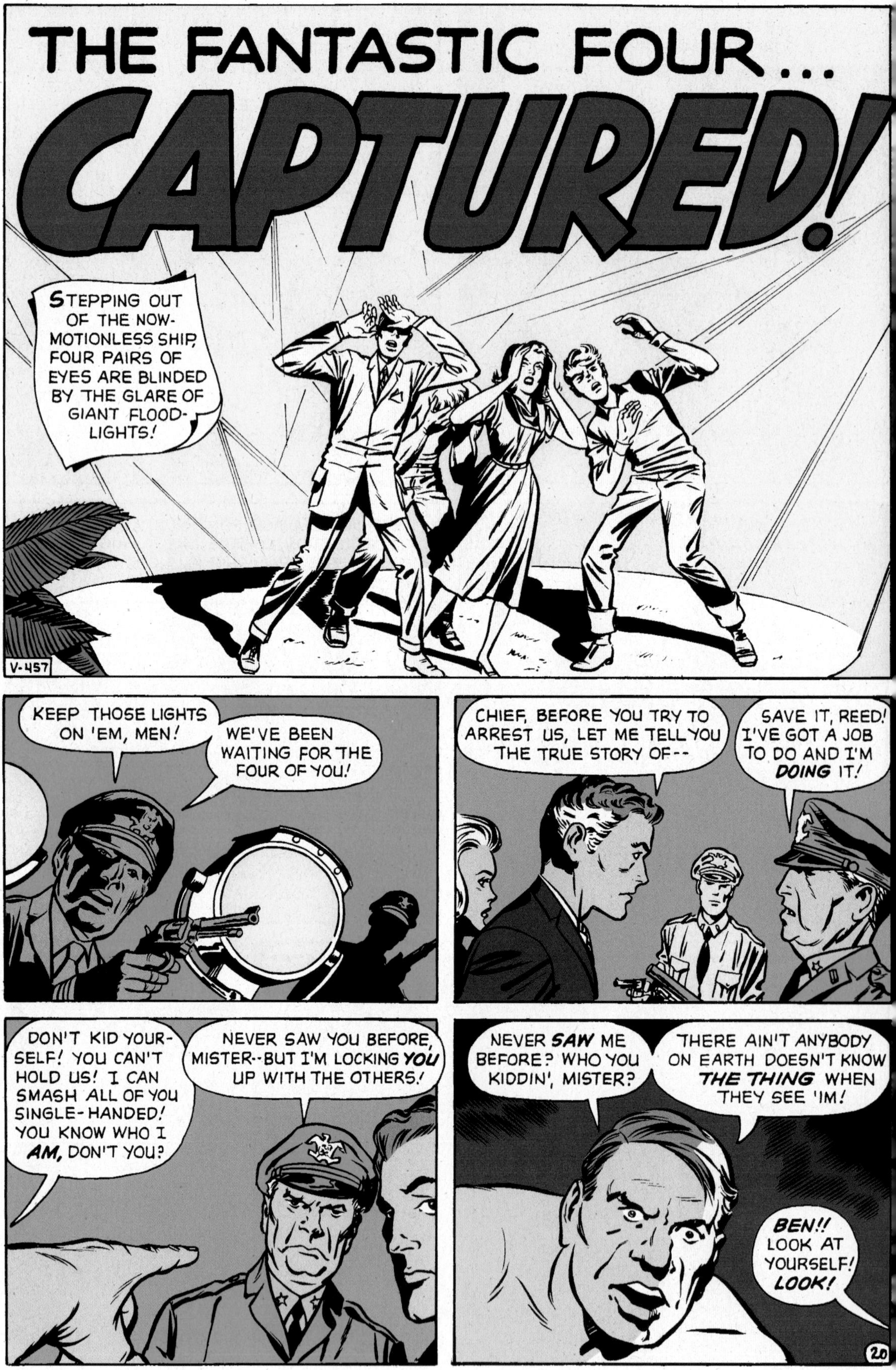
THE FANTASTIC FOUR...
CAPTURED!
STEPPING OUT OF THE NOW-MOTIONLESS SHIP, FOUR PAIRS OF EYES ARE BLINDED BY THE GLARE OF GIANT FLOOD-LIGHTS!
V-457
KEEP THOSE LIGHTS ON 'EM, MEN!
WE'VE BEEN WAITING FOR THE FOUR OF YOU!
CHIEF, BEFORE YOU TRY TO ARREST US, LET ME TELL YOU THE TRUE STORY OF--
SAVE IT, REED! I'VE GOT A JOB TO DO AND I'M DOING IT!
DON'T KID YOURSELF! YOU CAN'T HOLD US! I CAN SMASH ALL OF YOU SINGLE-HANDED! YOU KNOW WHO I AM, DON'T YOU?
NEVER SAW YOU BEFORE, MISTER--BUT I'M LOCKING YOU UP WITH THE OTHERS!
NEVER SAW ME BEFORE? WHO YOU KIDDIN', MISTER?
THERE AIN'T ANYBODY ON EARTH DOESN'T KNOW THE THING WHEN THEY SEE 'IM!
BEN!! LOOK AT YOURSELF! LOOK!
20

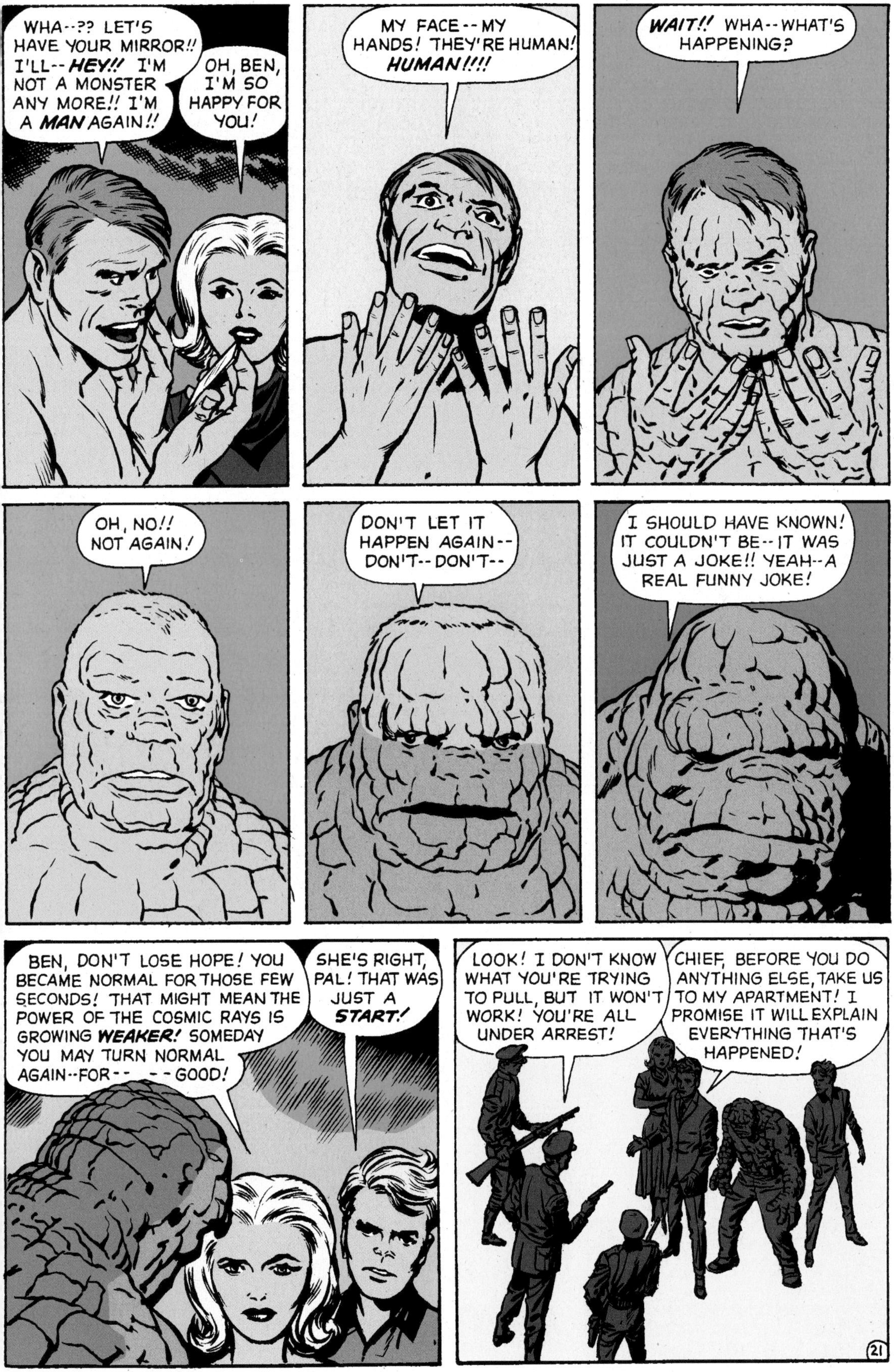

WHA--?? LET'S HAVE YOUR MIRROR!! I'LL--HEY!! I'M NOT A MONSTER ANY MORE!! I'M A MAN AGAIN!!
OH, BEN, I'M SO HAPPY FOR YOU!
MY FACE--MY HANDS! THEY'RE HUMAN! HUMAN!!!!
WAIT!! WHA--WHAT'S HAPPENING?
OH, NO!! NOT AGAIN!
DON'T LET IT HAPPEN AGAIN--DON'T--DON'T--
I SHOULD HAVE KNOWN! IT COULDN'T BE--IT WAS JUST A JOKE!! YEAH--A REAL FUNNY JOKE!
BEN, DON'T LOSE HOPE! YOU BECAME NORMAL FOR THOSE FEW SECONDS! THAT MIGHT MEAN THE POWER OF THE COSMIC RAYS IS GROWING WEAKER! SOMEDAY YOU MAY TURN NORMAL AGAIN--FOR-- --GOOD!
SHE'S RIGHT, PAL! THAT WAS JUST A START!
LOOK! I DON'T KNOW WHAT YOU'RE TRYING TO PULL, BUT IT WON'T WORK! YOU'RE ALL UNDER ARREST!
CHIEF, BEFORE YOU DO ANYTHING ELSE, TAKE US TO MY APARTMENT! I PROMISE IT WILL EXPLAIN EVERYTHING THAT'S HAPPENED!
21

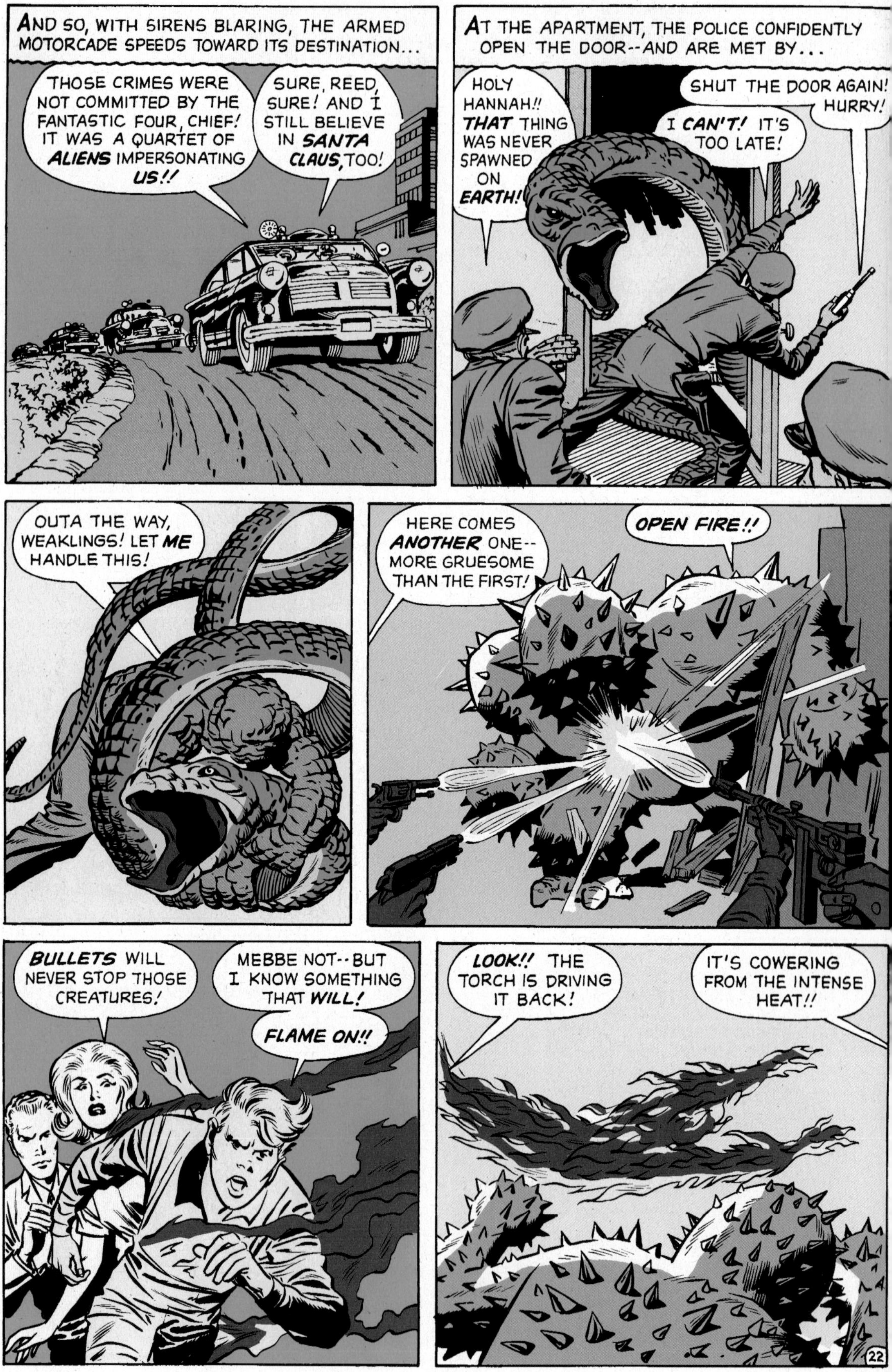
AND SO, WITH SIRENS BLARING, THE ARMED MOTORCADE SPEEDS TOWARD ITS DESTINATION...
THOSE CRIMES WERE NOT COMMITTED BY THE FANTASTIC FOUR, CHIEF! IT WAS A QUARTET OF ALIENS IMPERSONATING US!!
SURE, REED, SURE! AND I STILL BELIEVE IN SANTA CLAUS, TOO!
AT THE APARTMENT, THE POLICE CONFIDENTLY OPEN THE DOOR--AND ARE MET BY...
HOLY HANNAH!! THAT THING WAS NEVER SPAWNED ON EARTH!
SHUT THE DOOR AGAIN! HURRY!
I CAN'T! IT'S TOO LATE!
OUTA THE WAY, WEAKLINGS! LET ME HANDLE THIS!
HERE COMES ANOTHER ONE-- MORE GRUESOME THAN THE FIRST!
OPEN FIRE!!
BULLETS WILL NEVER STOP THOSE CREATURES!
MEBBE NOT--BUT I KNOW SOMETHING THAT WILL!
FLAME ON!!
LOOK!! THE TORCH IS DRIVING IT BACK!
IT'S COWERING FROM THE INTENSE HEAT!!
22

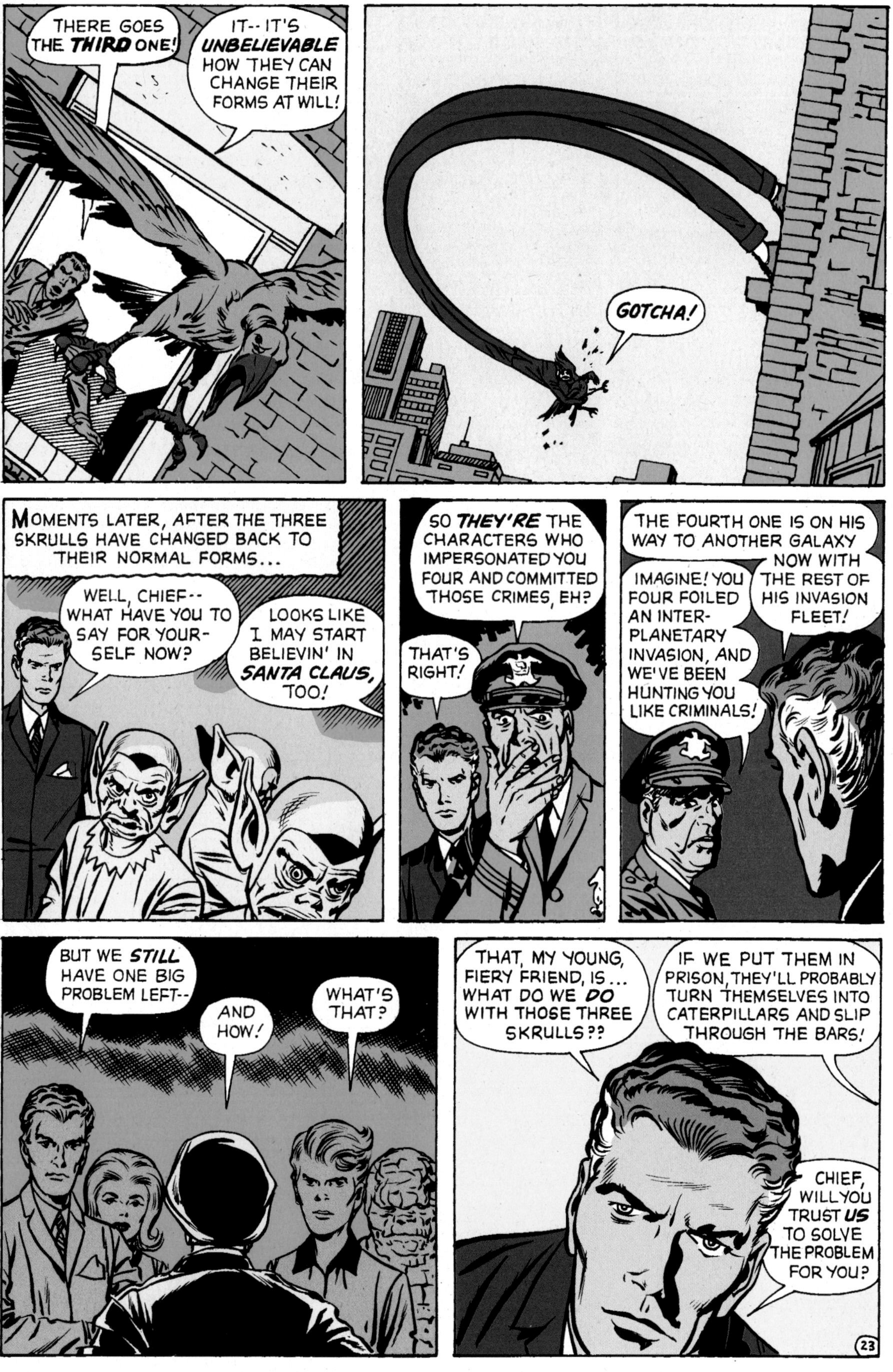
THERE GOES THE THIRD ONE!
IT-- IT'S UNBELIEVABLE HOW THEY CAN CHANGE THEIR FORMS AT WILL!
GOTCHA!
MOMENTS LATER, AFTER THE THREE SKRULLS HAVE CHANGED BACK TO THEIR NORMAL FORMS...
WELL, CHIEF-- WHAT HAVE YOU TO SAY FOR YOURSELF NOW?
LOOKS LIKE I MAY START BELIEVIN' IN SANTA CLAUS, TOO!
SO THEY'RE THE CHARACTERS WHO IMPERSONATED YOU FOUR AND COMMITTED THOSE CRIMES, EH?
THAT'S RIGHT!
THE FOURTH ONE IS ON HIS WAY TO ANOTHER GALAXY NOW WITH THE REST OF HIS INVASION FLEET!
IMAGINE! YOU FOUR FOILED AN INTER-PLANETARY INVASION, AND WE'VE BEEN HUNTING YOU LIKE CRIMINALS!
BUT WE STILL HAVE ONE BIG PROBLEM LEFT--
AND HOW!
WHAT'S THAT?
THAT, MY YOUNG, FIERY FRIEND, IS... WHAT DO WE DO WITH THOSE THREE SKRULLS??
IF WE PUT THEM IN PRISON, THEY'LL PROBABLY TURN THEMSELVES INTO CATERPILLARS AND SLIP THROUGH THE BARS!
CHIEF, WILL YOU TRUST US TO SOLVE THE PROBLEM FOR YOU?
23

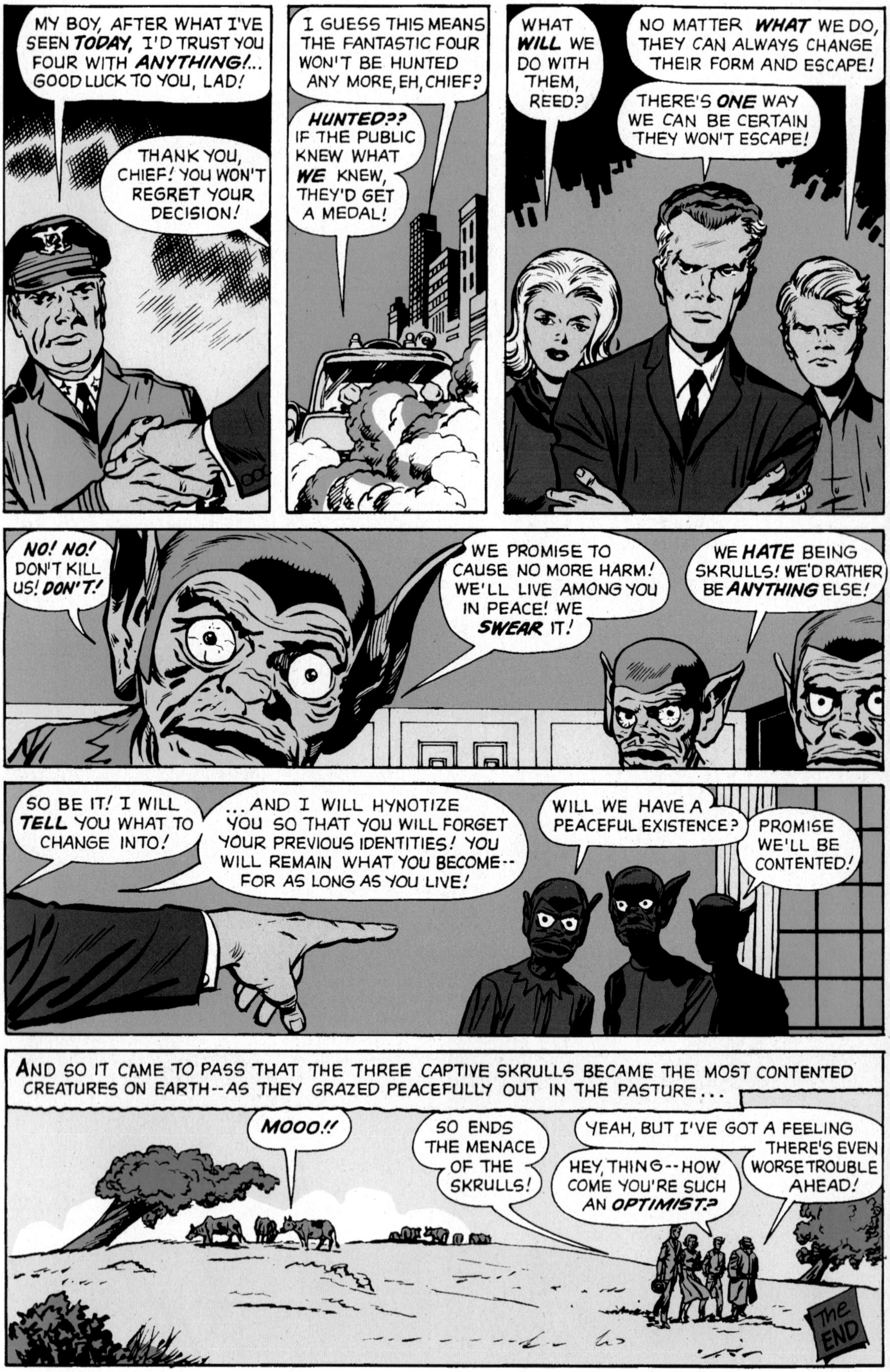
MY BOY, AFTER WHAT I'VE SEEN TODAY, I'D TRUST YOU FOUR WITH ANYTHING!... GOOD LUCK TO YOU, LAD!
THANK YOU, CHIEF! YOU WON'T REGRET YOUR DECISION!
I GUESS THIS MEANS THE FANTASTIC FOUR WON'T BE HUNTED ANY MORE, EH, CHIEF?
HUNTED?? IF THE PUBLIC KNEW WHAT WE KNEW, THEY'D GET A MEDAL!
WHAT WILL WE DO WITH THEM, REED?
NO MATTER WHAT WE DO, THEY CAN ALWAYS CHANGE THEIR FORM AND ESCAPE!
THERE'S ONE WAY WE CAN BE CERTAIN THEY WON'T ESCAPE!
NO! NO! DON'T KILL US! DON'T!
WE PROMISE TO CAUSE NO MORE HARM! WE'LL LIVE AMONG YOU IN PEACE! WE SWEAR IT!
WE HATE BEING SKRULLS! WE'D RATHER BE ANYTHING ELSE!
SO BE IT! I WILL TELL YOU WHAT TO CHANGE INTO!
...AND I WILL HYNOTIZE YOU SO THAT YOU WILL FORGET YOUR PREVIOUS IDENTITIES! YOU WILL REMAIN WHAT YOU BECOME-- FOR AS LONG AS YOU LIVE!
WILL WE HAVE A PEACEFUL EXISTENCE?
PROMISE WE'LL BE CONTENTED!
AND SO IT CAME TO PASS THAT THE THREE CAPTIVE SKRULLS BECAME THE MOST CONTENTED CREATURES ON EARTH--AS THEY GRAZED PEACEFULLY OUT IN THE PASTURE...
MOOO!!
SO ENDS THE MENACE OF THE SKRULLS!
YEAH, BUT I'VE GOT A FEELING THERE'S EVEN WORSE TROUBLE AHEAD!
HEY, THING--HOW COME YOU'RE SUCH AN OPTIMIST?
THE END

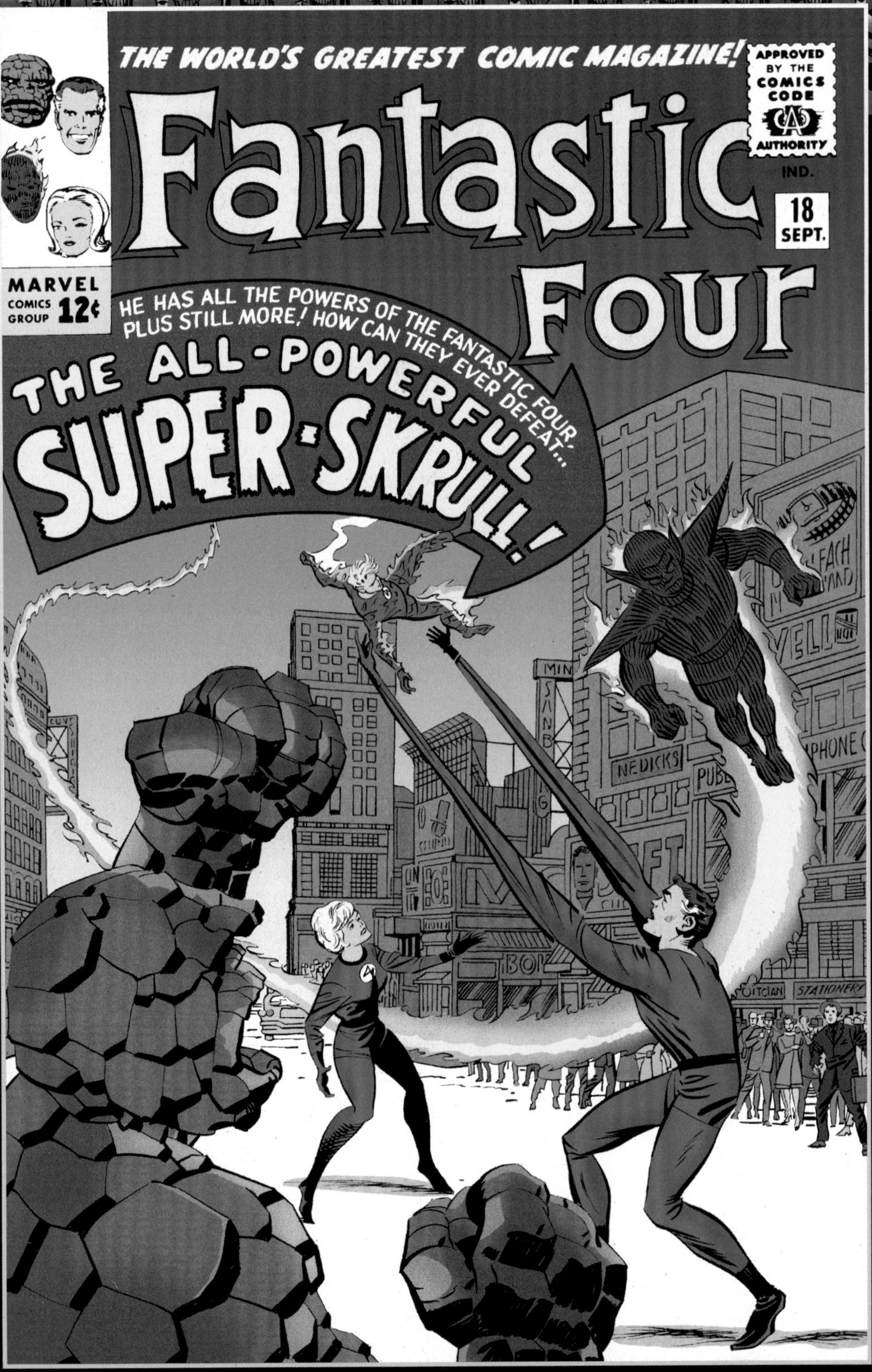
THE WORLD'S GREATEST COMIC MAGAZINE!
APPROVED BY THE COMICS CODE AUTHORITY
Fantastic Four
IND.
18 SEPT.
MARVEL COMICS GROUP 12¢
HE HAS ALL THE POWERS OF THE FANTASTIC FOUR, PLUS STILL MORE! HOW CAN THEY EVER DEFEAT...
THE ALL-POWERFUL SUPER-SKRULL!
NEDICKS
STATIONERY

FANTASTIC FOUR #18 (SEPTEMBER 1963)

After previously being defeated by the Fantastic Four, the Skrulls unleash their new ultimate weapon: the Super-Skrull, who has the combined powers of the FF!

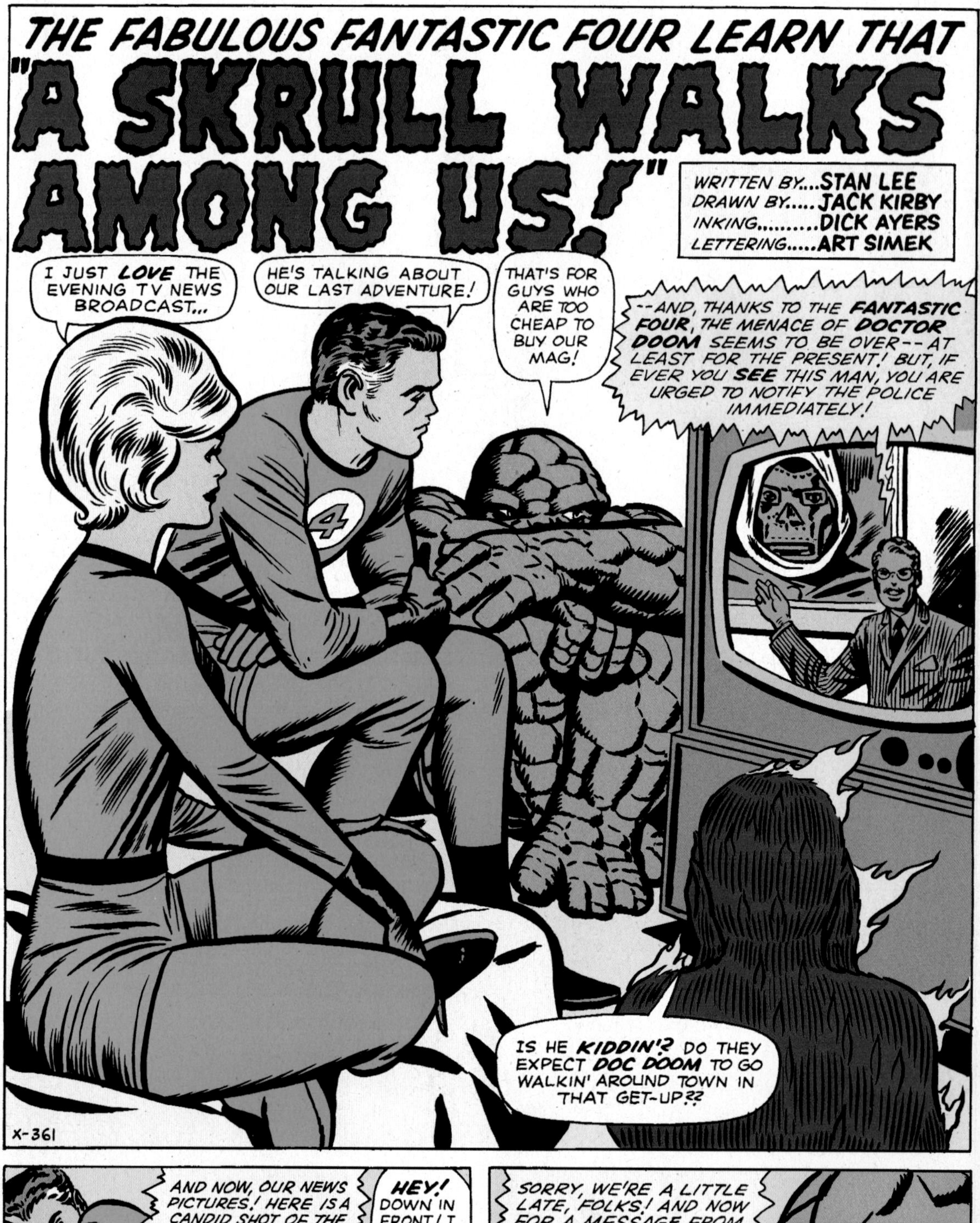
THE FABULOUS FANTASTIC FOUR LEARN THAT
"A SKRULL WALKS AMONG US!"
WRITTEN BY....STAN LEE
DRAWN BY.....JACK KIRBY
INKING..........DICK AYERS
LETTERING.....ART SIMEK
I JUST LOVE THE EVENING TV NEWS BROADCAST...
HE'S TALKING ABOUT OUR LAST ADVENTURE!
THAT'S FOR GUYS WHO ARE TOO CHEAP TO BUY OUR MAG!
--AND, THANKS TO THE FANTASTIC FOUR, THE MENACE OF DOCTOR DOOM SEEMS TO BE OVER--AT LEAST FOR THE PRESENT! BUT, IF EVER YOU SEE THIS MAN, YOU ARE URGED TO NOTIFY THE POLICE IMMEDIATELY!
IS HE KIDDIN'? DO THEY EXPECT DOC DOOM TO GO WALKIN' AROUND TOWN IN THAT GET-UP??
X-361

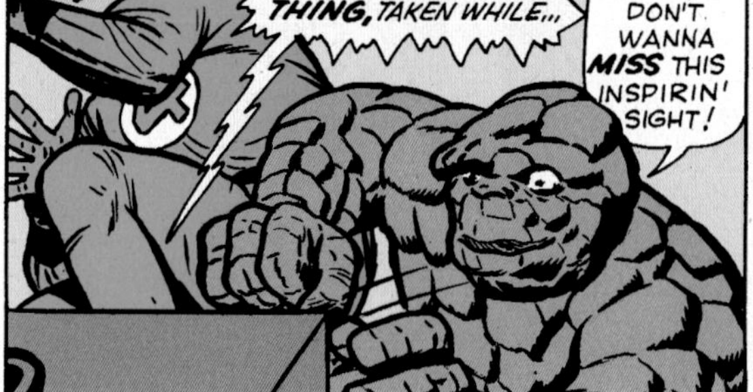
AND NOW, OUR NEWS PICTURES! HERE IS A CANDID SHOT OF THE THING, TAKEN WHILE...
HEY! DOWN IN FRONT! I DON'T WANNA MISS THIS INSPIRIN' SIGHT!

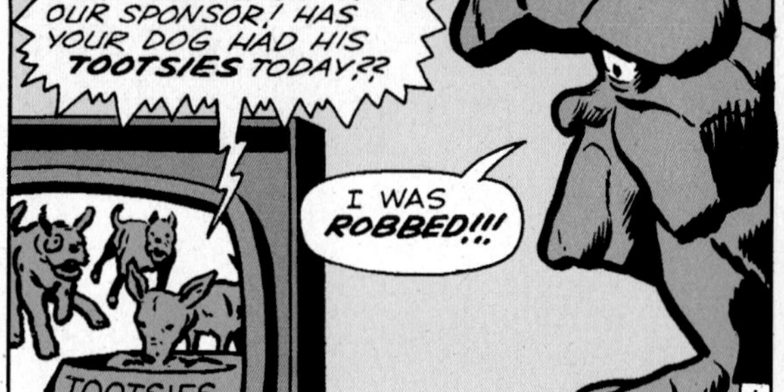
SORRY, WE'RE A LITTLE LATE, FOLKS! AND NOW FOR A MESSAGE FROM OUR SPONSOR! HAS YOUR DOG HAD HIS TOOTSIES TODAY??
I WAS ROBBED!!!
TOOTSIES
1

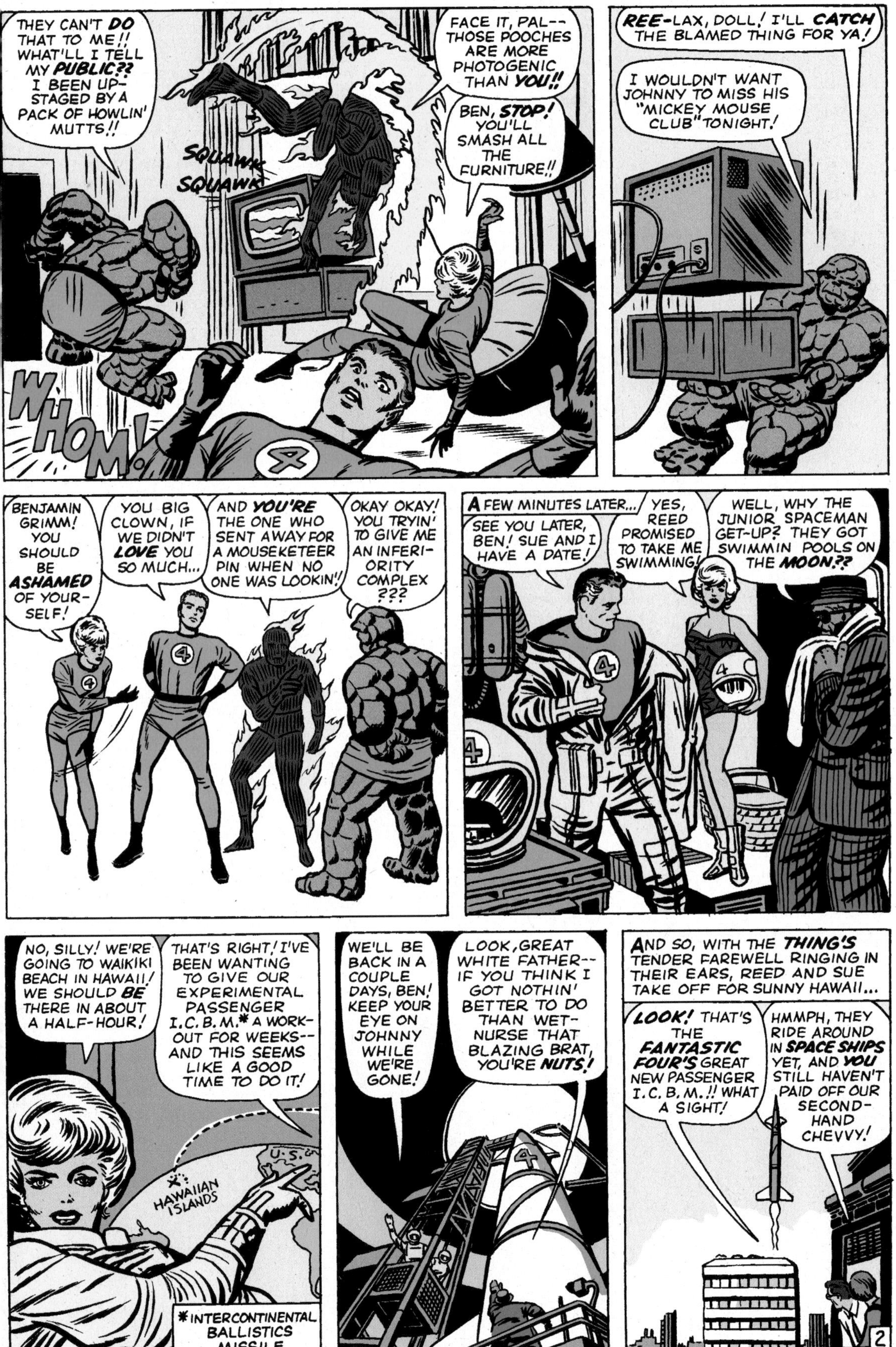

THEY CAN'T DO THAT TO ME!! WHAT'LL I TELL MY PUBLIC?? I BEEN UP-STAGED BY A PACK OF HOWLIN' MUTTS!!
FACE IT, PAL-- THOSE POOCHES ARE MORE PHOTOGENIC THAN YOU!!
BEN, STOP! YOU'LL SMASH ALL THE FURNITURE!!
SQUAWK
SQUAWK
WHOM!
REE-LAX, DOLL! I'LL CATCH THE BLAMED THING FOR YA!
I WOULDN'T WANT JOHNNY TO MISS HIS "MICKEY MOUSE CLUB" TONIGHT!
BENJAMIN GRIMM! YOU SHOULD BE ASHAMED OF YOURSELF!
YOU BIG CLOWN, IF WE DIDN'T LOVE YOU SO MUCH...
AND YOU'RE THE ONE WHO SENT AWAY FOR A MOUSEKETEER PIN WHEN NO ONE WAS LOOKIN'!
OKAY OKAY! YOU TRYIN' TO GIVE ME AN INFERIORITY COMPLEX ???
A FEW MINUTES LATER...
SEE YOU LATER, BEN! SUE AND I HAVE A DATE!
YES, REED PROMISED TO TAKE ME SWIMMING!
WELL, WHY THE JUNIOR SPACEMAN GET-UP? THEY GOT SWIMMIN POOLS ON THE MOON??
NO, SILLY! WE'RE GOING TO WAIKIKI BEACH IN HAWAII! WE SHOULD BE THERE IN ABOUT A HALF-HOUR!
THAT'S RIGHT! I'VE BEEN WANTING TO GIVE OUR EXPERIMENTAL PASSENGER I.C.B.M.* A WORK-OUT FOR WEEKS-- AND THIS SEEMS LIKE A GOOD TIME TO DO IT!
U.S.
HAWAIIAN ISLANDS
*INTERCONTINENTAL BALLISTICS MISSILE
WE'LL BE BACK IN A COUPLE DAYS, BEN! KEEP YOUR EYE ON JOHNNY WHILE WE'RE GONE!
LOOK, GREAT WHITE FATHER-- IF YOU THINK I GOT NOTHIN' BETTER TO DO THAN WET-NURSE THAT BLAZING BRAT, YOU'RE NUTS!
AND SO, WITH THE THING'S TENDER FAREWELL RINGING IN THEIR EARS, REED AND SUE TAKE OFF FOR SUNNY HAWAII...
LOOK! THAT'S THE FANTASTIC FOUR'S GREAT NEW PASSENGER I.C.B.M.!! WHAT A SIGHT!
HMMPH, THEY RIDE AROUND IN SPACE SHIPS YET, AND YOU STILL HAVEN'T PAID OFF OUR SECOND-HAND CHEVVY!
2

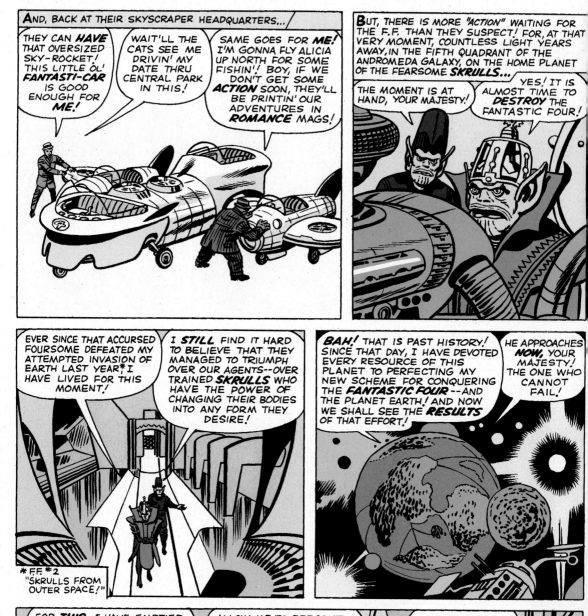

AND, BACK AT THEIR SKYSCRAPER HEADQUARTERS...

THEY CAN *HAVE* THAT OVERSIZED SKY-ROCKET! THIS LITTLE OL' *FANTASTI-CAR* IS GOOD ENOUGH FOR *ME!*

WAIT'LL THE CATS SEE ME DRIVIN' MY DATE THRU CENTRAL PARK IN THIS!

SAME GOES FOR *ME!* I'M GONNA FLY ALICIA UP NORTH FOR SOME FISHIN'! BOY, IF WE DON'T GET SOME *ACTION* SOON, THEY'LL BE PRINTIN' OUR ADVENTURES IN *ROMANCE* MAGS!

BUT, THERE IS MORE *"ACTION"* WAITING FOR THE F.F. THAN THEY SUSPECT! FOR, AT THAT VERY MOMENT, COUNTLESS LIGHT YEARS AWAY, IN THE FIFTH QUADRANT OF THE ANDROMEDA GALAXY, ON THE HOME PLANET OF THE FEARSOME *SKRULLS...*

THE MOMENT IS AT HAND, YOUR MAJESTY!

YES! IT IS ALMOST TIME TO *DESTROY* THE FANTASTIC FOUR!

EVER SINCE THAT ACCURSED FOURSOME DEFEATED MY ATTEMPTED INVASION OF EARTH LAST YEAR* I HAVE LIVED FOR THIS MOMENT!

I *STILL* FIND IT HARD TO BELIEVE THAT THEY MANAGED TO TRIUMPH OVER OUR AGENTS--OVER TRAINED *SKRULLS* WHO HAVE THE POWER OF CHANGING THEIR BODIES INTO ANY FORM THEY DESIRE!

*F.F. #2 "SKRULLS FROM OUTER SPACE!"

BAH! THAT IS PAST HISTORY! SINCE THAT DAY, I HAVE DEVOTED EVERY RESOURCE OF THIS PLANET TO PERFECTING MY NEW SCHEME FOR CONQUERING THE *FANTASTIC FOUR*--AND THE PLANET EARTH! AND NOW WE SHALL SEE THE *RESULTS* OF THAT EFFORT!

HE APPROACHES *NOW,* YOUR MAJESTY! THE ONE WHO CANNOT FAIL!

FOR *THIS,* I HAVE EMPTIED OUR TREASURY, DEVOTED ALL OUR SCIENTIFIC TALENTS, WORKED MY PEOPLE LIKE SLAVES--FOR *THIS* MOMENT!

ALLOW ME TO PRESENT THE MIGHTIEST WARRIOR IN THE KNOWN UNIVERSE-- THE *SUPER-SKRULL!!*

ALL HOMAGE TO YOUR SUPREME MAJESTY, SIRE! I AWAIT YOUR COMMANDS!

3

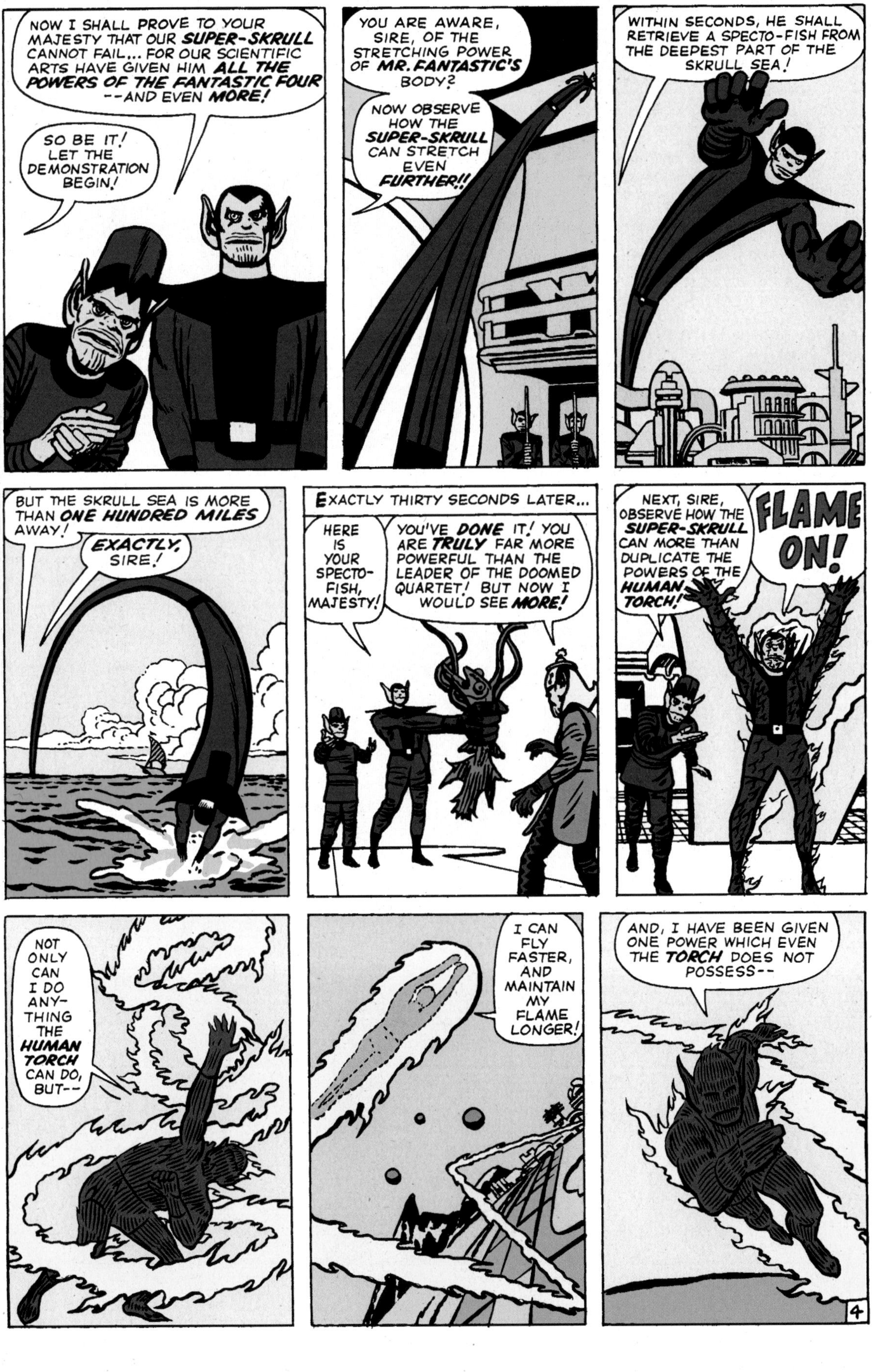

NOW I SHALL PROVE TO YOUR MAJESTY THAT OUR SUPER-SKRULL CANNOT FAIL... FOR OUR SCIENTIFIC ARTS HAVE GIVEN HIM ALL THE POWERS OF THE FANTASTIC FOUR --AND EVEN MORE!
SO BE IT! LET THE DEMONSTRATION BEGIN!
YOU ARE AWARE, SIRE, OF THE STRETCHING POWER OF MR. FANTASTIC'S BODY?
NOW OBSERVE HOW THE SUPER-SKRULL CAN STRETCH EVEN FURTHER!!
WITHIN SECONDS, HE SHALL RETRIEVE A SPECTO-FISH FROM THE DEEPEST PART OF THE SKRULL SEA!
BUT THE SKRULL SEA IS MORE THAN ONE HUNDRED MILES AWAY!
EXACTLY, SIRE!
EXACTLY THIRTY SECONDS LATER...
HERE IS YOUR SPECTO-FISH, MAJESTY!
YOU'VE DONE IT! YOU ARE TRULY FAR MORE POWERFUL THAN THE LEADER OF THE DOOMED QUARTET! BUT NOW I WOULD SEE MORE!
NEXT, SIRE, OBSERVE HOW THE SUPER-SKRULL CAN MORE THAN DUPLICATE THE POWERS OF THE HUMAN TORCH!
FLAME ON!
NOT ONLY CAN I DO ANY-THING THE HUMAN TORCH CAN DO, BUT--
I CAN FLY FASTER, AND MAINTAIN MY FLAME LONGER!
AND, I HAVE BEEN GIVEN ONE POWER WHICH EVEN THE TORCH DOES NOT POSSESS--

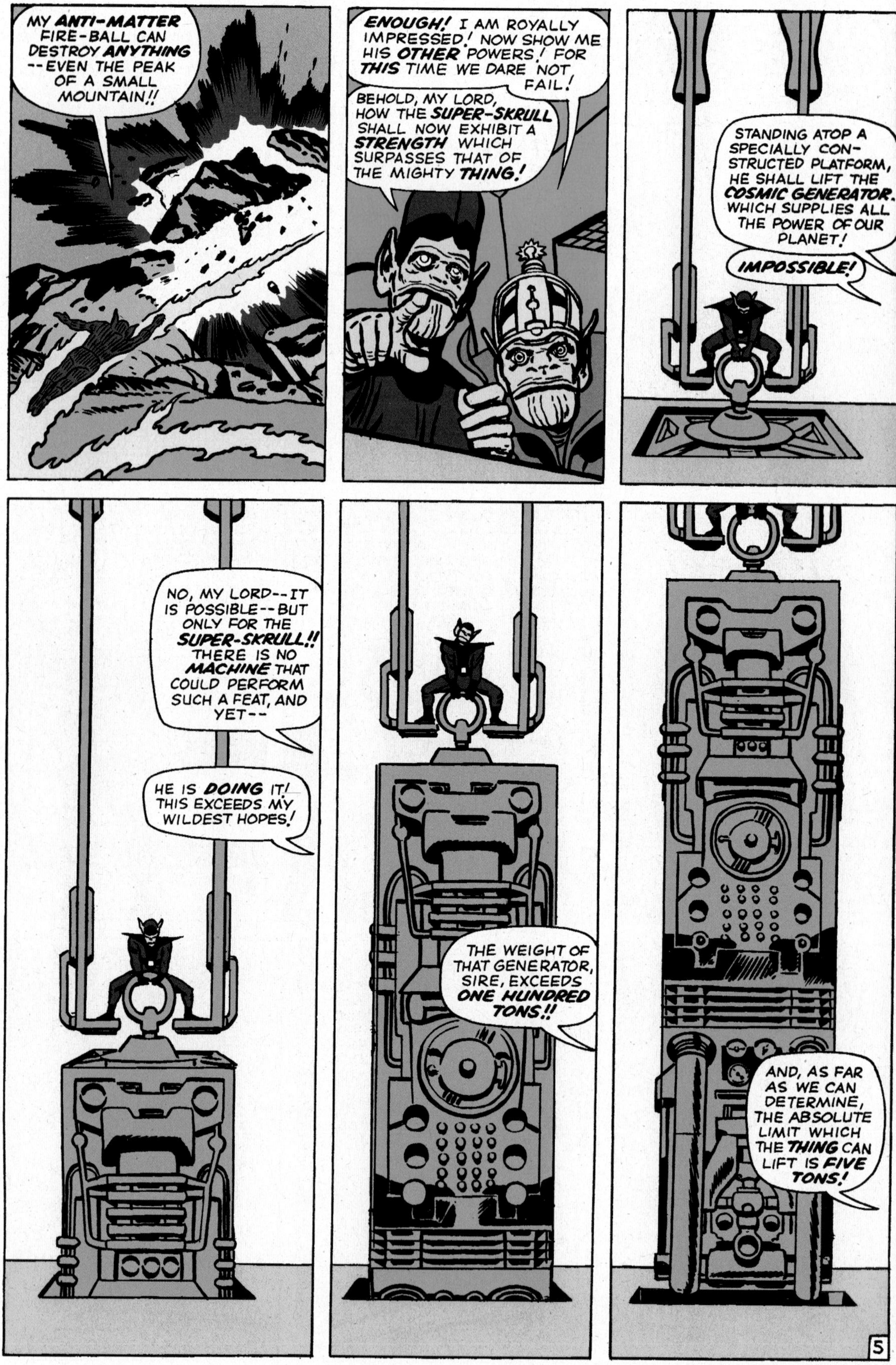
MY ANTI-MATTER FIRE-BALL CAN DESTROY ANYTHING --EVEN THE PEAK OF A SMALL MOUNTAIN!!
ENOUGH! I AM ROYALLY IMPRESSED! NOW SHOW ME HIS OTHER POWERS! FOR THIS TIME WE DARE NOT FAIL!
BEHOLD, MY LORD, HOW THE SUPER-SKRULL SHALL NOW EXHIBIT A STRENGTH WHICH SURPASSES THAT OF THE MIGHTY THING!
STANDING ATOP A SPECIALLY CON-STRUCTED PLATFORM, HE SHALL LIFT THE COSMIC GENERATOR, WHICH SUPPLIES ALL THE POWER OF OUR PLANET!
IMPOSSIBLE!
NO, MY LORD--IT IS POSSIBLE--BUT ONLY FOR THE SUPER-SKRULL!! THERE IS NO MACHINE THAT COULD PERFORM SUCH A FEAT, AND YET--
HE IS DOING IT! THIS EXCEEDS MY WILDEST HOPES!
THE WEIGHT OF THAT GENERATOR, SIRE, EXCEEDS ONE HUNDRED TONS!!
AND, AS FAR AS WE CAN DETERMINE, THE ABSOLUTE LIMIT WHICH THE THING CAN LIFT IS FIVE TONS!

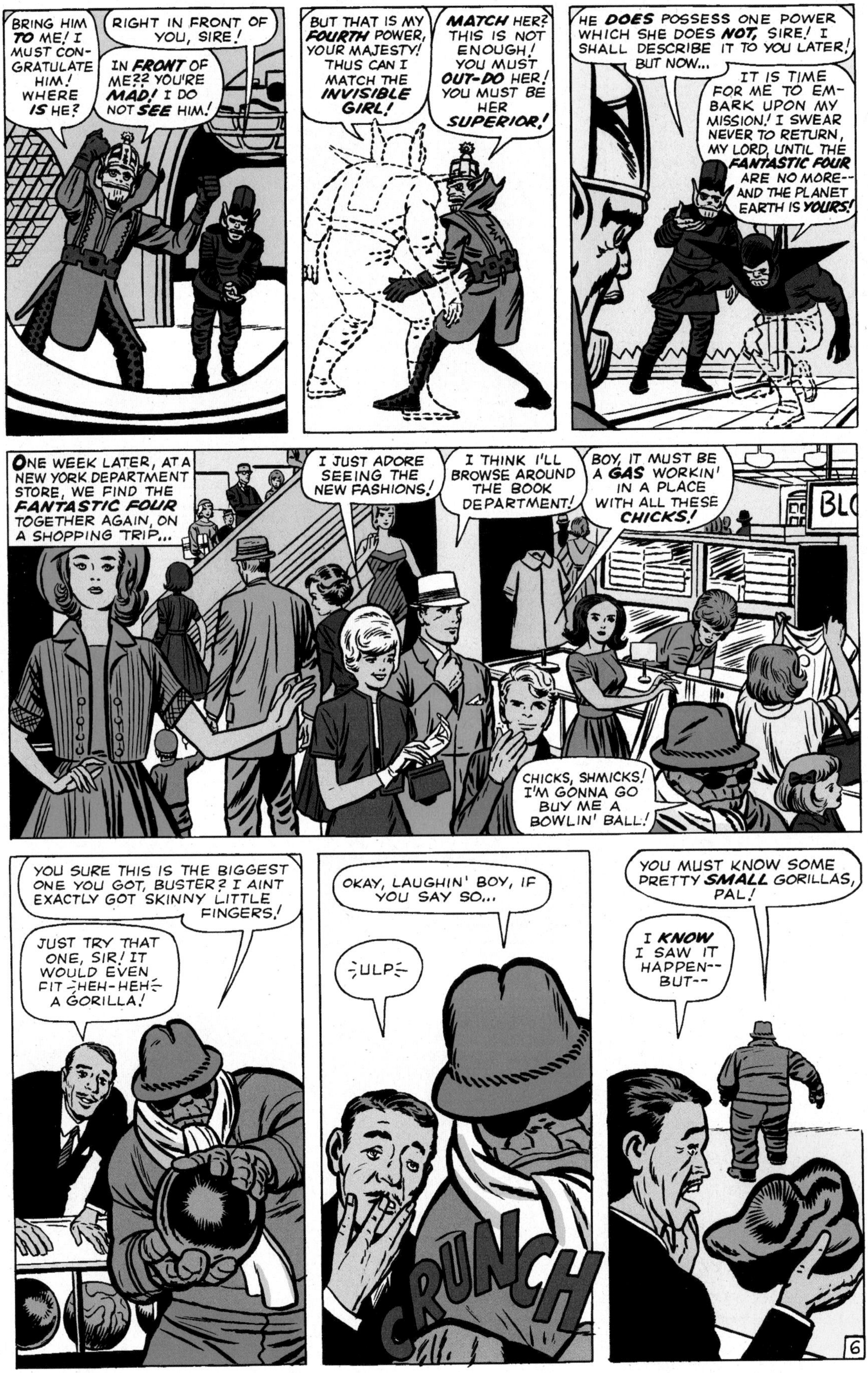

BRING HIM TO ME! I MUST CONGRATULATE HIM! WHERE IS HE?
RIGHT IN FRONT OF YOU, SIRE!
IN FRONT OF ME?? YOU'RE MAD! I DO NOT SEE HIM!
BUT THAT IS MY FOURTH POWER, YOUR MAJESTY! THUS CAN I MATCH THE INVISIBLE GIRL!
MATCH HER? THIS IS NOT ENOUGH! YOU MUST OUT-DO HER! YOU MUST BE HER SUPERIOR!
HE DOES POSSESS ONE POWER WHICH SHE DOES NOT, SIRE! I SHALL DESCRIBE IT TO YOU LATER! BUT NOW...
IT IS TIME FOR ME TO EMBARK UPON MY MISSION! I SWEAR NEVER TO RETURN, MY LORD, UNTIL THE FANTASTIC FOUR ARE NO MORE-- AND THE PLANET EARTH IS YOURS!
ONE WEEK LATER, AT A NEW YORK DEPARTMENT STORE, WE FIND THE FANTASTIC FOUR TOGETHER AGAIN, ON A SHOPPING TRIP...
I JUST ADORE SEEING THE NEW FASHIONS!
I THINK I'LL BROWSE AROUND THE BOOK DEPARTMENT!
BOY, IT MUST BE A GAS WORKIN' IN A PLACE WITH ALL THESE CHICKS!
BLO
CHICKS, SHMICKS! I'M GONNA GO BUY ME A BOWLIN' BALL!
YOU SURE THIS IS THE BIGGEST ONE YOU GOT, BUSTER? I AINT EXACTLY GOT SKINNY LITTLE FINGERS!
JUST TRY THAT ONE, SIR! IT WOULD EVEN FIT -HEH-HEH- A GORILLA!
OKAY, LAUGHIN' BOY, IF YOU SAY SO...
ULP
CRUNCH
YOU MUST KNOW SOME PRETTY SMALL GORILLAS, PAL!
I KNOW I SAW IT HAPPEN-- BUT--
6

MEANWHILE, DESPITE ALL THEIR PRECAUTIONS, SOME WELL-MEANING, SHARP-EYED ADMIRERS RECOGNIZE SUE, REED, AND JOHNNY, AND--

YEESH! WOTTA RACKET! THEY MUST BE GIVIN' AWAY FREE SAMPLES OF SOMETHIN'!

LET ME THRU! LET ME THRU!

I CAN'T SEE! I WANT TO GET CLOSER!

DON'T PUSH! DON'T SHOVE! ONE AT A TIME! KEEP BACK, FOLKS --PLEASE!

I WAS FIRST! OUT OF MY WAY! WHERE'S THE MANAGER?

BEN! DON'T JUST STAND THERE! GET US OUT OF HERE!

FOR THE LUVVA PETE! IT'S YOU!

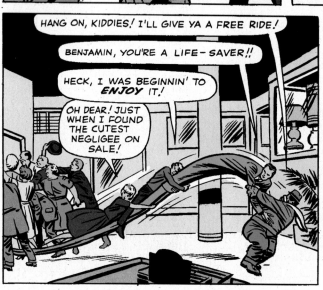

HANG ON, KIDDIES! I'LL GIVE YA A FREE RIDE!

BENJAMIN, YOU'RE A LIFE-SAVER!!

HECK, I WAS BEGINNIN' TO ENJOY IT!

OH DEAR! JUST WHEN I FOUND THE CUTEST NEGLIGEE ON SALE!

--WHEW!- LET'S GET OUT OF HERE BEFORE THEY FIND US AGAIN!

REED RICHARDS-- YOU'RE AN OLD SCAIRDY-CAT!

NAH! HE AINT SO OLD!

BOY! NEVER A DULL MOMENT!

BOYS! WAIT! LISTEN--

IT'S A SPECIAL BULLETIN COMIN' IN OVER THAT RADIO!

--AND TIMES SQUARE IS IN A STATE OF PANIC AND TURMOIL EVER SINCE THE ALIEN SPACE SHIP LANDED FIVE MINUTES AGO...

AN ALIEN SPACE SHIP-- IN TIMES SQUARE!!

IF THERE'S PANIC IN THE STREETS, THEN SOMETHING SERIOUS MUST BE WRONG!

NOW'S OUR CHANCE TO MAKE LIKE HEROES! WHAT'RE WE WAITIN' FOR?!!

7

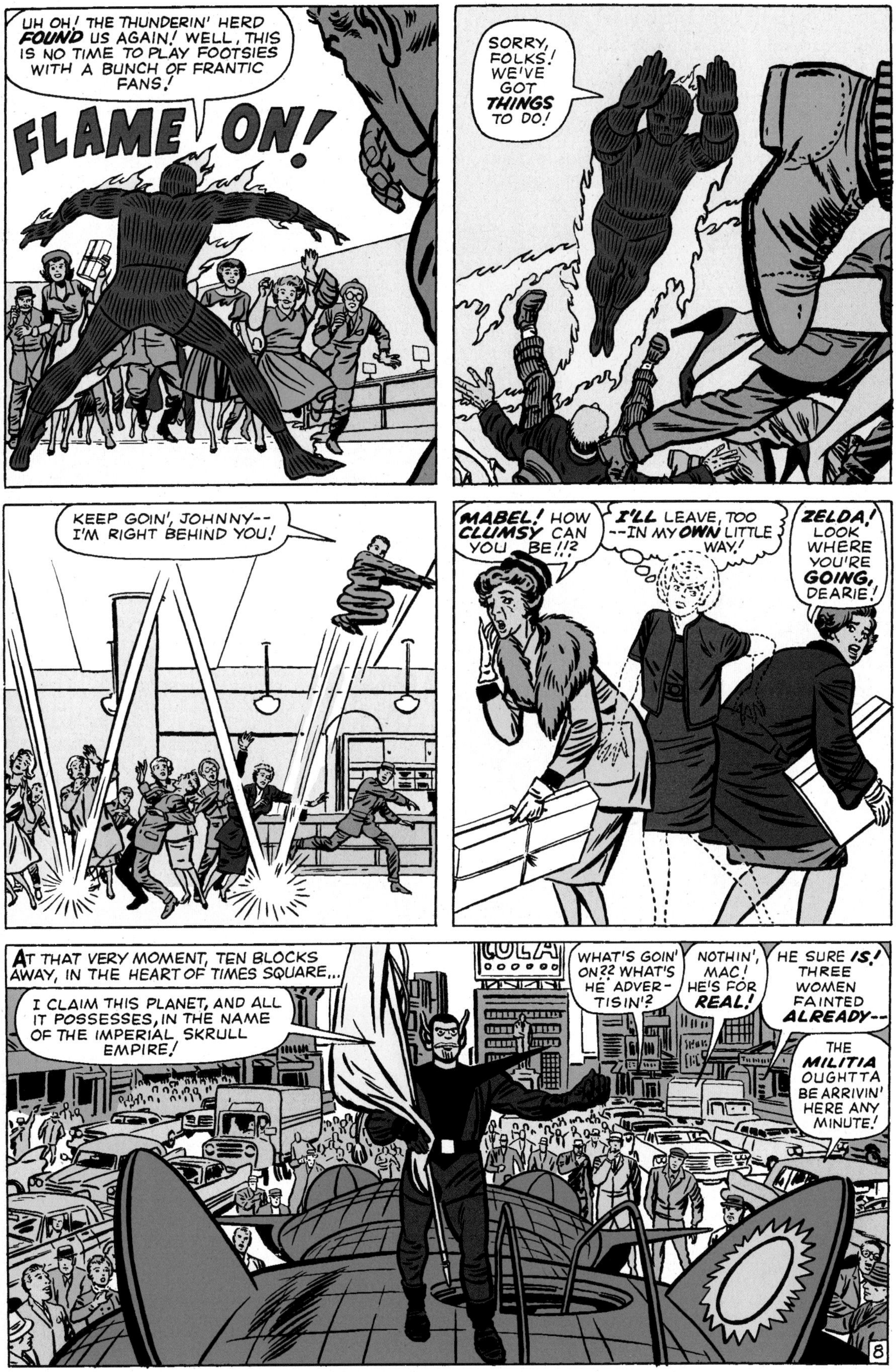
UH OH! THE THUNDERIN' HERD **FOUND** US AGAIN! WELL, THIS IS NO TIME TO PLAY FOOTSIES WITH A BUNCH OF FRANTIC FANS!
FLAME ON!
SORRY, FOLKS! WE'VE GOT **THINGS** TO DO!
KEEP GOIN', JOHNNY-- I'M RIGHT BEHIND YOU!
MABEL! HOW **CLUMSY** CAN YOU BE!!?
I'LL LEAVE, TOO --IN MY **OWN** LITTLE WAY!
ZELDA! LOOK WHERE YOU'RE **GOING,** DEARIE!
AT THAT VERY MOMENT, TEN BLOCKS AWAY, IN THE HEART OF TIMES SQUARE...
I CLAIM THIS PLANET, AND ALL IT POSSESSES, IN THE NAME OF THE IMPERIAL SKRULL EMPIRE!
WHAT'S GOIN' ON?? WHAT'S HE ADVER-TISIN'?
NOTHIN', MAC! HE'S FOR **REAL!**
HE SURE **IS!** THREE WOMEN FAINTED **ALREADY--**
THE **MILITIA** OUGHTTA BE ARRIVIN' HERE ANY MINUTE!
8

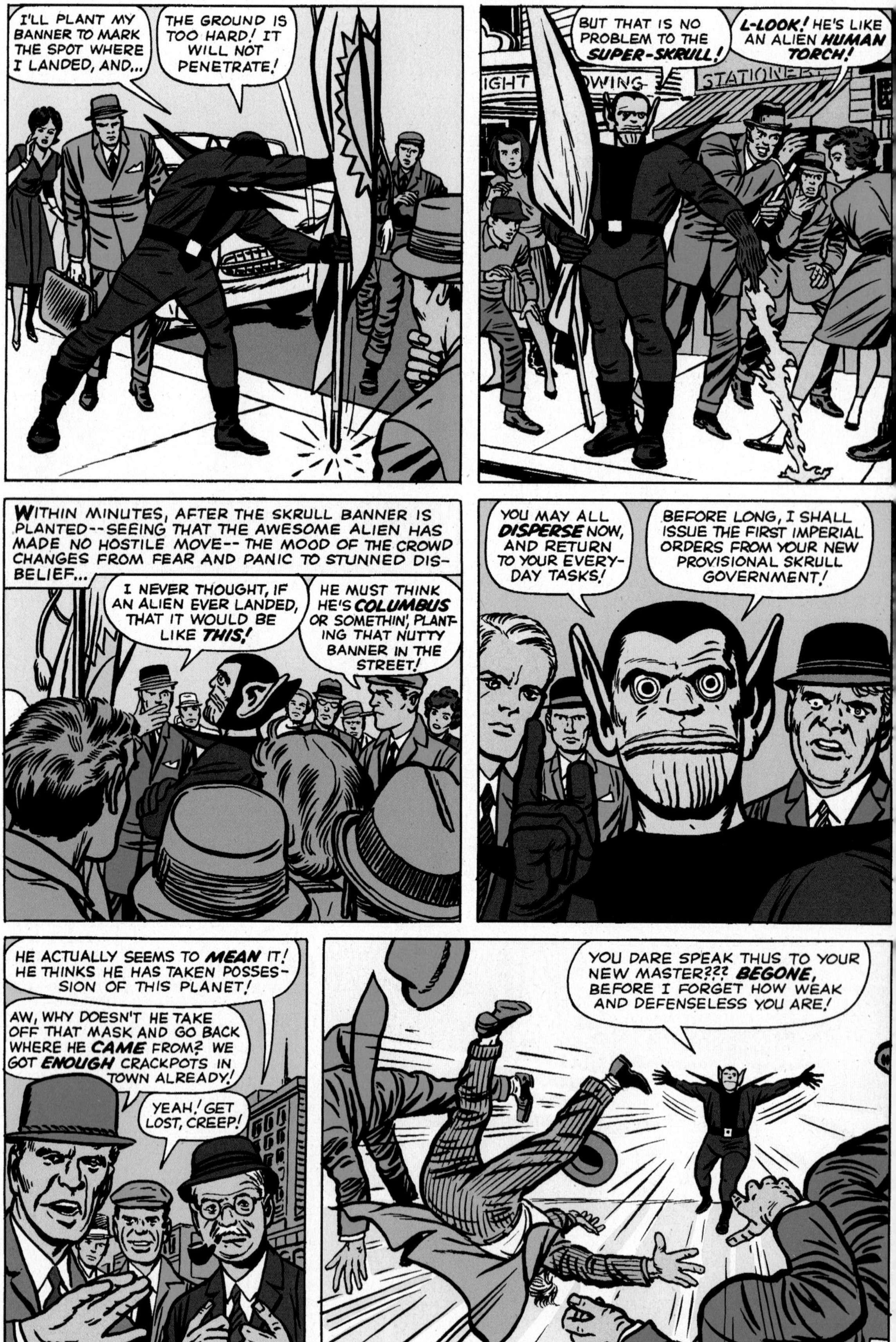

I'LL PLANT MY BANNER TO MARK THE SPOT WHERE I LANDED, AND...
THE GROUND IS TOO HARD! IT WILL NOT PENETRATE!
BUT THAT IS NO PROBLEM TO THE SUPER-SKRULL!
L-LOOK! HE'S LIKE AN ALIEN HUMAN TORCH!
WITHIN MINUTES, AFTER THE SKRULL BANNER IS PLANTED--SEEING THAT THE AWESOME ALIEN HAS MADE NO HOSTILE MOVE-- THE MOOD OF THE CROWD CHANGES FROM FEAR AND PANIC TO STUNNED DISBELIEF...
I NEVER THOUGHT, IF AN ALIEN EVER LANDED, THAT IT WOULD BE LIKE THIS!
HE MUST THINK HE'S COLUMBUS OR SOMETHIN', PLANTING THAT NUTTY BANNER IN THE STREET!
YOU MAY ALL DISPERSE NOW, AND RETURN TO YOUR EVERYDAY TASKS!
BEFORE LONG, I SHALL ISSUE THE FIRST IMPERIAL ORDERS FROM YOUR NEW PROVISIONAL SKRULL GOVERNMENT!
HE ACTUALLY SEEMS TO MEAN IT! HE THINKS HE HAS TAKEN POSSESSION OF THIS PLANET!
AW, WHY DOESN'T HE TAKE OFF THAT MASK AND GO BACK WHERE HE CAME FROM? WE GOT ENOUGH CRACKPOTS IN TOWN ALREADY!
YEAH! GET LOST, CREEP!
YOU DARE SPEAK THUS TO YOUR NEW MASTER??? BEGONE, BEFORE I FORGET HOW WEAK AND DEFENSELESS YOU ARE!
9

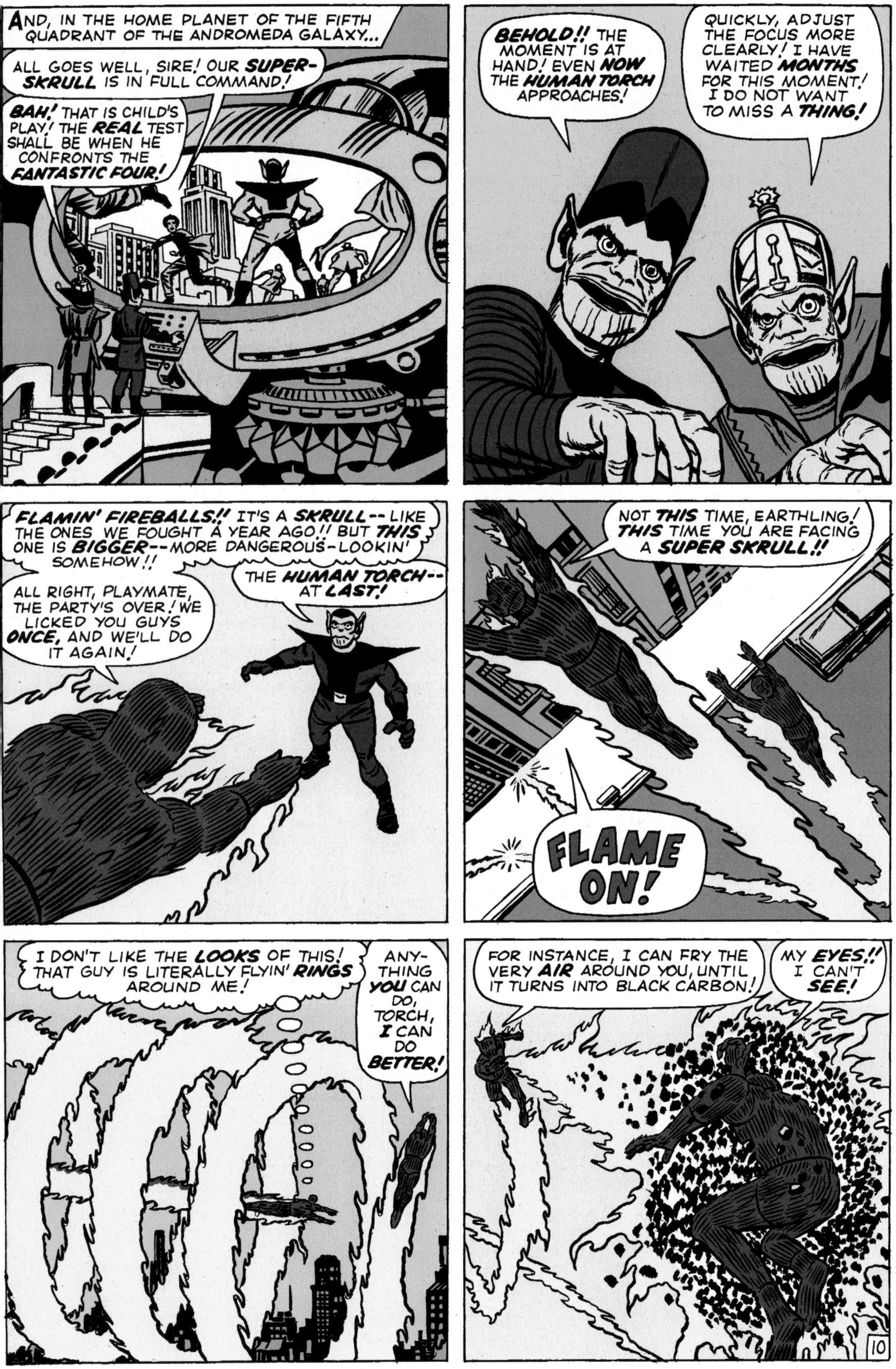
AND, IN THE HOME PLANET OF THE FIFTH QUADRANT OF THE ANDROMEDA GALAXY...
ALL GOES WELL, SIRE! OUR SUPER-SKRULL IS IN FULL COMMAND!
BAH! THAT IS CHILD'S PLAY! THE REAL TEST SHALL BE WHEN HE CONFRONTS THE FANTASTIC FOUR!
BEHOLD!! THE MOMENT IS AT HAND! EVEN NOW THE HUMAN TORCH APPROACHES!
QUICKLY, ADJUST THE FOCUS MORE CLEARLY! I HAVE WAITED MONTHS FOR THIS MOMENT! I DO NOT WANT TO MISS A THING!
FLAMIN' FIREBALLS!! IT'S A SKRULL--LIKE THE ONES WE FOUGHT A YEAR AGO!! BUT THIS ONE IS BIGGER--MORE DANGEROUS-LOOKIN' SOMEHOW!!
THE HUMAN TORCH--AT LAST!
ALL RIGHT, PLAYMATE, THE PARTY'S OVER! WE LICKED YOU GUYS ONCE, AND WE'LL DO IT AGAIN!
NOT THIS TIME, EARTHLING! THIS TIME YOU ARE FACING A SUPER SKRULL!!
FLAME ON!
I DON'T LIKE THE LOOKS OF THIS! THAT GUY IS LITERALLY FLYIN' RINGS AROUND ME!
ANYTHING YOU CAN DO, TORCH, I CAN DO BETTER!
FOR INSTANCE, I CAN FRY THE VERY AIR AROUND YOU, UNTIL IT TURNS INTO BLACK CARBON!
MY EYES!! I CAN'T SEE!
10

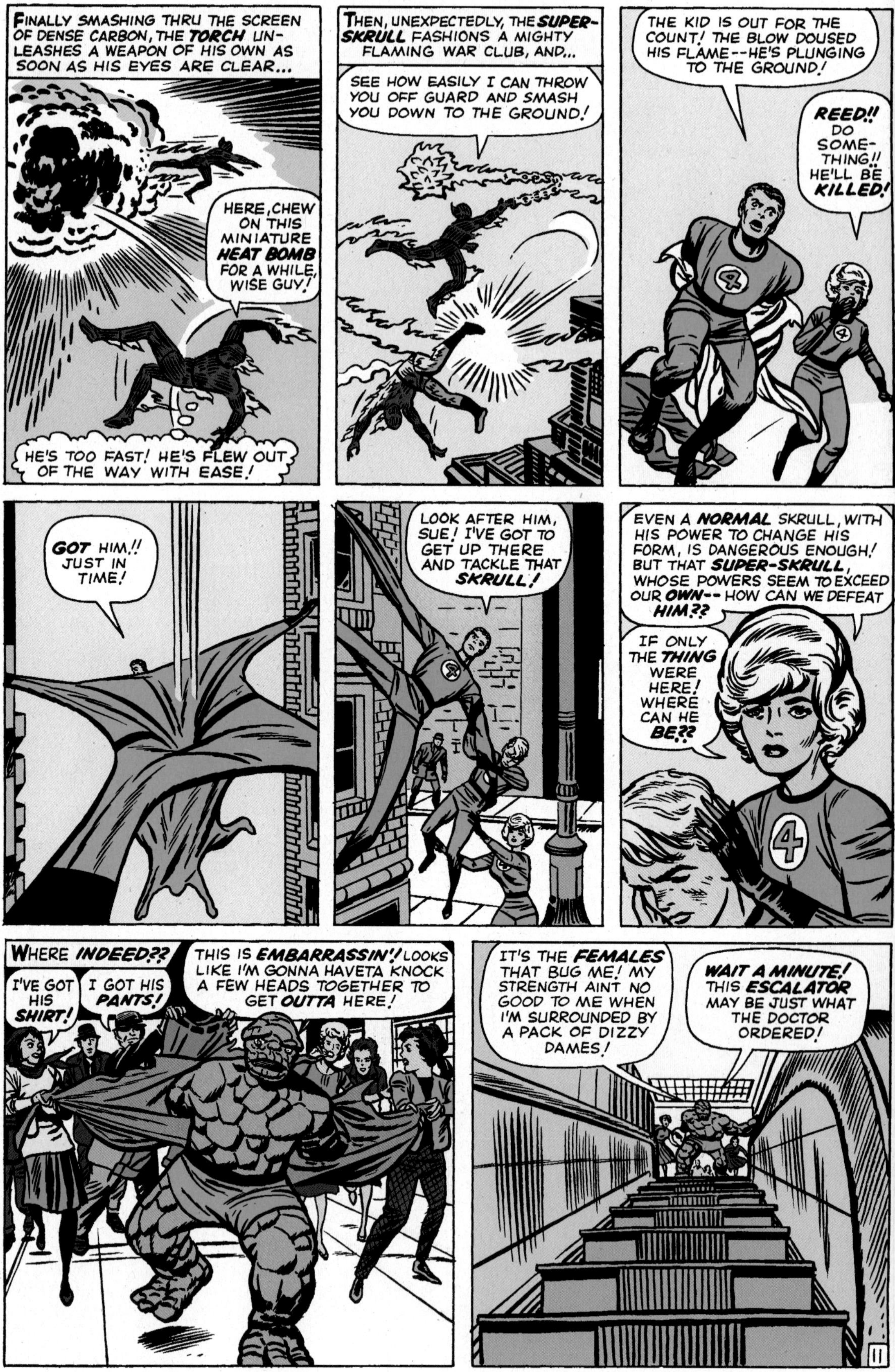

FINALLY SMASHING THRU THE SCREEN OF DENSE CARBON, THE TORCH UNLEASHES A WEAPON OF HIS OWN AS SOON AS HIS EYES ARE CLEAR...
HERE, CHEW ON THIS MINIATURE HEAT BOMB FOR A WHILE, WISE GUY!
HE'S TOO FAST! HE'S FLEW OUT OF THE WAY WITH EASE!
THEN, UNEXPECTEDLY, THE SUPER-SKRULL FASHIONS A MIGHTY FLAMING WAR CLUB, AND...
SEE HOW EASILY I CAN THROW YOU OFF GUARD AND SMASH YOU DOWN TO THE GROUND!
THE KID IS OUT FOR THE COUNT! THE BLOW DOUSED HIS FLAME--HE'S PLUNGING TO THE GROUND!
REED!! DO SOMETHING!! HE'LL BE KILLED!
GOT HIM!! JUST IN TIME!
LOOK AFTER HIM, SUE! I'VE GOT TO GET UP THERE AND TACKLE THAT SKRULL!
EVEN A NORMAL SKRULL, WITH HIS POWER TO CHANGE HIS FORM, IS DANGEROUS ENOUGH! BUT THAT SUPER-SKRULL, WHOSE POWERS SEEM TO EXCEED OUR OWN-- HOW CAN WE DEFEAT HIM??
IF ONLY THE THING WERE HERE! WHERE CAN HE BE??
WHERE INDEED??
I'VE GOT HIS SHIRT!
I GOT HIS PANTS!
THIS IS EMBARRASSIN'! LOOKS LIKE I'M GONNA HAVETA KNOCK A FEW HEADS TOGETHER TO GET OUTTA HERE!
IT'S THE FEMALES THAT BUG ME! MY STRENGTH AINT NO GOOD TO ME WHEN I'M SURROUNDED BY A PACK OF DIZZY DAMES!
WAIT A MINUTE! THIS ESCALATOR MAY BE JUST WHAT THE DOCTOR ORDERED!
11

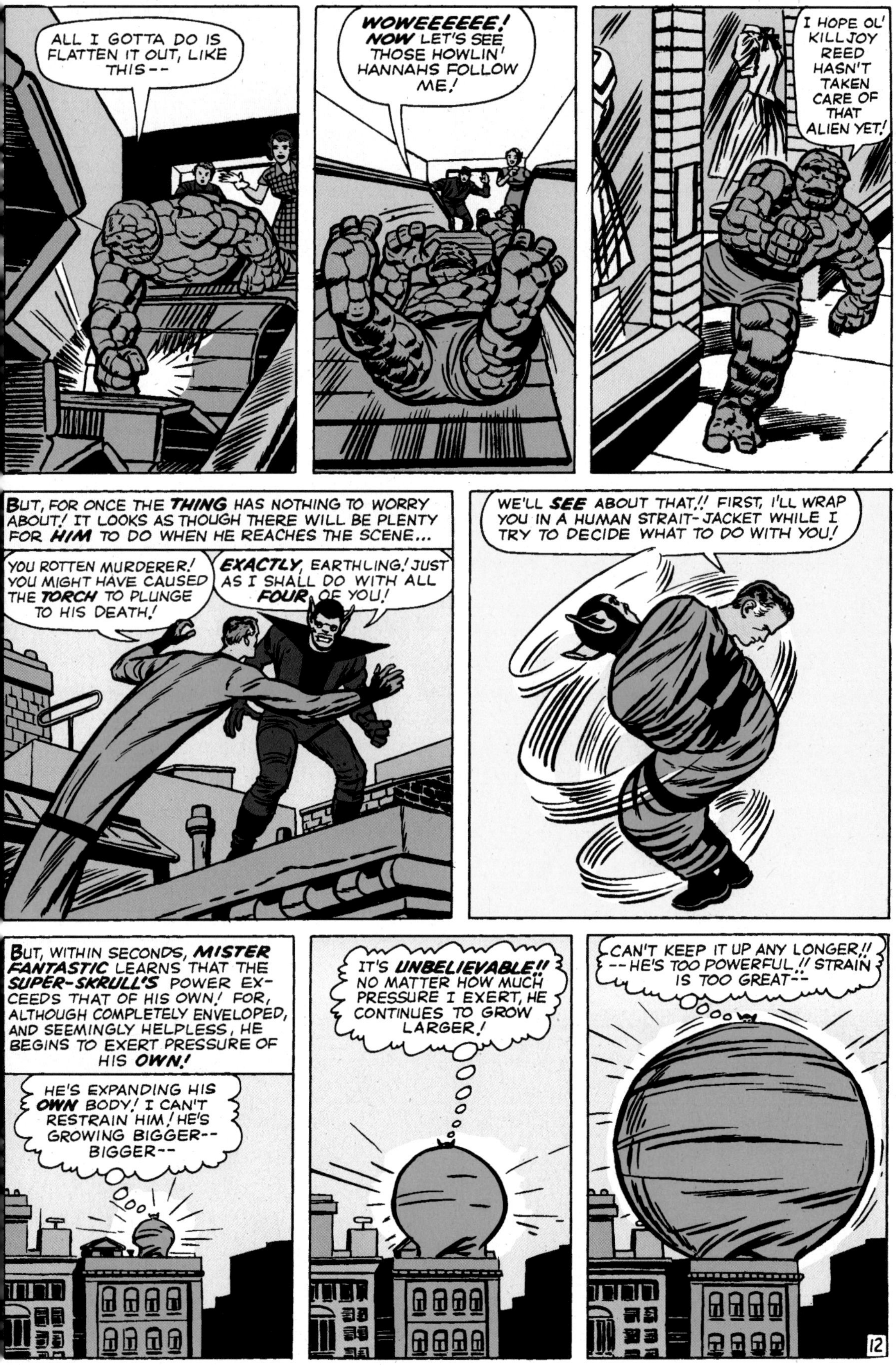
ALL I GOTTA DO IS FLATTEN IT OUT, LIKE THIS--
WOWEEEEEE! NOW LET'S SEE THOSE HOWLIN' HANNAHS FOLLOW ME!
I HOPE OL' KILLJOY REED HASN'T TAKEN CARE OF THAT ALIEN YET!
BUT, FOR ONCE THE THING HAS NOTHING TO WORRY ABOUT! IT LOOKS AS THOUGH THERE WILL BE PLENTY FOR HIM TO DO WHEN HE REACHES THE SCENE...
YOU ROTTEN MURDERER! YOU MIGHT HAVE CAUSED THE TORCH TO PLUNGE TO HIS DEATH!
EXACTLY, EARTHLING! JUST AS I SHALL DO WITH ALL FOUR OF YOU!
WE'LL SEE ABOUT THAT!! FIRST, I'LL WRAP YOU IN A HUMAN STRAIT-JACKET WHILE I TRY TO DECIDE WHAT TO DO WITH YOU!
BUT, WITHIN SECONDS, MISTER FANTASTIC LEARNS THAT THE SUPER-SKRULL'S POWER EXCEEDS THAT OF HIS OWN! FOR, ALTHOUGH COMPLETELY ENVELOPED, AND SEEMINGLY HELPLESS, HE BEGINS TO EXERT PRESSURE OF HIS OWN!
HE'S EXPANDING HIS OWN BODY! I CAN'T RESTRAIN HIM! HE'S GROWING BIGGER-- BIGGER--
IT'S UNBELIEVABLE!! NO MATTER HOW MUCH PRESSURE I EXERT, HE CONTINUES TO GROW LARGER!
CAN'T KEEP IT UP ANY LONGER!! --HE'S TOO POWERFUL!! STRAIN IS TOO GREAT--
12

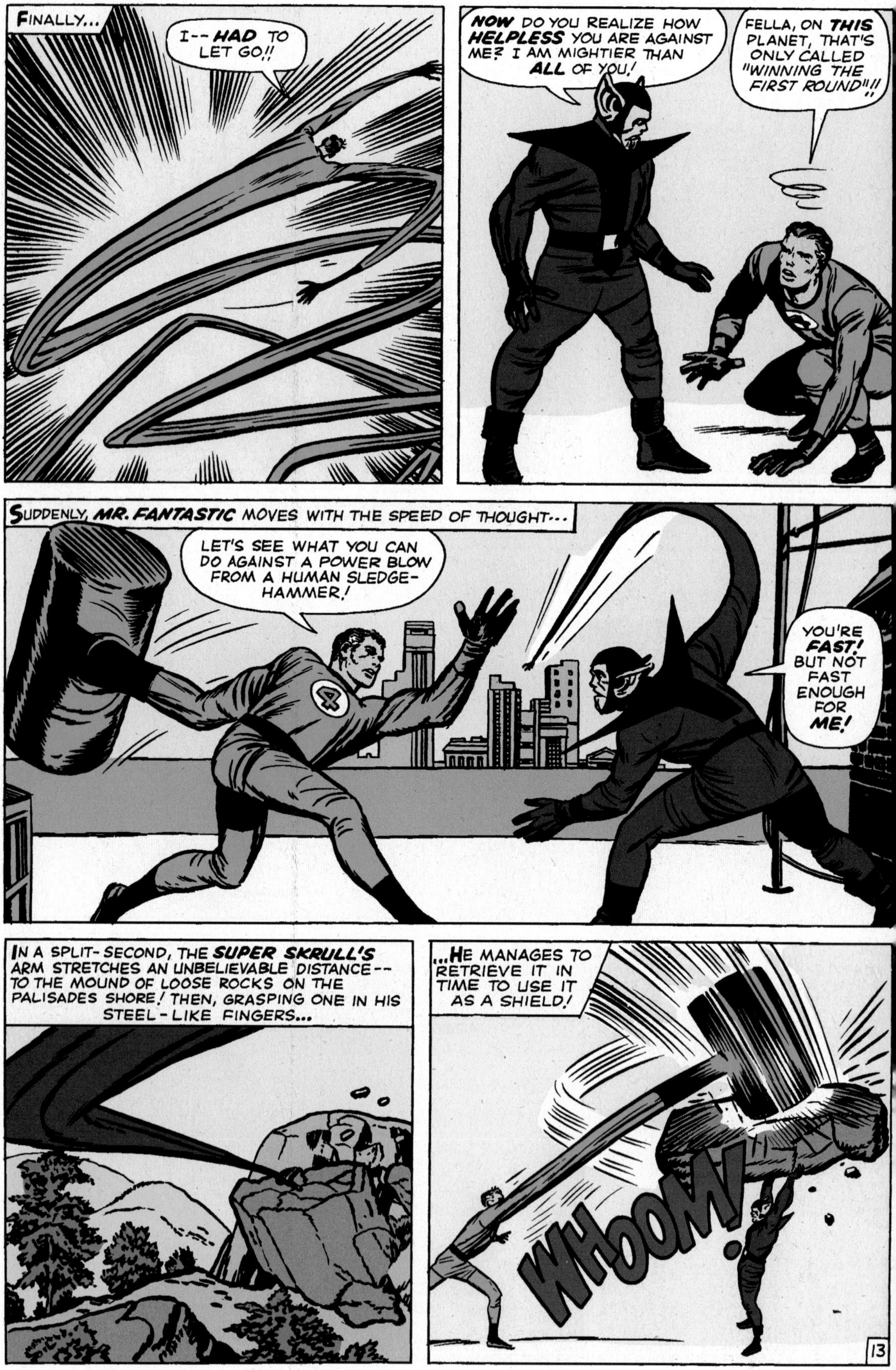
FINALLY...
I-- HAD TO LET GO!!
NOW DO YOU REALIZE HOW HELPLESS YOU ARE AGAINST ME? I AM MIGHTIER THAN ALL OF YOU!
FELLA, ON THIS PLANET, THAT'S ONLY CALLED "WINNING THE FIRST ROUND"!!
SUDDENLY, MR. FANTASTIC MOVES WITH THE SPEED OF THOUGHT...
LET'S SEE WHAT YOU CAN DO AGAINST A POWER BLOW FROM A HUMAN SLEDGE-HAMMER!
YOU'RE FAST! BUT NOT FAST ENOUGH FOR ME!
IN A SPLIT-SECOND, THE SUPER SKRULL'S ARM STRETCHES AN UNBELIEVABLE DISTANCE-- TO THE MOUND OF LOOSE ROCKS ON THE PALISADES SHORE! THEN, GRASPING ONE IN HIS STEEL-LIKE FINGERS...
...HE MANAGES TO RETRIEVE IT IN TIME TO USE IT AS A SHIELD!
WHOOM!
13

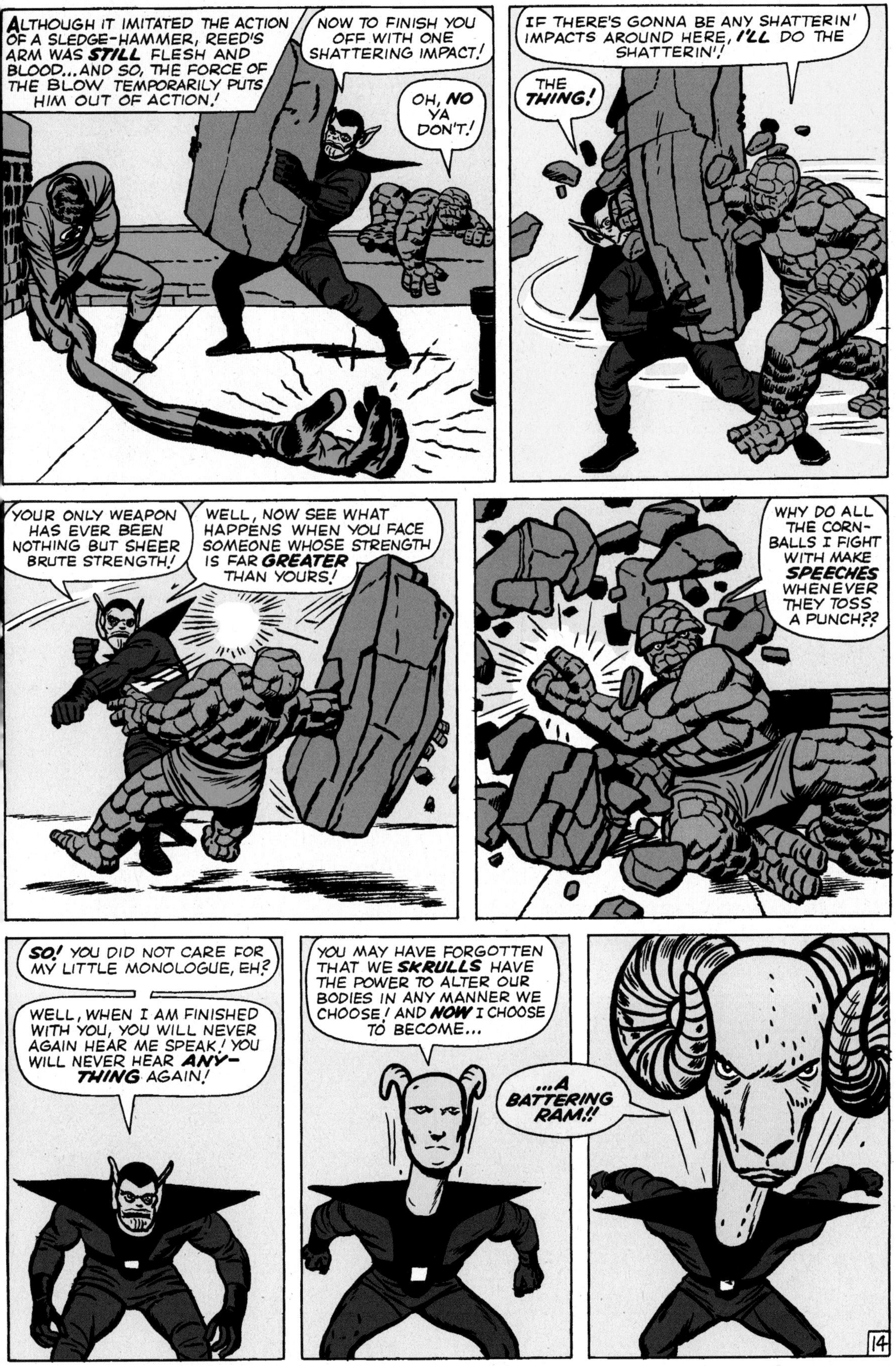
ALTHOUGH IT IMITATED THE ACTION OF A SLEDGE-HAMMER, REED'S ARM WAS STILL FLESH AND BLOOD... AND SO, THE FORCE OF THE BLOW TEMPORARILY PUTS HIM OUT OF ACTION!
NOW TO FINISH YOU OFF WITH ONE SHATTERING IMPACT!
OH, NO YA DON'T!
IF THERE'S GONNA BE ANY SHATTERIN' IMPACTS AROUND HERE, I'LL DO THE SHATTERIN'!
THE THING!
YOUR ONLY WEAPON HAS EVER BEEN NOTHING BUT SHEER BRUTE STRENGTH!
WELL, NOW SEE WHAT HAPPENS WHEN YOU FACE SOMEONE WHOSE STRENGTH IS FAR GREATER THAN YOURS!
WHY DO ALL THE CORN-BALLS I FIGHT WITH MAKE SPEECHES WHENEVER THEY TOSS A PUNCH??
SO! YOU DID NOT CARE FOR MY LITTLE MONOLOGUE, EH?
WELL, WHEN I AM FINISHED WITH YOU, YOU WILL NEVER AGAIN HEAR ME SPEAK! YOU WILL NEVER HEAR ANY-THING AGAIN!
YOU MAY HAVE FORGOTTEN THAT WE SKRULLS HAVE THE POWER TO ALTER OUR BODIES IN ANY MANNER WE CHOOSE! AND NOW I CHOOSE TO BECOME...
...A BATTERING RAM!!
14

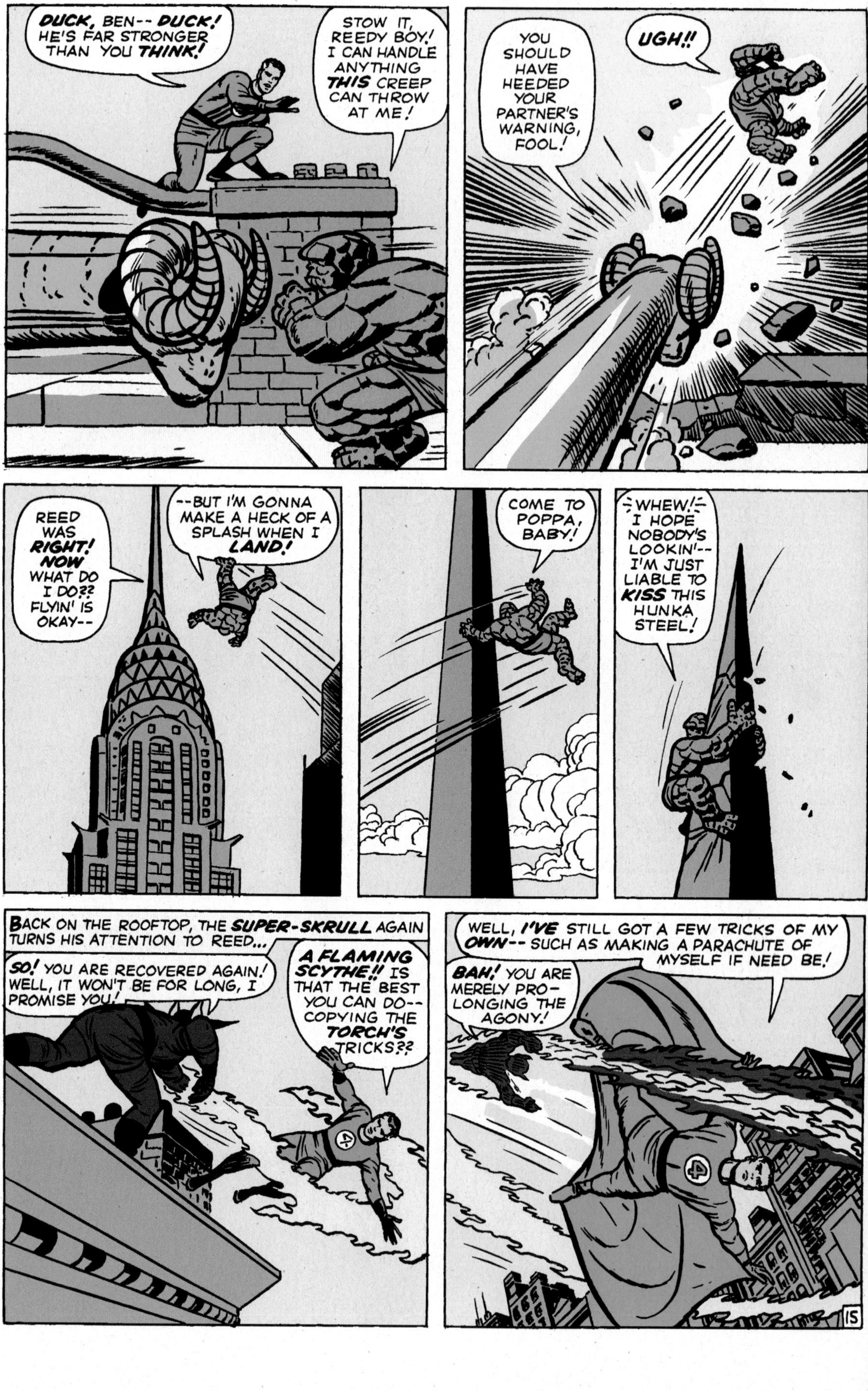

DUCK, BEN-- DUCK! HE'S FAR STRONGER THAN YOU THINK!
STOW IT, REEDY BOY! I CAN HANDLE ANYTHING THIS CREEP CAN THROW AT ME!
YOU SHOULD HAVE HEEDED YOUR PARTNER'S WARNING, FOOL!
UGH!!
REED WAS RIGHT! NOW WHAT DO I DO?? FLYIN' IS OKAY--
--BUT I'M GONNA MAKE A HECK OF A SPLASH WHEN I LAND!
COME TO POPPA, BABY!
WHEW! I HOPE NOBODY'S LOOKIN'-- I'M JUST LIABLE TO KISS THIS HUNKA STEEL!
BACK ON THE ROOFTOP, THE SUPER-SKRULL AGAIN TURNS HIS ATTENTION TO REED...
SO! YOU ARE RECOVERED AGAIN! WELL, IT WON'T BE FOR LONG, I PROMISE YOU!
A FLAMING SCYTHE!! IS THAT THE BEST YOU CAN DO-- COPYING THE TORCH'S TRICKS??
WELL, I'VE STILL GOT A FEW TRICKS OF MY OWN-- SUCH AS MAKING A PARACHUTE OF MYSELF IF NEED BE!
BAH! YOU ARE MERELY PRO-LONGING THE AGONY!
15

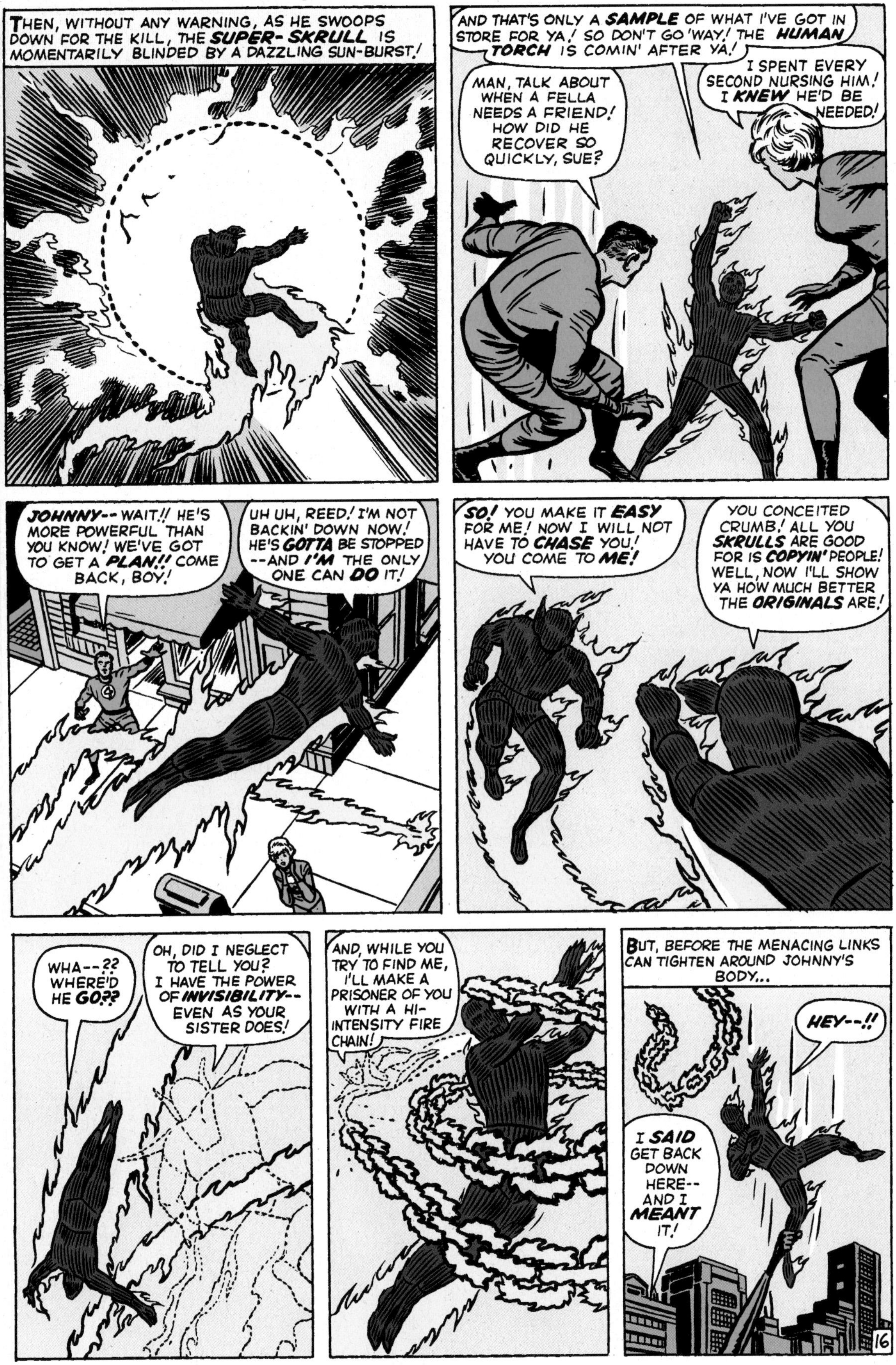
THEN, WITHOUT ANY WARNING, AS HE SWOOPS DOWN FOR THE KILL, THE SUPER-SKRULL IS MOMENTARILY BLINDED BY A DAZZLING SUN-BURST!
AND THAT'S ONLY A SAMPLE OF WHAT I'VE GOT IN STORE FOR YA! SO DON'T GO 'WAY! THE HUMAN TORCH IS COMIN' AFTER YA!
MAN, TALK ABOUT WHEN A FELLA NEEDS A FRIEND! HOW DID HE RECOVER SO QUICKLY, SUE?
I SPENT EVERY SECOND NURSING HIM! I KNEW HE'D BE NEEDED!
JOHNNY-- WAIT!! HE'S MORE POWERFUL THAN YOU KNOW! WE'VE GOT TO GET A PLAN!! COME BACK, BOY!
UH UH, REED! I'M NOT BACKIN' DOWN NOW! HE'S GOTTA BE STOPPED --AND I'M THE ONLY ONE CAN DO IT!
SO! YOU MAKE IT EASY FOR ME! NOW I WILL NOT HAVE TO CHASE YOU! YOU COME TO ME!
YOU CONCEITED CRUMB! ALL YOU SKRULLS ARE GOOD FOR IS COPYIN' PEOPLE! WELL, NOW I'LL SHOW YA HOW MUCH BETTER THE ORIGINALS ARE!
WHA--?? WHERE'D HE GO??
OH, DID I NEGLECT TO TELL YOU? I HAVE THE POWER OF INVISIBILITY-- EVEN AS YOUR SISTER DOES!
AND, WHILE YOU TRY TO FIND ME, I'LL MAKE A PRISONER OF YOU WITH A HI-INTENSITY FIRE CHAIN!
BUT, BEFORE THE MENACING LINKS CAN TIGHTEN AROUND JOHNNY'S BODY...
HEY--!!
I SAID GET BACK DOWN HERE-- AND I MEANT IT!
16

AWW, WHAT DID YOU DO *THAT* FOR? *SAY!* YOU BURNED YOURSELF ON MY LEG!

IT'LL BE ALL RIGHT, KID! I *HAD* TO DO IT! NONE OF US, ALONE, ARE A MATCH FOR THE *SKRULL!*

THIS IS *TERRIBLE!* I'VE NEVER FELT SO HELPLESS-- SO USELESS!

DON'T LET *THAT* BOTHER YOU, HONEY! WITH ALL OUR BLUSTER, *WE* HAVEN'T ACHIEVED ANY MORE THAN *YOU!* BUT-- WHERE IS THE *THING??*

LOOK, REED! UP THERE!

THIS IS MIGHTY *OBLIGIN'* OF YOU GUYS! I WAS BEGINNIN' TO FEEL LIKE A GOL-DANGED *WEATHER VANE* UP THERE!

N.Y.C. POLICE

WHAT *HAPPENED,* SKINNY? DIDJA GET RID OF OUR LITTLE PLAYMATE YET?

NO, BEN! WE'VE GOT TO GET TO OUR HEAD-QUARTERS AND MAP OUT A PLAN OF ACTION!

HURRY! HE MADE HIMSELF *INVISIBLE!* HE MIGHT BE *ANYWHERE!*

I *STILL* THINK YOU SHOULDA LET ME SLUG IT OUT WITH 'IM!

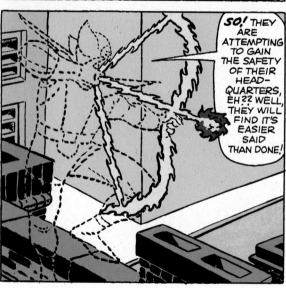

SO! THEY ARE ATTEMPTING TO GAIN THE SAFETY OF THEIR HEAD-QUARTERS, EH?? WELL, THEY WILL FIND IT'S EASIER SAID THAN DONE!

HA! DID YOU THINK TO EVADE ME THAT EASILY??

MOVE!! ALL OF YOU! HE'S SHOOTING *FIRE-ARROWS* AT US!

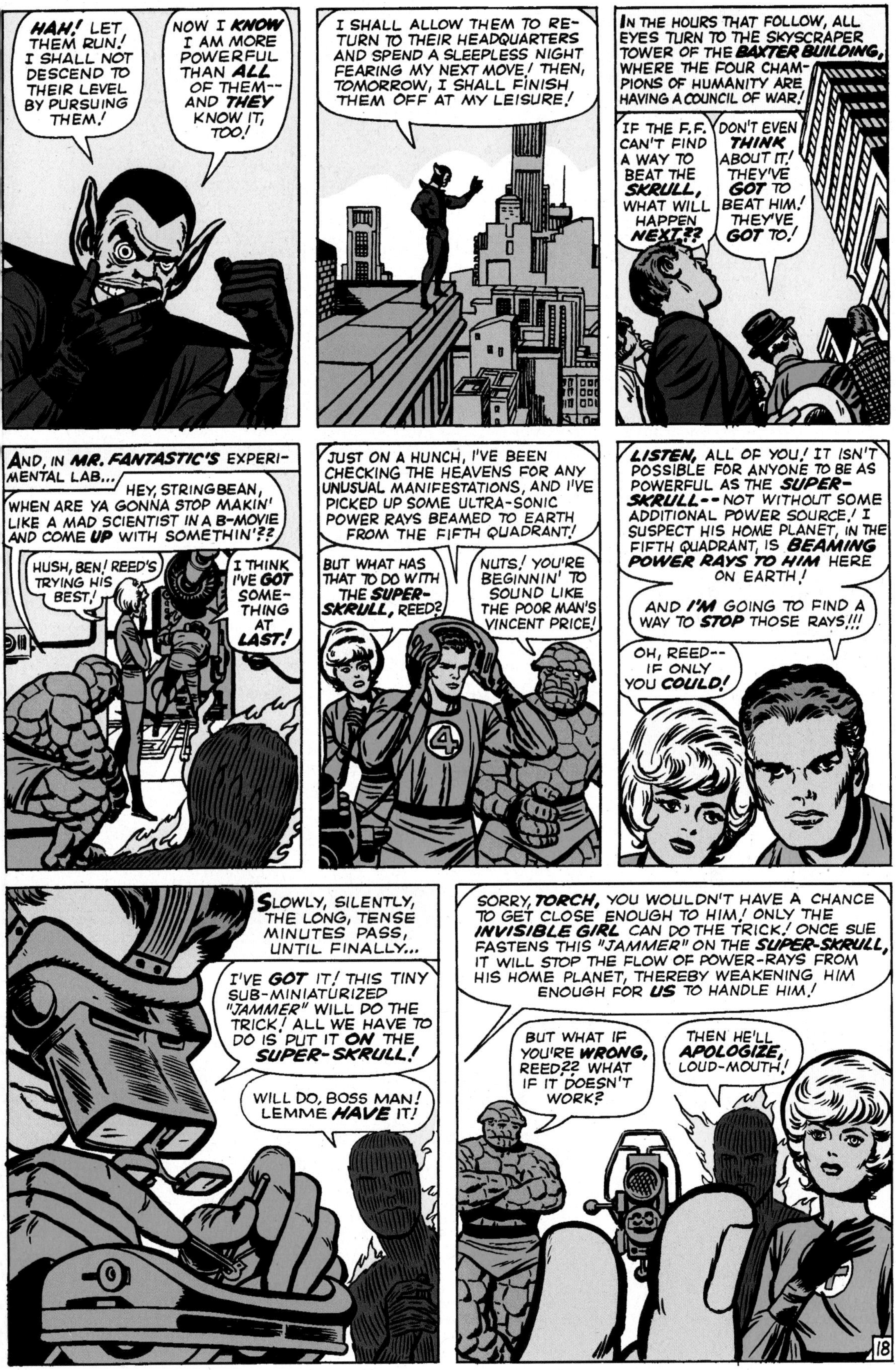
HAH! LET THEM RUN! I SHALL NOT DESCEND TO THEIR LEVEL BY PURSUING THEM!
NOW I KNOW I AM MORE POWERFUL THAN ALL OF THEM-- AND THEY KNOW IT, TOO!
I SHALL ALLOW THEM TO RETURN TO THEIR HEADQUARTERS AND SPEND A SLEEPLESS NIGHT FEARING MY NEXT MOVE! THEN, TOMORROW, I SHALL FINISH THEM OFF AT MY LEISURE!
IN THE HOURS THAT FOLLOW, ALL EYES TURN TO THE SKYSCRAPER TOWER OF THE BAXTER BUILDING, WHERE THE FOUR CHAMPIONS OF HUMANITY ARE HAVING A COUNCIL OF WAR!
IF THE F.F. CAN'T FIND A WAY TO BEAT THE SKRULL, WHAT WILL HAPPEN NEXT??
DON'T EVEN THINK ABOUT IT! THEY'VE GOT TO BEAT HIM! THEY'VE GOT TO!
AND, IN MR. FANTASTIC'S EXPERIMENTAL LAB...
HEY, STRINGBEAN, WHEN ARE YA GONNA STOP MAKIN' LIKE A MAD SCIENTIST IN A B-MOVIE AND COME UP WITH SOMETHIN'??
HUSH, BEN! REED'S TRYING HIS BEST!
I THINK I'VE GOT SOMETHING AT LAST!
JUST ON A HUNCH, I'VE BEEN CHECKING THE HEAVENS FOR ANY UNUSUAL MANIFESTATIONS, AND I'VE PICKED UP SOME ULTRA-SONIC POWER RAYS BEAMED TO EARTH FROM THE FIFTH QUADRANT!
BUT WHAT HAS THAT TO DO WITH THE SUPER-SKRULL, REED?
NUTS! YOU'RE BEGINNIN' TO SOUND LIKE THE POOR MAN'S VINCENT PRICE!
LISTEN, ALL OF YOU! IT ISN'T POSSIBLE FOR ANYONE TO BE AS POWERFUL AS THE SUPER-SKRULL-- NOT WITHOUT SOME ADDITIONAL POWER SOURCE! I SUSPECT HIS HOME PLANET, IN THE FIFTH QUADRANT, IS BEAMING POWER RAYS TO HIM HERE ON EARTH!
AND I'M GOING TO FIND A WAY TO STOP THOSE RAYS!!!
OH, REED-- IF ONLY YOU COULD!
SLOWLY, SILENTLY, THE LONG, TENSE MINUTES PASS, UNTIL FINALLY...
I'VE GOT IT! THIS TINY SUB-MINIATURIZED "JAMMER" WILL DO THE TRICK! ALL WE HAVE TO DO IS PUT IT ON THE SUPER-SKRULL!
WILL DO, BOSS MAN! LEMME HAVE IT!
SORRY, TORCH, YOU WOULDN'T HAVE A CHANCE TO GET CLOSE ENOUGH TO HIM! ONLY THE INVISIBLE GIRL CAN DO THE TRICK! ONCE SUE FASTENS THIS "JAMMER" ON THE SUPER-SKRULL, IT WILL STOP THE FLOW OF POWER-RAYS FROM HIS HOME PLANET, THEREBY WEAKENING HIM ENOUGH FOR US TO HANDLE HIM!
BUT WHAT IF YOU'RE WRONG, REED?? WHAT IF IT DOESN'T WORK?
THEN HE'LL APOLOGIZE, LOUD-MOUTH!
18

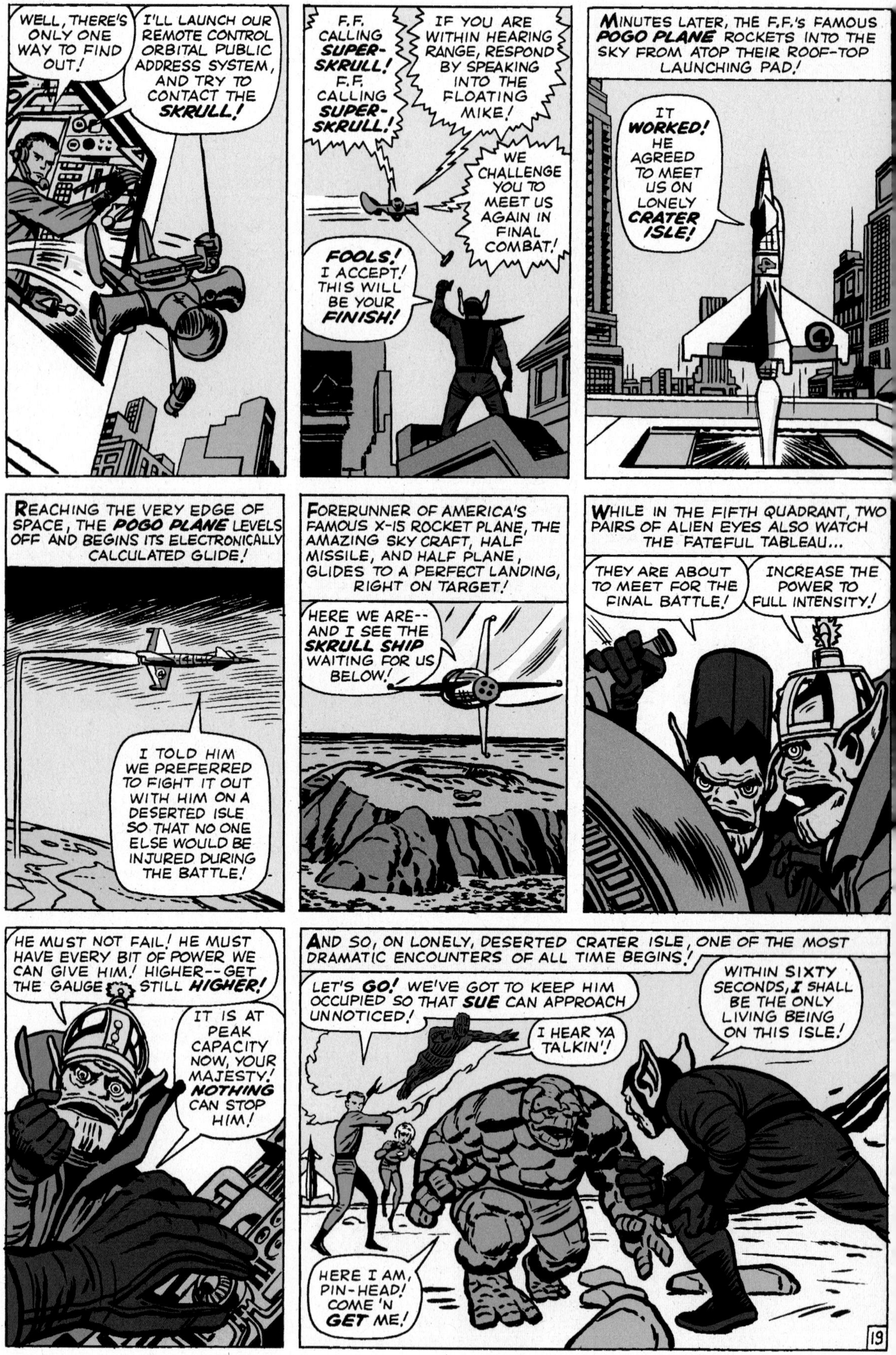

WELL, THERE'S ONLY ONE WAY TO FIND OUT!
I'LL LAUNCH OUR REMOTE CONTROL ORBITAL PUBLIC ADDRESS SYSTEM, AND TRY TO CONTACT THE SKRULL!
F.F. CALLING SUPER-SKRULL! F.F. CALLING SUPER-SKRULL!
IF YOU ARE WITHIN HEARING RANGE, RESPOND BY SPEAKING INTO THE FLOATING MIKE!
WE CHALLENGE YOU TO MEET US AGAIN IN FINAL COMBAT!
FOOLS! I ACCEPT! THIS WILL BE YOUR FINISH!
MINUTES LATER, THE F.F.'S FAMOUS POGO PLANE ROCKETS INTO THE SKY FROM ATOP THEIR ROOF-TOP LAUNCHING PAD!
IT WORKED! HE AGREED TO MEET US ON LONELY CRATER ISLE!
REACHING THE VERY EDGE OF SPACE, THE POGO PLANE LEVELS OFF AND BEGINS ITS ELECTRONICALLY CALCULATED GLIDE!
I TOLD HIM WE PREFERRED TO FIGHT IT OUT WITH HIM ON A DESERTED ISLE SO THAT NO ONE ELSE WOULD BE INJURED DURING THE BATTLE!
FORERUNNER OF AMERICA'S FAMOUS X-15 ROCKET PLANE, THE AMAZING SKY CRAFT, HALF MISSILE, AND HALF PLANE, GLIDES TO A PERFECT LANDING, RIGHT ON TARGET!
HERE WE ARE-- AND I SEE THE SKRULL SHIP WAITING FOR US BELOW!
WHILE IN THE FIFTH QUADRANT, TWO PAIRS OF ALIEN EYES ALSO WATCH THE FATEFUL TABLEAU...
THEY ARE ABOUT TO MEET FOR THE FINAL BATTLE!
INCREASE THE POWER TO FULL INTENSITY!
HE MUST NOT FAIL! HE MUST HAVE EVERY BIT OF POWER WE CAN GIVE HIM! HIGHER--GET THE GAUGE STILL HIGHER!
IT IS AT PEAK CAPACITY NOW, YOUR MAJESTY! NOTHING CAN STOP HIM!
AND SO, ON LONELY, DESERTED CRATER ISLE, ONE OF THE MOST DRAMATIC ENCOUNTERS OF ALL TIME BEGINS!
LET'S GO! WE'VE GOT TO KEEP HIM OCCUPIED SO THAT SUE CAN APPROACH UNNOTICED!
I HEAR YA TALKIN'!
WITHIN SIXTY SECONDS, I SHALL BE THE ONLY LIVING BEING ON THIS ISLE!
HERE I AM, PIN-HEAD! COME 'N GET ME!
19

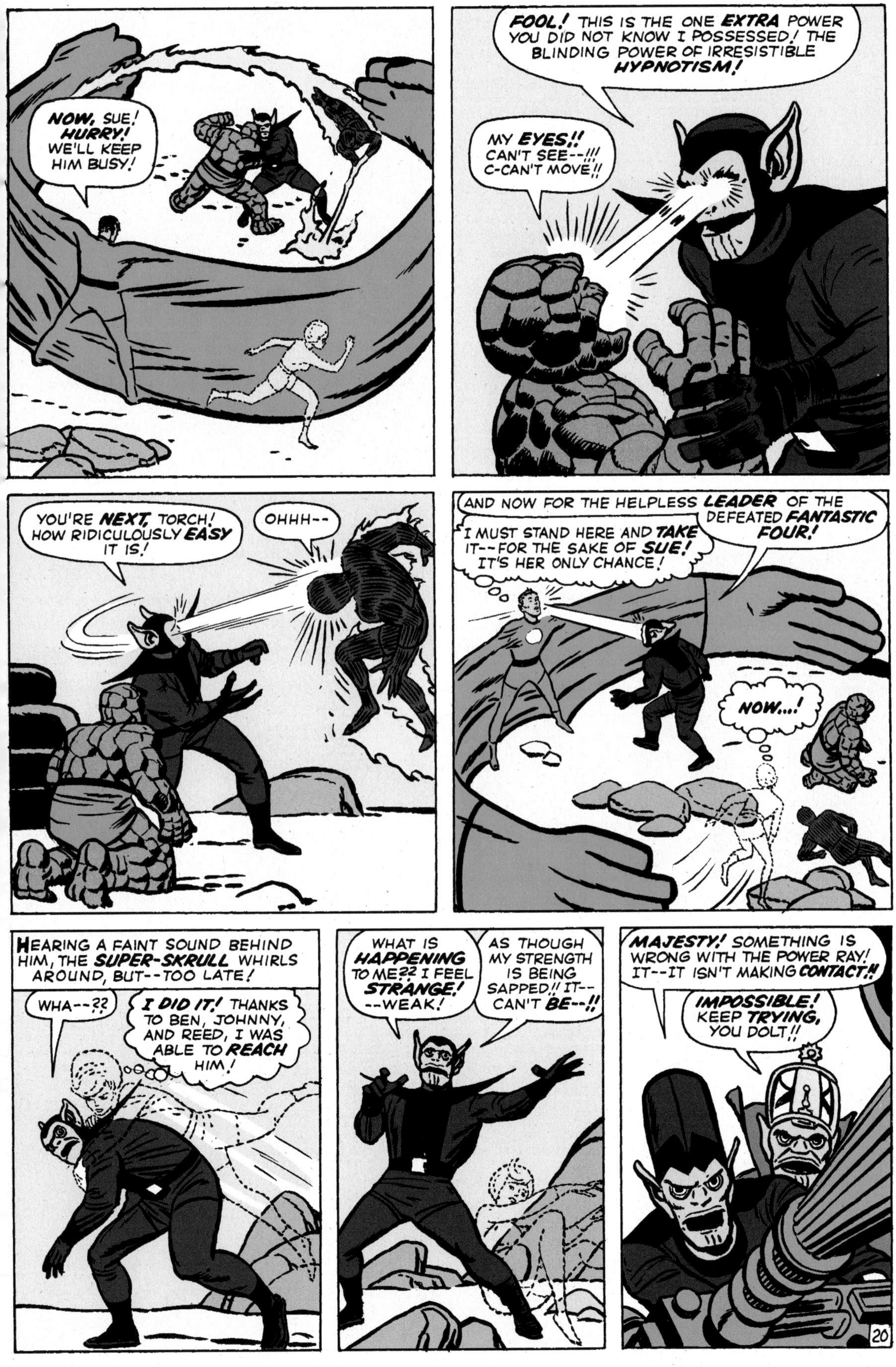
NOW, SUE! HURRY! WE'LL KEEP HIM BUSY!
FOOL! THIS IS THE ONE EXTRA POWER YOU DID NOT KNOW I POSSESSED! THE BLINDING POWER OF IRRESISTIBLE HYPNOTISM!
MY EYES!! CAN'T SEE--!!! C-CAN'T MOVE!!
YOU'RE NEXT, TORCH! HOW RIDICULOUSLY EASY IT IS!
OHHH--
AND NOW FOR THE HELPLESS LEADER OF THE DEFEATED FANTASTIC FOUR!
I MUST STAND HERE AND TAKE IT--FOR THE SAKE OF SUE! IT'S HER ONLY CHANCE!
NOW...!
HEARING A FAINT SOUND BEHIND HIM, THE SUPER-SKRULL WHIRLS AROUND, BUT--TOO LATE!
WHA--??
I DID IT! THANKS TO BEN, JOHNNY, AND REED, I WAS ABLE TO REACH HIM!
WHAT IS HAPPENING TO ME?? I FEEL STRANGE! --WEAK!
AS THOUGH MY STRENGTH IS BEING SAPPED!! IT--CAN'T BE--!!
MAJESTY! SOMETHING IS WRONG WITH THE POWER RAY! IT--IT ISN'T MAKING CONTACT!!
IMPOSSIBLE! KEEP TRYING, YOU DOLT!!
20

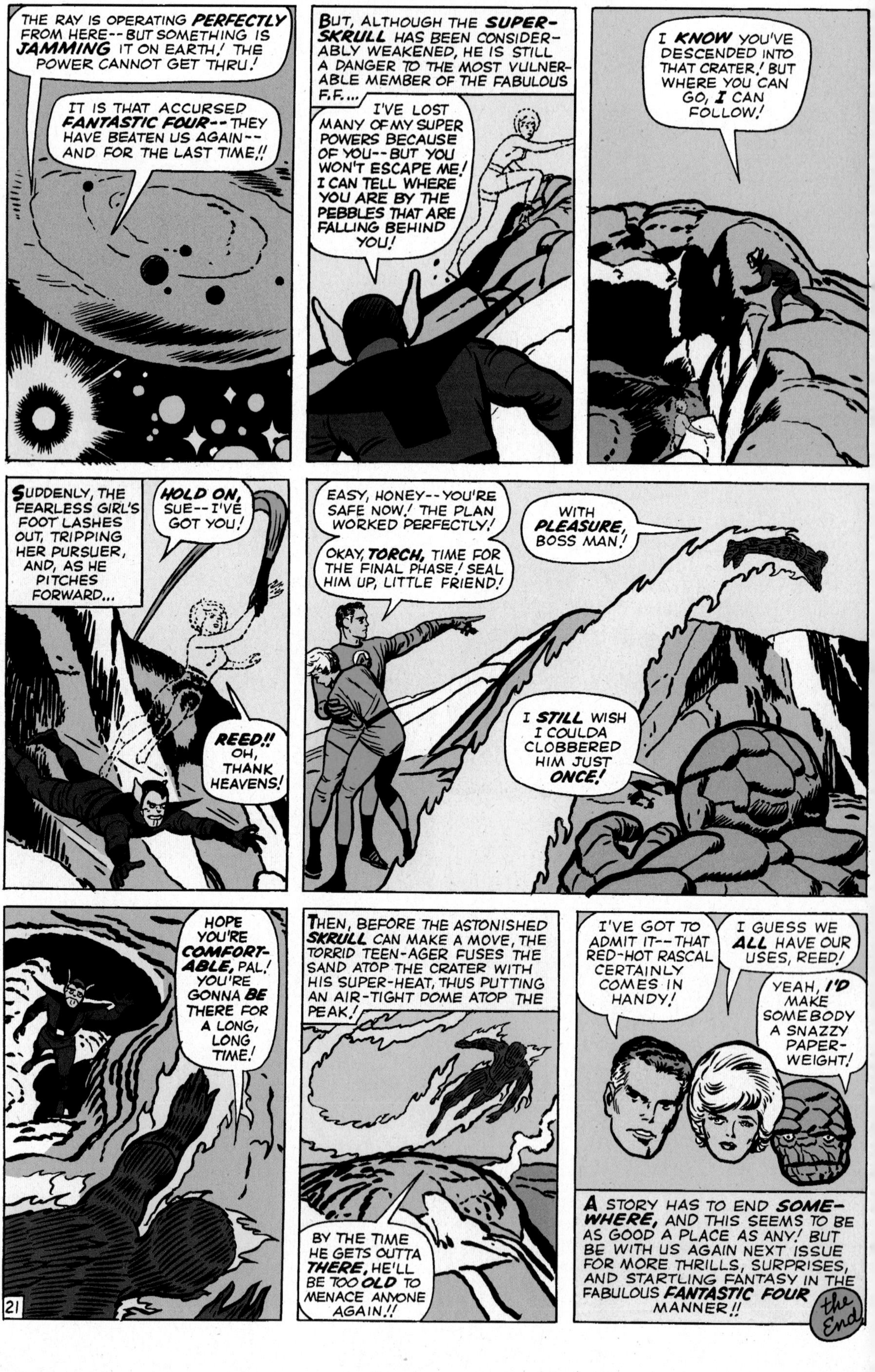
THE RAY IS OPERATING PERFECTLY FROM HERE--BUT SOMETHING IS JAMMING IT ON EARTH! THE POWER CANNOT GET THRU!
IT IS THAT ACCURSED FANTASTIC FOUR--THEY HAVE BEATEN US AGAIN--AND FOR THE LAST TIME!!
BUT, ALTHOUGH THE SUPER-SKRULL HAS BEEN CONSIDERABLY WEAKENED, HE IS STILL A DANGER TO THE MOST VULNERABLE MEMBER OF THE FABULOUS F.F....
I'VE LOST MANY OF MY SUPER POWERS BECAUSE OF YOU--BUT YOU WON'T ESCAPE ME! I CAN TELL WHERE YOU ARE BY THE PEBBLES THAT ARE FALLING BEHIND YOU!
I KNOW YOU'VE DESCENDED INTO THAT CRATER! BUT WHERE YOU CAN GO, I CAN FOLLOW!
SUDDENLY, THE FEARLESS GIRL'S FOOT LASHES OUT, TRIPPING HER PURSUER, AND, AS HE PITCHES FORWARD...
HOLD ON, SUE--I'VE GOT YOU!
REED!! OH, THANK HEAVENS!
EASY, HONEY--YOU'RE SAFE NOW! THE PLAN WORKED PERFECTLY!
OKAY, TORCH, TIME FOR THE FINAL PHASE! SEAL HIM UP, LITTLE FRIEND!
WITH PLEASURE, BOSS MAN!
I STILL WISH I COULDA CLOBBERED HIM JUST ONCE!
HOPE YOU'RE COMFORTABLE, PAL! YOU'RE GONNA BE THERE FOR A LONG, LONG TIME!
21
THEN, BEFORE THE ASTONISHED SKRULL CAN MAKE A MOVE, THE TORRID TEEN-AGER FUSES THE SAND ATOP THE CRATER WITH HIS SUPER-HEAT, THUS PUTTING AN AIR-TIGHT DOME ATOP THE PEAK!
BY THE TIME HE GETS OUTTA THERE, HE'LL BE TOO OLD TO MENACE ANYONE AGAIN!!
I'VE GOT TO ADMIT IT--THAT RED-HOT RASCAL CERTAINLY COMES IN HANDY!
I GUESS WE ALL HAVE OUR USES, REED!
YEAH, I'D MAKE SOMEBODY A SNAZZY PAPER-WEIGHT!
A STORY HAS TO END SOMEWHERE, AND THIS SEEMS TO BE AS GOOD A PLACE AS ANY! BUT BE WITH US AGAIN NEXT ISSUE FOR MORE THRILLS, SURPRISES, AND STARTLING FANTASY IN THE FABULOUS FANTASTIC FOUR MANNER!!
the End

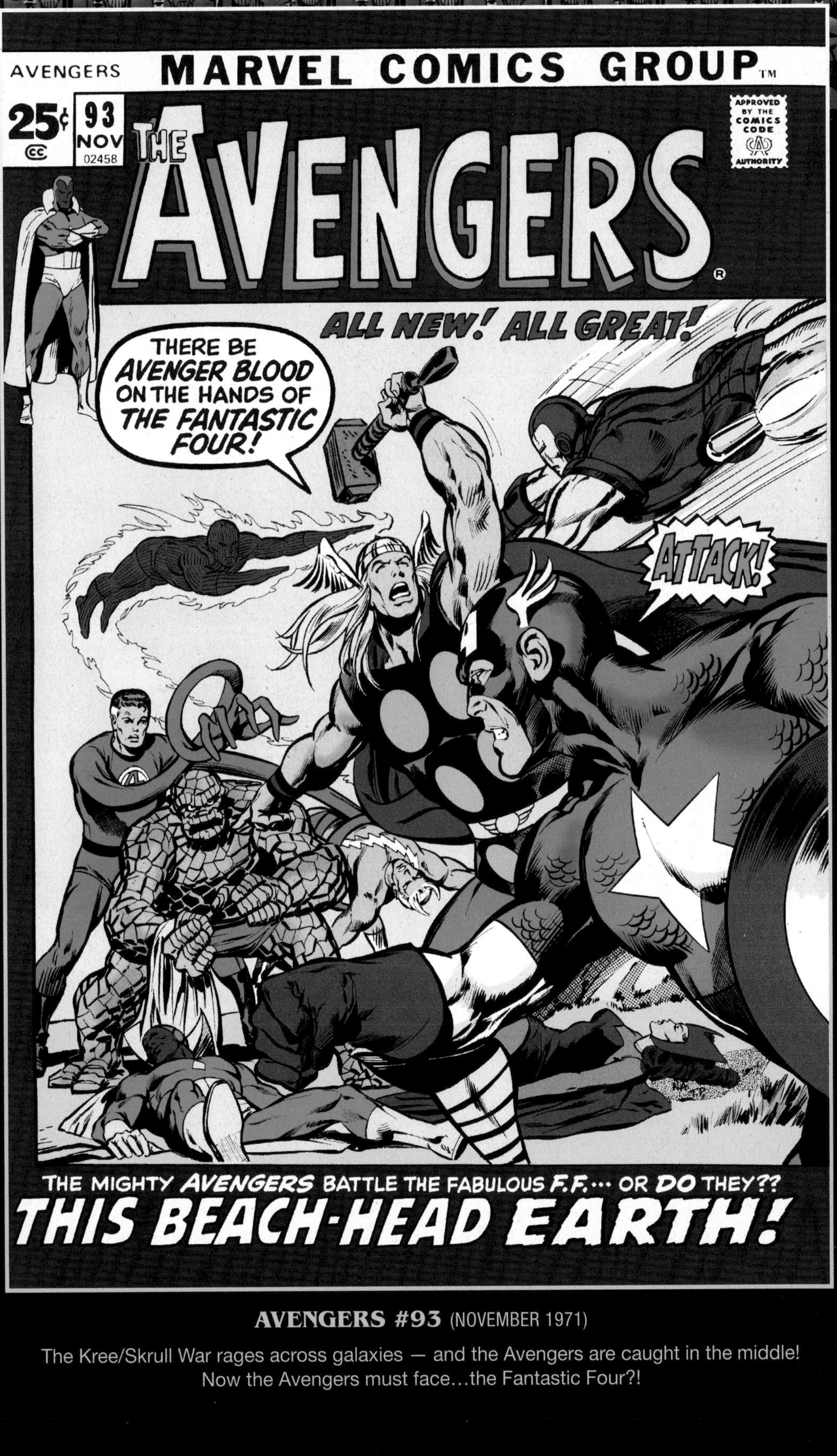
AVENGERS
MARVEL COMICS GROUP
25¢
93
NOV
02458
APPROVED BY THE COMICS CODE AUTHORITY
THE AVENGERS
ALL NEW! ALL GREAT!
THERE BE AVENGER BLOOD ON THE HANDS OF THE FANTASTIC FOUR!
ATTACK!
THE MIGHTY AVENGERS BATTLE THE FABULOUS F.F.... OR DO THEY??
THIS BEACH-HEAD EARTH!

AVENGERS #93 (NOVEMBER 1971)

The Kree/Skrull War rages across galaxies — and the Avengers are caught in the middle! Now the Avengers must face...the Fantastic Four?!

THE MIGHTY AVENGERS!®

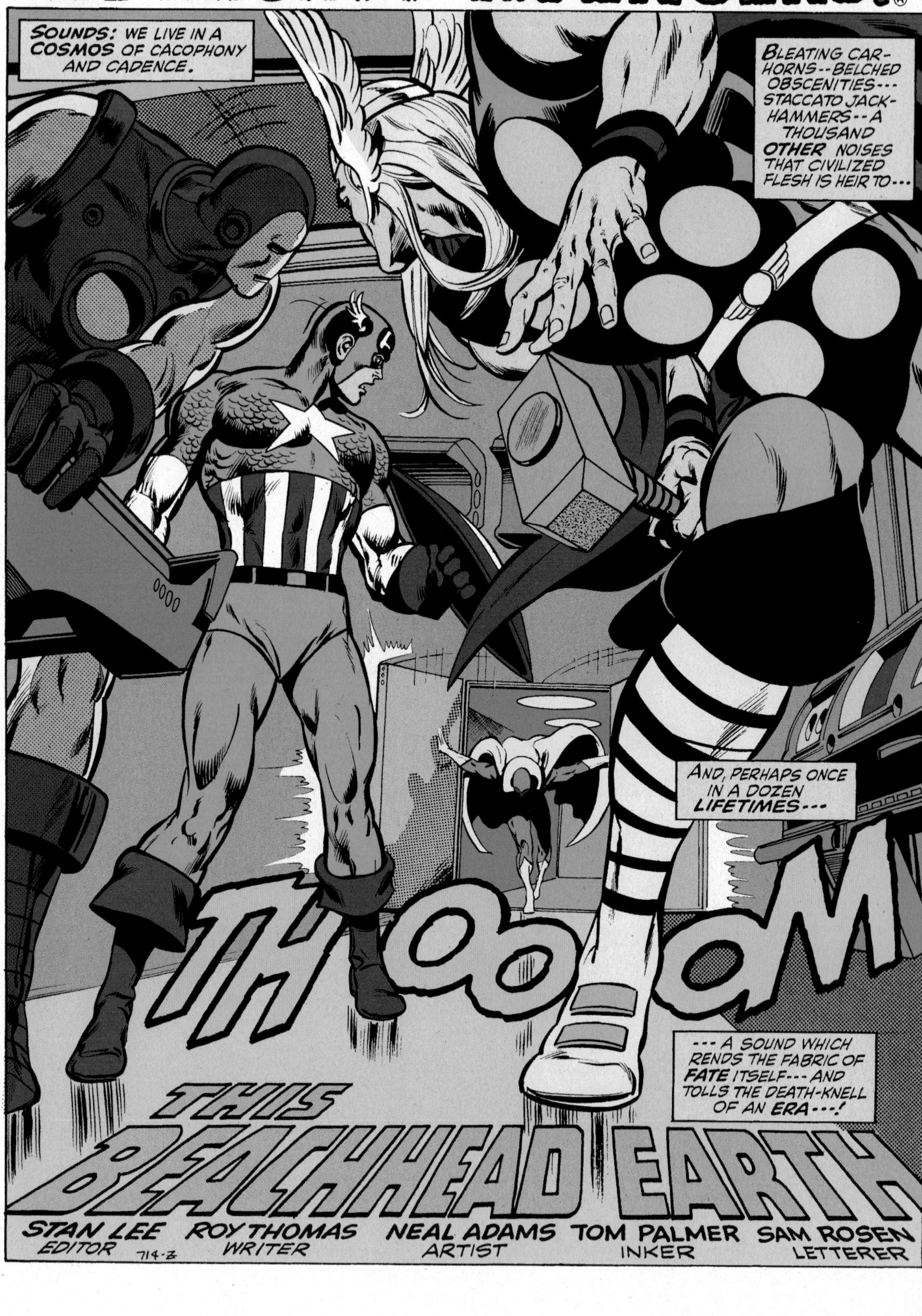

SOUNDS: WE LIVE IN A COSMOS OF CACOPHONY AND CADENCE.
BLEATING CAR-HORNS--BELCHED OBSCENITIES--- STACCATO JACK-HAMMERS--A THOUSAND OTHER NOISES THAT CIVILIZED FLESH IS HEIR TO---
AND, PERHAPS ONCE IN A DOZEN LIFETIMES---
THOOOM
---A SOUND WHICH RENDS THE FABRIC OF FATE ITSELF---AND TOLLS THE DEATH-KNELL OF AN ERA---!
THIS BEACHHEAD EARTH!
STAN LEE EDITOR
ROY THOMAS WRITER
NEAL ADAMS ARTIST
TOM PALMER INKER
SAM ROSEN LETTERER

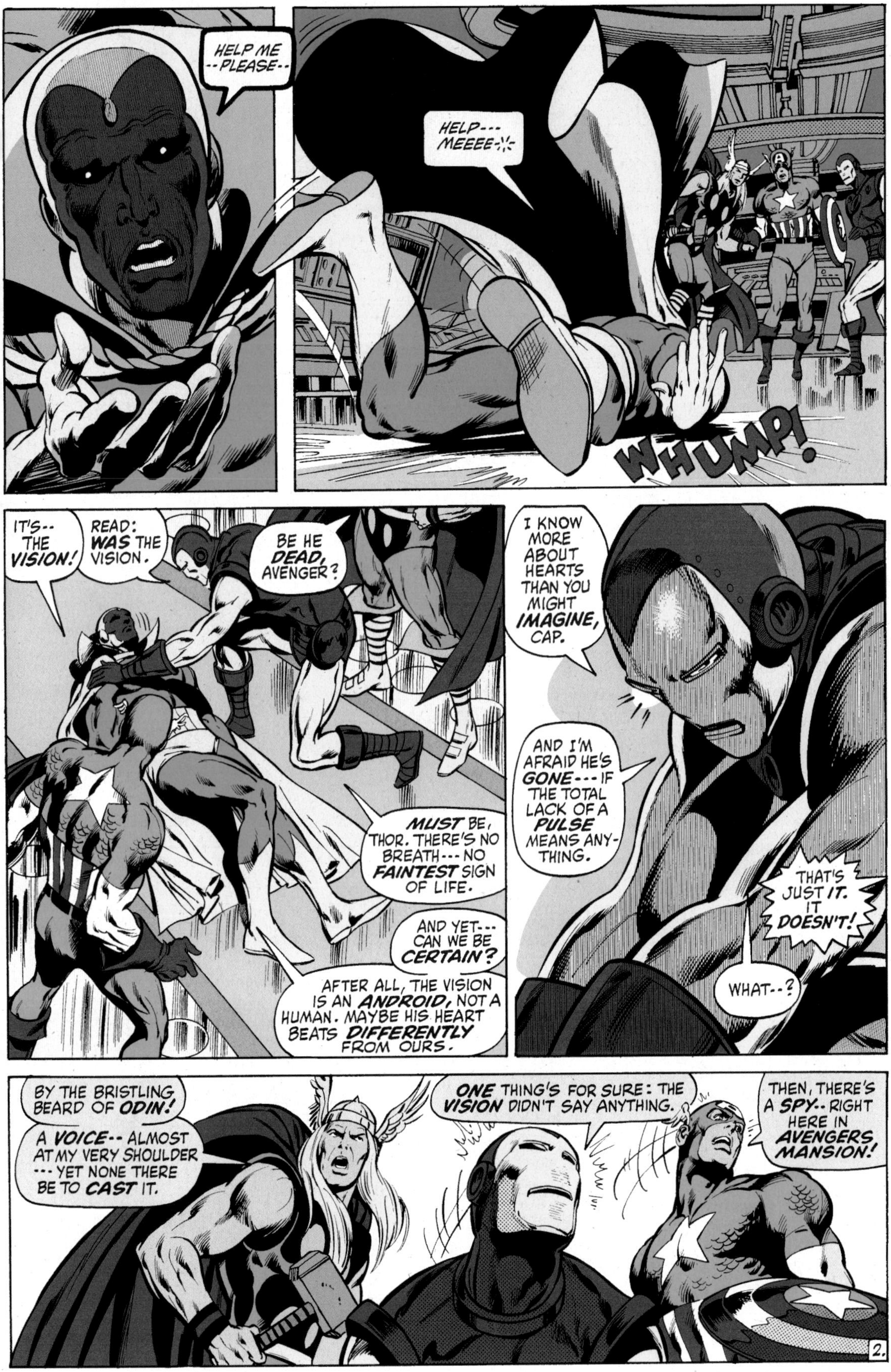
HELP ME --PLEASE--
HELP--- MEEEE-!-
WHUMP!
IT'S-- THE VISION!
READ: WAS THE VISION.
BE HE DEAD, AVENGER?
MUST BE, THOR. THERE'S NO BREATH--- NO FAINTEST SIGN OF LIFE.
AND YET--- CAN WE BE CERTAIN?
AFTER ALL, THE VISION IS AN ANDROID, NOT A HUMAN. MAYBE HIS HEART BEATS DIFFERENTLY FROM OURS.
I KNOW MORE ABOUT HEARTS THAN YOU MIGHT IMAGINE, CAP.
AND I'M AFRAID HE'S GONE--- IF THE TOTAL LACK OF A PULSE MEANS ANYTHING.
THAT'S JUST IT. IT DOESN'T!
WHAT--?
BY THE BRISTLING BEARD OF ODIN!
A VOICE-- ALMOST AT MY VERY SHOULDER --- YET NONE THERE BE TO CAST IT.
ONE THING'S FOR SURE: THE VISION DIDN'T SAY ANYTHING.
THEN, THERE'S A SPY-- RIGHT HERE IN AVENGERS MANSION!
2.

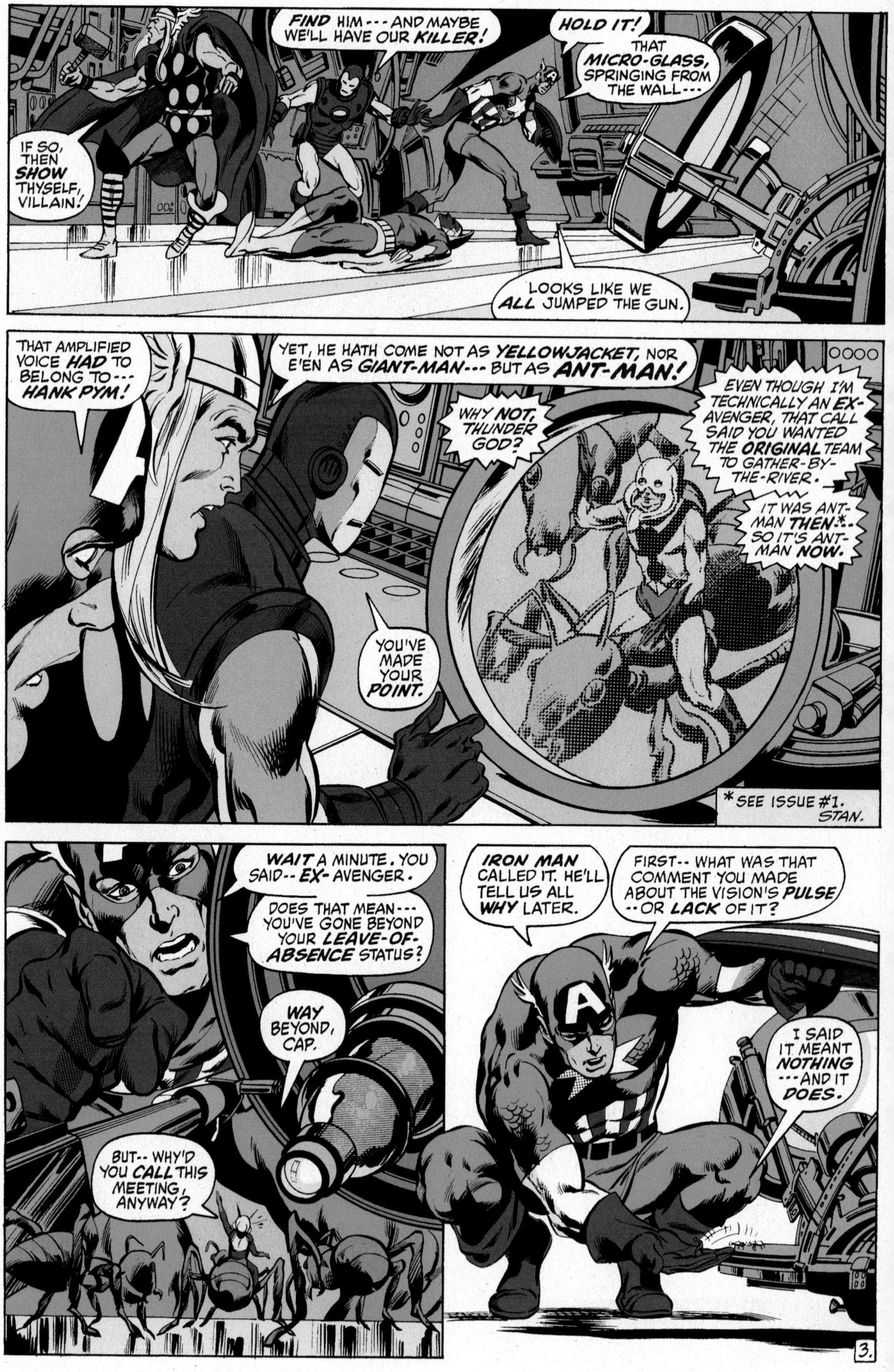
FIND HIM--- AND MAYBE WE'LL HAVE OUR KILLER!
IF SO, THEN SHOW THYSELF, VILLAIN!
HOLD IT!
THAT MICRO-GLASS, SPRINGING FROM THE WALL---
LOOKS LIKE WE ALL JUMPED THE GUN.
THAT AMPLIFIED VOICE HAD TO BELONG TO--- HANK PYM!
YET, HE HATH COME NOT AS YELLOWJACKET, NOR E'EN AS GIANT-MAN--- BUT AS ANT-MAN!
WHY NOT, THUNDER GOD?
EVEN THOUGH I'M TECHNICALLY AN EX-AVENGER, THAT CALL SAID YOU WANTED THE ORIGINAL TEAM TO GATHER-BY-THE-RIVER.
IT WAS ANT-MAN THEN*-- SO IT'S ANT-MAN NOW.
YOU'VE MADE YOUR POINT.
*SEE ISSUE #1. STAN.
WAIT A MINUTE. YOU SAID-- EX-AVENGER.
DOES THAT MEAN--- YOU'VE GONE BEYOND YOUR LEAVE-OF-ABSENCE STATUS?
WAY BEYOND, CAP.
BUT-- WHY'D YOU CALL THIS MEETING, ANYWAY?
IRON MAN CALLED IT. HE'LL TELL US ALL WHY LATER.
FIRST-- WHAT WAS THAT COMMENT YOU MADE ABOUT THE VISION'S PULSE --OR LACK OF IT?
I SAID IT MEANT NOTHING ---AND IT DOES.
3.

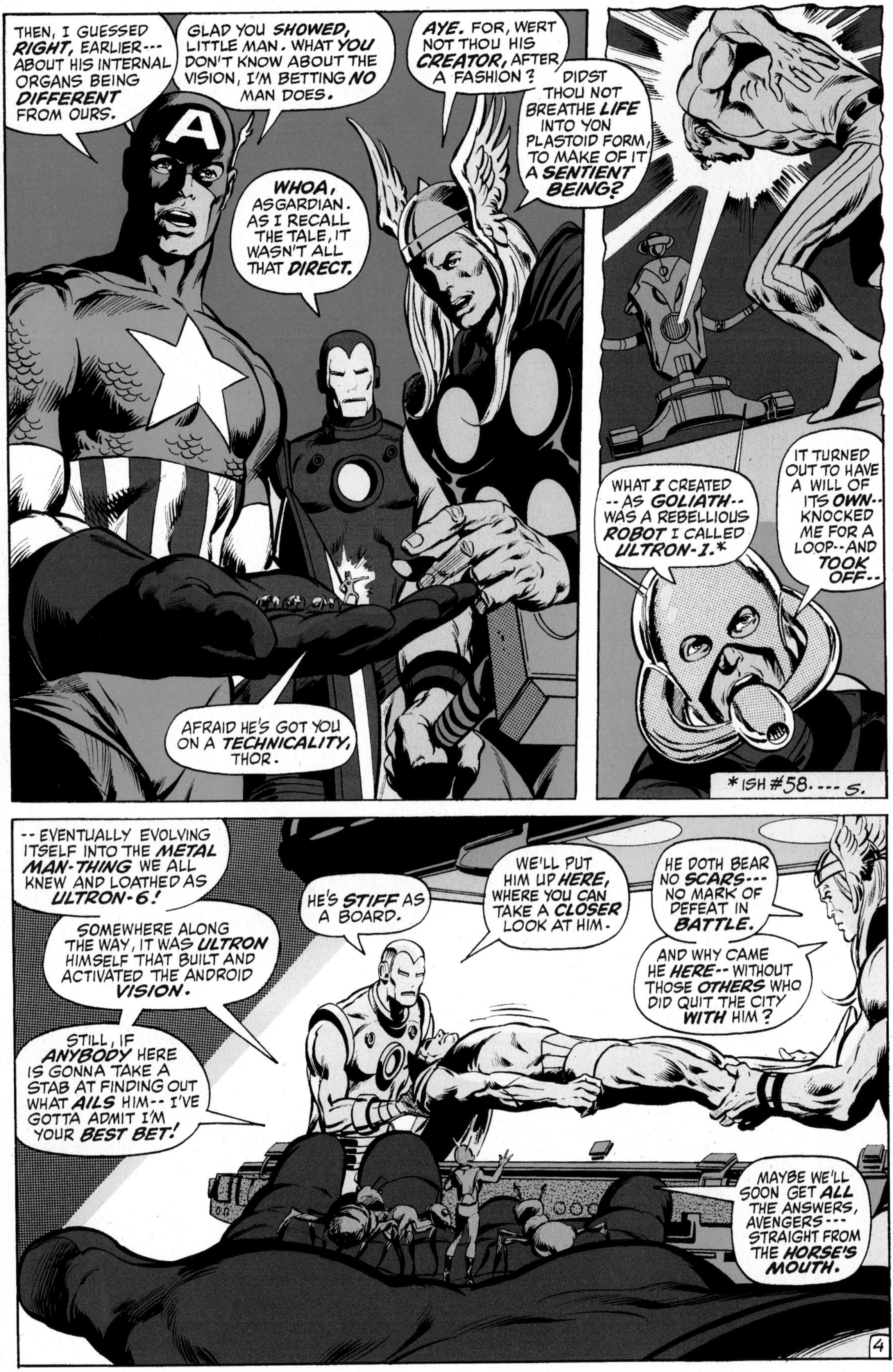
THEN, I GUESSED RIGHT, EARLIER--- ABOUT HIS INTERNAL ORGANS BEING DIFFERENT FROM OURS.
GLAD YOU SHOWED, LITTLE MAN. WHAT YOU DON'T KNOW ABOUT THE VISION, I'M BETTING NO MAN DOES.
AYE. FOR, WERT NOT THOU HIS CREATOR, AFTER A FASHION?
DIDST THOU NOT BREATHE LIFE INTO YON PLASTOID FORM, TO MAKE OF IT A SENTIENT BEING?
WHOA, ASGARDIAN. AS I RECALL THE TALE, IT WASN'T ALL THAT DIRECT.
AFRAID HE'S GOT YOU ON A TECHNICALITY, THOR.
WHAT I CREATED --AS GOLIATH-- WAS A REBELLIOUS ROBOT I CALLED ULTRON-1.*
IT TURNED OUT TO HAVE A WILL OF ITS OWN-- KNOCKED ME FOR A LOOP--AND TOOK OFF--
*ISH #58.---S.
--EVENTUALLY EVOLVING ITSELF INTO THE METAL MAN-THING WE ALL KNEW AND LOATHED AS ULTRON-6!
SOMEWHERE ALONG THE WAY, IT WAS ULTRON HIMSELF THAT BUILT AND ACTIVATED THE ANDROID VISION.
STILL, IF ANYBODY HERE IS GONNA TAKE A STAB AT FINDING OUT WHAT AILS HIM-- I'VE GOTTA ADMIT I'M YOUR BEST BET!
HE'S STIFF AS A BOARD.
WE'LL PUT HIM UP HERE, WHERE YOU CAN TAKE A CLOSER LOOK AT HIM.
HE DOTH BEAR NO SCARS--- NO MARK OF DEFEAT IN BATTLE.
AND WHY CAME HE HERE-- WITHOUT THOSE OTHERS WHO DID QUIT THE CITY WITH HIM?
MAYBE WE'LL SOON GET ALL THE ANSWERS, AVENGERS--- STRAIGHT FROM THE HORSE'S MOUTH.
4

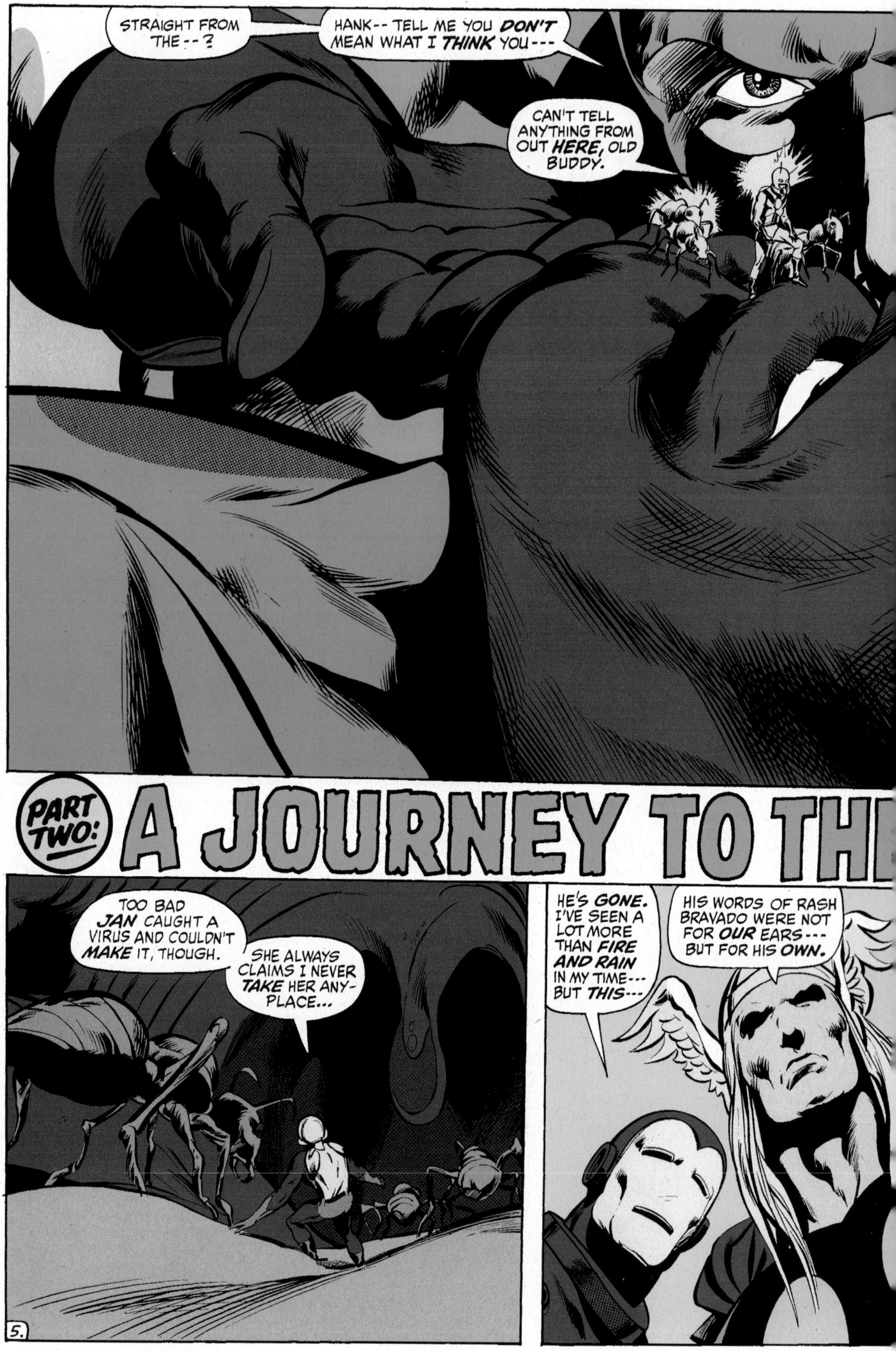

STRAIGHT FROM THE--?
HANK-- TELL ME YOU DON'T MEAN WHAT I THINK YOU---
CAN'T TELL ANYTHING FROM OUT HERE, OLD BUDDY.
PART TWO: A JOURNEY TO TH
TOO BAD JAN CAUGHT A VIRUS AND COULDN'T MAKE IT, THOUGH.
SHE ALWAYS CLAIMS I NEVER TAKE HER ANY-PLACE...
HE'S GONE. I'VE SEEN A LOT MORE THAN FIRE AND RAIN IN MY TIME--- BUT THIS---
HIS WORDS OF RASH BRAVADO WERE NOT FOR OUR EARS--- BUT FOR HIS OWN.
5.

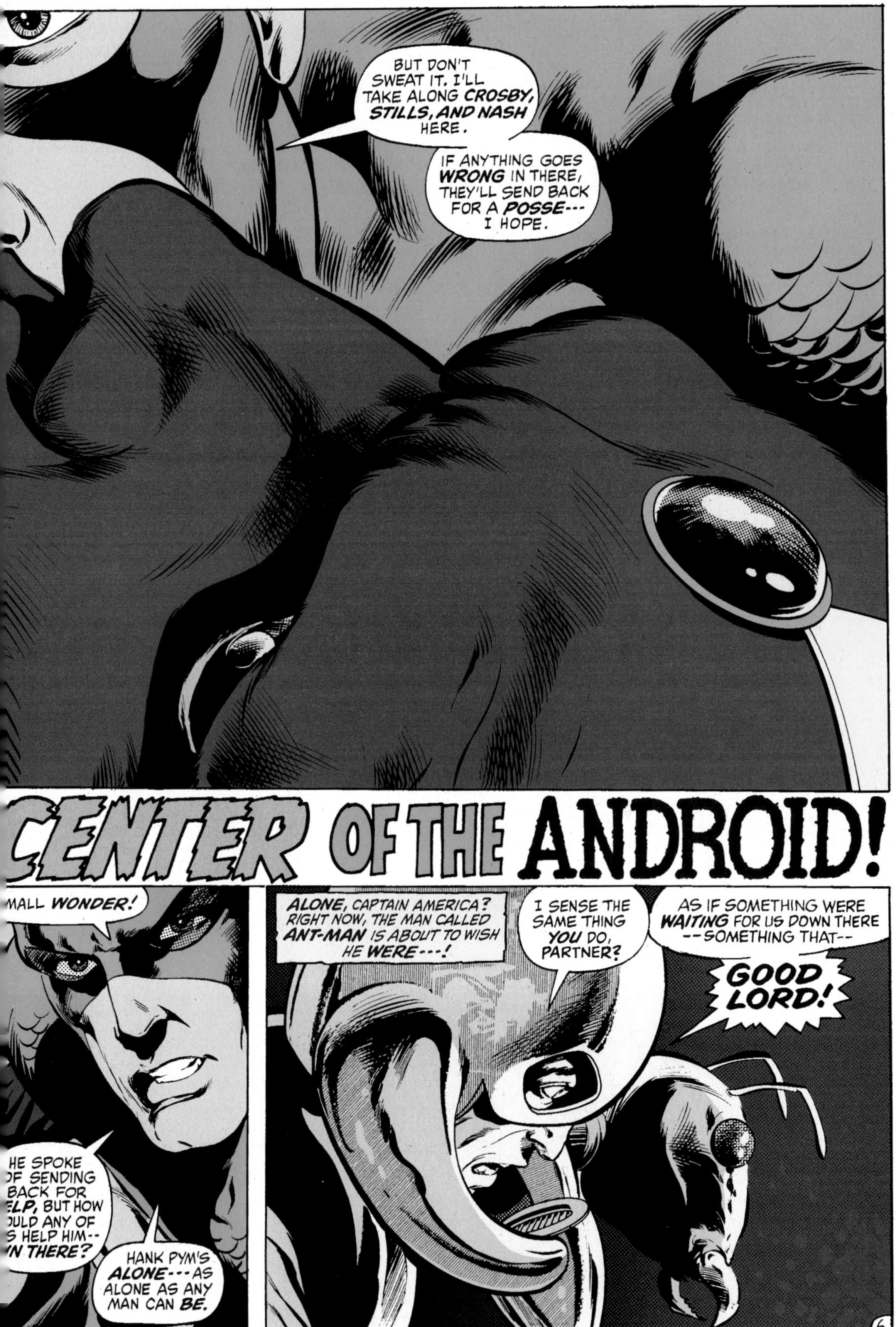

BUT DON'T SWEAT IT. I'LL TAKE ALONG CROSBY, STILLS, AND NASH HERE.
IF ANYTHING GOES WRONG IN THERE, THEY'LL SEND BACK FOR A POSSE--- I HOPE.
CENTER OF THE ANDROID!
MALL WONDER!
HE SPOKE
OF SENDING
BACK FOR
ELP, BUT HOW
OULD ANY OF
S HELP HIM--
N THERE?
HANK PYM'S ALONE---AS ALONE AS ANY MAN CAN BE.
ALONE, CAPTAIN AMERICA? RIGHT NOW, THE MAN CALLED ANT-MAN IS ABOUT TO WISH HE WERE---!
I SENSE THE SAME THING YOU DO, PARTNER?
AS IF SOMETHING WERE WAITING FOR US DOWN THERE --SOMETHING THAT--
GOOD LORD!
6.

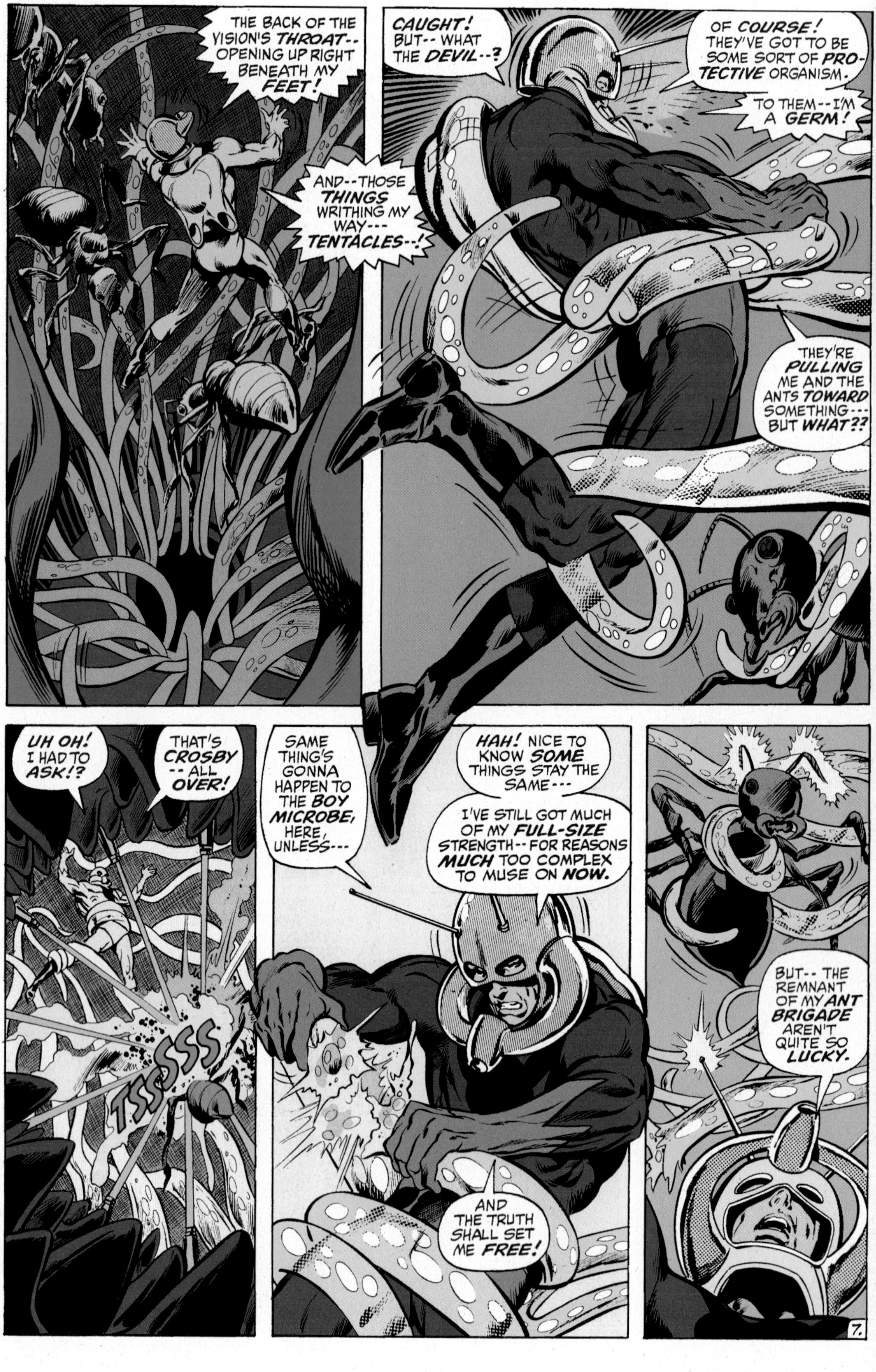
THE BACK OF THE VISION'S THROAT-- OPENING UP RIGHT BENEATH MY FEET!
AND--THOSE THINGS WRITHING MY WAY--- TENTACLES--!
CAUGHT! BUT-- WHAT THE DEVIL--?
OF COURSE! THEY'VE GOT TO BE SOME SORT OF PROTECTIVE ORGANISM.
TO THEM--I'M A GERM!
THEY'RE PULLING ME AND THE ANTS TOWARD SOMETHING--- BUT WHAT??
UH OH! I HAD TO ASK!?
THAT'S CROSBY --ALL OVER!
TSSSSSS
SAME THING'S GONNA HAPPEN TO THE BOY MICROBE, HERE, UNLESS---
HAH! NICE TO KNOW SOME THINGS STAY THE SAME---
I'VE STILL GOT MUCH OF MY FULL-SIZE STRENGTH--FOR REASONS MUCH TOO COMPLEX TO MUSE ON NOW.
AND THE TRUTH SHALL SET ME FREE!
BUT-- THE REMNANT OF MY ANT BRIGADE AREN'T QUITE SO LUCKY.
7.

HUMAN BEINGS ARE *FUNNY*-- THEY THINK NO LIVING THING BUT *THEMSELVES* CAPABLE OF FEELING *PAIN*.

THAT'S BECAUSE--- THEY'VE NEVER HEARD AN ANT *SCREAM*. WELL, *I* HAVE--

-- AND IT'S A SOUND TO *HAUNT* A LIFETIME WORTH OF DREAMS!

A SOUND LIKE LOST SOULS IN *TORMENT*-- OR THE WAILING OF A FORE-SAKEN *CHILD*---

--AND I DON'T *EVER* WANT TO HEAR THAT SOUND *AGAIN!*

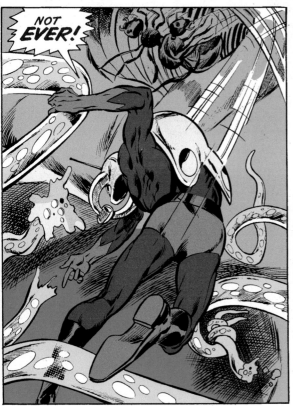

NOT EVER!

SO, *HEED* MY ELECTRONICALLY-BEAMED ORDERS, LITTLE FRIENDS-- AND *LEAVE* THE ANDROID'S BODY---*NOW!*

I CAN'T WATCH OUT FOR ONE BASHFUL *BIOCHEMIST* -- AND TWO *SIX-LEGGED* SIDEKICKS, TO BOOT--

WHERE *ANT-MAN* WALKS TODAY-- HE WALKS *ALONE!*

8

THAT BIT ABOUT "WALKING" WAS *FIGURATIVELY* SPEAKING, NATCH.

IN POINT OF FACT, IT'S TIME I GOT SOME USE OUT OF MY MINIATURIZED *BACK-PACK!*

STILL, I'VE *TIMED* THEM. THEY *BLAST AWAY* FOR FIVE SECONDS -- THEN *RECHARGE* FOR FIVE.

THOSE *SPRAYS* UP THERE ARE LIKE *ANTIBODIES* --- AND THEY'RE NOT GONNA TAKE *KINDLY* TO MY PASSING *THRU* ---

SO, WHILE IT'S *LULL- BEFORE- THE-STORM* TIME ---

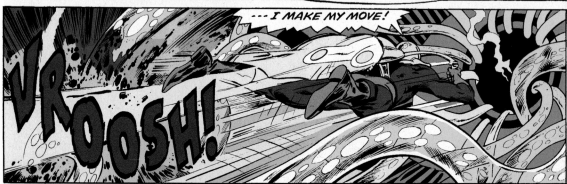

--- *I MAKE MY MOVE!*

VROOSH!

TSSSSS

CLOSE -- BUT NO *CIGAR.*

HMMM -- IF ALL THE VISION'S BODILY PROCESSES ARE *INTACT*, THAT *PROVES* MY POINT.

THE ONLY WAY TO TRULY *KILL* AN ANDROID -- IS TO *DISMANTLE* HIM.

THAT MEANS THE TROUBLE LIES IN -- HIS ARTIFICIAL *BRAIN.*

SOMEHOW, IT'S NOT MAKING *CONTACT* WITH THE REST OF HIS BODY.

NEXT STEP: A TWO-WAY *TRIP* TO THE CRANIAL CAVITY ---

--- WHICH MEANS GOING *FORWARD*, THEN *UP.*

Y'KNOW, ONLY THING *MISSING* SO FAR IS AN ASSISTANT WHO'S BUILT LIKE *RAQUEL WELCH.*

'COURSE, I'M A *HAPPILY- MARRIED* MAN --

BUT JUST THE *SAME*, I --

YEEEOWWW

ZOT!

9.

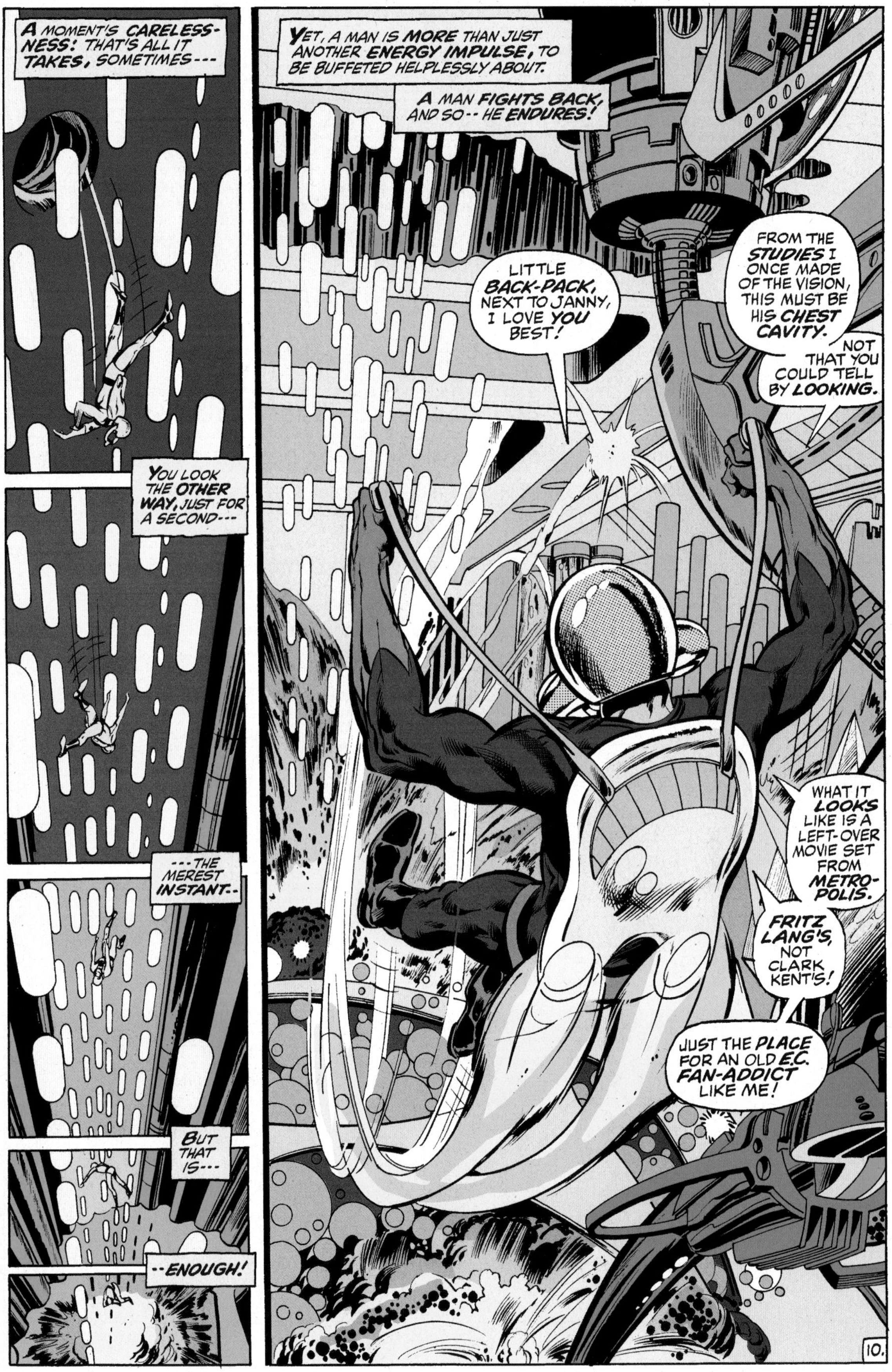
A MOMENT'S CARELESSNESS: THAT'S ALL IT TAKES, SOMETIMES---
YOU LOOK THE OTHER WAY, JUST FOR A SECOND---
---THE MEREST INSTANT--
BUT THAT IS---
--ENOUGH!
YET, A MAN IS MORE THAN JUST ANOTHER ENERGY IMPULSE, TO BE BUFFETED HELPLESSLY ABOUT.
A MAN FIGHTS BACK, AND SO-- HE ENDURES!
LITTLE BACK-PACK, NEXT TO JANNY, I LOVE YOU BEST!
FROM THE STUDIES I ONCE MADE OF THE VISION, THIS MUST BE HIS CHEST CAVITY.
NOT THAT YOU COULD TELL BY LOOKING.
WHAT IT LOOKS LIKE IS A LEFT-OVER MOVIE SET FROM METROPOLIS.
FRITZ LANG'S, NOT CLARK KENT'S!
JUST THE PLACE FOR AN OLD E.C. FAN-ADDICT LIKE ME!
10.

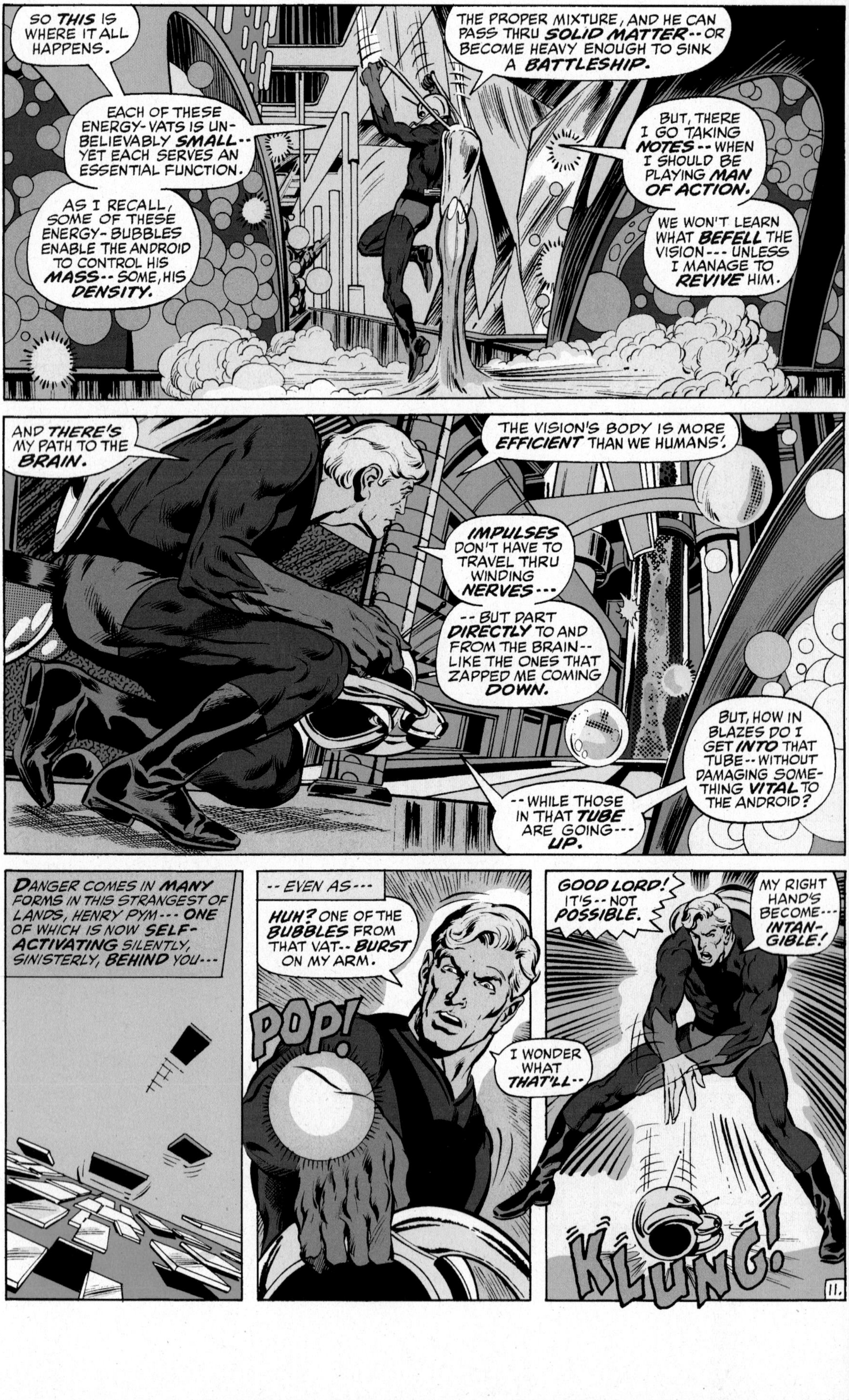
SO THIS IS WHERE IT ALL HAPPENS.
THE PROPER MIXTURE, AND HE CAN PASS THRU SOLID MATTER -- OR BECOME HEAVY ENOUGH TO SINK A BATTLESHIP.
EACH OF THESE ENERGY-VATS IS UNBELIEVABLY SMALL -- YET EACH SERVES AN ESSENTIAL FUNCTION.
AS I RECALL, SOME OF THESE ENERGY-BUBBLES ENABLE THE ANDROID TO CONTROL HIS MASS -- SOME, HIS DENSITY.
BUT, THERE I GO TAKING NOTES -- WHEN I SHOULD BE PLAYING MAN OF ACTION.
WE WON'T LEARN WHAT BEFELL THE VISION --- UNLESS I MANAGE TO REVIVE HIM.
AND THERE'S MY PATH TO THE BRAIN.
THE VISION'S BODY IS MORE EFFICIENT THAN WE HUMANS!
IMPULSES DON'T HAVE TO TRAVEL THRU WINDING NERVES ---
-- BUT DART DIRECTLY TO AND FROM THE BRAIN -- LIKE THE ONES THAT ZAPPED ME COMING DOWN.
-- WHILE THOSE IN THAT TUBE ARE GOING --- UP.
BUT, HOW IN BLAZES DO I GET INTO THAT TUBE -- WITHOUT DAMAGING SOMETHING VITAL TO THE ANDROID?
DANGER COMES IN MANY FORMS IN THIS STRANGEST OF LANDS, HENRY PYM --- ONE OF WHICH IS NOW SELF-ACTIVATING SILENTLY, SINISTERLY, BEHIND YOU ---
-- EVEN AS ---
HUH? ONE OF THE BUBBLES FROM THAT VAT -- BURST ON MY ARM.
POP!
I WONDER WHAT THAT'LL --
GOOD LORD! IT'S -- NOT POSSIBLE.
MY RIGHT HAND'S BECOME --- INTANGIBLE!
KLUNG!

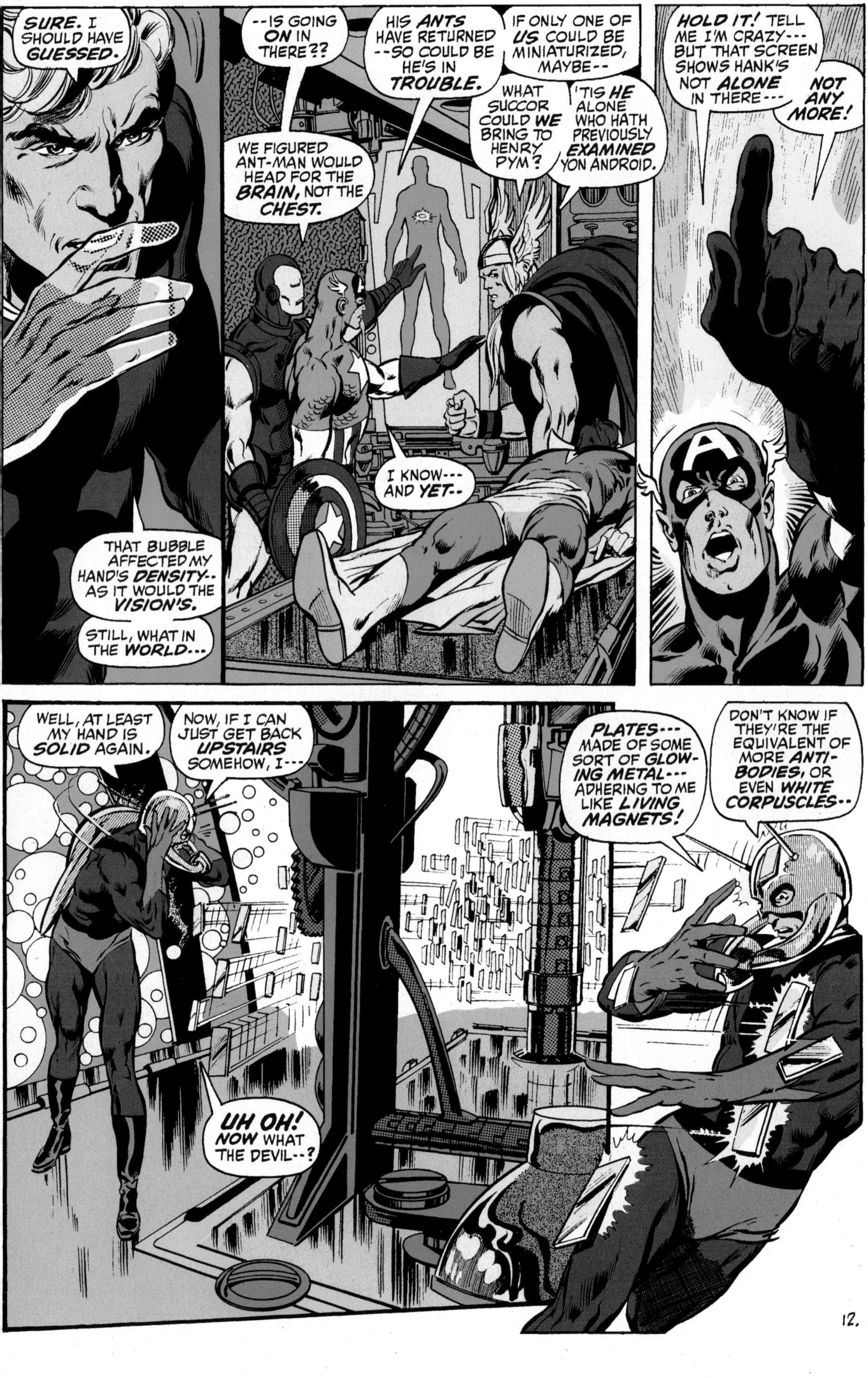
SURE. I SHOULD HAVE GUESSED.
THAT BUBBLE AFFECTED MY HAND'S DENSITY-- AS IT WOULD THE VISION'S.
STILL, WHAT IN THE WORLD...
--IS GOING ON IN THERE??
WE FIGURED ANT-MAN WOULD HEAD FOR THE BRAIN, NOT THE CHEST.
HIS ANTS HAVE RETURNED --SO COULD BE HE'S IN TROUBLE.
I KNOW--- AND YET--
IF ONLY ONE OF US COULD BE MINIATURIZED, MAYBE--
WHAT SUCCOR COULD WE BRING TO HENRY PYM?
'TIS HE ALONE WHO HATH PREVIOUSLY EXAMINED YON ANDROID.
HOLD IT! TELL ME I'M CRAZY--- BUT THAT SCREEN SHOWS HANK'S NOT ALONE IN THERE---
NOT ANY MORE!
WELL, AT LEAST MY HAND IS SOLID AGAIN.
NOW, IF I CAN JUST GET BACK UPSTAIRS SOMEHOW, I---
UH OH! NOW WHAT THE DEVIL--?
PLATES--- MADE OF SOME SORT OF GLOWING METAL--- ADHERING TO ME LIKE LIVING MAGNETS!
DON'T KNOW IF THEY'RE THE EQUIVALENT OF MORE ANTI-BODIES, OR EVEN WHITE CORPUSCLES--

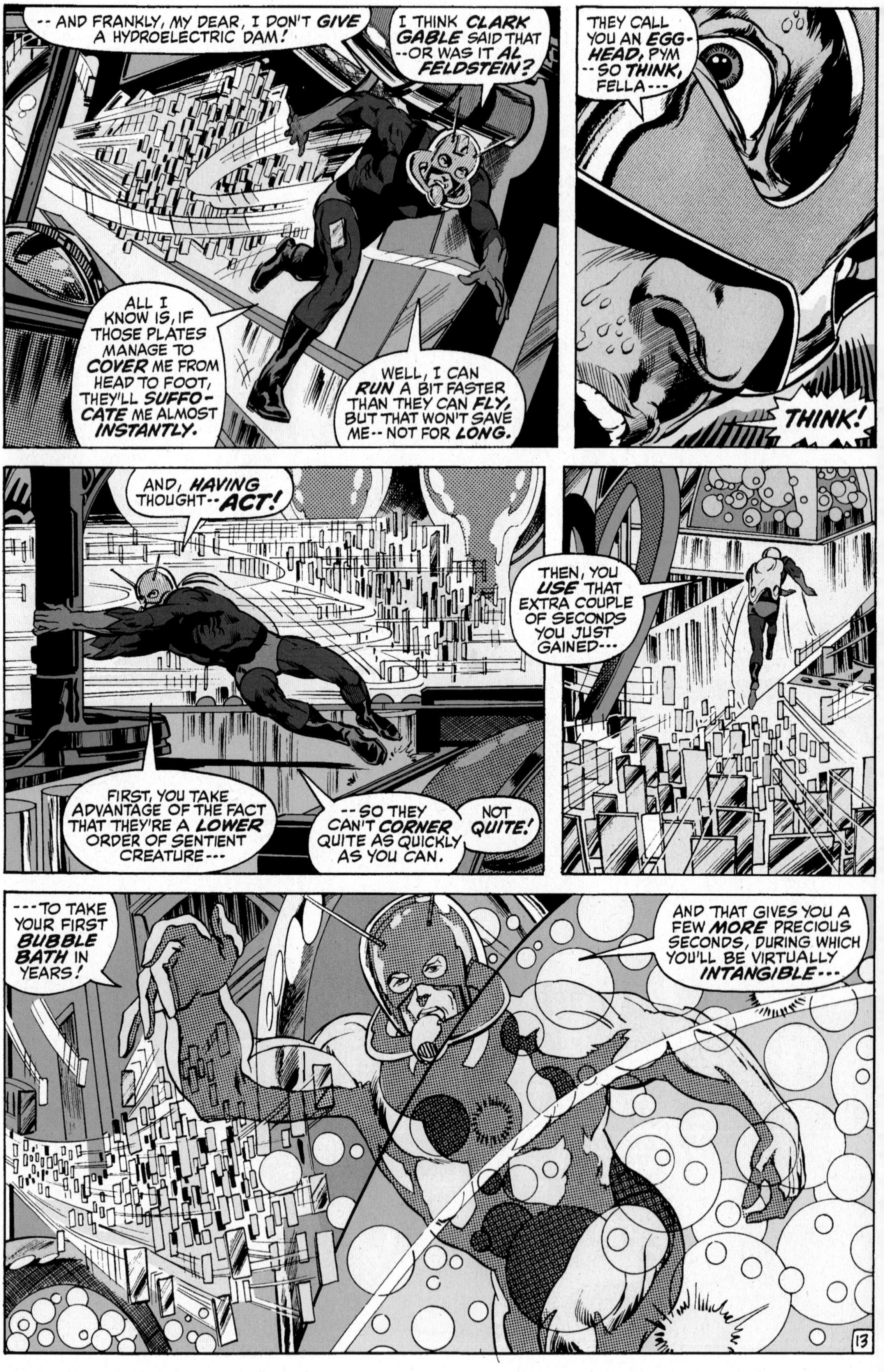
-- AND FRANKLY, MY DEAR, I DON'T GIVE A HYDROELECTRIC DAM!
I THINK CLARK GABLE SAID THAT --OR WAS IT AL FELDSTEIN?
ALL I KNOW IS, IF THOSE PLATES MANAGE TO COVER ME FROM HEAD TO FOOT, THEY'LL SUFFOCATE ME ALMOST INSTANTLY.
WELL, I CAN RUN A BIT FASTER THAN THEY CAN FLY, BUT THAT WON'T SAVE ME-- NOT FOR LONG.
THEY CALL YOU AN EGGHEAD, PYM --SO THINK, FELLA---
THINK!
AND, HAVING THOUGHT--ACT!
FIRST, YOU TAKE ADVANTAGE OF THE FACT THAT THEY'RE A LOWER ORDER OF SENTIENT CREATURE---
--SO THEY CAN'T CORNER QUITE AS QUICKLY AS YOU CAN.
NOT QUITE!
THEN, YOU USE THAT EXTRA COUPLE OF SECONDS YOU JUST GAINED---
---TO TAKE YOUR FIRST BUBBLE BATH IN YEARS!
AND THAT GIVES YOU A FEW MORE PRECIOUS SECONDS, DURING WHICH YOU'LL BE VIRTUALLY INTANGIBLE---
13

-- TO MAKE TRACKS FOR THIS FEEDER-TUBE, WHICH IS WHERE I WANTED TO GO IN THE FIRST PLACE.

'COURSE, IF ANY ONE PART OF MY LITTLE HYPOTHESIS IS WRONG--

SCRATCH ONE ANT-MAN!

HOO-HAH! THAT STOPPED 'EM. I DIDN'T THINK THE BUBBLES WOULD AFFECT THEM THE WAY THEY DID ME.

PLAK!

BUT-- ALL OF A SUDDEN--- CAN'T BREATHE!

NO OXYGEN-- IN HERE-- LIKE IN REST OF THE BODY--!

WELL, I'VE ADDED A FEW EXTRAS TO MY CYBERNETIC HELMET SINCE THE GOOD OLD DAYS--

SNIK

SNIK

-- INCLUDING AN OXYGEN UNIT, AND A PLEXIGLASS AIR-MASK.

THAT'S MORE LIKE IT.

NO NEED FOR MY BACK-PACK THIS TIME, EITHER.

ALL I HAVE TO DO IS STEP INTO THE IMPULSE-STREAM--

-- AND IT'S NEXT STEP HEAD CITY!

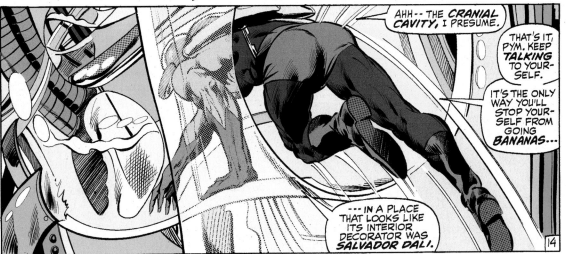

AHH-- THE CRANIAL CAVITY, I PRESUME.

THAT'S IT, PYM. KEEP TALKING TO YOURSELF.

IT'S THE ONLY WAY YOU'LL STOP YOURSELF FROM GOING BANANAS--

--- IN A PLACE THAT LOOKS LIKE ITS INTERIOR DECORATOR WAS SALVADOR DALI.

14

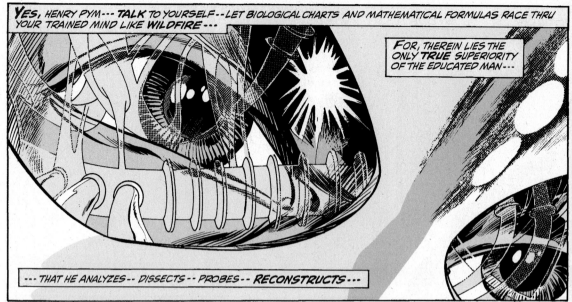

YES, HENRY PYM--- *TALK* TO YOURSELF--LET BIOLOGICAL CHARTS AND MATHEMATICAL FORMULAS RACE THRU YOUR TRAINED MIND LIKE *WILDFIRE*---

FOR, THEREIN LIES THE ONLY *TRUE* SUPERIORITY OF THE EDUCATED MAN---

--- THAT HE ANALYZES-- DISSECTS-- PROBES-- *RECONSTRUCTS*---

--TILL THE PIECES OF A MADDENING MECHANICAL *PUZZLE* FALL NEATLY INTO PLACE---

--- OR SO HE *HOPES!*

WELL, TIME TO *FISH*---

-- OR *CUT BAIT!*

THIS *WIRE*-- LOOSE, *DAMAGED*-- THE ONLY THING IN THE BRAIN-CASE THAT DOESN'T QUITE *FIT!*

I CAN *REPAIR* IT--- BUT IF I'M *WRONG*-- IF SOME NORMAL *AUTOMATIC* PROCESS DISCONNECTED IT---

-- I MAY CAUSE AN INTERNAL REACTION THAT'LL FINISH THE VISION FOR *GOOD.*

MOMENTS PASS--AN ETERNITY OF THEM-- THEN--

A *SOUND.* LIKE A GENTLE *HUMMING*-- STEADY, CONSTANT---

THAT MEANS --HIS BRAIN IS *WORKING* AGAIN.

THEN I'D BETTER *MOVE* IT, BEFORE-- *WHAT'S THIS* ??

A *MYSTERY* WITHIN AN ENIGMA, ANT-MAN-- ONE OF WHICH OUR READERS *MAY* LEARN ONE DAY---

15

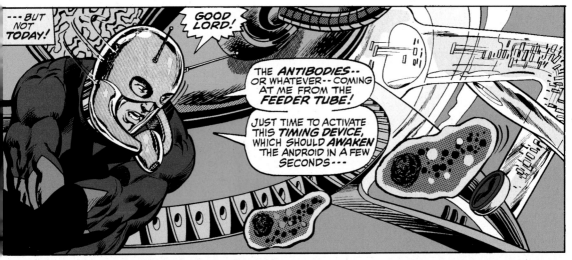

---BUT NOT TODAY!

GOOD LORD!

THE *ANTIBODIES*-- OR WHATEVER-- COMING AT ME FROM THE *FEEDER TUBE!*

JUST TIME TO ACTIVATE THIS *TIMING DEVICE,* WHICH SHOULD *AWAKEN* THE ANDROID IN A FEW SECONDS---

---THEN *RUN* LIKE THE DEVIL---

OTHERWISE, I'LL BE *TRAPPED* IN HERE WHEN THE VISION WAKES UP--

-- WHICH WOULD BE A DEFINITE *DISASTER.*

I MUST BE NEAR AN *ORIFICE.* THE HOT-PLATES ARE *TURNING BACK.*

-- AND PRAY THAT THIS REALLY IS THE *NASAL CAVITY* I *THINK* IT IS.

YEP-- EITHER THAT'S THE LIGHT OF *DAY* AHEAD---

-- OR ELSE THE VISION'S BEEN GOBBLING *FIREFLIES!*

THUS DO BRAVE MEN *JEST,* WHEN DEATH TURNS TAIL AND FLEES---AND THUS *ENDS* PERHAPS THE STRANGEST *RESCUE MISSION* IN HISTORY---

YET, IT MAY WELL BE THAT THIS HAS BEEN BUT A PALTRY *PROLOGUE*--- TO THE MOST *PORTENTOUS* AVENGERS SAGA OF *ALL*---!

16

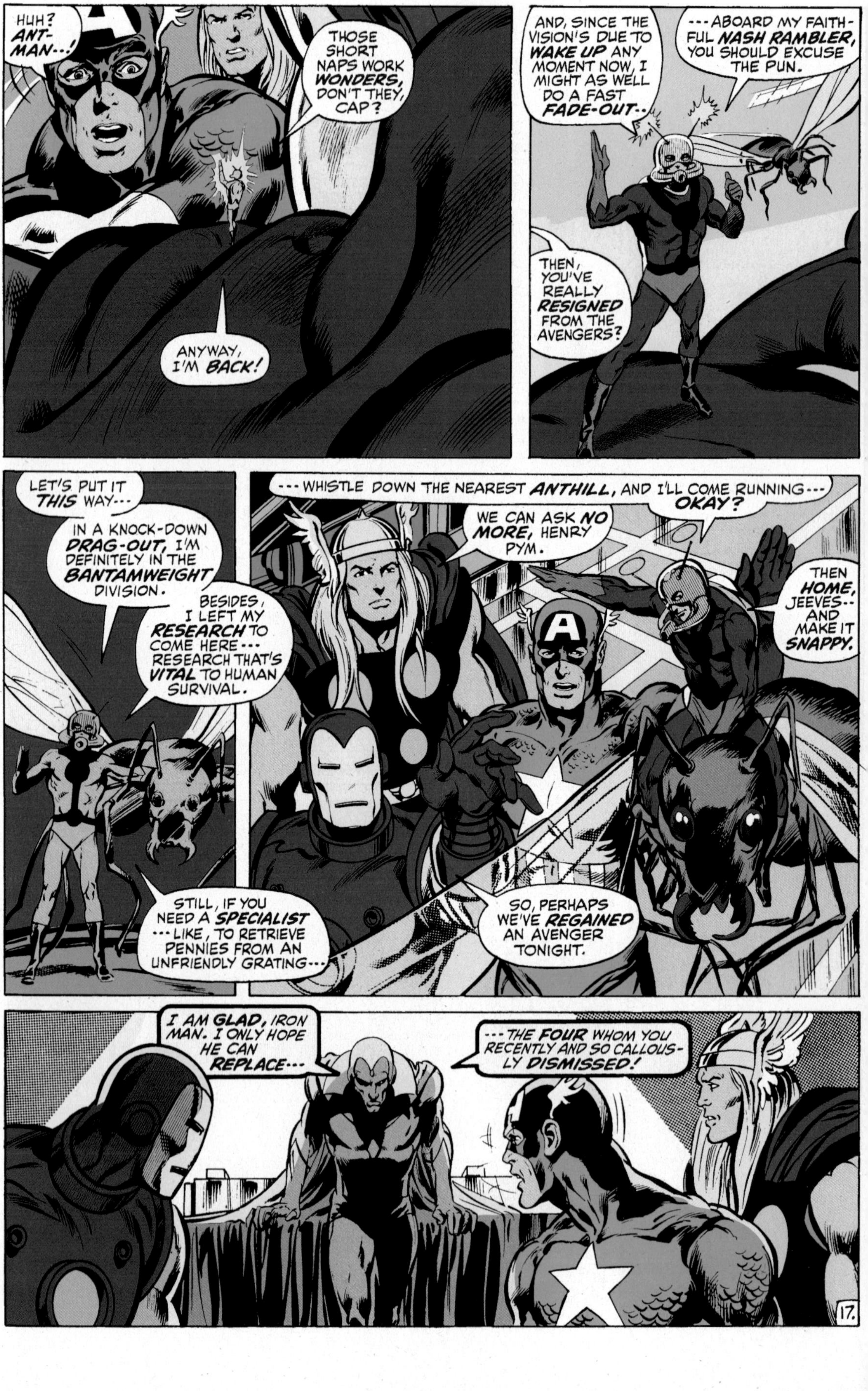
HUH? ANT-MAN--!
THOSE SHORT NAPS WORK WONDERS, DON'T THEY, CAP?
ANYWAY, I'M BACK!
AND, SINCE THE VISION'S DUE TO WAKE UP ANY MOMENT NOW, I MIGHT AS WELL DO A FAST FADE-OUT--
---ABOARD MY FAITHFUL NASH RAMBLER, YOU SHOULD EXCUSE THE PUN.
THEN, YOU'VE REALLY RESIGNED FROM THE AVENGERS?
LET'S PUT IT THIS WAY---
IN A KNOCK-DOWN DRAG-OUT, I'M DEFINITELY IN THE BANTAMWEIGHT DIVISION.
BESIDES, I LEFT MY RESEARCH TO COME HERE--- RESEARCH THAT'S VITAL TO HUMAN SURVIVAL.
STILL, IF YOU NEED A SPECIALIST ---LIKE, TO RETRIEVE PENNIES FROM AN UNFRIENDLY GRATING---
---WHISTLE DOWN THE NEAREST ANTHILL, AND I'LL COME RUNNING--- OKAY?
WE CAN ASK NO MORE, HENRY PYM.
THEN HOME, JEEVES-- AND MAKE IT SNAPPY.
SO, PERHAPS WE'VE REGAINED AN AVENGER TONIGHT.
I AM GLAD, IRON MAN. I ONLY HOPE HE CAN REPLACE---
---THE FOUR WHOM YOU RECENTLY AND SO CALLOUSLY DISMISSED!
17.

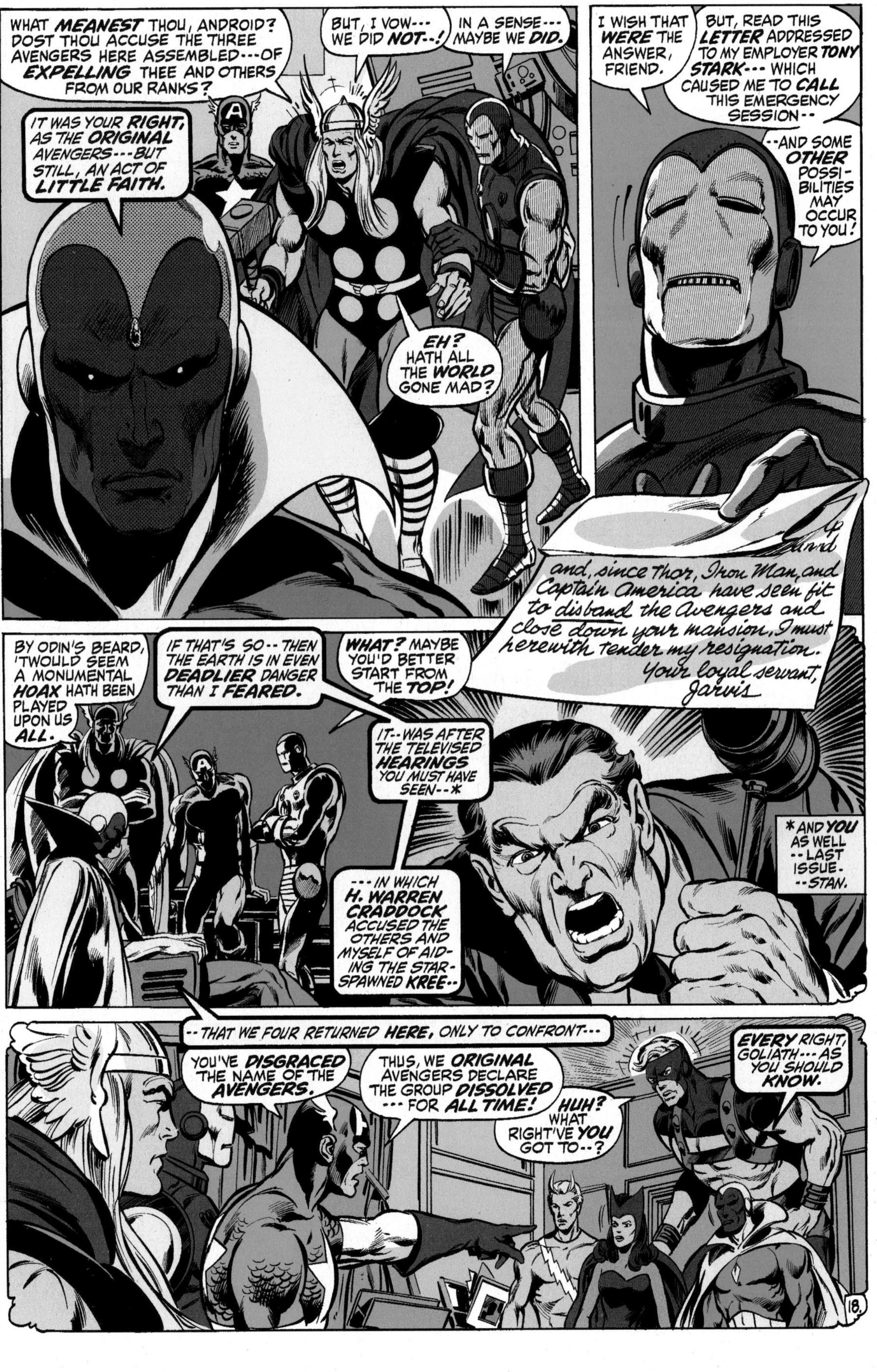

WHAT MEANEST THOU, ANDROID? DOST THOU ACCUSE THE THREE AVENGERS HERE ASSEMBLED---OF EXPELLING THEE AND OTHERS FROM OUR RANKS?
BUT, I VOW--- WE DID NOT--!
IN A SENSE--- MAYBE WE DID.
IT WAS YOUR RIGHT, AS THE ORIGINAL AVENGERS---BUT STILL, AN ACT OF LITTLE FAITH.
EH? HATH ALL THE WORLD GONE MAD?
I WISH THAT WERE THE ANSWER, FRIEND.
BUT, READ THIS LETTER ADDRESSED TO MY EMPLOYER TONY STARK--- WHICH CAUSED ME TO CALL THIS EMERGENCY SESSION--
--AND SOME OTHER POSSIBILITIES MAY OCCUR TO YOU!
and, since Thor, Iron Man, and Captain America have seen fit to disband the Avengers and close down your mansion, I must herewith tender my resignation.
Your loyal servant, Jarvis
BY ODIN'S BEARD, 'TWOULD SEEM A MONUMENTAL HOAX HATH BEEN PLAYED UPON US ALL.
IF THAT'S SO--THEN THE EARTH IS IN EVEN DEADLIER DANGER THAN I FEARED.
WHAT? MAYBE YOU'D BETTER START FROM THE TOP!
IT--WAS AFTER THE TELEVISED HEARINGS YOU MUST HAVE SEEN--*
---IN WHICH H. WARREN CRADDOCK ACCUSED THE OTHERS AND MYSELF OF AIDING THE STAR-SPAWNED KREE--
*AND YOU AS WELL--LAST ISSUE.--STAN.
--THAT WE FOUR RETURNED HERE, ONLY TO CONFRONT---
YOU'VE DISGRACED THE NAME OF THE AVENGERS.
THUS, WE ORIGINAL AVENGERS DECLARE THE GROUP DISSOLVED---FOR ALL TIME!
HUH? WHAT RIGHT'VE YOU GOT TO--?
EVERY RIGHT, GOLIATH--AS YOU SHOULD KNOW.
18.

"THEN, YOU-- OR YOUR *IMITATORS*--- DEPARTED, AND WE DID *LIKEWISE* SOON AFTER---"

SHEESH! WHY COULDN'T WE AT LEAST TAKE ONE LOUSY *QUINJET?*

THOSE SHIPS WERE MERELY *LEASED* TO US, CLINT--- BY *TONY STARK.*

WE'RE JUST LUCKY MY *CREDIT CARD* GOT US THIS *CAR.*

"YET, EVERYWHERE WE WENT, DARTING GLANCES OF *SUSPICION* FOLLOWED US--- FOR WERE WE NOT *ACCUSED* OF SHIELDING A PLANET'S *ENEMIES*--?"

"AND, AMONG *HUMANKIND,* IS NOT *ACCU- SATION*---THE SAME AS *CON- VICTION*--?"

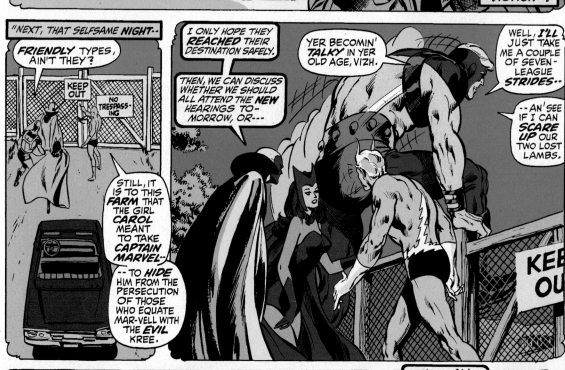

"NEXT, THAT SELFSAME *NIGHT*--

FRIENDLY TYPES, AIN'T THEY?

KEEP OUT

NO TRESPASS- ING

STILL, IT IS TO THIS *FARM* THAT THE GIRL *CAROL* MEANT TO TAKE *CAPTAIN MARVEL*--

-- TO *HIDE* HIM FROM THE *PERSECUTION* OF THOSE WHO EQUATE MAR-VELL WITH THE *EVIL* KREE.

I ONLY HOPE THEY *REACHED* THEIR DESTINATION SAFELY.

THEN, WE CAN DISCUSS WHETHER WE SHOULD ALL ATTEND THE *NEW* HEARINGS TO- MORROW, OR---

YER BECOMIN' *TALKY* IN YER OLD AGE, *VIZH.*

WELL, *I'LL* JUST TAKE ME A COUPLE OF SEVEN- LEAGUE *STRIDES*--

--AN' SEE IF I CAN *SCARE UP* OUR TWO LOST LAMBS.

KEE OU

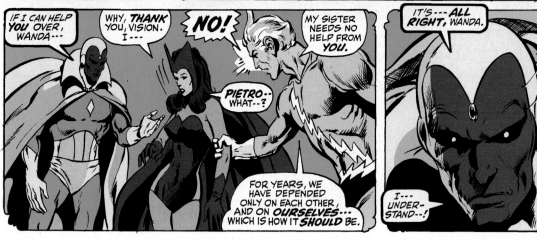

IF I CAN HELP *YOU* OVER, WANDA---

WHY, *THANK* YOU, VISION. I ---

NO!

PIETRO-- *WHAT*--?

MY SISTER NEEDS NO HELP FROM *YOU.*

FOR YEARS, WE HAVE DEPENDED ONLY ON EACH OTHER, AND ON *OURSELVES*--- WHICH IS HOW IT *SHOULD* BE.

IT'S--- *ALL RIGHT,* WANDA.

I--- UNDER- STAND--!

19.

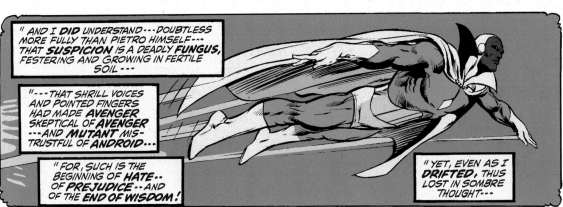

" AND I **DID** UNDERSTAND---DOUBTLESS MORE FULLY THAN PIETRO HIMSELF--- THAT **SUSPICION** IS A DEADLY **FUNGUS,** FESTERING AND GROWING IN FERTILE SOIL ---

"---THAT SHRILL VOICES AND POINTED FINGERS HAD MADE **AVENGER** SKEPTICAL OF **AVENGER** ---AND **MUTANT** MIS- TRUSTFUL OF **ANDROID**---

" FOR, SUCH IS THE BEGINNING OF **HATE**-- OF **PREJUDICE**--AND OF THE **END OF WISDOM!**

" YET, EVEN AS I **DRIFTED,** THUS LOST IN SOMBRE THOUGHT---

"--I SUDDENLY PASSED THRU THE **GATES OF HELL**--!

AARRR

ZZAKT!

PIETRO-- THOSE **RAYS** WHICH STRUCK THE VISION DOWN! **WHERE** DID THEY--?

THEY SHOT OUT SO **SWIFTLY,** I COULDN'T **SEE!**

IT'S GOOD THAT HE LANDED AMONG THESE HARMLESS **CATTLE,** SO THAT---

" 'HARMLESS **CATTLE!'** THAT IS THE MOMENT, AS IF BY SOME SINISTER **CUE**---

"-- THEY BEGAN TO--- **CHANGE**--!

20

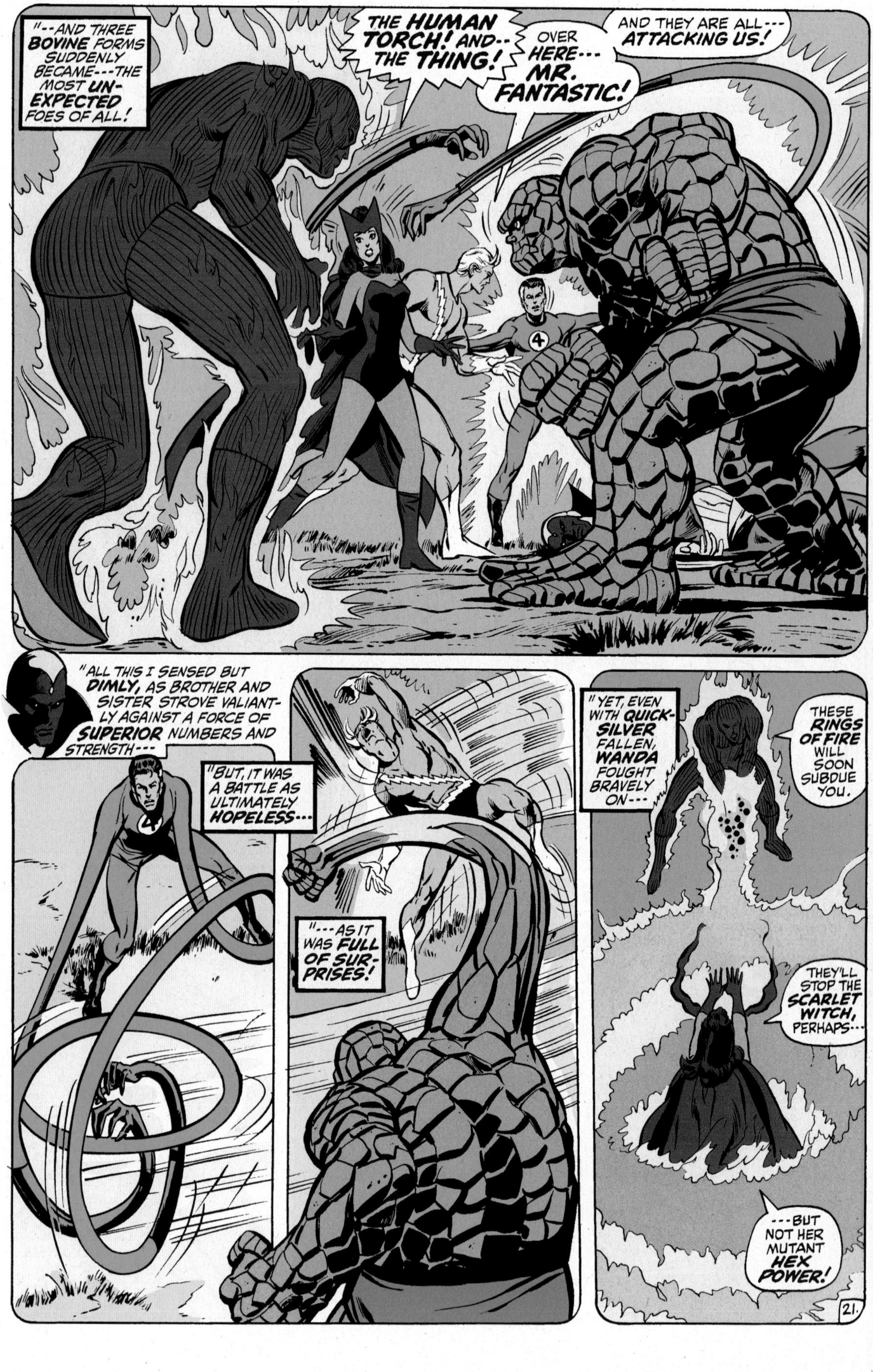

"--AND THREE BOVINE FORMS SUDDENLY BECAME---THE MOST UN-EXPECTED FOES OF ALL!
THE HUMAN TORCH! AND.. THE THING!
OVER HERE... MR. FANTASTIC!
AND THEY ARE ALL--- ATTACKING US!
"ALL THIS I SENSED BUT DIMLY, AS BROTHER AND SISTER STROVE VALIANT-LY AGAINST A FORCE OF SUPERIOR NUMBERS AND STRENGTH---
"BUT, IT WAS A BATTLE AS ULTIMATELY HOPELESS...
"---AS IT WAS FULL OF SUR-PRISES!
"YET, EVEN WITH QUICK-SILVER FALLEN, WANDA FOUGHT BRAVELY ON---
THESE RINGS OF FIRE WILL SOON SUBDUE YOU.
THEY'LL STOP THE SCARLET WITCH, PERHAPS---
---BUT NOT HER MUTANT HEX POWER!
21.

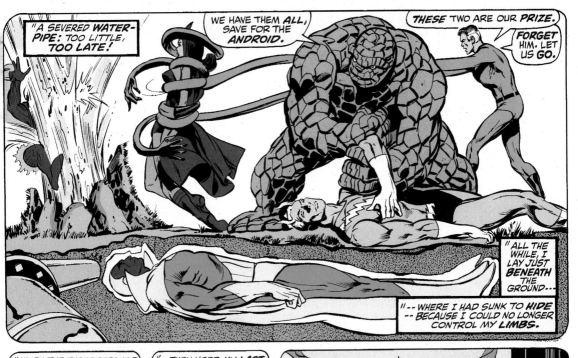

"A SEVERED WATER-PIPE: TOO LITTLE, TOO LATE!"

WE HAVE THEM ALL, SAVE FOR THE ANDROID.

THESE TWO ARE OUR PRIZE.

FORGET HIM. LET US GO.

"ALL THE WHILE, I LAY JUST BENEATH THE GROUND--"

"-- WHERE I HAD SUNK TO HIDE -- BECAUSE I COULD NO LONGER CONTROL MY LIMBS."

"WHEN THE THREE STRANGE-LINGS WERE GONE, I BE-CAME LIGHT ENOUGH TO RISE ONCE MORE FROM THE CLAMMY EARTH---"

"-- THEN USED MY LAST VESTIGE OF DENSITY-CONTROL TO STEER MYSELF SLOWLY, SURELY---"

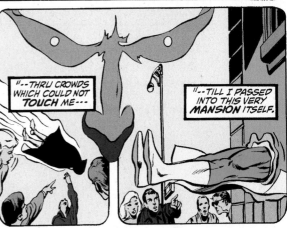

"--THRU CROWDS WHICH COULD NOT TOUCH ME---"

"--TILL I PASSED INTO THIS VERY MANSION ITSELF."

AND NOW, I AM WELL---FREE-- WHILE TWO COMRADES LIE IN MORTAL PERIL.

I MUST RETURN TO THAT FARM-- NOW!

BUT NOT ALONE--- AVENGER.

STILL--- WHO DID THEY FIGHT?

AYE! THAT, WE MUST AND SHALL LEARN.

FOR, THIS NIGHT HAVE WE A WRONG TO REDRESS ---A NAME TO AVENGE!

NOBLE WORDS. YET, SOME THINGS MAY LIE BEYOND REACH EVEN OF A GOD--!

22

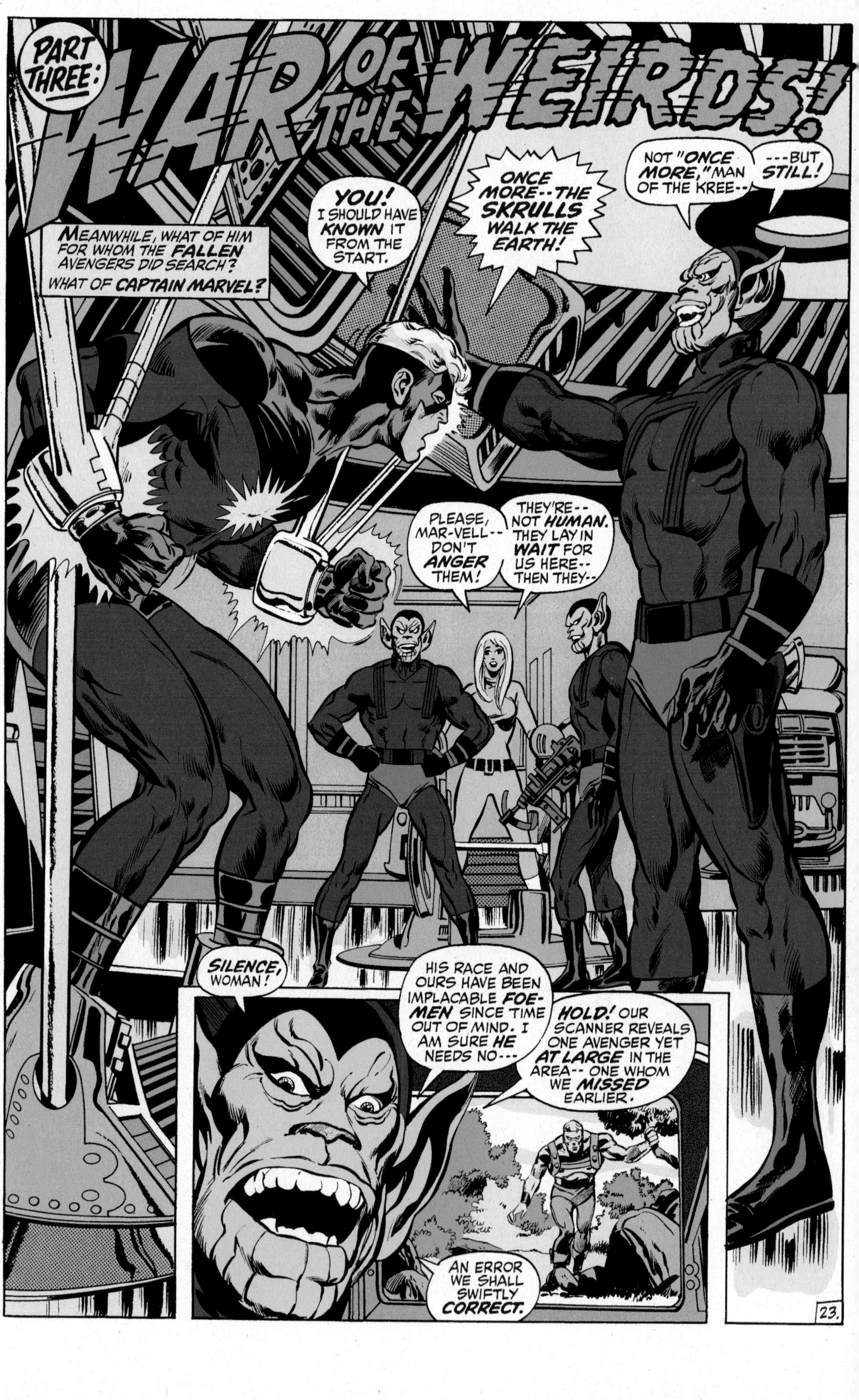
PART THREE:
WAR OF THE WEIRDS!
MEANWHILE, WHAT OF HIM FOR WHOM THE FALLEN AVENGERS DID SEARCH? WHAT OF CAPTAIN MARVEL?
YOU! I SHOULD HAVE KNOWN IT FROM THE START.
ONCE MORE--THE SKRULLS WALK THE EARTH!
NOT "ONCE MORE," MAN OF THE KREE--
---BUT STILL!
PLEASE, MAR-VELL-- DON'T ANGER THEM!
THEY'RE--NOT HUMAN. THEY LAY IN WAIT FOR US HERE--THEN THEY--
SILENCE, WOMAN!
HIS RACE AND OURS HAVE BEEN IMPLACABLE FOE-MEN SINCE TIME OUT OF MIND. I AM SURE HE NEEDS NO---
HOLD! OUR SCANNER REVEALS ONE AVENGER YET AT LARGE IN THE AREA-- ONE WHOM WE MISSED EARLIER.
AN ERROR WE SHALL SWIFTLY CORRECT.

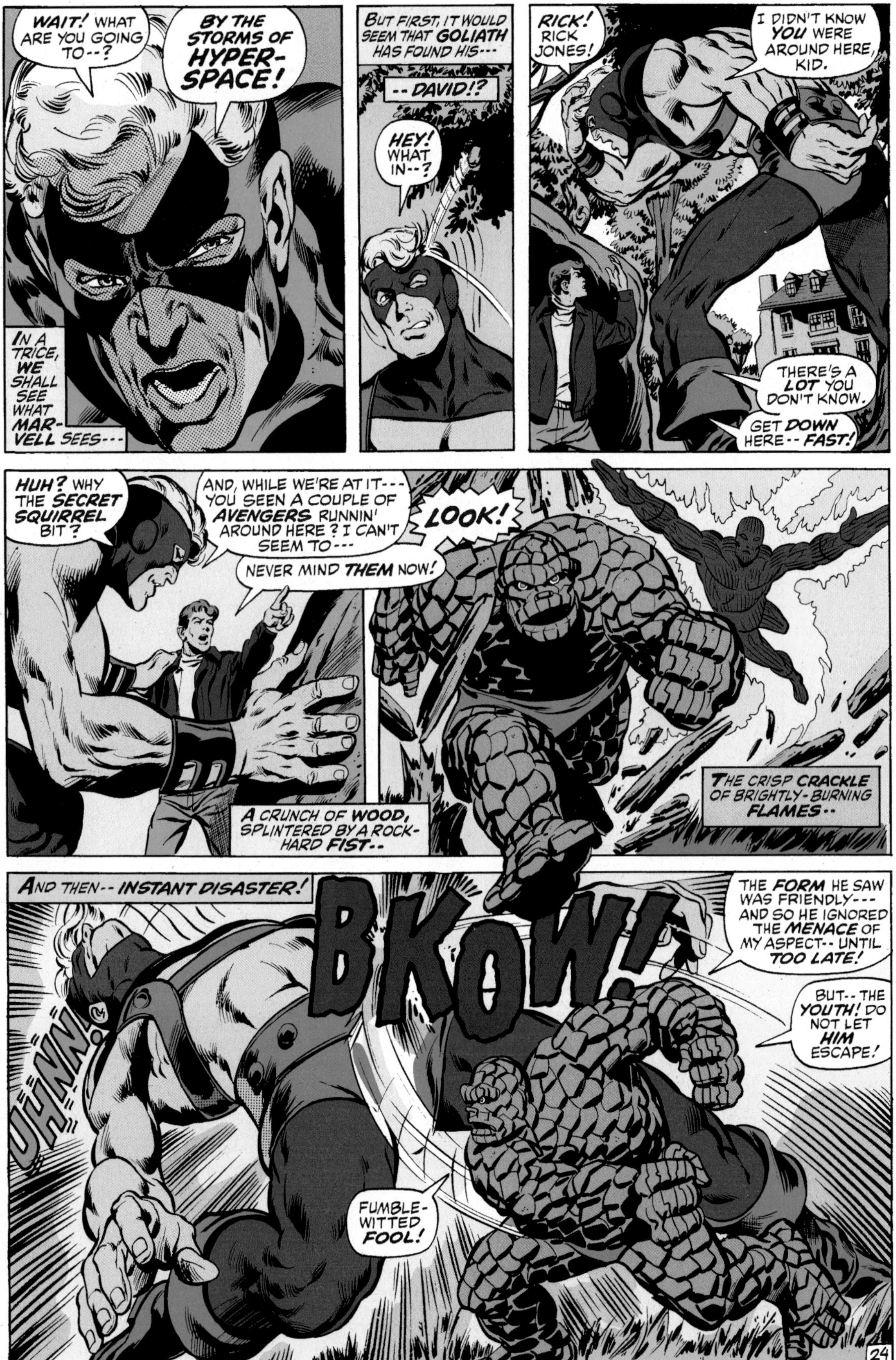
WAIT! WHAT ARE YOU GOING TO--?
BY THE STORMS OF HYPER-SPACE!
IN A TRICE, WE SHALL SEE WHAT MAR-VELL SEES---
BUT FIRST, IT WOULD SEEM THAT GOLIATH HAS FOUND HIS---
--DAVID!?
HEY! WHAT IN--?
RICK! RICK JONES!
I DIDN'T KNOW YOU WERE AROUND HERE, KID.
THERE'S A LOT YOU DON'T KNOW.
GET DOWN HERE--FAST!
HUH? WHY THE SECRET SQUIRREL BIT?
AND, WHILE WE'RE AT IT--- YOU SEEN A COUPLE OF AVENGERS RUNNIN' AROUND HERE? I CAN'T SEEM TO---
NEVER MIND THEM NOW!
LOOK!
A CRUNCH OF WOOD, SPLINTERED BY A ROCK-HARD FIST--
THE CRISP CRACKLE OF BRIGHTLY-BURNING FLAMES--
AND THEN--INSTANT DISASTER!
BKOW!
UHNN!
THE FORM HE SAW WAS FRIENDLY--- AND SO HE IGNORED THE MENACE OF MY ASPECT--UNTIL TOO LATE!
BUT--THE YOUTH! DO NOT LET HIM ESCAPE!
FUMBLE-WITTED FOOL!
24

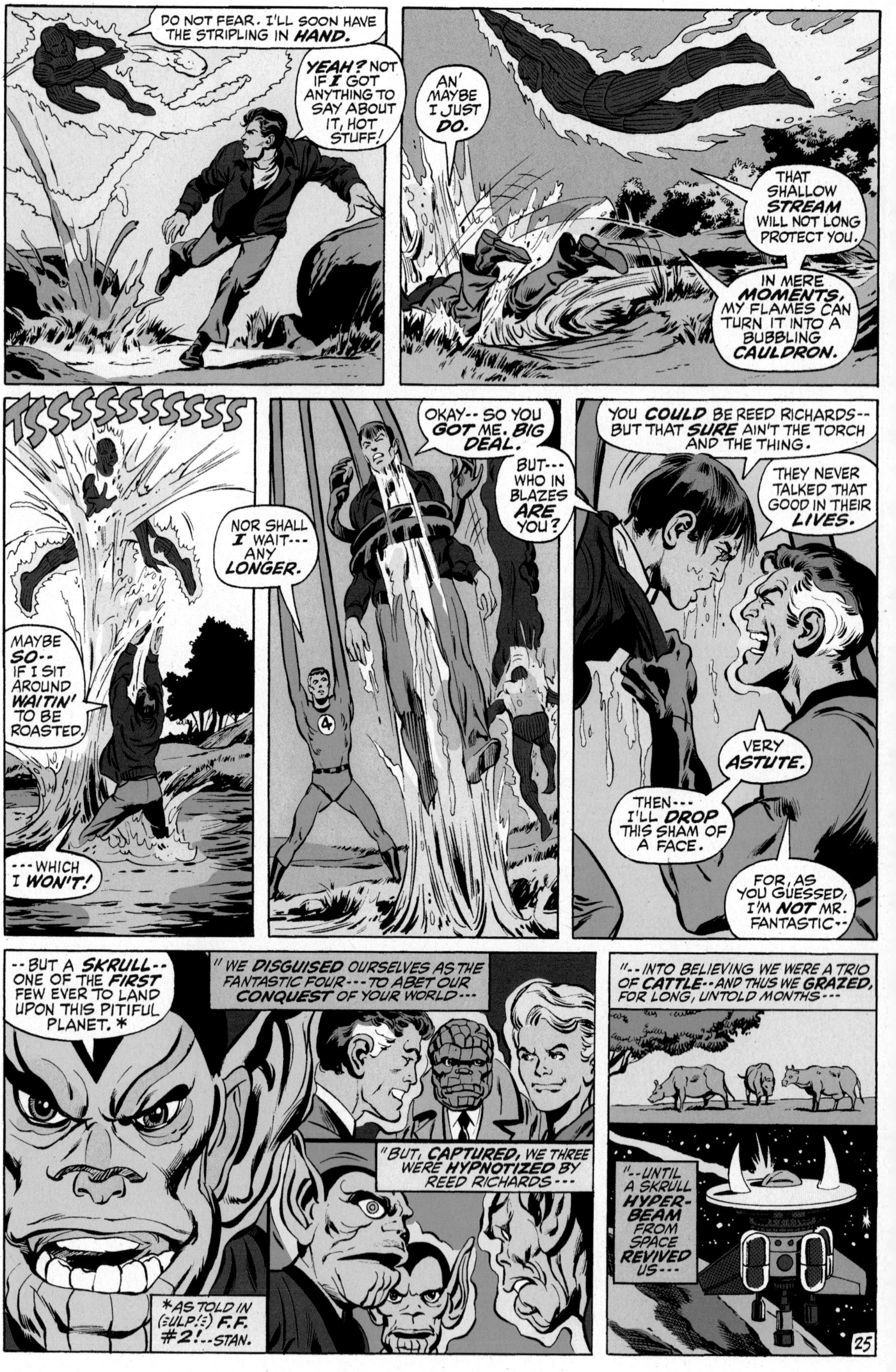
DO NOT FEAR. I'LL SOON HAVE THE STRIPLING IN HAND.
YEAH? NOT IF I GOT ANYTHING TO SAY ABOUT IT, HOT STUFF!
AN' MAYBE I JUST DO.
THAT SHALLOW STREAM WILL NOT LONG PROTECT YOU.
IN MERE MOMENTS, MY FLAMES CAN TURN IT INTO A BUBBLING CAULDRON.
TSSSSSSSSSS
NOR SHALL I WAIT--- ANY LONGER.
MAYBE SO-- IF I SIT AROUND WAITIN' TO BE ROASTED.
---WHICH I WON'T!
OKAY-- SO YOU GOT ME. BIG DEAL.
BUT--- WHO IN BLAZES ARE YOU?
YOU COULD BE REED RICHARDS-- BUT THAT SURE AIN'T THE TORCH AND THE THING.
THEY NEVER TALKED THAT GOOD IN THEIR LIVES.
VERY ASTUTE.
THEN--- I'LL DROP THIS SHAM OF A FACE.
FOR, AS YOU GUESSED, I'M NOT MR. FANTASTIC--
--BUT A SKRULL-- ONE OF THE FIRST FEW EVER TO LAND UPON THIS PITIFUL PLANET. *
*AS TOLD IN (GULP!) F.F. #2!--STAN.
"WE DISGUISED OURSELVES AS THE FANTASTIC FOUR---TO ABET OUR CONQUEST OF YOUR WORLD---
"BUT, CAPTURED, WE THREE WERE HYPNOTIZED BY REED RICHARDS---
"--INTO BELIEVING WE WERE A TRIO OF CATTLE--AND THUS WE GRAZED, FOR LONG, UNTOLD MONTHS---
"--UNTIL A SKRULL HYPER-BEAM FROM SPACE REVIVED US---
25

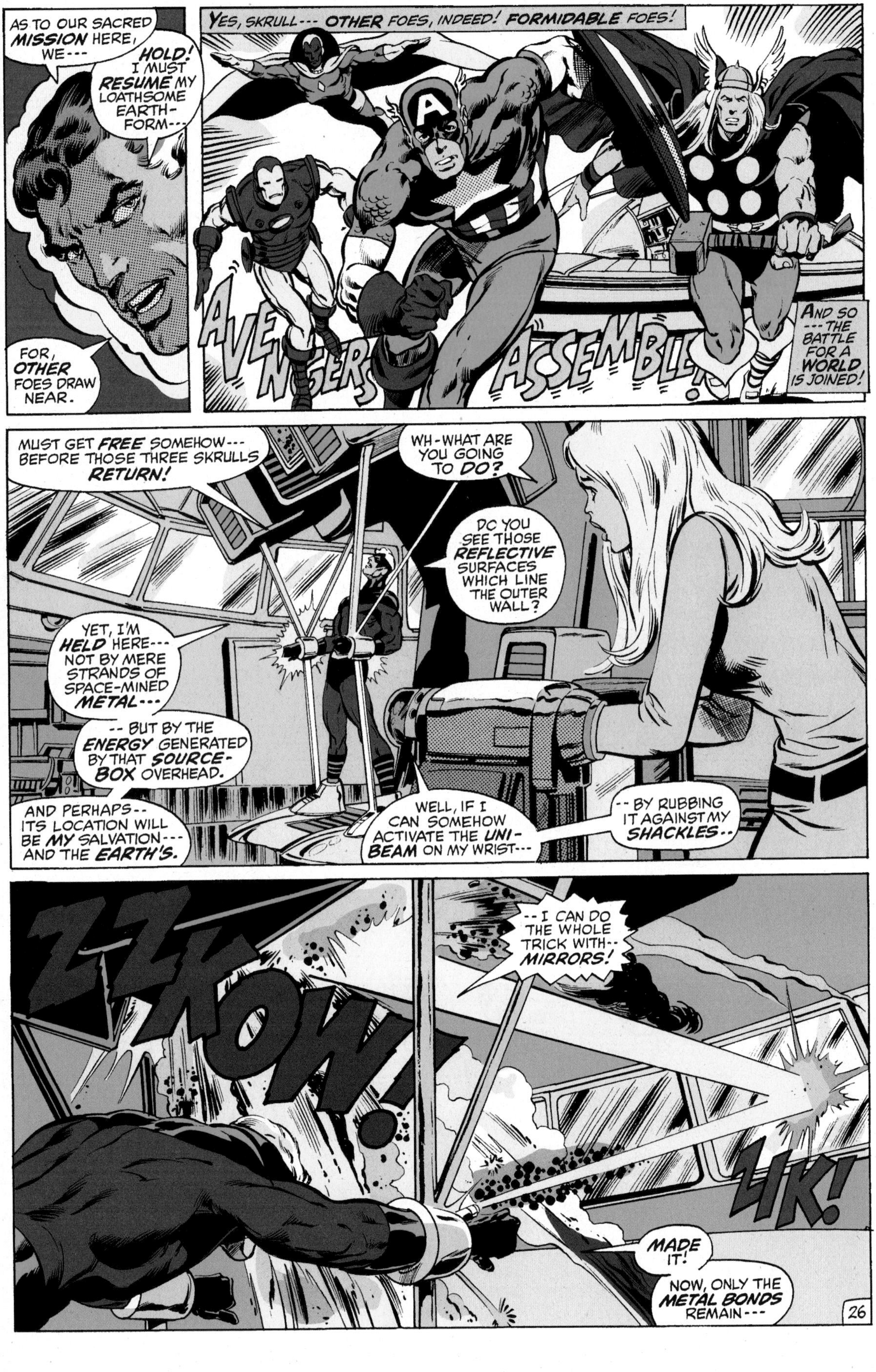

AS TO OUR SACRED MISSION HERE, WE---
HOLD! I MUST RESUME MY LOATHSOME EARTH-FORM---
FOR, OTHER FOES DRAW NEAR.
YES, SKRULL--- OTHER FOES, INDEED! FORMIDABLE FOES!
AVENGERS ASSEMBLE!
AND SO---THE BATTLE FOR A WORLD IS JOINED!
MUST GET FREE SOMEHOW--- BEFORE THOSE THREE SKRULLS RETURN!
WH-WHAT ARE YOU GOING TO DO?
YET, I'M HELD HERE--- NOT BY MERE STRANDS OF SPACE-MINED METAL---
-- BUT BY THE ENERGY GENERATED BY THAT SOURCE-BOX OVERHEAD.
AND PERHAPS-- ITS LOCATION WILL BE MY SALVATION--- AND THE EARTH'S.
DO YOU SEE THOSE REFLECTIVE SURFACES WHICH LINE THE OUTER WALL?
WELL, IF I CAN SOMEHOW ACTIVATE THE UNI-BEAM ON MY WRIST---
-- BY RUBBING IT AGAINST MY SHACKLES--
ZZKOW!
-- I CAN DO THE WHOLE TRICK WITH-- MIRRORS!
ZIK!
MADE IT!
NOW, ONLY THE METAL BONDS REMAIN---

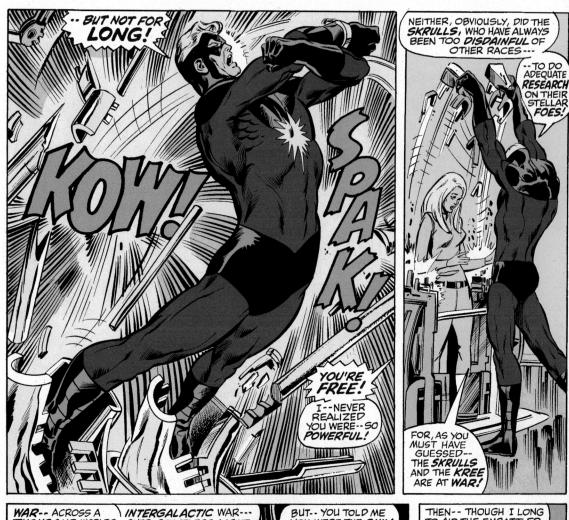

-- BUT NOT FOR **LONG!**

KOW!

SPAK!

YOU'RE FREE! I-- NEVER REALIZED YOU WERE-- SO **POWERFUL!**

NEITHER, OBVIOUSLY, DID THE **SKRULLS,** WHO HAVE ALWAYS BEEN TOO **DISDAINFUL** OF OTHER RACES---

--TO DO ADEQUATE **RESEARCH** ON THEIR STELLAR **FOES!**

FOR, AS YOU MUST HAVE GUESSED-- THE **SKRULLS** AND THE **KREE** ARE AT **WAR!**

WAR-- ACROSS A **THOUSAND** WORLDS WHOSE NAMES THEY SCARCELY KNOW!

INTERGALACTIC WAR--- OVER COUNTLESS **LIGHT-CENTURIES** OF DISTANCE!

BUT-- YOU TOLD ME YOU WERE THE **ONLY KREE** ON EARTH.

DOES THAT MEAN -- YOUR PEOPLE DO NOT **KNOW** THE SKRULLS ARE HERE?

YOU'RE **RIGHT.** I HADN'T **CONSIDERED** THAT.

THEN-- THOUGH I LONG TO AID THE EMBATTLED **AVENGERS** WITHOUT--- THERE IS SOMETHING **ELSE** I MUST DO.

FOR, **EXILE** THOUGH I BE-- FAR-FLUNG **OUTCAST** OF A UNIVERSE THAT OWNS ME **NOT**--

I AM STILL A **KREE.**

27

AN *OMNI-WAVE PROJECTOR*--- THAT IS THE *ONLY* ANSWER!

THAT ALONE CAN SEND AN *IN-STANTANEOUS* MESSAGE TO THE *KREE* GALAXY--ACROSS THE VOID OF *HYPER-SPACE!*

BUT-- WHY STAY *HERE*, ON THE *SKRULL* SHIP?

COULD AN EARTH-MAN BUILD A *RADIO* IF HE WERE STRANDED ON A *DESERT ISLE?*

ONLY *HERE* EXIST THE *TOOLS* FOR FORGING MY *UNI-BEAM* INTO THE PROPER FORM.

AND YET, THE SKRULLS WOULD GIVE *TEN PLANETS* FOR THE SECRET OF THE *OMNI-WAVE.*

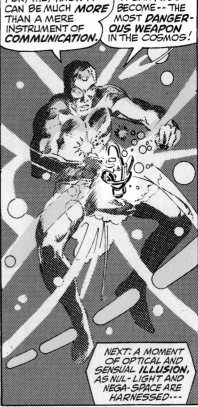

FOR, THEY KNOW IT CAN BE MUCH *MORE* THAN A MERE INSTRUMENT OF *COMMUNICATION.*

IT CAN ALSO BECOME-- THE MOST *DANGER-OUS WEAPON* IN THE COSMOS!

NEXT: A MOMENT OF OPTICAL AND SENSUAL *ILLUSION*, AS NUL-LIGHT AND NEGA-SPACE ARE HARNESSED---

`1:COMPU-SYSTEMS PRIMED FOR BLASTOFF...`

AMAZING! THESE GUYS CAN'T BE THE REAL F.F.!

AYE. BUT THEY *MATCH* OUR OLD FRIENDS-- FOR *POWER!*

KRAK!

THOOM!

28.

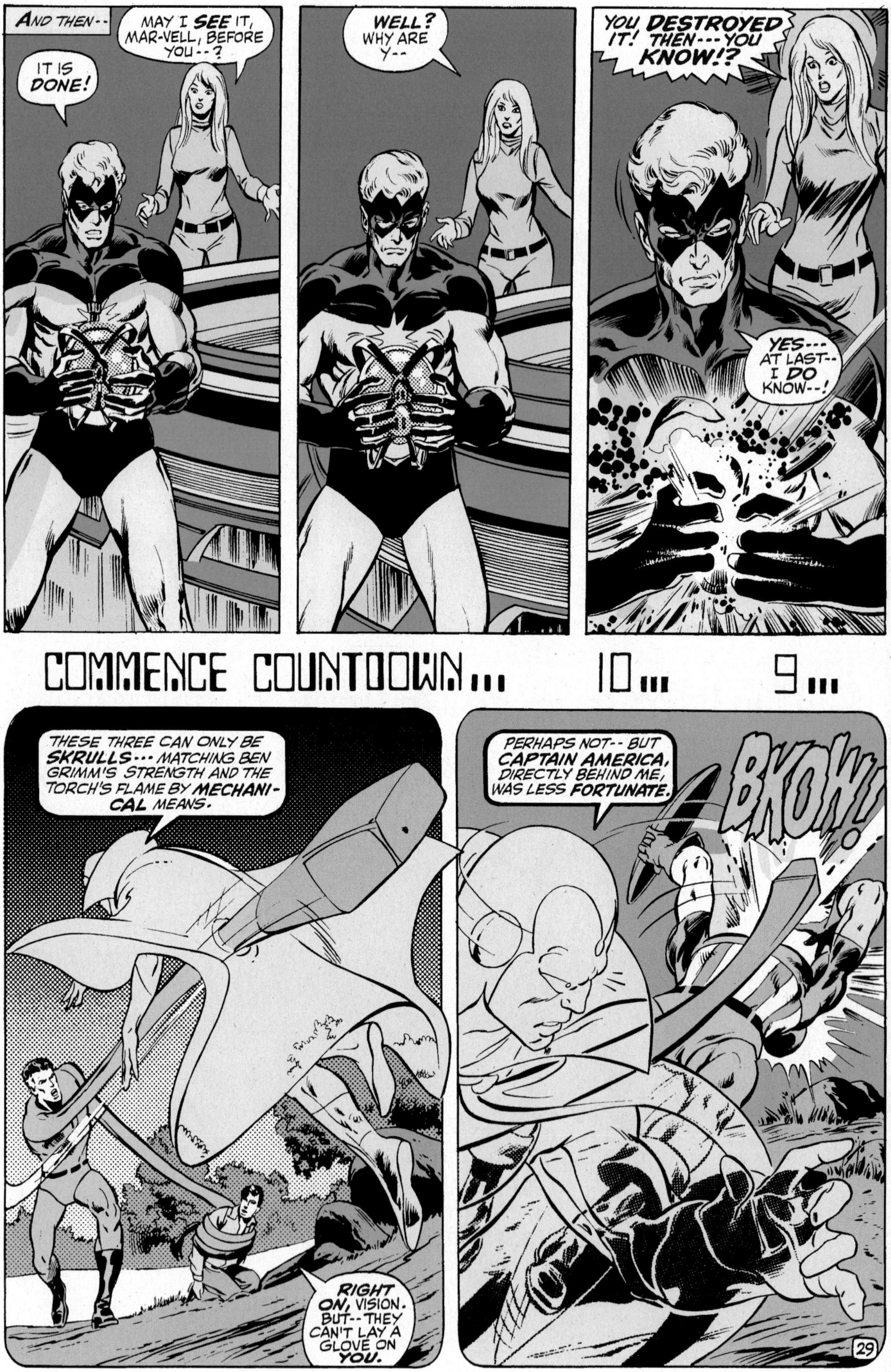
AND THEN--
IT IS DONE!
MAY I SEE IT, MAR-VELL, BEFORE YOU--?
WELL? WHY ARE Y--
YOU DESTROYED IT! THEN---YOU KNOW!?
YES--- AT LAST-- I DO KNOW--!
COMMENCE COUNTDOWN... 10... 9...
THESE THREE CAN ONLY BE SKRULLS--- MATCHING BEN GRIMM'S STRENGTH AND THE TORCH'S FLAME BY MECHANICAL MEANS.
RIGHT ON, VISION. BUT--THEY CAN'T LAY A GLOVE ON YOU.
PERHAPS NOT-- BUT CAPTAIN AMERICA, DIRECTLY BEHIND ME, WAS LESS FORTUNATE.
BKOW!
29

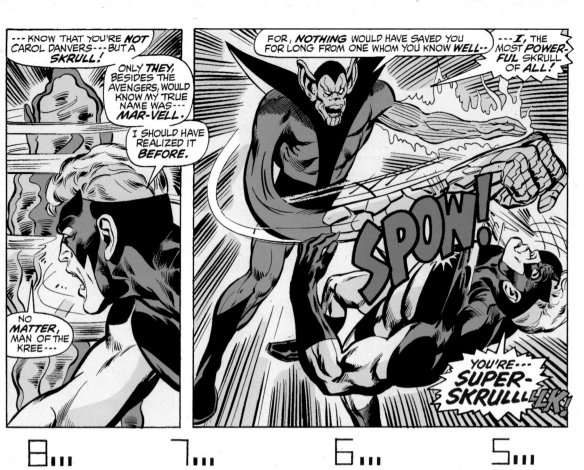

---KNOW THAT YOU'RE **NOT** CAROL DANVERS---BUT A **SKRULL!**

ONLY **THEY,** BESIDES THE AVENGERS, WOULD KNOW MY TRUE NAME WAS--- **MAR-VELL.**

I SHOULD HAVE REALIZED IT **BEFORE.**

NO **MATTER,** MAN OF THE KREE---

FOR, **NOTHING** WOULD HAVE SAVED YOU FOR LONG FROM ONE WHOM YOU KNOW **WELL**---

---**I,** THE MOST **POWERFUL** SKRULL OF **ALL!**

SPOW!

YOU'RE--- **SUPER-SKRULLL!**

EK!

8... 7... 6... 5...

DON'T COUNT ME OUT **YET,** AVENGER.

I CAN **STILL** TOSS A **MEAN** SHIELD!

UNGGH!

WAY TO **GO,** CAP!

WAK!

BUT-- LOOK AT **IRON MAN!**

SSSSSSS

BLAST IT! COULDN'T QUITE DODGE **BOTH** THOSE FIREBALLS!

BUT-- THAT ONE'S MELTING PART OF MY **CHESTPLATE**...AND IT--**HURTS**--!

30

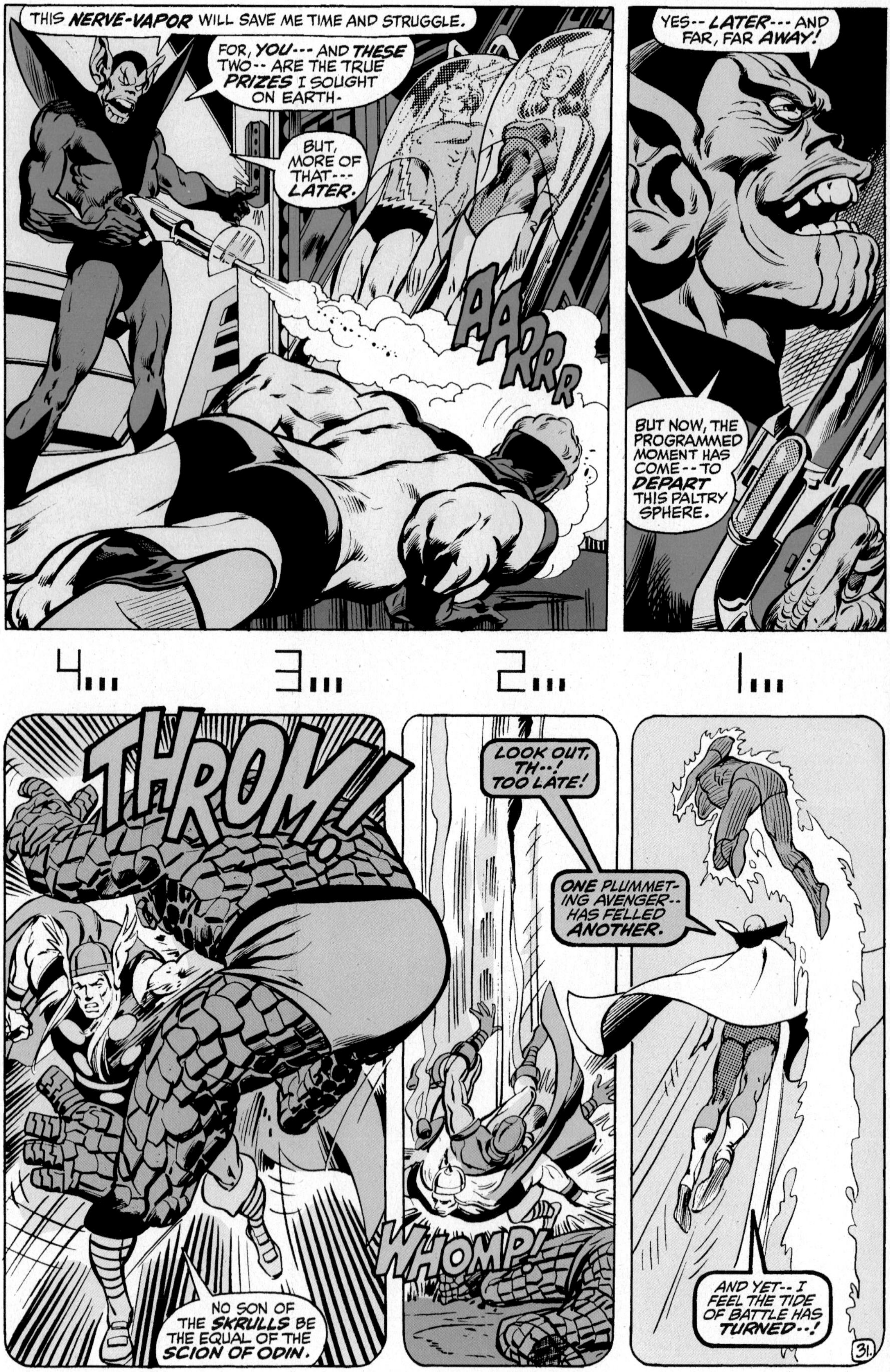
THIS NERVE-VAPOR WILL SAVE ME TIME AND STRUGGLE.
FOR, YOU--- AND THESE TWO-- ARE THE TRUE PRIZES I SOUGHT ON EARTH-
BUT, MORE OF THAT--- LATER.
AARRRR
YES-- LATER--- AND FAR, FAR AWAY!
BUT NOW, THE PROGRAMMED MOMENT HAS COME--TO DEPART THIS PALTRY SPHERE.
4...
3...
2...
1...
THROM!
NO SON OF THE SKRULLS BE THE EQUAL OF THE SCION OF ODIN.
LOOK OUT, TH--! TOO LATE!
ONE PLUMMETING AVENGER-- HAS FELLED ANOTHER.
WHOMP!
AND YET-- I FEEL THE TIDE OF BATTLE HAS TURNED--!

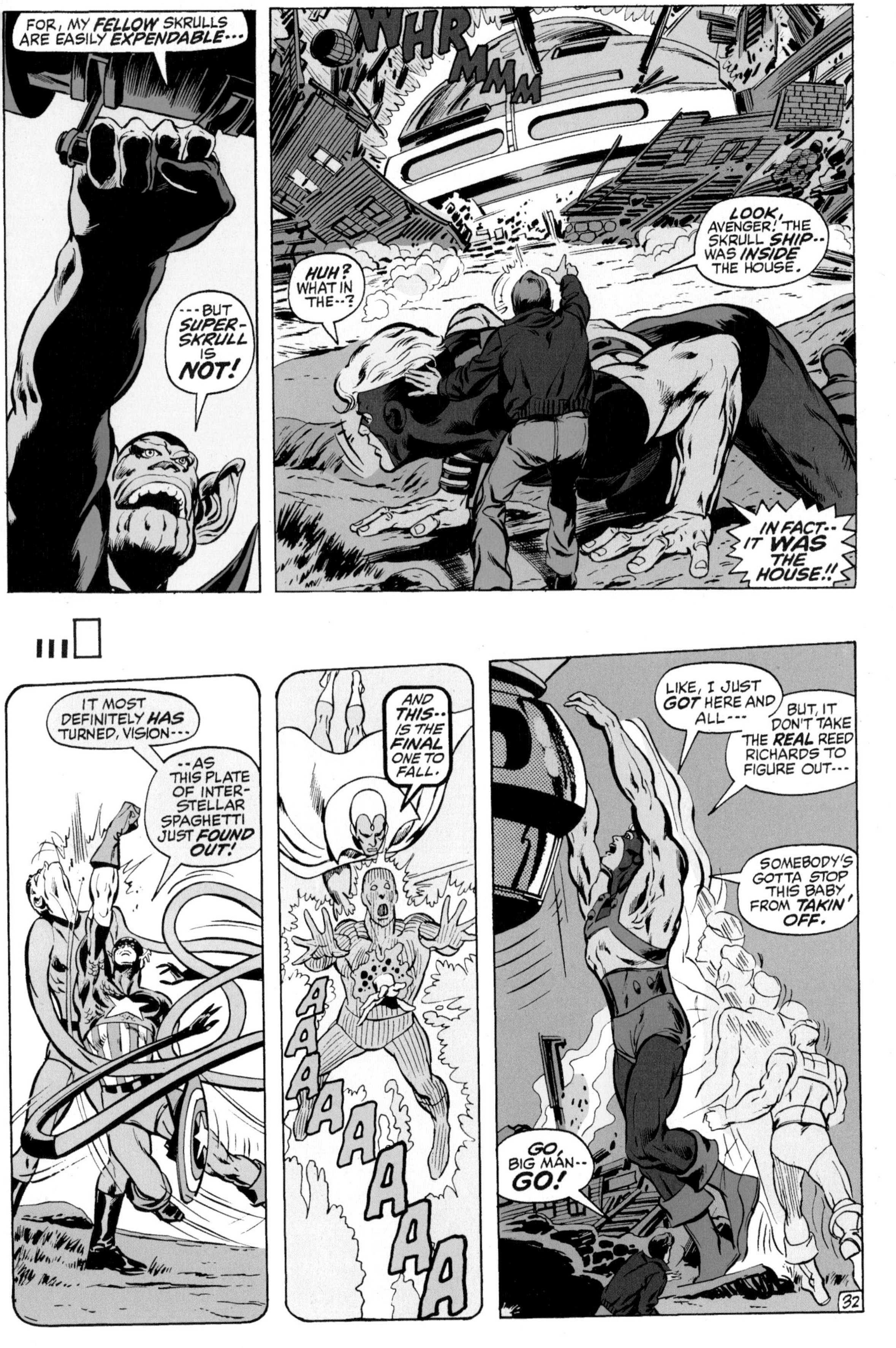

FOR, MY FELLOW SKRULLS ARE EASILY EXPENDABLE...
---BUT SUPER-SKRULL IS NOT!
WHRMMMM
HUH? WHAT IN THE--?
LOOK, AVENGER! THE SKRULL SHIP.. WAS INSIDE THE HOUSE.
IN FACT-- IT WAS THE HOUSE!!
IT MOST DEFINITELY HAS TURNED, VISION---
--AS THIS PLATE OF INTER-STELLAR SPAGHETTI JUST FOUND OUT!
AND THIS.. IS THE FINAL ONE TO FALL.
AAAAAAAAAAA
LIKE, I JUST GOT HERE AND ALL---
BUT, IT DON'T TAKE THE REAL REED RICHARDS TO FIGURE OUT---
SOMEBODY'S GOTTA STOP THIS BABY FROM TAKIN' OFF.
GO, BIG MAN-- GO!
32

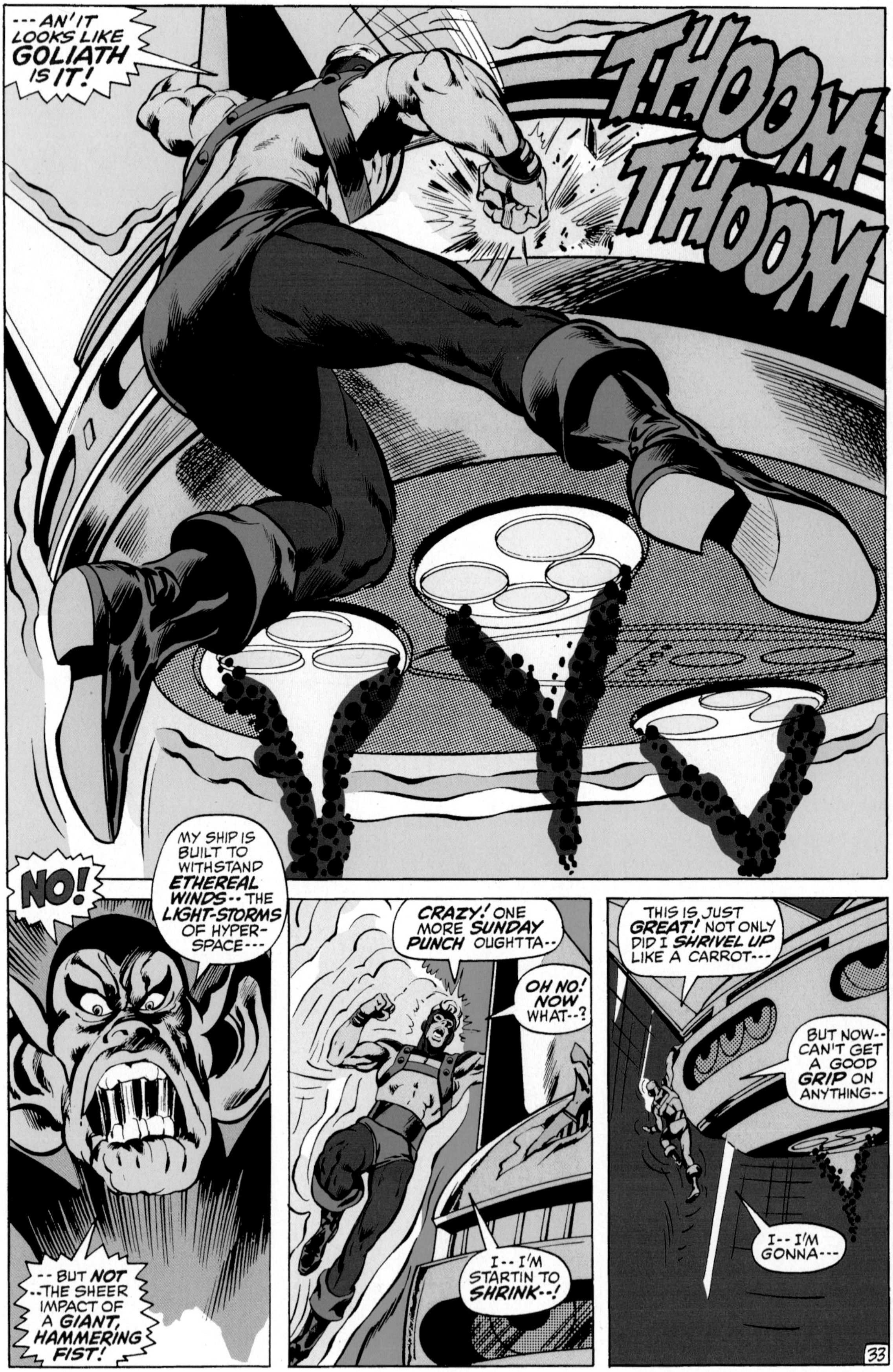

---AN' IT LOOKS LIKE GOLIATH IS IT!
THOOM THOOM
NO!
MY SHIP IS BUILT TO WITHSTAND ETHEREAL WINDS-- THE LIGHT-STORMS OF HYPER-SPACE---
--BUT NOT--THE SHEER IMPACT OF A GIANT, HAMMERING FIST!
CRAZY! ONE MORE SUNDAY PUNCH OUGHTTA--
OH NO! NOW WHAT--?
I--I'M STARTIN TO SHRINK--!
THIS IS JUST GREAT! NOT ONLY DID I SHRIVEL UP LIKE A CARROT---
BUT NOW--CAN'T GET A GOOD GRIP ON ANYTHING--
I--I'M GONNA---

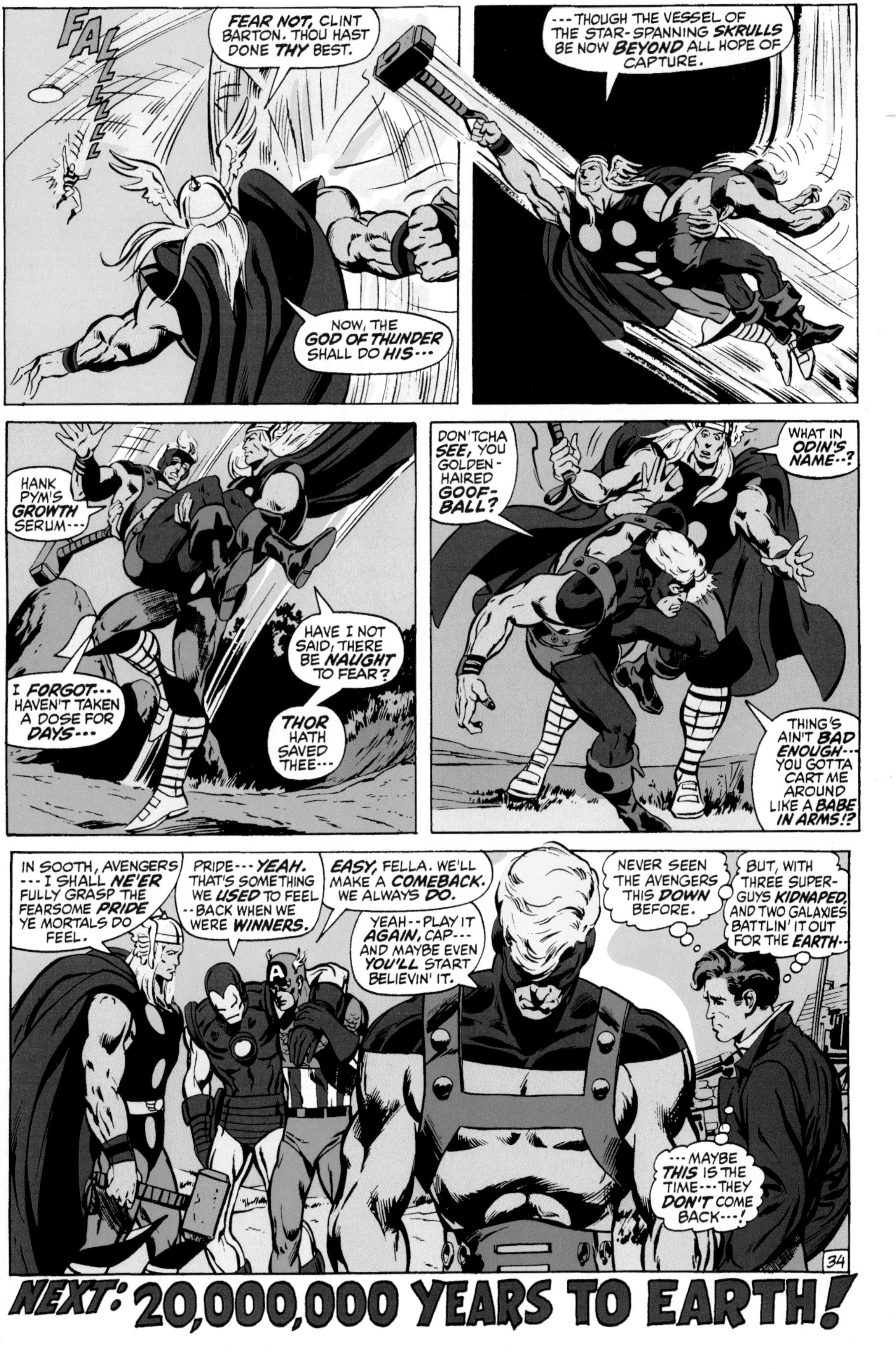
FALLLLLL
FEAR NOT, CLINT BARTON. THOU HAST DONE THY BEST.
NOW, THE GOD OF THUNDER SHALL DO HIS---
---THOUGH THE VESSEL OF THE STAR-SPANNING SKRULLS BE NOW BEYOND ALL HOPE OF CAPTURE.
HANK PYM'S GROWTH SERUM---
I FORGOT--- HAVEN'T TAKEN A DOSE FOR DAYS---
HAVE I NOT SAID, THERE BE NAUGHT TO FEAR?
THOR HATH SAVED THEE---
DON'TCHA SEE, YOU GOLDEN-HAIRED GOOF-BALL?
WHAT IN ODIN'S NAME--?
THING'S AIN'T BAD ENOUGH--- YOU GOTTA CART ME AROUND LIKE A BABE IN ARMS!?
IN SOOTH, AVENGERS --- I SHALL NE'ER FULLY GRASP THE FEARSOME PRIDE YE MORTALS DO FEEL.
PRIDE--- YEAH. THAT'S SOMETHING WE USED TO FEEL --BACK WHEN WE WERE WINNERS.
EASY, FELLA. WE'LL MAKE A COMEBACK. WE ALWAYS DO.
YEAH--PLAY IT AGAIN, CAP--- AND MAYBE EVEN YOU'LL START BELIEVIN' IT.
NEVER SEEN THE AVENGERS THIS DOWN BEFORE.
BUT, WITH THREE SUPER-GUYS KIDNAPED, AND TWO GALAXIES BATTLIN' IT OUT FOR THE EARTH--
---MAYBE THIS IS THE TIME--- THEY DON'T COME BACK---!
34
NEXT: 20,000,000 YEARS TO EARTH!

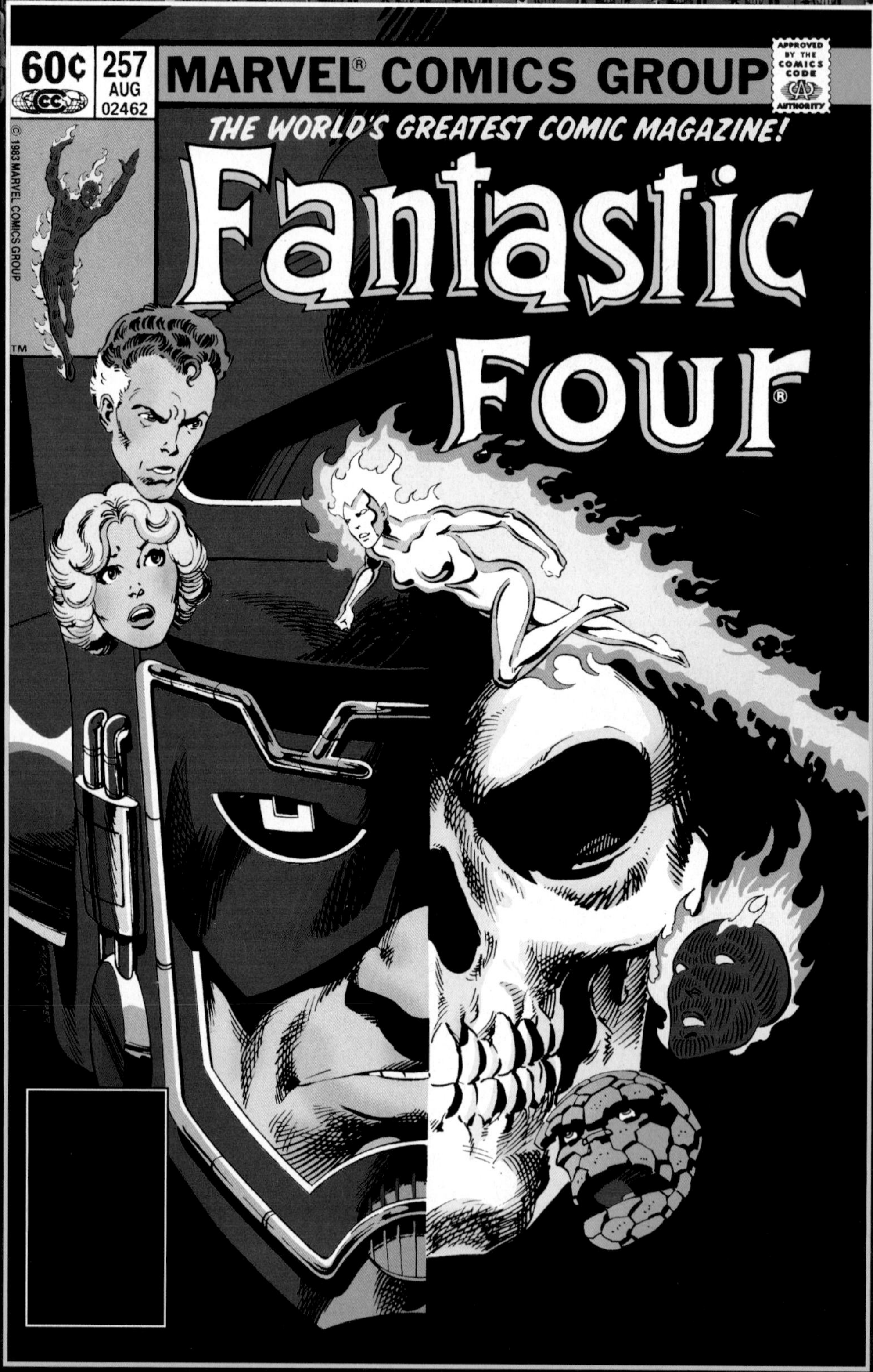
60¢
257
AUG
02462
MARVEL® COMICS GROUP
APPROVED BY THE COMICS CODE AUTHORITY
© 1983 MARVEL COMICS GROUP
THE WORLD'S GREATEST COMIC MAGAZINE!
Fantastic Four®
TM

FANTASTIC FOUR #257 (AUGUST 1983)

Tragedy strikes when Galactus, the Devourer of Words, arrives at the Skrull Throneworld.

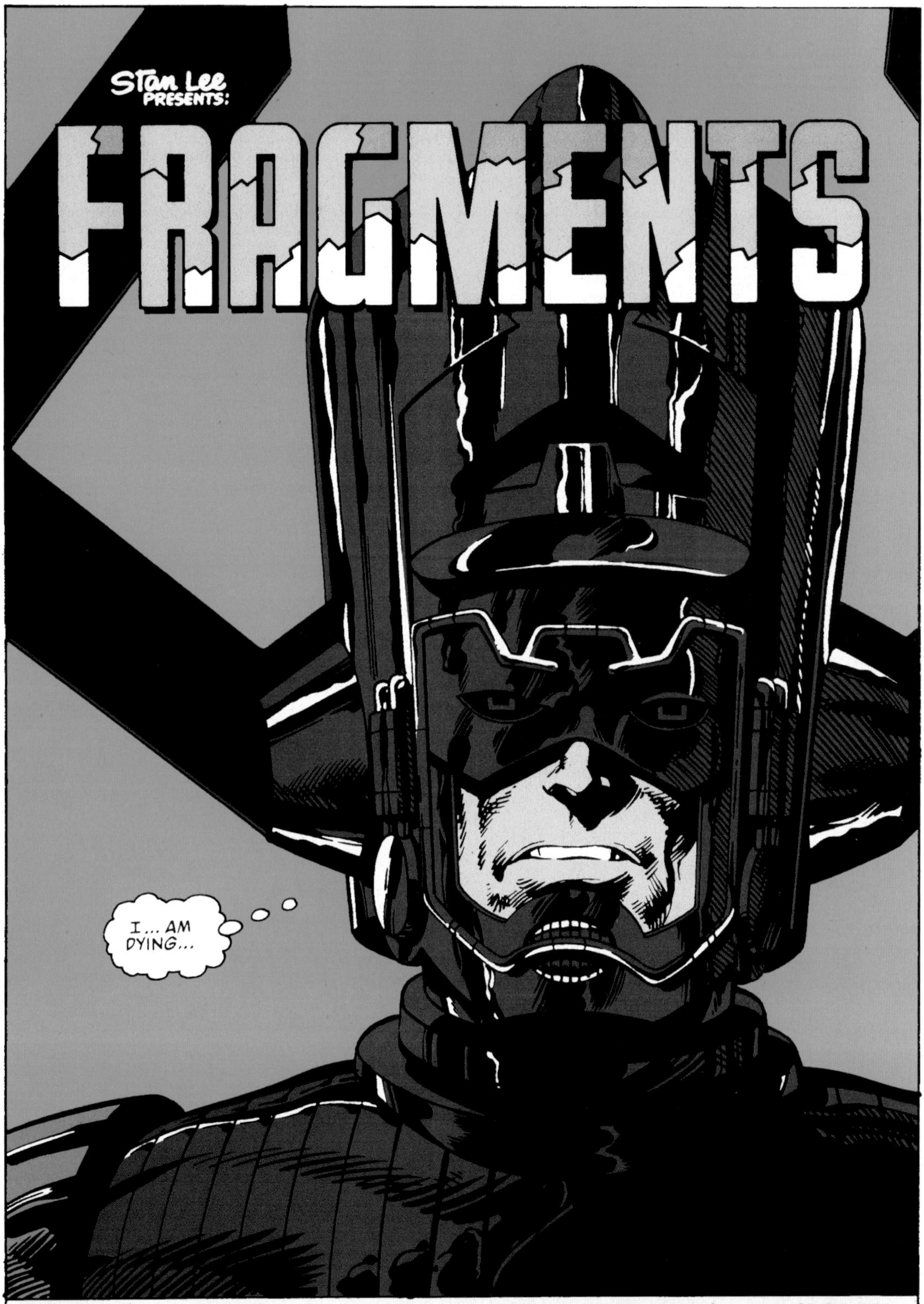

STAN LEE PRESENTS / JOHN BYRNE WRITING, DRAWING, INKING / GLYNIS WEIN COLORING / JIM NOVAK LETTERING / AL MILGROM EDITING / JIM SHOOTER EARTHLING

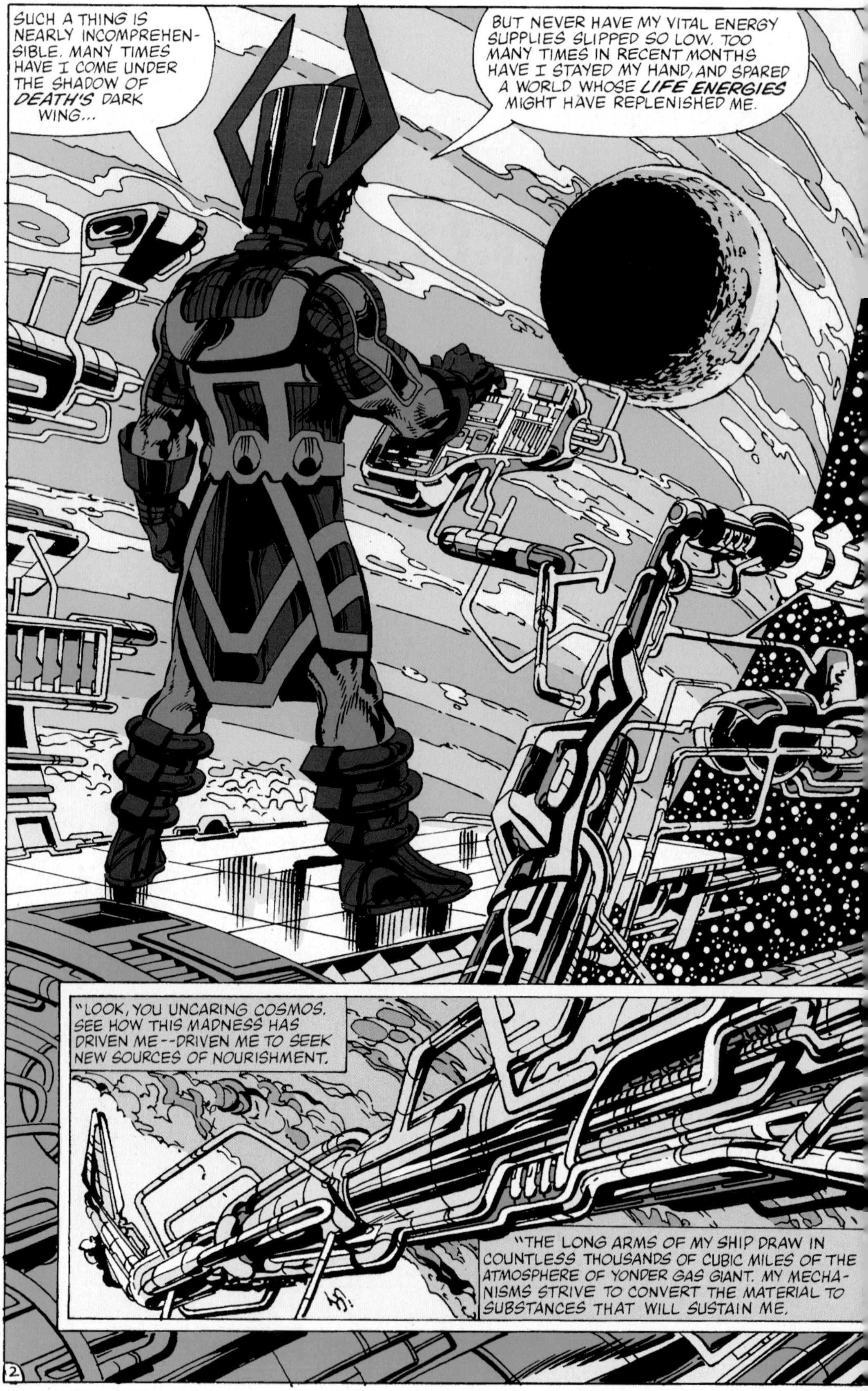
SUCH A THING IS NEARLY INCOMPREHENSIBLE. MANY TIMES HAVE I COME UNDER THE SHADOW OF DEATH'S DARK WING...
BUT NEVER HAVE MY VITAL ENERGY SUPPLIES SLIPPED SO LOW. TOO MANY TIMES IN RECENT MONTHS HAVE I STAYED MY HAND, AND SPARED A WORLD WHOSE LIFE ENERGIES MIGHT HAVE REPLENISHED ME.
"LOOK, YOU UNCARING COSMOS. SEE HOW THIS MADNESS HAS DRIVEN ME--DRIVEN ME TO SEEK NEW SOURCES OF NOURISHMENT.
"THE LONG ARMS OF MY SHIP DRAW IN COUNTLESS THOUSANDS OF CUBIC MILES OF THE ATMOSPHERE OF YONDER GAS GIANT. MY MECHANISMS STRIVE TO CONVERT THE MATERIAL TO SUBSTANCES THAT WILL SUSTAIN ME.

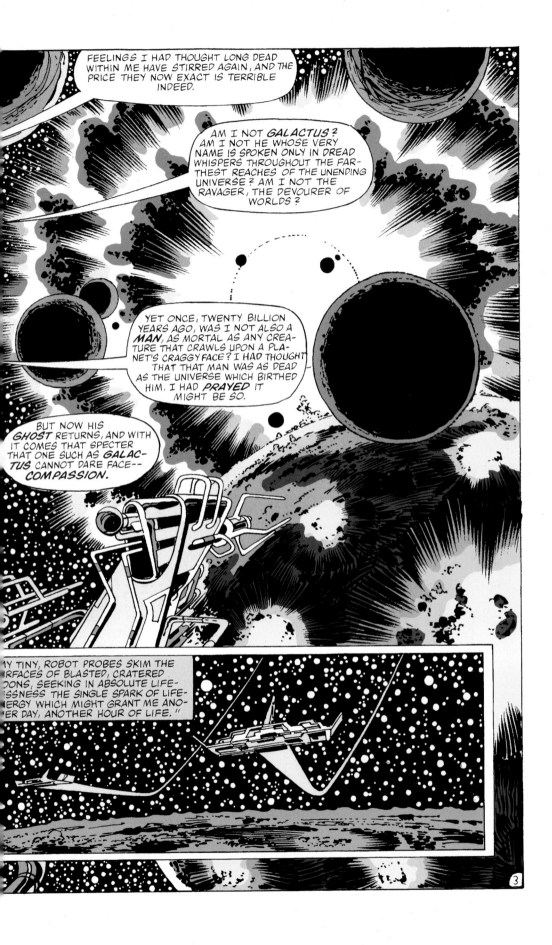

FEELINGS I HAD THOUGHT LONG DEAD WITHIN ME HAVE STIRRED AGAIN, AND THE PRICE THEY NOW EXACT IS TERRIBLE INDEED.

AM I NOT *GALACTUS*? AM I NOT HE WHOSE VERY NAME IS SPOKEN ONLY IN DREAD WHISPERS THROUGHOUT THE FARTHEST REACHES OF THE UNENDING UNIVERSE? AM I NOT THE RAVAGER, THE DEVOURER OF WORLDS?

YET ONCE, TWENTY BILLION YEARS AGO, WAS I NOT ALSO A *MAN*, AS MORTAL AS ANY CREATURE THAT CRAWLS UPON A PLANET'S CRAGGY FACE? I HAD THOUGHT THAT THAT MAN WAS AS DEAD AS THE UNIVERSE WHICH BIRTHED HIM. I HAD *PRAYED* IT MIGHT BE SO.

BUT NOW HIS *GHOST* RETURNS, AND WITH IT COMES THAT SPECTER THAT ONE SUCH AS *GALACTUS* CANNOT DARE FACE-- *COMPASSION*.

MY TINY, ROBOT PROBES SKIM THE SURFACES OF BLASTED, CRATERED MOONS, SEEKING IN ABSOLUTE LIFELESSNESS THE SINGLE SPARK OF LIFE-ENERGY WHICH MIGHT GRANT ME ANOTHER DAY, ANOTHER HOUR OF LIFE."

3

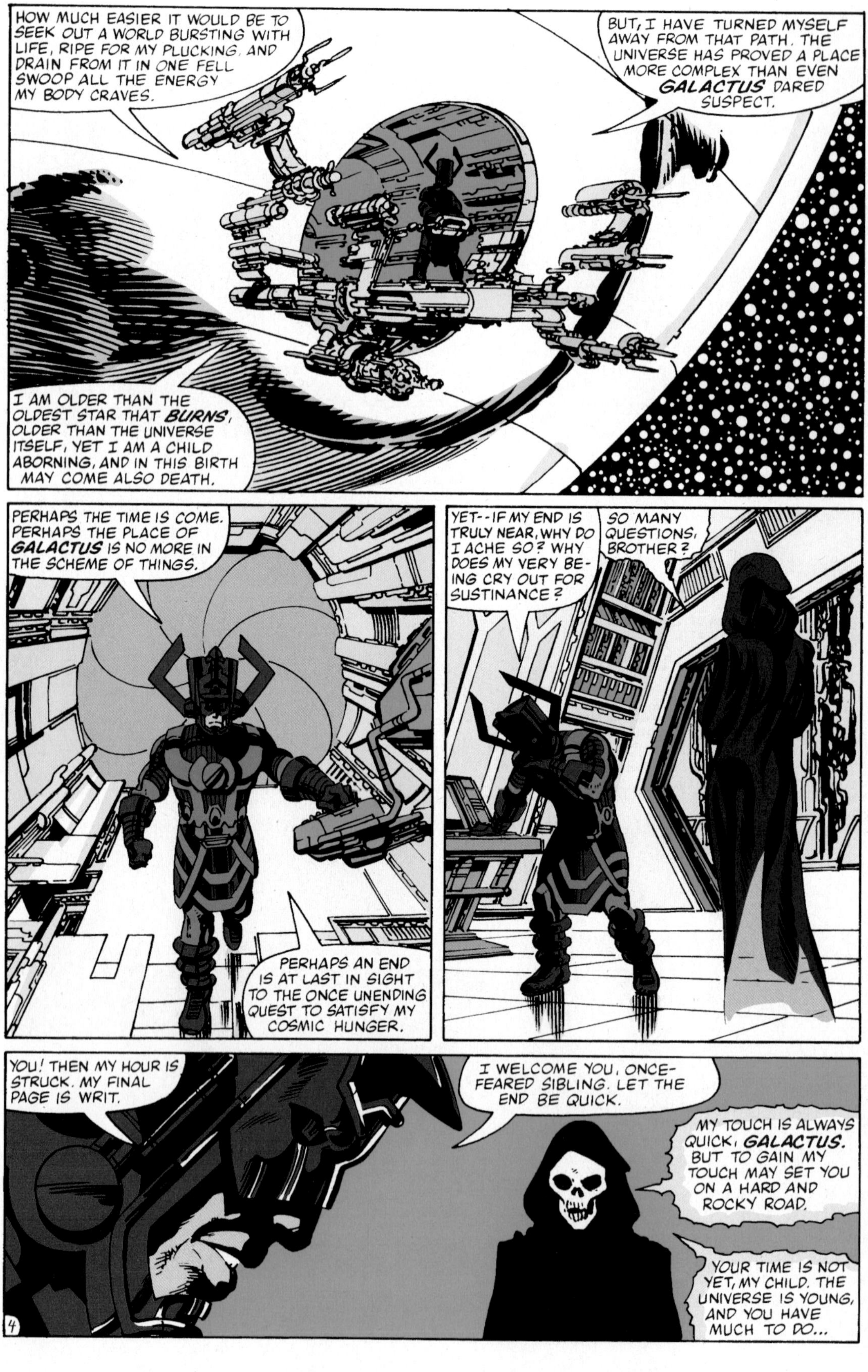
HOW MUCH EASIER IT WOULD BE TO SEEK OUT A WORLD BURSTING WITH LIFE, RIPE FOR MY PLUCKING, AND DRAIN FROM IT IN ONE FELL SWOOP ALL THE ENERGY MY BODY CRAVES.
BUT, I HAVE TURNED MYSELF AWAY FROM THAT PATH. THE UNIVERSE HAS PROVED A PLACE MORE COMPLEX THAN EVEN GALACTUS DARED SUSPECT.
I AM OLDER THAN THE OLDEST STAR THAT BURNS, OLDER THAN THE UNIVERSE ITSELF, YET I AM A CHILD ABORNING, AND IN THIS BIRTH MAY COME ALSO DEATH.
PERHAPS THE TIME IS COME. PERHAPS THE PLACE OF GALACTUS IS NO MORE IN THE SCHEME OF THINGS.
PERHAPS AN END IS AT LAST IN SIGHT TO THE ONCE UNENDING QUEST TO SATISFY MY COSMIC HUNGER.
YET--IF MY END IS TRULY NEAR, WHY DO I ACHE SO? WHY DOES MY VERY BEING CRY OUT FOR SUSTINANCE?
SO MANY QUESTIONS, BROTHER?
YOU! THEN MY HOUR IS STRUCK. MY FINAL PAGE IS WRIT.
I WELCOME YOU, ONCE-FEARED SIBLING. LET THE END BE QUICK.
MY TOUCH IS ALWAYS QUICK, GALACTUS. BUT TO GAIN MY TOUCH MAY SET YOU ON A HARD AND ROCKY ROAD.
YOUR TIME IS NOT YET, MY CHILD. THE UNIVERSE IS YOUNG, AND YOU HAVE MUCH TO DO...
4

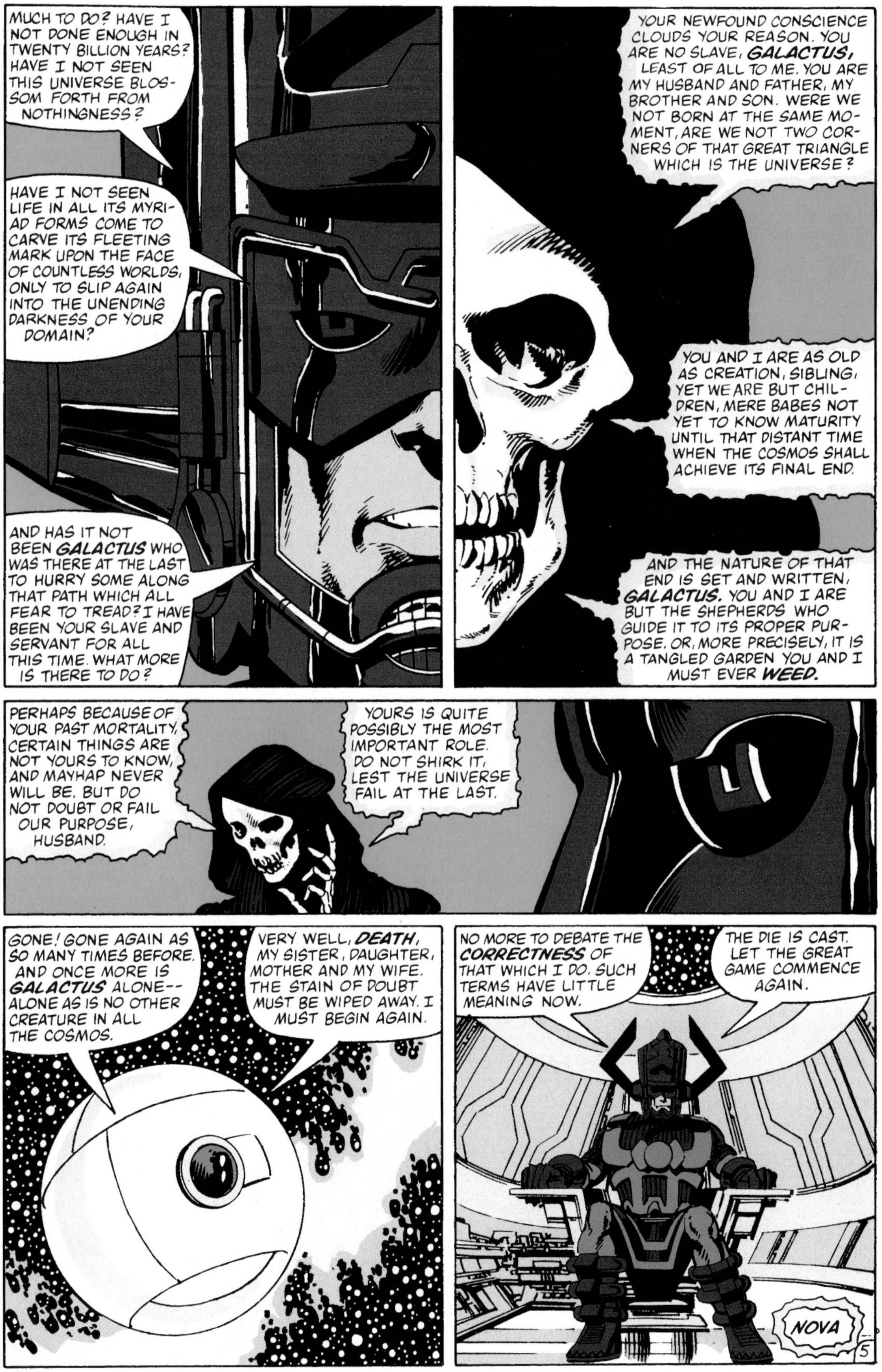
MUCH TO DO? HAVE I NOT DONE ENOUGH IN TWENTY BILLION YEARS? HAVE I NOT SEEN THIS UNIVERSE BLOSSOM FORTH FROM NOTHINGNESS?
HAVE I NOT SEEN LIFE IN ALL ITS MYRIAD FORMS COME TO CARVE ITS FLEETING MARK UPON THE FACE OF COUNTLESS WORLDS, ONLY TO SLIP AGAIN INTO THE UNENDING DARKNESS OF YOUR DOMAIN?
AND HAS IT NOT BEEN GALACTUS WHO WAS THERE AT THE LAST TO HURRY SOME ALONG THAT PATH WHICH ALL FEAR TO TREAD? I HAVE BEEN YOUR SLAVE AND SERVANT FOR ALL THIS TIME. WHAT MORE IS THERE TO DO?
YOUR NEWFOUND CONSCIENCE CLOUDS YOUR REASON. YOU ARE NO SLAVE, GALACTUS, LEAST OF ALL TO ME. YOU ARE MY HUSBAND AND FATHER, MY BROTHER AND SON. WERE WE NOT BORN AT THE SAME MOMENT, ARE WE NOT TWO CORNERS OF THAT GREAT TRIANGLE WHICH IS THE UNIVERSE?
YOU AND I ARE AS OLD AS CREATION, SIBLING, YET WE ARE BUT CHILDREN, MERE BABES NOT YET TO KNOW MATURITY UNTIL THAT DISTANT TIME WHEN THE COSMOS SHALL ACHIEVE ITS FINAL END.
AND THE NATURE OF THAT END IS SET AND WRITTEN, GALACTUS. YOU AND I ARE BUT THE SHEPHERDS WHO GUIDE IT TO ITS PROPER PURPOSE. OR, MORE PRECISELY, IT IS A TANGLED GARDEN YOU AND I MUST EVER WEED.
PERHAPS BECAUSE OF YOUR PAST MORTALITY, CERTAIN THINGS ARE NOT YOURS TO KNOW, AND MAYHAP NEVER WILL BE. BUT DO NOT DOUBT OR FAIL OUR PURPOSE, HUSBAND.
YOURS IS QUITE POSSIBLY THE MOST IMPORTANT ROLE. DO NOT SHIRK IT, LEST THE UNIVERSE FAIL AT THE LAST.
GONE! GONE AGAIN AS SO MANY TIMES BEFORE. AND ONCE MORE IS GALACTUS ALONE-- ALONE AS IS NO OTHER CREATURE IN ALL THE COSMOS.
VERY WELL, DEATH, MY SISTER, DAUGHTER, MOTHER AND MY WIFE. THE STAIN OF DOUBT MUST BE WIPED AWAY. I MUST BEGIN AGAIN.
NO MORE TO DEBATE THE CORRECTNESS OF THAT WHICH I DO. SUCH TERMS HAVE LITTLE MEANING NOW.
THE DIE IS CAST. LET THE GREAT GAME COMMENCE AGAIN.
NOVA
5

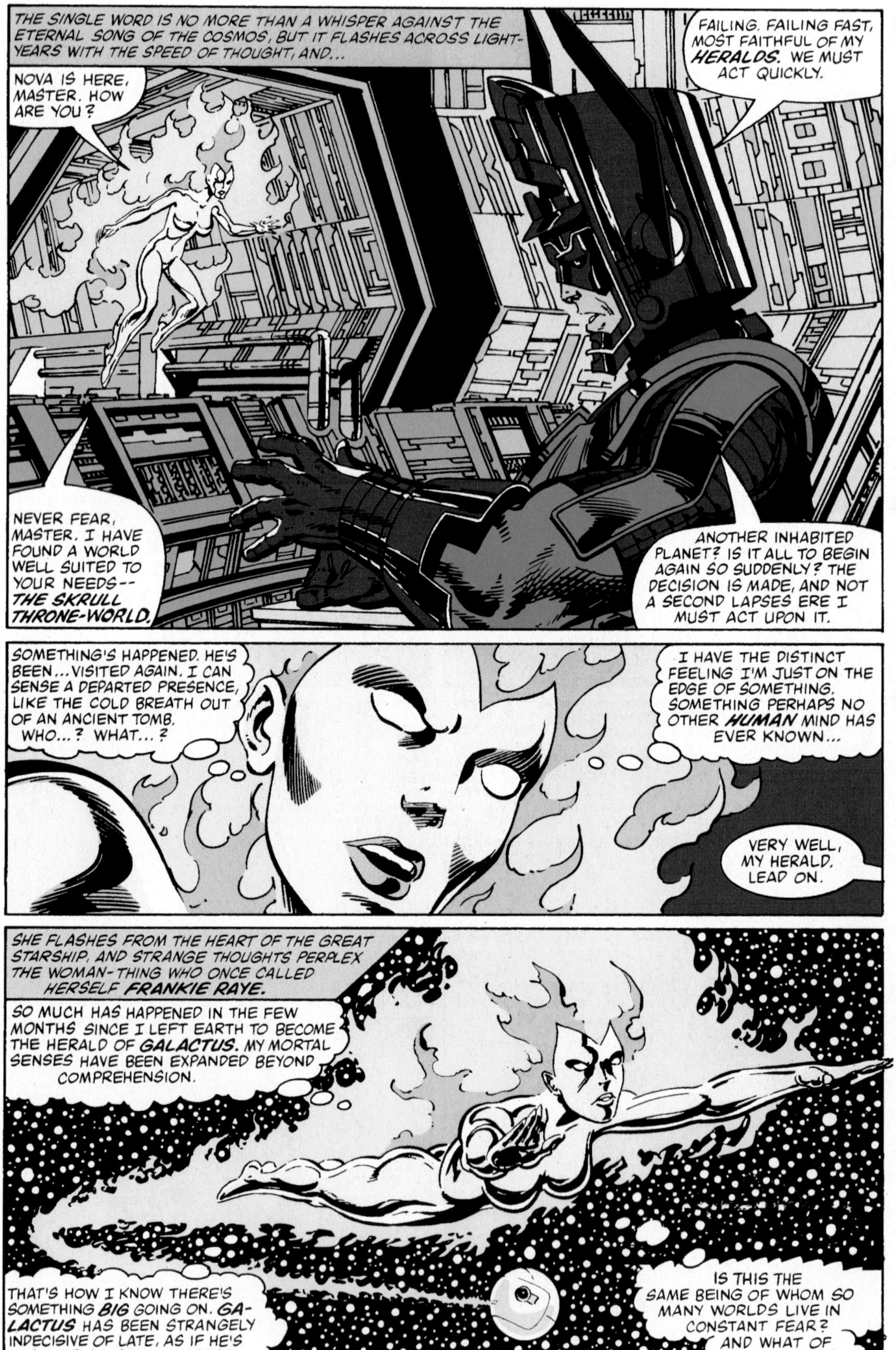
THE SINGLE WORD IS NO MORE THAN A WHISPER AGAINST THE ETERNAL SONG OF THE COSMOS, BUT IT FLASHES ACROSS LIGHT-YEARS WITH THE SPEED OF THOUGHT, AND...
NOVA IS HERE, MASTER. HOW ARE YOU?
FAILING. FAILING FAST, MOST FAITHFUL OF MY HERALDS. WE MUST ACT QUICKLY.
NEVER FEAR, MASTER. I HAVE FOUND A WORLD WELL SUITED TO YOUR NEEDS-- THE SKRULL THRONE-WORLD.
ANOTHER INHABITED PLANET? IS IT ALL TO BEGIN AGAIN SO SUDDENLY? THE DECISION IS MADE, AND NOT A SECOND LAPSES ERE I MUST ACT UPON IT.
SOMETHING'S HAPPENED. HE'S BEEN...VISITED AGAIN. I CAN SENSE A DEPARTED PRESENCE, LIKE THE COLD BREATH OUT OF AN ANCIENT TOMB. WHO...? WHAT...?
I HAVE THE DISTINCT FEELING I'M JUST ON THE EDGE OF SOMETHING. SOMETHING PERHAPS NO OTHER HUMAN MIND HAS EVER KNOWN...
VERY WELL, MY HERALD. LEAD ON.
SHE FLASHES FROM THE HEART OF THE GREAT STARSHIP, AND STRANGE THOUGHTS PERPLEX THE WOMAN-THING WHO ONCE CALLED HERSELF FRANKIE RAYE.
SO MUCH HAS HAPPENED IN THE FEW MONTHS SINCE I LEFT EARTH TO BECOME THE HERALD OF GALACTUS. MY MORTAL SENSES HAVE BEEN EXPANDED BEYOND COMPREHENSION.
THAT'S HOW I KNOW THERE'S SOMETHING BIG GOING ON. GALACTUS HAS BEEN STRANGELY INDECISIVE OF LATE, AS IF HE'S LOST HIS SENSE OF PURPOSE.
IS THIS THE SAME BEING OF WHOM SO MANY WORLDS LIVE IN CONSTANT FEAR? AND WHAT OF MY FEELINGS?
6

IT'S SHEER INSANITY TO EVEN CONSIDER FEELING THE WAY I DO. BUT I CAN'T HELP IT. *GALACTUS* IS LIKE NO MAN I'VE EVER KNOWN...

NOW, THERE'S A BRILLIANT OBSERVATION. *GALACTUS* IS LIKE NO MAN, *PERIOD*. I KNOW MY LIBERATED SISTERS BACK ON EARTH WOULD HAVE KITTENS, BUT I FIND HIM ABSOLUTELY IRRESISTABLE. HIS POWER. HIS ALMOST OMNISCIENT ALOOFNESS.

DO I DARE PUT THE WORD TO IT? AM I IN *LOVE* WITH *GALACTUS*?

A STRANGE THOUGHT TO BE SURE, AND PASSING QUICKLY FOR NOW AS THE BAREST CONCENTRATION WARPS TIME AND SPACE...

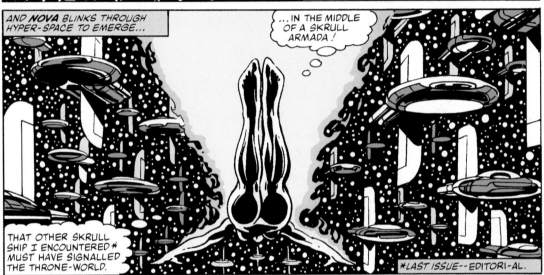

AND *NOVA* BLINKS THROUGH HYPER-SPACE TO EMERGE...

...IN THE MIDDLE OF A SKRULL ARMADA!

THAT OTHER SKRULL SHIP I ENCOUNTERED* MUST HAVE SIGNALLED THE THRONE-WORLD.

*LAST ISSUE--EDITORI-AL.

ABOARD THE SHIPS OF THE FLEET THE USUALLY LIMBER SKRULLS MOVE AWKWARDLY IN THEIR CUMBERSOME SPACE ARMOR.

AND *FEAR* SITS HEAVILY ON EVERY SHOULDER.

READY, WEAPONS OFFICER. STAND BY TO FIRE.

AT YOUR ORDER, COMMANDER...

THE WORD IS NEVER SPOKEN.

NOVA'S FLAME INTENSIFIES TO THE POWER OF HER NAMESAKE...

AND THE FIRST SKRULL SHIP PERISHES WITHOUT EVER KNOWING BATTLE.

THE FOOLS! DO THEY REALLY THINK THEY STAND A CHANCE AGAINST THE HERALD OF *GALACTUS*?

7

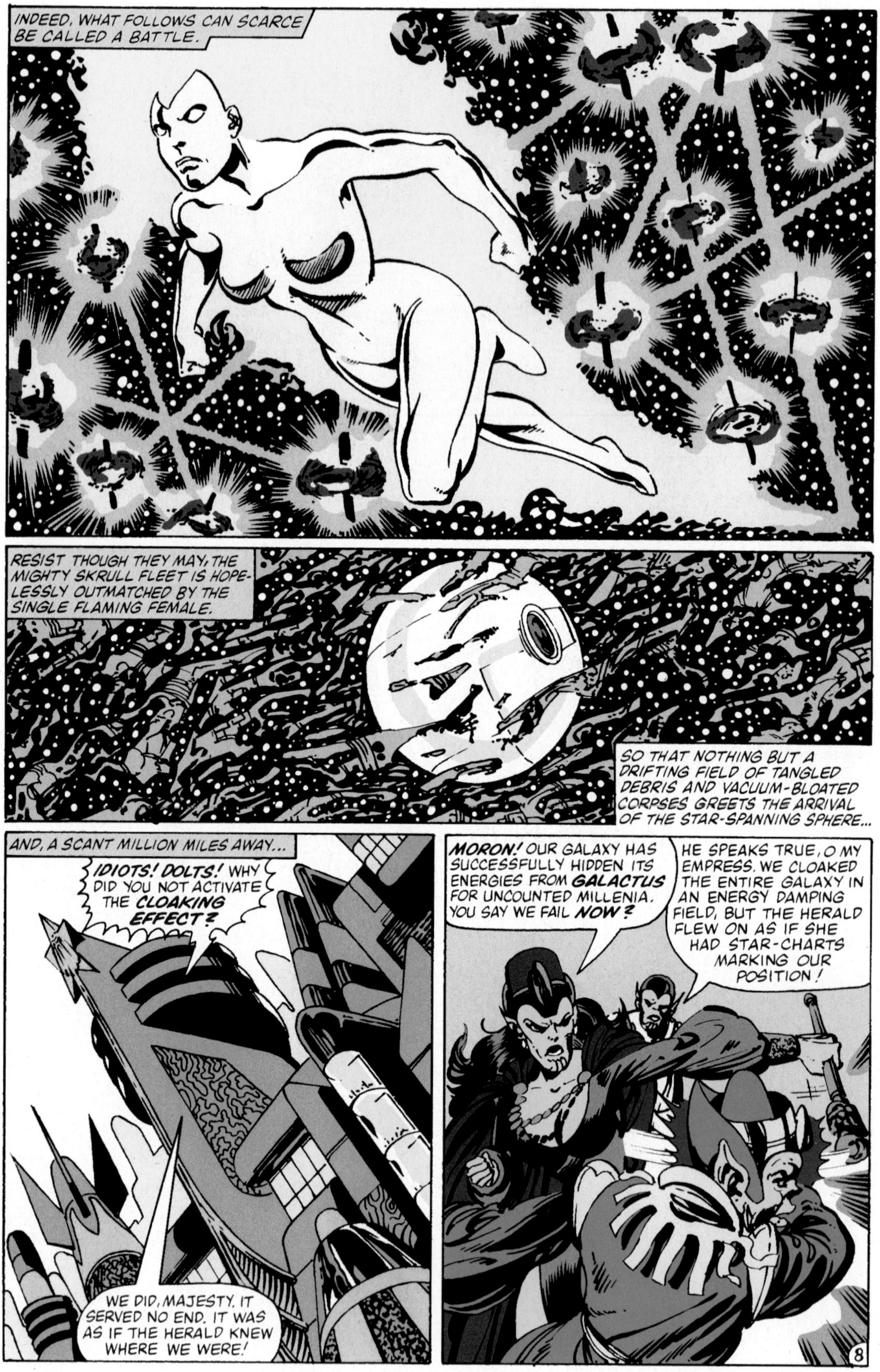

INDEED, WHAT FOLLOWS CAN SCARCE BE CALLED A BATTLE.
RESIST THOUGH THEY MAY, THE MIGHTY SKRULL FLEET IS HOPELESSLY OUTMATCHED BY THE SINGLE FLAMING FEMALE.
SO THAT NOTHING BUT A DRIFTING FIELD OF TANGLED DEBRIS AND VACUUM-BLOATED CORPSES GREETS THE ARRIVAL OF THE STAR-SPANNING SPHERE...
AND, A SCANT MILLION MILES AWAY...
IDIOTS! DOLTS! WHY DID YOU NOT ACTIVATE THE CLOAKING EFFECT?
WE DID, MAJESTY. IT SERVED NO END. IT WAS AS IF THE HERALD KNEW WHERE WE WERE!
MORON! OUR GALAXY HAS SUCCESSFULLY HIDDEN ITS ENERGIES FROM GALACTUS FOR UNCOUNTED MILLENIA. YOU SAY WE FAIL NOW?
HE SPEAKS TRUE, O MY EMPRESS. WE CLOAKED THE ENTIRE GALAXY IN AN ENERGY DAMPING FIELD, BUT THE HERALD FLEW ON AS IF SHE HAD STAR-CHARTS MARKING OUR POSITION!
8

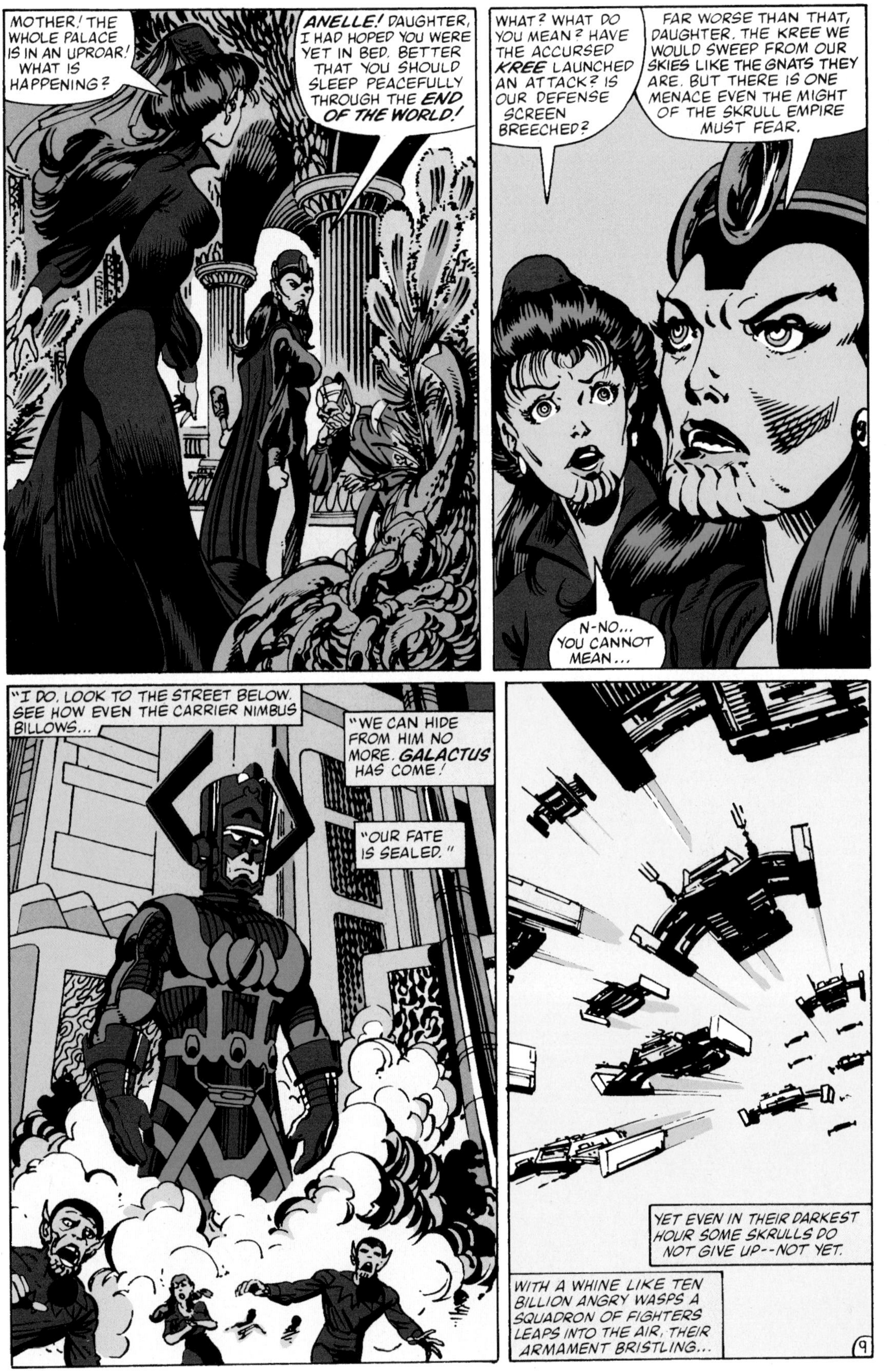
MOTHER! THE WHOLE PALACE IS IN AN UPROAR! WHAT IS HAPPENING?
ANELLE! DAUGHTER, I HAD HOPED YOU WERE YET IN BED. BETTER THAT YOU SHOULD SLEEP PEACEFULLY THROUGH THE END OF THE WORLD!
WHAT? WHAT DO YOU MEAN? HAVE THE ACCURSED KREE LAUNCHED AN ATTACK? IS OUR DEFENSE SCREEN BREECHED?
FAR WORSE THAN THAT, DAUGHTER. THE KREE WE WOULD SWEEP FROM OUR SKIES LIKE THE GNATS THEY ARE. BUT THERE IS ONE MENACE EVEN THE MIGHT OF THE SKRULL EMPIRE MUST FEAR.
N-NO... YOU CANNOT MEAN...
"I DO. LOOK TO THE STREET BELOW. SEE HOW EVEN THE CARRIER NIMBUS BILLOWS...
"WE CAN HIDE FROM HIM NO MORE. GALACTUS HAS COME!
"OUR FATE IS SEALED."
YET EVEN IN THEIR DARKEST HOUR SOME SKRULLS DO NOT GIVE UP--NOT YET.
WITH A WHINE LIKE TEN BILLION ANGRY WASPS A SQUADRON OF FIGHTERS LEAPS INTO THE AIR, THEIR ARMAMENT BRISTLING...
9

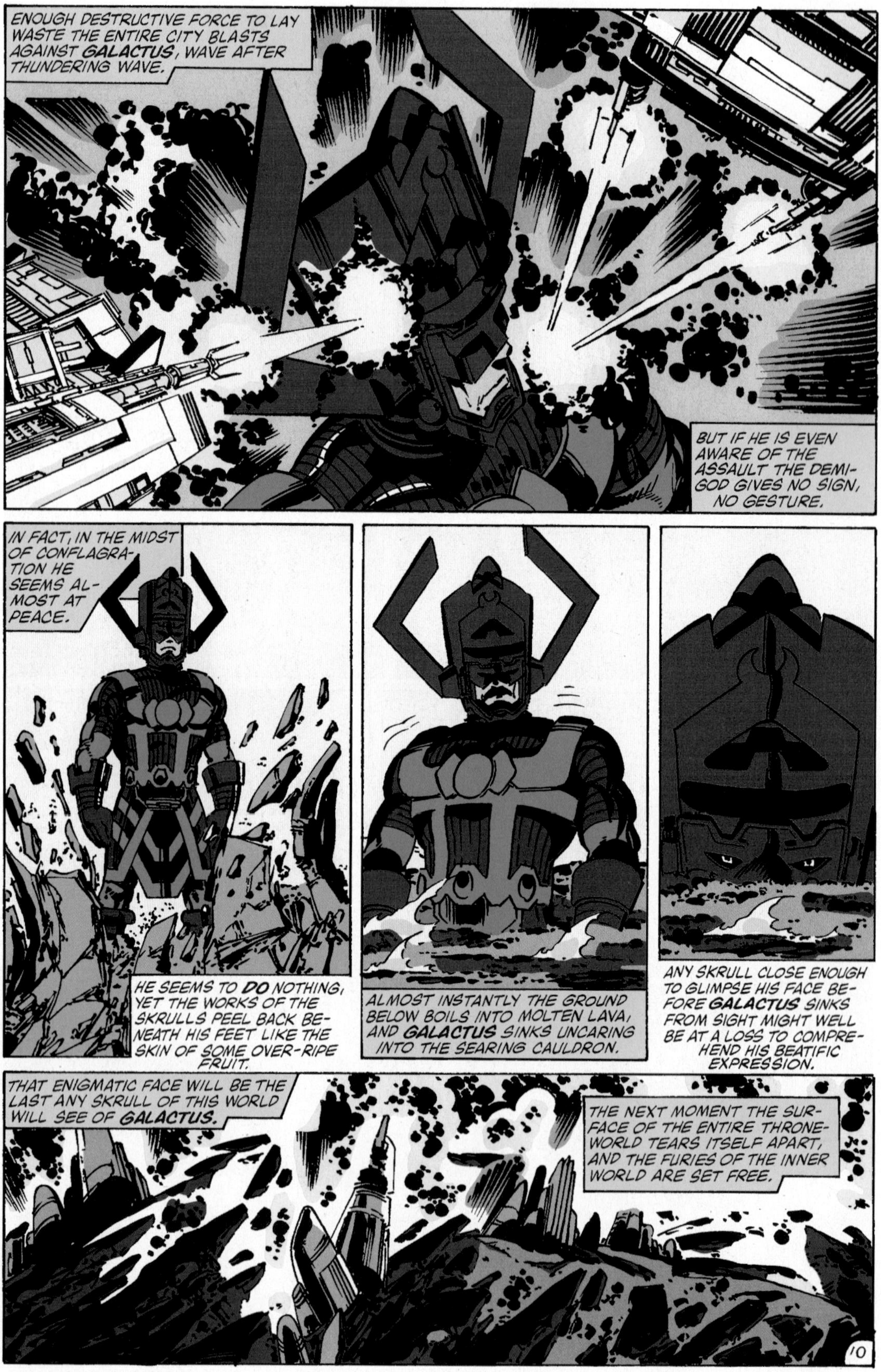
ENOUGH DESTRUCTIVE FORCE TO LAY WASTE THE ENTIRE CITY BLASTS AGAINST GALACTUS, WAVE AFTER THUNDERING WAVE.
BUT IF HE IS EVEN AWARE OF THE ASSAULT THE DEMI-GOD GIVES NO SIGN, NO GESTURE.
IN FACT, IN THE MIDST OF CONFLAGRATION HE SEEMS ALMOST AT PEACE.
HE SEEMS TO DO NOTHING, YET THE WORKS OF THE SKRULLS PEEL BACK BENEATH HIS FEET LIKE THE SKIN OF SOME OVER-RIPE FRUIT.
ALMOST INSTANTLY THE GROUND BELOW BOILS INTO MOLTEN LAVA, AND GALACTUS SINKS UNCARING INTO THE SEARING CAULDRON.
ANY SKRULL CLOSE ENOUGH TO GLIMPSE HIS FACE BEFORE GALACTUS SINKS FROM SIGHT MIGHT WELL BE AT A LOSS TO COMPREHEND HIS BEATIFIC EXPRESSION.
THAT ENIGMATIC FACE WILL BE THE LAST ANY SKRULL OF THIS WORLD WILL SEE OF GALACTUS.
THE NEXT MOMENT THE SURFACE OF THE ENTIRE THRONEWORLD TEARS ITSELF APART, AND THE FURIES OF THE INNER WORLD ARE SET FREE.
10

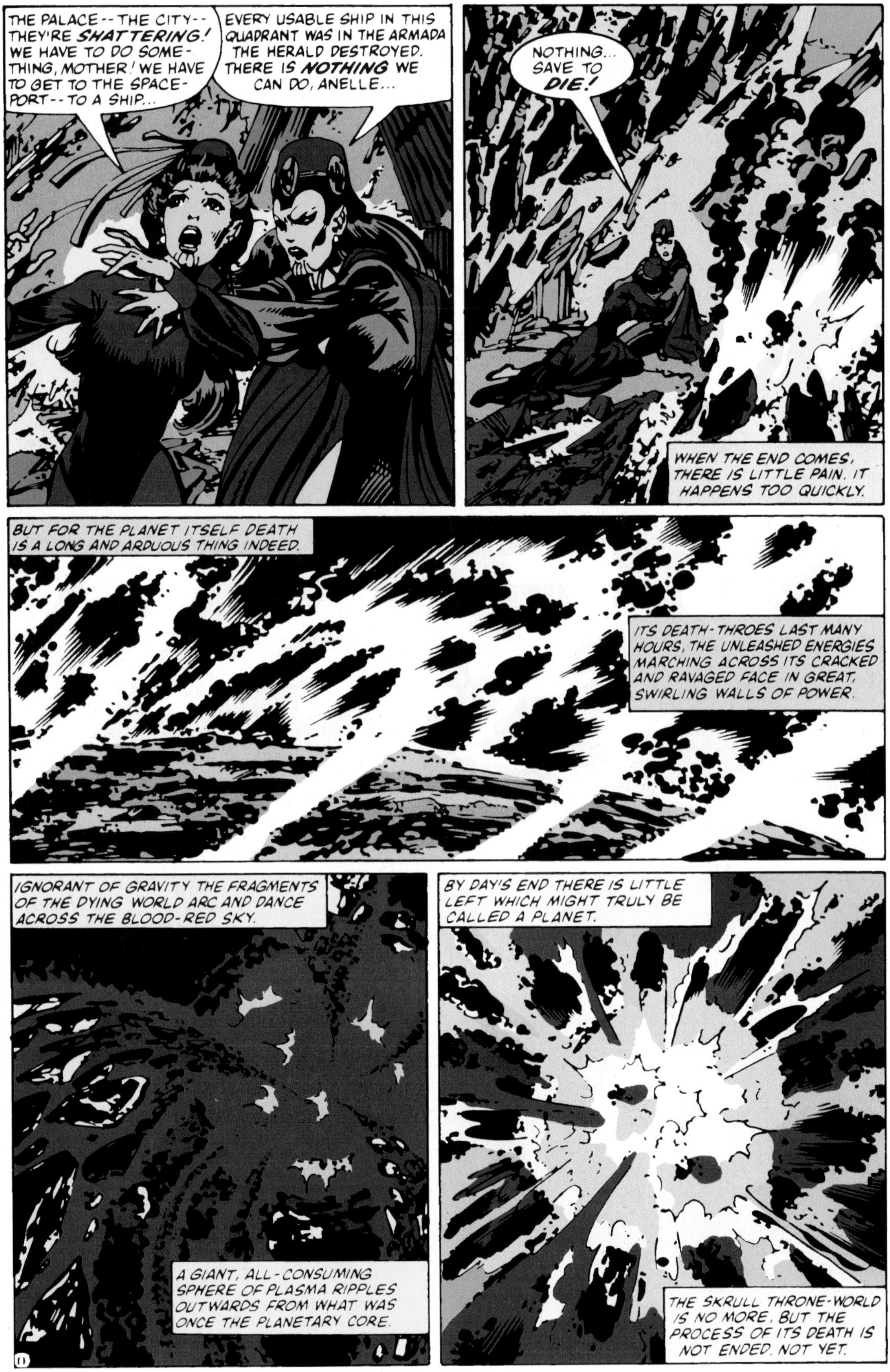
THE PALACE -- THE CITY -- THEY'RE SHATTERING! WE HAVE TO DO SOMETHING, MOTHER! WE HAVE TO GET TO THE SPACEPORT -- TO A SHIP...
EVERY USABLE SHIP IN THIS QUADRANT WAS IN THE ARMADA THE HERALD DESTROYED. THERE IS NOTHING WE CAN DO, ANELLE...
NOTHING... SAVE TO DIE!
WHEN THE END COMES, THERE IS LITTLE PAIN. IT HAPPENS TOO QUICKLY.
BUT FOR THE PLANET ITSELF DEATH IS A LONG AND ARDUOUS THING INDEED.
ITS DEATH-THROES LAST MANY HOURS, THE UNLEASHED ENERGIES MARCHING ACROSS ITS CRACKED AND RAVAGED FACE IN GREAT, SWIRLING WALLS OF POWER.
IGNORANT OF GRAVITY THE FRAGMENTS OF THE DYING WORLD ARC AND DANCE ACROSS THE BLOOD-RED SKY.
A GIANT, ALL-CONSUMING SPHERE OF PLASMA RIPPLES OUTWARDS FROM WHAT WAS ONCE THE PLANETARY CORE.
BY DAY'S END THERE IS LITTLE LEFT WHICH MIGHT TRULY BE CALLED A PLANET.
THE SKRULL THRONE-WORLD IS NO MORE, BUT THE PROCESS OF ITS DEATH IS NOT ENDED. NOT YET.

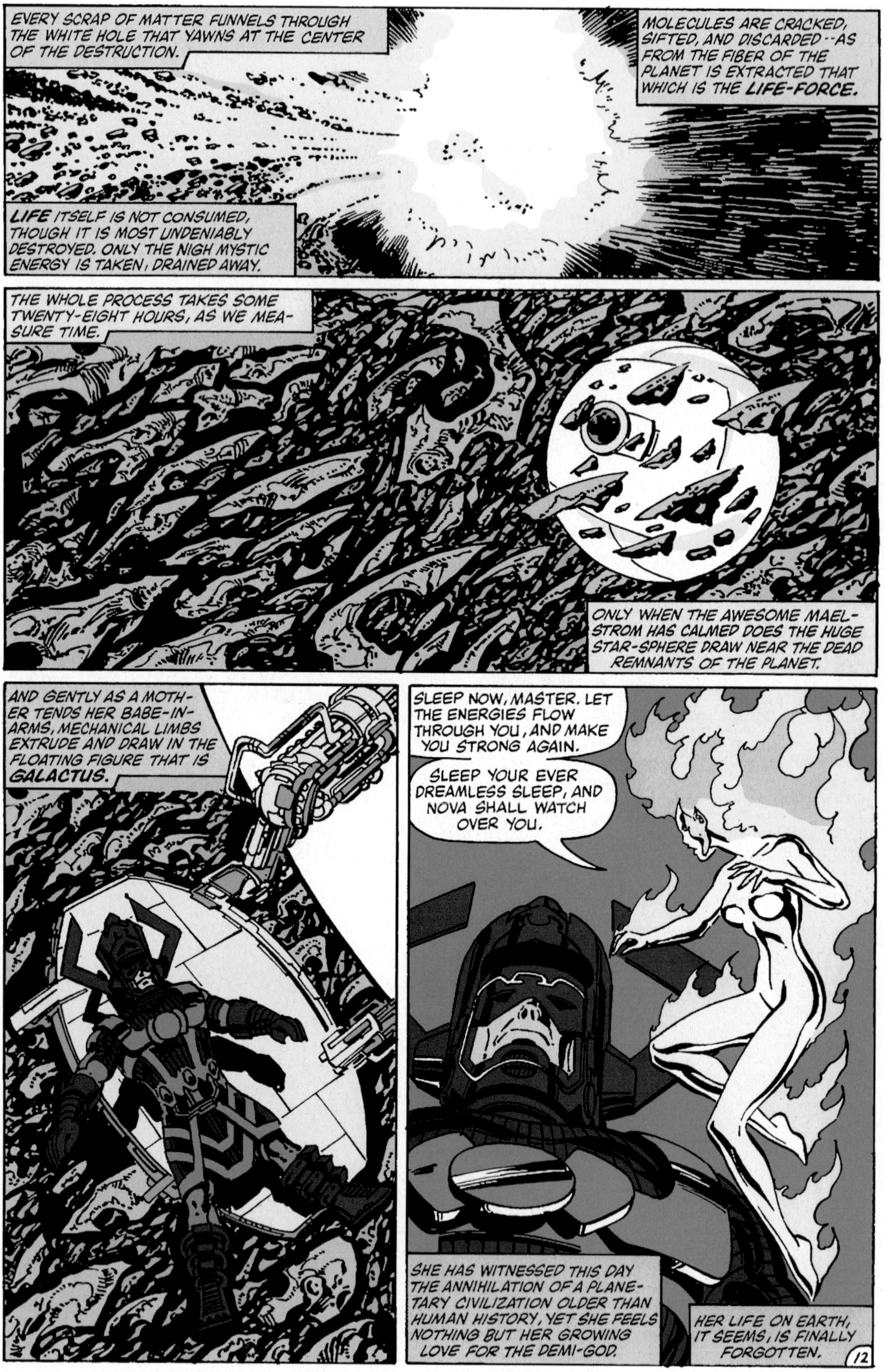
EVERY SCRAP OF MATTER FUNNELS THROUGH THE WHITE HOLE THAT YAWNS AT THE CENTER OF THE DESTRUCTION.
MOLECULES ARE CRACKED, SIFTED, AND DISCARDED--AS FROM THE FIBER OF THE PLANET IS EXTRACTED THAT WHICH IS THE LIFE-FORCE.
LIFE ITSELF IS NOT CONSUMED, THOUGH IT IS MOST UNDENIABLY DESTROYED. ONLY THE NIGH MYSTIC ENERGY IS TAKEN, DRAINED AWAY.
THE WHOLE PROCESS TAKES SOME TWENTY-EIGHT HOURS, AS WE MEASURE TIME.
ONLY WHEN THE AWESOME MAELSTROM HAS CALMED DOES THE HUGE STAR-SPHERE DRAW NEAR THE DEAD REMNANTS OF THE PLANET.
AND GENTLY AS A MOTHER TENDS HER BABE-IN-ARMS, MECHANICAL LIMBS EXTRUDE AND DRAW IN THE FLOATING FIGURE THAT IS GALACTUS.
SLEEP NOW, MASTER. LET THE ENERGIES FLOW THROUGH YOU, AND MAKE YOU STRONG AGAIN.
SLEEP YOUR EVER DREAMLESS SLEEP, AND NOVA SHALL WATCH OVER YOU.
SHE HAS WITNESSED THIS DAY THE ANNIHILATION OF A PLANETARY CIVILIZATION OLDER THAN HUMAN HISTORY, YET SHE FEELS NOTHING BUT HER GROWING LOVE FOR THE DEMI-GOD.
HER LIFE ON EARTH, IT SEEMS, IS FINALLY FORGOTTEN.

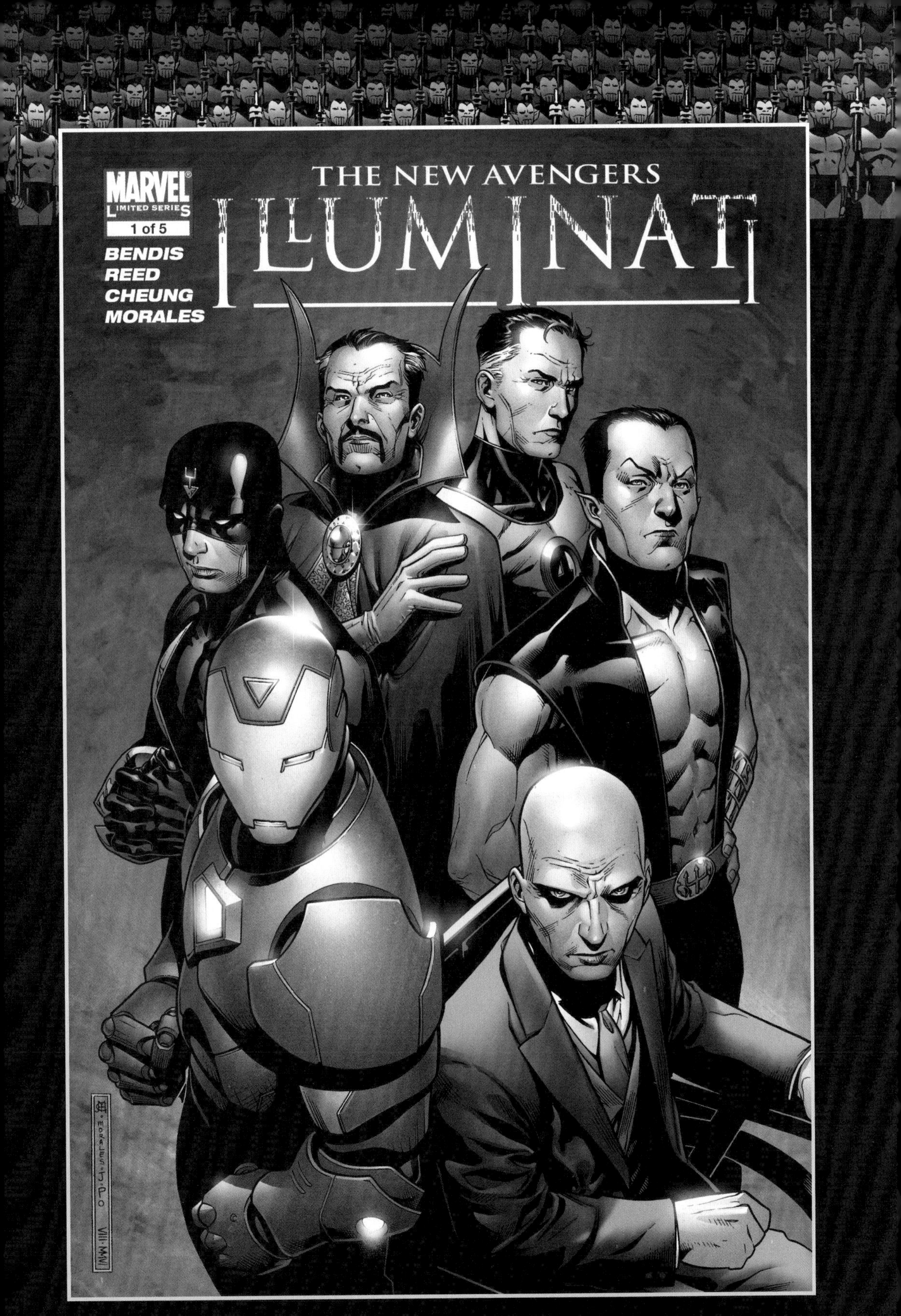
THE NEW AVENGERS
ILLUMINATI
MARVEL
LIMITED SERIES
1 of 5
BENDIS
REED
CHEUNG
MORALES

NEW AVENGERS: ILLUMINATI #1 (FEBRUARY 2007)

After the Kree/Skrull War, some of Earth's most powerful superhumans band together to protect the planet as *Secret Invasion* marches on the Marvel Universe.

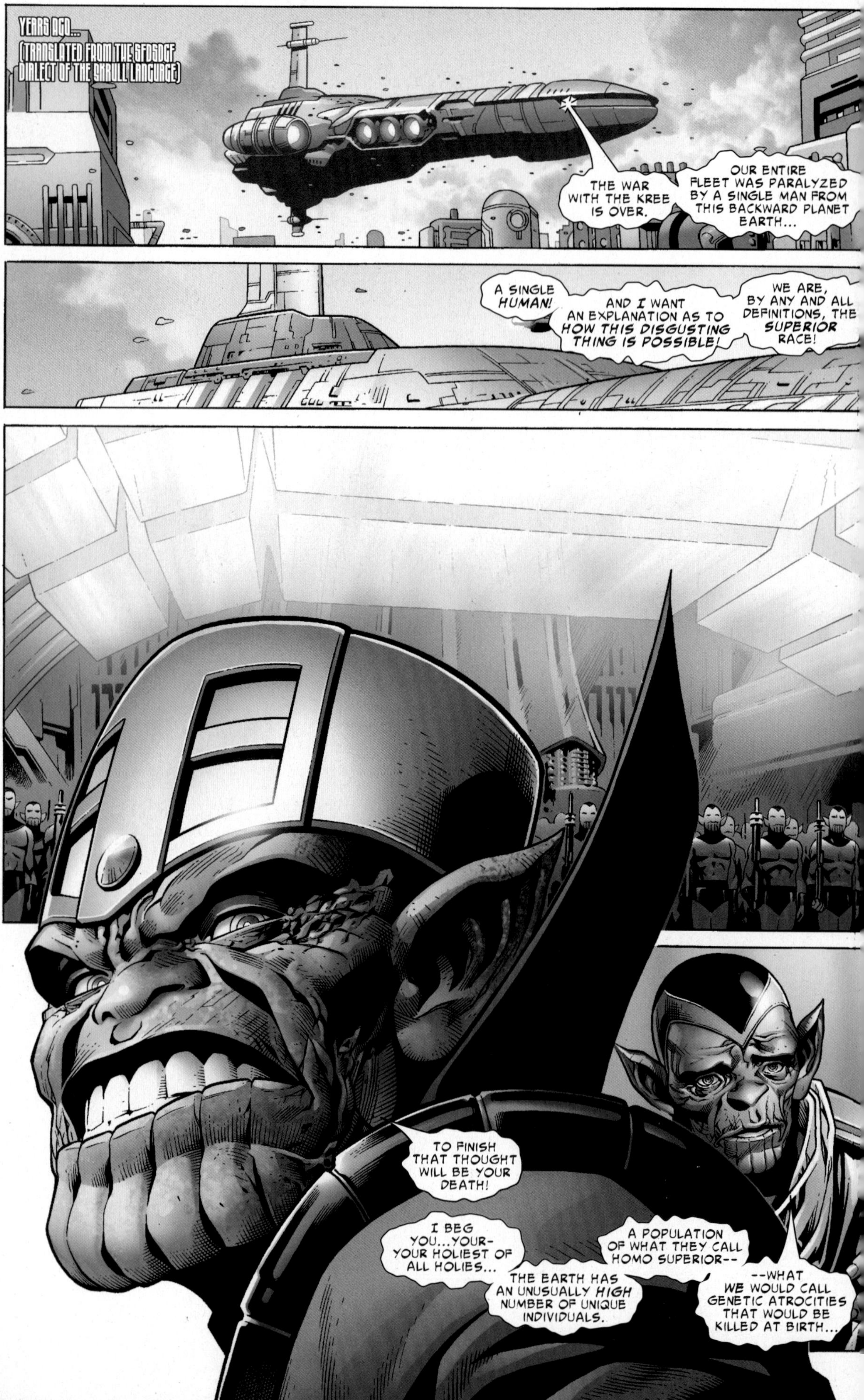

YEARS AGO...
(TRANSLATED FROM THE SFDSDGF DIALECT OF THE SKRULL LANGUAGE)
THE WAR WITH THE KREE IS OVER.
OUR ENTIRE FLEET WAS PARALYZED BY A SINGLE MAN FROM THIS BACKWARD PLANET EARTH...
A SINGLE HUMAN!
AND I WANT AN EXPLANATION AS TO HOW THIS DISGUSTING THING IS POSSIBLE!
WE ARE, BY ANY AND ALL DEFINITIONS, THE SUPERIOR RACE!
TO FINISH THAT THOUGHT WILL BE YOUR DEATH!
I BEG YOU...YOUR-YOUR HOLIEST OF ALL HOLIES...
THE EARTH HAS AN UNUSUALLY HIGH NUMBER OF UNIQUE INDIVIDUALS.
A POPULATION OF WHAT THEY CALL HOMO SUPERIOR--
--WHAT WE WOULD CALL GENETIC ATROCITIES THAT WOULD BE KILLED AT BIRTH...

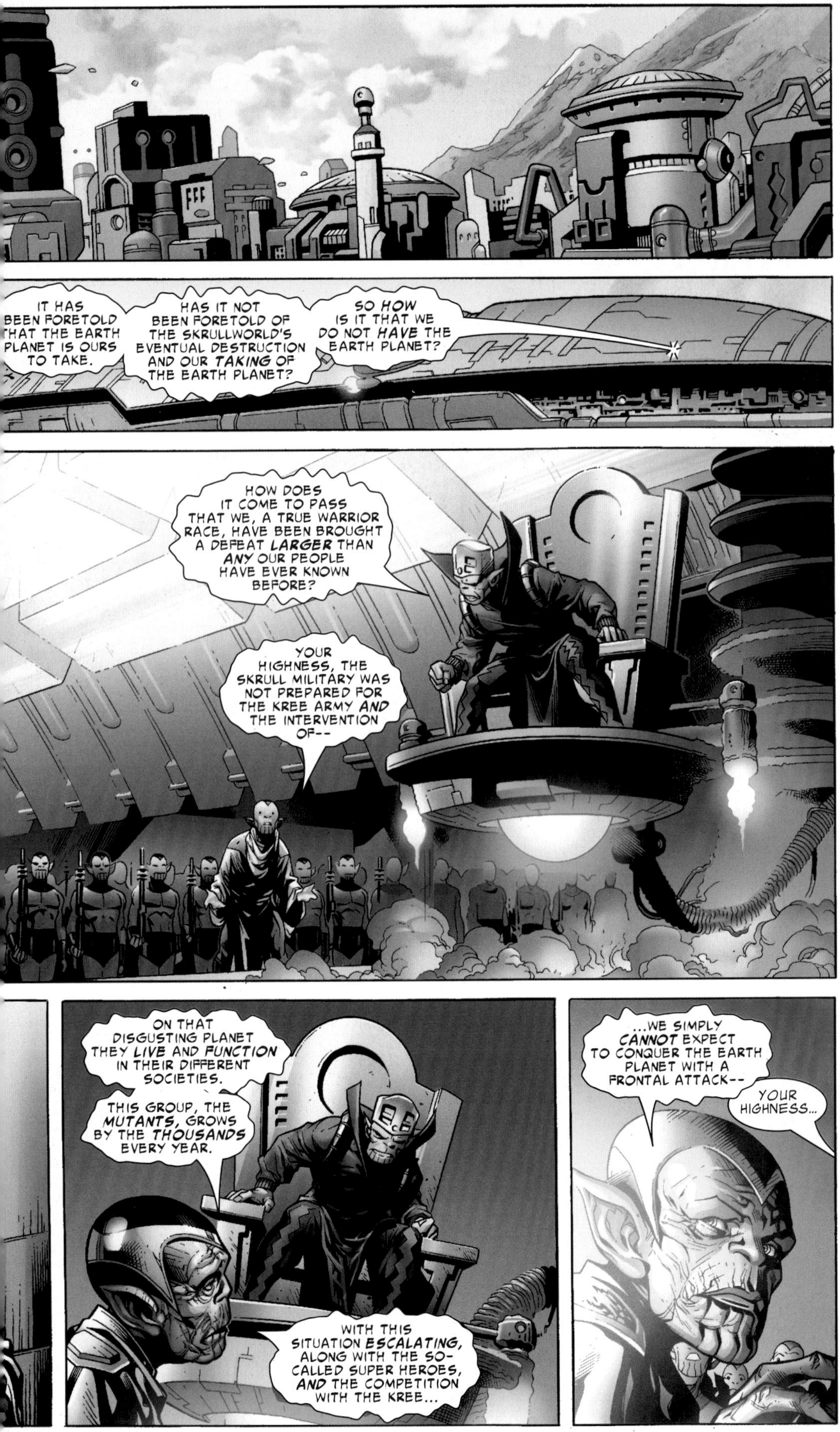
IT HAS BEEN FORETOLD THAT THE EARTH PLANET IS OURS TO TAKE.
HAS IT NOT BEEN FORETOLD OF THE SKRULLWORLD'S EVENTUAL DESTRUCTION AND OUR TAKING OF THE EARTH PLANET?
SO HOW IS IT THAT WE DO NOT HAVE THE EARTH PLANET?
HOW DOES IT COME TO PASS THAT WE, A TRUE WARRIOR RACE, HAVE BEEN BROUGHT A DEFEAT LARGER THAN ANY OUR PEOPLE HAVE EVER KNOWN BEFORE?
YOUR HIGHNESS, THE SKRULL MILITARY WAS NOT PREPARED FOR THE KREE ARMY AND THE INTERVENTION OF--
ON THAT DISGUSTING PLANET THEY LIVE AND FUNCTION IN THEIR DIFFERENT SOCIETIES.
THIS GROUP, THE MUTANTS, GROWS BY THE THOUSANDS EVERY YEAR.
WITH THIS SITUATION ESCALATING, ALONG WITH THE SO-CALLED SUPER HEROES, AND THE COMPETITION WITH THE KREE...
...WE SIMPLY CANNOT EXPECT TO CONQUER THE EARTH PLANET WITH A FRONTAL ATTACK--
YOUR HIGHNESS...

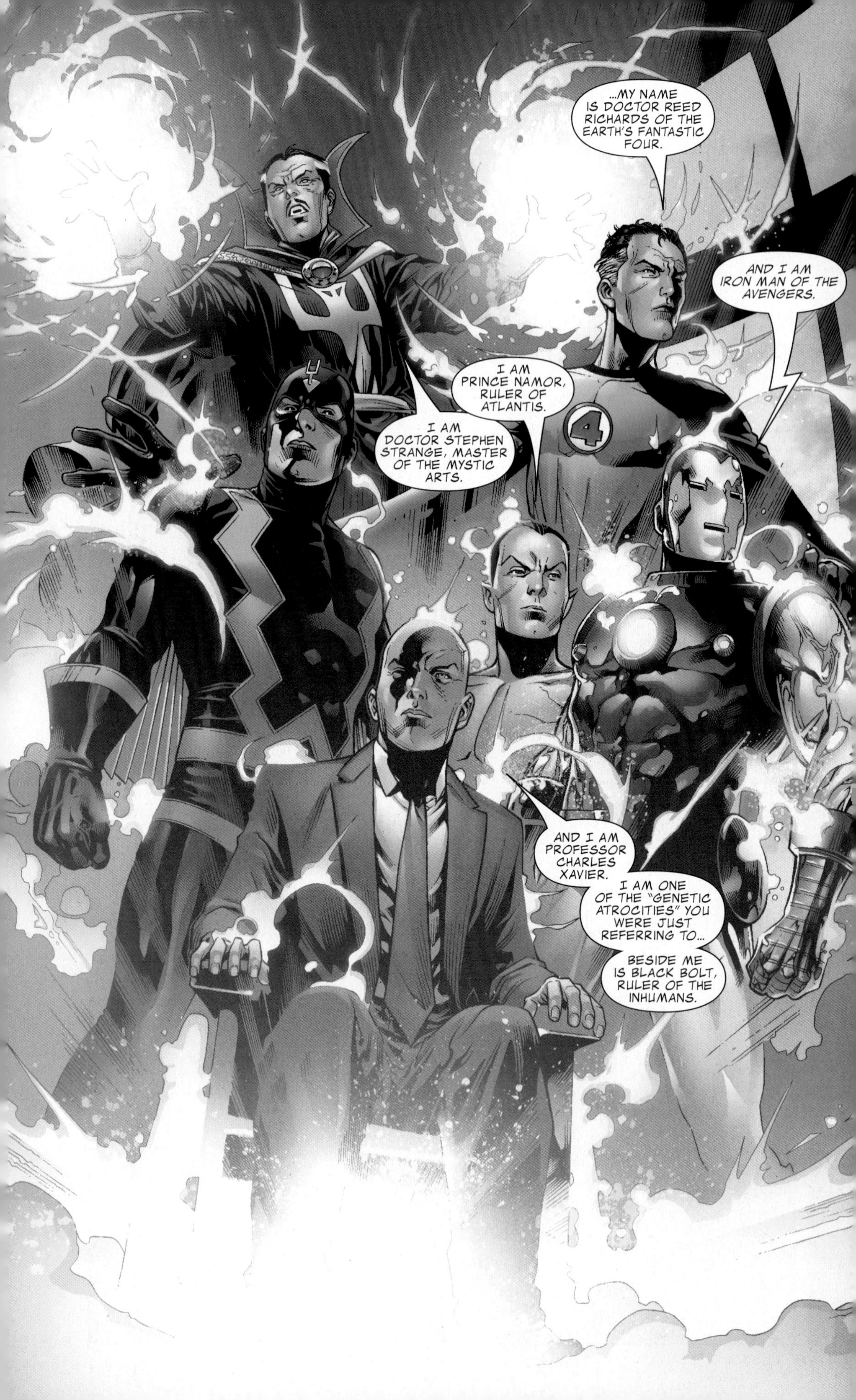
...MY NAME IS DOCTOR REED RICHARDS OF THE EARTH'S FANTASTIC FOUR.
AND I AM IRON MAN OF THE AVENGERS.
I AM PRINCE NAMOR, RULER OF ATLANTIS.
I AM DOCTOR STEPHEN STRANGE, MASTER OF THE MYSTIC ARTS.
AND I AM PROFESSOR CHARLES XAVIER.
I AM ONE OF THE "GENETIC ATROCITIES" YOU WERE JUST REFERRING TO...
BESIDE ME IS BLACK BOLT, RULER OF THE INHUMANS.

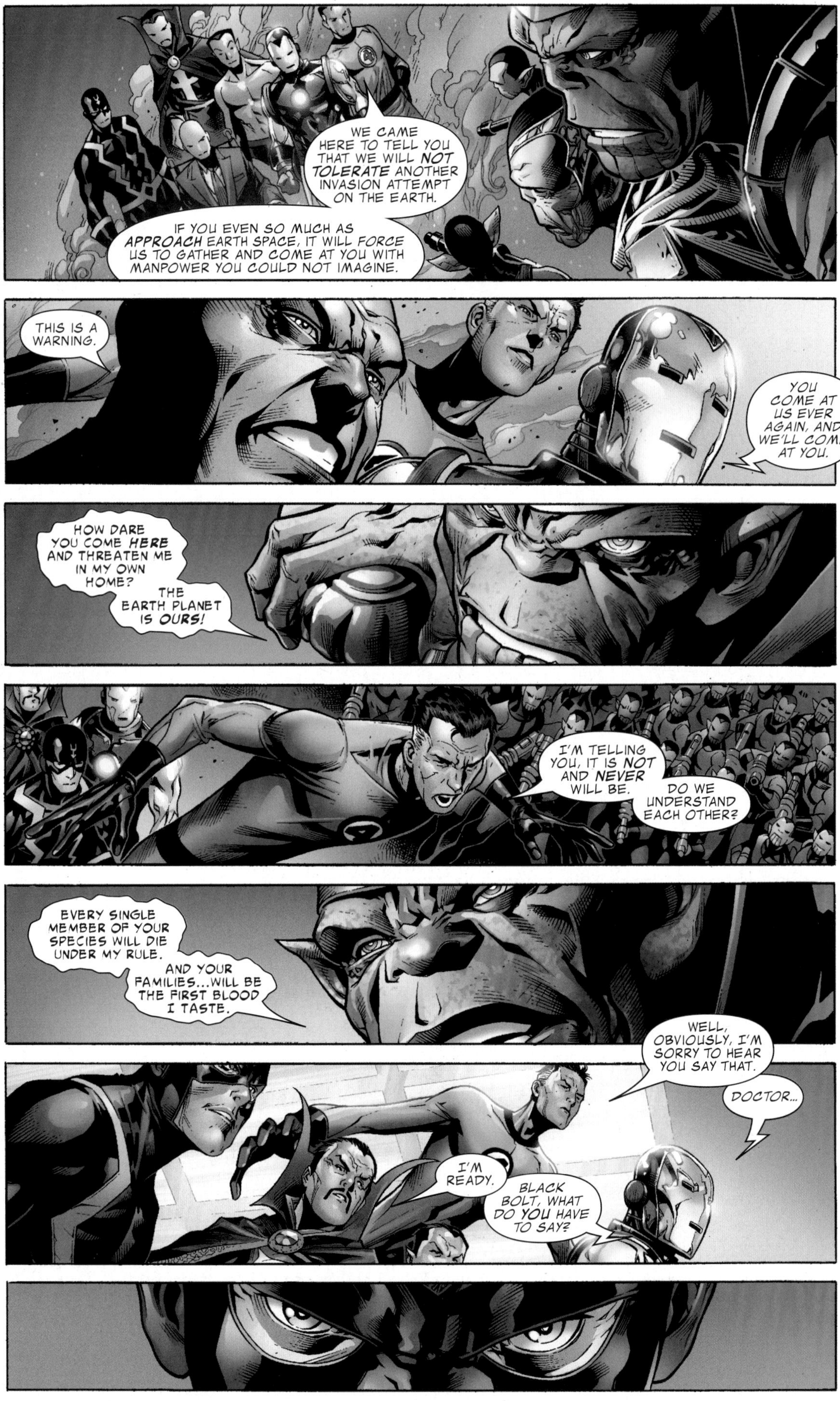
WE CAME HERE TO TELL YOU THAT WE WILL NOT TOLERATE ANOTHER INVASION ATTEMPT ON THE EARTH.
IF YOU EVEN SO MUCH AS APPROACH EARTH SPACE, IT WILL FORCE US TO GATHER AND COME AT YOU WITH MANPOWER YOU COULD NOT IMAGINE.
THIS IS A WARNING.
YOU COME AT US EVER AGAIN, AND WE'LL COME AT YOU.
HOW DARE YOU COME HERE AND THREATEN ME IN MY OWN HOME?
THE EARTH PLANET IS OURS!
I'M TELLING YOU, IT IS NOT AND NEVER WILL BE.
DO WE UNDERSTAND EACH OTHER?
EVERY SINGLE MEMBER OF YOUR SPECIES WILL DIE UNDER MY RULE.
AND YOUR FAMILIES...WILL BE THE FIRST BLOOD I TASTE.
WELL, OBVIOUSLY, I'M SORRY TO HEAR YOU SAY THAT.
DOCTOR...
I'M READY.
BLACK BOLT, WHAT DO YOU HAVE TO SAY?

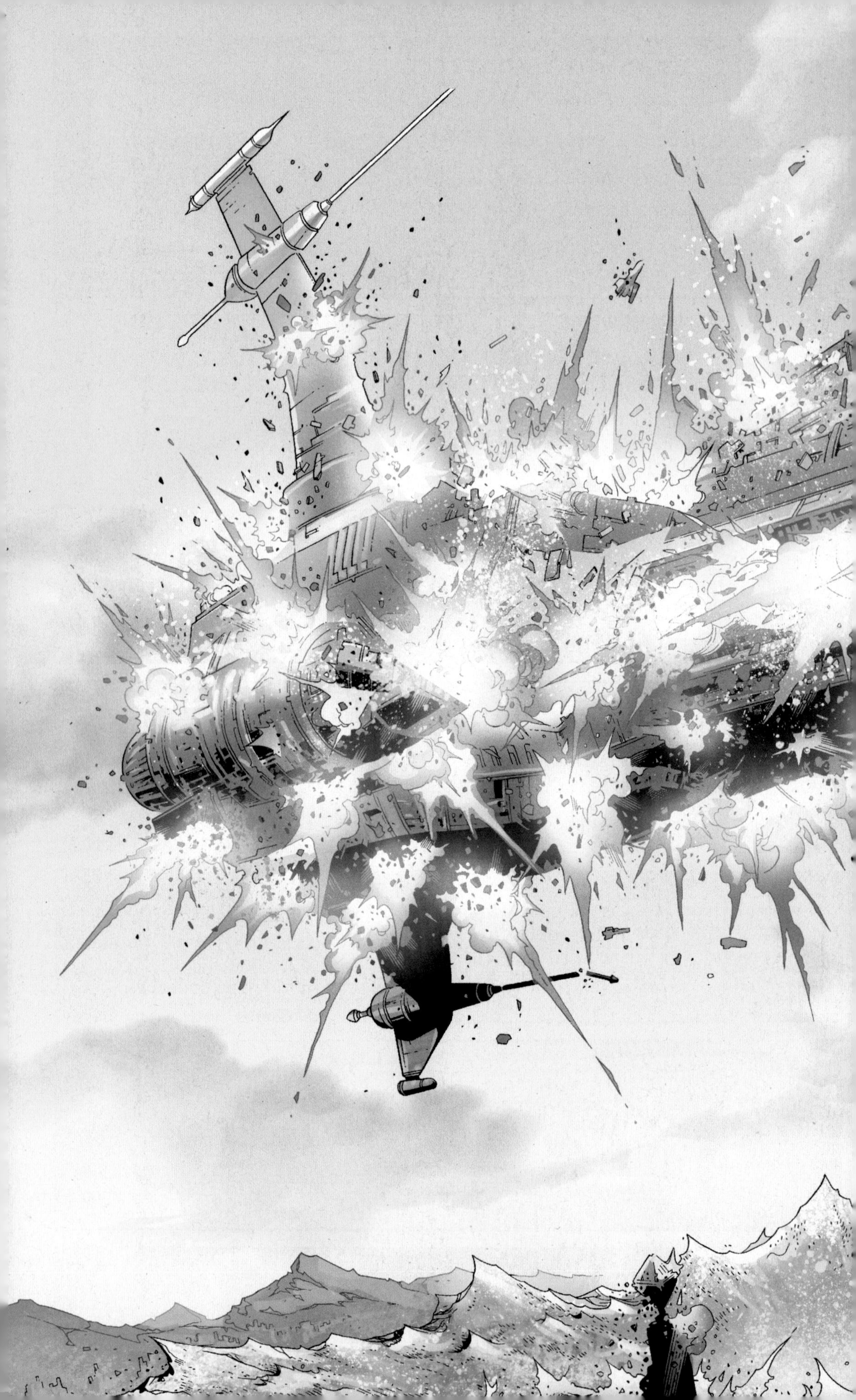

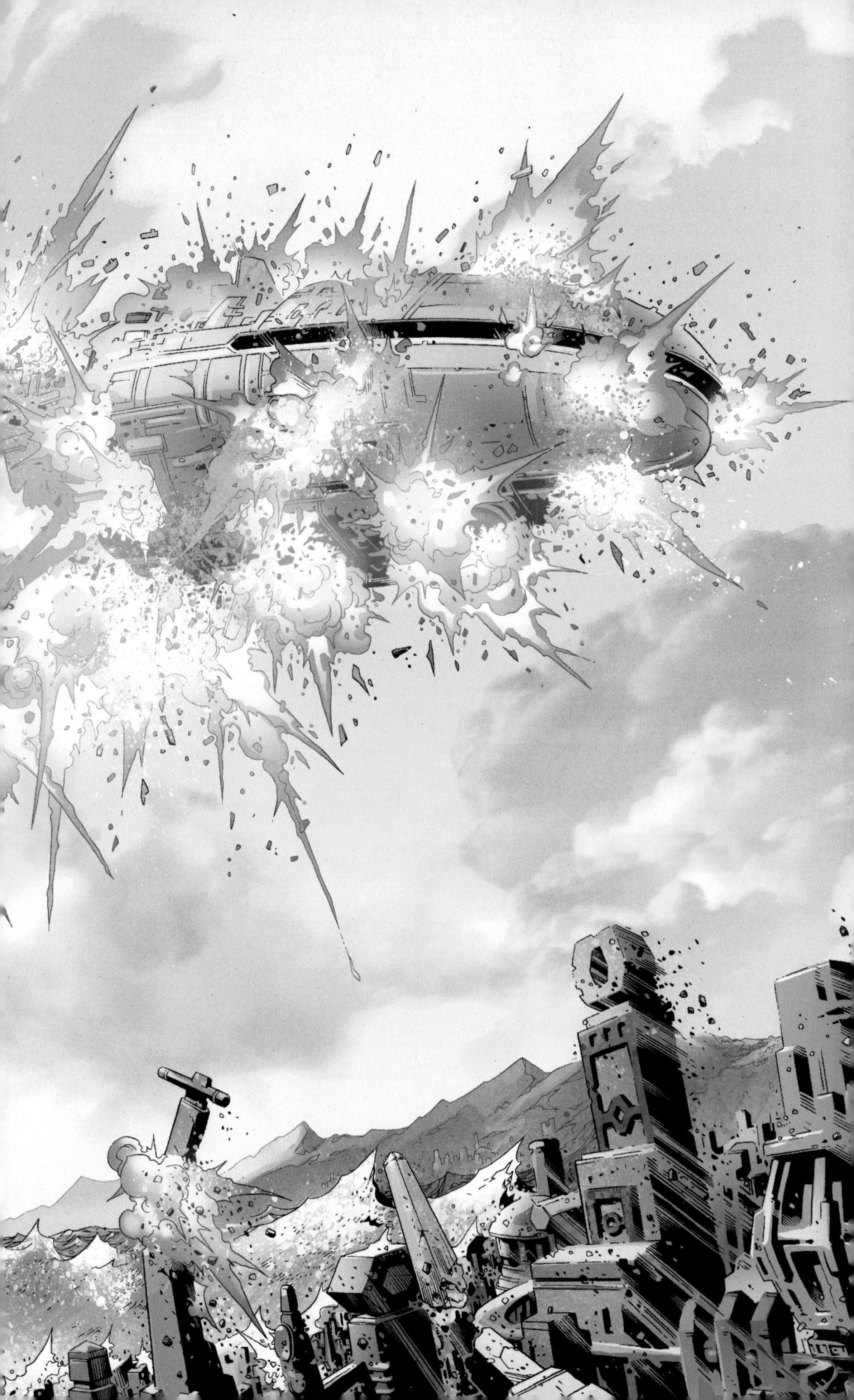

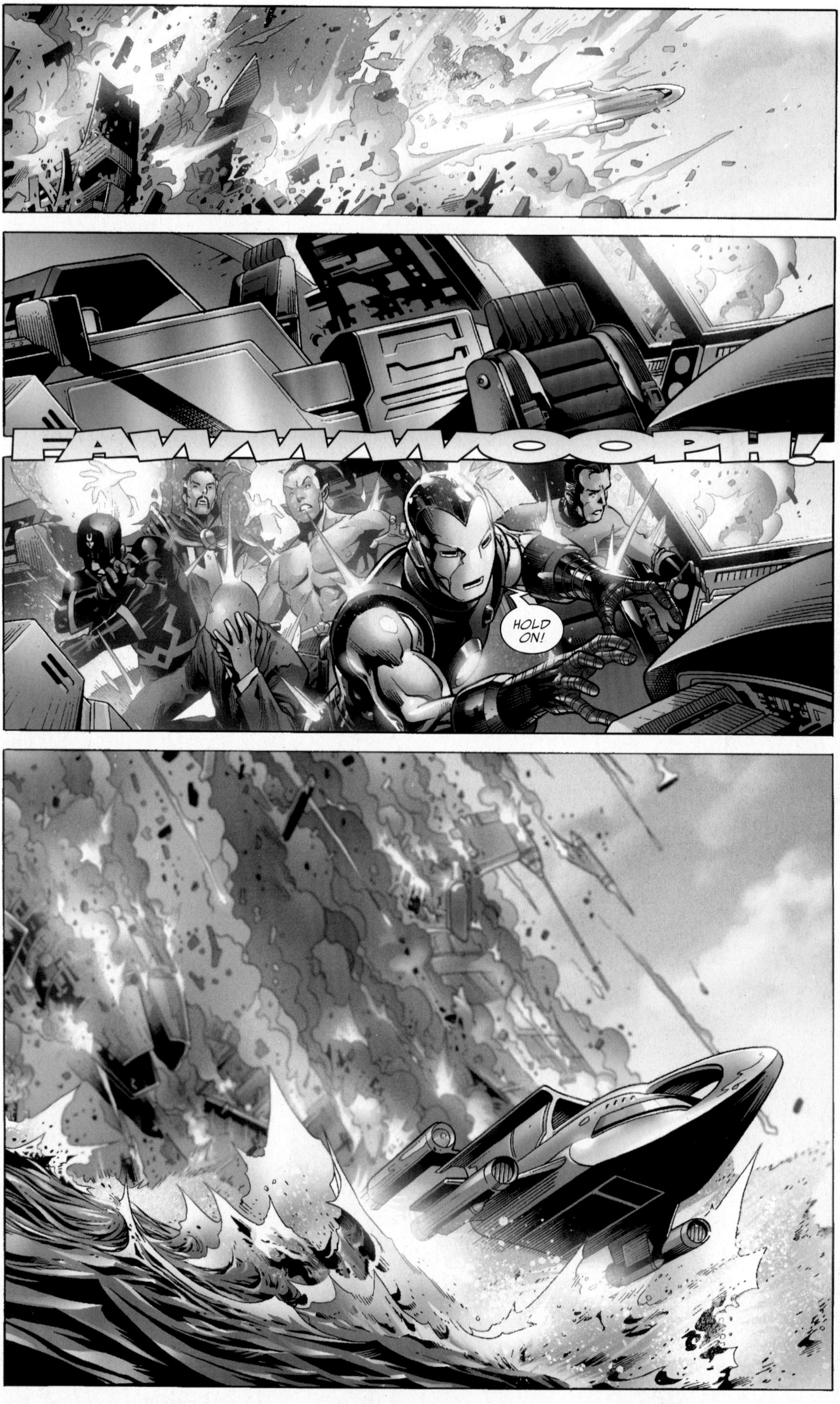
FAWWWWOOPH!
HOLD ON!

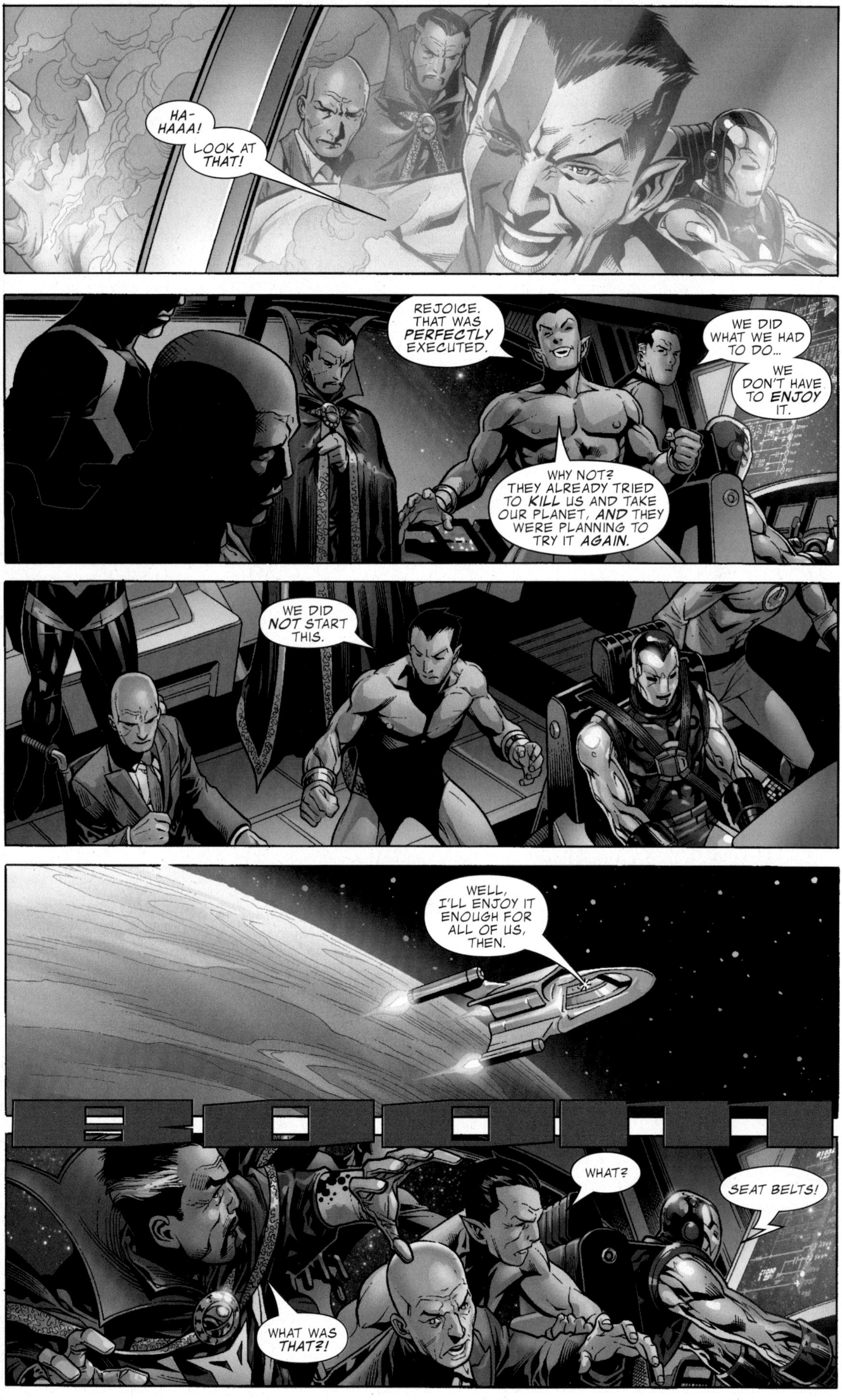
HA-HAAA!
LOOK AT THAT!
REJOICE. THAT WAS PERFECTLY EXECUTED.
WE DID WHAT WE HAD TO DO...
WE DON'T HAVE TO ENJOY IT.
WHY NOT? THEY ALREADY TRIED TO KILL US AND TAKE OUR PLANET, AND THEY WERE PLANNING TO TRY IT AGAIN.
WE DID NOT START THIS.
WELL, I'LL ENJOY IT ENOUGH FOR ALL OF US, THEN.
WHAT?
SEAT BELTS!
WHAT WAS THAT?!

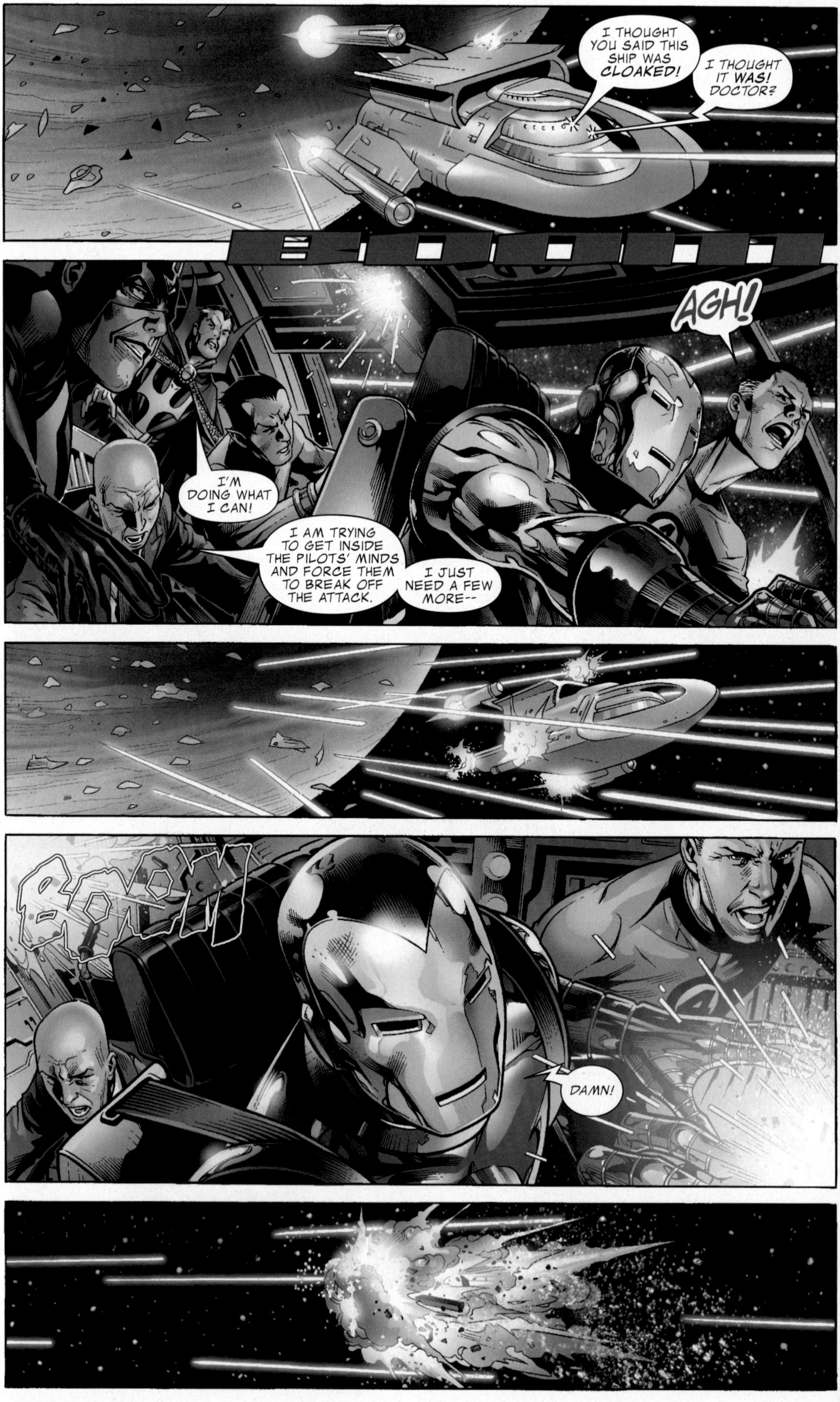
I THOUGHT YOU SAID THIS SHIP WAS CLOAKED!
I THOUGHT IT WAS! DOCTOR?
AGH!
I'M DOING WHAT I CAN!
I AM TRYING TO GET INSIDE THE PILOTS' MINDS AND FORCE THEM TO BREAK OFF THE ATTACK.
I JUST NEED A FEW MORE--
BOOM
DAMN!

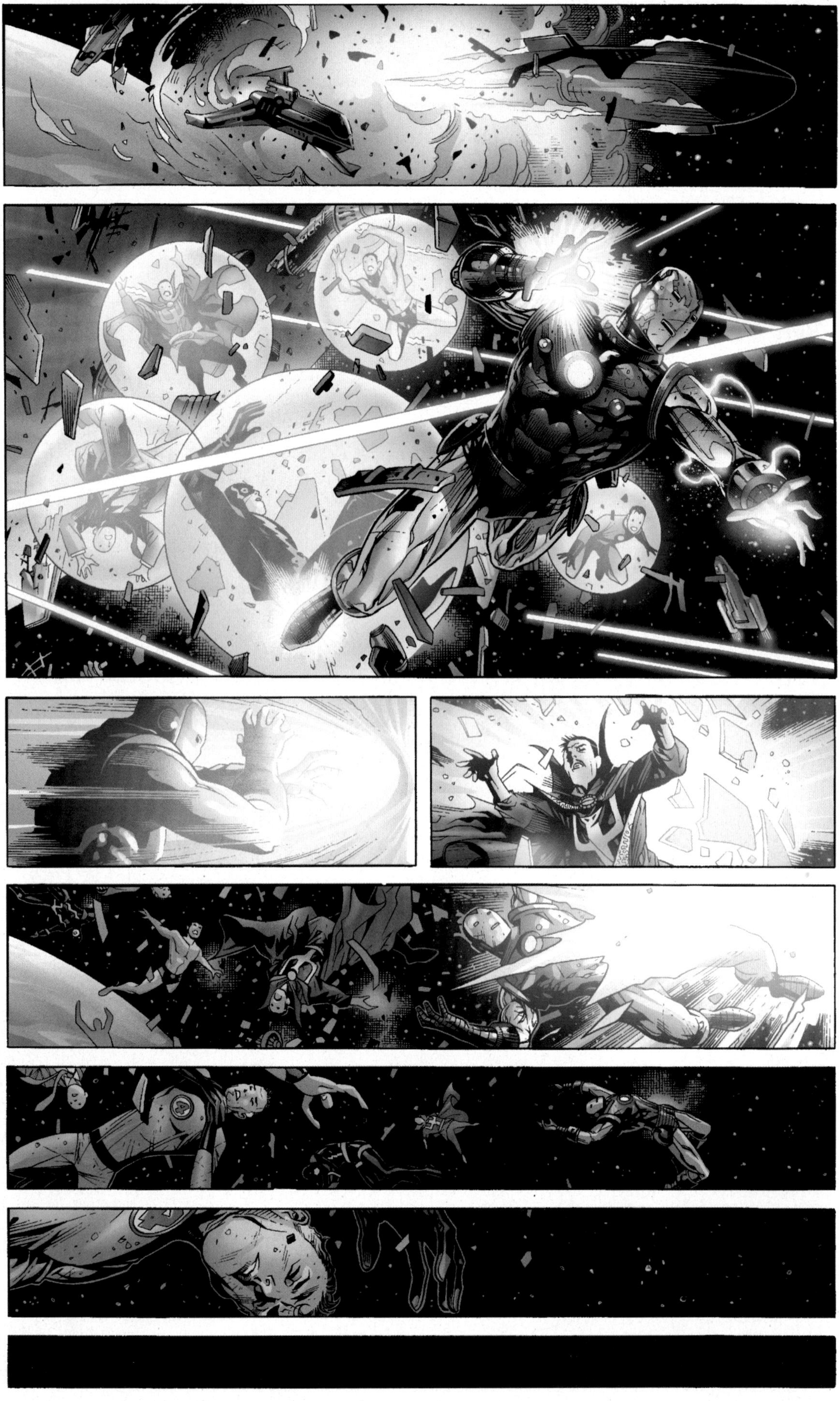

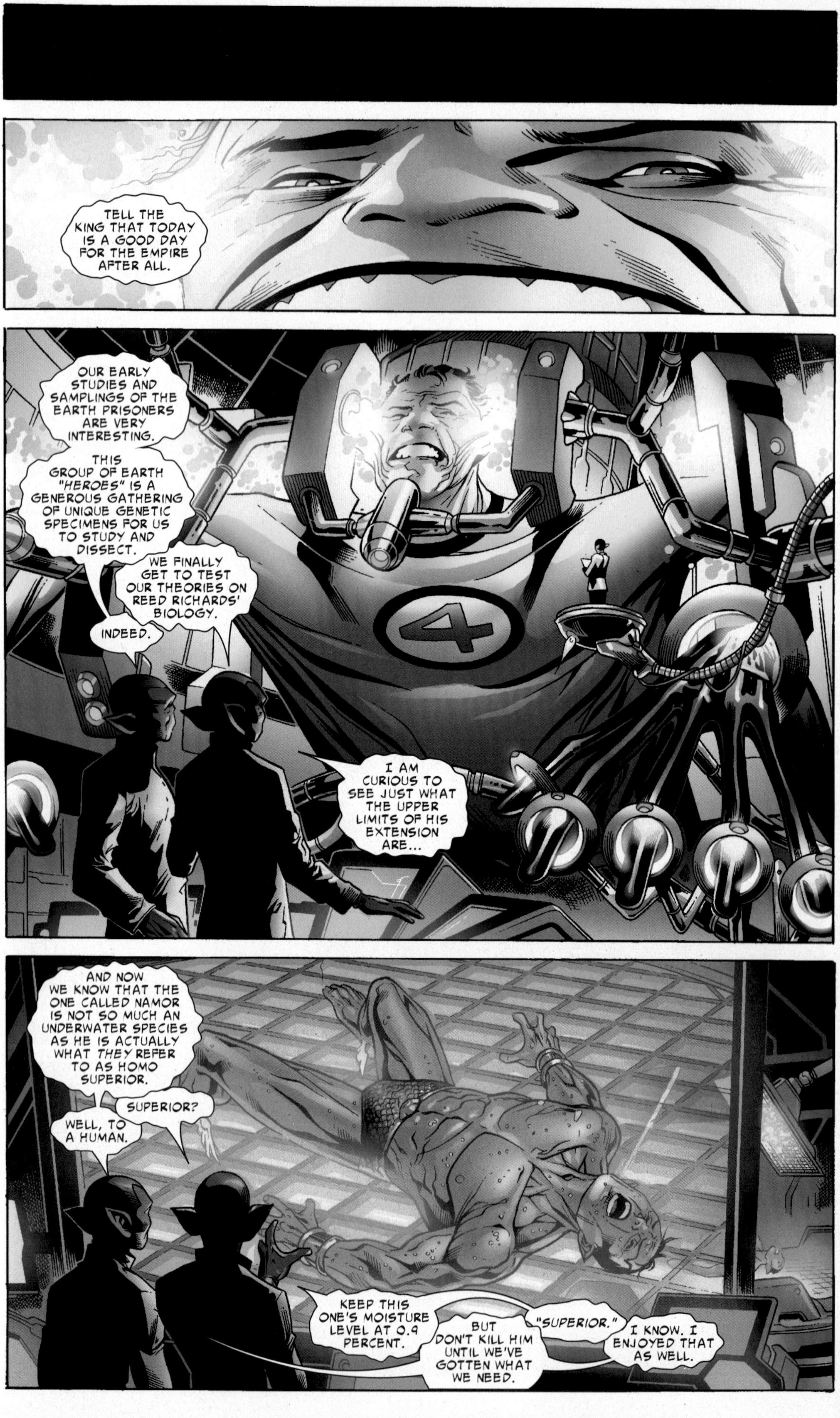
TELL THE KING THAT TODAY IS A GOOD DAY FOR THE EMPIRE AFTER ALL.
OUR EARLY STUDIES AND SAMPLINGS OF THE EARTH PRISONERS ARE VERY INTERESTING.
THIS GROUP OF EARTH "HEROES" IS A GENEROUS GATHERING OF UNIQUE GENETIC SPECIMENS FOR US TO STUDY AND DISSECT.
WE FINALLY GET TO TEST OUR THEORIES ON REED RICHARDS' BIOLOGY.
INDEED.
I AM CURIOUS TO SEE JUST WHAT THE UPPER LIMITS OF HIS EXTENSION ARE...
AND NOW WE KNOW THAT THE ONE CALLED NAMOR IS NOT SO MUCH AN UNDERWATER SPECIES AS HE IS ACTUALLY WHAT THEY REFER TO AS HOMO SUPERIOR.
SUPERIOR?
WELL, TO A HUMAN.
KEEP THIS ONE'S MOISTURE LEVEL AT 0.9 PERCENT.
BUT DON'T KILL HIM UNTIL WE'VE GOTTEN WHAT WE NEED.
"SUPERIOR."
I KNOW. I ENJOYED THAT AS WELL.

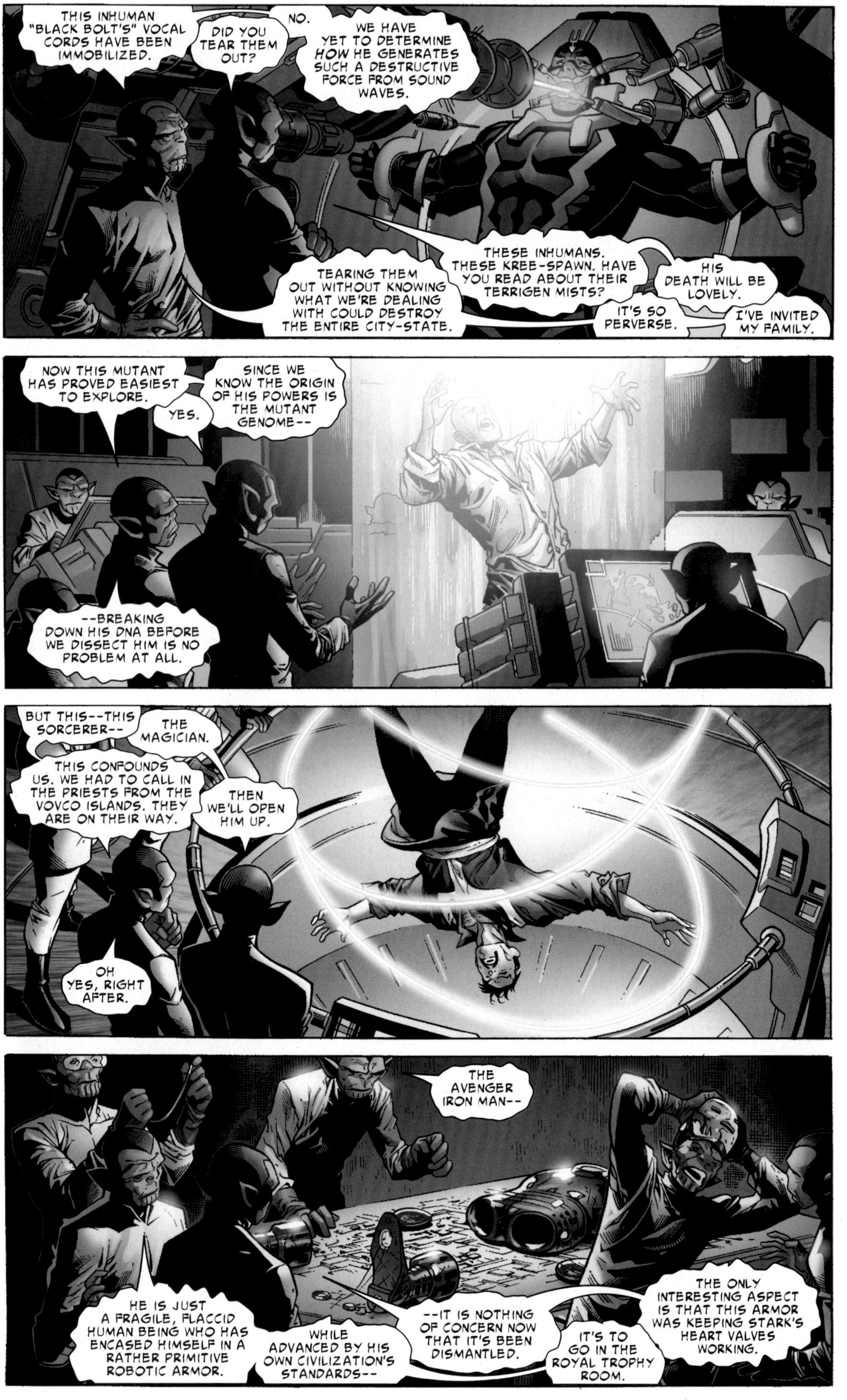

THIS INHUMAN "BLACK BOLT'S" VOCAL CORDS HAVE BEEN IMMOBILIZED.
DID YOU TEAR THEM OUT?
NO.
WE HAVE YET TO DETERMINE HOW HE GENERATES SUCH A DESTRUCTIVE FORCE FROM SOUND WAVES.
TEARING THEM OUT WITHOUT KNOWING WHAT WE'RE DEALING WITH COULD DESTROY THE ENTIRE CITY-STATE.
THESE INHUMANS. THESE KREE-SPAWN. HAVE YOU READ ABOUT THEIR TERRIGEN MISTS?
IT'S SO PERVERSE.
HIS DEATH WILL BE LOVELY.
I'VE INVITED MY FAMILY.
NOW THIS MUTANT HAS PROVED EASIEST TO EXPLORE.
YES.
SINCE WE KNOW THE ORIGIN OF HIS POWERS IS THE MUTANT GENOME--
--BREAKING DOWN HIS DNA BEFORE WE DISSECT HIM IS NO PROBLEM AT ALL.
BUT THIS--THIS SORCERER--
THE MAGICIAN.
THIS CONFOUNDS US. WE HAD TO CALL IN THE PRIESTS FROM THE VOVCO ISLANDS. THEY ARE ON THEIR WAY.
THEN WE'LL OPEN HIM UP.
OH YES, RIGHT AFTER.
THE AVENGER IRON MAN--
HE IS JUST A FRAGILE, FLACCID HUMAN BEING WHO HAS ENCASED HIMSELF IN A RATHER PRIMITIVE ROBOTIC ARMOR.
WHILE ADVANCED BY HIS OWN CIVILIZATION'S STANDARDS--
--IT IS NOTHING OF CONCERN NOW THAT IT'S BEEN DISMANTLED.
IT'S TO GO IN THE ROYAL TROPHY ROOM.
THE ONLY INTERESTING ASPECT IS THAT THIS ARMOR WAS KEEPING STARK'S HEART VALVES WORKING.

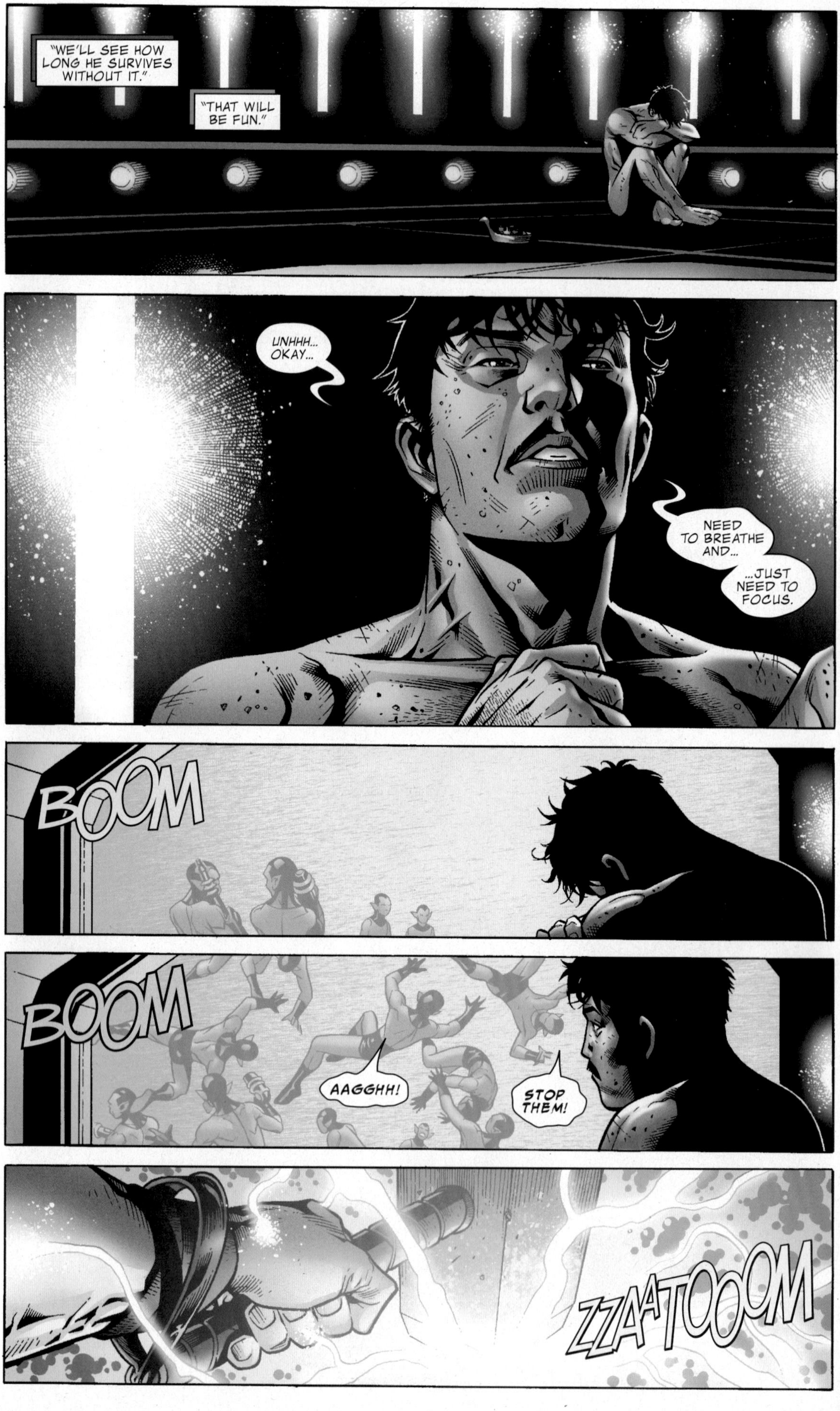
"WE'LL SEE HOW LONG HE SURVIVES WITHOUT IT."
"THAT WILL BE FUN."
UNHHH... OKAY...
NEED TO BREATHE AND...
...JUST NEED TO FOCUS.
BOOM
BOOM
AAGGHH!
STOP THEM!
ZZAATOOOM

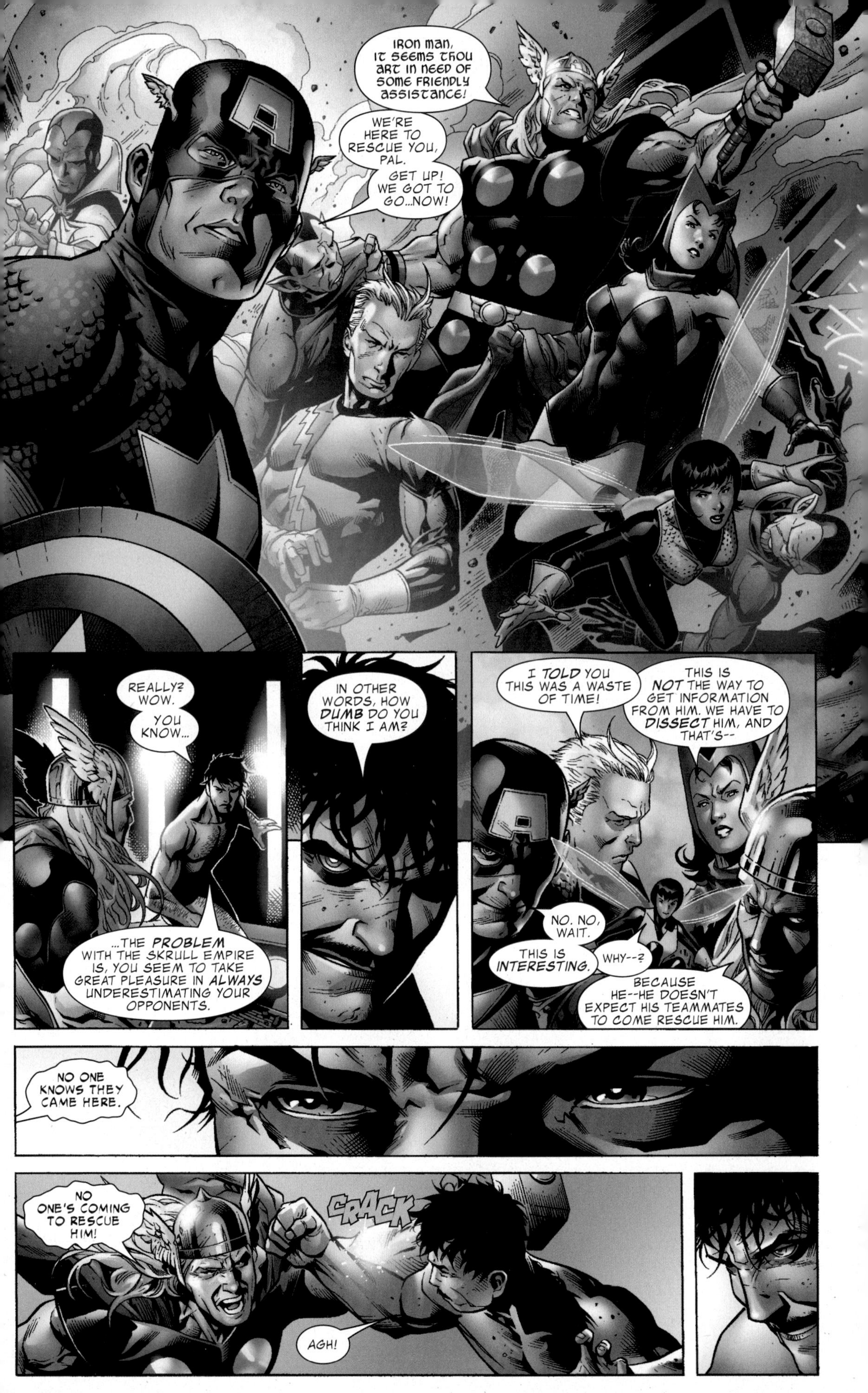
IRON MAN, IT SEEMS THOU ART IN NEED OF SOME FRIENDLY ASSISTANCE!
WE'RE HERE TO RESCUE YOU, PAL.
GET UP! WE GOT TO GO...NOW!
REALLY? WOW.
YOU KNOW...
...THE PROBLEM WITH THE SKRULL EMPIRE IS, YOU SEEM TO TAKE GREAT PLEASURE IN ALWAYS UNDERESTIMATING YOUR OPPONENTS.
IN OTHER WORDS, HOW DUMB DO YOU THINK I AM?
I TOLD YOU THIS WAS A WASTE OF TIME!
THIS IS NOT THE WAY TO GET INFORMATION FROM HIM. WE HAVE TO DISSECT HIM, AND THAT'S--
NO. NO, WAIT.
THIS IS INTERESTING.
WHY--?
BECAUSE HE--HE DOESN'T EXPECT HIS TEAMMATES TO COME RESCUE HIM.
NO ONE KNOWS THEY CAME HERE.
NO ONE'S COMING TO RESCUE HIM!
CRACK
AGH!

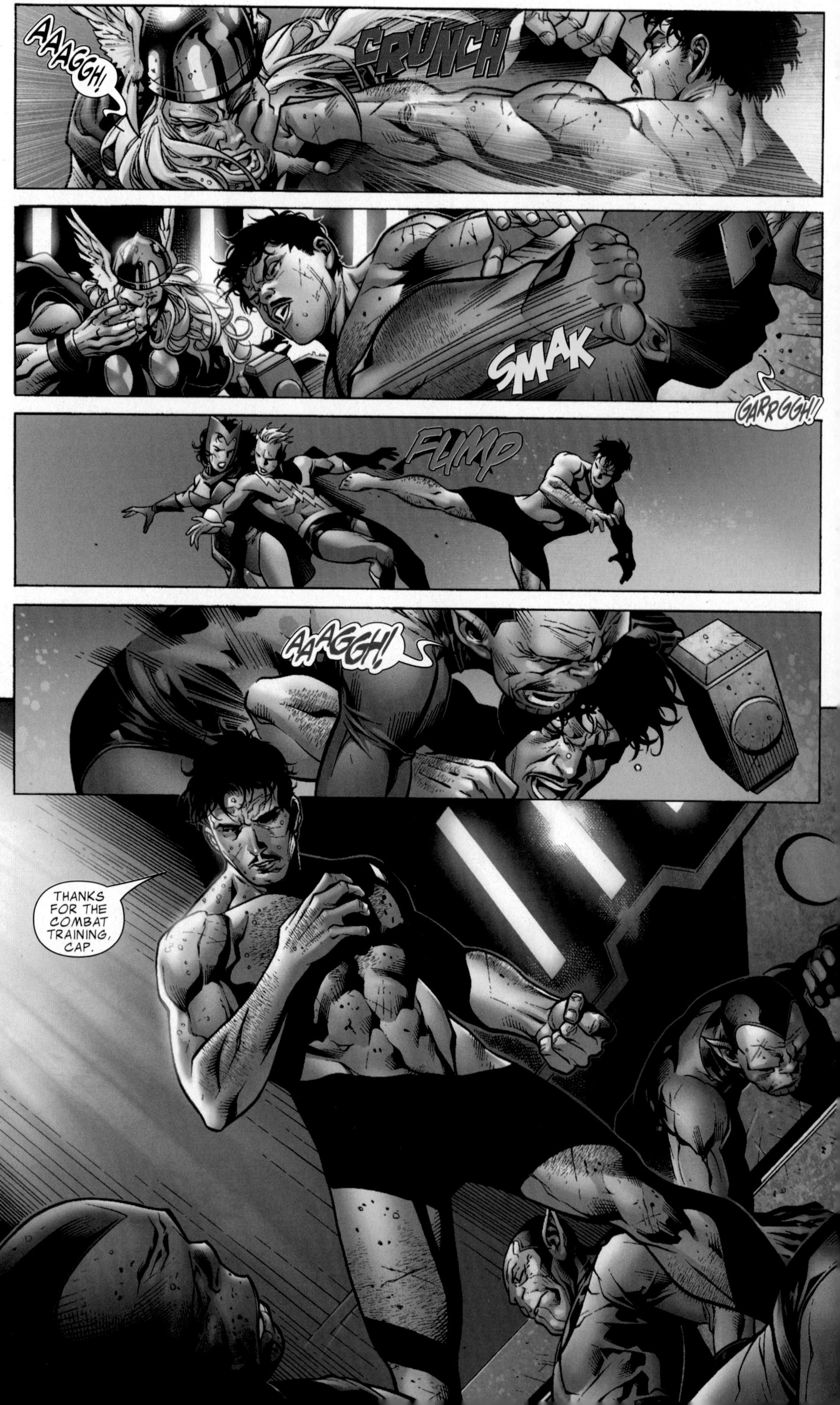
AAAGGH!
CRUNCH
SMAK
GARRGGH!
FLUMP
AAAGGH!
THANKS FOR THE COMBAT TRAINING, CAP.

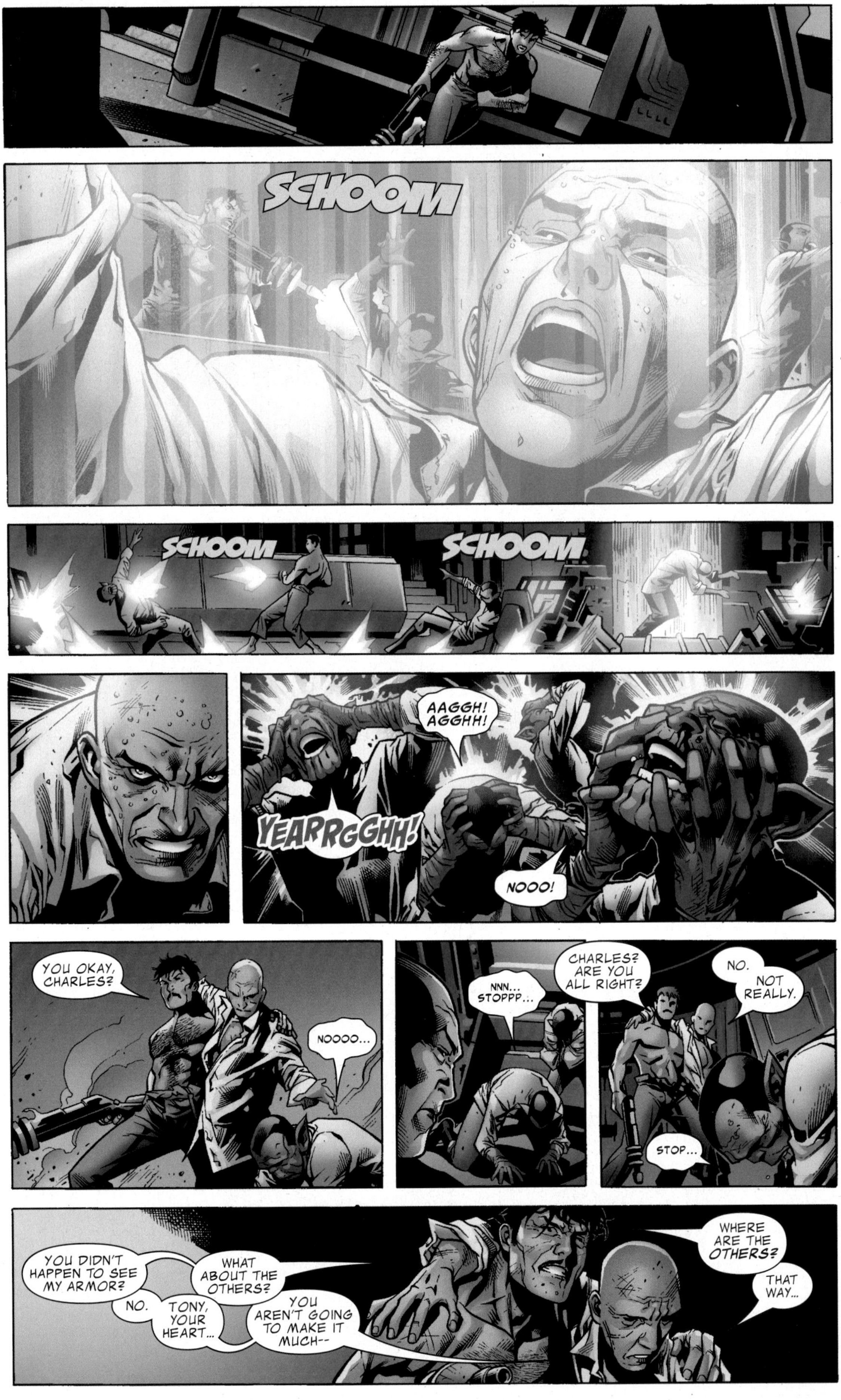
SCHOOM
SCHOOM
SCHOOM
AAGGH! AGGHH!
YEARRGGHH!
NOOO!
YOU OKAY, CHARLES?
NOOOO...
NNN... STOPPP...
CHARLES? ARE YOU ALL RIGHT?
NO. NOT REALLY.
STOP...
WHERE ARE THE OTHERS?
THAT WAY...
WHAT ABOUT THE OTHERS?
YOU AREN'T GOING TO MAKE IT MUCH--
TONY, YOUR HEART...
YOU DIDN'T HAPPEN TO SEE MY ARMOR?
NO.

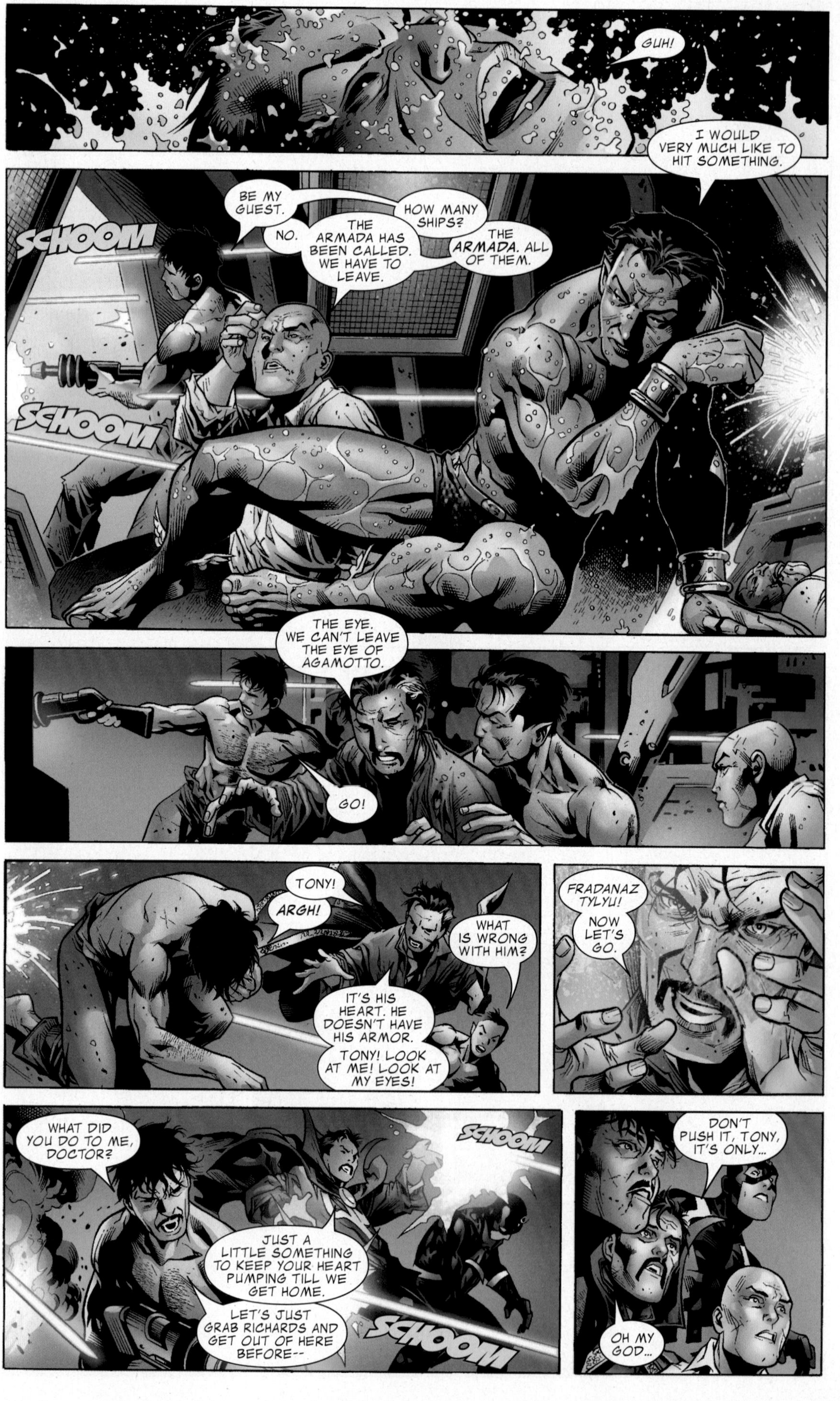
GUH!
I WOULD VERY MUCH LIKE TO HIT SOMETHING.
BE MY GUEST.
HOW MANY SHIPS?
NO.
THE ARMADA HAS BEEN CALLED. WE HAVE TO LEAVE.
THE ARMADA. ALL OF THEM.
SCHOOM
SCHOOM
THE EYE. WE CAN'T LEAVE THE EYE OF AGAMOTTO.
GO!
TONY!
ARGH!
WHAT IS WRONG WITH HIM?
IT'S HIS HEART. HE DOESN'T HAVE HIS ARMOR.
TONY! LOOK AT ME! LOOK AT MY EYES!
FRADANAZ TYLYU!
NOW LET'S GO.
WHAT DID YOU DO TO ME, DOCTOR?
SCHOOM
JUST A LITTLE SOMETHING TO KEEP YOUR HEART PUMPING TILL WE GET HOME.
LET'S JUST GRAB RICHARDS AND GET OUT OF HERE BEFORE--
SCHOOM
DON'T PUSH IT, TONY, IT'S ONLY...
OH MY GOD...

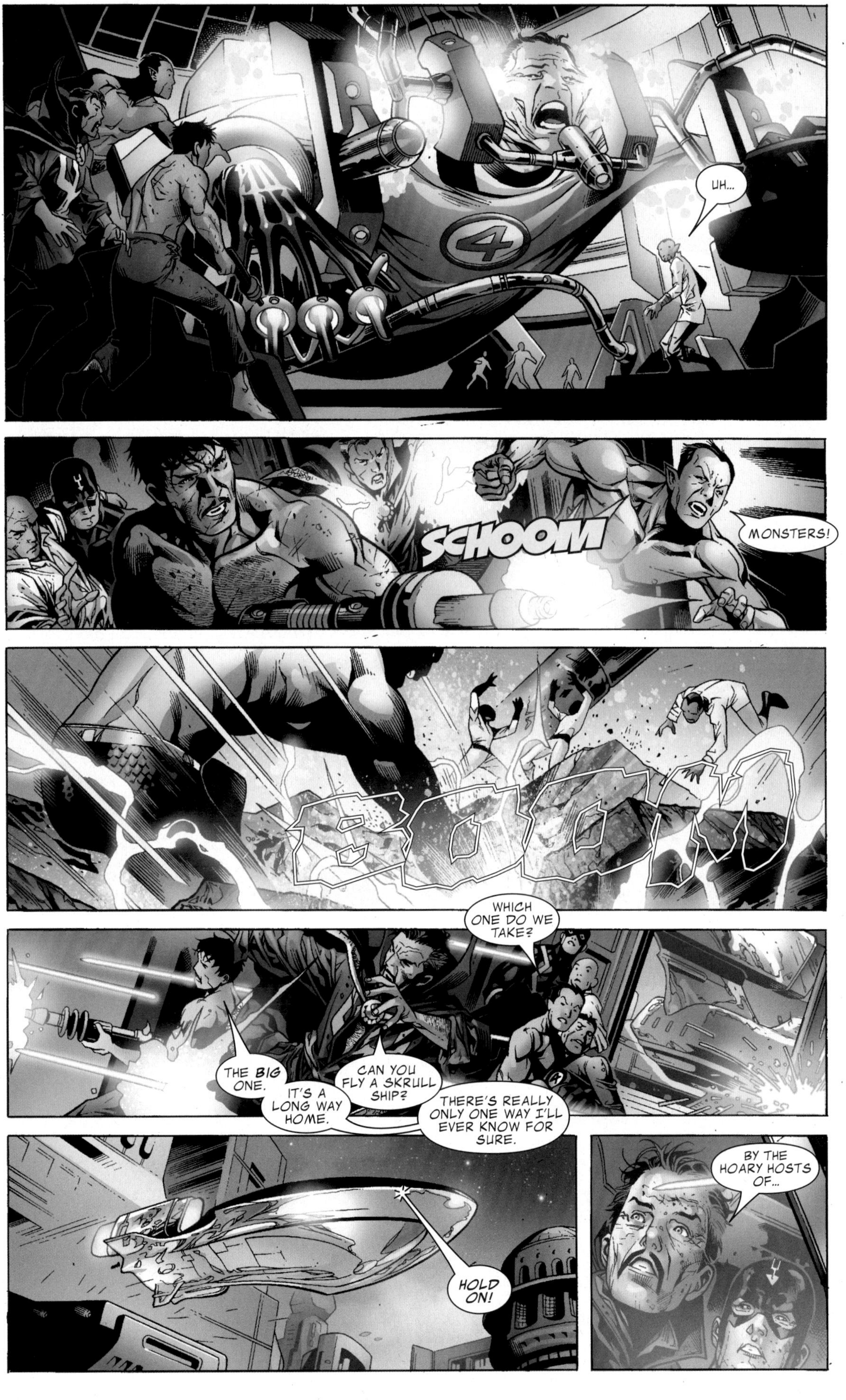
UH...
SCHOOM
MONSTERS!
BOOOM
WHICH ONE DO WE TAKE?
THE BIG ONE.
IT'S A LONG WAY HOME.
CAN YOU FLY A SKRULL SHIP?
THERE'S REALLY ONLY ONE WAY I'LL EVER KNOW FOR SURE.
HOLD ON!
BY THE HOARY HOSTS OF...

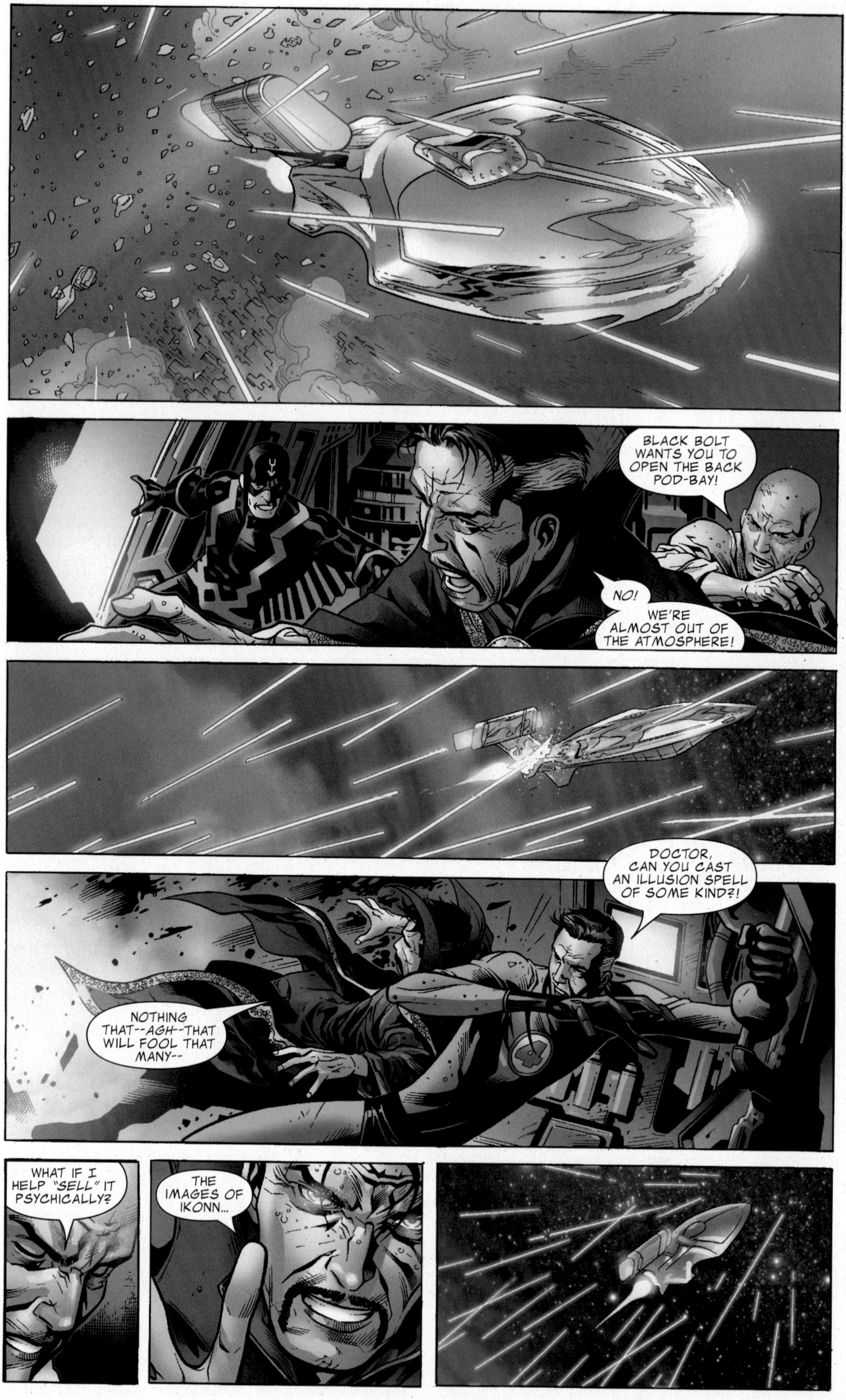
BLACK BOLT WANTS YOU TO OPEN THE BACK POD-BAY!
NO!
WE'RE ALMOST OUT OF THE ATMOSPHERE!
DOCTOR, CAN YOU CAST AN ILLUSION SPELL OF SOME KIND?!
NOTHING THAT--AGH--THAT WILL FOOL THAT MANY--
WHAT IF I HELP "SELL" IT PSYCHICALLY?
THE IMAGES OF IKONN...

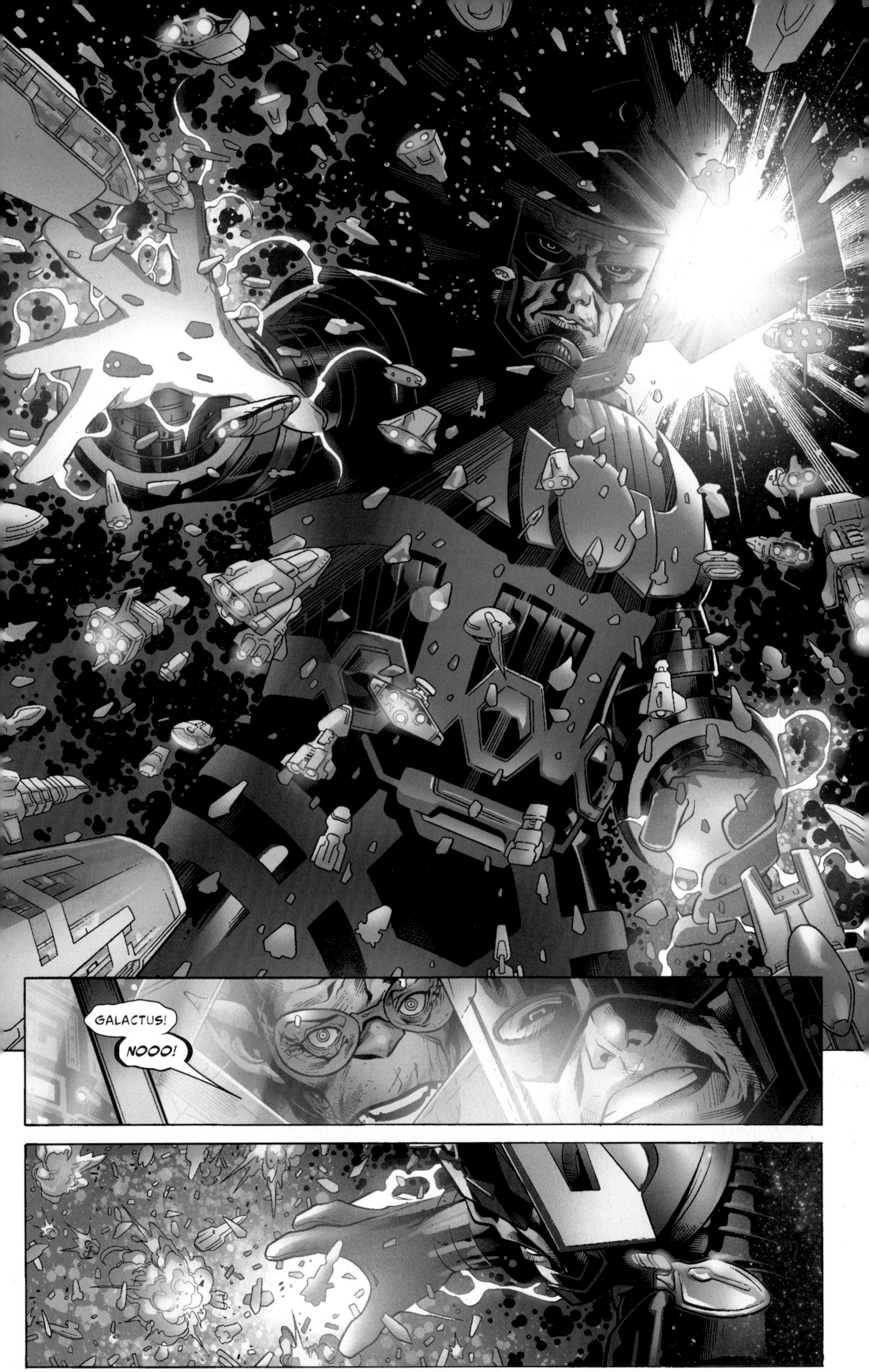
GALACTUS!
NOOO!

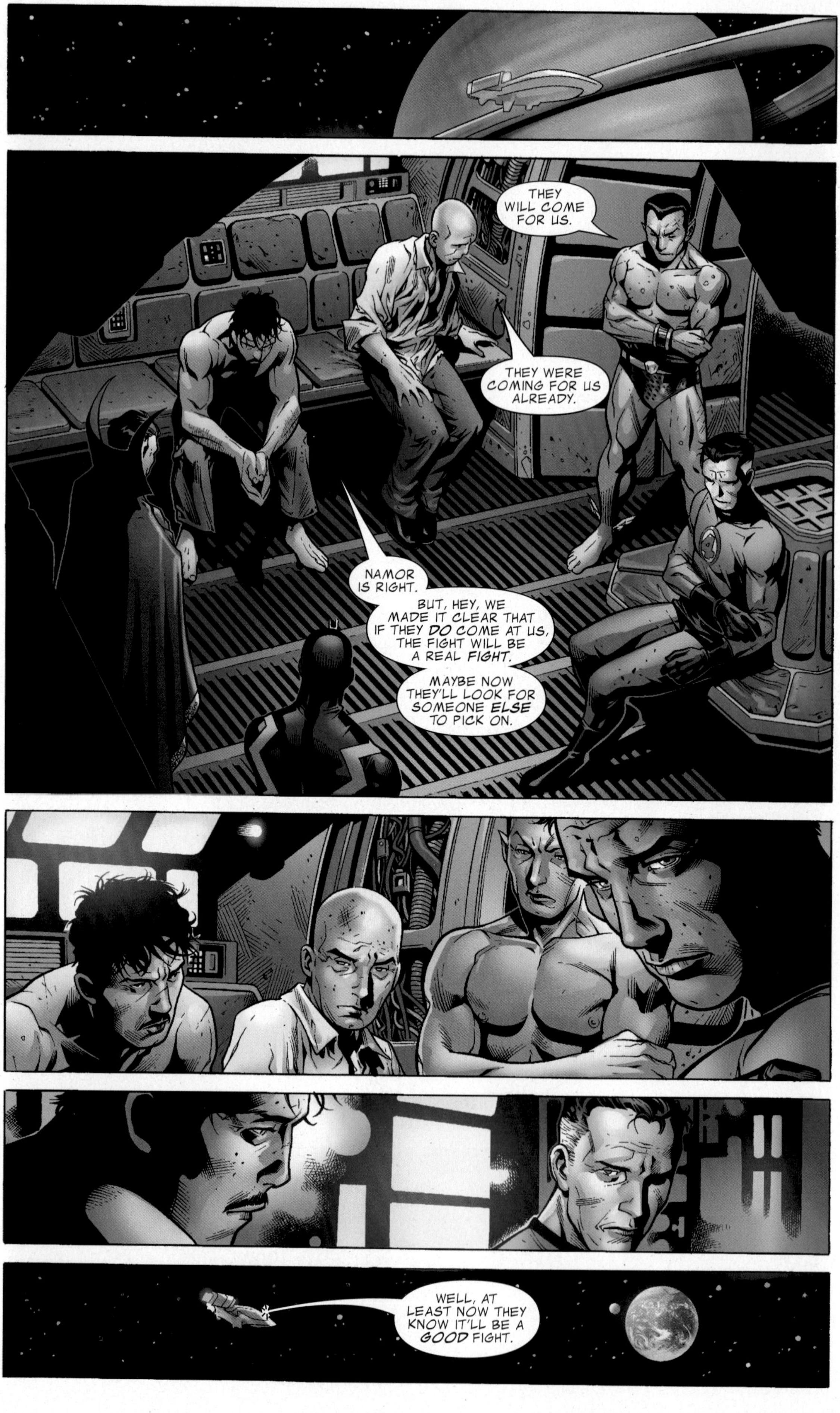
THEY WILL COME FOR US.
THEY WERE COMING FOR US ALREADY.
NAMOR IS RIGHT.
BUT, HEY, WE MADE IT CLEAR THAT IF THEY *DO* COME AT US, THE FIGHT WILL BE A REAL *FIGHT*.
MAYBE NOW THEY'LL LOOK FOR SOMEONE *ELSE* TO PICK ON.
WELL, AT LEAST NOW THEY KNOW IT'LL BE A *GOOD* FIGHT.

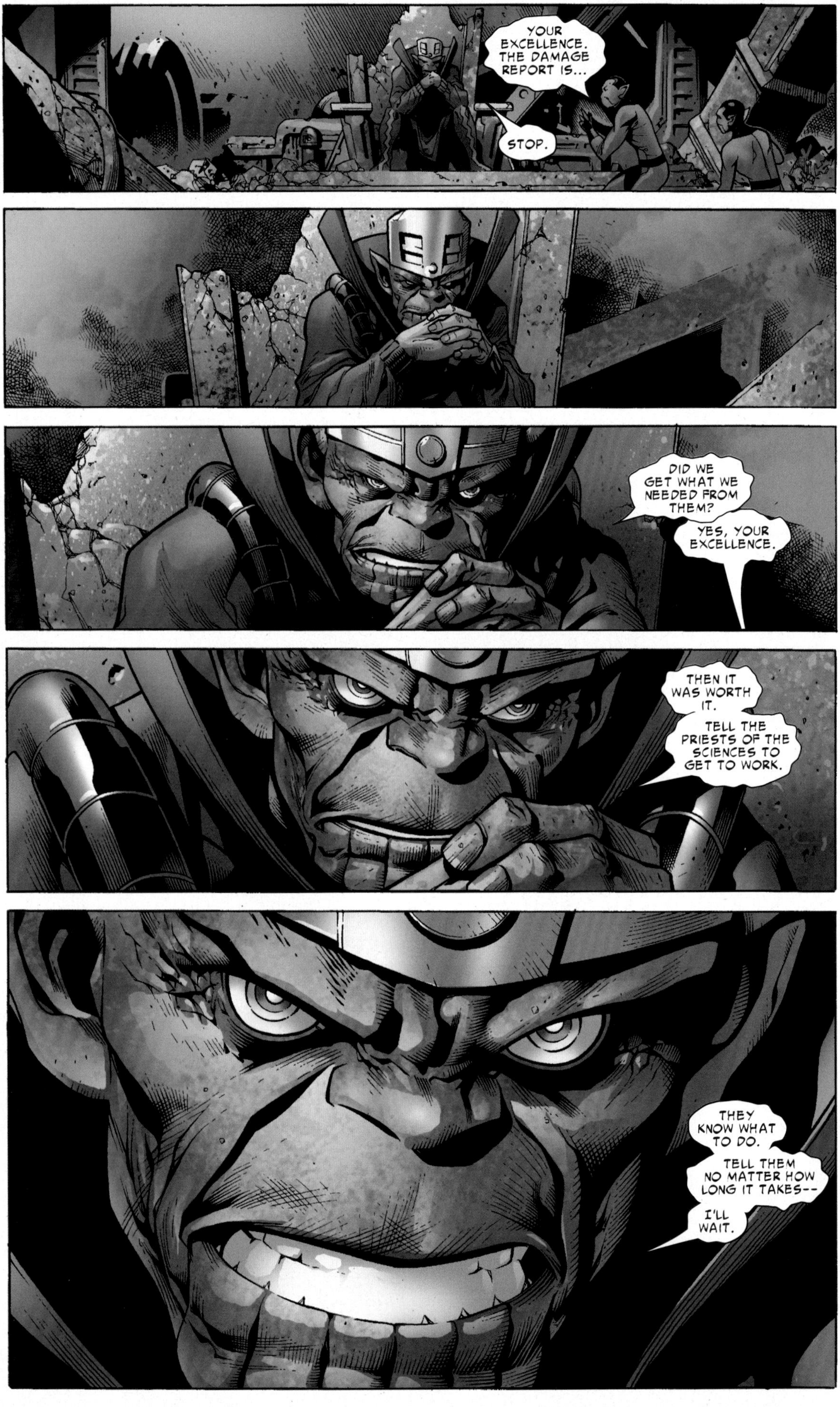
YOUR EXCELLENCE. THE DAMAGE REPORT IS...
STOP.
DID WE GET WHAT WE NEEDED FROM THEM?
YES, YOUR EXCELLENCE.
THEN IT WAS WORTH IT.
TELL THE PRIESTS OF THE SCIENCES TO GET TO WORK.
THEY KNOW WHAT TO DO.
TELL THEM NO MATTER HOW LONG IT TAKES--
I'LL WAIT.

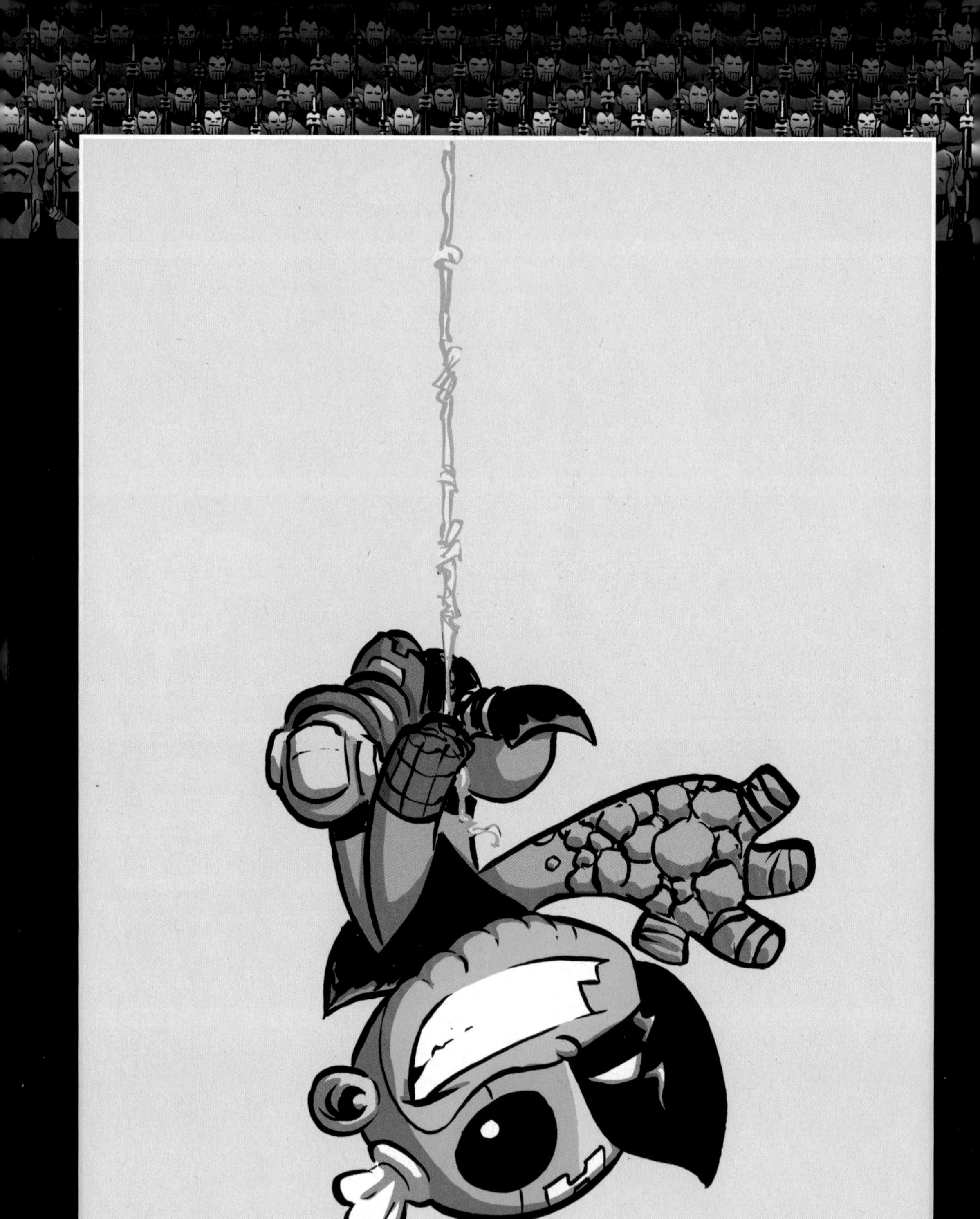
SY
19

SKOTTIE YOUNG MEET THE SKRULLS #1 VARIANT

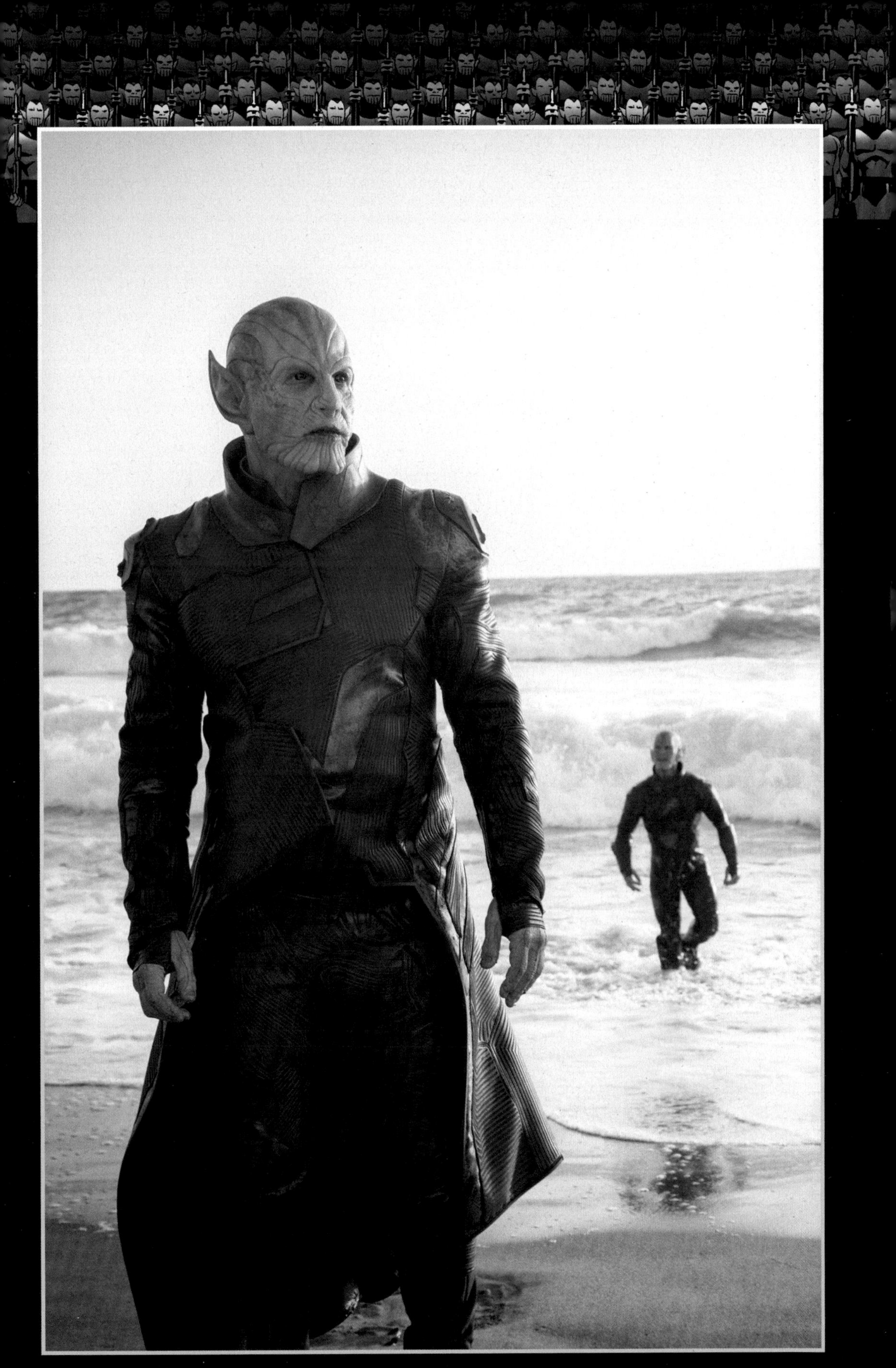

MEET THE SKRULLS #1 MOVIE VARIANT

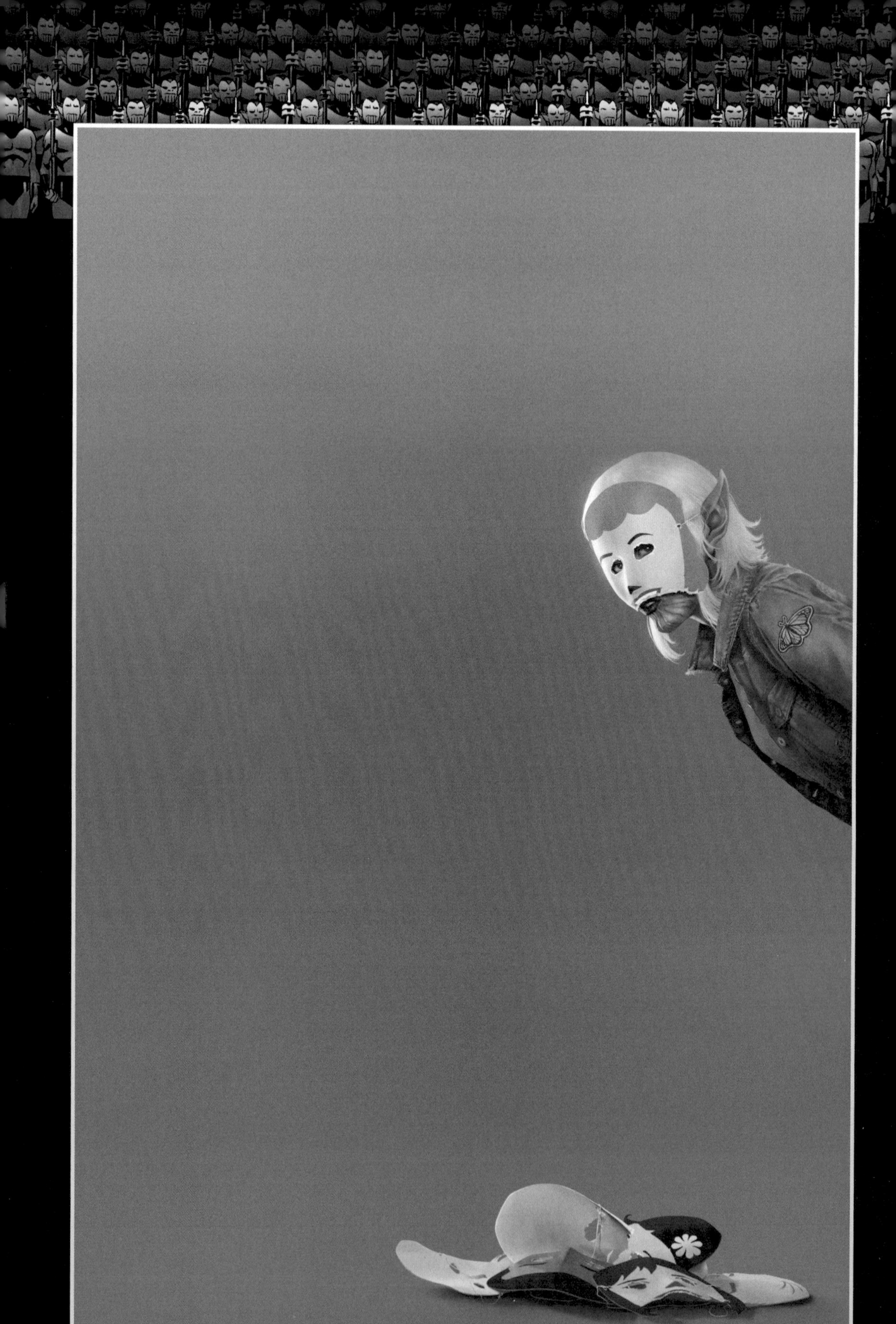

RAHZZAH MEET THE SKRULLS #2 VARIANT

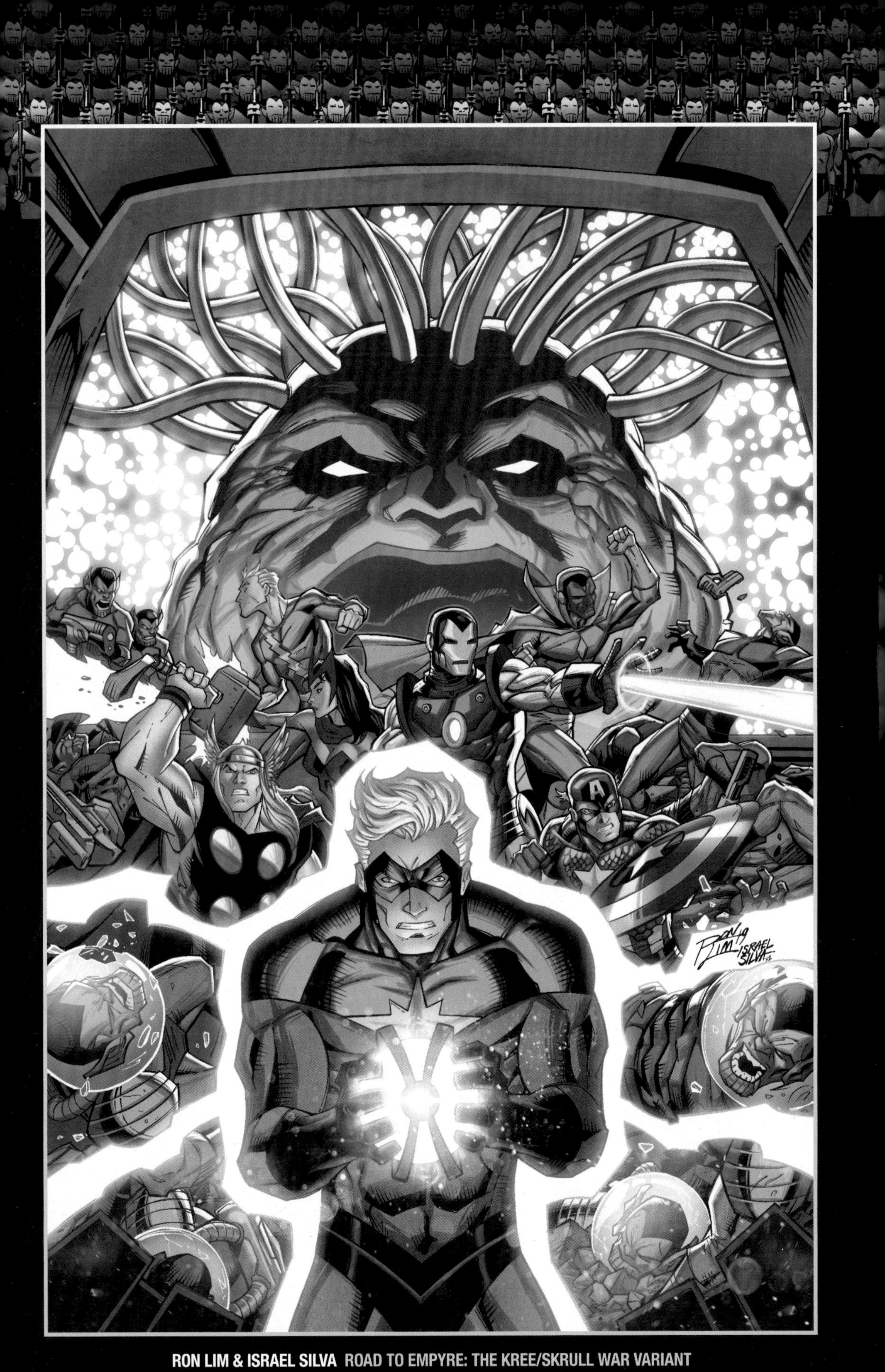

RON LIM & ISRAEL SILVA ROAD TO EMPYRE: THE KREE/SKRULL WAR VARIANT

THE END.

Well, sort of. My name is Nick Lowe, and I've been the lucky person who edited this book. Over the years, Robbie Thompson and I have talked about doing books that were really different from those we'd been working on, like SILK and SPIDEY and SPIDER-MAN/DEADPOOL. We talked about a lot of concepts to try to put together, but when he had the idea of a spy family of Skrulls, I was hooked and knew that Robbie's incredible voice for dialogue and characters' inner lives would make it sing. But I also knew it would be a tough sell. When I got a walk-through of the Captain Marvel film and the Skrulls' involvement, we jumped and got the book approved.

We talked about artists, and I can't remember whose idea it was to go to the incredible Niko Henrichon, but as soon as we thought of it we realized no one else could do it. From *Pride of Baghdad*, where I first saw his work, to DOCTOR STRANGE and NEW MUTANTS, where we got to work together, Niko showed he could draw anything. Usually when you say that, you mean big, crazy stuff, which Niko can certainly draw. But in this case, could he draw a family in their living room? Might be strange to say, but not every comic book artist can draw that and still have it be interesting. Niko excelled at it AND the big, crazy things he had to draw as well.

The incredible Assistant Editor Kathleen Wisneski (who is responsible for so much of what makes this book subtle and powerful) and I had just finished working with letterer Travis Lanham on PETER PARKER: THE SPECTACULAR SPIDER-MAN and wanted a new project with him. He is a tireless worker and so creative, so we knew we'd be in good hands. Travis delivered.

Lastly, we knew this wasn't a concept that would be easy to make jump off the shelves, so we needed the covers to be powerful. Luckily, one of the greatest cover artists of **ALL TIME**, Marcos Martin, came on board.

It was these people who brought the Warners to life and made their lives so rich, and I feel lucky to have spent these five issues with them. And now, it ends. This book and the Warners' story is over. There's no way that, over the next few years, you'll be spending time with one of your favorite characters in one of your favorite books and come across a reveal that it's actually Alice Warner. NO WAY is that going to happen. Their story is over. **THE END.**

Nick Lowe
Editor

This is for my family. Thank you for making me who I am.

Robbie Thompson